If it's APRIL 2007
and you are still using this Directory,
it's time to order the NEW Edition.

Please visit our website

www.cabells.com

or contact us at

Box 5428, Beaumont, Texas 77726-5428
(409) 898-0575
Fax (409) 866-9554
Email: publish@cabells.com

iv

Cabell's Directory of Publishing Opportunities in Accounting

TENTH EDITION 2006-2007

David W. E. Cabell, Editor-in-Chief
McNeese State University
Lake Charles, Louisiana

Deborah L. English, Executive Editor
Twyla J. George, Associate Editor
Lacey E. Earle, Associate Editor

To order additional copies
or electronic versions
visit our web site
www.cabells.com

or contact us at

Box 5428 Beaumont, Texas 77726-5428
(409) 898-0575 Fax (409) 866-9554

$99.95 U.S. for addresses in United States
Price includes shipping and handling for U.S.
Add $60 for surface mail to countries outside U.S.
Add $150 for air mail to countries outside U.S.

ISBN # 0-911753-31-1

Printed by Technical Communication Services, 110 West 12th Avenue, North Kansas City, MO 64116

Cover Design by Wayne Hale/Alphabet Soup, Inc.

TABLE OF CONTENTS

ii

iv

Preface

The objective of *Cabell's Directory of Publishing Opportunities in Accounting* is to help you publish your ideas.

The *Directory* contains the editor's name(s), address(es), phone number(s), and e-mail and web address(es) for over 180 journals.

To help you in selecting those journals that are most likely to publish your manuscripts the **Index** classifies the journals into twenty-four (**24**) different topic areas. In addition, the Index provides information on the journal's type of review process, number of external reviewers and acceptance rate.

To further assist you in organizing and preparing your manuscripts, the *Directory* includes extensive information on the style and format of most journals. If a journal has its own set of manuscript guidelines, a copy of these guidelines is published in the *Directory*. Also, each entry indicates the use of a standard set of publication guidelines by a journal. For example, some journals use the *Chicago Manual of Style* or the *Publication Manual of the American Psychological Association.*

Furthermore, the *Directory* describes the type of review process used by the editor(s) of a journal, type of review, number of reviewers, acceptance rate, time required for review, availability of reviewers comments, fees charged to review or publish the manuscript, copies required and manuscript topics. Information on the journal's readership is also provided.

Although this *Directory* focuses on journals in the specialized area of **Accounting**, other directories focus on **Economics and Finance**, **Management**, and **Marketing**. The division of business journals into these four directories more appropriately meets the researcher's need for publishing in his area of specialization.

The decision to place journals in their respective directory is based on the manuscript topics selected by the editor as well as the journals' guidelines for authors. If you wish to find the most current information on the *Directory*, visit **www.cabells.com**. Please contact us for the login registration procedure.

Also, the *Directory* includes a section titled **"What is a Refereed Article?"** which tends to emphasize the value of a blind review process and use of external reviewers. However, this section cautions individuals using these criteria to also consider a journal's reputation for quality. Additionally, it indicates that differences in acceptance rates may be the result of different methods used to calculate these percentages and the number of people associated with a particular area of specialization.

How To Use the Directory

TABLE OF CONTENTS
Table of Contents provides over 180 journals to help your locate a publication.

INDEX
Index classifies the journals according to twenty-four (24) different manuscript topics. It also includes information on the type of review, number of external reviewers, acceptance rate and page number of each journal.

ADDRESS FOR SUBMISSION
Address for Submission provides: the Editor's name(s), Mailing address(es), Telephone number(s), and E-mail and Web address(es).

PUBLICATION GUIDELINES
Manuscript Length refers to the length of the manuscript in terms of the number of double-spaced typescript pages.

Copies Required indicates the number of manuscript copies you should submit to the editor.

Computer Submission indicates whether the journal prefers hardcopy (paper) or electronic submissions such as disk, e-mail attachment, or a combination of methods.

Format refers to the type of word processing programs or computer programs the journal requires for reviewing the manuscript. Some examples of these programs are Microsoft Word, Word Perfect, or ASCII.

Fees to Review refers to whether the journal charges a fee to review the manuscript. Knowing this item permits the author to send the required funds with the manuscript.

Manuscript Style refers to the overall style guide the journal uses for text, references within the text and the bibliography. This is usually either the *Chicago Manual of Style* or the *Publication Manual of the American Psychological Association (APA)*.

REVIEW INFORMATION
Type of Review specifies blind, editorial, or optional review methods. A blind review indicates the reviewer(s) does not know who wrote the manuscript. An editorial review indicates the reviewer knows who wrote the manuscript. The term "optional" indicates the author may choose either one of these types of review.

No. of External Reviewers and *No. of In House Reviewers*
These two items refer to the number of reviewers who review the manuscript prior to making a decision regarding the publication of the manuscript. Although the editor attempted to determine whether the reviewers were on the staff of the journal or were outside reviewers, many of the respondents had trouble distinguishing between internal and external reviewers. Thus it may be more accurate to add these two categories and determine the total number of reviewers.

Acceptance Rate refers to the number of manuscripts accepted for publication relative to the number of manuscripts submitted within the last year. The method of calculating acceptance rates varies among journals.

Time to Review indicates the amount of time that passes between the submission of a manuscript and notification to the author regarding the results of the review process.

Reviewer's Comments indicates whether the author can obtain a copy of the reviewer's comments. In some cases, the author needs to request that the editor send these remarks.

Invited Articles indicates the percentage of articles for which the editor requests an individual to write specifically for publication in the journal. The percentage is the number of invited articles relative to the total number of articles that appeared in a journal within the past year.

Fees to Publish refers to whether the journal charges a fee to publish the manuscript. Knowing this item assists the author in his decision to place the manuscript into the review process.

CIRCULATION DATA
Reader indicates the predominant type of reader the publication seeks to attract. These are classified into researchers, businesspersons and academics.

Frequency of Issue indicates the number of times a journal will be published in a year.

Sponsor/Publisher indicates the journal's affiliation with a professional association, educational institution, governmental agency, and/or publishing company.

MANUSCRIPT TOPICS
Manuscript Topics indicates those subjects the journal emphasizes.

MANUSCRIPT GUIDELINES/COMMENTS
Manuscript Guidelines/Comments provides information on the journal's objectives, style and format for references and footnotes that the editor expects the author to follow in preparing his manuscript for submission.

How the Directory Helps You Publish

Although individuals must communicate their ideas in writing, the *Directory* helps the author determine which journal will most likely accept the manuscript. In making this decision, it is important to compare the characteristics of your manuscript and the needs of each journal. The following table provides a framework for making this comparison.

Information Provided by the Directory for Each Journal	Manuscript Characteristics
Topic(s) of Articles Manuscript Guidelines	Theme
Acceptance Rate Percentage of Invited Articles	Significance of Theme
Type of Reader	Methodology and Style
Circulation Review Process	Prestige
Number of Reviewers Availability of Reviewers Comments Time Required for Reviewer	Results of Review

This framework will help the author determine a small number of journals that will be interested in publishing the manuscript. The *Directory* can assist the author in determining these journals, yet a set of unwritten and written laws prevent simultaneous submission of a manuscript to more than one journal. However, a manuscript can be sent to another journal in the event of a rejection by any one publication.

Furthermore, copyright laws and editorial policy of a given publication often require the author to choose only one journal. Consequently, some journals will require the author to sign a statement indicating the manuscript is not presently under review by another publication.

Publication of the manuscript in the proceedings of a professional association does not prevent the author from sending it to a journal, however there usually are some restrictions attached. Most professional associations require that the author acknowledge the presentation of the manuscript at the associate meeting.

Since the author is limited to submission of a manuscript to only one journal and the review process for each journal requires a long period of time, contacting the editors of the journals may help the author determine the journal most likely to publish the manuscript.

To interest the editor the author should provide the following information:
- Topic, major idea or conclusion of the manuscript
- The subject sample, research setting conceptual framework, methodology type of organization or location
- The reasons why the author thinks the journal's readers would be interested in your proposed article
- Asks the editor to make comments or suggestions on the usefulness of this type of article to the journal

While contacting the editor is helpful in selecting a journal that will be likely to publish the manuscript, the author could use the *Directory* and the framework presented to develop a set of journals which would be likely to publish the manuscript.

Relating the Theme of the Manuscript to the Topics of Articles Published by Each Journal

To begin the processes of choosing editors to contact and/or submitting a manuscript, the author needs to examine the similarity between the theme of the manuscript and the editor's needs. The *Directory* describes these needs by listing the topics each publication considers important and the manuscript guidelines. To find those journals that publish manuscripts in any particular area, refer to the topic index.

In attempting to classify the theme, the author should limit his choice to a single discipline. With the increasing specialization in the academic world, it is unlikely that reviewers, editors, or readers will understand an article that requires knowledge of two different disciplines. If these groups do not understand a manuscript, the journal will reject it.

If a manuscript emphasizes an interdisciplinary approach, it is important to decide who will be reading the article. The approach should be to explain the theoretical concepts of one discipline to the specialist in another discipline. The author should not attempt to resolve theoretical issues present in his discipline and explain their implications for specialists in another discipline.

Although the discipline classifications indicate the number of journals interested in your manuscript topic, the manuscript guidelines help the author determine the journals that will most likely have the greatest interest in the manuscript. The manuscript guidelines provide a detailed statement of the criteria for judging manuscripts, the editorial objectives, the readership and the journal's content and approach. This information makes it possible to determine more precisely the congruence between the manuscript and the type of articles the journal publishes. **The *Directory* contains the manuscript guidelines for a large number of journals.**

The Relationship Between the Journal's Acceptance Rate and Significance of the Theme of the Manuscript

In addition to determining the similarity between the topic of the manuscript and the topic of articles published by the journal, an examination of the significance of the theme to the discipline is also an important criterion in selecting a journal. The journals with the lowest acceptance rate will tend to publish those manuscripts that make the most significant contributions to the advancement of the discipline. Since these journals receive a large number of manuscripts, the editors distinguish those manuscripts likely to make a significant contribution to the reader's knowledge.

Defining newness or the contribution of any one study to the understanding of a discipline is difficult. However, it is possible to gain some insights into this definition by asking the following questions:

1. Is the author stating the existence of a variable, trend or problem, not previously recognized by the literature?

2. Is the author testing the interactions of a different set of variables or events?

3. Is the author presenting a new technique to cope with a problem or test an idea not previously presented in the literature?

4. Is the author using a subject sample with different characteristics than previously presented in the literature?

If the manuscript does not satisfy one of the first two categories, it is unlikely that a journal with a low acceptance rate will accept it for publication. Thus, the author should send the manuscript to those journals where the acceptance rate is higher.

Although the *Directory* provides the acceptance rates of manuscripts for many different journals, it is important to examine the data on percentage of invited articles for each journal. A high acceptance rate may result because the editor has asked leaders in the discipline to write articles on a particular subject. These invited articles are usually accepted. Since the author of an unsolicited manuscript competes with the leaders in the discipline, the manuscript will have to make a significant contribution to receive the editor's approval.

The Relationship of the Manuscript's Style and Methodology to the Journal's Readership

Another factor in selecting the journal to receive the manuscript is the journal's readership. The readers of each journal include businesspersons, academics and researchers or a combination of these groups.

Since the most important goal for an author is to publish the manuscript, the author should consider the prestige of the journal only after the manuscript has a relatively high probability of being published by more than one journal. This probability is determined by the responses the author received from contact with the editors and the similarity between the finished manuscript and the needs of the journal.

The method of determining the prestige of a journal varies depending on its readership, review process and acceptance rate. If the readership is primarily businesspersons, the author should request the editor provide a media package that would contain the journal's circulation and an average reader profile.

In contrast, the prestige of journals whose readership is primarily academic is determined by the review process, the acceptance rate and the journal's reputation. The review process should be a blind review with two or three reviewers and the acceptance rate should be low. In addition, the journal should posses a reputation for quality.

The Possible Results of the Review Process and the Selection of a Journal to Receive the Manuscript

Despite the fact that a journal with lower prestige would most likely publish the article, the author might be willing to take a chance on a journal with a greater amount of prestige. Since this will decrease the chances of manuscript acceptance, the author should also consider the consequences of rejection. The consequences include the knowledge the author will gain from having his manuscript rejected.

To determine the amount of knowledge the author is likely to gain requires consideration of the number of reviewers the journal uses in the review process, the availability of the reviewer's comments and the time required for the review process. If the journal makes the reviewer's comments available to the author, this provides a great learning opportunity. Also, the more people that review the manuscript, the greater the author's knowledge will be concerning how to improve the present manuscript. Hopefully, the author will transfer the knowledge gained from writing this manuscript to future manuscripts.

Should the review process take a small amount of time relative to a long period of time, the author is provided with a greater opportunity to use this knowledge to revise the manuscript. To assist the author in determining those journals that provide a suitable learning opportunity, each journal in the *Directory* includes information on the number of reviewers, availability of reviewer's comments to the author and time required for review.

Sending the Manuscript

Before sending the manuscript to an editor, the author should write a cover letter, make sure the manuscript is correctly typed, the format conforms to the journal's guidelines and the necessary copies have been included. **The author should always keep a copy of the manuscript.**

The cover letter that is sent with the manuscript makes it easy for the editor to select reviewers and monitor the manuscript while it is in the review process. This letter should include the title of the manuscript, the author name(s), mailing address(es) phone and fax number(s) and e-mail addresses. In addition, this letter should provide a brief description of the manuscript theme, its applicability and significance to the journal's readership. Finally it should request a copy of the reviewer's comments regardless of whether the manuscript is accepted or rejected.

Receipt of the Reviewer's Comments

The reviewers may still reject the article although the author may have followed this procedure and taken every precaution to avoid rejection. When this occurs, the author's attitude should be focused on making those changes that would make the manuscript more understandable to the next editor, and/or reviewer. These changes may include providing additional information and/or presenting the topic in a more concise manner. Also, the author needs to determine whether some error occurred in selecting the journal to receive the manuscript. Regardless of the source of the errors, the author needs to make those changes that will improve the manuscript's chances of being accepted by the next journal to receive it.

Unless the journal specifically requests the author to revise the manuscript for publication, the author should not send the manuscript to the journal that first rejected it. In rejecting the manuscript, the reviewers implied that it could not be revised to meet their standards for publication. Thus, sending it back to them would not improve the likelihood that the manuscript will be accepted.

If your manuscript is accepted, go out and celebrate but write another one very quickly. When you find you're doing something right, keep doing it so you won't forget.

"What is a Refereed Article?"

With some exceptions a refereed article is one that is blind reviewed and has two external reviewers. The blind review requirement and the use of external reviewers are consistent with the research criteria of objectivity and of knowledge.

The use of a blind review process means that the author of the manuscript is not made known to the reviewer. With the large number of reviewers and journals, it is also likely that the name of the reviewers for a particular manuscript is not made known to the author. Thus, creating a double blind review process. Since the author and reviewers are frequently unknown, the manuscript is judged on its merits rather than on the reputation of the author and/or the author's influence on the reviewers.

The use of two (2) reviewers permits specialists familiar with research similar to that presented in the paper to judge whether the paper makes a contribution to the advancement of knowledge. When two reviewers are used it provides a broader perspective for evaluating the research. This perspective is further widened by the discussion between the editor and reviewers in seeking to reconcile these perspectives.

In contrast to these criteria, some journals that have attained a reputation for quality do not use either a blind review process or external reviewers. The most notable is *Harvard Business Review* that uses an editorial review process. Its reputation for quality results from its readership whose continual subscription attests to its quality.

In addition to these criteria, some researchers include the journal's acceptance rate in their definition of a refereed journal. However, the method of calculating acceptance rates varies among journals. Some journals use all manuscripts received as a base for computing this rate. Other journals allow the editor to choose which papers are sent to reviewers and calculate the acceptance rate on those that are reviewed that is less than the total manuscripts received. Also, many editors do not maintain accurate records on this data and provide only a rough estimate.

Furthermore, the number of people associated with a particular area of specialization influences the acceptance rate. If only a few people can write papers in an area, it tends to increase the journal's acceptance rate.

Although the type of review process and use of external reviewers is one possible definition of a refereed article, it is not the only criteria. Judging the usefulness of a journal to the advancement of knowledge requires the reader to be familiar with many journals in their specialization and make their own evaluation.

Abacus

ADDRESS FOR SUBMISSION:

Graeme W. Dean, Editor
Abacus
University of Sydney
School of Business
Discipline of Accounting
Faculty of Economics and Business
Sydney, 2006
N.S.W. Australia
Phone: 61-02-9351-3107
E-Mail: g.dean@econ.usyd.edu.au
Web: www.blackwellpublishing.com

PUBLICATION GUIDELINES:

Manuscript Length: 16-20
Copies Required: Three
Computer Submission:
Format: MS Word
Fees to Review: 50.00 US$

Manuscript Style:
 See Manuscript Guidelines

CIRCULATION DATA:

Reader: Academics
Frequency of Issue:
Sponsor/Publisher: Accounting Foundation,
 Univ. of Sydney / Blackwell Publishing,
 Inc.

REVIEW INFORMATION:

Type of Review: Blind Review
No. of External Reviewers: 2
No. of In House Reviewers: 1
Acceptance Rate:
Time to Review: 4 - 6 Months
Reviewers Comments: Yes
Invited Articles: 0-5%
Fees to Publish: 0.00 US$

MANUSCRIPT TOPICS:
Accounting Education; Accounting Information Systems; Accounting Theory & Practice; Auditing; Behavioral Accounting; Cost Accounting; Government & Non Profit Accounting; Tax Accounting

MANUSCRIPT GUIDELINES/COMMENTS:

Aims and Scope
Since 1965 *Abacus* has consistently provided a vehicle for the expression of independent and critical thought on matters of current academic and professional interest in accounting, finance and business. The journal reports current research; critically evaluates current developments in theory and practice; analyses the effects of the regulatory framework of accounting, finance and business; and explores alternatives to, and explanations of, past and current practices.

Instructions for Authors
1. Submission of a paper will be held to imply that paper has not been previously published and is not under consideration for publication elsewhere. Papers accepted for publication become copyright of the Accounting Foundation and authors will be asked to sign a transfer of copyright form. In signing the transfer of copyright it is assumed that authors have obtained

permission to use any copyright or previously published material. All authors must read and agree to the conditions outlined in the Copyright Assignment Form and must sign the Form or agree that the corresponding author can sign on their behalf. Articles cannot be published until a signed Copyright Assignment Form has been received. Authors can download the Form from http://www.blackwellpublishing.com/pdf/abacus.caf.pdf.

2. Submit three copies of manuscript together with a submission fee of US$50 (cheque/money order payable to 'Abacus, University of Sydney' - this fee is waived if you are a subscriber to *Abacus*) to:

> Professor Graeme Dean
> Accounting & Business Law
> University of Sydney
> Sydney
> NSW 2006
> Australia
> Phone: +612 9351 3107; Fax: +612 9351 6638
> e-mail: **g.dean@econ.usyd.edu.au**

To download payment form, please visit our website. After the paper has been accepted authors should supply papers as formatted text on disk. The disk copy will be used for printing. Any word processing package must be specified on the disk.

After the paper has been accepted, authors should supply papers as formatted text on disk. Any word processing format is acceptable. The hardware and the word processing package must be specified on the disk.

3. Use opaque quarto paper (207mm x 260mm) or A4 (210mm x 297mm); double space text; leave adequate (30mm) margins on both sides.

4. Place name of author in BLOCK capitals above title of the article. Give author's present position at the foot of the first page.

5. Use footnotes sparingly. Place them at the end of the manuscript, double spaced with an extra line between entries. Number footnotes consecutively throughout the text; use superior numbers without point, thus: '...money'. [3] Cite books and articles in the text thus: ... (Jones, 1962, p. 21).

For page reference numbers use p. 21, pp. 423-32, pp. 406-571, but pp. 11-13, pp. 115-119.

6. List books and articles cited in alphabetical order at the end of the manuscript. When listing books and articles, use the following forms respectively: Jones, A., *Depreciation of Assets*, Publisher & Co., 1962. Morrissey, L., 'Intangible Costs' in Morton Backer (ed.), *Modern Accounting Theory*, Prentice-Hall, 1966. Revsine, L. and J. Weygandt, 'Accounting for Inflation: The Controversy', *Journal of Accountancy*, October 1974. Smith, B., 'An Aspect of Depreciation', *The Journal of Accounting*, August 1965. Do not use brackets; use short titles for publishers unless it is essential to tracing.

7. Underline what is to be printed in italics. Use BLOCK capitals only for what is to be printed in capitals. Use italics and BLOCK capitals sparingly. Use the smallest number of styles for section headings; preferably side headings, in italics.

8. For quotations within the text use only single quotation marks, and double marks for quotes within quotes. Where quotations exceed four lines inset quoted material three spaces, but do not use quotation marks.

9. Do not use a point in standard abbreviations such as CPA, SEC but use points in U.K., U.S.A., and similar abbreviations. Date style e.g. 19 February 1966.

10. Use double dashes (--) to indicate dashes in the text, single dashes (-) for hyphens.

11. Use 'z' for such words as capitalize; 's' for the smaller number of words such as advise, analyse, comprise, enterprise (see *Oxford English Dictionary*).

12. Use the simplest possible form for mathematical symbols.

13. Keep tables to a minimum, but do not try to convey too much information, at the cost of simplicity, in any one table.

14. For book reviews use the following form for headnotes:
A. JONES. *Depreciation*, Publisher & Co., London 1966, vii + 212 pp.

4

Academy of Accounting and Financial Studies Journal

ADDRESS FOR SUBMISSION:

Current Editor / Check Website
Academy of Accounting and Financial
   Studies Journal
Digital Submission Through Website
Address other questions to:
   Jim or JoAnn Carland at # below
USA
Phone: 828-293-9151
E-Mail: info@alliedacademies.org
Web: www.alliedacademies.org

PUBLICATION GUIDELINES:

Manuscript Length: 16-20
Copies Required: Submit Through Web
Computer Submission: Yes
Format: MS Word, WordPerfect
Fees to Review: 0.00 US$

Manuscript Style:
   American Psychological Association

CIRCULATION DATA:

Reader: Academics
Frequency of Issue: 2 Times/Year
Sponsor/Publisher: Allied Academies, Inc.

REVIEW INFORMATION:

Type of Review: Blind Review
No. of External Reviewers: 3
No. of In House Reviewers: 2
Acceptance Rate: 21-30%
Time to Review: 3-4 Months
Reviewers Comments: Yes
Invited Articles: 0-5%
Fees to Publish: 75.00 US$ Membership

MANUSCRIPT TOPICS:
Accounting Information Systems; Accounting Theory & Practice; Auditing; Cost Accounting; Finance; Government & Non Profit Accounting; International Finance; Investments; Portfolio & Security Analysis; Tax Accounting

MANUSCRIPT GUIDELINES/COMMENTS:

The journal publishes theoretical or empirical research on any of the Manuscript Topics.

Comments. All authors of published manuscripts must be members of the appropriate academy affiliate of Allied Academies. The current membership fee is $75.00.

Editorial Policy Guidelines. The primary criterion upon which manuscripts are judged is whether the research advances the discipline. Key points include currency, interest and relevancy.

In order for a theoretical manuscript to advance the discipline, it must address the literature to support conclusions or models which extend knowledge and understanding. Consequently, referees pay particular attention to completeness of literature review and appropriateness of conclusions drawn from the review.

In order for an empirical manuscript to advance the discipline, it must employ appropriate and effective sampling and statistical analysis techniques, and must be grounded by a thorough literature review. Consequently, referees pay particular attention to the research methodology and to the conclusions drawn from statistical analyses and their consistency with the literature.

Academy of Educational Leadership Journal

ADDRESS FOR SUBMISSION:

Current Editor / Check Website
Academy of Educational Leadership Journal
Digital Submission Through Website
Address other questions to:
    Jim or JoAnn Carland at # below
USA
Phone: 828-293-9151
E-Mail: info@alliedacademies.org
Web: www.alliedacademies.org

CIRCULATION DATA:

Reader: Academics
Frequency of Issue: 2 Times/Year
Sponsor/Publisher: Allied Academies, Inc.

PUBLICATION GUIDELINES:

Manuscript Length: 16-20
Copies Required: Submit Through Web
Computer Submission: Yes
Format: MS Word, WordPerfect
Fees to Review: 0.00 US$

Manuscript Style:
    American Psychological Association

REVIEW INFORMATION:

Type of Review: Blind Review
No. of External Reviewers: 3
No. of In House Reviewers: 2
Acceptance Rate: 21-30%
Time to Review: 3-4 Months
Reviewers Comments: Yes
Invited Articles: 0-5%
Fees to Publish: 75.00 US$ Membership

MANUSCRIPT TOPICS:
Accounting Education; Business Education; Education; Educational Research; Teaching or Pedagogy

MANUSCRIPT GUIDELINES/COMMENTS:

The journal publishes theoretical or empirical research concerning any of the Manuscript Topics.

Comments. All authors of published manuscripts must be members of the appropriate academy affiliate of Allied Academies. The current membership fee is $75.00 U.S.

Editorial Policy Guidelines. The primary criterion upon which manuscripts are judged is whether the research advances the art and science of teaching. Key points include currency relevance and usefulness to educators.

In order for a theoretical manuscript to advance the discipline, it must address the literature to support conclusions or models which extend knowledge and understanding. Consequently, referees pay particular attention to completeness of literature review and appropriateness of conclusions drawn from the review.

In order for an empirical manuscript to advance the discipline, it must employ appropriate and effective sampling and statistical analysis techniques, and must be grounded by a thorough literature review. Consequently, referees pay particular attention to the research methodology and to the conclusions drawn from statistical analyses and their consistency with the literature.

Accounting & Business

ADDRESS FOR SUBMISSION:

John Prosser, Editor
Accounting & Business
10 Lincoln's Inn Fields
London, WC2A 3RP
UK
Phone: 00 44 (0)207 059 5966
E-Mail: john.prosser@accaglobal.com
Web: www.accaglobal.com/publications

CIRCULATION DATA:

Reader: Business Persons
Frequency of Issue: 10 Times/Year
Sponsor/Publisher: Association of
Chartered Certified Accountants

PUBLICATION GUIDELINES:

Manuscript Length: 6-10
Copies Required: One
Computer Submission: Yes
Format: MS Word e-mail
Fees to Review: 0.00 US$

Manuscript Style:
American Psychological Association

REVIEW INFORMATION:

Type of Review: Blind Review
No. of External Reviewers: No Reply
No. of In House Reviewers: No Reply
Acceptance Rate: 21-30%
Time to Review: 1 Month or Less
Reviewers Comments: No
Invited Articles: 60-70%
Fees to Publish: 0.00 US$

MANUSCRIPT TOPICS:
Accounting Information Systems; Accounting Theory & Practice; Auditing; Cost Accounting; International Economics & Trade; International Finance; Small Business Entrepreneurship; Social & Environmental Accounting

MANUSCRIPT GUIDELINES/COMMENTS:

Accounting & Business is ACCA's professional magazine, which is sent to all members and affiliates and circulates widely within the international business and accountancy community. It addresses critical issues in international accountancy and business and contains the latest in news analysis and features.

Accounting and Business Research

ADDRESS FOR SUBMISSION:

K.V. Peasnell, Editor
Accounting and Business Research
University of Lancaster
Management School
Lancaster, LA1 4YX
UK
Phone: 44 0 1524 593977
E-Mail: k.peasnell@lancaster.ac.uk
Web: www.accountancymag.co.uk

PUBLICATION GUIDELINES:

Manuscript Length: No Limits
Copies Required: Four
Computer Submission: Yes
Format: N/A
Fees to Review: 0.00 US$

Manuscript Style:
See Manuscript Guidelines

CIRCULATION DATA:

Reader: Academics
Frequency of Issue: Quarterly
Sponsor/Publisher: Cronor CCH Group

REVIEW INFORMATION:

Type of Review: Blind Review
No. of External Reviewers: 2
No. of In House Reviewers: 0
Acceptance Rate: 11-20%
Time to Review: 2 - 3 Months
Reviewers Comments: Yes
Invited Articles: 0%
Fees to Publish: 0.00 US$

MANUSCRIPT TOPICS:
Accounting Education; Accounting Information Systems; Accounting Theory & Practice; Auditing; Behavioral Accounting; Cost Accounting; Government & Non Profit Accounting; Tax Accounting

MANUSCRIPT GUIDELINES/COMMENTS:

General
Papers should be in English and consist of original unpublished work not currently being considered for publication elsewhere. They should be typed and double-spaced. **Four** copies should be submitted, together with a submission fee of £18 for subscribers or £36 for non-subscribers. In order to ensure an anonymous review, authors should not identify themselves, directly or indirectly. Experience has shown that papers that have already benefited from critical comment from colleagues at seminars or at conferences have a much better chance of acceptance. Where the research takes the form of field surveys or experiments, **four** copies of the instrument should be submitted. Where the paper shares data with another paper, **four** copies of the other paper must also be provided.

Submission Fee
A submission fee must accompany each paper submitted to *ABR*, except in the case of a resubmitted version of a previously submitted manuscript. The fee is £36, reduced to £18 where one or more of the authors is a personal subscriber to *ABR*.

Alternatively, the fee can be paid in advance in US dollars, $75 for non-subscribers and $37.50 for subscribers, or in other countries at the equivalent exchange value to the appropriate dollar amount. The submission fee should be paid by check or draft made payable to *Accounting and Business Research*. Payment cannot be made by credit card.

Presentation
A cover page should show the title of the paper, the author's name, title and affiliation, and any acknowledgements. The title of the paper, but not the author's name, should appear on the first page of the text. An abstract of 150-250 words should be provided on a separate page immediately preceding the text. Section headings should be numbered using Arabic numerals.

Tables and Figures
Each table and figure should bear an Arabic number and a title and should be referred to in the text. Sources should be clearly stated. Sufficient details should be provided in the heading and body of each table and figure to reduce to a minimum the need for cross-referencing by readers to other parts of the manuscript. Tables and figures should appear at the end of the paper, with its most appropriate placing noted in the paper itself. Diagrams and charts should be submitted in camera-ready form.

Footnotes
Footnotes should be used only in order to avoid interrupting the continuity of the text, and should not be used to excess. They should be numbered consecutively throughout the manuscript with superscript Arabic numerals. They should not be used in book reviews.

References
References should be listed at the end of the paper and referred to in the text as, for example, (Zefl, 1980: 24). Wherever appropriate, the reference should include a page or chapter number in the journal or book in question. Only works cited in the paper should be included in the list. Citations to institutional works should if possible employ acronyms or short titles. If an author's name is mentioned in the text it need not be repeated in the citation, e.g. 'Tippett and Whittington (1995: 209) state...'

In the list of references, titles of journals should omit an initial 'The' but should not otherwise be abbreviated. The entries should be arranged in alphabetical order by surname of the first author. Multiple works by the same author should be listed in chronological order of publication. Some examples are:

Accounting Standards Steering Committee (1975). *The Corporate Report*. London: ASC.
Tippett, M. and Whittington, G. (1995). 'An empirical evaluation of an induced theory of financial ratios'. *Accounting and Business Research*, 25 (Summer): 208-218.
Watts, R. L. and Zimmerman, J. L. (1986). *Positive Accounting Theory*. Englewood Cliffs, NJ: Prentice-Hall.

Style, Spelling and Notation

Abbreviations of institutional names should be written as, for example, FASB and not F.A.S.B; those of Latin terms should contain stops (thus i.e. not ie). Words such as 'realise' should be spelled with an 's' not a 'z'. Single quotations marks should be used, not double. Mathematical notation should be used only where it adds rigour and precision, and should be properly explained in the text. Equations should be numbered in parentheses, flush with the right-hand margin.

Accounting and Finance

ADDRESS FOR SUBMISSION:

Robert Faff, Editor
Accounting and Finance
Monash University
Department of Accounting and Finance
Building 11
Victoria, 3800
Australia
Phone: +61 3 9905 2387
E-Mail: robert.faff@buseco.monash.edu.au
Web: www.aaanz.org/afaanz_pub.htm

PUBLICATION GUIDELINES:

Manuscript Length: 26-30
Copies Required: One
Computer Submission: Yes Email
Format: Ms Word, PDF
Fees to Review: 90.00 US$

Manuscript Style:

CIRCULATION DATA:

Reader: Academics
Frequency of Issue: 4 Times/Year
Sponsor/Publisher: Accounting and Finance
    Association of Australia and New
    Zealand

REVIEW INFORMATION:

Type of Review: Blind Review
No. of External Reviewers: 2
No. of In House Reviewers: 0
Acceptance Rate: 21-30%
Time to Review: 1 - 2 Months
Reviewers Comments: Yes
Invited Articles: 0-5%
Fees to Publish: 0.00 US$

MANUSCRIPT TOPICS:

Accounting Education; Accounting Information Systems; Accounting Theory & Practice; Auditing; Econometrics; Financial Services; Government & Non Profit Accounting; Insurance; International Finance; Portfolio & Security Analysis; Real Estate; Tax Accounting

MANUSCRIPT GUIDELINES/COMMENTS:

Aims and Scope

This established journal publishes theoretical, empirical and experimental papers which significantly contribute to the disciplines of accounting and finance. Using a wide range of research methods including statistical analysis, analytical work, case studies, field research and historical analysis, articles examine significant research questions from a broad range of perspectives. Accounting and Finance applies economic, organizational and other theories to accounting and finance phenomena and publishes occasional special issues on themes such as on research methods in management accounting.

Accounting and Finance is essential reading for academics, graduate students and all those interested in research in accounting and finance. The journal is also widely read by practitioners in accounting, corporate finance, investments and merchant and investment banking.

Instructions to Authors
1. Electronic submission to the Editor, Professor Robert Faff, is required via email. Submission of a manuscript implies that it contains original unpublished work and is not submitted for publication elsewhere.

Please note the following:
* Electronic submissions can be in WORD or 'pdf' format.
* Submission email address is: **Robert.Faff@buseco.monash.edu.au**
* The submission fee ($132AUD), together with a photocopy of the submission letter sent to the Editor, should be posted directly to Effie Margiolis: Effie Margiolis, Executive Director, AFAANZ, GPO Box 2820 AA, Melbourne Vic 3001

Alternatively, three copies of the manuscript should be sent to:
Professor Robert Faff, Editor, /Accounting and Finance/, Department of Accounting and Finance, Monash University, PO Box 11E, Victoria, 3800, Australia.

2. Manuscripts should be double spaced, with wide margins, and printed on one side of the paper only. All pages should be numbered consecutively.

3. Titles and subtitles should be short. An example of these follows:
1. **Introduction**
2. **Theoretical background and hypothesis**
3. **Empirical tests**
   1. *Sample selection*
   2. *Measurement of variables*
4. **Results**
   1. *Univariate tests*
   2. *Multivariate tests*
5. **Summary and conclusions**

4. The first page of the manuscript should contain the following information: (i) the title; (ii) the name(s) and institutional affiliation(s) of the author(s); (iii) an abstract of not more than 100 words; (iv) a footnote giving the name, address, telephone number, fax number, and E-mail address of the corresponding author; (v) at least one classification code according to the Classification System for Journal Articles as used by the *Journal of Economic Literature*; (vi) up to five key words; (vii) a footnote of acknowledgments which should not be included in the consecutive numbering of footnotes.

5. Footnotes should be kept to a minimum and numbered consecutively throughout the text with superscript Arabic numerals. They should not include displayed formulae or tables.

6. Displayed formulae should be numbered consecutively throughout the manuscript as (1), (2), etc. against the right-hand margin of the page. Letters used as symbols should be set in italics unless they represent vector quantities in which case they should be bold. Do not use bold or italics for numerals and abbreviations for math functions (such as ln, S). Use italics for names of statistical tests (such as t-statistics, t-test, $t = 4.68$, F-test).

14

7. References to publications should be as follows: "Jones (1992)suggests that ..." or "This problem was noted earlier (see Smith,1990; Jones, 1992; Black and Cook 1990)" or "There are 128 companies using this accounting method (Green, 1995 p. 38)".

8. The list of references should appear at the end of the main text (after appendices, but before tables and figures). It should be double spaced and listed in alphabetical order. References should appear as follows:

For periodicals. Eddey, P.H., K.W. Lee, and S.L. Taylor, 1996, What motivates going private? An analysis of Australian firms, Accounting and Finance 36, 31-50.

For monographs. Cox, J.C. and M.Rubenstein, 1985, Options markets (Prentice-Hall, Englewood Cliffs, NJ).

For contributions to collective works. Nobes, C.W., 1988, The causes of financial reporting difficulties, in C.W. Nobes and R.H. Parker, eds., Issues in multinational accounting (Ethan Allan, Oxford) 29-42.

For working papers. Chua, W.F., B.K. Sidhu, and G.P. Whittred, 1985, The impact of industry regulation, taxation and corporate strategy on accounting method choice - Cash vs accrual accounting for tobacco licence fees, Working paper (University of New South Wales, Sydney, NSW).

For conference papers. Guilding, C., 1996, A contingency study of the adoption of competitor-focused accounting, Paper presented at AANZ Annual Conference, Christchurch.

9. Tables and figures should be numbered consecutively in the text in Arabic numerals and printed on separate sheets.

10. A submission fee (fee amount listed on website) is required per manuscript for a contributor who is not a member of AFAANZ (overseas contributors to send a bank draft in Australian currency). Cheques should be made payable to the Accounting Association of Australia and New Zealand.

11. If a manuscript is accepted for publication the author is requested to provide a copy of the paper on a 3.5 inch disk (preferably a Microsoft WORD file) as well as a printed copy. Data should be supplied so that figures can be reproduced using DeltaGraph.

Any manuscript which does not conform to the above instructions may be returned for the necessary revision before publication.

Page proofs will be sent to the corresponding author. Proofs should be corrected carefully; the responsibility for detecting errors lies with the author.

Accounting and the Public Interest

ADDRESS FOR SUBMISSION:

Jesse F. Dillard, Editor
Accounting and the Public Interest
Portland State University
School of Business
Portland, OR
USA
Phone: 503-725-2278
E-Mail: jdillard@pdx.edu
Web: http://aaahq.org/ic/browse.htm

PUBLICATION GUIDELINES:

Manuscript Length: 26-30
Copies Required: Electronic
Computer Submission: Yes Disk or Email
Format: MS Word
Fees to Review: 15.00 US$

Manuscript Style:
    Chicago Manual of Style

CIRCULATION DATA:

Reader: Academics
Frequency of Issue: Yearly / Ongoing
    Postings
Sponsor/Publisher: Public Interest Section
    of the American Accounting Association

REVIEW INFORMATION:

Type of Review: Blind Review
No. of External Reviewers: 2
No. of In House Reviewers: 0
Acceptance Rate: 11-20%
Time to Review: 1 - 2 Months
Reviewers Comments: Yes
Invited Articles: 0-5%
Fees to Publish: 0.00 US$

MANUSCRIPT TOPICS:

Accounting and the Public Interest; Accounting History; Accounting Information Systems; Accounting Theory & Practice; Auditing; Cost Accounting; Ethics; Gender & Diversity; Tax Accounting

MANUSCRIPT GUIDELINES/COMMENTS:

Editorial Policy and Style Information

Accounting and the Public Interest is an academic journal published by the Public Interest Section of the American Accounting Association. The journal, envisioned as innovative and eclectic, welcomes alternative theories and methodologies as well as the more traditional ones. The common element in this diversity is the requirement that the study and its findings be linked to the public interest by situating them within the historical, social, and political context, and ultimately providing guidance for responsible action. Responsible action can be promoted through research in all areas of accounting including, but not restricted to:

- financial accounting and auditing,
- accounting in organizations,
- social and environmental accounting,
- government and professional regulation,
- taxation,
- gender and diversity issues,

- professional and business ethics,
- information technology,
- accounting and business education, and
- governance of accounting organizations

Theoretical and empirical contributions, as well as literature reviews synthesizing the state of the art in specific areas are considered appropriate. Replications and reinterpretations of previous work will also be considered. This editorial policy intends to provide a publication outlet for accounting research taking a socially responsive, and responsible, perspective.

Review Process
Each manuscript submitted to *Accounting and the Public Interest* is subject to the following review procedures:
1. The manuscript is screened by the editor for general suitability.
2. If the manuscript passes the initial editorial screening, it will be blind-reviewed by at least two peer reviewers.
3. In light of the reviewers' recommendations, a decision will be made by the editor as to whether the article will be accepted as is, revised, or rejected. It is anticipated that the decision will be communicated to the author within four to six weeks after submission.
4. The process described above is a general one. The editor may, in some circumstances, vary this process at his or her discretion. Through its constructive and responsive editorial procedures, the journal aims to render research efforts relevant and rewarding for all concerned.

Submission Requirements
Manuscripts are expected to be original research that has not been previously published or not currently under review by another journal. If measurement instruments (questionnaires, case, interview plan, etc.) have been developed by the authors and are an integral part of the study, copies should be included with the manuscript. Manuscripts are to be submitted via email to **jdillard@pdx.edu** or mailed on a 3½-inch disk to the Editor. MS Word files are preferred. There is no submission fee for Public Interest Section members. A nonrefundable $15 fee will be charged to non-section members. AAA members may choose to have the fee applied toward section membership dues that are coincidentally $15/year. (The submission fee [membership fee] may be paid online to AAA or posted to the above address regardless of the method of manuscript submission. Checks are to be made out to Public Interest Section—AAA.) Please indicate how the submission fee requirement has been satisfied. Revisions must be submitted within 12 months from notification; otherwise the manuscript will be considered a new submission.

Style
Accounting and the Public Interest's manuscript preparation guidelines follow (with a slight modification) the B-format of *The Chicago Manual of Style* (14th ed.: University of Chicago Press). Another helpful guide to usage and style is *The Elements of Style*, William Strunk, Jr. and E. White (Macmillan). Spelling follows *Webster's International Dictionary*.

Format
1. All manuscripts should be double-spaced, except for indented quotations.
2. Manuscripts should be as concise as the subject matter and research method permit.
3. Margin settings should provide for at least 1-inch top, side, and bottom margins.
4. A cover page should include the title of the paper, the author's name, title and affiliation, any acknowledgments, and a footnote indicating whether the author is willing to share the data (see policy statement below).
5. All pages, including tables, appendices, and references, should be serially numbered.
6. Spell out numbers from one to ten, except when used in tables and lists, and when used with mathematical, statistical, scientific, or technical units and quantities, such as distances, weights, and measures. For example: *three days; 3 kilometers; 30 years.* All other numbers are expressed numerically.
7. In non-technical copy use the word *percent* in the text.
8. Use a hyphen to join unit modifiers or to clarify usage. For example: *a well-presented analysis; re-form.* See *Webster's* for correct usage.
9. Equations should be numbered in parentheses flush with the right-hand margin.
10. Headings should be arranged so that major headings are centered, bold, and capitalized. Second level headings should be flush left, bold, and both upper and lowercase. Third level headings should be flush left, bold, italic, and both upper and lower case. Fourth level headings should be paragraph indent, bold, and lower case. For example:

First Level Heading

Second Level Heading
Third Level Heading
    Fourth level heading. Text starts....

Abstract
An abstract of 100-200 words should be presented on a separate page immediately preceding the text. The Abstract should concisely inform the reader of the manuscript's topic, its method, and its conclusions. The Abstract is to be followed by four key words that will help in indexing the paper.

Tables and Figures
The author should note the following general requirements:
- Each table and figure (graphic) should bear an Arabic number and a complete title indicating the exact context of the table or figure.
- A reference to each graphic should be made in the text.
- Graphics should be reasonably interpretable without reference to the text.
- Source lines and notes should be included as necessary.

Documentation
Citations. Work cited should use the "author-date system" keyed to a list of works in the reference list (see below). Authors should make an effort to include the relevant page numbers in the cited works.

In the text, works are cited as follows: author's last name and date, without comma, in parentheses: for example, (Jones 1987), with two authors: (Jones and Freeman 1973); with

18

more than two: (Jones et al. 1985); with more than one source cited (Jones 1987; Freeman 1986); with two or more works by one author (Jones 1985, 1987).

Unless confusion would result, do not use "p." or "pp." before page numbers: for example (Jones 1987, 115).

When the reference list contains more than one work of an author published in the same year, the suffix a, b, etc. follows the date in the text citation: for example (Jones 1987a).

If the author's name is mentioned in the text, it need not be repeated in the citation: for example, "Jones (1987, 115) says....

Citations to institutional works should use acronyms or short titles where practicable: for example, AAA ASOBAT 1966; AICPA Cohen Commission Report 1977. Where brief, the full title of the institutional work might be shown in a citation: for example, ICAEW *The Corporate Report* 1975.

If the manuscript refers to statutes, legal treaties, or court cases, citations acceptable in law reviews should be used.

Reference list. Every manuscript must include a list of references containing only those works cited. Each entry should contain the data necessary for unambiguous identification. With the author-date system, use the following format recommended by *The Chicago Manual of Style*:
1. Arrange citations in alphabetical order according to surname of the first author or the name of the institution responsible for the citation.
2. Use the author's initials instead of proper names.
3. Date of publication should be placed immediately after the author's name.
4. Titles of journals should not be abbreviated.
5. Multiple works by the same author(s) in the same year are distinguished by letters after the date.

Sample entries are as follows:
American Accounting Association, Committee on Concepts and Standards for External Financial Reports. 1977. *Statement on Accounting Theory and Theory Acceptance.* Sarasota, FL: AAA.
Becker, H., and D. Fritsche. 1987. Business ethics: A cross-cultural comparison of managers' attitudes. *Journal of Business Ethics* 6: 289-295.
Bowman, R. 1980a. The importance of market-value measurement of debt in assessing leverage. 18 (Spring): 617-630
———. 1980b. The debt equivalence of leases: An empirical investigation. *The Accounting Review* 55 (April): 237-253.
Harry, J., and N. Goldner. 1972. The null relationship between teaching and research. *Sociology of Education* 45 (1): 47-60.
Hopwood, A., and P. Miller, eds. 1994. *Accounting as Social and Institutional Practice.* Cambridge, U.K.: Cambridge University Press.

Jensen, M., and C. Smith. 1985. Stockholder, manager, and creditor interests: Applications of agency theory. In *Recent Advances in Corporate Finance*, edited by E. Altman, and M. Subrahmanyam. Homewood, IL: Richard D. Irwin.

Munn, G., F. Garcia, and C. Woelfel, eds. 1991. *Encyclopedia of Banking and Finance.* 9th edition. Chicago, IL: St. James Press.

Murray, F. 1991. Technical rationality and the IS specialists: Power, discourse and identity. *Critical Perspectives on Accounting.* (March): 59-81.

Yuthas, K. 1996. Structuration theory and business ethics: Integration and emergence. Working paper, University of New Mexico.

Footnotes. Footnotes are not to be used for documentation. Textual footnotes should be used for extensions and useful excursions of information that if included in the body of the text might disrupt its continuity. Footnotes should be consecutively numbered throughout the manuscript with superscript Arabic numerals.

Policy on Reproduction

An objective of *Accounting and the Public Interest* is to promote wide dissemination of the results of scholarly inquiries into the broad field of accounting. Permission is hereby granted to reproduce any of the contents of *Accounting and the Public Interest* for use in courses of instruction as long as the source and the Public Interest Section as a member of the American Accounting Association copyright are indicated in any such reproductions. Written application must be made to the Editor for permission to reproduce any of the contents of *Accounting and the Public Interest* for use in other than courses of instruction—e.g., inclusion in books of readings or in any other such instances, the applicant must notify the author(s) in writing of the intended use of each reproduction. Normally, a charge will not be assessed for the waiver of copyright.

Except as otherwise noted in articles, the copyright has been transferred to the Public Interest Section of the American Accounting Association for all items appearing in this journal. Where the author(s) has (have) not transferred the copyright to the Public Interest Section of the American Accounting Association, applicants must seek permission to reproduce (for all purposes) directly from the author(s).

Policy on Data Availability

The following policy, adopted by the American Accounting Association, is applicable to all manuscripts submitted to *Accounting and the Public Interest.*

...authors are encouraged to make their data available for use by others.... Authors of articles that report data should footnote the status of data availability and, when pertinent, this should be accompanied by information on how the data may be obtained.

Accounting Education: An International Journal

ADDRESS FOR SUBMISSION:

Richard M. S. Wilson, Editor
Accounting Education: An International
    Journal
Loughborough University Business School
Loughborough
Leicestershire, LE11 3TU
UK
Phone: +44 1509 223120
E-Mail: r.m.wilson@lboro.ac.uk
Web: www.tandf.co.uk

PUBLICATION GUIDELINES:

Manuscript Length: 21-25
Copies Required: Four or Online
Computer Submission: Yes
Format: N/A
Fees to Review: 0.00 US$

Manuscript Style:
    See Manuscript Guidelines

CIRCULATION DATA:

Reader: Academics
Frequency of Issue: Quarterly
Sponsor/Publisher: Routledge (Taylor &
    Francis Ltd.)

REVIEW INFORMATION:

Type of Review: Blind Review
No. of External Reviewers: 3
No. of In House Reviewers: 2
Acceptance Rate: 21-30%
Time to Review: 2 - 3 Months
Reviewers Comments: Yes
Invited Articles: 0-5%
Fees to Publish: 0.00 US$

MANUSCRIPT TOPICS:
Accounting Education; Pedagogic Innovations; Teaching Resources

MANUSCRIPT GUIDELINES/COMMENTS:

Accounting Education: an international journal is the official education journal of the International Association for Accounting and Education Research (IAAER).

Aims and Scope
Accounting Education is a quarterly international journal devoted to publishing research-based papers and other information on key aspects of accounting education and training of relevance to practitioners, academics, trainers, students and professional bodies.

It is a forum for the exchange of ideas, experiences, opinions and research results relating to (a) the preparation of students/trainees for careers in public accounting, managerial accounting, financial management, corporate accounting, controllership, treasury management, financial analysis, internal auditing, and accounting in government and other non-commercial organizations; and (b) the continuing professional education of practitioners.

The coverage includes aspects of accounting education and training policy, curriculum issues, computing matters, and accounting research as it impinges on educational or training issues.

The journal seeks to make available innovative teaching resource material that can be used by readers in their own institutions. As a necessary corollary to this, the journal seeks to publish papers dealing with the effectiveness of accounting education or training.

In addition to publishing original papers the journal also includes exemplars and reviews relating to what we teach, how we teach it, and how effective our endeavours are in providing an adequate educational and training base for accounting practice.

Instructions for Authors
Note to Authors. Please make sure your contact address information is clearly visible on the **outside** of all packages you are sending to Editors.

Submission of papers
Manuscripts should be submitted (4 copies) with original figures to: Professor Richard M.S. Wilson. Loughborough University Business School, Loughborough, Leicestershire LE11 3TU, UK (Tel: +44 (0) 1509 223120: Fax: +44 (0) 1509 223991 Email: **R.M.Wilson@LBORO.ac.uk**). Submission of manuscripts online is encouraged. These should be prepared using a standard word processing package. Four printed copies are to be supplied with the disc and should match their contents exactly. All submissions will be subject to refereeing by experts in the field. There is no submission fee and no page charges. Only papers receiving favourable recommendations from the referees will be accepted for publication.

The Editor will be pleased to deal with enquiries from potential authors about papers they may be considering writing or submitting to *Accounting Education*. However, comments will not be given on drafts that have not been formally submitted.

MANUSCRIPT PREPARATION
Format and style
Manuscripts should be in English and typed (double-spaced) with a generous margin (at least 2.5 cm) at each edge of each page on one side of international A4 bond paper.

The first page (title page) should contain the title of the paper, authors' names and institutional affiliations. The address, telephone number, fax number, telex number and E-mail address (if available) of the author to whom decisions, proofs and offprints should be sent should also be given.

Authors should enclose a brief biographical outline with their submissions.

Abstract
The second page should include the papers title and an abstract (up to 150 words). The abstract should be an accurate representation of the papers contents. Major results, conclusions, and/or recommendations should be given with brief details of methods, etc.

There should be no indication (other than on the title page) of the identity of the author(s) or the authors (or authors) affiliations.

Keywords
Up to six keywords or descriptors that clearly describe the subject matter of the paper should be provided. These keywords will facilitate indexing as well as help in describing the subject matter for prospective readers.

References
Citations in the text should follow the Harvard scheme (i.e. name(s) of author(s) followed by the year of publication and page numbers where relevant, all in parenthesis). Where a source has more than two authors cite the first authors name and et al. For multiple citations in the same year use a, b and c immediately following the year of publication.

The reference section should only contain references cited in the text. These should be arranged in alphabetical order by surname of the first author (then chronologically). Each reference should contain full bibliographic details: journal titles should not be abbreviated. The following style is expected:

Gee, K.P. and Gray, R.H. (eds) (1990) The British Accounting Review Research Register. London: Academic Press. Novin A.M., Pearson, M.A. and Senge, S.V. (1990) Improving the curriculum for aspiring management accountants: the practitioners point of view. Journal of **Accounting Education** 6 (2) Fall, 207Ð24.

Walsh, A.I. (1988) The making of the chartered accountant. In D. Rowe (ed.) The Irish Chartered Accountant, pp. 155Ð73. Dublin: Gill and Macmillan.

Figures and tables
All figures and tables should be given titles, numbered consecutively in Arabic numerals, and referred to within the text. Labelling should be clear and of sufficient size to be legible after any necessary reduction. Lettering on line figures should usually be prepared with a 2:1 reduction in mind.

Permission to reproduce illustrations from other published work must be obtained by the author before submitting an article and any acknowledgement should be included in the figure captions.

Tables should be titled, numbered consecutively and independently of any figures, and referred to within the text.

Acknowledgements
Should appear at the end of the paper before the list of references.

Footnotes
Should be kept to a minimum and appear at the end of the paper on a separate page.

Mathematical notation

Mathematics should only be used if this contributes significantly to the clarity and economy of presentation, or is essential to the argument of a paper. Whenever possible authors should put mathematics in an appendix. The conclusions of articles using mathematics should be summarized in a form that is intelligible to non-mathematical readers of the Journal.

Early Electronic Offprints. Corresponding authors can now receive their article by e-mail as a complete PDF. This allows the author to print up to 50 copies, free of charge, and disseminate them to colleagues. In many cases this facility will be available up to two weeks prior to publication. Or, alternatively, corresponding authors will receive the traditional 50 offprints. A copy of the journal will be sent by post to all corresponding authors after publication. Additional copies of the journal can be purchased at the author's preferential rate of £15.00/$25.00 per copy.

Copyright matters

Manuscripts will only be considered for *Accounting Education* if they are unpublished and not being submitted for publication elsewhere. If previously published tables, illustrations or text exceeding 200 words are to be included then the copyright holders written permission should be obtained, and included with the submission. A clear statement should appear in the text if any material has been published elsewhere in a preliminary form.

Authors submitting articles with a view to publication warrant that the work is not an infringement of any existing copyright and agree to indemnify the publisher against any breach of such warranty.

Upon acceptance of a paper by *Accounting Education* the author(s) will be asked to transfer copyright, via a supplied form, to the publisher.

A fuller version of the notes for contributors can be obtained from the publisher's website.

Accounting Educator's Journal

ADDRESS FOR SUBMISSION:

Mark E. Friedman, Editor
Accounting Educator's Journal
University of Miami
Department of Accounting
301 Kossar/Epstein
5250 University Drive
Coral Gables, FL 33146-6531
USA
Phone: 305-284-6296
E-Mail: markfriedman@miami.edu
Web:

PUBLICATION GUIDELINES:

Manuscript Length: 11-15
Copies Required: Electronic
Computer Submission: Yes
Format: MS Word, pdf
Fees to Review: 40.00 US$

Manuscript Style:
    See Manuscript Guidelines

CIRCULATION DATA:

Reader: Academics
Frequency of Issue: 2 Times/Year
Sponsor/Publisher: Academy of Accounting
    Educators

REVIEW INFORMATION:

Type of Review: Blind Review
No. of External Reviewers: 2
No. of In House Reviewers: 0
Acceptance Rate: 21-30%
Time to Review: 2 - 3 Months
Reviewers Comments: Yes
Invited Articles: 0-5%
Fees to Publish: 0.00 US$

MANUSCRIPT TOPICS:
Accounting Education; Accounting Information Systems; Accounting Theory & Practice

MANUSCRIPT GUIDELINES/COMMENTS:

Editorial Policies
The *Accounting Educators' Journal* (*AEJ*) is a refereed academic journal intended to promote excellence in accounting education. The primary purpose of the journal is to provide a forum for accounting educators to communicate matters relevant to the design, delivery, and assessment of the accounting education process. The journal is particularly receptive to research that challenges and provides alternatives to existing approaches of identifying, measuring, and evaluating the outcomes of the classroom experience. The journal invites work that will enhance the capabilities of accounting educators to prepare students to enter and successfully remain in the complex, dynamic, and ever changing accounting profession.

The *AEJ* publishes a variety of intellectual work:
• findings of basic and applied research

- effective and innovative curriculum strategies, methods and techniques - including cases, software solutions and
- commentary, reports, descriptive studies, literature reviews, book reviews and software reviews as warrant

Editorial Procedures

Manuscripts will be evaluated by members of the editorial review board, under the direction of the Editor and the Associate Editors

Manuscript Guidelines/Comments

1. Manuscripts should include a cover page which indicates the author's name, address, affiliation and any acknowledgements. The author should not be identified anywhere else in the manuscript.

2. Manuscripts should include on a separate lead page an abstract not exceeding 150 words.

3. Topical headings should be in caps and centered. Subheadings should be flush with the left margin, underlined, and not in caps. Headings and subheadings should not be numbered.

4. Tables, figures, and exhibits should appear on separate pages. Each should be numbered and have a title.

5. Footnotes and references should appear at the end of the manuscript. However, every effort should be made to incorporate material into the body of the paper. The list of references should include only works actually cited.

Data Availability

Authors of manuscripts which are based on data analysis are encouraged to make data available to others interested in replicating or extending research in the area. Data-based manuscripts should include a reference or footnote describing the status of data availability and if available, the means by which the data may be obtained.

Reproduction

Permission is granted to reproduce any of the contents of *The Accounting Educators' Journal* for classroom use by individual subscribers. Please indicate the source and our copyright on any reproductions.

Written permission is required to reproduce any of these copyrighted materials in other media.

Accounting Forum

ADDRESS FOR SUBMISSION:

Glen Lehman, Editor
Accounting Forum
University of South Australia
School of Accounting
GPO Box 2471
Adelaide, SA 5001
Australia
Phone: 61-8-83020293
E-Mail: glen.lehman@unisa.edu.au
Web: www.elsevier.com

PUBLICATION GUIDELINES:

Manuscript Length: 16-20
Copies Required: Four
Computer Submission: No
Format:
Fees to Review: 0.00 US$

Manuscript Style:
    Chicago Manual of Style

CIRCULATION DATA:

Reader: Academics, Business Persons
Frequency of Issue: Quarterly
Sponsor/Publisher: Elsevier Inc.

REVIEW INFORMATION:

Type of Review: Blind Review
No. of External Reviewers: 2
No. of In House Reviewers: 0
Acceptance Rate: 11-20%
Time to Review: 2 - 3 Months
Reviewers Comments: Yes
Invited Articles: 0-5%
Fees to Publish: 0.00 US$

MANUSCRIPT TOPICS:
Accounting Theory & Practice

MANUSCRIPT GUIDELINES/COMMENTS:

Description

Accounting Forum publishes authoritative yet accessible articles which advance our knowledge of theory and practice in all areas of accounting, business finance and related subjects The journal both promotes greater understanding of the role of business in the global environment, and provides a forum for the intellectual exchange of academic research in business fields, particularly in the accounting profession. Covering a range of topical issues in accounting, business finance and related field, *Accounting Forum's* main areas of interest are: accounting theory; auditing; financial accounting; finance and accounting education; management accounting; small business; social and environmental; and taxation. Of equal interest to practitioners, academics, and students, each issue of the journal includes peer-reviewed articles, notes and comments, and an invaluable book review section.

GUIDE FOR AUTHORS

Submission of Papers. Authors in Australia, the UK and Australasia, please send your original manuscript to Glen Lehman, Editor, Accounting Forum, School of Accounting, University of South Australia, GPO Box 2471, Adelaide SA 5001, Australia (e-mail: **Glen.Lehman@unisa.edu.au**). Authors in the USA, Europe and the rest of the world should send their manuscripts to Professor Tony Tinker, Co-Editor, Accounting Forum, Baruch College: City University of New York, Box B12-236, 17 Lexington Avenue, New York, NY 10010, USA (e-mail: **TonyTinker@msn.com**). Four copies of the manuscript, including one set of high-quality original illustrations, suitable for direct reproduction, should be submitted. (Copies of the illustrations are acceptable for the other sets of manuscripts, as long as the quality permits refereeing.) In the case of manuscripts reporting on field surveys of experiments, two copies of the instrument (questionnaire, case, interview plan or the like) should be submitted.

General. It is essential to give a fax number and e-mail address when submitting a manuscript. Articles must be written in good English. Submission of an article implies that the work has not been published previously (except in the form of an abstract or as part of a published lecture or academic thesis), that it is not under consideration for publication elsewhere, and that its publication is approved by all Authors and tacitly or explicitly by the responsible authorities where the work was carried out, and that, if accepted, it will not be published elsewhere in the same form, in English or in any other language, without the written consent of the Publisher. Upon acceptance of an article, Authors will be asked to transfer copyright (for more information on copyright see http://authors.elsevier.com). This transfer will ensure the widest possible dissemination of information. A letter will be sent to the corresponding Author confirming receipt of the manuscript. A form facilitating transfer of copyright will be provided. If excerpts from other copyrighted works are included, the Author(s) must obtain written permission from the copyright owners and credit the source(s) in the article. Elsevier has preprinted forms for use by Authors in these cases: contact Elsevier's Rights Department, Oxford, UK; e-mail: permissions@elsevier.com phone: (+44) 1865 843830; fax: (+44) 1865 853333;. Requests may also be completed on-line via the Elsevier homepage (http://www.elsevier.com/locate/permissions).

Electronic Format Requirements for Accepted Articles

General points. We accept most wordprocessing formats, but Word, WordPerfect of LaTex is preferred. An electronic version of the text should be submitted together with the final hard copy of the manuscript. The electronic version must match the hardcopy exactly. Always keep a backup copy of the electronic file for reference and safety. Label storage media with you name, journal title, and software used. Save your files using the default extension of the program used. No changes to the accepted version are permissible without the explicit approval of the Editors. Electronic files can be stored on 3 inch diskette, ZIP-disk or CD (either MS-DOS or Macintosh).

Wordprocessor documents. It is important that the file be saved in the native format of the wordprocessor used. The text should be in single-column format. Keep the layout of the text as simple as possible. Most formatting codes will be removed and replaced on processing the article. In particular, do not use the wordprocessor's options to justify text or to hyphenate words. However, do use bold face, italics, subscripts, superscripts etc. Do not embed "graphically designed" equations or tables, but prepare these using the wordprocessor's facility. When preparing tables, if you are using a table grid, use only one grid for each individual table and a grid for each row. If no grid is used, use tabs, not spaces, to align columns. The electronic text should be prepared in a way very similar to that of conventional manuscripts (see also the Author Gateway's Quick Guide: http://authors.elsevier.com). Do not import the figures into the text file but, instead, indicate their approximate locations directly in the electronic text and on the manuscript. See also the section on Preparation of electronic illustrations. To avoid unnecessary errors you are strongly advised to use the "spellchecker" function of your wordprocessor. Although Elsevier can process most wordprocessor file formats, should your electronic file prove to be unusable, the article will be typeset from the hardcopy printout.

Preparation of Text
Presentation of manuscript. Please write your text in good English (American or British usage is accepted, but not a mixture of these). Italics are not to be used for expressions of Latin origin, for example, in vivo, et al., per se. Use decimal points (not commas); use a space for thousands (10 000 and above). Print the entire manuscript on one side of paper only, using double spacing and wide (3 cm) margins. (Avoid full justification, i.e., do not use a constant right-hand margin.) Ensure that each new paragraph is clearly indicated. Present tables and figure captions on separate pages at the end of the manuscript. If possible, consult a recent issue of the journal to become familiar with layout and conventions. Number all pages consecutively. Good quality print-outs with a font size of 12 or 10 pt are required. Provide the following data on the title page (in the order given).

Title. Concise and informative. Titles are often used in information-retrieved systems. Avoid abbreviations and formulae where possible.

Author Names and Affiliations. Where the family name may be ambiguous (e.g.., a double name), please indicate this clearly. Present the Author's affiliation addresses (where the actual work was done) below the names. Indicate all affiliations with a lower-case superscript letter immediately after the Author's name and in front of the appropriate address. Provide the full postal address of each affiliation including the country name, and, if available, the e-mail address of each Author.

Corresponding Author. Clearly indicate who is willing to handle correspondence at all stages of refereeing and publication, also post-publication. Ensure the telephone and fax numbers (with country and area code) are provided in addition to the e-mail address and the complete postal address.

Present/permanent address. If an Author has moved since the work described in the article was done, or was visiting at the time, a "Present address" (or "Permanent address") may be indicated as a footnote to that Author's name. The address at which the Author actually did the work must be retained as the main, affiliation address. Superscript Arabic numerals are used for such footnotes.

Abstract. A concise and factual abstract is required (maximum length 100 words). The abstract should state briefly the purpose of the research, the principal results and major conclusions. An abstract is often presented separate from the article, so it must be able to stand alone. References should therefore be avoided, but if essential, they must be cited in full, without reference to the reference list.

Keywords. Immediately after the abstract, provide a maximum of 6 keywords, avoiding general and plural terms and multiple concepts (avoid, for example, "and", "of"). Be sparing with abbreviations: only abbreviations firmly established in the field may be eligible. These keywords will be used for indexing purposes.

N.B. Acknowledgements. Collate acknowledgements in a separate section at the end of the article and do not, therefore, include them on the title page, as footnote to the title or otherwise.

Arrangement of the Article
Subdivision of the article. Divide your article into clearly defined and numbered sections. Subsections should be numbered 1.1 (then 1.1.1., 1.1.2., . . .), 1.2., etc. (the abstract is not included in section numbering). Use this numbering also for internal cross-referencing: do not just refer to "the text". Any subsections may be given a brief heading. Each heading on its own separate line.

Text. Follow this order when typing manuscripts: Title, Authors, Affiliations, Abstract, Keywords, Main text, Acknowledgements, Appendix, References, Figure Captions, Tables (and figures) should be kept separate from the rest of the manuscript (see instructions for illustrations below). The corresponding Author should be identified with an asterisk and footnote. All other footnotes (except table footnotes) should be identified with superscript Arabic numerals.

Appendices. If there is more than one appendix, they should be identified as A, B, etc. Formulae and equations in appendices should be given separate numbering: (Eq. A.1), (Eq. A.2), etc.: in a subsequent appendix (Eq. B.1) and so forth. Acknowledgements. Place acknowledgements, including information on grants received, before the references, in a separate section, and not as a footnote on the title page. References. See separate section, below.

Vitae. Include in the manuscript a short (maximum 50 words) biography of each Author.

References
Responsibility for the accuracy of bibliographic citations lies entirely with the Authors.

Citations in the text. Please ensure that every reference cited in the text is also present in the reference list (and vice versa). Any references cited in the abstract must be given in full. Unpublished results and personal communications are not recommended in the reference list, but may be mentioned in the text. If these references are included in the reference list they should follow the standard reference style of the journal and should include a substitution of the publication date with either "Unpublished results" or "Personal communication". Citation of a reference as 'in press' implies that the item has been accepted for publication.

30

Text. Citations in the text should follow the referencing style used by the American Psychological Association. You are referred to the *Publication Manual of the American Psychological Association*, Fifth Edition, ISBN 1-55798-790-4, copies of which may be ordered from http://wsw.apa..org/books/4200061. html or APA Order Dept., P.O.B. 2710, Hyattsville, MD 20784, USA or APA, 3 Henrietta Street, London, WC3E 8LU, UK. Details concerning this referencing style can also be found at:
http://humanities.byu.edu/linguistics/Henrichsen/APA/APA01.html.

List. References should be arranged first alphabetically and then further sorted chronologically if necessary. More than one reference from the same Author(s) in the same year must be identified by the letters "a", "b", "c" etc., placed after the year of publication.

Examples
Reference to a journal publication. Van der Geer, J., Hanraads, J.A.J., & Lupton, R.A. (2000). The art of writing a scientific article. Journal of Scientific Communications, 163, 51-59.

Reference to a book. Strunk, Jr.,W., & White, E.B. (1979). The elements of style (3rd ed.). New York: Macmillan (Chapter 4).

Reference to a chapter in an edited book. Mettam, G.R., & Adams, L.B. (1994). How to prepare an electronic version of your article. In B.S. Jones, & R.Z. Smith (Eds.), Introduction to the electronic age (pp. 281-304). New York: E-Publishing Inc.

Preparation of Illustrations
Preparation of electronic illustrations. Submitting your artwork in an electronic format helps us to produce your work to the best possible standards, ensuring accuracy, clarity and a high level of detail.

General points
- Always supply high-quality printouts of your artwork, in case conversion of the electronic artwork is problematic.
- Make sure you use uniform lettering and sizing of your original artwork.
- Save text in illustrations as "graphics" or enclose the font.
- Only use the following fonts in your illustrations: Arial, Courier, Times, Symbol.
- Number the illustrations according to their sequence in the text.
- Use a logical naming convention for your artwork files, and supply a separate listing of the files and the software used.
- Provide all illustrations as separate files and as hardcopy printouts on separate sheets.
- Provide captions to illustrations separately.
- Produce images near to the desired size of the printed version. Files can be stored on 3" inch diskette, ZIP-disk or CD (either MS-DOS or Macintosh). A detailed guide on electronic artwork is available on our website: http://authors.elsevier.com/artwork. You are urged to visit this site; some excerpts from the detailed information are given here.

Formats. Regardless of the application used, when your electronic artwork is finalised, please "save as" or convert the images to one of the following formats (Note the resolution requirements for line drawings, halftones, and line/halftone combinations are given below.):

- EPS: Vector drawings: embed the font or save the text as "graphics".
- TIFF: Colour or greyscale photographs (halftones): always use a minimum of 300 dpi.
- TIFF: Bitmapped line drawings line drawings: use a minimum of 1000 dpi.
- TIFF: Combinations bitmapped line/half-tone (colour or greyscale): a minimum of 500 dpi is required.
- DOC, XLS, or PPT: If your electronic artwork is created in any of these Microsoft Office applications please supply "as is".

Please do not:

- Supply embedded graphics in your wordprocessor (spreadsheet, presentation) documentation;
- Supply files that are optimised for screen use (like GIF, BMP, PICT, WPG); the resolution is too low;
- Supply files that are too low in resolution;
- Submit graphics that are disproportionately large for the content.

Non-electronic illustrations. Provide all illustrations as high-quality printouts, suitable for reproduction (which may include reduction) without retouching. Number illustrations consecutively in the order in which they are referred to in the text. They should accompany the manuscript, but should not be included within the text. Clearly mark all illustrations on the back (or - in case of line drawings - on the lower front side) with the figure number and the author's name and, in cases of ambiguity, the correct orientation. Mark the appropriate position of a figure in the article.

Captions. Ensure that each illustration has a caption. Supply captions on a separate sheet, not attached to the figure. A caption should compromise a brief title (not on the figure itself) and a description of the illustration. Keep text in the illustrations themselves to a minimum but explain all symbols and abbreviations used.

Line drawings. Supply high-quality printouts on white paper produced with black ink. The lettering and symbols, as well as other details, should have proportionate dimensions, so as to become illegible or unclear after possible reduction; in general, the figures should be designed for a reduction factor of two to three. The degree of reduction will be determined by the Publisher. Illustrations will not be enlarged. Consider the page format of the journal when designing the illustration. Photocopies are not suitable for reproduction. Do not use any type of shading on computer-generated.

Photographs (halftones). Please supply original photographs for reproduction, printed on glossy paper, very sharp and with good contrast. Remove non-essential areas of a photograph. Do not mount photographs unless they form part of a composite figure. Where necessary, insert a scale bar in the illustration (not below it), as opposed to giving a magnification factor in the legend. Note that photocopies of photographs are not acceptable.

32

Colour illustrations. Submit colour illustrations as original photographs, high-quality computer prints or transparencies, close to the size expected in publication, or as 35mm slides. Polaroid colour prints are not suitable. If, together with your accepted article, you submit usable colour figures then Elsevier will ensure, at no additional charge, that these figures will appear in colour on the web (e.g., ScienceDirect and other sites) regardless of whether or not these illustrations are reproduced in colour in the printed version. For colour reproduction in print, you will receive information regarding the costs from Elsevier after receipt of your accepted article. Please indicate your preference for colour in print or on the Web only.

Further information on the preparation of electronic artwork, please see:
http://authors.elsevier.com/artwork

Please note: Because of technical complications which can arise by converting colour figures to "grey scale" (for the printed version should you not opt for colour in print) please submit in addition usable black and white versions of all the colour illustrations.

Proofs

When your manuscript is received by the Publisher it is considered to be in its final form. Proofs are not to be regarded as "drafts". One set of page proofs in PDF format will be sent by e-mail to the corresponding Author, to be checked for typesetting/editing. No changes in, or additions to, the accepted (and subsequently edited) manuscript will be allowed at this stage. Proofreading is solely your responsibility. A form with queries from the copyeditor may accompany your proofs. Please answer all queries and make any corrections or additions required. Elsevier will do everything possible to get your article corrected and published as quickly and accurately as possible. In order to do this we need your help. When you receive the (PDF) proof of your article for correction, it is important to ensure that all of your corrections are sent back to us in one communication. Subsequent corrections will not be possible, so please ensure your first sending is complete. Note that this does not mean you have any less time to make your corrections, just that only one set of corrections will be accepted.

Offprints

Twenty five offprints will be supplied free of charge. Additional offprints can be ordered at a specially reduced rate using the order form sent to the corresponding author after the manuscript has been accepted. Orders for reprints (produced after publication of an article) will incur a 50% surcharge.

Accounting Historians Journal

ADDRESS FOR SUBMISSION:

Richard Fleischman, Editor
Accounting Historians Journal
John Carroll University
University Heights, OH 44122
USA
Phone: 216-397-4443
E-Mail: fleischman@jcu.edu
Web: http://accounting.rutgers.edu

PUBLICATION GUIDELINES:

Manuscript Length: 26-30
Copies Required: Electronic
Computer Submission: Yes Email Required
Format: MS Word
Fees to Review: 0.00 US$

Manuscript Style:
　See Manuscript Guidelines

CIRCULATION DATA:

Reader: Academics
Frequency of Issue: 2 Times/Year
Sponsor/Publisher: Academy of Accounting
　Historians

REVIEW INFORMATION:

Type of Review: Blind Review
No. of External Reviewers: 2
No. of In House Reviewers: 0
Acceptance Rate: 30%
Time to Review: 1-3 months
Reviewers Comments: Yes
Invited Articles: 6-10%
Fees to Publish: 0.00 US$

MANUSCRIPT TOPICS:

Accounting History; Accounting Information Systems; Accounting Theory & Practice; Auditing; Cost Accounting; Economic History; Government & Non Profit Accounting; International Economics & Trade; Tax Accounting

MANUSCRIPT GUIDELINES/COMMENTS:

Statement of Policy

The *Accounting Historians Journal* is an international journal that addresses the development of accounting thought and practice. *AHJ* embraces all subject matter related to accounting history, including but not limited to research that provides an historical perspective on contemporary accounting issues.

Authors may find the following guidelines helpful.

1. Authors should provide a clear specification of the research issue or problem addressed and the motivation for the study.

2. Authors should describe the method employed in the research, indicating the extent and manner in which they intend to employ the methodology. Manuscripts are encouraged that draw on a variety of conceptual frameworks and techniques, including those used in other social sciences.

3. Manuscripts that rely on primary sources should contain a statement specifying the original materials or data collected or analyzed and the rationale used in selection of those source materials. Authors should provide the reader information as to how these source materials may be accessed.

4. Authors who use a critical or new theoretical framework to examine prior historical interpretations of the development of accounting thought or practice should include a discussion of the rationale for use of that framework in the manuscript.

5. In performing all analyses, authors should be sensitive to and take adequate account of the social, political, and economic contexts of the time period examined and of other environmental factors.

6. While historians have long debated the ability to assign causation to particular factors, we encourage authors to address and evaluate the probable influences related to the problem or issue examined.

7. Authors should clearly state all their interpretations of results, and the conclusions they draw should be consistent with the original objectives of and data used in the study. Interpretations and conclusions should be clearly linked to the research problem. Authors also should state the implications of the study for future research.

Manuscripts should be in English and of acceptable style and organization for clarity of presentation. Submit three copies, typewritten, double-spaced on one side of 8 ½ X 11 inch (approx. 28.5 cm X 28.0 cm) white paper; paragraphs should be indented. Margins should be wide enough to facilitate editing and duplication. All pages, including bibliographic pages, should be serially numbered. Manuscripts should be run through a spell check software program or similar review prior to submission. [**Type of Review is double blind**]

Cover Sheet. The cover sheet should state the title of the paper, name(s) of author(s), affiliation(s), the address for future correspondence and the FAX number or EMAIL address (or both) of the author designated as the contact person for the manuscript.

Abstract. An abstract of not more than 100 words should accompany the manuscript on a separate page. The title, but not the name(s) of the author(s) should appear on the abstract page and on the first page of the manuscript.

Major Headings within the manuscript should be centered, unnumbered and capitalized. Subheadings should be on a separate line beginning flush with the left margin, italicized, with the first letter of major words capitalized. Text should follow immediately on the same line, separated from the header by a colon.

Tables, Figures and Exhibits should be numbered (Arabic), titled, and, when appropriate, referenced. Limited use of original documents can be accommodated in the Journal if authors can provide good quality reproductions. Important textual materials may be presented in both the original language and the English translation. Tables, and similar items must be discussed in the text and will not be included unless they lend support to the text.

Literature References
Footnotes should not be used for literature references. The work cited should be referenced using the author's name and date of publication in the body of the text, inside square brackets, i.e., Garner [1954, p. 33]. If the author's name is mentioned in the text, it need not be repeated, i.e., Garner [1954, p. 33] concluded.... If a reference has more than three authors, only the first name and "et al" should be used in the text citation. References to statutes, legal treatise or court cases should follow the accepted form of legal citation. All references to direct quotations should contain page numbers.

Content Footnotes
Content footnotes may be used sparingly to expand upon or comment upon the text itself. These should be numbered consecutively throughout the manuscript and should appear at the bottom of the page on which the reference appears.

Bibliography
A bibliography of works cited should appear at the end of the manuscript. The works cited should be listed alphabetically according to the surname of the first author. Information about books and journals should include the following information: **Books**—author(s), date of publication, title italicized, place of publication, and publisher (in parentheses); **Articles**—author(s), date of publication, title (with quotation marks), journal italicized, volume and number, page numbers. **Multiple works by an author** should be listed in chronological order; if multiple works appear in a single year, the suffix a, b, etc. should be used to identify each work.

For questions of style not covered above, authors should consult a style manual such as Turabian, Kate L. *A Manual for Writers of Term Papers, Theses and Dissertations*, published by the University of Chicago Press.

Diskette. When a manuscript has been accepted for publication, authors will be asked to submit a diskette with the final manuscript. The diskette should be prepared in IBM compatible ASCII file format.

Complimentary Copies and Reprints. Author(s) will be provided with 3 copies of the Journal issue in which the manuscript is published. Reprints may be ordered from the printer; the minimum order is 100. The printer will establish the price and bill the author(s) directly for the cost of the reprints.

Accounting History

ADDRESS FOR SUBMISSION:

Garry D. Carnegie, Editor
Accounting History
Melbourne University Private
School of Enterprise
Hawthorn, VIC 3122
Australia
Phone: 61 3 9810 3102
E-Mail: g.carnegie@muprivate.edu.au
Web: www.muprivate.edu.au/accounting
   history

PUBLICATION GUIDELINES:

Manuscript Length: 26-30
Copies Required: Three
Computer Submission: Yes Email Preferred
Format:
Fees to Review: 0.00 US$

Manuscript Style:
   See Manuscript Guidelines

CIRCULATION DATA:

Reader: Academics
Frequency of Issue: 3 Times/Year
Sponsor/Publisher: Academic Association

REVIEW INFORMATION:

Type of Review: Blind Review
No. of External Reviewers: 2
No. of In House Reviewers: 0
Acceptance Rate: 21-30%
Time to Review: 2 - 3 Months
Reviewers Comments: Yes
Invited Articles: 11-20%
Fees to Publish: 0.00 US$

MANUSCRIPT TOPICS:
Accounting History; Accounting Theory & Practice; Auditing; Cost Accounting; Economic History; Government & Non Profit Accounting

MANUSCRIPT GUIDELINES/COMMENTS:

Accounting History is sponsored by Accounting History Special Interest Group of the Accounting and Finance Association of Australia and New Zealand.

Editorial Policies
Accounting History aims to publish quality historical papers. These could be concerned with exploring the advent and development of accounting bodies, conventions, ideas, practices and rules. They should attempt to identify the individuals and also the local, time-specific environmental factors which affected accounting, and should endeavor to assess accounting's impact on organizational and social functioning.

Editorial Procedures
1. Address copies of all manuscripts and editorial correspondence to the Editor.

2. The cover of the manuscript should contain the following:
- Title of manuscript.
- Name of author(s), including the name of the corresponding author for co-authored papers.
- Institutional affiliation of author(s) including telephone, fax and email address(es).
- Date of submission and, where applicable, date(s) of resubmission.
- Any acknowledgement, not exceeding 50 words. An acknowledgement should not be included in the consecutive number of other notes.

3. An abstract of no more than 150 words should be presented, along with the title of the manuscript, on a separate page immediately preceding the text of the manuscript.

4. Manuscripts for review should be submitted electronically to the following address: **j.hyslop@muprivate.edu.au**. Manuscripts should be double-spaced, generally of not more than 8,500 words and all pages should be numbered. Manuscripts currently under review for publication in other outlets should not be submitted.

5. Headings should be formatted so that major headings are flush left, bold, lower case and two font sizes larger than the main text. Second level headings should be flush left, bold, lower case and same size as main text. Third level headings should be flush left, italics, lower case and same size as main text. For example:
1. **Flush left, bold, lower case, two font sizes larger than main text**
2. Flush left, bold, lower case, same size font as main text
3. *Flush left, italics, lower case, same size font as main text.*

6. Figures, tables, diagrams and appendices should be numbered consecutively and titled.

7. Notes should appear as endnotes and be numbered consecutively. They should begin on a separate page at the end of the manuscript.

8. References should appear in the text as West (2003) or West (2003, p.35). The full references should be typed on separate sheets and appear after any notes at the end of the manuscript. The following guidelines should be followed:

Books
West, B.P., (2003), *Professionalism and Accounting Rules*, London and New York: Routledge.

Contributions in Edited Books
Parker, L.D., (1997), "Practitioner Perspectives on Personal Conduct: Images from the World of Business, 1900-55", in Cooke, T.E. and Nobes, C.W. (eds.), *The Development of Accounting in an International Context: A Festschrift in Honour of R.H. Parker*, London: Routledge, pp.68-89.

Periodicals
Fleischman, R.K., (2004), "Confronting Moral Issues from Accounting's Dark Side", *Accounting History*, Vol.9, No.1, March, pp.7-23.

38

Conference Papers
Loft, A., (2003), "The Accounting Machine and its Woman Operator: Beyond the Boundaries of Accounting's History", The third *Accounting History* International Conference, Siena, September 2003.

9. When a paper is accepted for publication the authors are requested to provide an electronic copy of the accepted version of the paper. Submissions saved in text format (specifically ASCII text) are preferred. Microsoft Word (for Macintosh or PC compatibles) is the preferred word processing format.

Accounting Horizons

ADDRESS FOR SUBMISSION:

Robert C. Lipe, Managing Editor
Accounting Horizons
Carl A. Wood, Editorial Assistant
University of Oklahoma
Michael F. Price College of Business
307 West Brooks Street, Room 259
Norman, OK 73019-4004
USA
Phone: 405-325-4090
E-Mail: ahorizons@ou.edu
Web: http://aaahq.org

CIRCULATION DATA:

Reader: Business Persons, Academics
Frequency of Issue: Quarterly
Sponsor/Publisher: American Accounting
    Association

PUBLICATION GUIDELINES:

Manuscript Length: 7,000 Words
    Maximum
Copies Required: Two
Computer Submission: Yes
Format: MS Word or PDF
Fees to Review: 75.00 US$
    100.00 US$ Nonmembers of AAA

Manuscript Style:
    Chicago Manual of Style

REVIEW INFORMATION:

Type of Review: Blind Review
No. of External Reviewers: 2
No. of In House Reviewers: 1
Acceptance Rate: 11-20%
Time to Review: 2 - 3 Months
Reviewers Comments: Yes
Invited Articles: 6-10%
Fees to Publish: 0.00 US$

MANUSCRIPT TOPICS:
Accounting & Tax Policy; Accounting Theory & Practice; Auditing; Cost Accounting; Government & Non Profit Accounting; Tax Accounting

MANUSCRIPT GUIDELINES/COMMENTS:

Accounting Horizons is one of three association-wide journals published by the American Accounting Association (AAA). Each of the journals has a primary focus, and *Accounting Horizons'* primary objective is to publish papers focusing on the scholarship of integration and application. Building on the work of the Carnegie Foundation, we can define integration scholarship and application scholarship as follows:

- The *scholarship of integration* asks—What do research results mean to those who might benefit from those discoveries? Is it possible to interpret new discoveries in ways that provide a larger, more comprehensive understanding?
- The *scholarship of application* focuses on engagement and asks—How can knowledge be responsibly applied to consequential problems? Application is not a one-way street, as new intellectual understandings can arise out the very act of application ... theory and practice vitally interact and one renews the other.

With its focus on integration and application, *Accounting Horizons* seeks to communicate with a large and diverse audience. Its contents should be of interest to researchers, educators, practitioners, regulators, and students of accounting. Accordingly, papers submitted for publication in *Horizons* must address subjects that appeal to its readership's interests and must be written in a style that communicates effectively across those diverse groups. Technical terms, methodologies, and tabular presentations must be explained clearly. An appendix should be used for extensive methodological discussions. Because of *Horizons'* broad focus, the scope of acceptable manuscripts is also broad, and papers may deal with any aspect of accounting, including but not limited to:

- Accounting ethics
- Assurance services
- Financial reporting
- The impact of accounting on organizations and individual behavior
- Information systems
- Managerial accounting
- Regulation of the profession and related legal developments
- Risk management
- Taxation

Moving from these particulars to the overall, one of *Accounting Horizons'* paramount objectives is to establish a dialogue—a bridge of ideas—between accounting academics and the business community.

From time to time, think pieces, memorials, historical and other reviews, editorials, and original research relevant to current issues and the future of the accounting profession will be commissioned by the Editor. Ideas for such articles may come from the Associate Editors, the Executive Committee of the Association, or other sources. In addition, reviews of contemporary professional literature, commentaries on practice, and reports of current events will appear when developments warrant.

All submitted articles processed for publication will be peer reviewed. Articles that address an especially timely subject will be evaluated and refereed on an expedited basis to facilitate prompt publication if accepted.

Submission of Manuscripts
Authors should note the following guidelines for submitting manuscript:
1. Manuscripts currently under consideration by another journal or other publisher should not be submitted. The author must state that the work is not submitted or published elsewhere.

2. Manuscripts should be submitted via email to the *Accounting Horizons* office at **ahorizons@ou.edu**. A submission letter, a cover page (containing the name and affiliation of each author, a complete address, a phone number, and an email address for the corresponding author, and any acknowledgments that the authors wish to make) and the manuscript containing no author identification should be attached as separate files. Files must be in either Microsoft® Word or PDF format. Prior to the final revision, footnotes can be at the bottom of the page.

3. In the case of manuscripts reporting on field surveys or experiments, a copy of the instrument (questionnaire, case, interview plan, or the like) should be submitted. The document(s) should be submitted electronically as separate file attachments in the original email, but hard copies are acceptable if the electronic version is either unavailable or not in a format suitable electronic submission. Information in the instrument that might identify the authors must be deleted or masked.

4. Online payment of the submission fee (VISA or MasterCard) is preferred at https://aaahq.org/AAAforms/journals/horsubmit.cfm and must be made in U.S. funds for $75.00 for members or $100.00 for nonmembers of the AAA. The submission fee is nonrefundable.

5. Unless stipulated by the Editor, revisions must be submitted within 12 months from request, otherwise they will be considered new submissions.

6. The author should retain a copy of the paper.

7. The editor and his assistant can be reached using the information below:
Robert C. Lipe, Managing Editor
Carl A. Wood, Editorial Assistant
Michael F. Price College of Business
University of Oklahoma, 307 West Brooks Street, Room 259, Norman, OK 73019-4004
Phone: (405) 325-4090,   Fax: (405) 325-2539,   Email:**ahorizons@ou.edu**

Comments
Comments on articles previously published in *Accounting Horizons* will be considered for publication, subject to review by the Editorial Group, the author of the article being critiqued, and other reviewer(s) deemed necessary by the Editor. If a comment is accepted for publication, the original author will be invited to reply. All other editorial requirements, as enumerated above, also apply to proposed comments.

Manuscript Preparation and Style
The *Accounting Horizons* manuscript preparation guidelines follow (with a slight modification) documentation 2 of *The Chicago Manual of Style* (15th edition, University of Chicago Press). Another helpful guide to usage and style is *The Elements of Style*, by William Strunk, Jr., and E. B. White (Macmillan). Spelling follows *Merriam-Webster's Collegiate Dictionary*.

Format
1. All manuscripts should be typed in 12-point font on one side of 8½" × 11" good quality paper and be double-spaced, except for indented quotations.

2. Manuscripts should be as concise as the subject and research method permit. The Editorial Group asks authors to aim for 20 double-spaced pages total in their submissions. We recommend a limit of 30 pages in total for text, tables, references, and appendices, if applicable.

3. Margins should be at least one inch from top, bottom, and sides to facilitate editing and duplication.

4. To assure anonymous review, authors should not identify themselves directly or indirectly in their papers. Single authors should not use the editorial "we."

5. A separate file should contain the cover page. This page contains the name and affiliation of each author; a complete address, a phone number and an email address for the corresponding author; and any acknowledgments that the authors wish to make. The cover page must also have a footnote indicating whether the author would be willing to share the data (see last paragraph in this statement).

6. A synopsis of about 150–200 words should be presented on a separate page immediately preceding the text. The synopsis should be nonmathematical and include a readable summary of the research question, method, and the significance of the findings and contribution. The title, but not the author's name or other identification designations, should appear on the synopsis page.

7. All pages, including tables, appendices and references, should be serially numbered. The cover and synopsis pages are not numbered.

8. Spell out numbers from one to ten, except when used in tables and lists, and when used with mathematical, statistical, scientific or technical units and quantities, such as distances, weights and measures. For example: *three days; 3 kilometers; 30 years.* All other numbers are expressed numerically.

9. In non-technical text use the word *percent*; in tables and figures, the symbol % is used.

10. Use a hyphen to join unit modifiers or to clarify usage. For example: a well-presented analysis; re-form. See *Webster's* for correct usage.

11. Headings should be arranged so that major headings are centered, bold and capitalized. Second-level headings should be flush left, bold, and both upper and lower case. Third-level headings should be flush left, bold, italic, and both upper and lower case. Fourth-level headings should be paragraph indent, bold and lower case. Headings and subheadings should not be numbered. For example:

A CENTERED, BOLD, ALL CAPITALIZED, FIRST-LEVEL HEADING
A Flush Left, Bold, Upper and Lower Case, Second-Level Heading
A Flush Left, Bold, Italic, Upper and Lower Case, Third-Level Heading
A paragraph indent, bold, lower case, fourth-level heading. Text starts …

Tables and Figures
The author should note the following general requirements:

1. Each table and figure (graphic) should appear on a separate page and should be placed at the end of the text. Each should bear an Arabic number and a complete title indicating the exact contents of the table or figure.

2. A reference to each table or figure should be made in the text.

3. The author should indicate by marginal notation where each table or figure should be inserted in the text, e.g., (Insert Table X here).

4. Tables or figures should be reasonably interpretable without reference to the text.

5. Notes should be included as necessary.

6. Figures must be prepared in a form suitable for printing.

Mathematical Notation
Mathematical notation should be employed only where its rigor and precision are necessary, and in such circumstances authors should explain in the narrative format the principal operations performed. Notation should be avoided in footnotes. Displayed material should clearly indicate the alignment, superscripts, and subscripts. Equations should be numbered in parentheses flush with the right-hand margin.

Documentation
Citations. Work cited should use the "author-date system" keyed to a list of works in the reference list (see below). Authors should make an effort to include the relevant page numbers in the cited works.

1. In the text, works are cited as follows: author's last name and date, without comma, in parentheses: for example (Jones 1987); with two authors: (Jones and Freeman 1973); with more than two: (Jones et al. 1985); with more than one source cited together: (Jones 1987; Freeman 1986); with two or more works by one author: (Jones 1985, 1987).

2. Unless confusion would result, do not use "p." or "pp." before page numbers: Example: (Jones 1987, 115).

3. When the reference list contains more than one work of an author published in the same year, the suffix a, b, etc. follows the date in the text citation: Example: (Jones 1987a) or (Jones 1987a; Freeman 1985b).

4. If an author's name is mentioned in the text, it need not be repeated in the citation: for example, "Jones (1987, 115) says ..."

5. Citations to institutional works should use acronyms or short titles where practicable: for example, (AAA ASOBAT 1966); (AICPA *Cohen Commission Report* 1977). Where brief, the full title of an institutional work might be shown in a citation: for example, (ICAEW *The Corporate Report* 1975).

6. If the manuscript refers to statutes, legal treatises or court cases, citations acceptable in law reviews should be used.

Reference List. Every manuscript must include a list of references containing only those works cited. Each entry should contain all data necessary for unambiguous identification. With the author-date system, use the following format recommended by the *Chicago Manual*:

1. Arrange citations in alphabetical order according to surname of the first author or the name of the institution responsible for the citation.

2. Use authors' initials instead of proper names.

3. Dates of publication should be placed immediately after authors' names.

4. Titles of journals should not be abbreviated.

5. Multiple works by the same author(s) should be listed in chronological order of publication. Two or more works by the same author(s) in the same year are distinguished by letters after the date.

Footnotes. Footnotes are not to be used for documentation. Textual footnotes should be used only for extensions and useful excursions of information that if included in the body of the text might disrupt its continuity. Footnotes should be consecutively numbered throughout the manuscript with superscript Arabic numerals. Footnote text should be double-spaced and placed at the end of the article.

Policy on Reproduction
An objective of *Accounting Horizons* is to promote the wide dissemination of the results of systematic scholarly inquiries into the broad field of accounting.

Permission is hereby granted to reproduce any of the contents of *Horizons* for use in courses of instruction, as long as the source and American Accounting Association copyright are indicated in any such reproductions.

Written application must be made to the American Accounting Association, 5717 Bessie Drive, Sarasota, FL 34233-2399, for permission to reproduce any of the contents of *Horizons* for use in other than courses of instruction—e.g., inclusion in books of readings or in any other publications intended for general distribution. In consideration for the grant of permission by *Horizons* in such instances, the applicant must notify the author(s) in writing of the intended use to be made of each reproduction. Normally, *Horizons* will not assess a charge for the waiver of copyright.

Except where otherwise noted in articles, the copyright interest has been transferred to the American Accounting Association. Where the author(s) has (have) not transferred the copyright to the Association, applicants must seek permission to reproduce (for all purposes) directly from the author(s).

Policy on Data Availability
The following policy has been adopted by the Executive Committee in its April 1989 meeting. "An objective of (*The Accounting Review, Accounting Horizons, Issues in Accounting Education*) is to provide the widest possible dissemination of knowledge based on systematic scholarly inquiries into accounting as a field of professional, research and educational activity. As part of this process, authors are encouraged to make their data available for use by others in extending or replicating results reported in their articles. Authors of articles which report data dependent results should footnote the status of data availability and, when pertinent, this should be accompanied by information on how the data may be obtained."

Accounting Instructors' Report

ADDRESS FOR SUBMISSION:

Belverd E. Needles, Jr., Editor
Accounting Instructors' Report
Depaul University
School of Accountancy
1 East Jackson Blvd.
Chicago, IL 60604-2287
USA
Phone: 312-362-5130
E-Mail: bneedles@needles-powers.com
Web: http://college.hmco.com/accounting/
    resources/instructors/air/

PUBLICATION GUIDELINES:

Manuscript Length: 1-5
Copies Required: Two
Computer Submission: Yes
Format:
Fees to Review: 0.00 US$

Manuscript Style:

CIRCULATION DATA:

Reader: Academics
Frequency of Issue: 2 Times/Year
Sponsor/Publisher: Profit Oriented Corp.

REVIEW INFORMATION:

Type of Review: Blind Review
No. of External Reviewers: 1
No. of In House Reviewers: 1
Acceptance Rate: 21-30%
Time to Review: 4 - 6 Months
Reviewers Comments: No
Invited Articles: 6-10%
Fees to Publish: 0.00 US$

MANUSCRIPT TOPICS:
Accounting Education

MANUSCRIPT GUIDELINES/COMMENTS:

Submission Information
Essays, studies, and research of four to six double-spaced pages are sought from instructors of accounting at all levels.

The Accounting Instructors' Report is published twice a year to achieve the following objectives:

• To advance the teaching of accounting at the college level
• To provide a dissemination vehicle for information about teaching techniques

Papers to be considered for publication should be submitted to: Belverd E. Needles, Jr., Editor, AIR, School of Accountancy, DePaul University, 1 East Jackson Boulevard, Chicago, IL 60604-2287, Telephone: 847-441-9017, Fax: 847-441-9028

Accounting Research Journal

ADDRESS FOR SUBMISSION:

Tim Brailsford, Managing Editor
Accounting Research Journal
UQ Business School
University of Queensland
ST. LUCIA QLD 4072
Australia
Phone: 61 (7) 3365 6225
E-Mail: t.brailsford@business.uq.edu.au
Web: www.bus.qut.edu.au/schools/accoun
tancy/research/arj/about.jsp

PUBLICATION GUIDELINES:

Manuscript Length: N/A
Copies Required: Three
Computer Submission: Yes
Format: 3.5 disk
Fees to Review: 0.00 US$

Manuscript Style:
See Manuscript Guidelines

CIRCULATION DATA:

Reader: Academics
Frequency of Issue: 2 Times/Year
Sponsor/Publisher: QUT

REVIEW INFORMATION:

Type of Review: Blind Review
No. of External Reviewers: 2
No. of In House Reviewers: 1
Acceptance Rate: 21-30%
Time to Review: 1 - 2 Months
Reviewers Comments: Yes
Invited Articles: 0-5%
Fees to Publish: 0.00 US$

MANUSCRIPT TOPICS:
Accounting Information Systems; Accounting Theory & Practice; Auditing; Corporate Finance; Cost Accounting; Government & Non Profit Accounting; International Finance; Portfolio & Security Analysis; Tax Accounting

MANUSCRIPT GUIDELINES/COMMENTS:

Editorial Policy
The *Accounting Research Journal* is a fully refereed journal. All papers are subject to a peer review process involving at least one independent referee as well as consultation between relevant Editorial Board members and the Joint Editors.

The objective of the *Accounting Research Journal* is to provide a valuable forum for communication between the profession and academics on the research and practice of accounting, finance, auditing, commercial law and cognate disciplines. The editors would encourage submissions in any of the above areas, which have a practical and/or applied focus. In particular, work reporting the results of research conducted using data from Australia, New Zealand and other Asian-Pacific countries would be welcomed. However, this policy does not exclude the publication of theoretical works. The journal is committed to the dissemination of research findings to as wide an audience as possible. As a result, we strongly encourage authors to consider a wide and varied readership when writing papers.

Two types of articles are published in the *Accounting Research Journal*: (1) Main articles; and (2) Educational Notes.

Main Articles
These papers are written in an academic style, providing considerable detail about the issues at hand. The paper may be either theoretical or empirical or a combination of both. Work involving a case study approach is acceptable. In addition, well balanced review articles covering fundamental and/or topical areas relevant to the broad accounting discipline will be encouraged.

Educational Notes
These papers would involve issues or experiments which have accounting education (broadly defined) as their central focus. While these papers would normally be shorter than main articles, longer pieces may be justified depending on the specific topic area.

Submissions in any of these forms are warmly encouraged. The editors will endeavour to ensure a turn-around time of not more than 8 weeks in the first instance.

Submission of a paper implies that the material is original, unpublished work not under consideration for publication elsewhere and that the author/s agree that the copyright will be assigned to the QUT.

Manuscript Awards
An annual prize of $500 and a certificate will be awarded to the best manuscript published in the *Accounting Research Journal*. In addition, an annual prize of $200 and a certificate will be awarded to the best Educational Note manuscript published in the journal. The manuscript awards are voted on by the Editorial Board, excluding any Editorial Board members with a paper published in a given year. It is hoped that these awards might provide a worthwhile inducement for the submission of high quality research to the journal.

Preparation of Manuscripts
1. Manuscripts should be typed on one side of the paper only, double-spaced; all pages should be numbered.

2. Headings, Figures, Tables and Diagrams should be numbered consecutively and titled.

3. Footnotes should be numbered consecutively with superscript Arabic numerals. Footnotes must appear on the page they refer to and not on a separate sheet at the end of the manuscript.

4. References should appear in the text as Brown (1988) or Brown (1988, p. 120). The full references should be typed on separate sheets at the end of the manuscript. The following rules should be adopted:

Monographs
Brown, X.Y. (1988), *Advanced Commercial Law*, Brett Publishing Co., Brisbane.

Periodicals
Brown, X.Y. and Black, A.B. (1988), 'The Current Tax Law', *Journal of Taxation*, June, vol. 1, pp. 15-50.

5. Three copies of all manuscripts should be submitted.

6. Authors are requested to provide a copy of the paper on a 3.5 disk as well as a printed copy of the accepted version of the paper. Our equipment uses PC DOS with 360k floppy diskettes. The preferred word processing format is Microsoft Word.

Accounting Review (The)

ADDRESS FOR SUBMISSION:

Dan Dhaliwal, Editor
Accounting Review (The)
University of Arizona
Eller College of Management
Department of Accounting
McClelland 301, PO Box 210108
Tucson, AZ 85721-0108
USA
Phone: 520-626-0815
E-Mail: taruaz@email.arizona.edu
Web: http://aaahq.org/index.cfm

PUBLICATION GUIDELINES:

Manuscript Length: 26-30
Copies Required: One
Computer Submission: Yes
Format:
Fees to Review: 125.00 US$
 200.00 US$ AAA Nonmembers

Manuscript Style:
 See Manuscript Guidelines

CIRCULATION DATA:

Reader: Academics
Frequency of Issue: Quarterly
Sponsor/Publisher: American Accounting
 Association

REVIEW INFORMATION:

Type of Review: Blind Review
No. of External Reviewers: 2
No. of In House Reviewers: 0
Acceptance Rate: 11-15%
Time to Review: 2 - 3 Months
Reviewers Comments: Yes
Invited Articles: 0-5%
Fees to Publish: 0.00 US$

MANUSCRIPT TOPICS:
Accounting Theory & Practice; Auditing; Behavioral Accounting; Cost Accounting; Financial Accounting; Government & Non Profit Accounting; Managerial Accounting; Tax Accounting

MANUSCRIPT GUIDELINES/COMMENTS:

Editorial Policy and Style Information
According to the policies set by the Publications Committee (which were endorsed by the Executive Committee and were published in the Accounting Education News, June 1987), *The Accounting Review* "should be viewed as the premier journal for publishing articles reporting the results of accounting research and explaining and illustrating related research methodology. The scope of acceptable articles should embrace any research methodology and any accounting-related subject, as long as the articles meet the standards established for publication in the journal. No special sections should be necessary. The primary, but not exclusive, audience should be-as it is now-academicians, graduate students, and others interested in accounting research."

The primary criterion for publication in *The Accounting Review* is the significance of the contribution an article makes to the literature.

The efficiency and effectiveness of the editorial review process is critically dependent upon the actions of both the submitting authors and the reviewers. Authors accept the responsibility of preparing research papers at a level suitable for evaluation by independent reviewers. Such preparation, therefore, should include subjecting the manuscript to critique by colleagues and others and revising it accordingly prior to submission. The review process is not to be used as a means of obtaining feedback at early stages of developing the research.

Reviewers and associate editors are responsible for providing critically constructive and prompt evaluations of submitted research papers based on the significance of their contribution and on the rigor of analysis and presentation. Associate editors also make editorial recommendations to the editor.

Manuscript Preparation and Style
The Accounting Review's manuscript preparation guidelines follow (with a sight modification) the B-format of the *Chicago Manual of Style* (14th ed.; University of Chicago Press). Another helpful guide to usage and style is *The Elements of Style*, by William Strunk, Jr., and E. B. White (Macmillan). Spelling follows *Webster's Collegiate Dictionary*.

Format
1. All manuscripts should be typed on one side of 8 ½ x 11" good quality paper and be double-spaced, except for indented quotations.

2. Manuscripts should be as concise as the subject and research method permit, generally not to exceed 7,000 words.

3. Margins of at least one inch from top, bottom, and sides should facilitate editing and duplication.

4. To promote anonymous review, authors should not identify themselves directly or indirectly in their papers or in experimental test instruments included with the submission. Single authors should not use the editorial "we."

5. A cover page should show the title of the paper, the author's name, title and affiliation, email address, any acknowledgments, and a footnote indicating whether the author(s) would be willing to share the data (see last paragraph in this statement).

Pagination. All pages, including tables, appendices and references, should be serially numbered. The first section of the paper should be untitled and unnumbered. Major sections may be numbered in Roman numerals. Subsections should not be numbered.

Numbers. Spell out numbers from one to ten, except when used in tables and lists, and when used with mathematical, statistical, scientific, or technical units and quantities, such as distances, weights and measures. For example: three days; 3 kilometers; 30 years. All other numbers are expressed numerically.

Percentages and Decimal Fractions. In non-technical copy use the word percent in the text.

Hyphens. Use a hyphen to join unit modifiers or to clarify usage. For example: an up-to-date report; re-form. See *Webster's* for correct usage.

Keywords. The abstract is to be followed by four key words that will assist in indexing the paper.

Title Page
A title page stating the complete title, all author names and emails, and indicating the corresponding author should be presented on a separate page immediately preceding the abstract. Further, the title page should be saved in a separate file and given a filename that includes the word "titlepage".

Abstract / Introduction
An Abstract of approximately 100 words should be presented on a separate page immediately preceding the text. The Abstract should concisely inform the reader of the manuscript's topic, its methods, and its findings. Keywords and the Data Availability statements should follow the Abstract. The text of the paper should start with a section labeled "I. Introduction," which should provide more details about the paper's purpose, motivation, methodology, and findings. Both the Abstract and the Introduction should be relatively non-technical, yet clear enough for an informed reader to understand the manuscript's contribution. The manuscript's title, but neither the author's name nor other identification designations, should appear on the Abstract page.

Tables and Figures
The author should note the following general requirements:

1. Each table and figure (graphic) should appear on a separate page and should be placed at the end of the text. Each should bear an Arabic number and a complete title indicating the exact contents of the table or figure.

2. A reference to each graphic should be made in the text.

3. The author should indicate by marginal notation where each graphic should be inserted in the text.

4. Graphics should be reasonably interpreted without reference to the text.

5. Source lines and notes should be included as necessary.

Equations. Equations should be numbered in parentheses flush with the right-hand margin.

Documentation
Citations. Work cited should use the "author-date system" keyed to a list of works in the reference list (see below). Authors should make an effort to include the relevant page numbers in the cited works.

1. In the text, works are cited as follows: author's last name and date, without comma, in parentheses: for example, (Jones 1987); with two authors: (Jones and Freeman 1973); with more than two: (Jones et al. 1985); with more than one source cited together (Jones 1987; Freeman 1986); with two or more works by one author: (Jones 1985, 1987).

2. Unless confusion would result, do not use "p." or "pp." before page numbers: for example, (Jones 1987, 115).

3. When the reference list contains more than one work of an author published in the same year, the suffix a, b, etc., follows the date in the text citation: for example, (Jones 1987a) or (Jones 1987a; Freeman 1985b).

4. If an author's name is mentioned in the text, it need not be repeated in the citation; for example, "Jones (1987, 115) says...."

5. Citations to institutional works should use acronyms or short titles where practicable; for example, (AAA ASOBAT 1966); (AICPA Cohen Commission Report 1977). Where brief, the full title of an institutional work might be shown in a citation: for example, (ICAEW The Corporate Report 1975).

6. If the manuscript refers to statutes, legal treatises, or court cases, citations acceptable in law reviews should be used.

Reference List. Every manuscript must include a list of references containing only those works cited. Each entry should contain all data necessary for unambiguous identification. With the author-date system, use the following format recommended by the *Chicago Manual*:

1. Arrange citations in alphabetical order according to surname of the first author or the name of the institution responsible for the citation.

2. Use author's initials instead of proper names.

3. Date of publication should be placed immediately after author's name.

4. Titles of journals should not be abbreviated.

5. Multiple works by the same author(s) in the same year are distinguished by letters after the date.

6. Inclusive page numbers are treated as recommended in *Chicago Manual* section 8.67.

Footnotes. Footnotes are not used for documentation. Textual footnotes should be used only for extensions and useful excursions of information that if included in the body of the text might disrupt its continuity. Footnotes should be consecutively numbered throughout the manuscript with superscript Arabic numerals. Footnote text should be double-spaced and placed at the end of the article.

Submission of Manuscripts

Authors should note the following guidelines for submitting manuscripts:

1. Manuscripts currently under consideration by another journal or publisher should not be submitted. The author must state that the work is not submitted or published elsewhere.

2. In the case of manuscripts reporting on field surveys or experiments, Microsoft® Word or PDF files of the instrument (questionnaire, case, interview plan, or the like) should be submitted. Information that might identify the author(s) must be deleted from the instrument.

3. Online payment (Visa or MasterCard only) is preferred and must be in U.S. funds for $125.00 for members or $200.00 for nonmembers of the AAA. If unable to pay online, a check in U.S. funds, made payable to the American Accounting Association, may be sent to the editorial assistant at the address listed on this page. The submission fee is nonrefundable.

4. The author should retain a copy of the paper.

5. Revisions must be submitted within 12 months from request, otherwise they will be considered new submissions.

6. Final versions of papers accepted for publication MUST be submitted as Microsoft© Word files. No other format will be accepted. A hard copy printout must be furnished.

Editorial correspondence and all manuscripts should be sent to:
Attn: Kate Flynn Connolly, Editorial Assistant, TAR
Department of Accounting, University of Washington
Seattle, WA 98195-3200
Box 353200, Seattle, WA 98195-3200
Phone: (206) 616-3741;   Fax: (206) 685-9392
Email: **taruw@u.washington.edu**

Comments

Comments on articles previously published in *The Accounting Review* will be reviewed (anonymously) by two reviewers in sequence. The first reviewer will be the author of the original article being subjected to critique. If substance permits, a suitably revised comment will be sent to a second reviewer to determine its publishability in *The Accounting Review*. If a comment is accepted for publication, the original author will tie invited to reply. All other editorial requirements, as enumerated above, also apply to proposed comments.

Policy on Reproduction

An objective of *The Accounting Review* is to promote the wide dissemination of the results of systematic scholarly inquiries into the broad field of accounting. Permission is hereby granted to reproduce any of the contents of the *Review* for use in courses of instruction, as long as the source and American Accounting Association copyright are indicated in any such reproductions.

Policy on Data Availability
The following policy has been adopted by the Executive Committee in its April 1989 meeting. "An objective of (*The Accounting Review, Accounting Horizons, Issues in Accounting Education*) is to provide the widest possible dissemination of knowledge based on systematic scholarly inquiries into accounting as a field of professional research, and educational activity. As part of this process, authors are encouraged to make their data available for use by others in extending or replicating results reported in their articles. Authors of articles that report data dependent results should footnote the status of data availability and, when pertinent, this should be accompanied by information on how the data may be obtained."

Accounting, Auditing and Accountability Journal

ADDRESS FOR SUBMISSION:

Lee D. Parker, Joint Editor
Accounting, Auditing and Accountability
   Journal
University of Adelaide
School of Commerce
North Terrace
Adelaide, SA 5000,
Australia
Phone: 61-8 8303 4236
E-Mail: aaaj@commerce.adelaide.edu.au
Web: www.emeraldinsight.com/rpsv

PUBLICATION GUIDELINES:

Manuscript Length: 30+
Copies Required: Four
Computer Submission: Yes
Format: See Manuscript Guidelines
Fees to Review: 0.00 US$

Manuscript Style:
   See Manuscript Guidelines

CIRCULATION DATA:

Reader: Academics
Frequency of Issue: 6 Times/Year
Sponsor/Publisher: Emerald Group
   Publishing Limited

REVIEW INFORMATION:

Type of Review: Blind Review
No. of External Reviewers: 3+
No. of In House Reviewers: 2
Acceptance Rate: 20%
Time to Review: 3 - 4 Months
Reviewers Comments: Yes
Invited Articles: 0-5%
Fees to Publish: 0.00 US$

MANUSCRIPT TOPICS:
Accounting Theory & Practice; Auditing; Behavioral Accounting; Government & Non Profit Accounting

MANUSCRIPT GUIDELINES/COMMENTS:

Topics Include. Accounting in Third World; Accountability; Accounting & Accountability in the Public Sector; Accounting & Culture; Accounting & Gender and/or Feminist Theory; Accounting & Management Planning & Control; Accounting & Technology; Accounting & the Home; Accounting and the Public Interest; Accounting Communications; Accounting Policy & Standard Setting; Accounting Professions; Auditing/Accountability: Professional & Business Ethics; Corporate Governance; Corporate Regulation & Accountability; Critical Financial Analysis; Critical, Explanatory, Oral & Visual Approaches; Critical/Ethnographic Case Studies of Accounting in Action; Environmental Accounting; Intellectual Capital; International Accounting & Globalisation; Knowledge Management; Methodological & Theoretical Issues; New Forms of Accounting & Auditing; Non-Profit Organizations' Accountability; Risk Management; Social & Environmental Accounting

About the Journal

Articles submitted to *Accounting, Auditing & Accountability* should be original contributions and should not be under consideration for any other publication at the same time. Author's submitting articles for publication warrant that the work is not an infringement of any existing copyright and will indemnify the publisher against any breach of such warranty. For ease of dissemination and to ensure proper policing of use, papers and contributions become the legal copyright of the publisher unless otherwise agreed. Submissions should be sent to the Editor.

NOTES FOR CONTRIBUTORS

Copyright

Articles submitted to the journal should be original contributions and should not be under consideration for any other publication at the same time. Authors submitting articles for publication warrant that the work is not an infringement of any existing copyright and will indemnify the publisher against any breach of such warranty. For ease of dissemination and to ensure proper policing of use, papers and contributions become the legal copyright of the publisher unless otherwise agreed. Submissions should be sent to:

The Editor, Professor Lee D. Parker, Joint Editor,
Accounting, Auditing & Accountability Journal,
School of Commerce, University of Adelaide,
North Terrace, Adelaide, SA 5000, Australia.
Email: **aaaj@commerce.adelaide.edu.au**

Editorial objectives

The journal *Accounting, Auditing & Accountability* is dedicated to the advancement of accounting knowledge and provides a forum for the publication of high quality manuscripts concerning the interaction between accounting/auditing and their socio-economic and political environments. It therefore encourages critical analysis of policy and practice in these areas. Analysis could explore policy alternatives and provide new perspectives for the accounting discipline.

The problems of concern are international (in varying degree) and may have differing cultural, social and institutional structures. Analysis can be international, national or organization specific. It can be from a single, multi- or inter-disciplinary perspective.

Editorial criteria

Major criteria used to evaluate papers are:
1. Subject matter: must be of importance to the accounting discipline.
2. Research question: must fall within the journal's scope.
3. Research: well designed and executed.
4. Presentation: well written and conforming to the journal's style.

The reviewing process

Each paper submitted is subject to the following review procedures:
1. It is reviewed by the editor for general suitability for this publication.
2. If it is judged suitable two reviewers are selected and a double blind review process takes place.

3. Based on the recommendations of the reviewers, the editors then decide whether the particular article should be accepted as it is, revised or rejected.

Emerald Literati Editing Service
The Literati Club can recommend the services of a number of freelance copy editors, all themselves experienced authors, to contributors who wish to improve the standard of English in their paper before submission. This is particularly useful for those whose first language is not English.   http://www.emeraldinsight.com/literaticlub/editingservice.htm

Manuscript requirements
Three copies of the manuscript should be submitted in double line spacing with wide margins. All authors should be shown and author's details must be printed on a separate sheet and the author should not be identified anywhere else in the article.

As a guide, articles should be between 4,000 and 7,000 words in length. A title of not more than eight words should be provided. A brief autobiographical note should be supplied including full name, affiliation, e-mail address and full international contact details. Authors must supply an abstract of 100-150 words. Up to six keywords should be included which encapsulate the principal subjects covered by the article.

Where there is a methodology, it should be clearly described under a separate heading. Headings must be short, clearly defined and not numbered. Notes or Endnotes should be used only if absolutely necessary and must be identified in the text by consecutive numbers, enclosed in square brackets and listed at the end of the article.

Figures, charts and diagrams should be kept to a minimum. They should be provided both electronically and as good quality originals. They must be black and white with minimum shading and numbered consecutively using Arabic numerals.

Artwork should be either copied or pasted from the origination software into a blank Microsoft Word document, or saved and imported into a blank Microsoft Word document. Artwork created in MS PowerPoint is also acceptable. Artwork may be submitted in the following standard image formats: .eps - Postscript, .pdf - Adobe Acrobat portable document, .ai - Adobe Acrobat portable document, .wmf - Windows Metafile. If it is not possible to supply graphics in the formats listed above, authors should ensure that figures supplied as .tif, .gif, .jpeg, .bmp, .pcx, .pic, .pct are supplied as files of at least 300 dpi and at least 10cm wide.

In the text the position of a figure should be shown by typing on a separate line the words "take in Figure 2". Authors should supply succinct captions.

For photographic images good quality original *photographs* should be submitted. If submitted electronically they should be saved as tif files of at least 300dpi and at least 10cm wide. Their position in the text should be shown by typing on a separate line the words "take in Plate 2".

Tables should be kept to a minimum. They must be numbered consecutively with roman numerals and a brief title. In the text, the position of the table should be shown by typing on a separate line the words "take in Table IV".

Photos and illustrations must be supplied as good quality black and white original half tones with captions. Their position should be shown in the text by typing on a separate line the words "take in Plate 2".

References to other publications should be complete and in Harvard style. They should contain full bibliographical details and journal titles should not be abbreviated. For multiple citations in the same year use a, b, c immediately following the year of publication. References should be shown within the text by giving the author's last name followed by a comma and year of publication all in round brackets, e.g. (Fox, 1994). At the end of the article should be a reference list in alphabetical order as follows:

(a) *for books*
surname, initials and year of publication, title, publisher, place of publication, e.g. Casson, M. (1979), Alternatives to the Multinational Enterprise, Macmillan, London.

(b) *for chapter in edited book*
surname, initials and year, "title", editor's surname, initials, title, publisher, place, pages, e.g. Bessley, M. and Wilson, P. (1984), "Public policy and small firms in Britain", in Levicki, C. (Ed.), Small Business Theory and Policy, Croom Helm, London, pp.111-26. Please note that the chapter title must be underlined.

(c) *for articles*
surname, initials, year "title", journal, volume, number, pages, e.g. Fox, S. (1994) "Empowerment as a catalyst for change: an example from the food industry", Supply Chain Management, Vol 2 No 3, pp. 29-33.

If there is more than one author list surnames followed by initials. All authors should be shown.

Electronic sources should include the URL of the electronic site at which they may be found, as follows:
Neuman, B.C.(1995), "Security, payment, and privacy for network commerce", IEEE Journal on Selected Areas in Communications, Vol. 13 No.8, October, pp.1523-31. Available (IEEE SEPTEMBER) http://www.research.att.com/jsac/

Notes/Endnotes should be used only if absolutely necessary. They should, however, always be used for citing Web sites. They should be identified in the text by consecutive numbers enclosed in square brackets and listed at the end of the article. Please then provide full Web site addresses in the end list.

Final submission of the article
Once accepted for publication, the final version of the manuscript must be provided, accompanied by a 3.5" disk of the same version labeled with: disk format; author name(s); title of article; journal title; file name.

60

Each article must be accompanied by a completed and signed Journal Article Record Form available from the Editor or on http://www.emeraldinsight.com/literaticlub Authors should note that proofs are not supplied prior to publication.

The manuscript will be considered to be the definitive version of the article. The author must ensure that it is complete, grammatically correct and without spelling or typographical errors. In preparing the disk, please use one of the following preferred formats: Word, Word Perfect, Rich text format or TeX/LaTeX.

Technical assistance is available from Emerald's Literati Club on http://www.emeraldinsight.com/literaticlub or by contacting Mike Massey at Emerald, e-mail mmassey@emeraldinsight.com.

A summary of submission requirements:
- Good quality hard copy manuscript
- A labelled disk
- A brief professional biography of each author
- An abstract and keywords
- Figures, photos and graphics electronically and as good quality originals
- Harvard style references where appropriate
- A completed Journal Article Record form

Accounting, Business and Financial History

ADDRESS FOR SUBMISSION:

John Richard Edwards & Trevor Boyns, Eds
Accounting, Business and Financial History
Cardiff Business School
Accounting & Business History
  Research Unit
Colum Drive
Cardiff, CF10 3EU
UK
Phone: +2920 876658
E-Mail: edwardsjr@cardiff.ac.uk
  boyns@cardiff.ac.uk
Web: www.tandf.co.uk   and
    www.cf.ac.uk/carbs/research/abhru/
    index.html

PUBLICATION GUIDELINES:

Manuscript Length: 26-30
Copies Required: Three
Computer Submission: Yes
Format: MS Word
Fees to Review: 0.00 US$

Manuscript Style:
    See Manuscript Guidelines

CIRCULATION DATA:

Reader: Academics
Frequency of Issue: 3 Times/Year
Sponsor/Publisher: Routledge (Taylor &
  Francis Ltd.)

REVIEW INFORMATION:

Type of Review: Blind Review
No. of External Reviewers: 2
No. of In House Reviewers:
Acceptance Rate: 40%
Time to Review: 2 - 3 Months
Reviewers Comments: Yes
Invited Articles: 0-5%
Fees to Publish: 0.00 US$

MANUSCRIPT TOPICS:
Accounting Education; Accounting Information Systems; Accounting Theory & Practice;
Accounting, Business & Financial History; Auditing; Behavioral Accounting; Cost
Accounting; Economic Development; Economic History

MANUSCRIPT GUIDELINES/COMMENTS:

Aims & Scope
Accounting, Business & Financial History is a major journal which covers the areas of
accounting history, business history and financial history. As well as providing a valuable
international forum for investigating these areas, it aims to explore:
- the inter-relationship between accounting practices, financial markets and economic
  development
- the influence of accounting on business decision making
- the environment and social influences on the business and financial world

The special features of *ABFH* include:
- an on-going record and analysis of past developments in business and finance history
- explanations for present structures and practices
- a platform for solving current problems and predicting future developments

Notes for Contributors

1. Authors should submit three complete copies of their text, tables and figures, with any original illustrations, to: John Richard Edwards, Accounting and Business History Research Unit, Cardiff Business School CF10 3EU, UK. Where convenient please also supply an electronic version of your paper in Word format. Authors should note that evidence suggests that papers which have been enhanced as the result of the prior comment of colleagues and/or seminars and conferences stand a better chance of acceptance for publication.

2. The submission should include a cover page showing the author's name, the department where the work was done, an address for correspondence (including email), if different, and any acknowledgements.

3. Submissions should be in English, typed in double spacing with wide margins, on one side only of the paper, preferably of A4 size. The title, but not the author's name should appear on the first page of the manuscript.

4. Articles should normally be as concise as possible and preceded by an abstract of not more than 100 words and a list of up to 6 keywords for on-line searching purposes.

5. Within the manuscript there may be up to three levels of heading.

6. Tables and figures should not be inserted in the pages of the manuscript but should be on separate sheets. They should be numbered consecutively in Arabic numerals with a descriptive caption. The desired position in the text for each table and figure should be indicated in the margin of the manuscript.

7. Use the Harvard system of referencing which gives the name of the author and the date of publication as a key to the full bibliographical details which are set out in the list of references. When the author's name is mentioned in the text, the date is inserted in parentheses immediately after the name, as in 'Aldcroft (1964)'. When a less direct reference is made to one or more authors, both name and date are bracketed, with the references separated by a semicolon, as in 'several authors have noted this trend (Rimmer, 1960; Pollard, 1965; Mckendrick, 1970)'. Where appropriate, page numbers should also be provided '(Roberts, 1956: 56)'. When the reference is to a work of dual or multiple authorship, use 'Harvey and Press (1988)' or 'Yamey *et al.* (1963)' respectively. If an author has two references published in the same year, add lower case letters after the date to distinguish them, as in '(Johnson, 1984a, 1984b)'. Always use the minimum number of figures in page numbers, dates, etc., e.g. 22-4, 105-6 (but 112-13 for teen numbers) and 1968-9.

8. Direct quotations of 40 words or more should start on a separate line and be indented.

9. Footnotes should be used only where necessary to avoid interrupting the continuity of the text. They should be numbered consecutively using superscript Arabic numerals. They should appear at the end of the main text, immediately before the list of references.

10. Submissions should include a reference list, in alphabetical order, at the end of the article. The content and format should conform to the following examples.

Kennedy, W.P. (1987) *Industrial Structure: Capital Markets and the Origins of British Economic Decline*, (Cambridge: Cambridge University Press).

Chapman, S.D. (1985) British-based investment groups before 1914, *The Economic History Review*, 38(2), pp. 230-51.

Shannon, H.A. (1954) The limited companies of 1886-1883, in E.M. Carus-Wilson (Ed.) Essays in Economic History, pp. 380-415 (London: Edward Arnold)..

11. For any other matters of presentation not covered by the above notes, please refer to the usual custom and practice as indicated by the last few issues of the journal.

12. On acceptance for publication, authors will be requested to provide a copy of their paper in exact accordance with the conventions listed in the preceding notes. If the final version of the paper is *not* submitted in accordance with these conventions then publication may be delayed by the need to return manuscripts to authors for necessary revisions. Authors should note that, following acceptance for publication, they will be required to provide not only a hard copy of the final version, but also a copy on a virus-free disk, preferably in MS-Word 6 format, if possible. Authors will also be required to complete a Publishing Agreement form assigning copyright to the Publisher

13. Proofs will be sent for correction to a first-named author, unless otherwise requested. The difficulty and expense involved in making amendments at the page proof stage make it essential for authors to prepare their typescript carefully; any alteration to the original text is strongly discouraged.

14. It is a condition of publication that authors vest or license copyright in their articles, including abstracts, in Taylor & Francis Ltd. This enables us to ensure full copyright protection and to disseminate the article, and the journal, to the widest possible readership in print and electronic formats as appropriate. Authors may, of course, use the material elsewhere after publication providing that prior permission is obtained from Taylor & Francis Ltd. Authors are themselves responsible for obtaining permission to reproduce copyright material from other sources. To view the 'Copyright Transfer Frequently Asked Questions' please visit: http://www.tandf.co.uk/journals/copyright.asp

Accounting, Organizations and Society

ADDRESS FOR SUBMISSION:

Anthony G. Hopwood, Editor-in-Chief
Accounting, Organizations and Society
University of Oxford
Said Business School
Park End Street
Oxford, OX1 1HP
UK
Phone: 01865 288903
E-Mail: aos@sbs.ox.ac.uk
Web: www.elsevier.com

CIRCULATION DATA:

Reader: Academics
Frequency of Issue: 8 Times/Year
Sponsor/Publisher: Elsevier Inc.

PUBLICATION GUIDELINES:

Manuscript Length:
Copies Required: Two
Computer Submission: Yes Disk, Email
Format:
Fees to Review: 0.00 US$

Manuscript Style:
See Manuscript Guidelines

REVIEW INFORMATION:

Type of Review: Blind Review
No. of External Reviewers: 2
No. of In House Reviewers: 0
Acceptance Rate: 11-20%
Time to Review: 2 - 3 Months
Reviewers Comments: Yes
Invited Articles: 0-5%
Fees to Publish: 0.00 US$

MANUSCRIPT TOPICS:
Accounting Information Systems; Accounting Theory & Practice; Auditing; Behavioral Accounting; Economic History; Financial Services; Government & Non Profit Accounting

MANUSCRIPT GUIDELINES/COMMENTS:

Description
Accounting, Organizations & Society is a major international journal concerned with all aspects of the relationship between accounting and human behaviour, organizational structures and processes, and the changing social and political environment of the enterprise. Its unique focus covers such topics as: the social role of accounting, social accounting, social audit and accounting for scarce resources; the provision of accounting information to employees and trade unions and the development of participative information systems; processes influencing accounting innovations and the social and political aspects of accounting standard setting; behavioural studies of the users of accounting information; information processing views of organizations, and the relationship between accounting and other information systems and organizational structures and processes; organizational strategies for designing accounting and information systems; human resource accounting; cognitive aspects of accounting and decision-making processes, and the behavioural aspects of budgeting, planning and investment appraisal.

Audience
Researchers and students involved in behavioural, organizational and social aspects of accounting. personnel managers, information technologists.

GUIDE FOR AUTHORS
Submission of Papers
Authors are requested to submit their original manuscript and figures plus two copies to the Editor-in-Chief of *Accounting, Organizations and Society*: Anthony G. Hopwood, Said Business School, University of Oxford, Park End Street, Oxford OX1 1HP, UK.

Submission of a paper implies that it has not been published previously, that it is not under consideration for publication elsewhere, and that if accepted it will not be published elsewhere in the same form, in English or in any other language, without the written consent of the publisher. The contribution of the author(s) should be an original one and should in no way violate any existing copyright, and it should contain nothing of a libellous or scandalous nature.

Types of Contributions
Original papers; review articles; short communications; reports of conferences and meetings; book reviews; letters to the editor; forthcoming meetings; selected bibliography.

Manuscript Preparation
General. Manuscripts must be typewritten, double-spaced with wide margins on one side of white paper. Good quality printouts with a font size of 12 or 10 pt are required. A cover page should give the title of the manuscript, the author's name, position and institutional affiliation, and an acknowledgement, if desired. The title of the manuscript, but not the authors' names, should appear on the first page of the text. The corresponding author should be identified (include a Fax number and E-mail address). Full postal addresses must be given for all co-authors on the cover sheet. Authors should consult a recent issue of the journal for style if possible. An electronic copy of the paper should accompany the final version. The Editors reserve the right to adjust style to certain standards of uniformity. Authors should retain a copy of their manuscript since we cannot accept responsibility for damage or loss of papers. Original manuscripts are discarded one month after publication unless the Publisher is asked to return original material after use.

Abstract and Index. Three copies of an abstract not exceeding 80 words should accompany each manuscript submitted. Authors are also asked to supply a maximum of 10 keywords or phrases which will be used for indexing purposes.

Text. Follow this order when typing manuscripts: Title, Authors, Affiliations, Abstract, Keywords, Main text, Acknowledgements, Appendix, References, Vitae, Figure Captions and then Tables. Do not import the Figures or Tables into your text but supply them as separate files. The corresponding author should be identified with an asterisk and footnote. All other footnotes (except for table footnotes) should be identified with superscript Arabic numbers. Footnotes for clarification or elaboration should be used sparingly.

66

Research Instruments. If the manuscript refers to questionnaires or other research instruments which are not fully reproduced in the text, authors must also submit three copies of the complete research. Because of space limitations, questionnaires and other research instruments sometimes may not be fully reproduced in the published paper. When they are not fully reproduced a note must be inserted in the text of the paper indicating the address from which copies of the complete instrument are available.

References. All publications cited in the text should be present in a list of references following the text of the manuscript. The work should be cited by author's name and year of publication in the body of the text, e.g. (Watson, 1975); or when reference is made to a specific page (Wilkes & Harrison, 1975, p. 21). Where the author's name is included in the text, the name should not be repeated in the reference citation: e.g. "Angrist (1975, p. 79) says...". For identification purposes, the suffix a, b, etc. should follow the date when the bibliography contains more than one work published by an author in a single year. For 2-6 authors, all authors are to be listed at first citation, with "&" separating the last two authors. For more than six authors, use the first six authors followed by et al. In subsequent citations for three or more authors use author et al. in the text. The list of references should be arranged alphabetically by authors' names. The manuscript should be carefully checked to ensure that the spelling of authors' names and dates are exactly the same in the text as in the reference list. Each reference should contain full bibliographical details and journal titles should not be abbreviated. References should be given in the following form:

Abernathy, M., & Stoelwinder, J. (1996). The role of professional control in the management of complex organizations. *Accounting, Organizations and Society* 20, 1-17.

Bowen, D.E., & Schneider, B. (1988). Services, marketing and management: implications for organisational behaviour. In B.M. Straw, & L.L. Cummings, *Research in organisational behaviour*, vol. 10. Greenwich, CT: JAI Press.

Ericsson, K., & Simon, H. (1984). *Protocol analysis.* Cambridge, MA: The MIT Press.

Harper, R. (1989). An ethnography of accountants. Ph D Thesis. Department of Sociology, Manchester University.

Illustrations. All illustrations should be provided in camera-ready form, suitable for reproduction (which may include reduction) without retouching. Photographs, charts and diagrams are all to be referred to as "Figure(s)" and should be numbered consecutively in the order to which they are referred. They should accompany the manuscript, but should not be included within the text. All illustrations should be clearly marked on the back with the figure number and the author's name. All figures are to have a caption. Captions should be supplied on a separate sheet at the end of the paper. The author should clearly indicate in the text where he or she would like each figure to be placed.

Line drawings. Good quality printouts on white paper produced in black ink are required. All lettering, graph lines and points on graphs should be sufficiently large and bold to permit reproduction when the diagram has been reduced to a size suitable for inclusion in the journal.

Dye-line prints or photocopies are not suitable for reproduction. Do not use any type of shading on computer-generated illustrations.

Photographs. Original photographs must be supplied as they are to be reproduced (e.g. black and white or colour). If necessary, a scale should be marked on the photograph. Please note that photocopies of photographs are not acceptable.

Colour. Authors will be charged for colour at current printing costs.

Tables. Tables should be numbered consecutively and given a suitable caption and each table typed on a separate sheet. Footnotes to tables should be typed below the table and should be referred to by superscript lowercase letters. No vertical rules should be used. Tables should not duplicate results presented elsewhere in the manuscript, (e.g. in graphs). The author should clearly indicate in the text where he or she would like each table to be placed.

Electronic Submission
Authors should submit an electronic copy of the final version of their paper with the final version of the manuscript. The electronic copy should match the hardcopy exactly. Please specify what software was used, including which release, and what computer was used (IBM compatible PC or Apple Macintosh). Always keep a backup copy of the electronic file for reference and safety. Full details of electronic submission and formats can be obtained from http://www.elsevier.com/locate/disksub or from Author Services at Elsevier Science.

Proofs
Proofs will be sent to the author (first named author if no corresponding author is identified of multi-authored papers) and should be returned within 48 hours of receipt. Corrections should be restricted to typesetting errors; any others may be charged to the author. Any queries should be answered in full. Please note that authors are urged to check their proofs carefully before return, since the inclusion of late corrections cannot be guaranteed. Proofs are to be returned to the Log-in Department, Elsevier Science, Stover Court, Bampfylde Street, Exeter, Devon EX1 2AH, UK.

Offprints
Twenty-five offprints will be supplied free of charge. Offprints and copies of the issue can be ordered at a specially reduced rate using the order form sent to the corresponding author after the manuscript has been accepted. Orders for reprints (after publication) will incur a 50% surcharge.

Copyright
All authors must sign the "Transfer of Copyright" agreement before the article can be published. This transfer agreement enables Elsevier Science Ltd to protect the copyrighted material for the authors, but does not relinquish the author's proprietary rights. The copyright transfer covers the exclusive rights to reproduce and distribute the article, including reprints, photographic reproductions, microfilm or any other reproductions of similar nature and translations. This includes the right to adapt the article for use in conjunction with computer systems and programs, including reproduction or publication in machine-readable form and

incorporation in retrieval systems. Authors are responsible for obtaining from the copyright holder permission to reproduce any figures for which copyright exists.

Author Services
For queries relating to the general submission of manuscripts (including electronic text and artwork) and the status of accepted manuscripts, please contact Author Services, Log-in Department, Elsevier Science, The Boulevard, Langford Lane, Kidlington, Oxford OX5 1GB, UK. E-mail: authors@elsevier.co.uk, Fax: +44 (0) 1865 843905, Tel: +44 (0) 1865 843900. Authors can also keep track of the progress of their accepted article through our OASIS system on the Internet. For information on an article go to this Internet page and key in the corresponding author's name and the Elsevier reference number.

Advances in Accounting

ADDRESS FOR SUBMISSION:

Philip M. J. Reckers, Editor
Advances in Accounting
Arizona State University
W.P. Carey School of Business
Tempe, AZ 85287
USA
Phone: 602-965-2283
E-Mail: philip.reckers@asu.edu
Web: www.elsevier.com

CIRCULATION DATA:

Reader: Academics
Frequency of Issue: Yearly
Sponsor/Publisher: Elsevier Inc.

PUBLICATION GUIDELINES:

Manuscript Length: Any
Copies Required: Four
Computer Submission: Yes
Format:
Fees to Review: 50.00 US$

Manuscript Style:
    See Manuscript Guidelines

REVIEW INFORMATION:

Type of Review: Blind Review
No. of External Reviewers: 2
No. of In House Reviewers: 1
Acceptance Rate: 11-20%
Time to Review: 3 - 4 Months
Reviewers Comments: Yes
Invited Articles: 0-5%
Fees to Publish: 0.00 US$

MANUSCRIPT TOPICS:

Accounting Education; Accounting Information Systems; Accounting Theory & Practice; Auditing; Behavioral Accounting; Cost Accounting; Tax Accounting

MANUSCRIPT GUIDELINES/COMMENTS:

Advances in Accounting (AIA) is a professional publication whose purpose is to meet the information needs of both practitioners and academicians. We plan to publish thoughtful, well-developed articles on a variety of current topics in financial and management accounting, accounting education, auditing and accounting information systems.

Articles may range from empirical to analytical, from practice-based to the development of new techniques. Articles must be readable, relevant, and articles must be understandable and concise. To be relevant, articles must be related to problems facing the accounting and business community. To empirical reports, sound design and execution are critical. For theoretical treatises, reasonable assumptions and logical development are essential.

AIA welcomes all comments and encourages articles from practitioners and academicians. Editorial correspondence pertaining to manuscripts should be sent to Phillip M. J. Reckers.

Editorial Policy and Manuscripts Form Guidelines

1. Manuscripts should be typewritten and double-spaced on 8" x 11" white paper. Only one side of a page should be used. Margins should be set to facilitate editing and duplication except as noted:

A. Tables, figures and exhibits should appear on a separate page. Each should be numbered and have a title.

B. Footnotes should be presented by citing the author's name and the year of publication in the body of the text, e.g., Schwartz [1981]; Reckers and Pany [1980].

2. Manuscripts should include a cover page which indicated the author's name and affiliation.

3. Manuscripts should include on a separate lead page an abstract not exceeding 200 words. The author's name and affiliation should not appear on the abstract.

4. Topical headings and subheadings should be used. Main headings in the manuscript should be centered, secondary headings should be flush with the left-hand margin. (As a guide to usage and style, refer to William Strunk, Jr. and E.B. White, *The Elements of Style*.)

5. Manuscripts must include a list of references which contain only those works actually cited. (As a helpful guide in preparing a list of references, refer to Kate L. Turabian. *A Manual for Writers of Term Papers, Theses, and Dissertations*.)

6. In order to be assured of an anonymous review, authors should not identify themselves directly or indirectly. Reference to unpublished working papers and dissertations should be avoided. If necessary, authors may indicate that the reference is being withheld for the reasons cited above.

7. The author will be provided one complete volume of the *AIA* issue in which his or her manuscript appears and ten off-prints of the article.

8. Manuscripts currently under review by other publications should not be submitted. Complete reports of research presented at a national or regional conference of a professional association (e.g. AAA, DSI, etc.) and "State of the Art" papers are acceptable.

9. **Four** copies of each manuscript should be submitted to the Editor-in-Chief at the Arizona State University address. Copies of any and all research instruments also should be included.

For additional information regarding the type of manuscripts that are desired, see *AIA* Statement of Purpose.

Advances in Accounting Behavioral Research

ADDRESS FOR SUBMISSION:

Vicky Arnold, Editor
Advances in Accounting Behavioral
   Research
University of Central Florida
Dixon School of Accounting
PO Box 161400
Orlando, FL 32816-1400
USA
Phone: 407-823-5761
E-Mail: varnold@bus.ucf.edu
Web: www.elsevier.com

PUBLICATION GUIDELINES:

Manuscript Length: 30+
Copies Required: Electronic
Computer Submission: Yes
Format: MS Word
Fees to Review: 0.00 US$

Manuscript Style:
   American Psychological Association

CIRCULATION DATA:

Reader: Academics
Frequency of Issue: Yearly
Sponsor/Publisher: Elsevier Inc.

REVIEW INFORMATION:

Type of Review: Blind Review
No. of External Reviewers: 2
No. of In House Reviewers: 0
Acceptance Rate: 11-20%
Time to Review: 2 - 3 Months
Reviewers Comments: Yes
Invited Articles: 0-5%
Fees to Publish: 0.00 US$

MANUSCRIPT TOPICS:

Accounting Information Systems; Accounting Theory & Practice; Auditing; Behavioral Accounting; Behavioral Information Systems; Cost Accounting; Literature Reviews Relative to AIS; Tax Accounting

MANUSCRIPT GUIDELINES/COMMENTS:

The manuscript should include a Title Page, which should contain the following information:
1. the title,
2. the name(s) and institutional affiliations(s) of the author(s),
3. telephone number,
4. e-mail address,
5. fax number, and
6. an abstract of not more than 150 words.

This should be followed by the Main Text, Endnotes, Acknowledgements, Appendix, References, Figures, and Tables, Use times roman for all text and tables.

When typing
- Distinguish between the digit 1 and the letter l (also 0 and O)
- Use tabs for indents, not spaces.
- Display titles and headings in a consistent manner.
- Double space between all lines of the manuscript; single spacing is acceptable only on tables.

References should follow the APA (American Psychological Association) standard.

Begin each table or figure on a separate page. In text, indicate the approximate placement of each table by a clear break in the text, inserting "TABLE 1/FIGURE 1 ABOUT HERE". Set off by double spacing above and below. All figures and tables should be numbered consecutively (e.g. table 1, figure 1).

Please avoid the use of personal pronouns such as "I" and "we". Also, please use an active, rather than passive, writing style as much as possible.

Advances in Accounting Education

ADDRESS FOR SUBMISSION:

Bill Schwartz, Editor
Advances in Accounting Education
Indiana University - South Bend
School of Business and Economics
3147 Wiekamp Hall
1700 Mishawaka Avenue
South Bend, IN 46634-7111
USA
Phone: 574-520-4292
E-Mail: bschwart@iusb.edu
Web: www.elsevier.com/locate/series

PUBLICATION GUIDELINES:

Manuscript Length: No Reply
Copies Required: One
Computer Submission: Yes
Format: MS Word
Fees to Review: 35.00 US$

Manuscript Style:
      See Manuscript Guidelines

CIRCULATION DATA:

Reader: Academics
Frequency of Issue: Yearly
Sponsor/Publisher: Elsevier Inc.

REVIEW INFORMATION:

Type of Review: Blind Review
No. of External Reviewers: 2
No. of In House Reviewers: 0
Acceptance Rate: 21-30%
Time to Review: 1 - 2 Months
Reviewers Comments: Yes
Invited Articles: 0-5%
Fees to Publish: 0.00 US$

MANUSCRIPT TOPICS:
Accounting Education

MANUSCRIPT GUIDELINES/COMMENTS:

Description
Advances in Accounting Education is a refereed, academic research annual whose purpose is to meet the needs of individuals interested in the educational process. We publish thoughtful, well-developed articles that are readable, relevant and reliable. Articles are empirical and non-empirical with the emphasis on pedagogy explaining how teaching methods or curricula/programs can be improved.

Instructions to Authors
To be assured of an anonymous review, authors should NOT identify themselves directly or indirectly in the text of the paper. Authors should avoid reference to unpublished working papers and dissertations. If necessary, authors may indicate the reference is being withheld for the reasons cited here.

Authors ultimately must submit accepted manuscripts on an IBM compatible disk.

Authors should not submit manuscripts currently under review by other publications or manuscripts that have already been published (including proceedings from regional or national meetings). Please include a statement to that effect in the cover letter accompanying your submission. Authors can submit complete reports of research presented at regional or national meetings that they did not publish in the proceedings.

Authors should submit one copy of the manuscript by email attachment without a cover page and also the cover page in a separate attachment. Send one hard copy and the submission fee by regular mail. Empirical manuscripts go to:

Anthony H. Catanach
College of Commerce and Finance
Villanova University
Villanova, PA 19085-1678
USA
anthony.catanach@villanova.edu

Non-empirical manuscripts go to:
Bill N. Schwartz
School of Business and Economics
Indiana University South Bend
1700 Mishawaka Avenue
P.O. Box 7111
South Bend, IN 46634-7111
USA
bschwart@iusb.edu

The author should send a check for $35 made payable to *Accounting Education* each submission, whether it is the initial submission or a revision.

Detailed information on how to prepare your manuscript according to production requirements can be found at:

http://www.elsevier.com/homepage/authors/?main=/homepage/about/ita/getting_books_published.htm

Writing Guidelines
1. Each paper should include a cover sheet with names, addresses, telephone numbers, fax numbers, and e-mail address for all authors. The title page also should include an abbreviated title you should use as a running head (see item #six below). The running head should be no more than 70 characters, which includes all letters, punctuation and spaces between words.

2. The second page should consist of an Abstract of approximately 150-200 words.

3. You should begin the first page of the manuscript with the manuscript's title. DO NOT use the term "Introduction" or any other term at the beginning of the manuscript. Simply begin your discussion.

4. Use uniform margins of 1 ½ inches at the top, bottom, right and left of every page. Do not justify lines, leave the right margins uneven. *Do not* hyphenate words at the end of a line; let a line run short or long rather than break a word. Type no more than 25 lines of text per page.

5. Double space *among all* lines of text, which includes title, headings, quotations, figure captions, and all parts of tables.

6. After you have arranged the manuscript pages in correct order, number them consecutively, beginning with the title page. *Number all pages.* Place the number in the upper right-hand corner using Arabic numerals. Identify each manuscript page by typing an abbreviated title (header) above the page number.

7. We prefer **active** voice. Therefore, you can use the pronouns "we" and "I." Also, please avoid using a series of prepositional phrases. We strongly encourage you to use a grammar and spell checker on manuscripts before you submit to our journal.

8. All citations within your text should include page numbers. An appropriate citation is Schwartz (1994, 152) or Ketz (1995, 113-115). You do not need to cite six or seven references at once, particularly when the most recent references refer to earlier works. Please try to limit yourself to two or three citations at a time, preferably the most recent ones.

9. You should place page numbers for quotations along with the date of the material being cited. For example: According to Beaver (1987, 4), "Our knowledge of education research . . . and its potential limitations for accounting. . . ."

10. **Headings**. Use headings and subheadings liberally to break up your text and ease the reader's ability to follow your arguments and train of thought. First-level headings should be upper-case italics, bold face, and flush to the left margin. Second level headings should be in bold face italics, flush to the left margin with only the first letter of each primary word capitalized. Third-level headings should be flush to the left margin, in italics (but not bold face), with only the first letter of each primary word capitalized.

11. You should list any acknowledgments on a separate page immediately after your last page of text (before the *Notes* and *References* Sections). Type the word "Acknowledgment," centered, at the top of a new page; type the acknowledgment itself as a double-spaced, single paragraph.

12. You should try to incorporate endnote/footnote material into the body of the manuscript. When you have notes, place them on a separate section before your references. Begin notes on a separate page, with the word "Notes" centered at the top of the page. All notes should be double-spaced; indent the first line of each note five spaces.

13. Your reference pages should appear immediately after your "Notes" section (if any) and should include only works cited in the manuscript. The first page of this section should begin with the word "References" centered on the page. References to working papers are normally

76

not appropriate. All references must be available to the reader; however, reference to unpublished dissertations is acceptable.

14. You should label TABLES and FIGURES as such and number them consecutively (using Arabic numerals) in the order in which you mention them first in the text. Indicate the approximate placement of each table/figure by a clear break in the text, inserting:
TABLE (or FIGURE) 1 ABOUT HERE
set off double-spaced above and below. Tables should be placed after your References section: figures should follow tables. Double-space each table/figure and begin each on a separate page.

15. Parsimony is a highly desirable trait for manuscripts we publish. Be concise in making your points and arguments.

16. *Sample Book References*
Runkel, P. J. and J.E. McGrath. 1972. Research on human behavior. *A Systematic guide to method*. New York: Holt, Rinehart and Winston.

Smith, P. L. 1982. Measures of variance accounted for: Theory and Practice. Pp. 101-129 in *Statistical and methodological issues in psychology and social science research*, edited by G. Keren. Hillsdale, NJ: Erlbaum.

17. *Sample Journal References*
Abdolmohammadi, M. J., K. Menon, T. W. Oliver, and S. Umpathy. 1985. The role of the doctoral dissertation in accounting research careers. *Issues in Accounting Education*: 59-76.

Thompson, B. 1993. The use of statistical significance tests in research: Bootstrap and other methods. *Journal of Experimental Education* 61: 361-377.

Simon, H.A. 1980. The behavioral and social sciences. *Sciences* (July): 72-78.

Stout, D. E. and D. E. Wygal. 1994. An empirical evidence of test item sequencing effects in the managerial accounting classroom: Further evidence and extensions. Pp. 105-122 in *Advances in Accounting*, vol. 12, edited by Bill N. Schwartz. Greenwich, CT: JAI Press.

Advances in Environmental Accounting and Management

ADDRESS FOR SUBMISSION:

Bikki Jaggi, Co-Editor
Advances in Environmental Accounting and
   Management
Rutgers University
School of Business
Department of Accounting
Levin Building
New Brunswick, NJ 08903
USA
Phone: 732-445-3540
E-Mail: jaggi@rbsmail.rutgers.edu
   mfreedman@towson.edu
Web: www.elsevier.com

PUBLICATION GUIDELINES:

Manuscript Length: 16-50
Copies Required: Three
Computer Submission: Yes
Format:
Fees to Review: 0.00 US$

Manuscript Style:
   Chicago Manual of Style, Accounting
   Review

CIRCULATION DATA:

Reader: Academics
Frequency of Issue: Yearly
Sponsor/Publisher: Elsevier Inc.

REVIEW INFORMATION:

Type of Review: Blind Review
No. of External Reviewers: 2
No. of In House Reviewers: 1
Acceptance Rate: 20-30%
Time to Review: 2 - 3 Months
Reviewers Comments: Yes
Invited Articles: 0-5%
Fees to Publish: 0.00 US$

MANUSCRIPT TOPICS:
Accounting Theory & Practice; Cost Accounting; Environmental Accounting; Environmental Management; Public Policy Economics; Social Accounting

MANUSCRIPT GUIDELINES/COMMENTS:

Manuscripts, in triplicate, should be sent to **address for submission** above or to:
   Marty Freedman, Co-Editor
   Department of Accounting
   College of Business and Economics
   Towson University
   8000 York Rd.
   Towson, MD 21252
   E-mail: **mfreedman@towson.edu**
   Phone: 410-704-4143,   Fax: 410-704-3641

78

Advances in Environmental Accounting and Management invites manuscripts dealing with accounting and management perspectives of environmental issues. The Journal is devoted to examining different environmental aspects of manuscript decisions to meet the environmental information needs of various stakeholders, such as investors, creditors, employers, suppliers, customers, environmentalists, and the community. The Journal welcomes papers using traditional or alternative approaches, such as theoretical, empirical, applied, or critical approaches. Manuscripts dealing with case studies are also welcome.

Advances in International Accounting

ADDRESS FOR SUBMISSION:

J. Timothy Sale, Editor
Advances in International Accounting
University of Cincinnati
Department of Accounting
Mail Location 211
Cincinnati, OH 45221-0211
USA
Phone: 513-556-7062
E-Mail: tim.sale@uc.edu
Web: www.elsevier.com

CIRCULATION DATA:

Reader: Academics
Frequency of Issue: Yearly
Sponsor/Publisher: Elsevier Inc.

PUBLICATION GUIDELINES:

Manuscript Length: 26-30
Copies Required: Three
Computer Submission: Yes
Format: ASCII/only on acceptance
Fees to Review: 0.00 US$

Manuscript Style:
    See Manuscript Guidelines

REVIEW INFORMATION:

Type of Review: Blind Review
No. of External Reviewers: 2
No. of In House Reviewers: 1
Acceptance Rate: 50%
Time to Review: 2 - 3 Months
Reviewers Comments: Yes
Invited Articles: 0-5%
Fees to Publish: 0.00 US$

MANUSCRIPT TOPICS:
Accounting Information Systems; Accounting Theory & Practice; Auditing; Cost Accounting; Government & Non Profit Accounting; International Finance; Tax Accounting

MANUSCRIPT GUIDELINES/COMMENTS:

General Instructions
Paper. Type or print the manuscript on one side of standard-size, or European equivalent, paper. Do not use half sheets or strips of paper glued, taped, or stapled to the pages.

Type Element. The type must be dark, clear, and legible.

Double Spacing. Double space between all lines of the manuscript including headings, notes, references, quotations, and figure captions. Single-spacing is acceptable only on tables.

Permission To Reprint. If you are using material from a copyrighted work (e.g., tables, figures), you will need written permission from the copyright holder (in most cases the publisher) to use this material. It is the author's responsibility to obtain the reprint permission. A copy o the permission letter must accompany the manuscript.

80

Title Page. The title page includes 4 elements: (1) The title and subtitle, if any; (2) The author(s); (3) abbreviated title to be used as a running head consisting of a maximum of 70 characters, which includes all letters, punctuation, and spaces; (4) complete mailing address, phone, and fax numbers of each author.

Text. Begin the next on a new page. The sections of the text follow each other without a break.

Appendices. Begin each Appendix on a separate page, with the word "Appendix" and identifying capital letters centered at the top of the page. If there is only one Appendix, it is unnecessary to use an identifying letter.

Notes. Notes that are mentioned in text are numbered consecutively throughout the chapter. Begin notes on a separate page and **double space** them.

References. Each series has its own reference style, whether it be APA, ASA, or a style unique to its discipline. For the style you should use, please consult a previously published volume it the series.

References cited in text **must** appear in the reference list; conversely, each entry in the reference list **must** be cited in text. It is the author's responsibility to be sure that the text citation and reference list are identical.

Important. Foreign language volumes, parts, numbers, editions, and so on **must** be translated into their English equivalents. Both the original language and the English translation will appear in the references. Authors **must** transliterate or romanize languages that do not use Latin characters (e.g., Greek, Russian, Chinese, Arabic, etc.), along with their English translation. A comprehensive resource for this is a publication issued by the Library of Congress, titled: *ALA-LC Romanization Tables: Transliteration Schemes for Non-Roman Scripts*.

Tables. Tables are numbered consecutively in the order in which they are first mentioned in text. Begin each table on separate page. Do not write "the table above/below" or "the table on p. 32" because the position and page number of a table cannot be determined until the page is typeset. In text, indicate the approximate placement of each table by a clear break in the text, inserting: .

TABLE 1 ABOUT HERE

Set off by double-spacing above and below.

Figures. Figures are also numbered consecutively in the order in which they are first mentioned in text. Indicate the approximate placement of each figure by a clear break, inserting:

FIGURE 1 ABOUT HERE

Set off by double-spacing above and below. All figures must be submitted in a form suitable for reproduction by the printer without redrawing or retouching. Figures should be no larger than 4 x 6". If a figure exceeds this size, it should be large enough and sharp enough to be legible when reduced to fit the page.

Type all figure numbers and captions, double-spaced, on a separate page. When enclosing a figure in a box, please do not include the figure number and caption within the box, as these are set separately.

For identification by the production editor and the printer, please indicate your name and the figure number on the back of each figure. "Top" should be written on any figure that might accidentally be reproduced wrong side up. Neither staples nor paper clips should be used on any figure. Scotch tape should never be used to attach figure copy to another page as tape edges show up as black line in reproduction. Art will not be returned unless otherwise indicated.

Disk Preparation
1. Use a word processing program that is able to create an IBM compatible file. For technical (math, chemistry, etc.) Macintosh files are acceptable. (Macintosh files should be submitted on **high density** disks only.)

2. Use 3 ½ inch, double (low) density or high density disks (preferably high density).
Note. If you use double (low) density disks, be sure that the disk is formatted for double (low) density. If you use high density, be sure that the disk is formatted for high density. Unformatted or incorrectly formatted disks are unusable.

3. Structure the manuscript according to the Guidelines. Print one (1) copy for copy-editing/styling purposes. Be sure to **Double-Space** this copy. That includes the notes and references.

4. The entire chapter should be in one (1) file. **Do not** make separate files for text, notes, and references. If necessary, tables may go in a separate file.

5. All manuscripts must have **numbered pages**; all tables and figures must be placed **at the end of the chapters**; placement lines must be indicated for all tables and figures (e.g., PLACE FIGURE/TABLE X HERE).

6. Submit the word processing file with your printed copy. Please indicate on the disk which word processing program and version you have used (e.g., MS Word, WordPerfect 5.1, 6.0, 7.0, etc. Word Star, WordPerfect for Windows, MS Word for Windows, etc.).

7. All text files must be spell checked and stripped of any and all graphics (graphs, equations, charts, line drawings, illustrations, or tables). Text files must be marked as to the placement of **all** graphics. Please send a **separate** graphics file as either **tiff** (tagged image file format) or **eps** (encapsulated postscript) and indicate which format has been used on the disk. We will still require **camera-ready copy**, whether or not material is also supplied in a graphics file.

8. **PLEASE** be sure that the manuscript and disk submitted match. If the material on the disk has been updated, please print out a new copy of the manuscript to be sure you are submitting the correct version.

ELSEVIER SCIENCE LIMITED, The Boulevard, Langford Lane Kidlington, Oxford OX5 1GB England. Tel: (+44) (0) 1865843000, Fax (+44) (0) 1865843010, Web: http://www.elsevier.com.

Advances in Management Accounting

ADDRESS FOR SUBMISSION:

John Y. Lee, Editor
Advances in Management Accounting
Pace University
Lubin School of Business
Goldstein Center 218
861 Bedford Road
Pleasantville, NY 10570
USA
Phone: (914) 773-3443
E-Mail: jylee@pace.edu
Web: www.elsevier.com

PUBLICATION GUIDELINES:

Manuscript Length: 21-25
Copies Required: Four
Computer Submission: No
Format: N/A
Fees to Review: 25.00 US$

Manuscript Style:
    See Manuscript Guidelines

CIRCULATION DATA:

Reader: Business Persons, Academics
Frequency of Issue: Yearly
Sponsor/Publisher: Elsevier Inc.

REVIEW INFORMATION:

Type of Review: Blind Review
No. of External Reviewers: 2
No. of In House Reviewers: 1
Acceptance Rate: 21-30%
Time to Review: 1 - 2 Months
Reviewers Comments: Yes
Invited Articles: 0-5%
Fees to Publish: 0.00 US$

MANUSCRIPT TOPICS:
Accounting Information Systems; Cost Accounting; Managerial Accounting

MANUSCRIPT GUIDELINES/COMMENTS:

Statement of Purpose and Review Procedures
Advances in Management Accounting (AIMA) a professional journal whose purpose is to meet the information needs of both practitioners and academicians. We plan to publish thoughtful, well developed articles on a variety of current topics in management accounting, broadly defined.

Advances in Management Accounting is to be an annual publication of quality applied research in management accounting. The series will examine areas of management accounting, including performance evaluation systems, accounting for product costs, behavioral impacts on management accounting, and innovations in management accounting. Management accounting includes all systems designed to provide information for management decision making. Research methods will include survey research, field tests, corporate case studies, and modeling. Some speculative articles and survey pieces will be included where appropriate.

AIMA welcomes all comments and encourages articles from both practitioners and academicians.

Review Procedures
AIMA intends to provide authors with timely reviews clearly indicating the acceptance status of their manuscripts. The results of initial reviews normally will be reported to authors within eight weeks from the date the manuscript is received. Once a manuscript is tentatively accepted, the prospects for publication are excellent. The author(s) will be accepted to work with the corresponding Editor, who will act as a liaison between the author(s) and the reviewers to resolve areas of concern. To ensure publication, it is the author's responsibility to make necessary revisions in a timely and satisfactory manner.

Editorial Policy and Manuscript Form Guidelines
1. Manuscripts should be type written and double-spaced on 8 ½" by 11" white paper. Only one side of the paper should be used. Margins should be set to facilitate editing and duplication except as noted:

a. Tables, figures, and exhibits should appear on a separate page. Each should be numbered and have a title. b. Footnote should be presented by citing the author's name and the year of publication in the body of the text; for example, Ferreira (1998); Cooper and Kaplan (1998).

2. Manuscripts should include a cover page that indicates the author's name and affiliation.

3. Manuscripts should include on a separate lead page an abstract not exceeding 200 words. The author's name and affiliation should not appear on the abstract.

4. Topical headings and subheadings should be used. Main headings in the manuscript should be centered, secondary headings should be flush with the left hand margin. (As a guide to usage and style, refer to the William Strunk, Jr., and E.B. White, *The Elements of Style.)*

5. Manuscripts must include a list of references which contain only those works actually cited. (As a helpful guide in preparing a list of references, refer to Kate L. Turbian, *A Manual for Writers of Term Papers, Theses, and Dissertations.)*

6. In order to be assured of anonymous review, authors should not identify themselves directly or indirectly. Reference to unpublished working papers and dissertations should be avoided. If necessary, authors may indicate that the reference is being withheld for the reason cited above.

7. The author will be provided one complete volume of *AIMA* issue in which his or her manuscript appears and the senior author will receive 25 offprints of the article.

8. Manuscripts currently under review by other publications should not be submitted. Complete reports of research presented at a national or regional conference of a professional association and "State of the Art" papers are acceptable.

9. Four copies of each manuscript should be submitted to John Y. Lee at the address below under Guideline 13.

10. A submission fee of $25.00, made payable to Advances in Management Accounting, should be included with all submissions.

11. For additional information regarding the type of manuscripts that are desired, see "*AIMA* Statement of Purpose."

12. Final acceptance of all manuscripts requires typed and computer disk copies in the publisher's manuscript format.

13. Inquires concerning *Advances in Management Accounting* may be directed to either one of the two editors:

Marc J. Epstein
Jones Graduate School of Administration
Rice University
Houston, Texas 77251-1892

John Y. Lee
Lubin School of Business
Pace University
Pleasantville, NY 10570-2799

Advances in Public Interest Accounting

ADDRESS FOR SUBMISSION:

Cheryl R. Lehman, Editor
Advances in Public Interest Accounting
Hofstra University
Department of Accounting, Taxation and
  Legal Studies in Business
Weller Hall
Hempstead, NY 11549
USA
Phone: 516-463-6986 or 5684
E-Mail: cheryl.r.lehman@hofstra.edu
Web: www.elsevier.com

CIRCULATION DATA:

Reader: Academics
Frequency of Issue: Yearly
Sponsor/Publisher: Elsevier Inc.

PUBLICATION GUIDELINES:

Manuscript Length: Any
Copies Required: Four
Computer Submission: No
Format:
Fees to Review: 0.00 US$

Manuscript Style:
  See Manuscript Guidelines

REVIEW INFORMATION:

Type of Review: Blind Review
No. of External Reviewers: 2
No. of In House Reviewers: 0
Acceptance Rate: 21-30%
Time to Review: 2 - 3 Months
Reviewers Comments: Yes
Invited Articles: 10-20%
Fees to Publish: 0.00 US$

MANUSCRIPT TOPICS:

Accounting Education; Accounting Information Systems; Accounting Theory & Practice; Auditing; Behavioral Accounting; Cost Accounting; Economic Development; Financial Services; Government & Non Profit Accounting; International Economics & Trade; Public Policy Economics

MANUSCRIPT GUIDELINES/COMMENTS:

Topics Inculde. Corporate Governance, and Regulatory Spheres; Critical Accounting; Environmental Issues; Finance, Banking, and Accounting; Gender Issues in Accounting; Historical Perspectives; Global, International & Trade Dynamics; Public Policy; Race, Ethnicity, and Identity; Social Accounting; Social Power and Accounting; Technology and Systems.

1. *Advances in Public Interest Accounting* is a research publication with two major aims. First to provide a forum for researchers concerned with critically appraising and significantly transforming conventional accounting theory and practice, teaching and research. Second, to increase the social self-awareness of accounting practitioners, educators, and researchers, encouraging them to assume a greater responsibility for the profession's social role. We are

seeking original manuscripts that explore all facets of this broad agenda. Illustrative of these aims, authors are concerned with:

- expanding accounting's focus beyond the behavior of individual corporate entities, encompassing the conflicts of interest within the accounting-regulatory process and effected groups;
- exploring alternatives to traditional economic and sociology models, beyond conventional efficiency and profitability measures of corporate performance;
- recognizing and examining the influences of gender and feminist theory, class and race, on accounting practice, education, and research;
- incorporating the significance of accounting as a communicative practice, as social dialogue, and as a social arbiter;
- recognizing and examining the effect of accounting practice on environmental issues and on the externalities imposed on local and global communities;
- examining accounting's participation in multinational expansion, consolidations, and changing economies undergoing transformations, such as Eastern and Central Europe and the Former Soviet Union, and the European community;
- addressing the impact of new advances in information technologies.

3. Send four copies of prospective manuscripts to Cheryl Lehman, Hofstra University.

4. All manuscripts should be typewritten and double-spaced on 8 ½" x 11" white paper. Only one side of a page should be set to facilitate editing and publication except as noted:
a.   Tables, figures and exhibits should appear on a separate page. Each should be numbered and have a title;
b.   References should be presented by citing the author's name and the year of publication in the body of the text, e.g. Schwartz (1981); Reckers and Pany (1980).

6. Manuscripts should include a cover page which indicates the author's name and affiliation.

7. Manuscripts should include on a separate lead page the title and an abstract not exceeding 200 words. The author's name and affiliation should not appear on the abstract.

8. Topical headings and subheadings should be used. Main headings in the manuscript should be centered, secondary headings should be flush with the left-hand margin. (As a guide to usage and style, refer to William Strunk Jr. and E.B. White, *The Elements of Style*.)

9. Manuscripts must include a list of references which contain only those works actually cited. (As a helpful guide in preparing a list of references, refer to Kate L. Turabian, *A Manual for Writers of Term Papers, Theses, and Dissertations*.)

10. In order to be assured of an anonymous review, authors should not identify themselves directly or indirectly. Reference to unpublished working papers and dissertations should be avoided. If necessary, authors may indicate that the reference is being withheld for the reasons cited above.

11. The author will be provided one complete volume of the issue in which his or her manuscript appears and ten off-prints of the article.

12. Manuscripts currently under review by other publications should not be submitted. Complete reports of research presented at a national or regional conference of a professional association (e.g. AAA, AIDS etc.) and "State of the Art" papers are acceptable.

13. Four copies of each manuscript should be submitted to the General Editor, Cheryl R. Lehman. Ph.D.

14. Copies of any and all research instruments should be included.

Advances in Taxation

ADDRESS FOR SUBMISSION:

Suzanne Luttman, Editor
Advances in Taxation
Santa Clara University
Accounting Department
Santa Clara, CA 95053-0380
USA
Phone: 408-554-4897
E-Mail: sluttman@scu.edu
Web: scu.edu/business/accounting/ait.cfm

CIRCULATION DATA:

Reader: Academics
Frequency of Issue: Yearly
Sponsor/Publisher: JAI / Elsevier Inc.

PUBLICATION GUIDELINES:

Manuscript Length: 20+
Copies Required: Three
Computer Submission: No
Format: N/A
Fees to Review: 40.00 US$

Manuscript Style:
    See Manuscript Guidelines

REVIEW INFORMATION:

Type of Review: Blind Review
No. of External Reviewers: 2
No. of In House Reviewers: 0
Acceptance Rate: 21-30%
Time to Review: 2 - 3 Months
Reviewers Comments: Yes
Invited Articles: 0-5%
Fees to Publish: 0.00 US$

MANUSCRIPT TOPICS:

Accounting Education; Behavioral Accounting; Fiscal Policy; Macro Economics; Micro Economics; Monetary Policy; Public Policy Economics; Tax Accounting

MANUSCRIPT GUIDELINES/COMMENTS:

Advances in Taxation is a refereed academic tax journal published annually. Academic articles on any aspect of federal, state, local, or international taxation will be considered. These include, but are not limited to, compliance, education, law, planning, and policy. Interdisciplinary research involving economics, finance, or other areas is encouraged. Acceptable research methods include any analytical, behavioral, descriptive, legal, quantitative, survey, or theoretical approach appropriate to the project.

Manuscripts must be readable, relevant, and reliable. To be readable, articles must be understandable and concise. To be relevant, articles must be directly related to problems inherent in the system of taxation. To be reliable, conclusions must follow logically from the evidence and arguments presented. Sound research design and execution are critical for empirical studies. Reasonable assumptions and logical development are essential for theoretical manuscripts.

Submit three copies of the typed manuscript along with a $40 (U.S.) check made payable to *Advances in Taxation*. In the case of manuscripts reporting on field surveys or experiments, please also submit three copies of the research instrument. The submission fee is nonrefundable. On the cover page the author(s) should include name, affiliation, address, phone number, fax number, and e-mail address. Manuscripts currently under consideration by another journal or publisher should not be submitted.

Advances in Taxation is published by Elsevier, a well-regarded publisher of academic literature in a number of business and non-business fields. Subscription information may be obtained by calling 800-545-2522. *Advances* is available online through ScienceDirect.

1. Manuscripts should be typewritten and double-spaced on 8 ½" x 11" white paper. Only one side of a page should be used. Margins should be set to facilitate editing and duplication except as noted:

a. Tables, figures and exhibits should appear on a separate page. Each page should be numbered and have a separate title.

b. Literature citations should be presented by citing the author's name and the year of publication in the body of the text, for example, (Shevlin 1987); (Davis and Swenson 1988).

c. Textual footnotes should be used only for extensions for which the inclusion in the text might disrupt continuity. Footnotes should be numbered consecutively throughout the manuscript with subscript Arabic numbers and placed on a separate page at the end of the text.

2. Manuscripts should include a cover page which indicates the author's name, address, affiliation, phone number, fax number, and e-mail address.

3. Manuscripts should include on a separate lead page an abstract not exceeding 200 words. The title should appear on this page, but the author's name and affiliation should not appear on the abstract page.

4. The text should begin on a separate page and the title should appear on the first page of the text.

5. Manuscript inclusions should appear in the following order: cover page, abstract, text, appendices, notes, references, tables, figures, and exhibits.

6. The text should have a logical order; for example, introduction and statement of purpose, previous research, hypotheses, research method, results, limitations, and implications and conclusions.

7. Topical headings and subheadings should be used (but do not number the sections). Main headings in the manuscript should be centered and typed in uppercase. As a guide to usage and style, refer to William Strunk, Jr. and E.B. White, *The Elements of Style*.

8. Manuscripts must include a list of references which contain only those works actually cited. The entries should be arranged in alphabetical order according to the surname of the first author. Samples of entries are as follows:

Porcano, T.M. 1984. "The Perceived Effects of Tax Policy on Corporate Investment Intentions", **The Journal of the American Taxation Association** (Fall): 7-19.
Swenson, C.W., and M.L. Moore. 1987. Use of Input-Output Analysis in Tax Research. **Advances in Taxation** 1:49-84.

9. In order to be assured of an anonymous review, authors should not identify themselves directly or indirectly. Reference to unpublished working papers and dissertations should be avoided. If necessary, authors may indicate that the reference is being withheld for the reasons cited above.

10. Manuscripts currently under review by other publications should not be submitted. Complete reports of research presented at a national or regional conference of a professional association (e.g., AAA, ATA, etc.) are acceptable.

American Journal of Business and Economics

ADDRESS FOR SUBMISSION:

Alan S. Khade, Editor
American Journal of Business and
   Economics
PO Box 2536
Turlock, CA 95307
USA
Phone: 209-667-3074
E-Mail: Review@iabe.org
Web: www.iabe.org

PUBLICATION GUIDELINES:

Manuscript Length:
Copies Required: Two
Computer Submission: Yes Disk or Email
Format: MS Word
Fees to Review: 0.00 US$

Manuscript Style:
   Chicago Manual of Style

CIRCULATION DATA:

Reader: Academics, Business Persons
Frequency of Issue: 2 Times/Year
Sponsor/Publisher: International Academy
   of Business and Economics (IABE)

REVIEW INFORMATION:

Type of Review: Blind Review
No. of External Reviewers: 2
No. of In House Reviewers: 1
Acceptance Rate: 21-30%
Time to Review: 2 - 3 Months
Reviewers Comments: Yes
Invited Articles: 21-30%
Fees to Publish: 0.00 US$

MANUSCRIPT TOPICS:

Accounting Education; Accounting Information Systems; Accounting Theory & Practice; Auditing; Cost Accounting; Econometrics; Economic Development; Financial Services; Fiscal Policy; Industrial Organization; International Economics & Trade; International Finance; Macro Economics; Micro Economics; Monetary Policy; Portfolio & Security Analysis; Public Policy Economics; Tax Accounting

MANUSCRIPT GUIDELINES/COMMENTS:

Please use following manuscript Guidelines for submission of your papers for the review. Papers are reviewed on a continual basis throughout the year. Early Submissions are welcome! Please email your manuscript to Dr. Alan S. Khade at **Review@iabe.org**.

Copyright. Articles, papers, or cases submitted for publication should be original contributions and should not be under consideration for any other publication at the same time. Authors submitting articles/papers/cases for publication warrant that the work is not an infringement of any existing copyright, infringement of proprietary right, invasion of privacy, or libel and will indemnify, defend, and hold IABE or sponsor(s) harmless from any damages, expenses, and costs against any breach of such warranty. For ease of dissemination and to ensure proper policing of use papers/articles/cases and contributions become the legal copyright of the IABE unless otherwise agreed in writing.

General Information. These are submission instructions for review purpose only. Once your submission is accepted you will receive submission guidelines with your paper acceptance letter. The author(s) will be emailed result of the review process in about 6-8 weeks from submission date. Papers are reviewed and accepted on a continual basis. Submit your papers early for full considerations!

Typing. Paper must be laser printed/printable on 8.5" x 11" white sheets in Arial 10-point font single-spaced lines justify style in MS Word. All four margins must be 1" each.

First Page. Paper title not exceeding two lines must be CAPITALIZED AND CENTERED IN BOLD LETTERS. Author name and university/organizational affiliation of each author must be printed on one line each. Do NOT include titles such as Dr., Professor, Ph.D., department address email address etc. Please print the word "ABSTRACT" in capitalized bold letters left justified and double-spaced from last author's name/affiliation. Abstract should be in italic. Please see the sample manuscript.

All other Headings. All other section headings starting with INTRODUCTION must be numbered in capitalized bold letters left justified and double-spaced from last line above them. See the subsection headings in the sample manuscript.

Tables Figures and Charts. All tables, figures or charts must be inserted in the body of the manuscripts within the margins with headings/titles in centered CAPITALIZED BOLD letters.

References and Bibliography. All references listed in this section must be cited in the article and vice-versa. The reference citations in the text must be inserted in parentheses within sentences with author name followed by a comma and year of publication. Please follow the following formats:

Journal Articles
Khade Alan S. and Metlen Scott K. "An Application of Benchmarking in Dairy Industry" *International Journal of Benchmarking* Vol. III (4) 1996 17

Books
Harrison Norma and Samson D. Technology Management: Text and Cases McGraw-Hill Publishing New York 2002

Internet
Hesterbrink C. E-Business and ERP: Bringing two Paradigms together October 1999; PricewaterhouseCoopers *www.pwc.com*.

Author Profile(s). At the end of paper include author profile(s) not exceeding five lines each author including name highest degree/university/year current position/university and major achievements. For example:

Author Profile:
Dr. Tahi J. Gnepa earned his Ph.D. at the University of Wisconsin Madison in 1989. Currently he is a professor of international business at California State University Stanislaus and Managing Editor of Journal of International Business Strategy (JIBStrategy).

Manuscript. Absolutely no footnotes! Do not insert page numbers for the manuscript. Please do not forget to run spelling and grammar check for the completed paper. Save the manuscript on your diskette/CD or hard drive.

Electronic Submission. Send your submission as an MS Word file attachment to your Email to Dr. Alan S. Khade at **Review@iabe.org**.

ATA Journal of Legal Tax Research (The)

ADDRESS FOR SUBMISSION:

W.E. Seago, Editor
ATA Journal of Legal Tax Research (The)
Virginia Tech
Pamplin College of Business
Blacksburg, VA 24061-0101
USA
Phone: 540-231-6564
E-Mail: seago@vt.edu
Web: www.atasection.org

PUBLICATION GUIDELINES:

Manuscript Length: 26-30
Copies Required: Electronic
Computer Submission: Yes Email
Format:
Fees to Review: 50.00 US$

Manuscript Style:
   Chicago Manual of Style

CIRCULATION DATA:

Reader: Academics
Frequency of Issue: Yearly
Sponsor/Publisher: American Taxation
   Association (ATA)

REVIEW INFORMATION:

Type of Review: Blind Review
No. of External Reviewers: 2
No. of In House Reviewers: 2
Acceptance Rate: 21-30%
Time to Review: 1 - 2 Months
Reviewers Comments: Yes
Invited Articles: 0-5%
Fees to Publish: 0.00 US$

MANUSCRIPT TOPICS:
Tax Accounting

MANUSCRIPT GUIDELINES/COMMENTS:

Publication Information
The American Taxation Association announces a new electronic journal. *The ATA Journal of Legal Tax Research* publishes creative and innovative studies employing legal research methodologies that logically and clearly

- identify, describe and illuminate important current tax issues including the history, development and congressional intent of specific provisions,
- propose improvements in tax systems and unique solutions to problems,
- critically analyze proposed or recent tax rule changes from both technical and policy perspectives.

The ATA Journal of Legal Tax Research solicits unpublished manuscripts not currently under consideration by another journal or publisher. Each article will be published electronically as soon as the editor, based upon advice from referees, determines that the manuscript meets the objectives and standards set forth by the ATA and the journal's editorial board.

Review Process

Each manuscript submitted to *The ATA Journal of Legal Tax Research* is subject to the following review procedures:

- The manuscript is screened by the editor for general suitability.
- If the manuscript passes the initial editorial screening, it will be blind-reviewed by at least two reviewers.
- In light of the reviewers' recommendations, a decision will be made by the editor as to whether the article will be accepted as is, revised, or rejected. It is anticipated that the decision will be communicated to the author within four to six weeks after submission.

The process described above is a general one. The editor may, in some circumstances, vary this process at his or her discretion. Through its constructive and responsive editorial procedures, the journal aims to render research efforts relevant and rewarding for all concerned.

Submission Requirements

Manuscripts are expected to be original research that has not been previously published and is not currently under review by another journal. If measurement instruments (questionnaires, case, interview plan, etc.) have been developed by the authors and are an integral part of the study, copies should be included with the manuscript. Manuscripts are to be submitted via email to **weseago@vt.edu** as a MS Word file. A nonrefundable $50 fee must accompany each submission. The submission fee may be paid online to AAA or posted to W. E Seago, Pamplin College of Business, Virginia Poly Inst & State University, Blacksburg, VA 24061-0101.

Checks are to be made out to American Taxation Association - AAA. Please indicate how the submission fee requirement has been satisfied. Revisions must be submitted within 12 months from notification; otherwise the manuscript will be considered a new submission.

Style

The ATA Journal of Legal Tax Research manuscript preparation guidelines follow (with modifications) Documentation 1 of *The Chicago Manual of Style* (14th ed.: University of Chicago Press). Citations to authorities should be presented in accordance with *The Bluebook: A Uniform System of Citation* (17th ed.: Harvard Law Review Association). Spelling follows *Webster's International Dictionary*.

Format

1. All manuscripts should be double-spaced, except for indented quotations.
2. Margins settings should provide for at least one inch top, side, and bottom margins.
3. A cover page should include the title of the paper, the author's name, title and affiliation, any acknowledgments, and a footnote indicating whether the author is willing to share the data (see policy statement below).
4. All pages, including tables, appendices, and references, should be serially numbered.
5. Spell out numbers from one to ten, except when used in tables and lists, and when used with mathematical, statistical, scientific, or technical units and quantities, such as distances, weights and measures. For example: three days; 3 kilometers; 30 years. All other numbers are expressed numerically.
6. In non-technical copy use the word percent in the text.

7. Use a hyphen to join unit modifiers or to clarify usage. For example: a well-presented analysis; re-form. See *Webster's* for correct usage.
8. Equations should be numbered in parentheses flush with the right-hand margin.
9. Headings should be arranged so that major headings are centered, bold, and capitalized. Second level headings should be flush left, bold, and both upper and lowercase. Third level headings should be flush left, bold, italic, and both upper and lower case. Fourth level headings should be paragraph indent, bold, and lower case. Format Example:

FIRST LEVEL HEADING
Second Level Heading
Third Level Heading
Fourth level heading. Text starts

Abstract
An abstract of 100-200 words should be presented on a separate page immediately preceding the text. The Abstract should concisely inform the reader of the manuscript's topic, its method, and its findings. The Abstract is to be followed by four key words that will help in indexing the paper.

Tables and Figures
The author should note the following general requirements:
1. Each table and figure (graphic) should bear an Arabic number and a complete title indicating the exact context of the table or figure.
2. A reference to each graphic should be made in the text.
3. Graphics should be reasonably interpretable without reference to the text.
4. Source lines and notes should be included as necessary.

Documentation
Citations and Other Footnotes. Authorities should be cited in footnotes using *The Bluebook* (cited above) styles. Textual footnotes should be used for extensions and useful excursions of information that if included in the body of the text might disrupt its continuity. Footnotes should be consecutively numbered throughout the manuscript with superscript Arabic numerals.

Sample entries for legislative sources
An Internal Revenue Code Section: I.R.C. §61.
An enacted bill: H.R. 3838, 99th Cong., 2d Sess. (1986) (enacted)
Congressional committee report: H.R. Rep. No. 1043, 99th Cong., 2d Sess.11 (1985), 1985-1 C.B. 412.
Congressional hearing: *Senate Hearings before the Committee on Finance on Tax Reform Proposal* – 1, 99th Cong., 1st Sess. 3 (1985) (Statement of Sen. Chafee).

Sample entries for administrative sources
Treas. Reg. §1.162-4(a).
Rev. Rul. 83-137, 1983-2 C.B. 41.
Rev. Proc. 85-37, 1985-2 C.B. 66.
T.D. 7522, 1978-1 C.B. 59.

98

Priv. Ltr. Rul. 91-10-003 (March 15, 1991).

Tech. Adv. Mem. 85-04-005(September 18, 1985).

I.R.S. Notice 89-29, 1989-1 C.B. 33.

Sample entries for judicial sources
United State Supreme Court opinion: *United States v. Mitchell* 403 U.S. 190 (1971)
Regular Tax Court opinion: *Pope v. Commissioner*, 114 T.C. 789 (2000).
Memorandum Tax Court opinion: *Brown v. Commissioner*, 65 T.C.M. (CCH) 666 (1983), T.C.M. (RIA) ¶ 93.039.
Circuit Court of Appeals opinion: *White v. Commissioner*, 32 F.3d 108 (CA-6, 2000).
United States District Court opinion: *Grey v. United States*, 222 F.Supp. 109 (M.D. Georgia, 1955).
Court of Federal Claims opinion: *Green v. United States*, 405 F.2d 890 (Fed.Cl. 1993).

Sample entries for secondary sources
Laura E. Cunnignham, *National Health Insurance and the Medical Deduction*, 50 Tax L. Rev. 237, 244-6 (1964).
Michael R. Harper, *The Marvel of Medical Savings Accounts*, Wall St. J., January 23, 1998, at A-14.
Joel Slemrod & Jon Bakija, *Taxing Ourselves: A Citizen's Guide to the Great Debate over Tax Reform* 201 (Cambridge, Mass: MIT Press, 2d. ed., 2001).
Environmental Protection Agency, *Brownfields Tax Incentive Guidelines*, at http://www.epa.gov/brownfields.
Richard M. Horwood, *Corporate Reorganizations*, 52-3rd Tax Mgmt. Portfolio (BNA), at A-25 (2000).

Editor
W. Eugene Seago
Pamplin College of Business
Virginia Poly Inst & State University
Blackburg, VA 24061-0101
Phone: (540) 231-6564 Fax: (540) 231-2511
Email: **weseago@vt.edu**

Australian Accounting Review

ADDRESS FOR SUBMISSION:

Linda English, Editor
Australian Accounting Review
University of Sydney
Discipline of Accounting
and Business Law
NSW 2006,
Phone: (02) 9351 3900
E-Mail: l.english@econ.usyd.edu.au
Web: www.cpaaustralia.com.au

CIRCULATION DATA:

Reader: Academics
Frequency of Issue: 3 Times/Year
Sponsor/Publisher: CPA Australia

PUBLICATION GUIDELINES:

Manuscript Length: 21-25
Copies Required: Three
Computer Submission: Yes Email
Format: MS Word
Fees to Review: 0.00 US$

Manuscript Style:
  Uniform System of Citation (Harvard
  Blue Book)

REVIEW INFORMATION:

Type of Review: Blind Review
No. of External Reviewers: 2
No. of In House Reviewers:
Acceptance Rate: 50%
Time to Review: 2 - 3 Months
Reviewers Comments: Yes
Invited Articles: 50% +
Fees to Publish: 0.00 US$

MANUSCRIPT TOPICS:
Accounting Education; Accounting Information Systems; Accounting Theory & Practice; Auditing; Behavioral Accounting; Cost Accounting; Government & Non Profit Accounting; Tax Accounting

MANUSCRIPT GUIDELINES/COMMENTS:

1. Three copies of the manuscript should be sent to: Linda English, Editor, Australian Accounting Review, Discipline of Accounting and Business Law, The University of Sydney, NSW 2006, Australia. Submission of a manuscript implies that it contains original unpublished work and is not submitted for publication elsewhere.

2. Manuscripts should be double-spaced, with wide margins, and printed on one side of the paper only. All pages should be numbered consecutively.

3. The first page of the manuscript should contain the following information: (i) the title; (ii) the name/s and institutional affiliation/s of the author/s; (iii) an abstract of not more than 100 words; (iv) a footnote giving the name, address, telephone number, fax number, and email address of the corresponding author; (v) at least one classification code according to the Classification System for Journal Articles as used by the *Journal of Economic Literature*; (vi)

100

up to five key words; (vii) a footnote of acknowledgements which should not be included in the consecutive numbering of footnotes.

4. Footnotes should be kept to a minimum and numbered consecutively throughout the text with superscript Arabic numerals. They should not include displayed formulae or tables.

5. Displayed formulae should be numbered consecutively throughout the manuscript as (1), (2), etc. against the right-hand margin of the page. Letters used as symbols should be set in italics unless they represent vector quantities in which case they should be bold. Do not use bold or italics for numerals and abbreviations for math functions (such as $1n$, Σ). Use italics for names of statistical tests (such as t-statistics, t-test, $t = 4.68$, $F - test$).

Australian Accounting Review appreciates authors' adherence to the further style points set out below:

References in the body of the text should be as follows: "Jones (1992) suggests that . . ." or "This problem was noted earlier (see Smith 1990, Jones 1992, Black and Cook 1995)" or "There are 128 companies using this accounting method (Green 1995: 38)".

The list of references should appear at the end of the main text, after appendices but before tables and figures. It should be double-spaced and listed in alphabetical order. All co-authors' names are to be similarly listed in alphabetical order, ie., the use of et al is not acceptable. The following example illustrates the required style:

References
Australian Accounting Research Foundation, 1998, Accounting Theory Monograph No. 10 *Measurement in Financial Accounting*, AARF, Victoria.

Australian Accounting Standards Board, 1996, Australian Accounting Standard AASB 1033 *Presentation and Disclosure of Financial Instruments.*

Australian Society of Accountants, The Institute of Chartered Accountants in Australia and Accounting Standards Review Board, 1990, SAC 2 *Objective of General Purpose Financial Reporting.*

Barth, M.E., and W.R. Landsman, 1995, "Fundamental Issues Related to Using Fair Value Accounting for Financial Reporting", *Accounting Horizons*, December: 97-107.

Baxter, W.T., 1975, *Accounting Values and Inflation*, McGraw Hill, London.

Bell, P.W., 1982, Accounting Theory Monograph No. 1 "CVA, CCA, and CoCoA: How Fundamental are the Differences?", Australian Accounting Research Foundation, Melbourne.

Chambers, R.J., 1970, "Second Thoughts on Continuously Contemporary Accounting", Abacus, September: 39-55.

FASB, 1999a, Financial Accounting Series No. 195-A *Proposed Statement of Financial Accounting Concepts*, March.

FASB, 1999b, Financial Accounting Series No. 204-B *Preliminary Views on Major Issues Related to Reporting Financial Instruments and Certain Related Assets and Liabilities at Fair Value*, August.

Godfrey, J.M., 1994, "Foreign Currency Accounting Policies: The Impact of Asset Specificity", *Contemporary Accounting Research* 10, 2: 643-71.

International Accounting Standards Committee, 1995, IAS 32 *Financial Instruments: Presentation and Disclosure*.

International Accounting Standards Committee, 1997, "Accounting for Financial Assets and Liabilities", discussion paper, March.

Kerr, J. St.G., 1980, "Liabilities in a Current Value Accounting System", in D.M. Emanuel and I.C. Stewart (eds), *Essays in Honour of Trevor R. Johnston*, Auckland: 223-40.

Please note the following points:
- Titles of books, journals, monographs and newspapers in italics.
- Titles of articles, conference papers and working papers in quotation marks.
- Titles of standards, exposure drafts in italics.
- Provide volume number and issue number of journals, but omitting the words Vol. And No., as in the Godfrey example above; if unavailable, identify issue by month, season or quarter.
- Provide relevant page numbers preceded by a colon(:) only. Do not insert p. and pp.

Tables and figures should be numbered consecutively in the text in Arabic numerals and printed on separate pages.

If a manuscript is accepted for publication the author is required to provide one copy of the final version to the print setter, either in Microsoft Word on a 3.5-inch disk or as an attachment to an e-mail message; plus one hard copy to the Editor.

Manuscripts that do not conform to these requirements may be returned for revision.

Edited versions of papers will be sent to corresponding authors and should be checked carefully; there will be no further opportunity for amendments before publication.

Bank Accounting & Finance

ADDRESS FOR SUBMISSION:

Claire Greene, Editor
Bank Accounting & Finance
129 Everett Street
Concord, MA 01742
USA
Phone: 978-369-6285
E-Mail: clairegreene@verizon.net
Web: www.bankaccountingandfinance.com

CIRCULATION DATA:

Reader: Business Persons
Frequency of Issue: Bi-Monthly
Sponsor/Publisher: CCH Incorporated

PUBLICATION GUIDELINES:

Manuscript Length: 16-25
Copies Required: Two
Computer Submission: Yes
Format: IBM PC Compat, MS Word
Fees to Review: 0.00 US$

Manuscript Style:
 Chicago Manual of Style

REVIEW INFORMATION:

Type of Review: Blind Review
No. of External Reviewers: 2
No. of In House Reviewers: 1
Acceptance Rate: 50%
Time to Review: 1 - 2 Months
Reviewers Comments: Yes
Invited Articles: 50% +
Fees to Publish: 0.00 US$

MANUSCRIPT TOPICS:
Accounting Information Systems; Accounting Theory & Practice; Auditing; Bank Taxation; Cost Accounting; Financial Services; Insurance; Portfolio & Security Analysis; Risk Management; Tax Accounting

MANUSCRIPT GUIDELINES/COMMENTS:

Bank Accounting & Finance welcomes byline articles to be considered for publication. Bank Accounting & Finance is the first in-depth, practical magazine for bank accounting and financial officers. Readers are CFOs, treasurers, controllers, accountants, auditors, cashiers, and financial VPs.

Readers are interested in articles on topics including, but not limited to, the following:
- financial accounting
- management accounting
- capital planning
- profitability measurement
- asset/liability management
- liquidity issues
- treasury management and investment policy
- bank stock analysis

- risk management
- portfolio management
- new financial instruments and capital markets products
- cost control
- mergers and acquisitions
- technology
- reporting systems
- auditing and internal control
- regulation
- taxes

Case studies, surveys, and advice on implementing new accounting standards and regulations are particularly welcome. For a list of recent articles, see **www.bankaccountingandfinance.com.**

Articles should be practical, with concrete advice, illustrative anecdotes and examples, and a description of results readers might expect if they follow the author's recommendations. Articles generally run from 2,500 to 5,000 words (10 to 20 double-spaced typewritten pages).

Submission Guidelines
To propose an article, please contact editor Claire Greene before you start to write (voice 978-369-6285; fax 978-371-2961; **clairegreene@verizon.net**, 129 Everett St. Concord, MA 01742). She can help you tailor your idea to meet *Bank Accounting & Finance's* specific needs for manuscripts.

Charts and Graphs. If you have copied an Excel chart into a PowerPoint file, please provide both the PowerPoint file and the Excel file. If possible, avoid graphic special effects like shadow boxes and keep in mind that figures will be printed in black and white. If you used the Drawing function in Microsoft Word to make flow charts or other pictures, please copy your picture onto a PowerPoint slide and verify that the original Word layout has not been distorted. Please save charts other than PowerPoint or Excel as grayscale tifs with a resolution of 300 dpi or higher.

Subscriptions and Media Kits
For subscription and advertising information, 800 449-8114 To order reprints, Journal Reprint Services, (866) 863-9726 or www.journalreprint.com.

Bank Accounting & Finance is a publication of CCH Incorporated, 4025 W. Peterson Ave., Chicago, IL 60646 www.tax.cchgroup.com

Behavioral Research in Accounting

ADDRESS FOR SUBMISSION:

Bryan K. Church, Editor
Behavioral Research in Accounting
Georgia Institute of Technology
College of Management
Atlanta, GA 30332-0520
USA
Phone: 404-894-3907
E-Mail: bryan.church@mgt.gatech.edu
Web: http://business.baylor.edu/charles_
davis/abo/bria/authors.htm

PUBLICATION GUIDELINES:

Manuscript Length: 15-25
Copies Required: Electronic
Computer Submission: Yes
Format:
Fees to Review: 50.00 US$

Manuscript Style:
See Manuscript Guidelines

CIRCULATION DATA:

Reader: Academics
Frequency of Issue: Yearly
Sponsor/Publisher: Accounting, Behavior
and Organizations Section of American
Accounting Association

REVIEW INFORMATION:

Type of Review: Blind Review
No. of External Reviewers: 2
No. of In House Reviewers: 0
Acceptance Rate: 15-20%
Time to Review: 2 - 3 Months
Reviewers Comments: Yes
Invited Articles: 0-5%
Fees to Publish: 0.00 US$

MANUSCRIPT TOPICS:
Accounting Information Systems; Accounting Theory & Practice; Auditing; Behavioral Accounting Research; Cost Accounting; Econometrics; Government & Non Profit Accounting; Micro Economics; Tax Accounting

MANUSCRIPT GUIDELINES/COMMENTS:

Topics Include. Examples of manuscript topics include the interface of accounting, decision making, organizations, and the marketplace, auditor judgment, investor judgment, and tax-preparer judgment, among others.

Editorial Policies
Behavioral Research in Accounting is published by the Accounting, Behavior and Organizations Section of the American Accounting Association. Original research relating to accounting and how it affects and is affected by individuals and organizations will be considered for the journal. Theoretical papers and papers based upon empirical research (e.g., field, survey and experimental research) are appropriate. Replications of previously published studies will be considered. The primary audience of the journal is the membership of the Accounting, Behavior and Organizations Section of the American Accounting Association.

For a manuscript to be acceptable for publication, the research questions should be of interest to the intended readership, the research project should be well designed and well executed, and arguments or findings should be presented effectively and efficiently.

The Review Process

Each manuscript submitted to *Behavioral Research in Accounting* is subject to the following review procedures:

1. Each manuscript is reviewed by the editor for general suitability for this journal.

2. For those that are judged suitable, at least two reviewers are selected and a double-blind review process takes place.

3. Using recommendations of the reviewers, the editor will decide whether the particular manuscript should be accepted as is, revises or rejected for publications.

The process described above is a general process. In any particular case, deviations may occur from the steps described.

Submission of Manuscripts

Authors should note the following guidelines for submitting manuscripts:

1. Manuscripts currently under consideration by another journal or other publisher should not be submitted. The author must state that the work is not submitted or published elsewhere.

2. In the case of manuscripts reposting on field surveys or experiments, four copies of the instrument (questionnaire, case, interview plan, or the like) should be submitted.

3. Manuscripts should be submitted as Word or PDF files to **bryan.church@mgt.gatech.edu**. The submission fee can be paid online at:
   https://aaahq.org/AAAforms/journals/briasubmit.cfm.

Alternatively, the submission fee can be paid by check, for $50 in US funds payable to the American Accounting Association, sent to:

Professor Bryan K. Church
Editor, Behavioral Research in Accounting
College of Management
Georgia Institute of Technology
Atlanta, GA 30332-0520

The submission fee is nonrefundable.

4. The author should retain a copy of the paper.

5. Revisions must be submitted within 12 months from request, otherwise they will be considered new submissions.

Manuscript Preparation and Style

Behavioral Research in Accounting's manuscript preparation guidelines follow (with a slight modification) documentation 2 of the *Chicago Manual of Style* (14th ed.; University of Chicago Press). Another helpful guide to usage and style is *The Elements of Style*, by William Strunk, Jr., and E. B. White (Macmillan). Spelling follows *Webster's International Dictionary*.

Format

1. All manuscripts should be typed on one side of 8.5" x 11" good quality paper and be double-spaced, except for indented quotations.

2. Manuscripts should be as concise as the subject and research method permit, generally not to exceed 7,000 words.

3. Margins should be at least one inch from top, bottom, and sides to facilitate editing and duplication.

4. To assure an anonymous review, authors should not identify themselves directly or indirectly in their papers. Single authors should not use the editorial "we."

5. A cover page should the title of the paper, the author's name, title, and affiliation, and any acknowledgments, and a footnote indicating whether the author would be willing to share the data (see last paragraph in this statement).

6. All pages, including tables, appendices, and references, should be serially numbered.

7. Spell out numbers from one to ten, except when used in tables and lists, and when used with mathematical, statistical, scientific, or technical units and quantities, such as distances, weights, and measures. For example: *three days; 3 kilometers; 30 years*. All other numbers are expressed numerically. Generally when using approximate terms spell out the number, for example, *approximately thirty years*.

8. In nontechnical text use the word *percent*; in technical text the symbol % is used. (See the *Chicago Manual* for discussion of the correct usage.)

9. a. Use a hyphen (-) to join unit modifiers or to clarify usage. For example: *a well-presented analysis; re-form*. See *Webster's* for correct usage. b. En dash (-) is used between words indicating a duration, such as hourly time or months or years. No space on either side. c. Em dash (--) is used to indicate an abrupt change in thought, or where a period is strong and a comma is too weak. No space on either side.

10. The following will be Roman in all cases: i.e., e.g., ibid., et al., op. cit.

11. Initials: A. B. Smith (space between); States, etc.: U.S., U.K. (no space between).

12. When using "Big 5," "Big 6" or "Big 8," use Arabic figures (don't spell out).

13. Ellipsis should be used not periods, example: ... not . . . .

14. Use "SAS No. #" not "SAS #."

15. Use only one space after periods, colons, exclamation points, questions marks, quotation marks--any punctuation that separates two sentences.

16. a. Use real quotation marks--never inch marks: "and" not "and ". b. Use apostrophes, not foot marks: ' not '.

17. Punctuation used with quote marks: a. Commas and periods are always placed inside quotation marks. b. Colons and semicolons go outside the quotation marks. c. Question marks and exclamation points go in or out, depending on whether they belong to the material inside the quote or not. If they belong to the quoted material, they go inside the quote marks, and vice versa.

18. Punctuation and parentheses: Sentence punctuation goes after the closing parenthesis if what is inside the parentheses is part of the sentence (as this phrase is). This also applies to commas, semicolons, and colons. If what is inside the parentheses is an entire statement of its own, the ending punctuation should also be inside the parentheses.

19. Headings should be arranged so that major headings are centered, bold, and capitalized. Second level headings should be flush left, bold, and both upper and lower case. Third level headings should be flush left, bold, italic, and both upper and lower case. Fourth level headings should be paragraph indent, bold, and lower case. Headings and subheadings should not be numbered. For example:

A CENTERED, BOLD, ALL CAPITALIZED, FIRST LEVEL HEADING

A Flush Left, Bold, Upper and Lower Case, Second Level Heading
A Flush Left, Bold, Italic, Upper and Lower Case, Third Level Heading
A paragraph indent, bold, lower case, fourth level heading. Text starts...

Abstract
An abstract of 100-150 words should be presented on a separate page immediately preceding the text. The abstract should be nonmathematical and include a readable summary of the research question, method, and the significance of the findings and contribution. The title, but not the author's name or other identification designations, should appear on the abstract page.

Tables and Figures
The author should note the following general requirements:
1. Each table and figure (graphic) should appear on a separate page and should be placed at the end of the text. Each should bear an Arabic number and a complete title indicating the exact contents of the table or figure.

2. A reference to each table or figure should be made in the text.

3. The author should indicate by marginal notation where each table or figure should be inserted in the text, e.g., (Insert Table X here).

4. Tables or figures should be reasonably interpretable without reference to the text.

5. Source lines and notes should be included as necessary.

6. When information is not available, use "NA" capitalized with no slash between.

7. Figures must be prepared in a form suitable for printing.

Mathematical Notation
Mathematical notation should be employed only where its rigor and precision are necessary, and in such circumstances authors should explain in the narrative format the principal operations performed. Notation should be avoided in footnotes. Unusual symbols, particularly if handwritten, should be identified in the margin when they appear. Displayed materials should clearly indicate alignment, superscripts, and subscripts. Equations should be numbered in parentheses flush with the right-hand margin.

Documentation
Citations. Work cited should use the "author-date system" keyed to a list of works in the reference list (see below). Authors should make an effort to include the relevant page numbers in the cited works.

1. In the text, works are cited as follows: author's last name and date, without comma, in parentheses: for example, (Jones 1987); with two authors: (Jones and Freeman 1973); with more than two: (Jones et al. 1985); with more than one source cited together (Jones 1987; Freeman 1986); with two or more works by one author: (Jones 1985, 1987).

2. Unless confusion would result, do not use "p." or "pp." before page numbers, for example (Jones 1987, 115).

3. When the reference list contains more than one work of an author published in the same year, the suffix *a, b*, etc. follows the date in the text citation, for example (Jones 1987a) or (Jones 1987a; Freeman 1985b).

4. If an author's name is mentioned in the text, it need not be repeated in the citation, for example "Jones (1987, 115) says ..."

5. Citations to institutional works should employ acronyms or short titles where practicable, for example., [AAA ASOBAT 1966); (AICPA *Cohen Commission Report* 1977). Where brief, the full title of an institutional work might be shown in a citation, for example (ICAEW *The Corporate Report* 1975).

6. If the manuscript refers to statutes, legal treatises, or court cases, citations acceptable in law reviews should be used.

Reference List. Every manuscript must include a list of references containing only those works cited. Each entry should contain all data necessary for unambiguous identification. With the author-date system, use the following format recommended by the *Chicago Manual:*

1. Arrange citations in alphabetical order according to the surname of the first author or the name of the institution responsible for the citation.

2. Use author's initials instead of proper names.

3. In listing more than one name in references (Rayburn, L. and B. Harrelson, ...), there should always be a comma before "and."

4. Dates of publication should be placed immediately after author's names.

5. Titles of journals should not be abbreviated.

6. Multiple works by the same author(s) should be listed in chronological order of publication. Two or more works by the same author(s) should be listed in chronological order of publication. Two or more works by the same author(s) in the same year are distinguished by letters after the date.

Sample entries are as follows:

American Accounting Association, Committee on Concepts and Standards for External Financial Reports. 1977. *Statement of Accounting Theory and Theory Acceptance*, Sarasota, FL; AAA.

Bohrnstedt, G. W. 1970. Reliability and Validity Assessment in Attitude Measurement. In *Attitude Measurement,* edited by G. Summers, 80-99. Chicago, IL: Rand McNally.

Burgstahler, D. 1987. Inference from Empirical Research. *The Accounting Review* 62 (January): 203-214.

Chow, C. 1983. The Impacts of Accounting Regulation on Bondholder and Shareholder Wealth: The Case of the Securities Act. *The Accounting Review* 58 (3): 485-520.

Hunt, S. D., L. B. Chonko, and J. B. Wilcox. 1984. Ethical Problems of Marketing Researchers. *Journal of Marketing Research* (August): 304-324.

Maranell, G., ed. 1974. *Scaling: A Sourcebook of Behavioral Scientist*. Chicago, IL: Aldine Publishing Company.

Saaty, T. L. and L. G. Varga. 1984a. The Legitimacy of Rank Reversal, *Omega* 12: 513-516.

_____, and _____. 1984b. Inconsistency and Rank Reversal. *Journal of Mathematical Psychology* 28: 205-214.

Waterhouse, J. and A. Richardson. 1989 Behavioural Research Implications of the New Management Accounting Environment. Working paper, University of Alberta.

Footnotes. Footnotes should not be used for documentation. Textual footnotes should be used only for extensions and useful excursions of information that if included in the body of the text might disrupt its continuity. Footnotes should be double spaced and numbered consecutively throughout the manuscript with superscript Arabic numerals. Footnotes are placed at the end of the text.

Policy on Reproduction
An objective of *Behavioral Research in Accounting* is to promote the wide dissemination of the results of systematic scholarly inquiries into the broad field of accounting.

Permission if hereby granted to reproduce any of the contents of *BRIA* for use in courses of instruction, as long as the source and American Accounting Association copyright are indicated in any such reproductions.

Written application must be made to the Editor for permission to reproduce any of the contents of *BRIA* for use in other than courses of instruction--e.g., inclusion in books of readings or in any other such instances, the applicant must notify the author(s) in writing of the intended use of each reproduction. Normally, *BRIA* will not assess a charge for the waiver of copyright.

Except as otherwise noted in articles, the copyright has been transferred to the American Accounting Association for all items appearing in this journal. Where the author(s) has (have) not transferred the copyright to the American Accounting Association, applicants must seek permission to reproduce (for all purposes) directly from the author(s).

Policy on Data Availability
The following policy, adopted by the Executive Committee of the AAA in April 1989, is applicable to *all* manuscripts submitted to *Behavioral Research in Accounting*:

...Authors are encouraged to make their data available for use by others...Authors of articles which report data-dependent results should footnote the status of data availability and when pertinent, this should be accompanied by information on how the data may be obtained.

British Accounting Review (The)

ADDRESS FOR SUBMISSION:

Ruth Harkin, Editorial Assistant
British Accounting Review (The)
V. Beattie & C. Emmanuel, Editors
University of Glasgow
Department of Accounting and Finance
65-73 Southpark Avenue
Glasgow, G12 8LE
UK
Phone: +44 (0) 141 330 1939
E-Mail: BAR@gla.ac.uk
Web: www.elsevier.com

PUBLICATION GUIDELINES:

Manuscript Length: Up to 10,000 Words
Copies Required: Four
Computer Submission: Yes
Format: English - MS Word
Fees to Review: 0.00 US$

Manuscript Style:
    See Manuscript Guidelines

CIRCULATION DATA:

Reader: Academics
Frequency of Issue: Quarterly
Sponsor/Publisher: British Accounting
    Association (BAA) / Elsevier Inc.

REVIEW INFORMATION:

Type of Review: Blind Review
No. of External Reviewers: 2
No. of In House Reviewers: 1
Acceptance Rate: 10-15%
Time to Review: Over 3 Months
Reviewers Comments: Yes
Invited Articles: 0-5%
Fees to Publish: 0.00 US$

MANUSCRIPT TOPICS:
Accounting Information Systems; Accounting Theory & Practice; Auditing; Capital Budgeting; Corporate Finance; Cost Accounting; Government & Non Profit Accounting; International Finance; Portfolio & Security Analysis; Tax Accounting

MANUSCRIPT GUIDELINES/COMMENTS:

Description
Published by Elsevier for the British Accounting Association, the journal acts as a forum for communication throughout the world between members of the academic and professional community concerned with the research and teaching, at degree level and above, of accounting, finance, and cognate disciplines. The *British Accounting Review* carries three types of articles: main articles, review articles, and book reviews. Main articles are research reports, polemical articles, and state-of-the- art papers. Book reviews are commissioned by the book review editor, and notes and comments on the published articles are welcomed.

Guide for Authors
The *British Accounting Review* (*BAR*) is particularly concerned with the readability of papers. Prospective authors are asked to pay particular attention to the clarity of their communication.

112

Authors are reminded that the most common root causes for the rejection of a manuscript are the failure to expose the material as widely as possible before submission and failure to comply with the Editorial Policy and Notes for Contributors. Authors are asked to use mathematics only if it contributes to the clarity and economy of presentation or is an essential part of the argument. Authors are encouraged to put the mathematics in an appendix whenever possible.

Submission of a paper to *BAR* automatically implies that the manuscript is not concurrently under consideration for publication elsewhere. All papers submitted to *BAR* will normally only be published subject to review by double blind referees. In the interests of a fair review, authors should try and avoid the use of anything which would make their identity obvious. Referees are asked to comment upon the *originality, authority, comprehensiveness, contribution, interest* and *usefulness* of the submitted paper. All papers are also subjected to editorial review which covers style, quality of communication, and academic and scholarly content. The editors make every effort to give a decision on manuscripts as soon as possible. Electronic submission in Microsoft Word for consideration by *BAR* should be sent to **BAR@gla.ac.uk**. Alternatively, four hard copies may be sent to:

Ruth Harkin, Editorial Assistant,
The British Accounting Review
Department of Accounting and Finance
University of Glasgow, 65-73 Southpark Avenue
Glasgow G12 8LE
Tel: +44 (0) 141 330 1939 Fax: +44 (0) 141 330 4442

When supplying your final article you are required to submit your manuscript electronically using Microsoft Word.

Preparation of Manuscripts
Manuscripts must by typed in journal style on one side only of the paper (preferably A4), double spaced (including notes and references), with margins of at least 1 inch. Essential notes should be indicated by superscript figures in the text and collected in a single section placed before the references under a heading 'Notes'. Tables and figures should be attached on separate sheets at the end of the manuscript: their position should be indicated in the text. A short abstract should be included at the head of the paper.

Citations in the text should read thus: Brown & Smith (1975), or (Brown & Smith, 1975), or, for specific quotations, (Brown & Smith, 1975, 63-64). The conventions White (1975a), White (1975b) should be used if more than one publication by the same author(s) in a particular year is cited. Where there are three authors or more, all names should be given in the first citation; subsequently, use *et al*. References should be listed in full, alphabetically at the end of the paper in the following style:

Cohen, D., Dey, A., Lys, T., 2004. Trends in Earnings Management and Informativeness of Earnings Announcements in the Pre- and Post-Sarbanes Oxley Periods (Working Paper, Northwestern University), available on the internet at http://papers.ssrn.com/sol3/papers/cfm?abstract_id=568921.

Fairclough, N., 2003. Analysing Discourse: Textual Analysis for Social Research. Routledge, London.

Innes, J., Mitchell, F., Sinclair, D., 2000. Activity-based costing in the UK's largest companies: a comparison of 1994 and 1999 survey results. Management Accounting Research 11 (3), 349-362.

Ritchie, J., 1991. Enterprise cultures: a frame analysis. In: Burrows, R., (Ed.), Deciphering The Enterprise Culture. Routledge, London, 17-34.

Proofs and Offprints

Authors are expected to correct proofs quickly and not to make revisions on proofs; revisions made on proofs may be charged for by the editors. No payments are made to authors.

Authors submitting a manuscript do so on the understanding that if it is accepted for publication, exclusive copyright in the article, including the right to reproduce the article in all forms and media, shall be assigned exclusively to the Publisher. The transfer of copyright does not take effect until the manuscript is accepted for publication.

Exceptions

It is the policy of Elsevier that authors need not obtain permission in the following cases only: (1) to use their original figures or tables in their future works; (2) to make copies of their papers for use in their classroom teaching; and (3) to include their papers as part of their dissertations. In consideration for the assignment of copyright, the Publisher will supply 25 offprints of each paper. Further offprints may be ordered at extra cost; the offprint order form will be sent with the proofs. The Publisher will not put any limitation on the personal freedom of the author to use material contained in the paper in other works which may be published.

Business Case Journal

ADDRESS FOR SUBMISSION:

Martha C. Fransson, Associate Editor
Business Case Journal
Rensselaer Polytechnic Institute
Lally School of Management & Technology
Hartford Department
275 Windsor Street
Hartford, CT 06120-2991
USA
Phone: 860-548-7831
E-Mail: fransson@rh.edu
Web: www.sfcr.org

PUBLICATION GUIDELINES:

Manuscript Length:
Copies Required: Four
Computer Submission: Yes Disk or Email
Format: MS Word
Fees to Review: 0.00 US$

Manuscript Style:
    See Manuscript Guidelines

CIRCULATION DATA:

Reader: Academics
Frequency of Issue:
Sponsor/Publisher: Society for Case
    Research

REVIEW INFORMATION:

Type of Review: Blind Review
No. of External Reviewers: 3
No. of In House Reviewers: 1
Acceptance Rate: 11-20%
Time to Review: 4 - 6 Months
Reviewers Comments: Yes
Invited Articles: 0-5%
Fees to Publish: 50.00 US$

MANUSCRIPT TOPICS:

Accounting Education; Accounting Information Systems; Accounting Theory & Practice; Auditing; Behavioral Accounting; Cost Accounting; Industrial Organization; Insurance; International Finance; Portfolio & Security Analysis; Real Estate; Tax Accounting

MANUSCRIPT GUIDELINES/COMMENTS:

Editorial Policy
The *Business Case Journal* was established by the Society for Case Research to publish cases and research related to case writing or teaching with cases. All cases and teaching notes are subject to editorial review as well as to a triple blind review process. Acceptance rates have recently ranged from 10 to 20 percent. Historically, the *Business Case Journal* has focused on cases in which the student is place in the manager's position and asked to make recommendations appropriate to the context of the situation. The Editor refers to these as "decision cases." The *Journal* will also accept case studies. A case study is a description of a real situation. Authors must provide sufficient background information such that the student can evaluate how effectively the situation was managed. Teaching notes of these "descriptive cases" will require the student to analyze, assess, evaluate the situation, and determine if there was a more effective way to handle the situation.

The *Business Case Journal* has a preference for field-researched cases but will also consider cases based on substantial research from secondary sources. The *Journal* does not accept fictional or synthesized cases.

Cases or articles that have been published previously or are under review elsewhere will not be reviewed by the *Business Case Journal*. Cases may be released for other publications after a publication date has been set by the *Journal's* Editor. No part of a case or teaching note may be reproduced or used in any form or by any means without a written permission of the Society for Case Research.

Submissions are subject to an initial editorial review. Manuscripts that meet the minimum standards of the *Journal* will receive a blind review by at least two members of the Editorial Review Board.

Submission Guidelines
Send manuscripts for review to Associate Professor Martha C. Fransson, Associate Editor, Business Case Journal, c/o Rensselaer Polytechnic Institute, Lally School of M&T, Hartford Deptartment, 275 Windsor Street, Hartford, CT 06120-2991 or **Fransson@rh.edu**.

Microsoft Word is the only acceptable format.

Manuscripts must be double-spaced with 1" margins.

All tables, figures, and artwork must be incorporated into the manuscript or appropriately acknowledged as to location. (NOTE: The *BCJ* does not use Exhibits: it is either a Table or a Figure.)

If submitting hardcopies: You must send the following:
- A transmittal letter containing the name, affiliation, mailing address, phone number, and email address for each author. Be sure to note which author is the primary contact.
- A statement detailing your personal experience, or those of colleague, that have used the case in the classroom.
- Authors of cases based on field research must submit a copy of the written authorization for the use of the case from an appropriate officer in the subject organization before the case will be reviewed.
- Permission letters for the use of material that has previously been copy-righted must be submitted at this time. (NOTE: If it belongs to someone else or has been adapted from someone else, appropriate citation must be given!)
- Four (4) copies of the Case and four (4) copies of the Teaching Note (TN). (NOTE: There should be absolutely no reference to the author, co-authors, their affiliations, etc., on the case or TN.)
- If your case was previously presented elsewhere, i.e., the SCR summer workshop, include copies of the scribe notes or evaluation/critique sheets with your submission. It will preclude me from having to ask you for them.

116

If submitting electronically: You must send the following in separate files:

- Case (NOTE: There should be absolutely no reference to the author, co-authors, their affiliations, etc., on the case or TN.
- Teaching Note
- Letter of transmittal
- Statement of pre-submission classroom testing experience
- Permissions and Authorizations
- Scribe notes or evaluation sheets (See item 6 above.)

When your submission is tentatively accepted for publication, the primary author will receive detailed guidelines and instructions for the preparation of the Abstract, Case, and Teaching Note.

All authors of accepted cases must become members of the Society for Case Research prior to publication of the case in the *Business Case Journal*.

For additional information, visit our Web site (**www.sfcr.org**) or contact the Editor directly:
Associate Professor Martha C. Fransson
Associate Editor, The Business Case Journal
Rensselaer Polytechnic Institute
Lally School of Management & Technology
Hartford Department
275 Windsor Street
Hartford, CT 06120-2991
Tel.: 860-548-7831 Email: **Fransson@rh.edu**

Business Education Forum

ADDRESS FOR SUBMISSION:

Susan O'Brien, Editor
Business Education Forum
NBEA
1914 Association Drive
Reston, VA 20191-1596
USA
Phone: 703-860-8300
E-Mail:
Web: www.nbea.org

PUBLICATION GUIDELINES:

Manuscript Length: 6-10
Copies Required: Two
Computer Submission: No
Format: N/A
Fees to Review: 0.00 US$

Manuscript Style:
    American Psychological Association

CIRCULATION DATA:

Reader: Academics, Practicing Teachers,
    Administrators
Frequency of Issue: Quarterly
Sponsor/Publisher: National Business
    Education Association

REVIEW INFORMATION:

Type of Review: Editorial Review
No. of External Reviewers: 1
No. of In House Reviewers: 1
Acceptance Rate: 6-10%
Time to Review: 2 - 3 Months
Reviewers Comments: Yes
Invited Articles: 6-10%
Fees to Publish: 0.00 US$

MANUSCRIPT TOPICS:
Accounting Education

MANUSCRIPT GUIDELINES/COMMENTS:

Members of NBEA are encouraged to submit articles for publication in *Business Education Forum*. Here's what you need to know about writing for your association's journal.

What to Write
Write the kind of article you would like to read. *Business Education Forum* is geared toward teachers in the field of business education. The style of the publication is academic, and its aim is to improve learning for students or make teaching more effective and interesting. The information appearing in *Business Education Forum* should not be readily available in other magazines or journals. Ideas should be developed clearly and comprehensively with supporting graphs and tables, if necessary. Avoid excessive jargon in favor of concise, specific, and concrete prose. Use active, not passive, words and phrases. Be sure to proofread your article for errors in grammar, punctuation, and spelling. A list of references should be included. Do not use footnotes. The closing paragraph in each article should be summarizing in nature and worthy of emphasis.

Length of Copy
Your manuscript should run from 1,500 to 2,000 words, or six to eight pages of double-spaced copy, using a 12-point font.

Manuscript Format
Use standard, 8 ½ x 11 inches, white paper. Manuscripts should be legible and double-spaced, (except for long quotes of four or more lines). When printed, primary headings should be flush left and boldface on a single line. *The Publication Manual of the American Psychological Association* (Fifth Edition) should be consulted for further questions of style. For ease of editing, a disk version of your article, compatible with Microsoft Word for a PC, must be included.

Membership
In order to publish a manuscript in *Business Education Forum*, the author(s) must be a member of the NBEA. Articles must also be submitted exclusively to *Business Education Forum*; one article per year can be published by an author(s).

Acceptance
Please allow several months for your manuscript to be reviewed. Although *Business Education Forum* is not a refereed publication, the articles published are reviewed by a section editor who is a professional business educator and two NBEA staff editors. To speed up the review of your manuscript, please submit your article to the appropriate section editor.

Editing
Business Education Forum section editors often make suggestions for revisions to manuscripts accepted for publication. These suggestions can include cutting or adding material, as well as stylistic changes. Editors work in conjunction with the author(s) to make these changes, and, if time permits, changes are reviewed and approved by the author(s) before publication. A copyright release form is sent along as well. NBEA does not assume responsibility for the points of view or the opinions expressed by the author(s) unless such statements have been established by a resolution of the Association.

Photographs and Graphics
Tables, graphs, diagrams, and photographs should be used if they contribute to the article and enhance its clarity. Graphics, such as illustrations or photographs, may not be embedded in the word processing file; they must be submitted as a separate PC, EPS or TIFF, file.

Copyright Permission
Obtaining permission to use charts, photographs, or any book, magazine, or newspaper excerpts in an article is the author's responsibility.

Bylines
Authors should include their names, titles, and the schools where they teach. An e-mail address should also be provided, so that readers may contact the authors.

Examples

1. Byline for a single author
- Margaret Smith is an assistant professor at the University of Florida, Gainesville, Florida. She can be contacted via e-mail at msmith@uf.edu.

2. Bylines for multiple authors
- Elaine McPherson is an assistant professor at Boston College, in Boston, Massachusetts and can be contacted via e-mail at emcpherson@bc.edu. Brian Miller is a high school instructor at Delray High School in Delray Beach, Florida. His e-mail address is millerm@aol.com.

References

Authors should cite references in alphabetical order and in the following manner. References to periodicals should include:
- Author(s) with last name first, then first initial(s). (Year of publication). Article name. Journal title (in italics), Volume (Issue), Page number(s).

Examples

1. *Journal article, one author*
Baker, D. (1997). Business Software. *Business Journal*, 11, 31-34.

2. *Journal article, multiple authors*
Jensen, I., Polk, G., and Stevens, R. (1991). The Role of the Internet in Distance Learning. *The Journal of Technology*, 21, 201-209.

3. *Magazine article*
Skolnik, J. (1997, April 4). Statistics in Business. *Science*, 97, 151-156.

4. *References to books should include*:
Author(s) with last name first, then first initial(s) (Year of publication). Title of book (in italics). Place of publication: Publisher.

Examples

1. *References to entire books*
Allen, V., and Smith, J.P., (1982). *Modern Survey of Business*. New York: McGraw-Hill.

2. *Edited book*
Keller, S., and Tan A.S. (Eds.). (1994). *International Business in the New Millennium*. Boston: Allyn and Bacon, Inc.

3. *Books with a group author, such as a government agency, as publisher*
U.S. Bureau of Statistics. (1994). *Population Shifts in the United States*. Washington, D.C.: Author.

Online references should include: Author(s) with last name first, then first initial(s). (Date of access). Title of work. [Online]. Available: Specify path.

120

Examples

Dodge, B. (1997, May 5). The WebQuest Page. [Online]. Available:
http://edweb.sdsu.edu/courses/edtec597/aboutawebquests.html.

References to an NBEA yearbook should be formatted as follows:

- Smith, B. (1997). Evaluation: A Tool for Learning and Identifying Talent. In C. P.
  Brantley and B. J. Davis (Eds.), *The Changing Dimensions of Business Education.*
  Yearbook No. 35. (pp. 88-99). Reston, VA: National Business Education Association.

Sending Your Manuscript

Please submit two paper copies of your article and one disk, virus free and labeled with the software and operating system used. Remember to include your name, address, phone number, as well as fax number and e-mail address, if available. E-mail or fax cannot be used for submitting manuscripts. Your article should be sent to the appropriate section editor or to the Editor, NBEA, 1914 Association Drive, Reston, VA 20191-1596. For further information, call NBEA at 703-860-8300.

California Business Review

ADDRESS FOR SUBMISSION:

Bhavesh M. Patel, Editor
California Business Review
PO Box 2536
Ceres, CA 95307
USA
Phone: 440-582-5978
E-Mail: Review@iabe.org
Web: www.iabe.com

CIRCULATION DATA:

Reader: Academics, Business Persons
Frequency of Issue:
Sponsor/Publisher: CSU-ABE /
　International Academy of Business and
　Economics

PUBLICATION GUIDELINES:

Manuscript Length: 11-15
Copies Required: One
Computer Submission: Yes Disk or Email
Format: MS Word
Fees to Review: 0.00 US$

Manuscript Style:
　Chicago Manual of Style

REVIEW INFORMATION:

Type of Review: No Reply
No. of External Reviewers: 2
No. of In House Reviewers: 1
Acceptance Rate:
Time to Review: 1 - 2 Months
Reviewers Comments: Yes
Invited Articles: 30%
Fees to Publish: 0.00 US$

MANUSCRIPT TOPICS:

Accounting Information Systems; Accounting Theory & Practice; Auditing; Cost Accounting; Econometrics; Economic Development; Financial Services; Fiscal Policy; Government & Non Profit Accounting; Insurance; International Economics & Trade; International Finance; Macro Economics; Micro Economics; Monetary Policy; Portfolio & Security Analysis; Public Policy Economics; Real Estate; Regional Economics; Tax Accounting

MANUSCRIPT GUIDELINES/COMMENTS:

Please use following manuscript Guidelines for submission of your papers for the review. Papers are reviewed on a continual basis throughout the year. Early Submissions are welcome! Please email your manuscript to **Review@iabe.org**.

Copyright. Articles papers or cases submitted for publication should be original contributions and should not be under consideration for any other publication at the same time. Authors submitting articles/papers/cases for publication warrant that the work is not an infringement of any existing copyright infringement of proprietary right invasion of privacy or libel and will indemnify defend and hold IABE or sponsor(s) harmless from any damages expenses and costs against any breach of such warranty. For ease of dissemination and to ensure proper policing of use papers/articles/cases and contributions become the legal copyright of the IABE unless otherwise agreed in writing.

122

General Information. These are submission instructions for review purpose only. Once your submission is accepted you will receive submission guidelines with your paper acceptance letter. The author(s) will be emailed result of the review process in about 6-8 weeks from submission date. Papers are reviewed and accepted on a continual basis. Submit your papers early for full considerations!

Typing. Paper must be laser printed/printable on 8.5" x 11" white sheets in Arial 10-point font single-spaced lines justify style in MS Word. All four margins must be 1" each.

First Page. Paper title not exceeding two lines must be CAPITALIZED AND CENTERED IN BOLD LETTERS. Author name and university/organizational affiliation of each author must be printed on one line each. Do NOT include titles such as Dr., Professor, Ph.D., department address email address etc. Please print the word "ABSTRACT" in capitalized bold letters left justified and double-spaced from last author's name/affiliation. Abstract should be in italic. Please see the sample manuscript.

All other Headings. All other section headings starting with INTRODUCTION must be numbered in capitalized bold letters left justified and double-spaced from last line above them. See the subsection headings in the sample manuscript.

Tables Figures and Charts. All tables figures or charts must be inserted in the body of the manuscripts within the margins with headings/titles in centered CAPITALIZED BOLD letters.

References and Bibliography. All references listed in this section must be cited in the article and vice-versa. The reference citations in the text must be inserted in parentheses within sentences with author name followed by a comma and year of publication. Please follow the following formats:

Journal Articles
Khade Alan S. and Metlen Scott K. "An Application of Benchmarking in Dairy Industry" *International Journal of Benchmarking* Vol. III (4) 1996 17

Books
Harrison Norma and Samson D. Technology Management: Text and Cases McGraw-Hill Publishing New York 2002

Internet
Hesterbrink C. E-Business and ERP: Bringing two Paradigms together October 1999; PricewaterhouseCoopers *www.pwc.com*.

Author Profile(s). At the end of paper include author profile(s) not exceeding five lines each author including name highest degree/university/year current position/university and major achievements. For example:

Author Profile:
Dr. Tahi J. Gnepa earned his Ph.D. at the University of Wisconsin Madison in 1989. Currently he is a professor of international business at California State University Stanislaus and Managing Editor of Journal of International Business Strategy (JIBStrategy).

Manuscript. Absolutely no footnotes! Do not insert page numbers for the manuscript. Please do not forget to run spelling and grammar check for the completed paper. Save the manuscript on your diskette/CD or hard drive.

Electronic Submission. Send your submission as an MS Word file attachment to your Email to **Review@iabe.org**.

124

California Journal of Business Research

ADDRESS FOR SUBMISSION:

Alan S. Khade, Editor
California Journal of Business Research
983 Woodland Drive
Turlock, CA 95382-7281
USA
Phone: 209-667-3074
E-Mail: Review@iabe.org
Web: www.iabe.org

CIRCULATION DATA:

Reader: Academics, Business Persons
Frequency of Issue: 2 Times/Year
Sponsor/Publisher: CSU - Academy of
    Business and Economics / IABE

PUBLICATION GUIDELINES:

Manuscript Length: 11-15
Copies Required: One
Computer Submission: Yes Disk or Email
Format: MS Word
Fees to Review: 0.00 US$

Manuscript Style:
    Chicago Manual of Style

REVIEW INFORMATION:

Type of Review: Blind Review
No. of External Reviewers: 2
No. of In House Reviewers: 1
Acceptance Rate: 25%
Time to Review: 1 - 2 Months
Reviewers Comments: Yes
Invited Articles: 11-20%
Fees to Publish: 0.00 US$

MANUSCRIPT TOPICS:

Accounting; Accounting Information Systems; Accounting Theory & Practice; Auditing; Cost Accounting; E-Business; Economics; Finance; Tax Accounting

MANUSCRIPT GUIDELINES/COMMENTS:

The original, high-quality research papers and articles (not currently under review or published in other publications) on all topics related to business and economics will be considered for publication in *California Journal of Business Research (CJBR)*.

Copyright. Articles, papers, abstracts or cases submitted for publication should be original contributions and should not be under consideration for any other publication at the same time. Authors submitting articles/papers/abstracts/cases for publication warrant that the work is not an infringement of any existing copyright, infringement of proprietary right, invasion of privacy, or libel and will indemnify, defend, and hold IABE/AIBE harmless from any damages, expenses, and costs against any breach of such warranty. For ease of dissemination and to ensure proper policing of use, papers/articles/abstracts/cases and contributions become the legal copyright of the IABE/AIBE unless otherwise agreed in writing.

Typing. Paper must be laser printed on 8.5" x 11" white sheets in Arial 10-point font, single-spaced lines, justify style in MS Word. All four margins must be 1" each.

125

First Page. Paper title, not exceeding two lines, must be CAPITALIZED AND CENTERED IN BOLD LETTERS. Author name and university/organizational affiliation of each author must be printed on one line each. Do NOT include titles such as, Dr., Professor, Ph.D., department, address, email address etc. Please print the word "ABSTRACT" in capitalized bold letters, left justified, and double-spaced from last author's name/affiliation. Abstract should be in italic. Please see the sample manuscript.

All other Headings. All other section headings starting with INTRODUCTION must be numbered, in capitalized bold letters, left justified, and double-spaced from last line above them.

Tables, Figures, and Charts. All tables, figures or charts must be inserted in the body of the manuscripts within the margins with headings/titles in centered CAPITALIZED BOLD letters.

References and Bibliography. All references listed in this section must be cited in the article and vice-versa. The reference citations in the text must be inserted in parentheses within sentences with author name followed by a comma and year of publication. Please follow the following formats:

Journal Articles
Khade, Alan S. and Metlen, Scott K., "An Application of Benchmarking in Dairy Industry", *International Journal of Benchmarking*, Vol. III (4), 1996, 17-27.

Books
Harrison, Norma and Samson, D., Technology Management: Text and Cases, McGraw-Hill Publishing, New York, 2002.

Internet
Hesterbrink, C., E-Business and ERP: Bringing two Paradigms together, October 1999; PricewaterhouseCoopers, www.pwc.com.

Author Profile(s). At the end of paper, include author profile(s), not exceeding five lines each author, including name, highest degree/university/year, current position/university, and major achievements. For example:

Dr. Tahi Gnepa earned his Ph.D. at University of Wisconsin in 1989. Currently he is a professor of international business at California State University, Stanislaus, and Program Chair of the AIBE.

Manuscript. Absolutely no footnotes allowed! Please do not forget to run spelling and grammar check for the completed paper. Save the manuscript on a diskette and label the diskette with title of your paper, your name, and email address.

SUBMISSION
Submissions by Mail
1. Please mail the following items in a 9 x 12" envelope:
2. Two camera-ready laser-printed copies of the manuscript
3. Diskette containing your manuscript

Submissions by Email
Send your paper as an attachment to the email to **Review@iabe.org**

California Tax Lawyer

ADDRESS FOR SUBMISSION:

Sharyn M. Fisk, Editor
California Tax Lawyer
9150 Wilshire Blvd, Ste 300
Beverly Hills, CA 90212
USA
Phone: 310-281-3286
E-Mail: sf@taxlitigator.com
Web:

PUBLICATION GUIDELINES:

Manuscript Length: 1-10
Copies Required: One
Computer Submission: Yes Email
Format: WordPerfect or MS Word
Fees to Review: 0.00 US$

Manuscript Style:
  Chicago Manual of Style

CIRCULATION DATA:

Reader: Business Persons, Tax Atorneys
Frequency of Issue: Quarterly
Sponsor/Publisher: California State Bar
  Taxation Section

REVIEW INFORMATION:

Type of Review: Editorial Review
No. of External Reviewers: 0
No. of In House Reviewers: 1
Acceptance Rate: 50%
Time to Review: 1 - 2 Months
Reviewers Comments: Yes
Invited Articles: 50% +
Fees to Publish: 0.00 US$

MANUSCRIPT TOPICS:
Legal; Tax Accounting; Taxation

MANUSCRIPT GUIDELINES/COMMENTS:

Important. The Editor may reject materials which do not meet the following criteria:
- Type should be single spaced. DO NOT FORMAT YOUR DOCUMENT (i.e., full justification, hyphenation, forced page breaks, etc.) as this will have to be stripped out and reformatted for typesetting.
- Include author's name, title, firm, address, telephone number, fax number and e-mail address.
- If separate citations are required, use endnotes only, not footnotes.
- If required, graphics must be submitted in TIFF (Mac) or TIFF (PC) format, although some types of materials may be accepted in camera ready copy. Please discuss any proposed graphics in advance with the Editor.
- Please submit your articles via email to Articles Editor. The article must be in either WordPerfect or Word format.
- Previously published materials may not be submitted for publication in the *California Tax Lawyer* without the Editor's prior approval.

128

- The *California Tax Lawyer* may, without limitation, reproduce or reprint, or permit others to reproduce or reprint, all or any portion of any material published in the *California Tax Lawyer* on a nonexclusive basis without further approval by the author.
- The *California Tax Lawyer* will not guarantee that articles submitted for publication will be printed in the *California Tax Lawyer* and/or published in a specific issue. The Editor further reserves the right to reject an article for any reason at any time during the production process. Authors will be notified as quickly as possible of articles rejected for publication.
- Republication of articles accepted for publication in the *California Tax Lawyer* within 90 days of delivery of the relevant issue to readers without the prior approval of the Editor is strictly prohibited.

CONTENT OF ARTICLES
Substantive Articles
In each issue, the *California Tax Lawyer* publishes four to six significant articles concerning aspects of federal and state tax law that are of interest to California tax practitioners. Articles addressing federal tax issues should also address whether California has conformed to federal law. There is no page length limitation on technical articles, although the Editor may request authors to shorten articles if there are space limitations.

Short Substantive Updates
Is there a hot tax issue in any area that can be clarified or for which practical insight can be offered to practitioners who would otherwise not be aware? These should be no more than 1000 words in length. The *California Tax Lawyer* will not accept articles previously printed in other journals without the prior approval of the Editor.

Commentaries
Practitioners are invited to provide brief commentaries on new or proposed legislation or regulations, developments in the tax law, or upon other issues affecting California tax practitioners.

Calendar Items
These items are grouped by month and should be submitted for as early publication as possible. Include any event where you are trying to reach members of the Taxation Section.

The Editor reserves the right to reduce the length of any report or article in order to accommodate space limitations, provided authors will have the opportunity to retract items submitted for publication if changes are significant.

Next Publication Schedule
Deadlines for Submission of Articles	*California Tax Lawyer* Received by Readers
February15	March 15
May 15	June 15
August 15	September 15
November 15	December 15

Contributors will receive a proof of their article, via e-mail as soon as it is available. You will then have 2 business days to review your article for any changes and then e-mail those changes to the Articles Editor. Note: any changes made to the proof at this time will be limited to corrections of typographical errors and other minor modifications. The Editor reserves the right to reject excessive changes from the original copy of the article if the Editor determines that making such changes would delay distribution of the *California Tax Lawyer*.

Submit Substantive Articles to:
Sharyn M. Fisk - Articles Editor
Hochman, Salkin, Rettig, Toscher & Perez, PC
9150 Wilshire Blvd, Ste 300
Beverly Hills, CA 90212
Tel: (310) 281-3286, Fax: (310) 859-1430
Email: **sf@taxlitigator.com**

CAmagazine

ADDRESS FOR SUBMISSION:

Christian Bellavance, Editor-in-Chief
CAmagazine
Canadian Inst. of Chartered Accountants
277 Wellington Street, W.
Toronto, Ontario, M5V 3H2
Canada
Phone: 416-204-3246
E-Mail: camagazine@cica.ca
Web: www.camagazine.com

PUBLICATION GUIDELINES:

Manuscript Length: 11-15
Copies Required: One
Computer Submission: Yes
Format: Word for Win, WdPer, Text only
Fees to Review: 0.00 US$

Manuscript Style:
See Manuscript Guidelines

CIRCULATION DATA:

Reader: Business Persons, Canadian
Chartered Accountants, Finance & Tax
Professionals
Frequency of Issue: 10 Times/Year
Sponsor/Publisher: Canadian Institute of
Chartered Accountants

REVIEW INFORMATION:

Type of Review: Editorial Review
No. of External Reviewers: 1
No. of In House Reviewers: 2
Acceptance Rate: 6-10%
Time to Review: 1 - 2 Months
Reviewers Comments: No
Invited Articles: less than 50%
Fees to Publish: 0.00 US$

MANUSCRIPT TOPICS:

Accounting Education; Accounting Information Systems; Accounting Theory & Practice;
Auditing; Behavioral Accounting; Business Valuation; Cost Accounting; Econometrics;
Economic Development; Economic History; Financial Services; Fiscal Policy; Fraud;
Governance; Government & Non Profit Accounting; Human Resources; Industrial
Organization; Information Technology; Insolvency; Insurance; International Economics &
Trade; International Finance; Law; Macro Economics; Micro Economics; Monetary Policy;
Portfolio & Security Analysis; Public Policy Economics; Real Estate; Regional Economics;
Risk Management; Tax Accounting

MANUSCRIPT GUIDELINES/COMMENTS:

Material must be of specific interest to finance and tax professionals, accountants and
auditors.

Canadian Accounting Perspectives

ADDRESS FOR SUBMISSION:

Joel Amernic, Editor
Canadian Accounting Perspectives
University of Toronto
Joseph L. Rotman School of Management
105 St. George St.
Toronto, Ontario, M5S 3E6
Canada
Phone: 416-978-3796
E-Mail: cap@caaa.ca
Web: www.caaa.ca

CIRCULATION DATA:

Reader: Academics
Frequency of Issue: 2 Times/Year
Sponsor/Publisher: Canadian Academic
    Accounting Association

PUBLICATION GUIDELINES:

Manuscript Length: 11-30+
Copies Required: One
Computer Submission: Yes Disk, Email
Format: MS Word or pdf
Fees to Review: 75.00 CAN$ Member/Sub
    125.00 CAN$ Non-Member/Subscriber

Manuscript Style:
    Chicago Manual of Style

REVIEW INFORMATION:

Type of Review: Blind Review
No. of External Reviewers: 2
No. of In House Reviewers: 0
Acceptance Rate: 11-20%
Time to Review: 2 - 3 Months
Reviewers Comments: Yes
Invited Articles: 0-5%
Fees to Publish: 0.00 US$

MANUSCRIPT TOPICS:
Accounting Education; Accounting Information Systems; Accounting Theory & Practice; Applied Accounting Research; Auditing; Behavioral Accounting; Cost Accounting; Economic History; Financial Services; Government & Non Profit Accounting; Tax Accounting

MANUSCRIPT GUIDELINES/COMMENTS:

Papers should be written either in English or in French.

Format
Manuscripts should be typed, doubled-spaced, on one side of 8 ½ × 11 inch paper. Margins should be wide enough to facilitate editing and duplication. All pages, including endnotes, tables, figures, illustrations, appendices, and references should be serially numbered. In the text, when not in lists or tables, numbers from one through nine should be spelled out, except when used with mathematical, statistical, scientific, or technical units and quantities.

A cover page should contain the following information: title, author's name and affiliation, the present address, email, telephone, and fax number of the author to whom correspondence should be addressed, and acknowledgements and information on grants received. Authors should not identify themselves in the paper.

An abstract (maximum 250 words) should be presented on the page immediately preceding the text, should include the research question, method of examination, and principal findings, and should be followed by four keywords (to aid in indexing).

Footnotes should be used for extensions where inclusion in the body of the text might disrupt continuity. All footnotes should be automated, numbered consecutively with superscript Arabic numerals, and be the same size and formatting as the main text. Each table, figure, or illustration should be presented on a separate page and bear an Arabic number and title.

Accepted papers are to be prepared on disk using software acceptable to the managing editor, but disks need not be included at the point of initial submission. The data underlying all graphs should be supplied in separate files in ASCII or Excel format.

Disclosure
Together with the paper being submitted, authors are asked to include a copy of any other paper, whether or not published elsewhere, that shares data or modelling analysis with the submitted paper. The contribution of the submitted paper must be clearly distinguished from other such papers. If the submitted paper is based on an experiment, survey, or other data manipulations, participants or variables involved in that collection are reflected in the paper, authors are asked to include a memo describing and explaining the circumstances and estimating any effects on the results. The memo may be sent to reviewers.

Submission
Submit one hard copy and one electronic copy (Word or PDF) to:
Canadian Accounting Perspectives
Joel Amernic, Editor
Joseph L. Rotman School of Management
University of Toronto
105 St. George Street
Toronto, Ontario, Canada M5S 3E6

Inquiries can be addressed to the Editor by email: **cap@caaa.ca**

Please refer to the detailed *CAP* author guidelines on the website. Their usage is required for papers that have been accepted to the journal.

Canadian Tax Journal

ADDRESS FOR SUBMISSION:

Alan Macnaughton & Scott Wilkie, Editors
Canadian Tax Journal
Canadian Tax Foundation
595 Bay Street, Suite 1200
Toronto, M5G 2N5
Canada
Phone: 416-599-0283
E-Mail: lamalia@ctf.ca
Web: www.ctf.ca/publications/journal.asp

CIRCULATION DATA:

Reader: Academics, Business Persons
Frequency of Issue: Quarterly
Sponsor/Publisher: Canadian Tax
    Foundation

PUBLICATION GUIDELINES:

Manuscript Length: 30+
Copies Required: One
Computer Submission: Yes Email
Format: MS Word
Fees to Review: 0.00 US$

Manuscript Style:
    See Manuscript Guidelines

REVIEW INFORMATION:

Type of Review: Blind Review
No. of External Reviewers: 2
No. of In House Reviewers: 0
Acceptance Rate: 21-30%
Time to Review: 1 - 2 Months
Reviewers Comments: Yes
Invited Articles: 11-20%
Fees to Publish: 0.00 US$

MANUSCRIPT TOPICS:
Fiscal Policy; Tax Accounting

MANUSCRIPT GUIDELINES/COMMENTS:

The purpose of the Canadian Tax Foundation, as one of its Directors once stated, "should be to establish facts and verify theories in every possible aspect of taxation in Canada." As the principal research publication of the Canadian Tax Foundation since 1953, the *Canadian Tax Journal* continues to carry out this mandate. Opinions expressed in the *Journal* are not necessarily endorsed by the Foundation or its members.

The *Canadian Tax Journal* is published quarterly. It consists of main articles, the Policy Forum, features, short (1-2 page) correspondence, and sometimes invited papers from a conference or symposium.

Main articles are in-depth examinations of issues in taxation and public finance with particular relevance to Canada and generally concern tax policy, tax practice, and the understanding of the effects of taxes on decision-making. Authors are typically tax practitioners or university faculty in accounting, economics, law, finance, political science, or other academic disciplines. Main articles are typically 20 to 30 journal pages, which corresponds to 35 to 55 double-spaced pages.

Each main article submission is sent out for comment to at least two experts in the area of the submission, most of whom are drawn from the Editorial Board (see our web page). The final decision on publication is made by the editors.

Policy Forum is a venue for informed commentary and expressions of opinion on issues of tax policy and broad issues of the conduct of tax practice. Contributions are invited by the editors.

Features are regular sections of the *Journal* on particular topics, which are mostly aspects of tax practice. Contributions are invited by feature editors.

Main articles, as well as contributions to Policy Forum and features, may be in English or French and should not have been submitted or published elsewhere. Submissions should be original work and should not be capable of being construed as plagiarizing any other published work. The preferred method of submission is by e-mail as an attachment in Word. E-mail inquires are welcome: address them to the managing editor, Laurel Amalia, at **lamalia@ctf.ca**

Persons considering submitting main articles on tax practice topics may wish to submit a proposal with curriculum vitae before writing commences to ensure that the topic would be of interest to *Journal* readers and does not overlap with other material that is in preparation or in press.

Detailed instructions to authors are available on the web at:
http://ww.ctf.ca/publications/journal.asp.

Full text of the entire *Journal* since 1991, including features, is available though our electronic product TaxFind. This product also contains a detailed index of the *Journal*. The *Journal* is also indexed in EconLit, ABI Inform, LegalTrac, CCH Canadian's Income Tax Research Index, Carswell's Income Tax References, and many other products.

CASE Journal (The)

ADDRESS FOR SUBMISSION:

Herbert Sherman, Editor
CASE Journal (The)
Division of Business
239 Montauk Highway
Southampton, NY 11968
USA
Phone: 631-287-8285
E-Mail: hsherman@southampton.liu.edu
Web:

CIRCULATION DATA:

Reader: Academics, Practitioner
Frequency of Issue: 2 - 3 Times/Year
Sponsor/Publisher: The CASE Association

PUBLICATION GUIDELINES:

Manuscript Length: 16-20
Copies Required: Electronic
Computer Submission: Yes Email
Format: MS Word, Office 2000
Fees to Review: 0.00 US$

Manuscript Style:
American Psychological Association

REVIEW INFORMATION:

Type of Review: Blind Review
No. of External Reviewers: 2
No. of In House Reviewers: 0
Acceptance Rate: 21-30%
Time to Review: 1 - 2 Months
Reviewers Comments: Yes
Invited Articles: No Reply
Fees to Publish: Member Only

MANUSCRIPT TOPICS:

Accounting Education; Accounting Information Systems; Accounting Theory & Practice; Auditing; Behavioral Accounting; Cost Accounting; Econometrics; Economic Development; Financial Services; Fiscal Policy; Government & Non Profit Accounting; Industrial Organization; Insurance; International Economics & Trade; International Finance; Macro Economics; Micro Economics; Monetary Policy; Portfolio & Security Analysis; Public Policy Economics; Real Estate; Regional Economics; Tax Accounting; Topics Covering the Above

MANUSCRIPT GUIDELINES/COMMENTS:

The audience for this journal includes both practitioners and academics and thus encourages submissions from a broad range of individuals.

Scholarly Works. Cases with teaching notes; conceptual papers and papers reporting original research as well as the applied implications of others' research in terms of case teaching, research, and instruction; and creative learning, research and writing methods are encouraged. We request that submitters of empirical research provide appropriate data set analyses to allow for meta-studies (i.e. correlations matrices and chi-alphas). Because of the broad appeal of the journal to practitioners and academics, *The CASE Journal* will not refuse to review a case or an article solely on the basis of format. However, if a case or paper is accepted, the final version for publication will be expected to adhere to the publication and manuscript

136

guidelines. Cases and papers may be returned due to issues relating to writing style and grammar. Consideration will be given to both primary and secondary case studies.

Cases. Those wishing to submit a case for potential publication should submit the entire case along with the completed teaching notes for review. If accepted for publication, only the case will be published along with a note for interested readers to contact the case author for the teaching notes. All review and publishing rules which apply to scholarly articles also apply for cases. Also, upon acceptance for publication, *The CASE Journal* requires that the author(s) submit a signed letter of liability (sample available upon request) release prior to publication.

Initial Submission. *The CASE Journal* blind-reviews submissions, and all manuscripts submitted are to be original, unpublished and not under consideration by any other publishing source. To ensure the blind review, there should be no author-identifying information in the text or references. An abstract of 150 words or fewer should accompany the paper. This journal will only accept on-line submissions. Send one (1) copy to the editor by e-mail in MS-Word and/or IBM text format. Exhibits, tables and illustrations should be integrated into the manuscript file. A separate title page must accompany the paper and include the title of the paper and all pertinent author information (i.e. name, affiliation, address, telephone number, FAX number, and E-mail address). If any portion of the manuscript has been presented in other formats (conferences, workshops, speeches, etc.), it should be so noted on the title page.

Copyright. Authors submitting articles and cases for potential publication in *The CASE Journal* warrant that the work is not an infringement on any existing copyright and will indemnify the publisher against any breach of such warranty. Upon acceptance for publication, authors must convey copyright ownership to *The CASE Journal* by submitting a transferal letter signed and dated by all authors which contains the following language: "in consideration of *The CASE Journal* acting to review, edit, and publish <title of submission>, the author(s) undersigned hereby transfer(s), assign(s), or otherwise convey(s) all copyright ownership to *The CASE Journal*."

Circulation Data
Reader. Academic and Practitioner
Frequency of Issue. 2-3 times per year (September, January and April based upon available accepted manuscripts)
Copies per Issue. N/A - Internet publication
Subscription Price. Free (non-members will be charged a download fee.)
Publishing Fee. None. However, at least one of the publishing authors must be a member of the CASE Association ($10 membership fee)
Sponsorship. Professional Association

Case Research Journal

ADDRESS FOR SUBMISSION:

Lew G. Brown, Editor
Case Research Journal
ELECTRONIC SUBMISSION ONLY
University of North Carolina, Greensboro
PO Box 26165
Greensboro, NC 27402-6165
USA
Phone: 336-334-4539
E-Mail: crj@uncg.edu
Web: www.NACRA.net

CIRCULATION DATA:

Reader: Academics
Frequency of Issue: Quarterly
Sponsor/Publisher: North American Case
  Research Association (NACRA)

PUBLICATION GUIDELINES:

Manuscript Length: Any
Copies Required: Online
Computer Submission: Yes Required
Format: See Website
Fees to Review: Member Req.

Manuscript Style:
, Turabian

REVIEW INFORMATION:

Type of Review: Blind Review
No. of External Reviewers: 3
No. of In House Reviewers: 1
Acceptance Rate: 11-20%
Time to Review: 2 - 3 Months
Reviewers Comments: Yes
Invited Articles: 0-5%
Fees to Publish: 0.00 US$

MANUSCRIPT TOPICS:
Accounting Theory & Practice; Cost Accounting; Tax Accounting

MANUSCRIPT GUIDELINES/COMMENTS:

Editorial Comments. The type of review is double-blind. The reviewers' comments are comprehensive. No fees are charged to review the manuscript; however, at least one author must belong to North American Case Research Association. See **www.NACRA.net** for membership information.

Manuscript Topics. The *Case Research Journal* publishes outstanding decision-focused teaching cases drawn from field research in real organizations. Published cases deal with important issues in all administration-related disciplines, including business, health care, education, technology, hospitality management, and public administration. The *Journal* emphasizes cases based on field research, but the editor may accept secondary-sourced cases in rare circumstances. Occasionally, the *Journal* publishes papers concerning case research, case writing, or case teaching.

Previously published cases or articles (except those appearing in NACRA Proceedings or workshop presentations) are not eligible for consideration. Cases must not be under simultaneous consideration for textbook adoption. The *Journal* does not accept fictional works or cases synthesized from author experience.

Manuscript Guidelines

1. The North American Case Research Association (NACRA), publisher of the *Case Research Journal*, encourages the widest possible reproduction and use of the cases developed through its workshops and the *Journal's* review process, always with appropriate notice of copyright.

2. All other rights, including the right to use the cases in printed or electronically produced textbooks, are reserved to NACRA and the authors, who share copyright for these purposes. NACRA charges permission fees for these publication rights, in order to fund its continuing faculty-development programs.

3. Cases must be accompanied by a comprehensive "Instructor's Manual," which identifies the case's intended course(s), audience, and the specific teaching objectives; lists assignment questions for student preparation; and analyzes each question. The Manual should discuss the research methodology for gathering case data and should state what disguises (if any) have been imposed. If possible, authors should include an epilogue or follow-on information about the decision actually taken.

4. Figures and Tables essential to student understanding of the case content should be embedded in the text and numbered separately. Exhibits should be grouped at the end of the case.

5. Wherever possible, citations should be embedded in the text, with bibliographic information restricted to a "Reference List" at the end of the case. All exhibits should state their sources in detail.

6. No author identification should appear in either the case or the Instructor's Manual.

7. The corresponding author's cover letter should include the following paragraph:
In submitting this case to the *Case Research Journal* for widespread distribution in print and electronic media, I (we) certify that it is original work, based on real events in a real organization. It has not been published and is not under review elsewhere. Copyright holders have given written permission for the use of any material not permitted by the "Fair Use Doctrine." Where research has included field interviews, the host organization has signed a release authorizing the publication of the case and all data gathered with understandings of confidentiality.

8. The following notice should appear at the bottom of the first page of the manuscript:
"Review copy for use of the *Case Research Journal*. Not for reproduction or distribution. Dated (date of submission)."

9. It is expected that at least one author will be a member of the North American Case Research Association. Membership applications are available from the editor or from NACRA's treasurer. See **www.NACRA.net**.

Catalyst: The Leading Edge of Ohio Business (Ohio CPA Journal)

ADDRESS FOR SUBMISSION:

Sandy Spieker, Editor
Catalyst: The Leading Edge of Ohio
   Business (Ohio CPA Journal)
535 Metro Place South
Dublin, OH 43017
USA
Phone: 614-764-2727
E-Mail: sspieker@ohio-cpa.com
Web: www.ohioscpa.com

CIRCULATION DATA:

Reader: Business Persons
Frequency of Issue: Monthly
Sponsor/Publisher:

PUBLICATION GUIDELINES:

Manuscript Length: 1-5
Copies Required:
Computer Submission: Yes Disk, Email
Format: MS Word preferred
Fees to Review: 0.00 US$

Manuscript Style:
   Associated Press Stylebook

REVIEW INFORMATION:

Type of Review: Editorial Review
No. of External Reviewers: 1
No. of In House Reviewers: 3+
Acceptance Rate: 11-20%
Time to Review: 4 - 6 Months
Reviewers Comments: Yes
Invited Articles: 50% +
Fees to Publish: 0.00 US$

MANUSCRIPT TOPICS:
Accounting Information Systems; Accounting Theory & Practice; Auditing; Cost Accounting; Financial Services; Government & Non Profit Accounting; Industrial Organization; Insurance; International Economics & Trade; International Finance; Portfolio & Security Analysis; Tax Accounting

MANUSCRIPT GUIDELINES/COMMENTS:

The Magazine and Format. Are your insights unique, sound, compelling, and relevant to CPAs in their roles as leaders, advisors, and managers? Can you offer the readership in-depth knowledge and insight into Ohio business issues?

If the answer is yes, these guidelines can make the publication process simpler. To author an article for *Catalyst* you must understand our audience.

The Magazine and Its Audience. *Catalyst* is a unique bimonthly magazine written specifically for CPAs, Ohio's key business and thought leaders, and those they serve. It provides timely coverage of issues and trends pertinent to Ohio business, along with in-depth industry-related articles.

140

The subjects include:

- accounting
- financial reporting
- personal financial planning
- technology
- professional development
- ethics and fraud
- related business issues

The majority of our readers are members of The Ohio Society of CPAs, primarily decision makers and staff level employees. The professional experience of our membership ranges greatly. Staff size varies significantly from one (the sole practitioner) to several hundred (large local or national firm).

Nearly 50 percent of the magazine's readers work in industry in positions from staff accountant to chief financial officer. Nearly 40 percent of readers are in public practice, in firms ranging in size from a sole practitioner to an international firm of several hundred. Just under 10 percent of our readers are sole practitioners and a great many others work in small or midsize firms. The remainder, almost 4 percent, are government personnel, educators or students.

Format
The magazine's format consists of one cover article and six to eight feature articles on other business issues. These articles focus on current events, select business news, and special interest topics. Articles are written by freelance writers, Society members, and staff and industry experts.

Because our magazine's readers have a variety of interests that require diverse editorial content, articles should have broad appeal. Those based on studies or surveys should be brief, focus on the conclusions drawn from the research, analyze the impact on the profession, and offer insights or advice that will be useful to readers. Articles that are entirely theoretical or are derived wholly from secondary sources are rarely accepted. All articles MUST include an executive summary with an overview of all pertinent points.

We highly recommend contacting the editor at the Society before preparing any materials to discuss the topics and possible timeline.

Authors should identify which segments of the readership their article addresses and their objectives in writing it. The more the editors know about the author's intent and targeted audience, the easier it is to judge an article's appropriateness. Thus, the larger the audience served, the more likely an article will be accepted.

Length and Style
Diversity. The CPA profession and Ohio business market is increasingly diverse and we want our magazine to reflect that diversity. The more sources, the better. Short, lively quotes are

desirable. Please also provide contact information – mailing and e-mail address, and phone and fax number – for all persons profiled or quoted in your article.

Length. We accept articles from one to three pages of our publication (950 to 2,000 words). We also publish one-page columns on various subjects. Some columns will appear in every issue, while others will appear on a rotating basis. Columns should be a maximum of 800 words. Careful monitoring of word lengths allows the editors to make maximum use of limited editorial space and therefore to ensure the presentation of a variety of topics that address the interests of our diverse readership. Submitted articles that do not meet the length specifications may not be accepted.

Style. Articles should be of a practical nature, offer guidance in complex situations, methods to implement in practice, or help resolve questions arising in practice.

Numbers from one through nine should be spelled out, except where decimals are used, used as a percentage, or where the numbers are in tabular form. Numbers 10 and above should be written numerically. The article should be written in third person and non-sexist language. Articles by one author should not employ the editorial "we."

We recommend *The Elements of Style* by William Strunk, Jr., and E. B. White (published in paperback by Macmillan Publishing Co., Inc.) as a guide to style and usage. The Ohio Society also follows the *Associated Press Style Guide* for all of our publications.

Executive Summary. All articles should include an executive summary with an overview of pertinent points. The executive summary should be an encapsulation of the key points of the article – and provide an abstract of the article and its message. The executive summary should present a clear and concise overview of the issue addressed and the conclusion that was reached in the article. It should not be longer than 150 words.

Content and Citations
Article Content. The first paragraph should say what the article is about and why the reader would be interested in it. Include essential background information on the topic here. Relate the rest of the article to the subject mentioned in the introductory paragraph. If you must include technical jargon or complicated terms in the text, follow them with brief explanations. Weave essential references into the narrative; do not use footnotes or endnotes.

Reference List. When the article cites other literature, a list of references must be included at the end of the text. References must be complete bibliography references, including page or paragraph numbers. Arrange entries alphabetically by surname of the first author. Works without authors should also be listed alphabetically. Multiple works by the same author(s) are listed in publication date order. Samples of entries are:

American Institute of Certified Public Accountants. Report of the Study on Establishment of Accounting Principles, Establishing Accounting Principles (1972).

Sprouse, R. T., "Accounting for What-You-May-Call-Its," Journal of Accountancy (August 1966), pp. 45-54.

Literature Citations. To cite sources of references, use square brackets in the body of the text to enclose the author's name and page number, if appropriate. If two references were published in one year, use a, b, c to indicate which work listed in the reference list is referred to, e.g. [Armstrong, 1977]; [Sprouse and Moonitz, 1962, p. 2]; [Hendriksen, 1973a]. Citations to professional publications should employ acronyms where practical, e.g., [APB Opinion No. 30]; (SFAS No 95]. If an author's name is mentioned in the text, it should not be repeated in the citation, e.g., "Armstrong [1977, p. 40] says . . ."

If a reference has three or more authors, list only the last name of the first author followed by "et al."

References to statutes, legal treatises or court cases should use citations acceptable in law reviews.

Requirements and Deadlines
Article Requirements. One copy of the article should be submitted in electronic format. The Ohio Society does request but does not require copyright assignment or transfer from authors; however, we request first publication rights. A publication release form is required to be filled out by all authors upon submission.

In addition, manuscripts should adhere to the following specifications:
- Font: Arial
- Size: 10 pt
- Spacing: Double
- Ink: Black
- Justification: Left

All submissions should include:
- A headline (title)
- An executive summary
- A byline
- Author photo
- Author's bio
- Final word count
- Indication of whether the article has been previously published.
- Disclosure of any financial, professional or other interests the writer has in the products or services described.

Editorial Deadlines. Deadlines are subject to change.

The Editorial and Review Process
Submit all articles on an exclusive basis. If an article has been submitted to any other publication, it should not be submitted and will not be considered.

Editorial advisers are used to assist in selecting material for publication. This group of advisers consists of professionals with broad experience and those with particular expertise in various specialties.

Articles submitted will undergo a very rigid review. Acceptance is based on practicality, readability, technical soundness, originality and interest to readers.

Once an article is accepted, an editor contacts the author to discuss any recommended changes. After revisions, the article is edited to conform to our magazine's style. The author receives a final manuscript for review and final approval. The author cannot rewrite at this time, but can make essential changes or corrections. Authors are given a proposed publication date. There are no payments of honoraria for published articles. However, as a token of appreciation, authors of feature articles receive five complimentary copies of the issue.

Authors will assure that any and all submitted materials are their own work and not copyrighted or under any legal restriction for publication.

All information that appears in the magazine is current as of approximately three weeks prior to mailing (when the printing process begins).

Biography of Author(s). "About the author" bios are welcome for articles contributed by industry experts who would like professional recognition and/or to share contact information with readers. Bio content should not exceed 25 words and should include the following information:
- Name(s), title(s), employer(s)
- Complete address and business telephone number

Submission Checklist. Be sure that your contact, whether it is a column coordinator, staff member, or the editorial board chairperson, has seen and approved the article or column before it is sent to the editor.
- Submit article on an exclusive basis. The Ohio Society of CPAs reserves all copyrights for article submissions.
- Send electronic copy.
- Do not send electronic artwork unless it has already been discussed with an editor.
- Include examples and/or case study(s).

Editors. To discuss an article or idea with the editor, contact Sandy Spieker at: **sspieker@ohio-cpa.com.**

Clarion Business and Economic Review

ADDRESS FOR SUBMISSION:

Rod D. Raehsler, Editor
Clarion Business and Economic Review
Clarion University
College of Business Administration
Bureau of Business & Economic Research
333 Dana Still Hall
Clarion, PA 16214
USA
Phone: 814-393-2627
E-Mail: raehsler@clarion.edu
Web:

PUBLICATION GUIDELINES:

Manuscript Length: 16-20
Copies Required: Two
Computer Submission: Yes Disk or Email
Format: MS Word
Fees to Review: 5.00 US$

Manuscript Style:
    Chicago Manual of Style

CIRCULATION DATA:

Reader: Business Persons, Academics
Frequency of Issue: 2 Times/Year
Sponsor/Publisher: Bureau of Business and
    Economic Research, Clarion University

REVIEW INFORMATION:

Type of Review: Blind Review
No. of External Reviewers: 1
No. of In House Reviewers: 2
Acceptance Rate: 50%
Time to Review: 2 - 3 Months
Reviewers Comments: Yes
Invited Articles: 0-5%
Fees to Publish: 0.00 US$

MANUSCRIPT TOPICS:
Accounting Education; Accounting Theory & Practice; Cost Accounting; Economic Development; Government & Non Profit Accounting; Industrial Organization; Marketing; Micro Economics; Public Policy Economics; Real Estate; Regional Economics

MANUSCRIPT GUIDELINES/COMMENTS:

Publication Guidelines
The *Clarion Business and Economic Review* is published by Clarion University Publications as a service to the university and business community. It is sponsored by the Bureau of Business and Economic Research and the College of Business Administration.

Contents of *Review* materials reflect the views of the authors and do not necessarily represent the views of members of the Bureau of Business and Economic Research, the College of Business Administration or Clarion University of Pennsylvania. The Editorial Board and Clarion University are not in any way responsible for the views expressed by contributors.

The *Review* welcomes the submission of articles on topics relating to business, economics, and development. In addition to articles, the *Review* invites authors to submit shorter works, such as book reviews, commentaries, recent developments, and bibliographies.

To be considered for publication, manuscripts should be typewritten and double-spaced. Submissions should be sent accompanied by a duplicate of the manuscript on a 3.5" floppy diskette preferably in Corel WordPerfect 8.0 or MSWord.

Please address manuscripts to:
Rod Raeshler & LeGene Quesenberry, Co-editors
The Clarion Business and Economic Review
Clarion University of Pennsylvania
Clarion, PA 16214

CMA Management Magazine

ADDRESS FOR SUBMISSION:

Rob Colman, Editor
CMA Management Magazine
CMA Canada
Mississauga Executive Center
1 Robert Speck Parkway, Suite 1400
Mississauga, ON L4Z 3M3
Canada
Phone: 905-949-3109
E-Mail: rcolman@cma-canada.org
Web: www.managementmag.com

CIRCULATION DATA:

Reader: Business Persons, Financial
   Executives
Frequency of Issue: 9 Times/Year
Sponsor/Publisher: CMA Canada

PUBLICATION GUIDELINES:

Manuscript Length: 1-5 2,000 Words
Copies Required: Two
Computer Submission: Yes Email
Format: MS Word
Fees to Review: 0.00 US$

Manuscript Style:
   See Manuscript Guidelines, Canadian
   Press Style Book

REVIEW INFORMATION:

Type of Review: Blind Review
No. of External Reviewers: 1
No. of In House Reviewers: 1
Acceptance Rate: 21-30%
Time to Review: 2 - 3 Months
Reviewers Comments: No
Invited Articles: 50% +
Fees to Publish: 0.00 US$

MANUSCRIPT TOPICS:
Accounting Education; Accounting Theory & Practice; Cost Accounting; Economic Development; Economic History; Fiscal Policy; Government & Non Profit Accounting; International Economics & Trade; International Finance; Monetary Policy; Public Policy Economics; Regional Economics; Strategic Management Policy

MANUSCRIPT GUIDELINES/COMMENTS:

1. Management accountants are involved in most aspects of business from an accounting and managerial perspective.

2. Articles should be brief (about 1500 words), readable and practical, illustrating how organizations can do things better (more cheaply, with good quality and economy of personnel). Management accountants are members of the management team providing information (not necessarily financial) for strategic, tactical and operational decisions. Their contribution is based on in-depth knowledge about what information is required and how it must be organized and presented to improve such decisions. Therefore, most aspects of business are of interest to them.

3. We especially like case study types of articles, featuring interviews with management, accounting and other authorities; articles of new developments in computers and software, management methods, accounting practices, etc.; articles on news and trends in management accounting and management, taxes, legislation, etc.

4. Articles should be readable and interesting, with the minimum of footnotes and references, as well as business jargon.

Writer's Guidelines
CMA Management is a magazine that addresses strategic business ideas and is distributed 9 times per year to Certified Management Accountants (CMAs) and other strategic financial management professionals. It is published by CMA Canada, the organization that designates and supports CMAs. *CMA Management's* editorial content is assigned three months in advance of publication date. Please review a copy of the magazine before submitting an editorial idea. Submit your article idea in writing (two to three paragraphs), or the complete article, to:

Robert Colman,
Editor CMA Management
CMA Canada
Mississauga Executive Center
1 Robert Speck Parkway, Suite 1400
Mississauga, ON L4Z 3M3
Tel: 905-949-3109
Fax: 905-949-0888
rcolman@cma-canada.org

Submitting a Story Idea
For feature-length stories, please indicate for which issue you believe your story would be a good fit. There is no specific focus for regular columns, and ideas submitted for a column may be placed in any issue.

Please describe the issues your article will address and why these issues are important/relevant to management professionals. Please also include a short bio of yourself or the potential author, outlining the previously published articles (if any) and/or the author's area of expertise.

Columns are a maximum of 700-1200 words and include these topics:
- Management Trends
- HR
- Business Strategies
- Government Issues
- Information Technology
- Global View
- Tax tips
- Money Management
- Media Bites (review of books and articles in other publications)
- Book Reviews

Feature articles are 1,500 to 3,000 words and include topics ranging from human resource management and e-business strategies, to performance measurement and ethics.

Articles that are most likely to be accepted are those that address current management topics of interest to management professionals, and include the viewpoints of at least two to three experts or sources. Our readers value articles that are educational and interesting. Technical or academic-style writing will not be accepted.

Articles that offer real-life examples of end-user applications (i.e., case studies) are also of interest to our readers, and articles that provide critical analyses should also contain possible solutions to the problems presented.

Please note that we will not accept any articles that merely serve as promotional pieces for a company (i.e., advertorial). All self-serving phrases will be edited out of the story as the editor sees fit.

Accepted articles must be either e-mailed to the editor as an attachment, or sent on disk. Faxed copies will not be accepted. Please feel free to contribute graphics or photos with your article. Electronic images must have a minimum resolution of 300 dots-per-inch.

We require at least three to four weeks to decide whether an editorial idea is suitable.

Coastal Business Journal

ADDRESS FOR SUBMISSION:

David A. DeCenzo, Editor
Coastal Business Journal
Coastal Carolina University
Wall College of Business
PO Box 261954
Conway, SC 29528
USA
Phone: 843-349-2640
E-Mail: ddcenzo@coastal.edu
Web: www.coastal.edu/business/cbj/

PUBLICATION GUIDELINES:

Manuscript Length: 11-15
Copies Required: Three
Computer Submission: Yes Disk, Email
Format: MS Word, WordPerfect
Fees to Review: 0.00 US$

Manuscript Style:
, Hybird

CIRCULATION DATA:

Reader: Business Persons, Academics, A
   mix of Applied Researchers
Frequency of Issue: 1-2 Times/Year
Sponsor/Publisher: Wall College of
   Business, Coastal Carolina University

REVIEW INFORMATION:

Type of Review: Blind Review
No. of External Reviewers: 8
No. of In House Reviewers: 11
Acceptance Rate: 37.5%
Time to Review: 4-9 Months
Reviewers Comments: Yes
Invited Articles: 6-10%
Fees to Publish: 0.00 US$

MANUSCRIPT TOPICS:
Accounting Information Systems; Coastal Economic Issues; Cost Accounting; Tourism & Hospitality Research

MANUSCRIPT GUIDELINES/COMMENTS:

We encourage you to submit your paper via an e-mail attachment to the Editor, David A. DeCenzo (**ddecenzo@coastal.edu**) in either Word or WordPerfect. However, if you prefer, you may submit your paper in a more traditional fashion by sending three (3) printed copies along with a copy on diskette. On the diskette, write the paper title and author(s). Please note that diskettes will not be returned.

Regardless of the submission method you choose, please ensure that you follow the conventions listed below. Submissions which do not conform to the following guidelines will be returned and will not be considered for publication.

Font. Times New Roman, 12 pt.

Margins. Indent paragraphs five (5) spaces. Leave a line after each paragraph. Set the margins as follows: left, right, and top: 1 inch; bottom, 1.25 inches.

150

Spacing. Single space the body of the paper. Double-space before and after first- and second-level headings. Triple space between the title and before and after the author(s).

Page Numbers. Please turn page numbering off. Pencil in page numbers on hard copies if you wish.

Title. Bold faced and centered at the top of the first page.

Authors and Affiliations. Centered, bold-faced and single-spaced beginning three lines below the title. Do not use titles such as Dr., Professor, etc.

Abstract. Begin the paper with an abstract of approximately 100 words. Type the word **ABSTRACT** in all capital letters, bold-faced and centered three lines below the author(s) and affiliation(s). The text of the abstract should be in *italics*.

Headings. Show first-level headings centered, bold-faced and in capital letters. Show second-level headings flush with the left margin, bold faced, in upper and lower case letters.

Body. Single space throughout, leaving one space between paragraphs. Text should be full-justified.

Tables and Figures. Include all tables and figures in the body of the text as close as possible to their reference.

Footnotes. Do NOT use footnotes. Give references within the text showing the last name and year of publication.

References. List references at the end of the paper in alphabetical order. Center the word **References** at the beginning of the list in bold-faced, capital letters.

About the Author(s). Immediately following the list of references, include a short paragraph about the author(s), including such information as education, titles, recognitions, other publications, etc.

Please submit your paper to:
Dr. David A. DeCenzo, Editor
The Coastal Business Journal
Coastal Carolina University, Wall College of Business
P.O. Box 261954, Conway, SC 29528
Phone: (843) 349-2640,   Fax: (843) 349-2455
Email: **ddecenzo@coastal.edu**

Commentaries on the Law of Accounting & Finance

ADDRESS FOR SUBMISSION:

Robert W. McGee, Editor
Commentaries on the Law of Accounting &
   Finance
Dumont Inst. for Public Policy Research
Andreas School of Business
Barry University
11300 Northeast Second Avenue
Miami Shores, FL 33161
USA
Phone: 305-899-3525
E-Mail: bob414@hotmail.com
Web:

PUBLICATION GUIDELINES:

Manuscript Length: 16-30+
Copies Required: Three
Computer Submission: Yes
Format: Law Review
Fees to Review: 0.00 US$

Manuscript Style:
   Uniform System of Citation (Harvard
   Blue Book)

CIRCULATION DATA:

Reader: Academics
Frequency of Issue: Yearly
Sponsor/Publisher: Dumont Institute for
   Public Policy Research

REVIEW INFORMATION:

Type of Review: Blind Review
No. of External Reviewers: 2
No. of In House Reviewers: 1
Acceptance Rate: 50%
Time to Review: 1 Month or Less
Reviewers Comments: Yes
Invited Articles: 11-20%
Fees to Publish: 0.00 US$

MANUSCRIPT TOPICS:

Accounting Law, Finance Law; Accounting Theory & Practice; Corporate Governance; Fiscal Policy; International Finance; Public Finance; Public Policy Economics; Tax Accounting

MANUSCRIPT GUIDELINES/COMMENTS:

Law review format--any length will be considered. Most manuscripts accepted are between 15-40 pages.

Copyright. *Commentaries on the Law of Accounting & Finance* retains the right to publish articles in any format without compensation to the authors. Authors retain the right to reprint without permission of this journal. Anyone may distribute copies of any article for classroom use without permission, provided the source is clearly indicated, unless the article indicates that the author retains the copyright, in which case the author's permission must first be obtained. Reprints for inclusion in a book or other publication require permission of the Journal.

Construction Management and Economics

ADDRESS FOR SUBMISSION:

Will P. Hughes, Editor
Construction Management and Economics
University of Reading
School of Construction Management
and Engineering
PO Box 219
Reading, RG6 6AW
UK
Phone: 44 118 378 8982
E-Mail: w.p.hughes@reading.ac.uk
Web: www.tandf.co.uk

PUBLICATION GUIDELINES:

Manuscript Length: 11-15
Copies Required: Four
Computer Submission: Yes Disk or Email
Format: MS Word, WordPerfect, Rich Text
Fees to Review: 0.00 US$

Manuscript Style:
    Uniform System of Citation (Harvard
    Blue Book)

CIRCULATION DATA:

Reader: Academics
Frequency of Issue: 10 Times/Year
Sponsor/Publisher: Taylor & Francis, Ltd /
    Spon Press

REVIEW INFORMATION:

Type of Review: Blind Review
No. of External Reviewers: 3+
No. of In House Reviewers: 0
Acceptance Rate: 50%
Time to Review: 2 - 3 Months
Reviewers Comments: Yes
Invited Articles: 0-5%
Fees to Publish: 0.00 US$

MANUSCRIPT TOPICS:
Construction Management; Econometrics; Economic History; Industrial Organization; International Economics & Trade; Macro Economics; Real Estate

MANUSCRIPT GUIDELINES/COMMENTS:

1. Submission
Authors should submit their paper as an e-mail attachment (in Microsoft Word or Rich Text Format) to: **W.P.Hughes@reading.ac.uk**. Alternatively, authors should send four copies of their papers (with floppy disk) to facilitate refereeing with original artwork to: Dr Will Hughes, School of Construction Management and Engineering, University of Reading, PO Box 219, Whiteknights, Reading RG6 6AW, UK. It will be assumed that the authors will keep a copy. Papers will be anonymously refereed by acknowledged experts in the subject. Only those receiving favourable recommendations from the referees will be accepted for publication. If an author is uncertain about whether a paper is suitable for publication in the Journal, it is acceptable to submit a synopsis first.

2. Effective communication

The paper should be written and arranged in a style that is succinct and easily followed. An informative but short title, a concise abstract with keywords, and a well-written introduction will help to achieve this. Simple language, short sentences and a good use of headings all help to communicate information more effectively. Discursive treatment of the subject matter is discouraged. Figures should be used to aid the clarity of the paper. The reader should be carefully guided through the paper. Always think about your reader.

3. Manuscript - papers

a. **Length**. although there is no length limitation, papers should fall within the range of 2000-5000 words. Authors are requested to state how many words their paper contains. The manuscript must be in English, typed in double spacing on one side of A4 paper only, with a 4 cm margin on the left-hand side. The pages should be numbered consecutively. There should be no loose addenda or notes or other explanatory material. The manuscript should be arranged under headings and subheadings.

b. **Title page**. the first page of the manuscript must contain the full title, the affiliation(s) and address(es) of the author(s), a running title of not more than 75 characters and spaces, and the name and address of the author who will be responsible for correspondence and correcting proofs.

c. **Abstract and keywords**. an abstract and up to five keywords for the purposes of indexing should be included, preferably on the title page. The abstract must not exceed 200 words and must precis the paper giving a clear indication of the conclusions it contains. Keywords must be carefully selected to facilitate readers' search.

d. **Illustrations**. illustrations must accompany the manuscript but should not be included in the text. Photographs, standard forms, and charts should be referred to as 'Figure 1', 'Figure 2' etc. They should be numbered in the order in which they are referred to in the text.

Illustrations should be submitted in a form ready for reproduction. Figures will normally be reduced in size on reproduction and authors should draw with this in mind. With a reduction scale of 2:1 in mind the authors should use lines not less than 0.25 mm thick, and upper and lower case lettering, the capital of which should be 4 mm high. To keep within the type area of the Journal, drawings for a 2:1 reduction should not exceed 280 mm in width. If you draw for any reduction other than 2:1 please indicate your intentions.

Photographs should be black and white glossy prints. Each should have written lightly on the back the author's name, the figure number and an indication of which is top. Where lettering is to appear on the photograph, two prints should be supplied, one of which should be left unlettered.

e. **Measurements**. metric units should be used; if other units are used then metric equivalents should be given in parentheses.

154

f. **References**. the Harvard system is used. References in the text should be quoted in the following manner: Smith (1975) or (Brown and Green, 1976) or if there are more than two authors, Jones et al. (1980). References should be collected at the end of the paper in alphabetical order by the first author's surname. If references to the same author have the same year, they should be differentiated by using 1980a and 1980b etc. The style should follow the examples below:

Ranasinghe, M. and Russell, A.D. (1993) Elicitation of subjective probabilities for economic risk analysis. Construction Management and Economics, 11(5), 326-40.

Reynolds, C.E. and Steedman, J.C. (1988) Reinforced Concrete Designer's Handbook, 10th Edn. E & FN Spon, London.

Barrett, S. (1981) Implementation of public policy, in Policy and Action, Barrett, S. and Fudge, C. (eds), Chapman & Hall, London, pp. 1-33.

If no person is named as the author the body should be used - for example: Royal Institution of Chartered Surveyors (1980) Report on Urban Planning Methods, London.

g. **Endnotes**. a limited number of explanatory endnotes is permissible. These should be numbered 1, 2, 3, consecutively in the text and denoted by superscripts. They should be typed on a separate sheet of paper at the end of the text. Endnotes should not be used for academic or project citations.

4. Manuscripts - short papers or notes
Short papers or notes should be as short as possible, and should not be longer than 2000 words. The specifications from the previous section apply in all respects. Short papers or notes may offer comments on other papers published by this Journal, as well as offer original contributions.

5. Proofs
Proofs will be sent to the corresponding author for correction. The difficulty and expense involved in making amendments at proof stage makes it essential for authors to prepare their manuscript carefully: any alterations to the original text are strongly discouraged. Our aim is rapid publication: this will be helped if authors provide good copy following the above instructions, and return their proofs as quickly as possible.

6. **Early Electronic Offprints**. Corresponding authors can now receive their article by e-mail as a complete PDF. This allows the author to print up to 50 copies, free of charge, and disseminate them to colleagues. In many cases this facility will be available up to two weeks prior to publication. Or, alternatively, corresponding authors will receive the traditional 50 offprints. A copy of the journal will be sent by post to all corresponding authors after publication. Additional copies of the journal can be purchased at the author's preferential rate of £15.00/$25.00 per copy.

7. Copyright

Submission of an article to this Journal is taken to imply that it represents original, unpublished work, not under consideration for publication elsewhere. Authors will be asked to transfer the copyright for their papers to the publisher if and when the article is accepted for publication, using the form provided. The copyright covers the exclusive rights to reproduce and distribute the article, including reprints, photographic reproductions, microfilm or any reproduction of a similar nature, and translations. Permission to publish illustrations must be obtained by the author before submission and any acknowledgements should be included in the figure captions.

Authors' Charter

To help authors to understand the editorial process, which has developed over the years, and which we intend to continue improving, this document makes explicit our policies and procedures.

As soon as we receive your paper, we will enter the details on our database and allocate a unique reference number. Within seven days, we will write to you advising you of the manuscript ID. The editor will check that the paper is appropriate for this journal in terms of word count, scope and research focus. Some papers will be returned to authors without being refereed if they do not pass these initial tests.

We will remove your name and address from the paper and send it to a minimum of four referees who will be familiar with your topic. If this is done by electronic mail, we will remove all means of identification that your computer has inserted. Any referee who has not responded within two weeks of our request will be sent a reminder. Second and final reminders are sent at weekly intervals, followed by a cancellation of our request if the review has not arrived after seven weeks. If necessary, we will find more referees, but in this case we will write to you informing you of the delay.

The editor will decide whether to accept or reject your paper, based on the advice from the referees. Referees do not decide the fate of papers; rather, they provide advice and suggestions. Since individual referees are being asked to volunteer personal impressions, it is unlikely that their views will all match. The most compelling view is not necessarily the majority view, but the strength of the argument advanced by the referee, or by the author in his or her response. If your paper requires revision, the editor will tell you whether the changes needed are minor or major. Minor changes will be checked by the editor, major by the referees. In cases of major revision, the paper may require further changes after the referees have seen it and may still be rejected at this point.

The decision on your paper will be taken within one week of the receipt of sufficient reviews. This decision will be sent to you within three days. If your paper is rejected, you will be told why. About half of all papers submitted are ultimately rejected.

When you are invited to respond to the referees by revising your paper, we ask you to let us know the date by which we can expect your response. Thus, you decide how long you need, and no reminders will be sent to you until the date you have chosen has passed. If we do not hear from you, and in the case of minor changes, we will assume that one month is enough.

156

Then reminders will be sent to you, followed by a cancellation if we have heard nothing after seven weeks. If you receive a letter cancelling our request to revise, it means that the status of your paper has been changed from 'under revision' to 'withdrawn' and the file is closed. In this case we will not initiate any further communication with you, but we will hold on to the file for twelve months before disposing of it.

After acceptance, the paper is forwarded to the publishers and it enters the production process, which is managed from the publisher's office. The amount of time it takes between acceptance and publication depends on the queue of papers awaiting publication, but is a minimum of four months. During this time, papers are copy-edited, checked with authors and editors, typeset, printed, bound and distributed. After copy-editing, the publishers will send a galley proof (usually by e-mail) to the authors to check that the text and figures have been prepared for publication properly. The position in the queue is determined by the date the manuscript was first submitted, not the date of acceptance. Each issue of the journal is made up two months before it appears in print, and papers are chosen primarily by their position in the queue, but with a view to achieving some kind of spread between topics, regions and institutions.

We will continue striving to maintain the highest editorial standards and seek to publish the best research in our field.

Contemporary Accounting Research

ADDRESS FOR SUBMISSION:

Gordon D. Richardson, Editor
Contemporary Accounting Research
University of Toronto
Joseph L. Rotman School of Management
105 St. George Street
Toronto
Ontario, M5S 3E6
Canada
Phone: 416-946-8601
E-Mail: car@caaa.ca
Web: www.caaa.ca

CIRCULATION DATA:

Reader: Academics
Frequency of Issue: Quarterly
Sponsor/Publisher: Canadian Academic
   Accounting Association

PUBLICATION GUIDELINES:

Manuscript Length: 16-30+
Copies Required: One
Computer Submission: Yes Online
Format:
Fees to Review: 165.00 US$ Non-Mbr/Sub
   100.00 US$ CAAA Mbr/CAR Subscr.

Manuscript Style:
   Chicago Manual of Style

REVIEW INFORMATION:

Type of Review: Blind Review
No. of External Reviewers: 2
No. of In House Reviewers: 0
Acceptance Rate: 11-20%
Time to Review: 2 - 3 Months
Reviewers Comments: Yes
Invited Articles: 0-5%
Fees to Publish: 0.00 US$

MANUSCRIPT TOPICS:

Accounting Education; Accounting Information Systems; Accounting Theory & Practice; Auditing; Behavioral Accounting; Cost Accounting; Econometrics; Government & Non Profit Accounting; Tax Accounting

MANUSCRIPT GUIDELINES/COMMENTS:

CAR accepts articles written either in English or in French.

Only papers containing original, unpublished work, which is not being considered for publication elsewhere, will be received.

Manuscripts should be submitted electronically using *CAR's* online submission and peer review system at: **https://www.editorialmanager.com/car/** .

In addition to submitting online, authors are required to mail one hard copy of the manuscript to the editorial office (address below) with the appropriate submission fee. Manuscripts reporting on field surveys or experiments should be accompanied by copies of the research instrument.

158

The submission fees are as follows: $100 for CAAA members and CAR subscribers, and $165 for nonmembers/nonsubscribers (dollar amounts are in Canadian funds in Canada and in US funds elsewhere). Cheques should be made payable to: The Canadian Academic Accounting Association (CAAA) and mailed to the address below.

Submission fee payments are accepted also by VISA or MasterCard. To authorize a credit card payment, provide the credit card information (cardholder name, number, and expiry date) in a letter and mail it to the address below, or email to: **submissionfees@caaa.ca**.

Manuscripts should be directed to:
Professor Gordon Richardson
Editor, Contemporary Accounting Research University of Toronto
Joseph Rotman School of Management 105 St. George Street
Toronto, Ontario M5S 3E6 Canada
Phone: 416-946-8601 Fax: 416-971-3048
https://www.editorialmanager. com/car/
For assistance, contact: **editorialassistant@caaa.ca**

Format
Manuscripts must be typed, double-spaced on one side of standard 8 ½" x 11" paper. Margins should be 1 ½" on all sides.

All pages, including endnotes, tables, figures, illustrations, appendices, and references, should be numbered sequentially.

A cover page for hard copy (only) submissions must contain the following information:
• title;
• author's name and affiliation;
• address, phone, fax, and email numbers of the person to whom correspondence should be addressed; and acknowledgements and information on grants received.
• Note: For online submissions, the cover page will not be necessary because you will submit this information as a step in the online process. Your cover page should be saved as a separate file so that it is not included when you upload the manuscript online (the manuscript must be a "blind" copy for review purposes).

An abstract of not more than 250 words must be presented on the second page immediately following the cover page. The abstract should include the research question, method of examination, and principal findings, and should be followed by four keywords and up to five JEL descriptors (to aid in indexing).

Endnotes should be used for extensions where inclusion in the body of the text might disrupt continuity. All endnotes should be numbered consecutively, presented together separately on pages immediately following the text. The endnotes should be referred to throughout the text with superscript Arabic numerals; not by using the automated endnote/footnote command.

Each table, figure, or illustration must be presented on a separate (numbered) page, following the text, each bearing both an Arabic numeral and a title.

Accepted papers are to be prepared on disk using software acceptable to the managing editor, but initial submissions should be in either Word or PDF format and a disk should accompany the hard copy. The data underlying all graphs should be supplied in separate files in ASCII or Excel format.

Disclosure
Together with the paper being submitted, authors are asked to include a copy of any other paper, whether or not published elsewhere, that shares data or modeling analysis with the submitted paper. The contribution of the submitted manuscript must be clearly distinguishable from other such papers. If the submitted paper is based on an experiment, survey, or other data manipulations, participants, or variables involved in that collection are reflected in the paper, authors are asked to include a memo describing and explaining the circumstances and estimating any effects on the results. The memo may be sent to reviewers. All reviews are blind reviews.

Papers Accepted for Publication
The detailed *CAR* author guidelines are available now online at the CAAA website. Their usage is required for papers that have been accepted for publication in the journal.

160

Cooperative Accountant (The)

ADDRESS FOR SUBMISSION:

Frank M. Messina, Editor
Cooperative Accountant (The)
University of Alabama at Birmingham
Dept of Accounting & Information Systems
BEC 305C
1530 3rd Avenue South - UAB Station
Birmingham, AL 35294-4460
USA
Phone: 205-934-8827
E-Mail: fmessina@uab.edu
Web: www.business.uab.edu/faculty

CIRCULATION DATA:

Reader: Academics, Business Persons
Frequency of Issue: Quarterly
Sponsor/Publisher: National Society of
  Accountants for Cooperatives

PUBLICATION GUIDELINES:

Manuscript Length: 6-15
Copies Required: Three
Computer Submission: Yes Email Preferred
Format: MS Word
Fees to Review: 0.00 US$

Manuscript Style:

REVIEW INFORMATION:

Type of Review: Blind Review
No. of External Reviewers: 2
No. of In House Reviewers: 1
Acceptance Rate: 21-30%
Time to Review: 4 - 6 Months
Reviewers Comments: Yes
Invited Articles: 11-20%
Fees to Publish: 0.00 US$

MANUSCRIPT TOPICS:
Accounting Information Systems; Accounting Theory & Practice; Auditing; Cooperative-Based Issues; International Economics & Trade; Monetary Policy; Tax Accounting

MANUSCRIPT GUIDELINES/COMMENTS:

Submissions and inquires should be directed to Editor Frank M. Messina at:
fmessina@uab.edu or by phone at 205-934-8827.

Corporate Taxation

ADDRESS FOR SUBMISSION:

Eugene M. Krader, Managing Editor
Corporate Taxation
RIA Group
395 Hudson Street
New York, NY 10014
USA
Phone: 212-807-2295
E-Mail: eugene.krader@riag.com
Web: www.riahome.com/journals

CIRCULATION DATA:

Reader: , Lawyers & Accountants
Frequency of Issue: Bi-Monthly
Sponsor/Publisher: RIA Group

PUBLICATION GUIDELINES:

Manuscript Length: 20+
Copies Required: Two
Computer Submission: Yes
Format:
Fees to Review: 0.00 US$

Manuscript Style:
    Chicago Manual of Style

REVIEW INFORMATION:

Type of Review: Editorial Review
No. of External Reviewers: 1
No. of In House Reviewers: 1
Acceptance Rate: 21-30%
Time to Review: 2 - 3 Months
Reviewers Comments: Yes
Invited Articles: 21-30%
Fees to Publish: 0.00 US$

MANUSCRIPT TOPICS:
Accounting Information Systems; Accounting Theory & Practice; Auditing; Corporate Taxation; Cost Accounting; Tax Accounting

MANUSCRIPT GUIDELINES/COMMENTS:

The journal used by top practitioners, *Corporate Taxation* identifies and implements optimal tax strategies. Written by professionals for professionals, this journal provides authoritative analysis and guidance from leading experts in corporate taxation.

Published six times per year, each issue delivers timely, in-depth coverage of such topics as:
• Corporate organizations and reorganizations
• Compensation and fringe benefits
• International developments
• Consolidated returns
• and more

Corporate Taxation keeps you informed of the latest legislation, rulings, regulations and cases that affect the taxation of corporations. It discusses new opportunities and warns against pitfalls that impact day-to-day and long-range planning. Every issue brings you in-depth analysis of the latest tax problems and concerns of corporate tax practitioners, together with the solutions and approaches used by the country's foremost experts.

CPA Journal

ADDRESS FOR SUBMISSION:

Thomas W. Morris, Managing Editor
CPA Journal
3 Park Avenue, 18th Floor
New York, NY 10016
USA
Phone: 212-719-8300
E-Mail: twmorris@nysscpa.org
Web: www.cpajournal.com

CIRCULATION DATA:

Reader: Business Persons, CPAs
Frequency of Issue: Monthly
Sponsor/Publisher: New York State Society
of CPAs

PUBLICATION GUIDELINES:

Manuscript Length: 2,500-4,000 Words
Copies Required: Electronic
Computer Submission: Yes Preferred
Format: MS Word or RTF
Fees to Review: 0.00 US$

Manuscript Style:
, NY Public Library

REVIEW INFORMATION:

Type of Review: Blind Review
No. of External Reviewers: 2
No. of In House Reviewers: 2
Acceptance Rate: 65%
Time to Review: 2 Months
Reviewers Comments: Yes
Invited Articles: 6-10%
Fees to Publish: 0.00 US$

MANUSCRIPT TOPICS:

Accounting Information Systems; Accounting Theory & Practice; Auditing; Cost Accounting; Government & Non Profit Accounting; International Economics & Trade; Portfolio & Security Analysis; Regional Economics; Tax Accounting

MANUSCRIPT GUIDELINES/COMMENTS:

The CPA Journal accepts manuscripts for review in the following areas:
Accounting & Auditing
- Financial Reporting
- SEC Reporting
- Government Accounting

Taxation
- Federal
- State & Local (New York, Connecticut, New Jersey)
- Estates & Trusts
- Flow-through Entities

Technology
- E-filing Taxes
- Computerized CPA Exam
- Accounting Software
- Internet
- E-Commerce

Management
- Human Resources
- Controllership
- Budgeting
- Practice Development

Finance
- Personal Financial Planning
- Corporate Finance
- Employee Benefit Plans

Responsibilities & Leadership
- Ethics
- Education
- Professional Development

The format of *The CPA Journal* encompasses three types of submission:
- Manuscripts of general interest to most reader -generally between 3,000 and 4,500 words.
- Manuscripts of specific, technical interest-generally between 500 and 3,000 words.
- Manuscripts that express an opinion, perspective, or viewpoint about a matter of importance to CPAs--between 250 and 2,500 words.

Authors should submit manuscripts electronically in Microsoft Word, WordPerfect, or simple text format to **CPAJ-Editors@nysscpa.org**. Alternatively, authors can send a diskette with their manuscript and a print out to Submissions, The CPA Journal, 3 Park Ave., 18th Floor, New York, N.Y. 10016-5991. Receipt of a manuscript will be acknowledged via e-mail within one week. It is important for authors to include complete contact information (name, affiliation, street address, telephone and fax numbers, and e-mail address) and brief biographical information (including relevant professional certifications and academic degrees) within a cover sheet. To facilitate the impartial review of the manuscript, there should be no personal or identifying information within the body of the manuscript.

Manuscripts reporting research should focus on the results rather than the methodology. *The Journal* does not publish articles whose major contribution consists of pure research or of research methodology applications. Authors whose manuscripts rely on a research study should address a readership of interested, first-year graduate students with a professional understanding of the topic. Because *The Journal's* readership consists of members in both public and private practice, with diverse backgrounds and specialties, manuscripts should not presume a certain background or mindset. For technical articles of 2,000 words or longer, a brief summary of 100-125 words is helpful.

Authors writing at the request of NYSSCPA technical committees should submit the manuscript to the designated committee representatives for technical review rather than directly to the editors. Such authors should review and follow these writers guidelines. Members of NYSSCPA technical committees developing manuscripts for *The CPA Journal* are requested to specify their committee affiliation when submitting manuscripts and confirm the committee's approval of the submission.

The Journal editors manage the review process and make the final decision regarding acceptance, rejection, or revision based on independent, blind reviews by two members of *The CPA Journal's* editorial board, editorial review board, or ad hoc reviewers. The manuscript is evaluated on the basis of its relevance, timeliness, interest level to The Journal readers, readability, practicality, and comprehensiveness. The typical review, from receipt of the manuscript to final decision typically takes six to eight weeks, although this timeframe varies considerably.

The Journal follows *The New York Public Library Writer's Guide to Style and Usage*. Please refer to this style manual (which is broadly similar to the *Chicago Manual of Style*) before submitting a manuscript. *The Journal's* preferred writing style has the following characteristics:

- Direct, declarative statements
- Active voice
- Tight reasoning
- Third-person narrative perspective, except in the case of opinion, commentary, or perspective submissions.

Please visit the archives at the website, and read published articles for examples of articles that reflect *The Journal's* style.

The editors of *The Journal* schedule articles for publication approximately three months before the issue appears. For example, the editors determine the contents for the January issue of *The Journal* in the first week of October. The production process for *The Journal* takes about 45 days after the editors have completed editing for length, style, and clarity of expression, which takes approximately 30 days. The editors fax preliminary page proofs to authors for their review of the final edited text approximately one month before publication.

At the time a manuscript is accepted, the editors will send an author agreement that specifies the terms of publication, including a grant of copyright to *The CPA Journal* for both print and Internet publication, and for possible awarding of CPE credit to readers of the article upon completion of an examination administered by the publishers.

Critical Issues in Environmental Taxation

ADDRESS FOR SUBMISSION:

Lawrence Kreiser, Co-Editor
Critical Issues in Environmental Taxation
Cleveland State University
Department of Accounting
2121 Euclid Avenue
Cleveland, OH 44115-2214
USA
Phone: 216-687-3670
E-Mail: l.kreiser@csuohio.edu
Web: www.richmondlawtax.com

PUBLICATION GUIDELINES:

Manuscript Length: 15-25
Copies Required: One
Computer Submission: Yes Disk or Email
Format: MS Word
Fees to Review: 0.00 US$

Manuscript Style:
, Any acceptable manuscript style

CIRCULATION DATA:

Reader: Academics, Government Officials,
 Accountants, Lawyers
Frequency of Issue: Yearly
Sponsor/Publisher: Richmond Law & Tax
 Ltd., UK

REVIEW INFORMATION:

Type of Review: Blind Review
No. of External Reviewers: 4
No. of In House Reviewers: 1
Acceptance Rate: 25%
Time to Review: 1 - 2 Months
Reviewers Comments: No
Invited Articles: Less than 10%
Fees to Publish: 0.00 US$

MANUSCRIPT TOPICS:
Environmental Taxation Issues; Fiscal Policy; Public Policy Economics

MANUSCRIPT GUIDELINES/COMMENTS:

Manuscripts accepted for publication in *Critical Issues in Environmental Taxation* deal with insights and analysis for achieving environmental goals through tax policy. We prefer computer submission of manuscripts that are double-spaced and written in any acceptable manuscript style. Manuscripts should deal with topics that are timely and of regional, national, or international interest. Authors will receive one copy of the publication.

Final versions of papers submitted for publication must meet the following requirements in addition to any requirements described in a letter of acceptance.

1. **Format.** Documents must be submitted in Microsoft Word with a minimum of formatting other than embedded footnotes. Any graphs or charts must be submitted as separate files with clear indications where they should be placed in the text.

2. **English.** The text must be written in clear, fluent English so that readers will not be able to distinguish authors who use English as a first language from those who use English as a

second language. The editors encourage any authors who are not fluent in English to engage their own editors who can help them to meet this standard for the final paper.

3. **Abstracts**. If the paper starts with an abstract, the abstract must be eliminated from the paper by the author prior to final submission.

4. **Author's Credentials**. A footnote following the author's name should indicate the author's professional title, affiliation (without abbreviations) and email address.

5. **Copyright**. The author(s) must be the sole owner(s) of the complete copyright and all other rights in the paper (apart from copyright material not owned by the author but included in the paper with the permission of the copyright holders). The author(s) have the responsibility for obtaining any necessary copyright permissions.

6. **Exclusive Publication**. The author has not previously published the manuscript in another publication and will not publish the manuscript in any other publication without the express permission of the editors.

7. **Publisher's Requirements**. The author must respond to the Publisher (Richmond Law & Tax Ltd.) promptly when receiving requests to review proofs and sign publication agreements.

Critical Perspectives on Accounting

ADDRESS FOR SUBMISSION:

Tony Tinker, Co-Editor
Critical Perspectives on Accounting
City Univesity of New York
Baruch College
Box B:12:236
One Baruch Way
New York, NY 10010-5585
USA
Phone: 646-312-3175
E-Mail: tony_tinker@baruch.cuny.edu
Web: www.sciencedirect.com/science/
journal/10452354

PUBLICATION GUIDELINES:

Manuscript Length: 20+
Copies Required: Four
Computer Submission: Yes Required
Format:
Fees to Review: 0.00 US$

Manuscript Style:
Chicago Manual of Style

CIRCULATION DATA:

Reader: Academics
Frequency of Issue: 8 Times/Year
Sponsor/Publisher: Elsevier Inc.

REVIEW INFORMATION:

Type of Review: Blind Review
No. of External Reviewers: 3
No. of In House Reviewers: 3
Acceptance Rate: 6-10%
Time to Review: 2 - 3 Months
Reviewers Comments: Yes
Invited Articles: 0-5%
Fees to Publish: 0.00 US$

MANUSCRIPT TOPICS:

Accounting Education; Accounting Information Systems; Accounting Theory & Practice; Auditing; Behavioral Accounting; Cost Accounting; Financial Services; Government & Non Profit Accounting; Industrial Organization; International Economics & Trade

MANUSCRIPT GUIDELINES/COMMENTS:

Critical Perspectives on Accounting aims to provide a forum for the growing number of accounting researchers and practitioners who realize that conventional theory and practice is ill-suited to the challenges of the modern environment, and that accounting practices and corporate behavior are inextricably connected with many allocative, distributive, social and ecological problems of our era. From such concerns, a new literature is emerging that seeks to reformulate corporate, social and political activity, and the theoretical practical means by which we apprehend and affect that activity.

Specific issues that the journal will address include, but are not limited to, the following:
• Studies involving the political economy of accounting, critical accounting, radical accounting, and accounting's implication in the exercise of power

- Financial accounting's role in the processes of international capital formation, including its impact on stock market stability and international banking activities
- Management accounting's role in organizing the labor process
- The relationship between accounting and the state in various social formation
- Studies of accounting's historical role, as a means of "remembering" the subject's social and conflictual character
- The role of accounting in establishing "real" democracy at work and other domains of life
- Accounting's adjudicative function in international exchanges, such as that of the third world debt
- Antagonisms between the social and private character of accounting, such as conflicts of interest in the audit process
- The identification of new constituencies for radical and critical accounting information
- Accounting's involvement in gender and class conflicts in the workplace
- The interplay between accounting, social conflict, industrialization, bureaucracy and technocracy
- Reappraisals of the role of accounting as a science and technology
- Accounting's implication in the management conflict around state enterprises
- Critical reviews of "useful" scientific knowledge about organizations

INSTRUCTIONS TO AUTHORS
Notes of Guidance to Contributors
Authors submitting papers for publication warrant that the work does not infringe any existing copyright and does not contain material of a libelous or scandalous nature. Further, the author indemnifies the publisher and editors against any branch of such warranty.

Format and Style
Chicago Manual of Style
Manuscripts are to be typewritten double spaced on one side (preferably international-size A4). Authors should include four copies of:
- an abstract not exceeding 150 words - it should summarize the purpose, methodology, and major conclusions of the article;
- 10 key words or phrases that can be used for indexing purposes;
- a short biographical sketch for each of the authors, together with their addresses and phone numbers.

The cover page of the manuscript should include the title, the author's name(s), position and institutional affiliation, and any acknowledgements. Only the title should appear on the next page of the manuscript and on the abstract. Footnotes, identified in the text by a numeral that is superscripted, should not include literature citations, and should be listed at the end of the paper, before the bibliography.

Literature citations in the text should include the author's name, the year of publication, and the specific page numbers if required (e.g., Mickey and Donald, 1968; p. 24). For more than two authors, the citation should be abbreviated as follows: (Kramdon et al., 1988, p. 1). Multiple citations of the same author(s) in the same year should be distinguished in the text

170

(and in the bibliography) by a, b, c, etc. and followed by the year of publication. The bibliography should only include references cited in the text and should be arranged in the alphabetical order according to the surname of the first author. Full bibliographical details are required. The following style is required for:
1. articles;
2. books;
3. citations from edited books;
4. translated books;
5. reference to a report.

1. DuBoff, R.B., and Herman, E.S., "Alfred Chandler's New Business History: A Review", Politics & Society, Vol. 10, No. 1, 1980, pp. 87-110.

2. Anderson, P., *Considerations On Western Marxism* (London: New Left Review Books,1976).

3. Hall, S., "The Little Caesars of Social Democracy", in Hall, S. and Jacques, M., (eds) The Politics of Thatcherism, pp. 309-322, (London: Lawrence & Wishart, 1983).

4. Adorno, T.W., Negative Dialektik (Frankfurt: Suhrkamp, 1968). Negative Dialectics, E.B. Ashton (trans) (New York: Seabury Press,1973).

5. Joint WHO Committee on Multinational Expansion. *The Role Of The Multinational In Health And Safety Developments* (Geneva: World Health Organisation, 1982, Technical Report Series 503).

Charts, Diagrams And Figures
These should all be called figures, numbered consecutively in Arabic numerals, with a brief title in capitals and labeled axes. The text should clearly indicate where the figure is to appear. Each figure should be submitted on a separate sheet of paper and be suitable for direct reproduction.

Tables
Tables should be numbered consecutively and independently of figures. Tables should be labeled with Roman numerals, a brief descriptive title, and headings down and across. The text should indicate clearly where each table is to appear. Each table should be submitted on a separate sheet of paper and be suitable for direct reproduction.

Proofs and Copies
Page proofs should be checked by the author and returned to the publisher within 48 hours. Only printer's typographical errors should be corrected at this stage; any substantive changes other than these will be charged to the author. The Editors reserve the right to publish a paper without the author's own corrections in cases of undue delay in returning the proofs.

Notes for Reviewers and Authors
The journal aims to provide a prompt and informative response to authors. Manuscripts that pass an initial preliminary screening will be sent to two blind reviews. It is policy to offer

authors constructive and supportive reviews and thus, as far as possible, reviewers will be encouraged to stress in their review what additional work would be necessary to bring a submission to publication standard.

Reprints
50 reprints of each paper are supplied free of charge. In the case of multiple authored papers, they will be sent to the first named author. Additional quantities may be ordered at the time the proofs are checked, on the form provided. There are no page charges.

Submission Requirements
Only manuscripts not under consideration elsewhere should be submitted. Copies of questionnaires and other research instruments should be included with the submission. However, space limitations may preclude the publication of this material. When they are not reproduced a note should be included indicating an address where readers may obtain a complete copy of the instruments.

Four copies of each manuscript should be submitted to the Editor.

Decision Sciences

ADDRESS FOR SUBMISSION:

Vicki Smith-Daniels, Editor
Decision Sciences
Arizona State University
W. P. Carey School of Business
Department of Supply Chain Management
PO Box 874706
Tempe, AZ 85287-4706
USA
Phone: 480-965-1152
E-Mail: decisionsciences@asu.edu
Web: www.blackwellpublishing.com; and
https://wpcarey.asu.edu/DSJOnline

PUBLICATION GUIDELINES:

Manuscript Length: 40 Pages Maximum
Copies Required: Electronic
Computer Submission: Yes Required
Format: Adobe PDF
Fees to Review: 0.00 US$

Manuscript Style:
See Manuscript Guidelines

CIRCULATION DATA:

Reader: Academics
Frequency of Issue: Quarterly
Sponsor/Publisher: Decision Sciences
Institute / Blackwell Publishing, Inc.

REVIEW INFORMATION:

Type of Review: Blind Review
No. of External Reviewers: 3
No. of In House Reviewers: 2
Acceptance Rate: 11-20%
Time to Review: 2 - 3 Months
Reviewers Comments: Yes
Invited Articles: 0-5%
Fees to Publish: 0.00 US$

MANUSCRIPT TOPICS:
Accounting Information Systems; Behavioral Accounting; Cost Accounting; Industrial Organization

MANUSCRIPT GUIDELINES/COMMENTS:

Editorial Statement of Purpose
Decision Sciences, a premier journal of the Decision Sciences Institute, publishes scholarly research about decision making within the boundaries of an organization, as well as decisions involving inter-firm coordination. The journal promotes research advancing decision making at the interfaces of business functions and organizational boundaries. The journal also seeks articles extending established lines of work assuming the results of the research have the potential to substantially impact either decision making theory or industry practice. Ground-breaking research articles that enhance managerial understanding of decision making processes and stimulate further research in multi-disciplinary domains are particularly encouraged. *Decision Sciences* recognizes that a delicate balance must be maintained between publishing traditional scholarly research and promoting novel, seminal research in new frontiers.

Through its focus on contemporary decision problems, the journal welcomes articles utilizing diverse research approaches that address the many complex phenomena of the decision making process. By publishing articles with theoretical, empirical, and analytical research methods, *Decision Sciences* recognizes that business scholars often share a common interest in gaining greater insights into complex decision problems, independent of research methods. The journal encourages research examining different types of decision problems ranging from strategic to operational that occur in various forms including inter-organizational, group-based, and technology-enabled. Since approaches to decision making may differ in different economies and cultures, *Decision Sciences* encourages articles advancing decision making theory and practices around the globe.

Articles published in *Decision Sciences* must meet high standards of research rigor and originality, while embracing managerial relevance, not only in the research problem studied, but also in their impact on enhanced decision making. The journal also publishes notes dealing with technical and methodological issues as well as theoretically-driven review and integration articles, particularly those focusing on an emerging topic or redirection of a line of research.

Further information about *Decision Sciences'* Mission, Editorial Statement of Purpose and Editorial Policies is available at *DSJ Online*, the journal's submission, review, and evaluation website at **https://wpcarey.asu.edu/DSJOnline/index.cfm**.

Submission
All manuscript submissions for consideration for publication in *Decision Sciences Journal* must be made electronically to *DSJ Online* at https://wpcarey.asu.edu/DSJOnline/index.cfm. The editorial team, including Editor Vicki Smith-Daniels and Managing Editor Jeanne Elliott, can be reached most expeditiously by email at **decisionsciences@asu.edu**, or can be reached by mail or telephone at (480) 965-1152.

Submission of a manuscript certifies that none of the contents are copyrighted, published or accepted for publication in another journal, under review by another journal, or submitted to another journal while under review by *Decision Sciences*.

Editorial Policies
Decision Sciences distinguishes itself as a business journal with an explicit focus on decision making. While this purpose may appear to encompass a broad-based spectrum of articles, the implementation of the journal's aims will be directed towards the needs of its research community. In the past, *Decision Sciences* scholars have come from the operations management, information systems, technology management, and quantitative methods disciplines. In the future, articles published in the journal will continue to address the needs of these disciplines, but will devote greater attention to decision making that spans the boundaries of business disciplines and integrates theoretical perspectives across the research domains. Expanding these targeted disciplines to also include perspectives from accounting, economics, finance, marketing, organization behavior, and strategy will be encouraged by the Editorial Team in their review and decision processes.

To be responsive to the changing needs of its research community, *Decision Sciences* maintains a flexible keyword reviewing system that allows the addition of new keyword groups and areas. Two categories of keywords are available for identifying the research areas and expertise needed to complete a comprehensive review of a manuscript: Topic Areas and Methodological Areas. Topic Areas are organized around different themes including:

- *Decision Making Type* (Inter-organizational, Organizational, Collaborative, and Individual)
- *Cross-Functional Processes* (E-Business, Knowledge Management, International Business, Product/System/Service Development, Supply Chain Management, System/Process/Service Design, and Technology and Innovation)
- *Cross-Functional Interfaces* (Accounting, Information Systems, Marketing, Operations, Organizational Behavior, Strategy, Supply Chain, etc.)
- *Functional Perspectives* (Accounting, Finance, Information Management and Systems, Marketing, Operations, Organizational Behavior, and Strategic Management)
- *Industry Areas* (Airlines, Biotechnology, Financial Services, Health Care, Manufacturing, etc.)

To promote more intense interactions between the targeted disciplines, cross-functional processes with commonality in the decision problem are grouped together. For example, Product/System/Service Development share similar decision making processes and are known to be influenced by similar phenomenon.

Methodological areas embrace the diversity of methodological approaches to decision making used by scholars in the *Decision Sciences* research community. Major areas include:

- Algorithm Development
- Chaotic Systems
- Computer Science Methods
- Economic Methods
- Empirical Methods
- Forecasting Methods
- Game Theory
- Interpretive Studies
- Longitudinal Studies
- Multi-Criteria Decision Making Methods
- Probabilistic Models
- Programming Methods
- Simulation Methods
- Statistical Methods
- Theoretical Foundations

A listing of the specific sub-areas within each Topic and Methodological Area can be located in *DSJ Online's* Author Information Center.

All articles must address a well-known or emerging decision problem that is of interest and concern to practicing decision makers. It is the responsibility of the authors to demonstrate the managerial relevance of the decision studied as well as to explain the managerial implications of the research results. If an article satisfies the high standards of research rigor necessary for publication, yet does not fully develop the managerial relevance and implications of the research study, the editorial decision will be to return the manuscript with encouragement to revise and submit a new manuscript for consideration to the journal.

Manuscript Policies

Decision Sciences strives to provide constructive and developmental reviews to authors within approximately two months. To accomplish this meaningful objective, the journal maintains strict policies for manuscript submissions and the reviewing process.

In order to ensure that as many worthy papers as possible appear in each issue, manuscripts submitted to *Decision Sciences* should not exceed more than 40 double-spaced pages excluding references, appendixes, tables, and figures. Preparation guidelines containing required style guidelines should be reviewed before submission of a manuscript. All manuscripts for publication consideration must be submitted electronically in the Author Center. As a rule, *Decision Sciences* does not accept resubmissions of rejected manuscripts, unless the revised manuscript represents a substantially different research contribution.

Authors submitting their manuscript to *DSJ* for publication consideration must certify that: (a) none of the contents of their manuscript has been copyrighted, published, or accepted for publication by another journal, or is under review by another journal; (b) authors whose manuscripts utilize data that are reported in any other manuscript, published or not, are required to inform the editor at the time of submission in a cover letter explaining the duplication; (c) this manuscript uses appropriate citations for the reproduction of someone else's original words or expression of ideas; (d) this manuscript has not been previously submitted to *DSJ* for review; (e) all working papers, prior drafts, and/or final version of submitted manuscripts that are posted on a website will be taken down during the review process. When a paper is accepted for publication, authors must provide an electronic copy of the final version in Word or TeX.

Review Process

Decision Sciences considers it is the highest honor to receive a manuscript for publication consideration from prospective author(s). As such, the review process is designed to promote expedited reviews, developmental feedback, and a service culture of professionalism and collegiality.

Decision Sciences maintains a double-blind review process where the authors, reviewers, and associate editor are anonymous. All manuscripts go through a comprehensive evaluation by at least two reviewers, an Associate Editor, and a final evaluation by the Editor. Incoming manuscripts are screened against the "Preparation Guidelines" before being sent out for review. Manuscripts that are outside of the journal's mission will be returned immediately after a review by the Editor, and if appropriate, an Associate Editor. The Editor makes the final decision to accept, reject, or invite a revision. If the author(s) select to revise and resubmit the manuscript, the revision is sent back to an Associate Editor, who reviews the manuscript, and may on occasion, request additional reviews, before making a recommendation to the Editor. Manuscripts will be evaluated on a number of critical dimensions including: (a) appropriateness of the topics/issues, (b) relevance in advancing decision making in the academic community, (c) managerial significance and potential impact on practicing managers, (d) conceptual and methodological rigor, (e) clarity of presentation and readability, and (f) intellectual stimulation. To promote the highest quality reviews that are of value to authors and align with the journal's mission, all reviews are evaluated by members of the Editorial Team. Associate Editors rate reviewers and the Editor rates Associate Editors on five dimensions including comprehensiveness, accuracy, professionalism, developmental value, and overall performance. These ratings are used to continuously improve the quality of the reviewing process.

The Editorial Team strives to respond to all authors within two months of an initial submission, and within one month for a revision. If a second revision is necessary, the expected turnaround time should be less than one month. To realize these goals, *Decision Sciences* lists up-to-date turnaround times on its web site and also reports individual turnaround times to members of its Editorial Team on a regular basis. Every quarter, the Editorial Team evaluates past performance and identifies areas for improvement in the reviewing process. To further reinforce the need for responsive and high-quality reviews, members of the Editorial team serve a two-year commitment, renewable at the end of the year. Additional two-year extensions are available for those members that desire to remain on the Editorial Team. By limiting editorial terms to shorter durations, while at the same time offering the flexibility to extend their appointments, *Decision Sciences* recognizes that the quality of the editorial review process can suffer when members of its Editorial Team are diverted to other scholarly activities. The rotation of the Editorial Team allows for new members as needed and for reviewers with the interest and expertise to serve as Associate Editors to be afforded this opportunity.

Defense Acquisition Review Journal

ADDRESS FOR SUBMISSION:

Norene Taylor, Managing Editor
Defense Acquisition Review Journal
Defense Acquisition University
Attn: OP-VAP
9820 Belvoir Road, Suite 3
Fort Belvoir, VA 22060-5565
USA
Phone: 703-805-3801
E-Mail: norene.taylor@dau.mil
Web: www.dau.mil/pubs/arqtoc.asp

PUBLICATION GUIDELINES:

Manuscript Length: See Guidelines
Copies Required: Two
Computer Submission: Yes
Format: MS Word
Fees to Review: 0.00 US$

Manuscript Style:
American Psychological Association

CIRCULATION DATA:

Reader: Business Persons
Frequency of Issue: Quarterly
Sponsor/Publisher: Defense Acquisition
University

REVIEW INFORMATION:

Type of Review: Blind Review
No. of External Reviewers: 2
No. of In House Reviewers: 1
Acceptance Rate: 11-20%
Time to Review: 6-9 Months
Reviewers Comments: Yes
Invited Articles: 0-5%
Fees to Publish: 0.00 US$

MANUSCRIPT TOPICS:
Accounting Information Systems; Acquisition Initiatives; Acquisition Related Topics; Fiscal Policy; Procurement-Related Topics; Weapons (Procurement)

MANUSCRIPT GUIDELINES/COMMENTS:

Topics Include. Areas of Defense Acquisition as follows: Business, Contracting, Earned Value, Financial, and Program Management; Cost and Risk Analysis; Knowledge Sharing; Communities of Practice; Systems Engineering, Transformation, and Leadership, Performance Based Logistics, and Lean.

The *Defense Acquisition Review Journal* (*ARJ*) is a scholarly peer-reviewed journal published by the Defense Acquisition University (DAU). All submissions receive a blind review to ensure impartial evaluation.

In General. We encourage prospective authors to co-author with others to add depth to their submissions. It is recommended that a mentor be selected who has published before or has expertise in the subject presented in the manuscript.

Authors should become familiar with the construction of previous *ARJs* and adhere to the use of end-notes versus footnotes, formatting of bibliographies, and the use of designated style guides. It is also the responsibility of the corresponding author to furnish government agency/employer clearance with each submission.

Submissions
We welcome submissions from anyone involved in the defense acquisition process. Defense acquisition is defined as the conceptualization, initiation, design, development, testing, contracting, production, deployment, logistic support, modification, and disposal of weapons and other systems, supplies, or services needed by the Defense Department, or intended for use to support military missions.

Research Articles
Manuscripts should reflect research or empirically supported experience in one or more of the afore-mentioned areas of acquisition. Research, lessons learned or tutorial articles should not exceed 4,500 words. Opinion articles should be limited to 1,500 words. Research articles are characterized by a systematic inquiry into a subject to discover/revise facts or theories.

Manuscript Sections
A brief abstract provides a comprehensive summary of the article and must accompany your submission. Abstracts give readers the opportunity to quickly review an articles' content and also allow information services to index and retrieve articles.

The introduction, which should not be labeled, opens the body of the paper and states the problem being studied and the rationale for the research undertaken.

The methods section should include a detailed methodology that clearly describes work performed. Al-though it is appropriate to refer to previous publications in this section, the author should provide enough information so that the experienced reader need not read earlier works to gain an understanding of the methodology.

The results section should concisely summarize findings of the research and follow the train of thought established in the methods section. This section should not refer to previous publications, but should be devoted solely to the current findings of the author.

The discussion section should emphasize the major findings of the study and its significance. Information presented in the aforementioned sections should not be repeated.

Research Considerations
Contributors should also consider the following questions in reviewing their research-based articles prior to submission:
- Is the research question significant?
- Are research instruments reliable and valid?
- Are outcomes measured in a way clearly related to the variables under study?
- Does the research design fully and unambiguously test the hypothesis?
- Did you build needed controls into the study?

Contributors of research-based submissions are also reminded they should share any materials and methodologies necessary to verify their conclusions.

Criteria for Tutorials
Tutorials should provide special instruction or knowledge relevant to an area of defense acquisition to be of benefit to the Department of Defense Acquisition, Technology and Logistics Workforce.

Topics for submission should rely on or be derived from observation or experiment, rather than theory. The submission should provide knowledge in a particular area for a particular purpose.

Opinion Criteria
Opinion articles should reflect judgments based on the special knowledge of the expert. Opinion articles should be based on observable phenomena and presented in a factual manner; that is, submissions should imply detachment. The observation and judgment should not reflect the author's personal feelings or thoughts. Nevertheless, an opinion piece should clearly express a fresh point of view, rather than negatively criticize the view of another previous author.

Manuscript Style
We will require you to recast your last version of the manuscript, especially citations (endnotes instead of footnotes) into the format required in two specific style manuals. The *ARJ* follows the author (date) form of citation. We expect you to use the *Publication Manual of the American Psychological Association* (5th Edition), and the *Chicago Manual of Style* (15th Edition).

Contributors are encouraged to seek the advice of a reference librarian in completing citations of government documents because standard formulas of citations may provide incomplete information in reference to government works. Helpful guidance is also available in Garner, D. L. and Smith, D. H., 1993, *The Complete Guide to Citing Government Documents: A Manual for Writers and Librarians* (Rev. Ed.), Bethesda, MD: Congressional Information Service, Inc.

Copyright Information
The *ARJ* is a publication of the United States Government and as such is not copyrighted. Because the *ARJ* is posted on the DAU home page, we will not accept copyrighted articles that require special posting requirements or restrictions. If we do publish your copyrighted article, we will print only the usual caveats. The work of federal employees undertaken as part of their official duties is not subject to copyright except in rare cases.

In citing the work of others, it is the contributor's responsibility to obtain permission from a copyright holder if the proposed use exceeds the fair use provisions of the law (see U.S. Government Printing Office, 1994, Circular 92: Copyright Law of the United States of America, p. 15, Washington, DC: Author). Contributors will be required to submit a copy of the written permission to the Managing Editor before publication.

180

Copyright Policy
We reserve the right to decline any article that falls into these problem copyright categories:
- The author cannot obtain official permission to use previously copyrighted material in the article.
- The author will not allow DAU to post the article with the rest of the *ARJ* issue on our home page.
- The author requires that unusual copyright notices be posted with the article.
- To publish the article requires copyright payment by DAU Press.

Manuscript Format
Pages should be double-spaced and organized in the following order: title page, abstract, body, reference list, author's note (if any), and figures or tables. Figures or tables should not be inserted (or embedded, etc.) into the text, but segregated (one to a page) following the text. If material is submitted on a computer diskette, each figure or table should be saved to a separate, exportable file (i.e., a readable EPS file). For additional information on the preparation of figures or tables, see CBE Scientific Illustration Committee, 1988, Illustrating Science: Standards for Publication, Bethesda, MD: Council of Biology Editors, Inc. Please restructure briefing charts and slides to a look similar to those in previous issues of the *ARJ*.

The author (or corresponding author in cases of multiple authorships) should attach to the manuscript a signed cover letter that provides all of the authors' names, addresses, telephone and fax numbers, and e-mail addresses. The letter should verify that the sub-mission is an original product of the author; that it has not been published before; and that it is not under consideration by another publication. Details about the manuscript should also be included in this letter: for example, title, word length, a description of the computer application programs, and file names used on enclosed diskettes, etc.

Please send us a cover letter; biographical sketch for each author (not to exceed 70 words); head and shoulder print(s) or digitized photo(s) (saved at 300 pixels per inch, at least 3 X 2 inches, and as a TIFF file); prints of photos will be accepted and returned upon request, one copy of the printed manuscript; and any diskettes. These items should be sturdily packaged and mailed to: Department of Defense, Defense Acquisition University, Attn: DAU Press (*ARJ* Managing Editor), Suite 3, 9820 Belvoir Road, Fort Belvoir, VA 22060-5565.

In most cases, the author will be notified that the submission has been received within 48 hours of its arrival. Following an initial review, submissions will be referred to referees and for subsequent consideration by the Executive Editor, *ARJ*.

Contributors may direct their questions to the Managing Editor, *ARJ*, at the address shown above, or by calling (703) 805-3801 (fax: (703) 805-2917), or via the Internet at:
norene.taylor@dau.mil.

Derivatives: Financial Products Report

ADDRESS FOR SUBMISSION:

Barbara Campbell, Managing Editor
Derivatives: Financial Products Report
RIA Group
395 Hudson Street - 4th Floor
New York, NY 10014
USA
Phone: 212-807-2182
E-Mail: barbara.campbell@thomson.com
Web: www.riahome.com

CIRCULATION DATA:

Reader: Business Persons
Frequency of Issue: Monthly
Sponsor/Publisher: RIA Group

PUBLICATION GUIDELINES:

Manuscript Length: 6-10
Copies Required: One
Computer Submission: Yes Email
Format: MS Word
Fees to Review: 0.00 US$

Manuscript Style:
    Chicago Manual of Style

REVIEW INFORMATION:

Type of Review: Editorial Review
No. of External Reviewers: 1
No. of In House Reviewers: 2
Acceptance Rate: 90%
Time to Review: 1 Month or Less
Reviewers Comments: Yes
Invited Articles: 50% +
Fees to Publish: 0.00 US$

MANUSCRIPT TOPICS:
Financial Services; Tax Accounting

MANUSCRIPT GUIDELINES/COMMENTS:

Topics Include. Financial products; Corporate tax shelters; US & International Accounting (involving derivatives and financial products); Hedging strategies; CFTC/SEC/OCC Regulation (financial products); FASB proposals (e.g., FAS 133, FIN 46R); Tax arbitrage; ISDA documentation; Securitization; Equity, debt, or currency derivatives; Regulation in financial centers

Derivatives Financial Products Report analyzes the tax, accounting and regulatory issues in the rapidly changing world of financial instruments. With coverage of rules and announcements from the IRS, the SEC, FASB, as well as from key court decisions, the *Report* gives investors and their advisors the tools needed to plan the most profitable investment strategies.

Aspiring Authors
Derivatives Financial Products Report welcomes articles offering practical information and planning strategies regarding derivatives and sophisticated financial instruments and transactions. Articles should focus on matters of importance to practitioners regarding

182

transactions that are being or can be used in financial activities and transactions. Topic areas include tax and regulation of financial instruments, accounting for financial transactions, financial engineering and product design, and developments within international regulatory bodies (IOSCO, BIS, OECD) and industry groups (ISDA, IASC). Articles should not focus on theoretical or policy matters.

To be considered for publication, articles must be sent to us exclusively and are subject to review by the editorial staff of *Derivatives Report* and members of the editorial board. If accepted for publication, the manuscript will be edited for stylistic conformity. Manuscripts generally run between 10 and 20 pages in length. An electronic version, which can be sent as an attached e-mail file, is also required.

To submit articles, or for more information, please contact:
Derivatives Financial Products Report
Barbara Campbell, Managing Editor
RIA
395 Hudson Street
New York, NY 10014
Phone: (212) 807-2182 Fax: (212) 337-4207
E-mail: **barbara.campbell@Thomson.com**

European Accounting Review

ADDRESS FOR SUBMISSION:

Kari Lukka, Editor
European Accounting Review
Turku School of Economics and
Business Administration
Rehtorinpellonkatu 3
FIN 20500 Turku,
Finland
Phone: 35 8 2 3383 315
E-Mail: kari.lukka@tukkk.fi
Web: www.eaa-online.org/pub/ear.com

CIRCULATION DATA:

Reader: Academics
Frequency of Issue: Quarterly
Sponsor/Publisher: Routledge (Taylor &
Francis Ltd.)

PUBLICATION GUIDELINES:

Manuscript Length: Any
Copies Required: One
Computer Submission: Yes Email
Format:
Fees to Review: 0.00 US$

Manuscript Style:
    Uniform System of Citation (Harvard
    Blue Book)

REVIEW INFORMATION:

Type of Review: Blind Review
No. of External Reviewers: 2
No. of In House Reviewers: 0
Acceptance Rate: 21-30%
Time to Review: 2 - 3 Months
Reviewers Comments:
Invited Articles: 6-10%
Fees to Publish: 0.00 US$

MANUSCRIPT TOPICS:
Accounting Education; Accounting Information Systems; Accounting Theory & Practice;
Auditing; Behavioral Accounting; Capital Market Based Accounting; Cost Accounting;
Financial Reporting; Government & Non Profit Accounting; Management Accounting; Tax
Accounting

MANUSCRIPT GUIDELINES/COMMENTS:

Aims and Scope. *European Accounting Review* is the international scholarly journal of the
European Accounting Association. Devoted to the advancement of accounting knowledge, it
provides a forum for the publication of high quality accounting research manuscripts. The
journal acknowledges its European origins and the distinctive variety of the European
accounting research community. Conscious of these origins, *European Accounting Review*
emphasises openness and flexibility, not only regarding the substantive issues of accounting
research, but also with respect to paradigms, methodologies and styles of conducting that
research. Though European Accounting Review is a truly international journal, it also holds a
unique position as it is the only accounting journal to provide a European forum for the
reporting of accounting research. The advent of e.g. the single European market and the
consequent harmonisation of accounting standards and regulations has shown the need for a
European forum for accounting research.

184

Instructions for Authors
Note to Authors. Please make sure your contact address information is clearly visible on the outside of all packages you are sending to Editors.

Submission of Articles
Authors should submit their article by e-mail in MS Word format to the Editor of *EAR*, Prof. Kari Lukka, at **kari.lukka@tukkk.fi** including an abstract and six keywords suitable for indexing and online search purposes. In addition, one complete copy of the article should be mailed as a hardcopy to the Editor (Turku School of Economics and Business Administration, Rehtorinpellonkatu 3, FIN-20500 Turku, Finland). Original copies of any illustrations should be provided. It will be assumed that the authors will keep a copy of their paper.

Submission of a paper to the journal will be taken to imply that it presents original, unpublished work not under consideration for publication elsewhere. By submitting a manuscript, the authors agree that the copyright has been assigned to the European Accounting Association. All articles will be double blind refereed.

The major aim of the journal is to publish scholarly articles, which fulfill the highest quality standards of academic accounting research. Occasionally research notes and commentaries on topical issues are published as well. In addition, special sections of articles may be published on topics of particular interest. The journal also has a book review section.

The Manuscript
Submissions should be made in the English language. They should be typed in double spacing with wide margins, on one side only of the paper, preferably of A4 size. The manuscript should have a separate cover page, giving the title of the manuscript, the authors' names, positions and institutional affiliations, and an acknowledgement if desired. The title of the manuscript (but not the authors' names) and the abstract (of no more than 200 words) should appear on the first page of the text. Furthermore, to assist objectivity, the author should avoid any reference to himself or herself which would enable identification by referees.

Articles should normally be as concise as possible and preceded by an abstract of not more than 200 words.

Tables and figures should not be inserted in the pages of the manuscript but should be on separate sheets. They should be numbered consecutively in Arabic numerals with a descriptive caption. The desired position in the text for each table and figure should be indicated in the manuscript. Permission to reproduce copyright material must be obtained by the authors before submission and any acknowledgements should be included in the typescript or captions as appropriate.

Notes should be used only where necessary to avoid interrupting the continuity of the text. They should be numbered consecutively and placed at the end of the article before the bibliographic references.

If an article is accepted for publication, authors are requested to send an electronic version of their paper to Dr Markus Granlund, either via e-mail as an attached file (markus.granlund@tukkk.fi) or on disk by ordinary mail (Turku School of Economics and Business Administration, Rehtorinpellonkatu 3, FIN-20500 Turku, Finland). They are asked to ensure that the electronic version is exactly the same as the accepted final version of the article, and to provide details of the make and model of the computer and the name and version of the word-processing package used.

References

The Harvard system uses the name of the author and the date of publication as a key to the full bibliographical details which are set out in the references.

When the author's name is mentioned in the text, the date is inserted in parentheses immediately after the name, as in 'Fitchew (1990)'. When a less direct reference is made to one or more authors, both name and date are bracketed, with the references separated by a semi-colon, as in 'several authors have noted this trend (Roberts, 1990; Brunsson, 1990; Johnson, 1987)'.

When the reference is to a work of dual or multiple authorship, use only surnames or the abbreviated form, as in 'Johnson and Kaplan (1987)' or '*Jones et al.* (1976)'. If an author has two references published in the same year, add lower-case letters after the date to distinguish them, as in 'Roberts (1990a, 1990b)'.

The date of publication used is the date of the source you have referred to. However, when using a republished book, a translation or a modern edition of an older edition, also give the date of the original publication, as in Flint (1988/1968), in order to place the work chronologically and locate it in the reference list. When using a reprinted article, cite date of original publication only, as this both places the work chronologically and locates it in the reference list. (See Format of reference lists for forms of citation in reference list.)

Page numbers are indicated by inserting the relevant numbers after the date, separated from the date by a colon and with no other punctuation, as in 'Provasoli (1989: 56)' or 'Casey and Bartczak (1985: 423)'. Always use the minimum number of figures in page numbers, dates, etc., e.g. 22-4, 101-2, 1968-9; but for 'teen numbers use 13-14, 1914-18, etc.

When references are made to institutions or works whose official title is not English, the following procedure should apply:
(a) institutions should always be referred to by their full official native title when first mentioned in the text, and by that title or an abbreviation of it thereafter. An English translation may be included, if appropriate, at the first mention, e.g. 'standard setting is the responsibility of the Conseil National de la Comptabilité (CNC - National Accounting Council). The CNC consists of . . .';

(b) articles, book titles, etc., which have been published other than in English should be referred to, where appropriate, using their original title [with English translation provided in brackets];

186

(c) where a quotation is used in the text, this should be an English translation, with the foreign language appended as a footnote if this is essential for an understanding of the point, e.g. 'It is a little different to the extent that it does not consider accounting exclusively as a technique of capturing, recording and manipulating information' (Colasse, 1991 translation).

Format of Reference Lists and Bibliographies
Submissions should include a reference list whose content and format conforms to the following examples. Note: secondary lines are indented; authors' names are given in full; page numbers are required for articles in readers, journals and magazines; where relevant, translator and date of first publication of a book, and original date of reprinted article, are noted.

Book
Bromwich, M. (1985) *The Economics of Standard Setting*. London: Prentice-Hall/ICAEW.

Multiple author
Bruns, W. J. and Kaplan, R. S. (eds) (1987) *Accounting and Management: Field Study Perspectives*. Boston, MA: Harvard Business School Press.

Article in edited volume
Kaplan, R. S. (1985) 'Accounting lag: the obsolescence of cost accounting systems', in Clark, K. and Lorenze, C. (eds) *Technology and Productivity: the Uneasy Alliance*. Boston, MA: Harvard Business School Press, pp. 195-226.

Article in journal
Ordelheide, D. (1993) 'The true and fair view: impact on and of the Fourth Directive', *European Accounting Review*, 2(1): 81-90.

Report
Fitchew, G. E. (1990) 'Summing up', in Commission of the European Communities, *The Future of Harmonization of Accounting Standards Within the European Communities*. Brussels.

Article in newspaper
The Times Literary Supplement (1991) 'The year that shook the world', 23 August 1991: 9.

Unpublished
Zito, A. (1994) 'Epistemic communities in European policy-making', Ph.D. dissertation, Department of Political Science, University of Pittsburgh.

NB: If referring to a revised or second edition, cite only edition used.

Proofs
Page proofs will be sent for correction to the first-named author, unless otherwise requested. The difficulty and expense involved in making amendments at the page-proof stage make it essential for authors to prepare their typescript carefully: any alteration to the original text is strongly discouraged. Authors should correct printers' errors in red; minimal alterations of their own should be in black.

Early Electronic Offprints. Corresponding authors can now receive their article by e-mail as a complete PDF. This allows the author to print up to 50 copies, free of charge, and disseminate them to colleagues. In many cases this facility will be available up to two weeks prior to publication. Or, alternatively, corresponding authors will receive the traditional 50 offprints. A copy of the journal will be sent by post to all corresponding authors after publication. Additional copies of the journal can be purchased at the author's preferential rate of £15.00/$25.00 per copy.

In addition to aiming at providing professional and constructive reviews for the submitted manuscripts, *European Accounting Review* also wishes to promote speedy evaluation processes. From now on, the journal will increase transparency in this regard in two ways. Firstly, we will start publishing annually a few key statistics indicating the speed *EAR* has been able to provide the Editor's first letter, offering feedback to the submitting author(s). Normally this letter is based on the peer review reports the Editor has asked for and received; in rare occasions of direct rejection this Editor's letter has been sent without asking for peer reviews. Secondly, starting from Vol.10 (year 2001), we will start publishing information related to each published article indicating the length of the process the manuscript has gone through.

188

Exempt Organization Tax Review (The)

ADDRESS FOR SUBMISSION:

Frederick W. Stokeld, Editor
Exempt Organization Tax Review (The)
Tax Analysts
6830 N. Fairfax Drive
Arlington, VA 22213
USA
Phone: 703-533-4670
E-Mail: fstokeld@tax.org
Web: www.tax.org

CIRCULATION DATA:

Reader: , Tax law practitioners
Frequency of Issue: Monthly
Sponsor/Publisher: Tax Analysts

PUBLICATION GUIDELINES:

Manuscript Length: Any
Copies Required: One
Computer Submission: Yes
Format: MS Word, WordPerfect
Fees to Review: 0.00 US$

Manuscript Style:
  Chicago Manual of Style

REVIEW INFORMATION:

Type of Review: Editorial Review
No. of External Reviewers: 0
No. of In House Reviewers: 1
Acceptance Rate: 50%
Time to Review: 1 Month or Less
Reviewers Comments: No
Invited Articles: 11-20%
Fees to Publish: 0.00 US$

MANUSCRIPT TOPICS:
Government & Non Profit Accounting; Nonprofit Tax Law

MANUSCRIPT GUIDELINES/COMMENTS:

See website. **www.tax.org**

Financial Accountability & Management

ADDRESS FOR SUBMISSION:

Irvine Lapsley, Editor
Financial Accountability & Management
University of Edinburgh
Management School
50 George Square
Edinburgh, EH8 9JY
UK
Phone: +44(0) 131 650 3790/1
E-Mail: I.Lapsley@ed.ac.uk
Web:

CIRCULATION DATA:

Reader: Business Persons, Academics
Frequency of Issue: Quarterly
Sponsor/Publisher: CIPFA

PUBLICATION GUIDELINES:

Manuscript Length: 26-30
Copies Required: Four
Computer Submission: Yes Disk, Email
Format: MS Word
Fees to Review: 0.00 US$

Manuscript Style:
    See Manuscript Guidelines

REVIEW INFORMATION:

Type of Review: Blind Review
No. of External Reviewers: 2
No. of In House Reviewers: 0
Acceptance Rate: 11-20%
Time to Review: 2 - 3 Months
Reviewers Comments: Yes
Invited Articles: 0-5%
Fees to Publish: 0.00 US$

MANUSCRIPT TOPICS:
Accounting Education; Accounting Theory & Practice; Auditing; Government & Non Profit Accounting

MANUSCRIPT GUIDELINES/COMMENTS:

All manuscripts submitted for review should be sent to the Editor, Professor Irvine Lapsley (see above for address). Both the Editor and the Associate Editors, June Pallot (Asian-Pacific), and Dana Forgione (North America) are happy to respond to informal enquiries about the suitability of papers for possible publication. Manuscripts are considered on the understanding that they are original, unpublished works not currently under consideration for publication elsewhere. The receipt of manuscripts will be acknowledged, but the editors and publishers can accept no responsibility for any loss or non-return of manuscripts.

Suitable manuscripts will be given anonymous double-blind review, following which a copy of any review report will be supplied together with the editors' decision. As regards papers accepted for publication, the author(s) will be asked to transfer copyright to the publishers. Authors are requested to follow *FAM's* manuscript and style requirements closely, to minimise later delay or redrafting. In particular, authors should draft their papers and footnotes etc. to avoid identifying themselves directly or indirectly, to help ensure a fair

190

review. *FAM* seeks to stimulate the flow of papers submitted for possible publication. To this end and until further notice no submission fees or publication fees will be required for papers sent for editorial consideration.

Manuscript Requirements

Manuscripts may be up to 9,000 words in length, or occasionally 10,000 if justifiable, inclusive of reference lists and the space equivalence taken up by illustrations. Submit four photocopies of the manuscript, typed double-spaced (preferably on international-size A4 paper). On the title page include the names, titles and institutional affiliations of the author(s), and also the complete correspondence address of the designated author to whom decisions, proofs, reprint requests and readers' enquiries should be sent. Also provide a running title of fewer than 50 characters and spaces, which will appear on alternate pages in the journal. If the paper is to include any acknowledgements these should be typed as a footnote on the title page. The second page should repeat the full title of the paper (but not the author(s)' names) and contain the Abstract of the paper, not exceeding 100 words for full-length papers, or 60 words for shorter Notes, Comments Replies or Rejoinders. Immediately below the Abstract, enter the heading **Keywords:**, followed by a listing of up to five most relevant keywords. The third page may repeat the full title of the paper (but not the author(s)' names) and here the text proper begins. The main text should be followed by any appendices, by any footnotes (which should be kept to the essential minimum, identified in the text by superscript numerals and listed together at the end, not separately at the bottom of each page), and by the list of source references (see below). Tables and figures should be numbered in order of their appearance with Arabic numerals, and each should have a concise descriptive title (and source, where relevant).

References

Citation in the text is by name(s) of author(s), followed by year of publication (and page numbers where relevant) in parentheses. For references authored by more than two contributors use the first author's name and 'et al'. For multiple citations in the same year use a, b, c immediately following the year of publication. The source reference list should be typed in alphabetical order, and in accord with the following examples of style:

Beattie, V.A. and M J. Jones (1992a), *Certified Research Report 31: The Communication of Information Using Graphs*
  in *Corporate Annual Reports*, Certified Accounts Education Trust (London).
_____(1992b), 'The Use and Abuse of Graphs in Annual Reports: A Theoretical Framework and Empirical Study',
  Accounting and Business Research (Autumn), pp. 291-303.
Bourn, M. and M. Ezzamel (1986), 'Costing and Budgeting in the National Health Service', *Financial Accountability*
  & Management, Vol. 2, No. 1 (Spring), pp. 53-71.
Jones R. and M. Pendlebury (1992), *Public Sector Accounting*, 3rd edn. (Pitman).
Propper, C. (1993), 'Quasi-Markets Contracts and Quality in Health and Social Care: The US Experience',in J.
  Le Grand and W. Bartlett (eds.), *Quasi Markets and Social Policy* (Macmillan, London).
Teece, D. etal. (1990), 'Firm Capabilities, Resources and the Concept of Strategy', CCC Working Paper No. 90-8.

Mathematical and Statistical Material

Mathematical notation should be used only when its rigour and precision are essential to comprehension, and authors should explain in narrative format the principal operations performed. Preferably detailed mathematical proofs and statistical support should be relegated to appendices. Any equations used should be numbered sequentially in parentheses positioned flush with the right-hand margin. Whilst the journal does not wish to publish unnecessary mathematical or statistical detail, or specimen questionnaires, supplementary information of these kinds may be of assistance to the editors and reviewers in assessing papers, and authors are invited to submit such supporting evidence as separate documents clearly marked as being for information rather than publication. Authors may include a footnote to inform readers that copies of questionnaires, supporting mathematical/ statistical analysis, or other detail are available on request from the published address for correspondence.

Proofs and Offprints

The designated author will receive proofs, which should be corrected and returned within ten days of receipt. This author is responsible for proofreading the manuscript: the editors/ publishers are not responsible for any error not marked by the author on the proofs. Corrections to proofs are limited to rectifying errors: no substantial author's changes can be allowed at this stage unless agreement to pay full costs is communicated with the return of proofs. Similarly, offprints in excess of the twenty-five free copies automatically supplied to the designated author (for sharing among any co-authors) must be ordered at the time of the return of proofs, in accord with the instructions and price list accompanying the proofs.

Comments and Replies

The journal welcomes non-trivial Comments on papers previously published in *FAM*. To avoid publishing Comments based on misunderstandings, and to obtain Replies quickly so that they can be published simultaneously with the Comments, it is required that draft Comments should be sent to the original authors for their reactions, prior to any formal submission to the editors for publication.

Financial Counseling and Planning

ADDRESS FOR SUBMISSION:

Sandra Helmick, Editor
Financial Counseling and Planning
Oregon State University
Room 206 Bates Hall
Corvallis, OR 07331-5102
USA
Phone: 541-737-0944
E-Mail: fcp@oregonstate.edu
Web: http://afcpe.org

CIRCULATION DATA:

Reader: Academics, Financial Advisors
Frequency of Issue: 2 Times/Year
Sponsor/Publisher: Association for
   Financial Couseling and Planning
   Education

PUBLICATION GUIDELINES:

Manuscript Length: 16-20
Copies Required: Four (If mailed)
Computer Submission: Yes Preferred
Format: MS Word
Fees to Review: 0.00 US$

Manuscript Style:
   American Psychological Association

REVIEW INFORMATION:

Type of Review: Blind Review
No. of External Reviewers: 3
No. of In House Reviewers: 0
Acceptance Rate: 25%
Time to Review: 2 - 3 Months
Reviewers Comments: Yes
Invited Articles: 0-5%
Fees to Publish: 0.00 US$

MANUSCRIPT TOPICS:
Econometrics; Financial Counseling Theory; Financial Decision Making; Insurance; Portfolio & Security Analysis; Real Estate; Retirement Planning; Tax Accounting

MANUSCRIPT GUIDELINES/COMMENTS:

Guidelines for Submission of Manuscripts
Financial Counseling and Planning is a journal for educators and practicing financial planners and counselors. The journal includes both reports of research and descriptions of proven approaches to education and practice. Readers expect to find detailed recommendations for education and practice in journal articles. Refer to the AFCPE website for current instructions and specifications for journal article submission.   **http://www.afcpe.org**

Manuscripts submitted should not be currently under review by another journal, but it is acceptable to submit papers that have been presented at conferences, even if they have been published in conference proceedings. If journal publication might precede the conference, you should check with the conference chair before submission to this journal.

Submissions should be electronic but mailed copies (four) are accepted. Author names should not be included in the manuscript file. There should be a separate file with title, author names and detailed contact information, including an e-mail address submitted separately from the manuscript file.

Note. to save time after acceptance, it may be worthwhile to study the **Guidelines for Submission of Accepted Manuscripts**. For instance, a version of *APA style* is used in the journal. However, it is acceptable to submit manuscripts for review in other formats.

It the manuscript is accepted for publication, it is the author's responsibility to submit a manuscript file in a Word document as an attached file in an email message. The **Guidelines for Submission of Accepted Manuscripts** should be followed as closely as possible, including the journal's version of *APA style* for references.

- Manuscripts should be submitted in electronic form. Word documents are preferred; other formats may be accepted with approval of the Editor. Send submissions to: **fcp@oregonstate.edu**
- The manuscript should contain no information that identifies the author(s). In a separate file, submit the cover page that includes authors' names and contact information (title, address, phone, fax, and e-mail) for each.
- At time of submission, you will receive a *manuscript submission form* to document and describe any previous submission for publication.
- Follow *APA style* for tables and references (except use *italics* instead of underline in references).
- Use endnotes (if needed) rather than footnotes; footnotes are used only to identify the authors in the published article.
- Follow the text material with (in this order, if needed) appendices, endnotes, references. Tables may be positioned at the end of references in submitted manuscripts; they will be positioned in the text prior to publication.
- Headers and footers will be added by the Editor prior to publication.
- Headings should be as follows:

First Order Heading Centered (no space before paragraph)
Second order heading flush left.
Third order heading precedes text.

- Graphics should be embedded in the document file, not submitted in paper form.
- Tables must be formatted to be printed in portrait mode, not landscape.

Questions regarding manuscript submission and review are welcomed by the Editor, Sandra Helmick, Bates Hall, Oregon State University, Corvallis, OR 97331. Phone: (541) 738-9769, Fax: (541)737-5579, Email: **fcp@oregonstate.edu**

194

Fraud Magazine

ADDRESS FOR SUBMISSION:

Dick Carozza, Editor
Fraud Magazine
Assn. of Certified Fraud Examiners
The Gregor Building
716 West Avenue
Austin, TX 78701
USA
Phone: 800-245-3321
E-Mail: dcarozza@cfenet.com
Web: www.acfe.com

CIRCULATION DATA:

Reader: Business Persons
Frequency of Issue: Bi-Monthly
Sponsor/Publisher: Association of Certified
  Fraud Examiners

PUBLICATION GUIDELINES:

Manuscript Length: 11-15
Copies Required: Three
Computer Submission: Yes
Format: Ms Word, WordPerfect, Mac
Fees to Review: 0.00 US$

Manuscript Style:
  Associated Press Stylebook

REVIEW INFORMATION:

Type of Review: Blind Review
No. of External Reviewers: 13
No. of In House Reviewers: 3+
Acceptance Rate: 11-20%
Time to Review: 2 - 3 Months
Reviewers Comments: No
Invited Articles: 0-5%
Fees to Publish: 0.00 US$

MANUSCRIPT TOPICS:
Auditing; Fraud Examination

MANUSCRIPT GUIDELINES/COMMENTS:

Publisher
Association of Certified Fraud Examiners
The Gregor Building - 716 West Avenue
Austin, TX 78701-2727 USA
Tel: (800) 245-3321(U.S. and Canada) Tel.: +1 (512) 478-9070 (other)
www.CFEnet.com   dcarozza@CFEnet.com

Purpose
Fraud Magazine is a 72-page, four-color magazine published bi-monthly by the Association of Certified Fraud Examiners (ACFE) as a service to its members and others interested in the deterrence and detection of fraud and white-collar crime. Articles published in *Fraud Magazine* cover a variety of topics related to white-collar crime, including forensic accounting; fraud investigation techniques; white-collar crime statutes, legislation, and regulatory issues; computer and management information systems abuse; and industry-specific concerns such as insurance, healthcare, and financial institution fraud.

Audience
Articles published in *Fraud Magazine* are directed at a wide range of professionals globally who have an interest in white-collar crime, including fraud examiners, internal auditors, forensic accountants, loss prevention professionals, investigators, law enforcement officials, financial officers, and academicians. Most readers are Certified Fraud Examiners, who have been granted the professional designation by the Association of Certified Fraud Examiners, and Associate Members of the Association.

Queries
The editors encourage contributors to submit completed articles. However, query letters, outlines, or summaries will be accepted for consideration.

Style
Material for *Fraud Magazine* should be written in a clear, straightforward style. Though some papers by academicians are accepted, Fraud Magazine is not an academic journal; scholarly formats and styles should be avoided. Readers want articles and columns containing practical principles they can apply immediately in their positions and careers.

Because the ACFE is a growing global entity, the best material will be of interest to readers worldwide and will provide insights and fraud examination techniques that those readers can apply. Contributors should focus on a specific type of fraud and the techniques used to prevent, detect, or investigate it. Country-specific statutes, references, abbreviations, and jargon should be avoided when possible by replacing them with globally understandable terms. When use of such terms is unavoidable, they should be explained to assist readers unfamiliar with those terms.

Contributors should use short sentences and paragraphs, similar to magazine and newspaper styles. Articles should lead off with an interesting case example of the fraud discussed. The remainder of the text will show how the fraud is investigated and resolved.

Successful articles contain strong examples, anecdotes, current facts and figures, and sound approaches to solving problems in the detection and deterrence of white-collar crime. Major points should be supported and adequately analyzed. Materials rejected by *Fraud Magazine* reviewers are often overly broad; inappropriate in tone; written for the wrong audience; too short; inadequately supported or researched; too "U.S.-centric"; deal with topics, approaches, or techniques that are elementary to experienced fraud examiners; are promotional sales pieces; or concentrate on just one case history or "war story" without supplying applicable fraud examination techniques.

Commercialism
Submitted articles should not be linked to proprietary products or procedures unless the article is an excerpt from a book. Specific commercial services, products, or organizations should not be written about unless they are necessary to the article, such as a review of fraud examination software or a publication.

Articles shouldn't promote the author's firm or product (they aren't advertising sales pieces) but should contain practical, transferable concepts backed up case histories.

Article Preparation

When submitting a draft article that has been approved for publication, the contributor(s) should provide a full name, academic or professional title, academic degrees, professional credentials, complete address (including e-mail), and telephone and fax numbers.

Articles are normally six to 12 pages in length, or from 1,500 to 4,000 words. However, shorter items, ranging from a couple of paragraphs to 1,200 words, may also be accepted for use in combination with other such pieces, particularly if they communicate insightful tips and techniques, which fraud examiners can use.

Please double space between lines and have only one character space between sentences. Please set all articles in 12 point type.

Footnotes should be used sparingly, designated numerically in the text, and be placed on a separate page at the end of the manuscript. Footnotes should follow this format:

Books
Full name(s) of contributor(s), title of book, publisher, city of publisher, year published, page(s) of reference.

Articles
Full name(s) of contributor(s), title of article, title of periodical, issue date, volume and number, page(s) of article.

Contributors should suggest titles for their articles. In most cases, the editors will reword titles to fit style and space constraints.

Be sure to check with your supervisor to see if your contribution needs to be reviewed by your entity's management. Disclaimers are allowed in articles.

Graphics

Computer-generated tables, charts, and graphs should be used where possible to help emphasize and clarify points in the article, and to provide graphic interest. Reproduced or hand-drawn exhibits may be acceptable. Artwork need not be camera-ready. The information in exhibits should be kept as simple and readable as possible.

Tables, charts, and graphs should be cited in the text. Contributors should refer to them as exhibits, and number them consecutively. The exhibit should include a brief title as well. For example, "Exhibit 1: ABC Co. Statement of Income."

Submission Format

Contributors should e-mail contributions as attachments to **dcarozza@cfenet.com**. To ensure an anonymous and impartial review, contributor(s) name(s), affiliations, biographies, and other identifying information should be deleted from the copy. (Those details will be added if the material is accepted for publication.)

Contributors should also submit résumés or curriculum vitae with their draft articles.

Review Process
Contributors should allow approximately four to eight weeks for the review process. The editors and members of a peer board review manuscripts submitted to *Fraud Magazine*. Reviewers consider each manuscript on the basis of technical accuracy, usefulness to readers, and timeliness.

If reviewers believe material is not appropriate for *Fraud Magazine*, an editor will notify the contributor(s) by letter, telephone, or e-mail. If reviewers believe additional clarification or information is needed before the material can be evaluated, an editor will ask the contributor(s) to make changes before reviewers make a final decision.

If the editors accept a draft article, editors will notify the contributor(s) by letter, telephone, or e-mail. The editors and contributor(s) then will work closely on preparing the material for publication. The editors will send a final version of the article to the contributor(s) before the art director designs the magazine issue.

Author Compensation
Fraud Magazine generally does not pay contributors for providing material. Contributors receive five complimentary copies of the issue in which their articles appear. Contributors may make reprints at no charge. However, they must place the following copyright permission line on the first page of every copy:

Reprinted with permission from the xxxxx/xxxxx 20XX issue of Fraud Magazine, a publication of the Association of Certified Fraud Examiners in Austin, Texas ©20XX.

Publication Scheduling
Fraud Magazine operates on a two- to four-month lead schedule. That is, the staff begins planning an issue approximately four months before the publication date. When combined with the time needed for editing and review, six or more months may elapse from the time material is received until it is published.

Other factors affecting the publication date are the existing backlog of manuscripts already accepted, the subject matter of the material (an article on a similar topic may have appeared recently), or an issue's theme.

Copyright
The Association of Certified Fraud Examiners assumes sole copyright of any article published in *Fraud Magazine*. *Fraud Magazine* follows a policy of exclusive publication. Permission of the publisher is required before an article can be copied or reproduced. Requests for reprinting an article must be directed in writing to the publisher or editor.

Global Business and Economics Review

ADDRESS FOR SUBMISSION:

Demetri Kantarelis, Editor
Global Business and Economics Review
Assumption College
Department of Economics & Global Studies
500 Salisbury Street
Worcester, MA 01609-1296
USA
Phone:
E-Mail: dkan@besiweb.com
Web: www.inderscience.com/gber

CIRCULATION DATA:

Reader: Academics, Business persons,
Policy Makers
Frequency of Issue: Quarterly
Sponsor/Publisher: Inderscience Enterprises
Limited

PUBLICATION GUIDELINES:

Manuscript Length: 21-25
Copies Required: Three
Computer Submission: Yes Disk, Email
Format: MS Word
Fees to Review: 0.00 US$

Manuscript Style:
See Manuscript Guidelines

REVIEW INFORMATION:

Type of Review: Blind Review
No. of External Reviewers: 3+
No. of In House Reviewers: 0
Acceptance Rate: 0-5%
Time to Review: 2 - 3 Months
Reviewers Comments: Yes
Invited Articles: 11-20%
Fees to Publish: 0.00 US$

MANUSCRIPT TOPICS:

Accounting Education; Accounting Information Systems; Accounting Theory & Practice; Auditing; Behavioral Accounting; Cost Accounting; Econometrics; Economic Development; Economic History; Financial Services; Fiscal Policy; Government & Non Profit Accounting; Industrial Organization; Insurance; International Economics & Trade; International Finance; Macro Economics; Micro Economics; Monetary Policy; Portfolio & Security Analysis; Public Policy Economics; Real Estate; Regional Economics; Tax Accounting

MANUSCRIPT GUIDELINES/COMMENTS:

Business & Economic Society International (B&ESI) submission address: B&ESI/GBER, 64 Holden Street, Worcester, MA 01605-3109 USA

The *GBER* is an international refereed journal for the presentation, discussion and analysis of advanced concepts, initial treatments and fundamental research in all fields of Business and Economics. Priority is given to insightful policy oriented articles that deal with the implications of the increasingly global business activity, especially written for the educated lay-person. The *GBER* welcomes contributions from academicians, corporate executives, staff members of research institutions, international organisations and government officials.

Objectives
The objectives of the journal are to serve as a medium of open discussion for everyone interested in Business and Economics problems and to facilitate communication between Practitioners and Business/Economics Academicians as they pursue excellence in practice, teaching and research in an increasingly global environment.

Readership
Primarily, Practitioners and Academicians in Business/Economics; secondarily, Practitioners and Academicians in other fields of inquiry who desire to learn about Business and Economics in a global context.

Contents
GBER publishes original papers, review papers, case studies, and book reviews. Special Issues devoted to topics in vogue will occasionally be published.

Subject Coverage
- Accounting
- Management science
- Marketing
- Finance and international finance
- Business ethics
- Quantitative methods
- Business statistics/econometrics
- Business law/law and economics
- Entrepreneurship
- Business and economics education
- Microeconomics
- Government regulation
- Industrial organisation
- Game theory
- International trade
- Labour economics/human resources
- Economic growth and development
- Behavioural and health economics
- Environmental business/economics
- Macroeconomics
- Monetary economics
- Government finance
- Urban, rural and regional economics
- Other – any business or economics discipline

Specific Notes for Authors
All papers are refereed through a double blind process. A guide for authors, sample copies and other relevant information for submitting papers are available on the Papers Submission section under Author Guidelines.

To submit a paper, please go to Submission of Papers. This is our preferred route for submitting papers; please use it if at all possible. However, if you experience any problems submitting papers in this way, an alternative route is suggested below.

Submitted papers should not have been previously published nor be currently under consideration for publication elsewhere.

As an alternative to using the Submission of Papers site, you may send THREE copies of each manuscript (in hard copy) or one copy in the form of an MS Word file attached to an e-mail (details of both formats in Author Guidelines) to Demetri Kantarelis, with a copy to:
Editor-in-Chief
IEL Editorial Office
PO Box 735
Olney, Bucks MK46 5WB
UK
Fax: +44 1234-240515
E-mail: **gber@inderscience.com**

Please include in your submission the title of the Journal.

Submission of Papers
Papers, case studies, technical and conference reports, etc. are invited for submission, together with a brief abstract (100-150 words) and 1-10 keywords that reflect the content. Authors may wish to send in advance abstracts of proposed papers along with cover letters/e-mails (see requirements below). Please refer to notes for intending authors for more detailed guidance.

Please submit your manuscript with a cover letter/e-mail containing the following imperative statements:
1. Title and the central theme of the article.

2. Journal for which publication is intended.

3. Which subject/theme of the Journal the material fits.

4. Why the material is important in its field and why the material should be published in this Journal.

5. Nomination of up to four recognized experts who would be considered appropriate to review the submission. Please state:
• The names, title, addresses, phone, fax, and email addresses of these reviewers
• The expertise of each reviewer relating to your paper
• Your relationship with each of them.

6. The fact that the manuscript contains original unpublished work and is not being submitted for publication elsewhere.

Note that
Any non-English speaking author should have his/her paper proofread by a professional technical writer for grammatical and spelling corrections as well as the readability of the paper, before submitting it to the Editor.

A complete submission must include the following components in three separate MS-Word/Word for Windows files, plus hard copy with high quality black and white artwork for all figures, as indicated.
- The cover letter complying to the format of the sample letter
- The title page, including authors' full mailing, e-mail addresses and biographical details, attached to each of the hard copies
- One hard copy of the manuscript (title, abstract, keywords, article, references) without authors' names unless they are in the References section
- An electronic copy of the manuscript containing all details
- A hard copy of the Assignment of Copyright statement, duly signed.

These files should be submitted to the Editor-in-Chief.

Papers may also be sent directly to the relevant Editor, with copies to the Editorial Office, abov.e Each paper submitted to Inderscience Enterprises Limited is subject to the following review procedure:
- It is reviewed by the editor for general suitability for this publication.
- If it is judged suitable, two reviewers are selected and a double-blind review process takes place
- Based on the recommendations of the reviewers, the editor then decides whether the particular article should be acceptable as it is, revised or rejected.

NOTES FOR INTENDING AUTHORS
Formal Conditions of Acceptance
- Papers will only be published in English.
- Each typescript must be accompanied by a statement that it has not been submitted for publication elsewhere in English.
- Previous presentation at a conference, or publication in another language, should be disclosed.
- All papers are refereed, and the Editor-in-Chief reserves the right to refuse any typescript, whether on invitation or otherwise, and to make suggestions and/or modifications before publication.
- Typescripts which have been accepted become the property of the publisher. It is a condition of acceptance that copyright shall be vested in the publisher.
- The publisher shall furnish authors of accepted papers with proofs for the correction of printing errors. The proofs shall be returned within 14 calendar days of submittal. The publishers shall not be held responsible for errors which are the result of authors' oversights.

Typescript Preparation
- The original typescript should be submitted electronically in A4 size format, with double-spaced typing preferred and a wide margin on the left, following the submission requirements described on the *Journal*'s website.
- A final paper which would exceed 7000 words or occupy more than 20 pages of the *Journal* may be returned for abridgement.
- A complete typescript should include, in the following order: *title, author(s), address(es), abstract, keywords, biographical notes, introduction, text, acknowledgements, references and notes, tables, figure captions, figures.*

Electronic Copy
- The preferred word processing program is Microsoft's Word or Word for Windows.
- Figures in the final accepted manuscript may be included in the electronic text file and also provided as separate files, but must also be accompanied by high-resolution hard copy printout.

International Context
- It should not be assumed that the reader is familiar with specific national institutions or corporations.
- Countries and groupings of countries should be referred to by their full title (for example, 'China', 'Europe' and 'America' are all ambiguous).
- Special attention should be paid to identifying units of currency by nationality.
- Acronyms should be translated in full into English. (See also 'Translated works' below.)

Title, Abstract, Keywords, Addresses, Biographical Notes
Please assist us by following these guidelines:
- Title . as short as possible
- Abstract. approximately 100 words, maximum 150
- Keywords . approximately 10 words or phrases
- Address . position, department, name of institution, full postal address
- Biographical notes . approximately 100 words per author, maximum 150.

References and Notes
- Inderscience journals use the Harvard (name and date) short reference system for citations in the text with a detailed alphabetical list at the end of the paper. For example, 'Hamel (2000) suggests..' or 'Nonaka and Takeuchi (1995) found that...' or 'A study of economic change (Nelson and Winter, 1982) has shown that..'.
- Footnotes should be avoided, but any short, succinct notes making a specific point, may be placed in number order following the alphabetical list of references.
- References should be made only to works that are published, accepted for publication (not merely 'submitted'), or available through libraries or institutions. Any other source should be qualified by a note regarding availability.
- Full reference should include *all authors' names and initials, year of publication, title of paper, title of publication* (<u>underlined</u>), *volume and issue number* (of a journal), *publisher and form* (book, conference proceedings), *page numbers.*

Figures

- All illustrations, whether diagrams or photographs, are referred to as Figures. They should be black and white, not colour, and numbered sequentially. Please place them at the end of the paper, rather than interspersed in text.
- Originals of line diagrams will be photographically reduced and used directly. All artwork for figures must be black and white and prepared to the highest possible standards. Bear in mind that lettering may be reduced in size by a factor of 2 or 3, and that fine lines may disappear.

Translated Works

- Difficulty often arises in translating acronyms, so it is best to spell out an acronym in English (for example, IIRP—French personal income tax).
- Similarly, labels and suffixes need careful attention where the letters refer to words which have been translated.
- The names of mathematical functions may change in translation—check against an English or American mathematical reference text.

Units of Measurement

- Inderscience journal follows the *Système International* for units of measurement.
- Imperial units will be converted, except where conversion would affect the meaning of a statement, or imply a greater or lesser degree of accuracy.

Appendix 1: Sample Cover Letter/E-mail [the example used is the *IJEB*]

January 1, 2003
Dear Editor of the *[please type in journal title or acronym]*:

Enclosed is a paper, entitled "**Mobile Agents for Network Management.**" Please accept it as a candidate for publication in the *[journal title]*. Below are our responses to your submission requirements.

1. Title and the central theme of the article.

Paper title. "**Mobile Agents for Network Management.**" This study reviews the concepts of mobile agents and distributed network management system. It proposes a mobile agent-based implementation framework and creates a prototype system to demonstrate the superior performance of a mobile agent-based network over the conventional client-server architecture in a large network environment.

2. Which subject/theme of the Journal the material fits

New enabling technologies (if no matching subject/theme, enter 'Subject highly related to *[subject of journal]* but not listed by *[please type in journal title or acronym]*)

3. Why the material is important in its field and why the material should be published in [please type in journal title or acronym]?

The necessity of having an effective computer network is rapidly growing alongside the implementation of information technology. Finding an appropriate network management system has become increasingly important today's distributed environment. However, the conventional centralized architecture, which routinely requests the status information of local units by the central server, is not sufficient to manage the growing requests. Recently, a new framework that uses mobile agent technology to assist the distributed management has emerged. The mobile agent reduces network traffic, distributes management tasks, and improves operational performance. Given today's bandwidth demand over the Internet, it is important for the *[journal title/acronym]* readers to understand this technology and its benefits. This study gives a real-life example of how to use mobile agents for distributed network management. It is the first in the literature that reports the analysis of network performance based on an operational prototype of mobile agent-based distributed network. We strongly believe the contribution of this study warrants its publication in the *[journal title/acronym]*.

4. Names, addresses, and email addresses of four expert referees.

Prof. Dr. William Gates
Chair Professor of Information Technology
321 Johnson Hall
Premier University Lancaster, NY 00012
-6666, USA
phone: +1-888-888-8888
fax: +1-888-888-8886
e-mail: wgates@lancaster.edu
Expertise: published a related paper
("TCP/IP and OSI: Four Strategies
for Interconnection") in CACM, 38(3),
pp. 188-198. Relationship: I met Dr. Gate
only once at a conference in 1999. I didn't
know him personally.

Assoc Prof. Dr. John Adams
Director of Network Research Center
College of Business Australian University
123, Harbor Drive Sydney,
Australia 56789
phone: +61-8-8888-8888
fax: +61-8-8888-8886
e-mail: jadams@au.edu.au
Expertise: published a related paper
("Creating Mobile Agents") in IEEE
TOSE, 18(8), pp. 88-98.
Relationship: None. I have never
met Dr. Adams.

Assoc Prof. Dr. Chia-Ho Chen
Chair of MIS Department
College of Management
Open University
888, Putong Road
Keelung, Taiwan 100
phone: +886-2-8888-8888
fax: +886-2-8888-8886
e-mail: chchen@ou.edu.tw
Expertise: published a related paper
("Network Management for E-Commerce")
in IJ Electronic Business, 1(4), pp. 18-28.
Relationship: Former professor, dissertation
chairman.

Mr. Frank Young
Partner, ABC Consulting
888, Seashore Highway
Won Kok, Kowloon
Hong Kong
phone: +852-8888-8888
fax: +852-8888-8886
e-mail: fyoung@abcc.com
Expertise: Mr. Young provides
consulting services extensively to his
clients regarding network management
practices. Relationship: I have worked
with Mr. Young in several consulting
projects in the past three years.

Finally, this paper is our original unpublished work and it has not been submitted to any other journal for reviews.

Sincerely,

Johnny Smith

For further detailed instructions please see **www.inderscience.com**.

Global Perspectives on Accounting Education

ADDRESS FOR SUBMISSION:

Dennis Bline, Editor
Global Perspectives on Accounting
    Education
Bryant University
Accounting Department
Faculty Suite A
1150 Douglas Pike
Smithfield, RI 02917
USA
Phone: 401-232-6402
E-Mail: gpae@bryant.edu
Web: www.gpae.bryant.edu

CIRCULATION DATA:

Reader: Academics
Frequency of Issue: Posted as accepted.
Sponsor/Publisher:

PUBLICATION GUIDELINES:

Manuscript Length: Submit Electronic
Copies Required: Electronic
Computer Submission: Yes Email
Format: MS Word, WordPerfect or ASCII
Fees to Review: 50.00 US$

Manuscript Style:
    See Manuscript Guidelines

REVIEW INFORMATION:

Type of Review: Blind Review
No. of External Reviewers: 2
No. of In House Reviewers: 1
Acceptance Rate: 11-20%
Time to Review: 2 - 3 Months
Reviewers Comments: Yes
Invited Articles: 0-5%
Fees to Publish: 0.00 US$

MANUSCRIPT TOPICS:
Accounting Education

MANUSCRIPT GUIDELINES/COMMENTS:

Topics Include. Course Innovation; Pedagogy; Instructional Resources; Replicated Studies; Accounting Faculty Issues (e.g., Productivity, Evaluation, Promotion); Technology in Accounting Education

About the Journal
Global Perspectives on Accounting Education is an academic, peer-reviewed journal that publishes research and instructional resources relevant to accounting faculty and accounting education worldwide. The journal welcomes manuscripts from any and all countries. Manuscripts can make either a direct or indirect contribution to accounting education to be considered for publication. An example of an indirect contribution could be a study that bridges education in accounting and other disciplines. The journal also welcomes studies replicating prior published works to assess the generalizability of existing literature.

Submitted articles should fit one of the following three categories:

- Empirical articles - these articles will include data analysis (e.g., experimental research and survey). Types of manuscripts considered in this section include, but are not limited to, those investigating teaching assessment, faculty issues such as promotion and tenure, experimental studies such as different teaching methods, and psychometric investigations of instruments used to gather data. Authors must provide sufficient information to allow knowledgeable readers to fully understand the manner in which the study was conducted and the analysis performed. This information includes survey instruments used to gather data, tests conducted pertaining to non-response bias, validity, and internal consistency, and discussions of control measures implemented in experimental studies.

- Non-empirical articles - types of manuscripts considered in this section include, but are not limited to, those investigating curriculum issues such as innovative presentations of subject matter in class and educational cases. Authors must adequately document teaching innovations including solutions illustrating how the teaching innovation differs from traditional presentation. Education cases must include a complete set of teaching notes accompanied by any necessary supplemental tables or schedules to document computations.

- Replication studies - these articles will include a complete or partial replication of a previously published study and may include an extension beyond the replication. Authors are encouraged to contact the author of a replicated study to ensure the replication is valid. The author of the replicated study will be asked to be a third reviewer. Authors must describe how the replication study is similar and/or different from the previously published study. Authors should present results in the same manner as the previously published study for comparison purposes. Presentation of additional results is also permitted. Of particular interest to the journal are replication studies across geographic boundaries testing the generalizability of findings.

Submission of Manuscripts
1. Manuscripts may not be currently under consideration by any other publication outlet.

2. A nonrefundable submission fee of $50 in U.S. funds is required for manuscripts to be reviewed. The submission fee can be paid by credit card or check.

To pay by credit card, click on the PayPal icon on the journals webpage. Checks should be made payable to *Global Perspectives on Accounting Education* and mailed to the address below.

3. All submissions and correspondence should be made to the editor at **gpae@bryant.edu**. The editor can also be reached by phone at (401) 232-6402, or by fax at (401) 232-6319.

4. Revisions must be submitted within 12 months of the initial editorial decision date; otherwise the manuscript will be considered a new submission.

Manuscript Preparation
1. Manuscripts should be formatted for an 8½" x 11" (or A4) page with 1" margins.

2. Manuscript text should be double spaced except for indented quotes.

3. Authors should not identify themselves directly or indirectly.

4. Two files should be electronically submitted to **gpae@bryant.edu** in Word, WordPerfect, or ASCII format. The cover page file should contain the title of the paper, the author's name, title, affiliation, acknowledgments, and footnote regarding the author's willingness to share the data. The manuscript file should contain the abstract, body of the manuscript, references, appendixes, tables, figures, exhibits, and footnotes.

5. The abstract for empirical and replication manuscripts should present the study's purpose, main method of analysis, and primary results. The abstract for non-empirical manuscripts should present the paper's purpose and the subject area. The abstract should be 100-150 words.

6. All pages, including appendices, are to be serially numbered.

7. Headings should be arranged as follows:

LEVEL ONE, CENTERED, BOLD, ALL CAPITAL
Level Two, Flush Left, Bold, Upper and Lower Case
Level Three, Flush Left, Italicized, Upper and Lower Case
Level Four, indented, bold, lower case. Immediately followed by the text

8. Tables, Figures, Exhibits, and Appendixes should conform to the following:
a.   Tables, Figures, Exhibits, and Appendixes should be placed at the end of the manuscript. Each should be numbered and include a title indicating the contents of the table or figure.
b.   Each table, figure, exhibit, and appendix must be referenced in the body of the text.
c.   Tables, figures, and exhibits should be interpretable without reference to the text.

9. Citations. Works cited will be indicated with the (Author, year) notation unless the author's name is used in the sentence then the citation is Author (year). Page numbers are to be included (Author, year. p. xx) where direct quotes are used. Citation examples:
a.   One author: (Chasteen, 2002)
b.   Two authors: (Almer and Kaplan, 2002)
c.   Three or more authors: (Fogarty et al., 2000)
d.   More than one work cited: (Fogarty et al., 2000; Almer and Kaplan, 2002)
e.   Two or more works by one author: (Ponemon, 1992; 1993)
f.   Two or more works by one author in the same year: Bernardi (1994a; 1994b)
g.   Quote: (Thorne, 2000. p. 151)
h.   Author's name used in the sentence: Thorne (2000)

10. Reference List. Authors must include a reference list containing only those works cited in the manuscript. References must contain the information necessary to identify the work.
a.   Order items in the reference list alphabetically by the surname of the first author or the organization responsible for the citation.

b.   Use authors' initials in place of proper names.

c.   Journal titles should not be abbreviated.

d.   Multiple works by the same author are to be listed chronologically.

e.   Multiple works by the same author in the same year are to be indicated by letters after the publication date.

f.   Reference examples:

Almer, E. D., and S. E. Kaplan. 2002. The Effects of Flexible Work Arrangements on Stressors, Burnout, and Behavioral Job Outcomes in Public Accounting. *Behavioral Research In Accounting* (Vol. 14) 1-34.

Bernardi, R. 1994a. Fraud Detection: The Effect of Client Integrity and Competence and Auditor Cognitive Style. *Auditing: A Journal of Practice & Theory* (Supplement) 68-97.

---, 1994b. Validating Research Results When Cronbach's Alpha is Below .70: A Methodological Procedure. *Educational and Psychological Measurement* (Vol. 54) 766-776.

Chasteen, L. G. 2002. Equity Method Accounting and Intercompany Transactions. *Issues in Accounting Education* (Vol. 17, No. 2) 185-196.

Financial Accounting Standards Board. 1982. *Related Party Disclosures.* Statement of Financial Accounting Standards No. 57. (Norwalk, CT: FASB).

Fogarty, T. J., J. Singh, G. K. Rhoads, R. K. Moore. 2000. Antecedents and Consequences of Burnout in Accounting: Beyond the Role Stress Model. *Behavioral Research In Accounting* (Vol. 12) 31-67.

May, C. B., and G. S. May. 2003. *Effective Writing: A Handbook for Accountants.* (New Jersey, Prentice Hall).

Ponemon, L. 1992. Auditor Under Reporting of Time and Moral Reasoning: An Experimental Lab Study. *Contemporary Accounting Research* (Vol. 9) 171-189.

---, 1993. The Influence of Ethical Reasoning on Auditors' Perception of Management's Competence and Integrity. *Advances in Accounting* (Vol. 11) 1-29.

Thorne, L. 2000. The Development of Two Measures to Assess Accountants' Prescriptive and Deliberative Moral Reasoning. *Behavioral Research in Accounting* (Vol. 12) 139-169.

Harvard Business Review

ADDRESS FOR SUBMISSION:

Editor
Harvard Business Review
60 Harvard Way
Boston, MA 02163
USA
Phone: 617-783-7400
E-Mail: hbr_editorial@hbsp.harvard.edu
Web: www.hbsp.harvard.edu

PUBLICATION GUIDELINES:

Manuscript Length: See Guidelines
Copies Required: See Guidelines
Computer Submission:
Format:
Fees to Review: 0.00 US$

Manuscript Style:
Chicago Manual of Style

CIRCULATION DATA:

Reader: Business Persons
Frequency of Issue: Bi-Monthly
Sponsor/Publisher: Harvard University

REVIEW INFORMATION:

Type of Review: Editorial Review
No. of External Reviewers: 0
No. of In House Reviewers: 3+
Acceptance Rate: 0-5%
Time to Review: 1 - 2 Months
Reviewers Comments: No
Invited Articles: 31-50%
Fees to Publish: 0.00 US$

MANUSCRIPT TOPICS:
Accounting Information Systems; Accounting Theory & Practice; Auditing; Cost Accounting; Government & Non Profit Accounting; Tax Accounting

MANUSCRIPT GUIDELINES/COMMENTS:

The *Harvard Business Review* has one goal: to be the source of the best new ideas for people creating, leading, and transforming business. Since its founding in 1922, *HBR* has a proud tradition of being the world's preeminent business magazine, publishing cutting-edge, authoritative thinking on the key issues facing managers.

HBR's articles cover a wide range of topics that are relevant to different industries, sectors, management functions, and geographic locations. They focus on such areas as strategy, leadership, teams, entrepreneurship, marketing, manufacturing, career management, and the war for talent. While the topics may very, all *HBR* articles share certain characteristics. They are written for senior executive by experts whose authority comes from careful analysis study, and experience. In addition, the ideas presented in these articles have been tested in the real world of business and can be translated into action.

HBR readers are business executives in organizations of all sizes and kinds. Their interests – in improving performance, in learning and benefiting from the thinking and experience of experts–shape what *HBR* editors look for when reviewing submissions. Proposals for articles that demonstrate clear and bold thinking, fresh and useful ideas, accessible and jargon-free expressions, and unambiguous authority and expertise are those most likely to meet our readers' needs.

The best way to inquire about *HBR's* potential interest in a topic is to prepare a three to four page summary. It can be submitted by mail or electronically and should answer the following questions:

1. What is the central message of the article you propose to write? Moreover, what is new, useful, counterintuitive, or important about your idea?
2. What are the real-world implications of the proposed article? Can the central message be applied in businesses today, and if so, how?
3. Who is the audience for your article? Why should a busy manager stop and read it?
4. What kind of research have you conducted to support the argument or logic in your article?
5. What academic, professional, or personal experience will you draw on to make your argument convincing? In other words, what is the source of your authority?

After you have answered these questions, please write an introduction to the articles, three to four paragraphs long, that lays out your main argument and suggests the structure of the manuscript that will follow.

Each issue of *HBR* contains both feature articles and departments:

- Each feature is an in-depth, rigorous presentation of breakthrough thinking and its application in the real world of business. They offer breakthrough ideas to help business leaders establish an intellectual agenda for discussion—and change—within their companies.
- The **Forethought** department is a survey of ideas, trends, people, and practices on the business horizon. Each issue contains approximately six Forethought pieces, including brief interviews, charts, opinion pieces, and short (750 words) discussions of provocative research.
- The *HBR* **Case Study** is a fictional account of a business dilemma with advice from four experts on how to "solve" that dilemma. The case study often focuses on difficult personal and interpersonal crises.
- The **First Person** department consists of personal business stories that contain lessons for executives.
- *HBR* **at Large** presents incisive reportage on business trends, phenomena, companies, or individuals.
- **Different Voice** features people from outside of business whose ideas hold salient lessons for those within.
- **Best Practice** articles present in-depth descriptions of the how and why behind successful business practices.
- **Tool Kits** provide a nuts-and-bolts explanation of a highly useful business tool that can be translated into action at many companies.
- **Big Picture** explores broad economic, social, political, or demographic trends affecting business.

- **The Entrepreneur** is a new section in *HBR*. As the title suggests, these articles tackle the particular challenges involved in starting up new businesses.
- **Frontiers** is a forum for forward-looking articles that explore exciting new trends or developments affecting business.
- **Managing Yourself** explores new ideas about the personal development of managers and leaders.

HBR readers are business executives in organizations of all sizes and kinds. Their interests —in improving performance, in learning and benefiting from the thinking and experience of experts—shape what *HBR* editors look for when reviewing submissions. Proposals for articles that demonstrate clear and bold thinking, fresh and useful ideas, accessible and jargon-free expression, and unambiguous authority and expertise are those most likely to meet our readers' needs.

Please email the proposal to: **hbr_editiorial@hbsp.harvard.edu**.

HBR deeply appreciates the time and energy required to prepare a proposal for our publication, and we are grateful to you for that investment. While we do receive many submissions, we are always looking for new sources of important, eminently useful ideas. We thank you again for your interest.

ICFAI Journal of Audit Practice (The)

ADDRESS FOR SUBMISSION:

E. N. Murthy, Editor
ICFAI Journal of Audit Practice (The)
The ICFAI University Press
#6-3-354/1 Stellar Sphinx, Road No. 1
Banjara Hills, Panjagutta
Hyderabad 500 082
Andhra Pradesh,
India
Phone: +91 (40) 23430-431 to 436
E-Mail: awjap@icfai.org
  gpadmavathi@icfai.org
  info@icfaipress.org
Web: www.icfaipress.org

PUBLICATION GUIDELINES:

Manuscript Length: 30+
Copies Required: Two
Computer Submission: Yes Disk, Email,
  Web
Format: MS Word
Fees to Review: 0.00 US$

Manuscript Style:
  See Manuscript Guidelines

CIRCULATION DATA:

Reader: Academics
Frequency of Issue: Quarterly
Sponsor/Publisher: ICFAI University Press

REVIEW INFORMATION:

Type of Review: Blind Review
No. of External Reviewers: 2
No. of In House Reviewers: 2
Acceptance Rate: 50%
Time to Review: 2 - 3 Months
Reviewers Comments: Yes
Invited Articles: 31-50%
Fees to Publish: 0.00 US$

MANUSCRIPT TOPICS:
Auditing

MANUSCRIPT GUIDELINES/COMMENTS:

The ICFAI Journal of Audit Practice is a quarterly journal that focuses on internal audit, audit of financial statements, audit education, cost audit, tax audit, audit standards and assurances, social audit, environmental audit and quality audit.

This journal contributes to our advancement of knowledge in auditing, addresses the changing function of an auditor, the contemporary areas in auditing requiring attention and the constructive influence they have on the companies, corporate governance, the investors and public at large. It brings the vast amount of research and thoughts in the area of auditing taking place globally and adds to the Knowledge bank of public, particularly the Academicians & Researchers. The journal also provides a platform for cutting-edge research for accountants, finance professionals and auditors.

Given the corporate scandals and the call for more transparent accounting, the profession of accountancy, the profession of auditing has been witnessing a significant transformation.· Auditing as a discipline is receiving more attention from academicians and Researchers. The editorials address various issues in accounting and auditing receiving attention and the various hot and controversial topics from audit planning to Auditor independence.

Information to Authors

Manuscripts submitted for publication should be in English and typed in double space only on one side of the paper with a wide margin. Footnotes should be listed consecutively in the text with superscript Arabic numerals. All footnotes typed in double space should be given separately at the end of the text. In the case of bibliographical and footnotes, references should be on a separate sheet. Authors are solely responsible for obtaining permission from original sources for longer quotations and any other material they wish to cite in their texts. The following format should be used for referring books, articles in Journals etc. in the reference.

Maurice D. Levi, International Finance, (International Edition, Finance Series, McGraw – Hill publication Co., 1990)

Berndt, E.R. and Christensen, L.R. (1973). "The Translog Function and The Substitution of Equipment, Structures and Labor in U.S. manufacturing 1929-68". Journal of Econometrics, March.

All tables must be consecutively numbered using Arabic numerals with appropriate titles. The title of the tables should not be underlined. All notes to tables should be given at the bottom of the respective table. The articles should end with a non-technical summary statement of the conclusion.

Diagrams, graphs, charts should be drawn in black ink on a glossy white paper with all axes clearly positioned.

A brief resume of the author/authors should accompany the research articles.

Please note that articles will be published in both print form and in the Internet edition. The Journal cannot be held responsible for unauthorized use of its contents.

Softcopy (MS Word is the choice of format) of the article/paper should be sent by e-mail in addition to the hardcopy of the manuscripts.

Articles are accepted for publication on the understanding that these contain original unpublished work not submitted for publication anywhere else. Papers presented/submitted in a conference/seminar must be clearly indicated at the bottom of the first page and the author should specify with whom the copyright rests.

Articles are processed through a blind referral system by experts in the subject areas. To ensure anonymity, the writer's name, designation and other details should only appear on the first page along with the title of the article.

All the manuscripts should be addressed to:
The Editor,
The ICFAI Journal of Audit Practice
The ICFAI University Press, 6-3-354/1, Stellar Sphinx,
Road No. 1, Banjara Hills, Panjagutta,
Hyderabad – 500 082, Andhra Pradesh, India.
Tel: +91 (40) 23430-448 to 451;
Fax: +91 (40) 23430-447
Email: **awjap@icfai.org**
Website: **www.icfaipress.org**

IDBA Journal of Information Technology

ADDRESS FOR SUBMISSION:

Kamal N Agarwal, Dinesh K Sharma, Co-
Eds
IDBA Journal of Information Technology
15319 Briarcliff Manor Way
Burtonsville, MD 20866
USA
Phone: 301-476-7562
E-Mail: kagarwal1@yahoo.com
  kagarwal@howard.edu
  dksharma@mail.umes.edu
Web: www.idba.us

PUBLICATION GUIDELINES:

Manuscript Length: 16-20
Copies Required: One
Computer Submission: Yes Email
Format: MS Word
Fees to Review: 0.00 US$

Manuscript Style:
  American Psychological Association

CIRCULATION DATA:

Reader: Business Persons, Academics
Frequency of Issue: Yearly
Sponsor/Publisher: International Digital
  Business Academy (IDBA)

REVIEW INFORMATION:

Type of Review: Blind Review
No. of External Reviewers: 2
No. of In House Reviewers: 0
Acceptance Rate: New J
Time to Review: 2 - 3 Months
Reviewers Comments: Yes
Invited Articles: New J
Fees to Publish: 50.00 US$

MANUSCRIPT TOPICS:
Accounting Information Systems; Government & Non Profit Accounting

MANUSCRIPT GUIDELINES/COMMENTS:

Please note that guidelines are being provided to the authors of accepted papers so that they can prepare their manuscripts for publication in the *IDBA Journal of Digital Business Review* or other IDBA journals focused on other issues. You may use these guidelines at the moment to start on your manuscript. Authors are encouraged to use these guidelines to submit manuscripts for review at the initial stage as well for conferences and journals.

Introduction. These "Manuscript Guidelines" are for papers that are accepted for publication in the Conference related IDBA journals and presentations. All IDBA conference papers and papers published in IDBA journals are peer-reviewed, hence classifying these publications as "double blind peer-reviewed". Authors should follow the guidelines very closely in order to maintain the publication consistency in terms of style, appearance, and so forth. If authors fail to follow these guidelines, the Editor reserves the right to reject publication of those papers in IDBA conference specific journals or IDBA other publications.

Please use the instruction sheet as an example or guide. Please note how the title and author information is displayed below:

BUSINESS CONTINUITY PLAN AND DISASTER RECOVERY
Kamal Nayan Agarwal, Howard University, USA

(As shown above, for each author on one separate, single-spaced, centered line: First Name Last Name, Institution, Country. DO NOT INCLUDE TITLES, such as Dr., Professor, and Prof.)

Page Size. Preferably 8 ½" x 11" or nearest size (NO LEGAL SIZE or SMALLER THAN 8 ½ X 11)

Page Limit. All manuscripts are limited to FOUR (4) pages. (There will be a charge of $50 for each additional page which must be paid with your submission. Your manuscript will not be published if you fail to pay for additional pages.)

Margins. 1" on all four sides (top, bottom, left and right).

Title. Preferably short manuscript title, centered, all capital letters, bold, 14 point Times New Roman

Author. Immediately following paper title, single-spaced, centered, bold, 10 point Times New Roman. On a separate line for each author: First Name, Last Name, Institution, Country e-mail address.

Headings. Preferably short. Left flushed, all capital letters, bold, 10 point Times New Roman.

Text/Body. 10 point Times New Roman, left flushed, no indention. Paragraphs begin at left margin and right justified. DO NOT NUMBER PAGES. Pages will be numbered consecutively at the time of publication by the Editor. However, use pencil lightly at bottom right corner to indicate page sequence/numbers that can be easily erased later on.

Spacings. All text SINGLE-SPACED, between paragraphs use Double Space.

Abstract. Begin your manuscript with an abstract of about 100 words, providing an overview of your research objectives, methodology, findings, etc. Include ABSTRACT as heading, left flushed and triple-spaced below the last author's name, affiliation, country, and e-mail.

Citations and References. The use of citations and references should be as limited as possible in order to save space. Only the most important sources should be cited and listed. Unlisted references should not be cited, and listed references must be cited in the body. Within your text, reference citations should consist of the author's last name and date of publication enclosed within parentheses. Example: (Agarwal, 2001). Do not use footnotes in your text.

218

All materials cited should be listed in an alphabetical order under the heading of REFERENCES starting at left margin. Do not number references. There should be double space between the REFERENCES heading and the first reference listing and between the two listings thereafter. However, each reference should be single-spaced.

Example of journal article
Garg, Rajendar K. (1996), "The Influence of positive and negative wording and issue involvement on responses to likert scales in Marketing Research", Journal of the Market Research Society, Vol. 38, No. 3, 235-246.

Example of a book
Turban, Efrain et al., (2004), *Electronic Commerce*, Prentice Hall, 2004

Tables and Figures. Tables and figures should be placed close to where they are cited, and they should be high quality and camera-ready. They should be placed flush with the left-hand margin and have proper numbering, headings and other notations.

Submission Deadline. Please follow the submission deadlines. For the final paper submission for publication, camera-ready copies and registration materials/fees must be received.

Items to Submit. Submit the following items:
1. Registration fee (in US$ payable to International Digital Business Academy or IDBA) please note that no paper will be published or placed in the program until the registration fee is received. See Instructions for Payments for remitting your fee.
2. Two CAMERA-READY copies of your manuscript (supported by a piece of cardboard)
3. Two copies of a cover sheet, containing your title and each author's name, organizational affiliation, physical address, telephone numbers, fax numbers, e-mail address, etc.
4. A 3 ½" DISKETTE (1.44 MB), or CD, containing an electronic file of your manuscript, a file of your abstract, and a file of your cover sheet in MS Word format. (Please make sure you diskette or CD is virus-free and contains no other files.)

Contact. For questions or information, send an e-mail to **kagarwal1@yahoo.com**.

Where to Send Manuscripts, Etc. Mail the items listed above to:
International Digital Business Academy
15319 Briarcliff Manor Way
Burtonsville, MD 20866, USA

Information Systems Control Journal (IS Audit & Control Journal)

ADDRESS FOR SUBMISSION:

Jen Blader, Publications Manager
Information Systems Control Journal (IS
    Audit & Control Journal)
Info. Systems Audit and Control Assoc.
3701 Algonquin Road, Suite 1010
Rolling Meadows, IL 60008
USA
Phone: 847-590-7458
E-Mail: publication@isaca.org
Web: www.isaca.org

PUBLICATION GUIDELINES:

Manuscript Length: 8-10
Copies Required: One
Computer Submission: Yes
Format: ASCII, MS Word, WP:PC or MAC
Fees to Review: 0.00 US$

Manuscript Style:
    See Manuscript Guidelines

CIRCULATION DATA:

Reader: Business Persons
Frequency of Issue: Bi-Monthly
Sponsor/Publisher: Information Systems
    Audit and Control Association (ISACA)

REVIEW INFORMATION:

Type of Review: Editorial Review
No. of External Reviewers: 3+
No. of In House Reviewers: 2
Acceptance Rate: 50%
Time to Review: 2 - 3 Months
Reviewers Comments: See Below
Invited Articles: 50% +
Fees to Publish: 0.00 US$

MANUSCRIPT TOPICS:
Accounting Information Systems; Auditing; Computer Security

MANUSCRIPT GUIDELINES/COMMENTS:

The *Information Systems Control Journal* is a bi-monthly publication of the Information Systems Audit and Control Association (ISACA). The *Journal* provides professional development information to those spearheading IT governance and those involved with information systems audit, control and security. This leading industry publication is read by more than 28,000 professionals in over 100 countries around the world. This select audience includes members of the Information Systems Audit and Control Association, subscribers, university libraries worldwide, and copies circulated within organizations in diverse industries.

The *Journal* provides important information on industry advancements and professional development to those involved in the IS audit, control and security community. Each issue gives significant attention to a single topic, but touches on other topics of interest as well, to ensure well-rounded coverage.

Editorial Calendar

We invite you to submit articles on any topics that are part of the *Journal's* editorial calendars which can be found on our website at **http://www.isaca.org**.

Why Invest in Being Published?

Publishing an article in the *Information Systems Control Journal* offers you several benefits. It places your name in front of your peers, establishes you as an expert in a technical area of IS audit and control, and enables you to exchange ideas with your colleagues.

Who May Write and About What?

Authors should cover either new developments in the field or in-depth technically oriented subjects. Major features should have broad appeal and focus on practical matters; purely theoretical material is not solicited. Authors are not required to be association members.

The *Information Systems Control Journal* predominantly publishes original manuscripts. However, in some cases, finished manuscripts also will be considered. Advertising and public relations agency submissions are considered only if the submissions are objective, balanced and cite examples from US as well as non-US countries.

Our Reader Profile

The *Information Systems Control Journal's* approximately 28,000 readers are practitioners, managers and senior executives in 100 countries around the world. The circulation list is a combination of association members and paid subscribers, which includes university, corporate and government libraries worldwide.

According to a recent reader survey:

- Over half of the *Journal* readers hold the job titles of IS auditor, IS audit manager or IS consultant. Other well-represented titles among the readership include audit director, IS security manager, external audit partner/manager, external auditor and internal auditor.
- Nearly two-thirds of *Journal* readers work in companies with more than 1,000 employees; over half work in companies with between one and seven IS audit staff on site.
- Two-thirds of *Journal* readers read three of the last four issues of the magazine; three-quarters read more than half of every issue.
- Thirty-five percent pass their copy of the *Journal* along to at least three other people. More than 80 percent save their copies for future reference.
- Eighty-six percent of readers express satisfaction with the *Journal's* ability to provide them information they need in their jobs. An equal number believe the technical level of the *Journal* is just right.

Types of Articles Accepted

Articles may be factual recitations of research or experiential findings, or they may express the author's opinion on a topic pertinent to *Journal* readers. (Opinion articles will be clearly identified as such.) Articles should be from two to eight double-spaced pages in length. Articles may be edited for length and appropriateness of content for our readers.

A strong article will co-mingle the pertinent facts with references to personal experience, and use anecdotes to illustrate the author's key points. Quotations from other experts involved also add to the article's depth. Please obtain quotes and add perspective from as broad a mix of countries as possible, in recognition of the international nature of the *Journal* readership.

Articles based on surveys or questionnaires must indicate when and where the study was done, relate the number of respondents, and include a brief analysis of the results and an evaluation of the significance of the results.

Authors are strongly encouraged to include exhibits, graphics and artwork for an article. They will assist the reader in comprehending and retaining the information in your article. Such items are treated as text manuscripts requiring the same warranties and assignments. Art files should be submitted separately from the text, in tif or gif format.

Book reviews are printed occasionally to provide an impartial evaluation to our readers. While reviews are generally assigned to authors by the *Journal* staff, review submissions from an independent source are sometimes accepted. Review articles should be from two to four double-spaced pages. Product illustrations or photographs are helpful, submitted separately from the text, in tif or gif format. To request a copy of the guidelines for writing a book review, please e-mail **jblader@isaca.org**.

Submission Requirements
The following guidelines must be followed when formatting a document for submission to the *Journal*:
- Electronic submissions in Microsoft Word are preferable.
- These documents parameters must be followed:
  - Turn off the hyphenation.
  - Double-space lines.
  - Number pages number in the upper right corner.
  - Turn off the right justify option.
  - Do not use automation headers/footers.
  - Turn off track changes.
  - Select standard printer specs.
  - Avoid special characters or keys. (For example, for indents use the TAB rather than the indent key.)
- Article length should be from four to 10 pages, double-spaced. Articles may be edited for length and appropriateness of content for *Journal* readers.
- Use endnotes at the end of the article, rather than footnotes, to credit sources.
- Include a brief biography including current position, background, professional affiliations, and books or articles published.
- Submit material in English. Articles written in both English and other languages are encouraged after discussion with the publications manager **jblader@isaca.org**.

Review Process
Manuscripts submitted to the *Journal* are acknowledged by the staff upon receipt. Manuscripts are subject to review by one or more members of the *Journal* Editorial Committee of the Information Systems Audit and Control Association.

The review process generally takes four to six weeks, depending on the length of the article and its complexity. When the review process is complete, authors will be informed of the reviewers' comments and recommendations regarding publication.

Each article published in the *Journal* becomes part of the *Journal's* overall copyright, as specified in the "Author Warranty and Copyright Assignment" form that authors are asked to sign.

Accepted articles are usually published within three to six months of their acceptance. Published authors receive three copies of the issue. Additional copies may be received upon request. There is no honorarium for *Journal* authors.

Manuscripts for publication in the *Information Systems Control Journal* are edited according to *The New York Times Manual of Style and Usage*. Significant content revisions are returned to the author to be made.

Copyright and Reprints
The Information Systems Audit and Control Association obtains first international serial rights to any published manuscript in the *Information Systems Control Journal*. While every effort is made to preserve the author's (or authors') style, the *Journal* Editorial Committee and staff reserve the right to edit articles.

Article reprints are available after publication. For more information, contact the *Journal's* publications manager, **jblader@isaca.org**.

Send Your Article to...
Please e-mail manuscripts as Microsoft Word attachments, and illustrations as a tif or gif attachment, to: **jblader@isaca.org**

A Checklist for Success
Helpful Hints for Getting Published
Drafting a manuscript takes time and practice. Crafting an article to fit a publication's style requires an eye for editorial detail. Here are some tips regarding the *Information Systems Control Journal* that will help prospective authors become published:

- Keep the readers in mind. Remember that while the readers are a sophisticated audience, both in technical training and in education, they also are busy. Be concise when expressing ideas and use subheadings to break up the text and make skimming easier.
- Follow a journalistic style. Provide details that illustrate the position expressed in the article and follow a logical progression of ideas. Vary sentence lengths to make reading easier and to engage the reader.
- Write in the active voice using active verbs. (For example, use "Write the sentence..." rather than "The sentence should be written...".)

- Use specific examples and case histories to illustrate points, but be careful not to promote an individual, company, product or service.
- Address readers clearly. Avoid unnecessarily complex vocabulary, clichés and excessive jargon.
- Use bullets to make points easier to read.
- Provide a summary of the major points of the article at the end.
- If the article becomes too long, consider separating some of the copy to form a sidebar. Sidebars should include supporting facts or data and should be no longer than 250 words.
- Provide supporting tables, figures, charts or artwork along with the manuscript. Indicators of the location of supporting illustrations should be included in the text, so the Journal staff will know where to place them, but the actual art itself should be submitted in a tif or gif file, separate from the text. Captions should be included that explain the relevance and significance of these supporting items.
- Please do not submit articles with automatic headers and footers or track changes functions engaged.
- Give the article a final edit to eliminate unnecessary words. Make sure paragraphs flow smoothly and logically.

Intelligent Systems in Accounting, Finance and Management

ADDRESS FOR SUBMISSION:

Bob Berry, Editor
Intelligent Systems in Accounting, Finance
  and Management
University of Nottingham
Nottingham University Business School
Nottingham, NG8 1BB
UK
Phone: 44 (0) 115 951 5256
E-Mail: robert.berry@nottingham.ac.uk
  bob.berry@nottingham.ac.uk
Web: www3.interscience.wiley.com

PUBLICATION GUIDELINES:

Manuscript Length: 21-25
Copies Required: Three
Computer Submission: Yes Email
Format: MS Word
Fees to Review: 0.00 US$

Manuscript Style:
  Chicago Manual of Style

CIRCULATION DATA:

Reader: Academics
Frequency of Issue: Quarterly
Sponsor/Publisher: John Wiley & Sons, Inc.

REVIEW INFORMATION:

Type of Review: Blind Review
No. of External Reviewers: 2
No. of In House Reviewers: 0
Acceptance Rate: 11-20%
Time to Review: 2 - 3 Months
Reviewers Comments: Yes
Invited Articles: 0-5%
Fees to Publish: 0.00 US$

MANUSCRIPT TOPICS:
Accounting Information Systems; Auditing; Capital Budgeting; Cost Accounting; Econometrics; Electronic Commerce; Enterprise Information Systems; Finance Information Systems; Tax Accounting

MANUSCRIPT GUIDELINES/COMMENTS:

Intelligent Systems in Accounting, Finance and Management publishes original material concerned with all aspects of intelligent systems in business, finance and management – based applications. It is devoted to the improvement and development of the theory and practice of intelligent system design, development and implementation. It is concerned with what is necessary to move systems out of the lab and what happens when they are moved out of the lab into organizational settings. The journal is designed to appeal both to academics and to practitioners.

Published papers can investigate a number of different issues, including 'research perspectives,' emerging technologies, existing technologies, verification and validation, cognitive models, cognitive science, impact of intelligent systems of organizations, integration of different technologies such as databases and intelligent systems. The prospective author is referred to the editorial in Volume 1 Number 1, for more detailed comments. We also welcome shorter submissions and news items from the business world. Periodically, book reviews, research comments, and notes also will be published.

Overall, the journal provides a communication forum for advancing the theory and practice of the application of advancing the theory and practice of the application of intelligent systems in business and other organizational settings.

Initial Manuscript Submission. Submit five copies of the manuscript (including copies of tables and illustrations) to Bob Berry, Boots Professor of Accounting & Finance, Nottingham University Business School, University of Nottingham, Nottingham, NG8 1BB, United Kingdom.

Authors must also supply
- a Copyright Transfer Agreement with original signature - without this, we are unable to accept the submission,
- permission letters - it is the author's responsibility to obtain written permission to reproduce (in all media, including electronic) material which has appeared in another publication and
- an electronic copy of the final version (see section below).

Submission of a manuscript will be held to imply that it contains original unpublished work and is not being submitted for publication elsewhere at the same time. Submitted material will not be returned to the author, unless specifically requested.

Electronic submission. The electronic copy of the final, revised manuscript must be sent to the Editor **together with** the paper copy. Disks should be PC or Mac formatted; write on the disk the software package used, the name of the author and the name of the journal. We are able to use most word processing packages, but prefer Word or WordPerfect and TeX or one of its derivatives.

Illustrations must be submitted in electronic format where possible. Save each figure as a separate file, in **TIFF** or **EPS** format preferably, and include the source file. Write on the disk the software package used to create them; we favor dedicated illustration packages over tools such as Excel or PowerPoint.

Manuscript style. The language of the journal is English. All submissions including book reviews must have a title, be printed on one side of the paper, be double-line spaced and have a margin of 3cm all round. Illustrations and tables must be printed on separate sheets, and not be incorporated into the text.
- The **title page** must list the full title, short title of up to 70 characters and names and affiliations of all authors. Give the full address, including email, telephone and fax, of the author who is to check the proofs.
- Include the name(s) of any sponsor(s) of the research contained in the paper, along with **grant number(s)**.

226

- Supply an abstract of up to 150 words for all articles [except book reviews]. An abstract is a concise summary of the whole paper, not just the conclusions, and is understandable without reference to the rest of the paper. It should contain no citation to other published work.
- Include up to five **keywords** that describe your paper for indexing purposes.
- Include also a brief autobiography (50 to 100 words) for each author, together with a black and white glossy photograph suitable for reproduction within the journal.

Reference style. References should be quoted in the text as name and year and listed at the end of the paper alphabetically. Where reference is made to more than one work by the same author published in the same year, identify each citation in the text as follows: (Collins, 1998a), (Collins, 1998b). Where three or more authors are listed in the reference list, please cite in the text as (Collins *et al.*, 1998)

All references must be complete and accurate. Online citations should include date of access. If necessary, cite unpublished or personal work in the text but do not include it in the reference list. References should be listed in the following style:

Denna EL, Hansen JV, Meservy RD, Wood LE. 1992. Case-based reasoning and risk assessment in audit judgment. *Intelligent Systems in Accounting, Finance and Management* 1(3): 163-171.

Chan S, Govindan M, Picard JY, Leschiutta E. 199 3. *EDI for Managers, and Auditors.* Electronic Data Interchange Council of Canada: Toronto, Ontario.

Sprague R, Benbast I, El Sawy O, King D Hill TR Sol H Todd P. 1992. Technology environments to support decision processes. In *Information arid Decision Processes,* Stohr E, Konsynski B (eds). IEEE Computer Society Press: Los Alamitos, CA; 167-204.

The Geriatric Website. 1999. http://www.wiley.com/oap/ [1 April 1999]

Illustrations. Supply each illustration on a separate sheet, with the lead author's name and the figure number, with the top of the figure indicated, on the reverse. Supply original **photographs**; photocopies or previously printed material will not be used. Line artwork must be high-quality laser output (not photocopies). Tints are not acceptable; lettering must be of a reasonable size that would still be clearly legible upon reduction, and consistent within each figure and set of figures. Supply artwork at the intended size for printing. The artwork must be sized to the text width of 7cm (single column) and 15cm (double column).

The cost of printing **color** illustrations in the journal will be charged to the author. There is a charge for printing color illustrations of approximately £700 per page. If color illustrations are supplied electronically in either **TIFF** or **EPS** format, they **may** be used in the PDF of the article at no cost to the author, even if this illustration was printed in black and white in the journal. The PDF will appear on the *Wiley InterScience* site.

Copyright. To enable the publisher to disseminate the author's work to the fullest extent, the author must sign a Copyright Transfer Agreement, transferring copyright in the article from the author to the publisher, and submit the original signed agreement with the article presented for publication. A copy of the agreement to be used (which may be photocopied) can be found in the first issue of each volume of *Intelligent Systems in Accounting, Finance and Management*. Copies may also be obtained from the journal editor or publisher, or may be printed from this website.

Further Information. Proofs will be sent to the author for checking. This stage is to be used only to correct errors that may have been introduced during the production process. Prompt return of the corrected proofs, preferably within two days of receipt, will minimize the risk of the paper being held over to a later issue. Twenty-five complimentary offprints will be provided to the author who checked the proofs, unless otherwise indicated. Further offprints and copies of the journal may be ordered. There is no page charge to authors.

Internal Auditing

ADDRESS FOR SUBMISSION:

Andrea Kingston, Editor
Internal Auditing
195 Dartmouth St. #2
Rochester, NY 14607
USA
Phone: 585-244-5709
E-Mail: andrea.kingston@thomson.com
Web: www.ria.thomson.com/journals

CIRCULATION DATA:

Reader: Academics, Internal Auditors, CPA
  Firms
Frequency of Issue: Bi-Monthly
Sponsor/Publisher: RIA / Warren, Gorham
  & Lamont

PUBLICATION GUIDELINES:

Manuscript Length: 2,000-6,000 Words
Copies Required: Electronic
Computer Submission: Yes Preferred
Format: MS Word (any version)
Fees to Review: 0.00 US$

Manuscript Style:
  Chicago Manual of Style

REVIEW INFORMATION:

Type of Review: Editorial Review
No. of External Reviewers: 0
No. of In House Reviewers: 1
Acceptance Rate: 75%
Time to Review: 2 - 3 Weeks
Reviewers Comments: Upon Request
Invited Articles: 11-20%
Fees to Publish: 0.00 US$

MANUSCRIPT TOPICS:
Auditing; Corporate Governance; Ethics; Financial Reporting; Information Technology;
Internal Auditing

MANUSCRIPT GUIDELINES/COMMENTS:

About the Journal
Internal Auditing seeks articles that are primarily practice-oriented and that will be of interest
to those in the internal auditing profession. The intent of *Internal Auditing* is to provide
operational and implementational guidance to internal auditors, with a strong emphasis on a
"how to" approach. Analysis of current developments and trends, results of original research,
case studies, professional standards and issues, and practical advice are all appropriate topics.
Short opinion pieces are also welcome. *Internal Auditing* is published bimonthly in both print
and electronic formats on an annual, paid subscription basis.

It is expected that most articles be in the range of 8 to 30 typed, double-spaced pages (i.e.,
2,000 to 6,000 words), but the subject matter should be the final determinant of length.

Internal Auditing publishes articles only if they have not yet appeared or been accepted for
publication elsewhere.

Manuscript Format Requirements
1. All manuscript copy should be typed, double-spaced, in a PC-compatible word-processing document (preferably Microsoft Word). Manuscripts can be submitted via an e-mail attachment, on diskette, or on CD-ROM. E-mail submission is preferred.

2. All footnotes or references should be typed on a separate page at the end of the manuscript (i.e., they should appear as unembedded endnotes). They should be limited to identification of sources referred to in the text and should include complete information on the source and publisher, including publisher location. References to websites should include the full name of the website, the author of the site's content (if known), and the date the site was accessed.

3. Please keep in mind that *Internal Auditing's* readers are a diverse group with a wide variety of experience and interests. The use of technical or professional jargon and acronyms should be kept to a minimum. Relatively obscure terminology (especially in articles dealing with information technology) should be clearly defined in plain English within the body of the article (not in a footnote).

4. All illustrations, tables, charts, and exhibits should be numbered, provided with a suitable legend, and protected with cardboard if mailed. Whenever possible, electronic versions of the illustrations should be provided with the manuscript.

What to Include
1. Include each author's complete contact information, including address, phone number, fax number, and e-mail address.

2. Include a brief, one-paragraph biography for each author.

3. If substantial material from other sources is included as part of the article, written reprint permission from those sources must accompany the article. Brief quotes from cited sources are not included in this requirement.

Please contact Andrea Kingston via e-mail (**andrea.kingston@thomson.com**) or by calling (585) 244-5709 if you have any questions.

All manuscripts should be sent in an **electronic format** either via e-mail, on diskette, or on CD-ROM to the editor at the address above. E-mail submission is preferred.

What to Expect
Receipt of the manuscript will be acknowledged at the editor's earliest convenience. A final decision on publishing the article is usually reached within two to three weeks, at which time the author will be notified. Please note that publication is at the editor's discretion and is not currently subject to a blind or peer review. It is possible that a blind review will be available for academic authors *by request only*. When in doubt, the submitting author should inquire about the review process currently used. Administrators or accrediting committees who are evaluating publication records should contact the editor if necessary to establish the type of review process used.

If the article is accepted for publication, the editor will send a publishing agreement letter to each author. This brief document must be signed and returned to the editor in a timely manner in order for the article to be published.

Once the issue is printed and mailed, three complimentary copies will be sent to each contributing author.

Internal Auditor

ADDRESS FOR SUBMISSION:

Dave Salierno, Managing Editor
Internal Auditor
The Institute of Internal Auditors
247 Maitland Avenue
Altamonte Springs, FL 32701-4201
USA
Phone: 407-937-1234
E-Mail: ascott@theiia.org
Web: www.theiia.org

CIRCULATION DATA:

Reader: Business Persons
Frequency of Issue: Bi-Monthly
Sponsor/Publisher: The Institute of Internal
    Auditors

PUBLICATION GUIDELINES:

Manuscript Length: 10
Copies Required: Four
Computer Submission: Yes Disk, Email
Format: MS Word
Fees to Review: 0.00 US$

Manuscript Style:
    American Psychological Association

REVIEW INFORMATION:

Type of Review: Blind Review
No. of External Reviewers: 3
No. of In House Reviewers: 3
Acceptance Rate: 21-30%
Time to Review: 2 - 3 Months
Reviewers Comments: No Reply
Invited Articles: 20%
Fees to Publish: 0.00 US$

MANUSCRIPT TOPICS:
Auditing; Corporate Governance; Internal Control; Risk

MANUSCRIPT GUIDELINES/COMMENTS:

Internal Auditor is the professional magazine of The Institute of Internal Auditors and the world's leading publication covering the internal auditing profession. Around the globe, the magazine's readership includes internal auditors; executives and managers in private industry, nonprofit organizations, and government; and professionals in related fields, such as public accounting, education, information systems, and security. *Internal Auditor* provides articles and information on:

• Current auditing techniques and applications.
• Information systems auditing.
• Internal controls and quality assurance.
• Corporate governance.
• Significant research.
• Practical case studies.
• Professional standards.
• General business skills and practices, such as developing communication skills, improving management relations, and hiring and training new staff.

- Updates on professional concerns and trends, such as salaries and reporting relationships.
- Current events that impact the internal auditing profession, such as actions by legislative bodies and other professional organizations.

The magazine's emphasis is on sharing timely, helpful information - indispensable information - for professionals who want to keep pace with the diverse, dynamic field of internal auditing. Information from *Internal Auditor* may be reprinted with the appropriate permission.

Internal Auditor is published six times per year. The editorial content of *Internal Auditor* is divided into two segments: articles and departments. Departments include: Letters, Roundtable, Fraud Findings, In My Opinion, Computers & Auditing, Contract Corner, and Back to Basics.

Editorial Lineup
The *Internal Auditor* Editorial Calendar is distributed to those interested in the special focus of each issue. Of course, articles on other topics are also published in each issue.

Writers Guidelines
The Editorial Content of *Internal Auditor* is divided into two segments: articles and departments. Potential authors with good ideas and information to share need to decide whether their subjects should be explored in depth—and are thus more appropriate to an article format—or whether the submission would work better in one of *Internal Auditor's* departments.

Authors include practitioners who are usually internal auditors but not always; they include senior management; academics, many of whom are involved in relevant research; consultants; and others. Slightly more than 20 percent of *Internal Auditor's* readers are from regions other than North America, so submitted manuscripts should reflect the magazine's global focus.

Feature Articles
One basic criterion for any good manuscript is whether or not the author has something of value to say: Does the manuscript provide information others might need or value? The best catalyst for a good article is likely to come from one's own internal audit experiences. Individuals who have found a way to audit a new high-risk area or to simplify report writing, for example, have information others want and will avidly read. Successful writers put themselves in the position of the readers and think about what the readers want to know about the topic, not only what they as writers want to say about it.

Because writing an article requires a considerable investment of time and energy, potential writers may want to review back issues of *Internal Auditor* to get an idea of the types of material generally published, as well as the general editorial tone and article construction. Authors are also invited to write or call an *Internal Auditor* editor to discuss a particular topic. Editors are always searching for good material and good authors, and such inquiries are usually of value to both the writer and the staff.

Submitting a Feature
Feature manuscripts usually run about 2,500 words, plus exhibits, but can be more or less depending on content. Articles should be submitted in hardcopy as well as on disk, preferably in a Microsoft Word or WordPerfect format. All submissions should be sent to Editor, Internal Auditor, 247 Maitland Ave., Altamonte Springs, FL 32701-4201. The name, address, and telephone number of the author are necessary, even when the manuscript is submitted through an IIA chapter.

Review Process
The review process for manuscripts submitted to *Internal Auditor* generally takes about 8 to 10 weeks. As soon as the manuscript is received, an acknowledgment is sent to the author. Three members of the editorial policy review board, selected for their knowledge of the topic, receive a "blind" copy of the manuscript. They evaluate the manuscript based on:

- Interest to auditors.
- Quality of writing.
- Global perspective.
- Technical soundness.
- Timeliness.
- Originality.

Once the reviewers have made their recommendations, the editor evaluates their comments, makes the final decision on whether to publish, and notifies the author. If an article has been rejected, the author is usually given a consensus comment from the reviewers' critiques. Sometimes the author is asked to rewrite the article and submit it again.

For several reasons, one being that *Internal Auditor* is a bimonthly publication, there may be a substantial time lapse between date of acceptance and date of publication. Accepted articles are filed according to their date of acceptance, but they may not always be published in precise chronological order because of special editorial considerations, an issue focusing on a special theme, for example.

Once the article has been scheduled for publication, the author is notified that the editing process has begun. The editor may suggest changes that are minor or fairly extensive, based on several considerations. The author is sent a copy of the edited manuscript so that any inaccuracies can be corrected before publication. Dialogue between the editor and the author is part of the final editorial process.

234

International Journal of Accounting

ADDRESS FOR SUBMISSION:

Rashad Abdel-khalik, Editor
International Journal of Accounting
University of Illinois
CIREA
320 Wohlers Hall
1206 South Street
Champaign, IL 61820
USA
Phone: 217-333-4545
E-Mail: ciera@uiuc.edu
Web: www.business.uiuc.edu/ciera/

PUBLICATION GUIDELINES:

Manuscript Length: 26-30+
Copies Required: Electronic
Computer Submission: Yes Email
Format: MS Word
Fees to Review: 0.00 US$

Manuscript Style:
Chicago Manual of Style

CIRCULATION DATA:

Reader: Academics
Frequency of Issue: Quarterly
Sponsor/Publisher: Elsevier Inc. / The
Zimmerman Center for International
Education and Research in Accounting

REVIEW INFORMATION:

Type of Review: Blind Review
No. of External Reviewers: 2
No. of In House Reviewers: 0
Acceptance Rate: 11-20%
Time to Review: 2 - 3 Months
Reviewers Comments: Yes
Invited Articles: 0-5%
Fees to Publish: 0.00 US$

MANUSCRIPT TOPICS:
Accounting Theory & Practice; Auditing; Behavioral Accounting; Cost Accounting; Government & Non Profit Accounting; Tax Accounting

MANUSCRIPT GUIDELINES/COMMENTS:

Aims and Scope
The International Journal of Accounting (IJA) aims at publishing accounting research that contributes to the analyses and understanding of international business conditions and transactions. The editors of *IJA* encourage authors to submit high quality research that studies accounting as a subsystem of the cultural, economic and institutional factors of different nations. Other than occasional commissioning of papers on specific topics, the editors of *IJA* will select publishable manuscripts after going through the normal refereeing process.

1. Manuscripts should be submitted electronically to **ciera@uiuc.edu** in a WORD version document.

2. All manuscripts must be double-spaced and numbered consecutively, including an abstract of approximately 100 words, and key words for indexing consistent with JLE Index.

Submitted papers must be neither previously published nor submitted elsewhere. Authors are responsible for obtaining permission from the copyright holder (usually the publisher) to use any lengthy quotations, illustrations, or tables from another source.

3. Books to be reviewed should be sent to Hervé Stolowy, HEC School of Management, Department of Accounting and Management Control, 1, rue de la Libération – 78351, Jouy-in-Josas Cedex, France.

4. The author's full name, affiliation, and e-mail address should appear on the title page only.

5. All tables, figures and illustrations should accompany the manuscript each typed on a separate sheet. Captions should clearly identify the contents of tables and charts. All should be referred to in text and indication given as to location. For example:

TABLE 1 ABOUT HERE

6. Footnotes should be numbered consecutively throughout the manuscript with superscript Arabic numerals. They should be collected in a separate file at the end of the text.

7. References should be cited in the text as follows:

Schweikart and O'Conner (1989) agree with this method. Other studies have found similar results (Schweikart and O'Conner, 1989: Smith, 1991).

On a separate Reference page(s), each cited work should appear, double-spaced, in alphabetical order as follows:

Journal Articles
    Barth, M. E., Clinch, G. J., and Shibano, T. (1999). International accounting harmonization and global equity markets. *Journal of Accounting and Economics*, 26, 201-235.

Books
    Neter, J., Wasserman, W., & Whitmore, G. A. (1993). *Applied Statistics* (4th ed.). Needham Heights, MA: Allyn & Bacon.

    Hofstede, G., and Schrueder, H. (1987). A joint reply to Montagna. In: B. Cushing (Ed.), *Accounting and Culture* (pp. 29-30). Sarasota, FL: American Accounting Association

Upon acceptance the author is to submit one copy of the approved manuscript on a spellchecked. The accuracy of the final draft and proofs is the responsibility of the author.

236

International Journal of Accounting Information Systems

ADDRESS FOR SUBMISSION:

Steve G. Sutton, Editor
International Journal of Accounting
  Information Systems
ELECTRONIC SUBMISSION ONLY
University of Central Florida
School of Accountancy
Orlando, FL 32816
USA
Phone: 407-823-2871
E-Mail: ijais@business.uconn.edu
  ijais@bus.ucf.edu
Web: www.ijais.org

CIRCULATION DATA:

Reader: Academics, Practitioners
Frequency of Issue: Quarterly
Sponsor/Publisher: Elsevier Inc.

PUBLICATION GUIDELINES:

Manuscript Length:
Copies Required: Electronic
Computer Submission: Yes Preferred
Format: MS Word
Fees to Review: 0.00 US$

Manuscript Style:
  See Manuscript Guidelines

REVIEW INFORMATION:

Type of Review: Blind Review
No. of External Reviewers: 2
No. of In House Reviewers: 1
Acceptance Rate: 11-20%
Time to Review: 2 - 3 Months
Reviewers Comments: Yes
Invited Articles: 0-5%
Fees to Publish: 0.00 US$

MANUSCRIPT TOPICS:
Accounting Information Systems; Accounting Theory & Practice; Auditing; Behavioral Accounting

MANUSCRIPT GUIDELINES/COMMENTS:

Description
The *International Journal of Accounting Information Systems* will publish thoughtful, well developed articles that examine the rapidly evolving relationship between accounting and information technology. Articles may range from empirical to analytical, from practice-based to the development of new techniques, but must be related to problems facing the integration of accounting and information technology. The journal will address (but will not limit itself to) the following specific issues: control and auditability of information systems; management of information technology; artificial intelligence research in accounting; development issues in accounting and information systems; human factors issues related to information technology; development of theories related to information technology; methodological issues in information technology research; information systems validation; human-computer

interaction research in accounting information systems. The journal welcomes and encourages articles from both practitioners and academicians.

Guide for Authors
International Journal of Accounting Information Systems is an academic and professional publication whose purpose is to meet the information needs of both practitioners and academicians. The journal publishes thoughtful, well-developed articles that examine the rapidly evolving relationship between accounting and information technology. Articles may range from empirical to analytical, from practice-based to the development of new techniques. Articles must be readable and logically integrated. To be reliable, conclusions must follow logically from the evidence and arguments presented. For empirical reports, sound design and execution are critical. For theoretical treatises, reasonable assumptions and logical development are essential. Relevant articles must be related to problems facing the integration of accounting and information technology.

Specific issues that the journal addresses include, but are not limited to, the following:
- Information systems assurance
- Control and auditability of information systems
- Management of information technology
- Artificial intelligence research in accounting
- Development issues in accounting and information systems
- Human factors issues related to information technology
- Development of theories related to information technology
- Methodological issues in information technology research
- Information systems validation
- Human-computer interaction research in accounting information systems

All manuscripts should be submitted to:
Dr. Steve G. Sutton
School of Business Administration - U41A
University of Connecticut
368 Fairfield Road
Storrs, CT 06269-2041
USA

Manuscripts are submitted with the understanding that they are original, unpublished works and are not being submitted elsewhere. All manuscripts are double-blind refereed and refereed by an associate editor in blind for the first round.

Manuscript. Electronic submission is preferred. Manuscript and instruments should be forwarded as attachments to **ijais@bus.ucf.edu**. If electronic submission is not possible submit the original and three photocopies of the manuscript, typed double-spaced on 8 ½ x 11 in. bond paper. On the title page include names and addresses of authors, academic or professional affiliations, and the complete address of the author to whom proofs and reprint requests should be sent. Also provide a running title of less than 45 characters and spaces, which will appear on alternate pages in the journal. Include an Abstract and list Key Words

238

that best code the contents of the article for indexing purposes. The text proper begins on the following page and ends with a citation of acknowledgments, whenever appropriate. References, tabular material, figure captions, and footnotes follow. Tables and figures are numbered in order of their appearance with Arabic numerals and each should have a brief descriptive title. Footnotes to the text are numbered consecutively with superior Arabic numerals.

Computer Disks. Authors are encouraged to submit a 3 ½" HD/DD computer disk to the editorial office. Please observe the following criteria. When your paper has been refereed, revised if necessary, and accepted, send a disk containing the final version with the final hard copy. Make certain that the disk and hard copy match exactly. Specify what software was used, including which release, e.g. WordPerfect 6.1. Specify what computer was used (IBM compatible PC, Apple Macintosh, etc.) The article file should include all textual material (text, references, tables, figure captions, etc.) and separate illustration files, if available. The file should follow the general instructions on style/arrangement and, in particular, the reference style of this journal as given in the Information for Authors. The file should be single spaced and should use the wrap-around end-of-line feature, i.e. returns at the end of paragraphs only. Place two returns after every element, such as title, headings, paragraphs, figure and table callouts. Be sure to keep a back-up disk for reference and safety.

Mathematical Notation. Use typewritten letters, numbers, and symbols whenever possible. Identify boldface, script letters, etc. at their first occurrence. Distinguish between one and the letter "l" and between zero and the letter "O" whenever confusion might result.

References. Citation in the text is by name(s) of authors, followed by year of publication in parentheses. For references authored by more than two contributors use first author's name and et al. For multiple citation in the same year use a, b, c after year of publication. The reference list should be typed alphabetically according to the following style.

Journal Article
Morrison A.J., Roth K. A taxonomy of business-level strategies in global industries. *Strategic Management Journal* 1992;13:399--418.

Book
Adler, N. *International dimensions of organized behavior.* Boston: PWS Kent, 1991.

Book Chapter
Root, F.R. Some reflections on the evolution of international business as a field of study; From periphery to center. In: D. Nigh, B. Toyne, eds. *International business: Institutions and the dissemination of knowledge.* Columbia (SC): University of South Carolina Press, 1994: 742--745.

Illustrations. Unmounted, glossy, black-and-white photographs or India Ink drawings on white paper should accompany the original copy of the manuscript. Photocopies are suitable for the other three copies of the manuscript. To facilitate identification and processing, on the back of each figure write the number, first author's name, and indicate which side is the top. Captions appear on a separate page.

Proofs and Reprints. The corresponding author will receive proofs, which should be corrected and returned within ten days of receipt or the article will be published without author's corrections. The author is responsible for proofreading the manuscript; the publisher is not responsible for any error not marked by the author on proof. Corrections on proof are limited to printer's errors; no substantial author changes are allowed at this stage. Reprints may be ordered prior to publication; consult the price list accompanying proofs.

Copyright. Upon acceptance of an article by the journal, the author(s) will be asked to transfer copyright of the article to the publisher, Elsevier Science Inc. This transfer will ensure the widest possible dissemination of information under the U.S. Copyright law.

International Journal of Accounting, Auditing and Performance Evaluation

ADDRESS FOR SUBMISSION:

Prem Lal Joshi, Editor-in-Chief
International Journal of Accounting,
   Auditing and Performance Evaluation
University of Bahrain
Business Administration
Department of Accounting
PO Box 32038
Kingdom of Bahrain, 32038
Bahrain
Phone: 00973-17643701
E-Mail: joshi@buss.uob.bh
   prem@acadjoshi.com
Web: www.inderscience.com/ijaape

PUBLICATION GUIDELINES:

Manuscript Length: 26-30
Copies Required: Three
Computer Submission: Yes Email
Format: MS Word
Fees to Review: 0.00 US$

Manuscript Style:
   See Manuscript Guidelines

CIRCULATION DATA:

Reader: Academics, Business Persons
Frequency of Issue: Quarterly
Sponsor/Publisher: Inderscience Enterprises
   Limited

REVIEW INFORMATION:

Type of Review: No Reply
No. of External Reviewers: 3
No. of In House Reviewers:
Acceptance Rate: 10-12%
Time to Review: 2-4 Months
Reviewers Comments: Yes (rigorous
   review)
Invited Articles: 0-10%
Fees to Publish: 0.00 US$

MANUSCRIPT TOPICS:

Accounting Education; Accounting Information Systems; Accounting Theory & Practice; Auditing; Behavioral Accounting; Cost Accounting; Financial Accounting; Financial Management; Financial Services; Government & Non Profit Accounting; International Accounting; Management Accounting; Performance Evaluation; Tax Accounting

MANUSCRIPT GUIDELINES/COMMENTS:

IJAAPE publishes original scholarly papers across the whole spectrum of: financial accounting, managerial accounting, accounting education, auditing, taxation, public sector accounting, capital market and accounting, accounting information systems, performance evaluation, corporate governance, ethics, and financial management. All methodologies, such as analytical, empirical, behavioural, surveys, and case studies are welcome.

IJAAPE encourages contributions especially from emerging markets and economies in transition and studies whose results are applicable across nation states or capable of being adapted to the different accounting and business environments.

Objectives
The primary mission of *IJAAPE* is to create an intellectual and practitioner forum for the exchange of information, knowledge, insights and evidence in the rapidly changing field of accounting, auditing and performance evaluation, from both developed and developing countries, thus representing cross-cultural accounting research.

Readership
The *IJAAPE* readership comprises academics, practitioners, consultants, and research students with an interest in research in the field of accounting, auditing, and performance evaluation systems.

Contents
Besides original papers, etc., *IJAAPE* also has a practitioner forum which aims at publishing case-based studies from practitioners, in particular. It will also publish book reviews. Occasionally, special issues of the journal dedicated to specific themes and topics may be commissioned.

Subject Coverage
Financial Accounting and International Accounting
- Compliance with IASs in emerging and transitioning economies
- IASs and accountant judgment
- Creative accounting and quality of financial reporting
- Financial reporting and capital markets and stock market returns
- Earnings management and shareholder reactions
- Corporate governance practices in the developing and developed worlds: a cross-comparison
- Communication and financial reporting on the internet
- Rule based accounting versus principle based accounting
- Accounting practices for financial instruments
- Financial reporting in emerging economies and those in transition
- International accounting harmonisation strategies
- Social and environmental reporting in Asia and Europe: cross-comparisons
- Financial reporting and adoption of IASs by SMEs
- Cultural impact on financial reporting
- Disclosure of financial forecasts in annual reports
- Accounting practices for intellectual capital and other intangible assets
- Segmental reporting
- International taxation and transfer pricing
- Assessing, measuring, reporting and managing risk in accounting

Auditing
- Audit quality and auditor skills
- Non-audit services and auditor independence
- Auditor judgment
- Audit planning
- Audit committees in developing countries
- Determinants of audit fees
- Audit risks, fraud detection and auditors, auditors' liabilities
- Forensic accounting and auditing
- Board composition, non-executive directors and corporate financial performance
- Value added auditing
- Internal control and internal auditing
- Audit expectations gap
- Systems audit
- International auditing standards
- True and fair view applications
- Assessing, measuring and managing risk in auditing

Performance Measurement and Management Accounting
- Balanced scorecards and performance evaluation
- Non-financial performance measurement
- Performance measurement practices of multinational corporations
- Performance evaluation in service and public sector organisations
- Relationship between performance evaluation and the achievement of organizational objectives
- Measurement and management of intellectual capital
- Changing role of accountants in the new technological era
- Activity-based costing and activity-based management
- Just-in-time and accounting implications
- Quality costs and reporting
- Target costing and strategic cost management practices
- Corporate budgeting practices in emerging capital markets
- Budgetary participation and budgetary slack studies
- Capital budgeting for advanced manufacturing technology
- Profitability analysis, revenue driver analysis, promotional effectiveness, and other approaches to integrate accounting information and marketing
- Assessing, measuring and managing risk in performance evaluation

AIS and Others
- Control, security, and audit of accounting information systems
- Accounting and e-business
- ERP and e-commerce interactions with accounting information systems
- XML and XBRL applications in accounting
- Privacy and security issues in accounting information systems

- Applications of artificial intelligence techniques and emerging technologies in accounting research, practice, and education
- Professional skills versus professional ethics
- International dispersion/diffusion of financial and management accounting practices
- Accounting education in developing countries

Specific Notes for Authors

All papers are refereed through a double blind process. A guide for authors, sample copies and other relevant information for submitting papers are available on the Papers Submission section under Author Guidelines.

To submit a paper, please go to Submission of Papers at:
   http://www.inderscience.com/papers

This is our preferred route for submitting papers; please use it if at all possible. However, if you experience any problems submitting papers in this way, an alternative route is suggested below.

Submitted papers should not have been previously published nor be currently under consideration for publication elsewhere.

As an alternative to using the Submission of Papers site, you may send ONE copy of each manuscript (in hard copy) or one copy in the form of an MS Word file attached to an e-mail (details of both formats in Author Guidelines) to Prof. Prem Lal Joshi, below, with a copy to:
   Editor-in-Chief
   IEL Editorial Office
   PO Box 735
   Olney, Bucks MK46 5WB
   UK
   Fax: +44 1234-240515 E-mail: **ijaape@inderscience.com**

Typescript Preparation

The original typescript should be submitted electronically in A4 size format, with double-spaced typing preferred and a wide margin on the left, following the submission requirements described on the *Journal's* website.

A final paper which would exceed 7000 words or occupy more than 20 pages of the *Journal* may be returned for abridgement.

Three files should be included together in the electronic version emailed:
- **File 1**. The title of the paper, plus the names, affiliation and complete addresses, e–mail and fax number of authors, and an abstract , keywords and brief biographical notes about authors

- **File 2**. The text of the paper, including text, acknowledgements, references and notes, tables, figure captions, figures, but without the names of authors or their biographical notes

- **File 3**. The cover letter which includes answers to questions about the relevance of the paper to the submitted journal and nominations of four experts in the subject of the paper who may be used as referees, unknown to the authors and from a different country to their own together with the Author Agreement, which may be downloaded from the website.

All papers must be written in UK English.

If English is not your first language, please ask an English-speaking colleague to proofread your paper.

Electronic Copy
The preferred word processing program is Microsoft's Word or Word for Windows. A general Word template is available for your use. If you have used LaTex format (and there is a LaTex template available), please convert it to PDF format. To ensure that those reviewing your manuscript will be able to view it, you must save your LaTex file as a PDF file.

Figures in the final accepted manuscript may be included in the electronic text file and also provided as separate files, but must also be accompanied by high-resolution hard copy printout.

International Context
It should not be assumed that the reader is familiar with specific national institutions or corporations. Authors are encouraged to approach their chosen topic with an international perspective.

Countries and groupings of countries should be referred to by their full title (for example, 'China', 'Europe' and 'America' are all ambiguous).

Special attention should be paid to identifying units of currency by nationality.

Acronyms should be translated in full into English. (See also 'Translated works' below.)

Title, Abstract, Keywords, Addresses, Biographical Notes
Please assist us by following these guidelines:
- Title: as short as possible
- Abstract: approximately 100 words, maximum 150
- Keywords: approximately 10 words or phrases
- Address: position, department, name of institution, full postal address
- Biographical notes: approximately 100 words per author, maximum 150.

References and Notes
Inderscience journals use the Harvard (name and date) short reference system for citations in the text with a detailed alphabetical list at the end of the paper. For example 'Hamel (2000) suggests …' or 'Nonaka and Takeuchi (1995) found that …' or 'A study of economic change (Nelson and Winter, 1982) has shown that …'.

Footnotes should be avoided, but any short, succinct notes making a specific point, may be placed in number order following the alphabetical list of references.

References should be made only to works that are published, accepted for publication (not merely 'submitted'), or available through libraries or institutions. Any other source should be qualified by a note regarding availability.

Full reference should include all authors' names and initials, date of publication, title of paper, title of publication (italics), volume and issue number (of a journal), publisher and form (books, conference proceedings), page numbers.

[N.B. Some of the sample copies have references in our previous Numerical format; please use our new Harvard format above for all references now]

Figures
All illustrations, whether diagrams or photographs, are referred to as Figures. They should be black and white, not colour, and numbered sequentially. Please place them at the end of the paper, rather than interspersed in text.

Originals of line diagrams will be reduced and used directly, so please prepare them to the highest possible standards. Bear in mind that lettering may be reduced in size by a factor of 2 or 3, and that fine lines may disappear. Electronic copies of the figures are also required.

Translated Works
Difficulty often arises in translating acronyms, so it is best to spell out an acronym in English (for example, IIRP - French personal income tax).

Similarly, labels and suffixes need careful attention where the letters refer to words which have been translated.

The names of mathematical functions may change in translation - check against an English or American mathematical reference text.

Units of Measurement
Inderscience journals follow the Système International for units of measurement.

Imperial units will be converted, except where conversion would affect the meaning of a statement, or imply a greater or lesser degree of accuracy.

246

Submission Preparation Checklist (All items required)
The submission has not been previously published in English nor is it before another journal for consideration; or an explanation has been provided in Comments to the Editor.

The text meets the formatting requirements outlined in the Author Guidelines section.

The submission file is in Microsoft Word, RTF or PDF document file format.

I have identified four experts (names, full addresses and expertise) in the subject of my paper who may be used as referees. These experts are personally unknown to the authors and at least two of them are from a different country from the author(s).

I have prepared the cover letter and printed and completed the required Author Agreement (Copyright) document.

IMPORTANT Because my article will be peer reviewed, I have removed all kind of author identification (names and affiliations) from the file that I am submitting and I am going to upload in Step 3. Also, I have removed any ACKNOWLEDGEMENT from paper.

International Journal of Auditing

ADDRESS FOR SUBMISSION:

Stuart Turley, General Editor
International Journal of Auditing
University of Manchester
Manchester Business School
Oxford Road
Manchester, M13 9PL
UK
Phone: 44 (0) 161 2754015
E-Mail: ija@manchester.ac.uk
Web: www.blackwellpublishing.com

CIRCULATION DATA:

Reader: Academics
Frequency of Issue: 3 Times/Year
Sponsor/Publisher: Blackwell Publishing,
   Inc.

PUBLICATION GUIDELINES:

Manuscript Length: 21-25
Copies Required: Two
Computer Submission: Yes Disk, Email
Format: MS Word
Fees to Review: 0.00 US$

Manuscript Style:
   See Manuscript Guidelines

REVIEW INFORMATION:

Type of Review: Blind Review
No. of External Reviewers: 2
No. of In House Reviewers:
Acceptance Rate: 33%
Time to Review: 2 - 3 Months
Reviewers Comments: Yes
Invited Articles: 0-5%
Fees to Publish: 0.00 US$

MANUSCRIPT TOPICS:
Auditing

MANUSCRIPT GUIDELINES/COMMENTS:

International Journal of Auditing sets out to be a high quality specialist journal carrying articles over a broad spectrum of auditing. Its primary aim is to communicate clearly to an international readership the results of original auditing research conducted in practice and in research institutions. The results of research conducted jointly by academics and practitioners are particularly welcome. Submitted articles should have an international appeal either due to the research topic transcending national frontiers, or due to the clear potential for readers to apply the results, perhaps with adaptation, to their local environments. While articles must be methodologically sound, any research orientation is acceptable - for instance papers may have an analytical and statistical, behavioural, economic and financial (including agency theory), sociological and critical, or historical basis. The editors consider articles for publication which fit into one or more of the following subject categories:
- The audit of financial statements
- Public sector/governmental auditing
- Internal auditing
- Audit education, including case studies

248

- Audit aspects of corporate governance, including audit committees
- The new audit agendas including quality, environment, social and vfm auditing, ethical issues and state: profession relationships
- Articles which are reflective rather than empirical in nature are considered for publication, if they fall into one of the above categories - so long as they extend the frontiers of knowledge and understanding about audit theory or practice.

Submission of Articles
Two copies of any manuscript for consideration should be sent on single-sided paper and on diskette to: Chris Gould, IJA Editorial Assistant, Accounting and Finance Division, Manchester Business School, University of Manchester, Oxford Road, Manchester M13 9PL, United Kingdom. The author's name(s), title(s) of their academic department(s), and institution(s) of affiliation should appear on a sheet separate from the title of the paper and separate from any text. It is a condition of our consideration of a ms for inclusion in *International Journal of Auditing* that the author(s) write a covering note confirming that it has not been published previously and will not be simultaneously under consideration for publication elsewhere. It is important the author(s)' covering note includes full address, phone and fax numbers.

Submitted and resubmitted ms's are "blind read" by two referees reporting to one of the journal's editors. We undertake, wherever possible, to give a decision on a ms within eight weeks of receipt.

Authors submitting a ms do so on the basis that if it is accepted for publication, exclusive copyright in the paper shall be assigned to the Publisher; no article will be accepted for publication without satisfactory completion of a standard form which will be supplied for this purpose. In consideration for the assignment of copyright, the Publisher will supply 9 offprints of each paper and further offprints may be ordered at the time of acceptance at extra cost. Authors are free to use their own material in other publications written or edited by themselves provided that when they do this they make proper acknowledgements to the *Journal* and to the Publisher.

No responsibility is taken for damages or loss of papers submitted. Papers will not normally be returned unless this is specially requested.

Preparation of Copy
The ms (including notes and references) should be 1½ line spacing in A4 (210 x 297mm) or Letter (8 ½ x 11 inches) format and should include:
- 10 Key words or phrases which can be used for indexing;
- An Abstract of not more than 150 words summarising the purpose, methodology and major conclusions;
- A Summary of not more than 500 words to provide the reader with a non-technical overview of the contents of the article;
- Author(s) mini profile(s) (maximum three sentences for each profile).

Readability is a key criterion for acceptance in *International Journal of Auditing*. Mathematics should only be included if it is essential - in which case preferably in Appendix form. Essential Notes should be indicated by superscripts in the text and provided in a single section just before the References at the end of the ms. Citations in the text should be given in abbreviated form allowing the reader to readily relate the citation to the full reference at the end of the article. A citation in the text should be embedded in the text in one of these forms:

'Innes (1990) showed that ...'
'It has been shown that .... (Innes, 1990)'
'Until recently ... (Ng & Tai (1994))'

References
The last section of the ms should be the References - in alphabetical order by first word, in this form:

Boritz J.E. (1992). The use of artificial intelligence in auditing. *In Proceedings of the XIV World Congress of Accountants on the Accountant's Role in a Global Economy* (Washington, October), New York, The International Federation of Accountants. pp 19E-1 - 19E-48.

Innes, J. (1990), 'External management auditing of companies: a survey of bankers', *Accounting, Auditing & Accountability Journal*, Vol.3, No. 1, pp. 18-37.

Lee, T.A. (1993), *Corporate Audit Theory*, (1st edn) London: Chapman & Hall, p. 174.

Ng, P.P.H. & Tai, B.Y.K. (1994), An empirical examination of the determinants of audit delay in Hong Kong. *The British Accounting Review*, 26, March, pp. 43-59.

It is the responsibility of the authors to obtain and supply with the manuscript written permission to use material from copyrighted sources.

Hyperlinks
It is the authors' responsibility to check any web links included within ms's for accuracy and longevity.

Figures
In the text, figures should be referred to as: see Figure 1 or Figures 2 and 3 etc. Their approximate location in the text should be indicated as follows: Insert Fig 1 about here. Line drawings should be submitted on a separate sheet at the same size as the intended printed version (so no enlargement or reduction is required), maximum width 154 mm. Lettering on the artwork should be set in 8pt type. Computer-generated artwork must be submitted as laser printed output at a resolution of 600 dots per inch on high quality paper. Tints are to be avoided; hatching should be used instead. Drawn artwork should be carefully lettered and drawn in black ink. Provide copies as well as originals. Drawings should be clearly identified on the back with the figure number and author's name. Artwork on disk is preferred on 3.5" PC or Macintosh format in a dedicated drawing package such as Adobe Illustrator or Macromedia Freehand (not presentation, spreadsheet or database packages). Each graphic should be in a separate file, should conform to the information above and be supplied as a

250

source (original) file as well as an ASCII .EPS file, if different. Provide hard copy print out of each figure, clearly identified.

Electronic Submission
When a paper is submitted in its final form and has been accepted for publication, it should be supplied on diskette preferably in Word format.

The disk must be accompanied by a hard copy printout. If the disk and the paper differ, the paper copy will be treated as the definitive version.

Proofs
Authors are given sight of the proofs of their articles and are expected to make corrections quickly. Changes at the proof stage should be limited to correcting typesetting errors.

Payments
No payments are made to authors and no charges to authors are made with the exception that revisions to content at the proof stage may be charged to the authors.

International Journal of Business and Public Administration

ADDRESS FOR SUBMISSION:

Abdalla Hagen, Editor
International Journal of Business and Public
    Administration
Grambling State University
College of Business
Department of Management
PO Box 295
Ruston, LA 71273
USA
Phone: 318-255-1491
E-Mail: conference@iabpad.com
Web: www.iabpad.com

PUBLICATION GUIDELINES:

Manuscript Length: 15 Pages
Copies Required: Electronic
Computer Submission: Yes Email
Format: MS Word
Fees to Review: 25.00 US$

Manuscript Style:
    American Psychological Association

CIRCULATION DATA:

Reader: Academics, Business Persons,
    Practitioners
Frequency of Issue: 3 Times/Year
Sponsor/Publisher: The International
    Academy of Business and Public
    Administration Disciplines (IABPAD)

REVIEW INFORMATION:

Type of Review: Blind Review
No. of External Reviewers: 2
No. of In House Reviewers: 0
Acceptance Rate: 10-20%
Time to Review: 3-6 Months
Reviewers Comments: Yes
Invited Articles:
Fees to Publish: 15.00 US$ Per Page
    25.00 US$ Additional per Coauthor

MANUSCRIPT TOPICS:

Accounting Education; Accounting Information Systems; Accounting Theory & Practice; Auditing; Cost Accounting; Government & Non Profit Accounting; Insurance; Tax Accounting

MANUSCRIPT GUIDELINES/COMMENTS:

Manuscript Length
Initial submission of manuscripts should not exceed 20 double-spaced pages. After acceptance, manuscripts should not exceed 15 single-spaced pages. A sample of journal publication will be emailed to authors of accepted papers in order to follow.

Submission
Submission of papers is electronically via email to **conference@iabpad.com**. Submissions are double-blind peer-reviewed. By submitting a paper authors are certifying that the work is original, is not being considered for publication elsewhere, has not been accepted for publication or previously published, and is not copyrighted.

Publication Fee
There is a $15 USD publication fee per page, and 25 USD per coauthor.

First Page
- The title of all papers should be centered, not to exceed three lines, and typed in caps on the first page. It should be 16 point font, Times New Roman and single spaced.
- The authors' names followed by affiliations should be centered, single-spaced, and typed beginning on the second line below the title. Use 12-point type.

Abstract
The abstract heading should appear two line spaces below author(s), centered, and italicized in 12-point font. The abstract text for a paper should appear one-line space below the abstract heading, indented 0.5 from the left and right margins. It should be italicized in a 10-point font, Times New Roman, and should not exceed 150 words.

Paper Typing
- All papers must be typed in Microsoft Word using Times New Roman and a 12-point font.
- All papers must be typed, single-spaced, on regular 8.5" x 11" paper, and fully justified.
- Margins should be set to 1-inch top, bottom, left, and right
- Page number should be in the bottom right
- No headers and footers
- Use *italics* in place of underlines
- Indent all paragraphs 1/2 inch and do not skip lines between paragraphs
- All major headings should be bold, centered, capitalized, set to 12-point font, and with one space around headings.
- All sub-headings should be bold, left justified with an initial capital for each word (Title case), set to 12-point font. Leave one line space above and below each sub-heading.
- The heading of acknowledgment should be centered and bold and placed before references.

Tables and Figures
All tables and figures should be typed in Microsoft Word and incorporated into the body of the text within the margins. They should be placed as close as possible to the location in the text where they are first cited. For each table or figure, center (1, 2, 3, etc) and identification above the table or figure. The identification labels should be under the **number** of "Table" or "Figure" centered, typed in intial cap for each word (Title case). Tables or figures not produced by authors should be documented by sources (references) written below such tables or figures.

Math and Equations
Use words in regular text, not math. For example, "We surveyed 100 managers," not "We surveyed n = 100 managers." "We used chi-squares to evaluate coefficients," not "We used X^2s." You can report statistical results using symbols in parentheses. Display and number only equations you mention in your work. Equation numbers should be between parentheses and flush with the right margin.

Footnotes and Endnotes
Do not use any footnotes or endnotes.

Reference Format
- References should be placed at the end of the manuscript and should include only those actually cited in the text.
- Each reference should have a 0.5-inch indentation on the second line. Leave one line space between references.
- The style guidelines for references must follow the Publications Manual of the American Psychological Association. Titles of journals or books will be italicized instead of underlined. Below are some examples:

Journal Articles
Paivio, A. (1988). Perceptual comparisons through the mind's eye. Memory and Cognition, 3(5), 653-668.

Richard, M. D. & Allaway, W. (1993). Service quality attributes and choice behavior. Journal of Services Marketing, 7, 59-68.

Schneider, B., Parkington, J. J., & Buxton, V. M. (1980). Employee and customer perceptions of service in banks. Administrative Science Quarterly, 25, 252-267.

Chapter in Book
Hartley, J.T., Harker, J.O., & Walsh, D.A. (1980). Contemporary issues and new directions in adult development. In L.W. Poon (Ed.), Aging in the 1980's (pp. 234-278). Washington, DC: American Psychological Association.

Book
Bernstein, T.M. (1965). The careful writer: a modern guide to English usage. New York: Atheneum.

Letheridege, S., & Cannon, C.R. (Eds.). (1980). Bilingual education: teaching English as a second language. New York: Praeger.

Internet Articles or Abstracts Based on a Printed Source
Smith, R. (1998). TQM in Australian manufacturing businesses [Electronic version]/Quality Journal, 5, 117-123.

Articles or Abstracts in an Internet-Only Journal
Frederickson, B.L. (2000, March 7). Cultivating positive emotions to optimize health and well being. Prevention & Treatment, 3, Article (or Abstract) 001 a. Retrieved November 20, 2000 from http://www.preventiontreatment.com/frederickson.html.

254

Report From an Organization on Its Web Site
Canarie, Inc. (1997, September 27 or n.d. if no date is available). Towards a Canadian health
IWAY: Vision, opportunities and fixture steps. Retrieved November 8, 2000, from
http://www.canada.org/iway.html.

Editorial Guidelines
The *International Journal of Business and Public Administration* (*IJBPA*) is a publication of
the International Academy of Business and Public Administration Disciplines (IABPAD).
Manuscripts presented at the IABPAD conferences are invited from faculty in business and
public administration colleges and professionals of private and public organizations. Only
original manuscripts can be considered for publication in the journal. All submissions will be
subject to double-blind peer-review. All authors are requested to strictly follow the above
manuscript guidelines.

International Journal of Government Auditing

ADDRESS FOR SUBMISSION:

Don R. Drach, Editor
International Journal of Government
    Auditing
International Organization
    of Supreme Audit Institution
U.S. General Accounting Office
441 G Street, N.W., Room 7814
Washington, DC 20548
USA
Phone: 202-512-4707
E-Mail: millerp@gao.gov
    drachd@gao.gov
Web: www.intosai.org

PUBLICATION GUIDELINES:

Manuscript Length: 6-10
Copies Required: Two
Computer Submission: Yes
Format: MS Word 97
Fees to Review: 0.00 US$

Manuscript Style:

CIRCULATION DATA:

Reader: Business Persons,
    Auditors/Financial Managers
Frequency of Issue: Quarterly
Sponsor/Publisher: International
    Organization of Supreme Audit
    Institutions

REVIEW INFORMATION:

Type of Review: Editorial Review
No. of External Reviewers: 2
No. of In House Reviewers: 1
Acceptance Rate: 11-20%
Time to Review: 2 - 3 Months
Reviewers Comments: No Reply
Invited Articles: 11-20%
Fees to Publish: 0.00 US$

MANUSCRIPT TOPICS:
Accounting Information Systems; Auditing; Econometrics; Fiscal Policy; International Development; Public Sector Auditing and Accounting

MANUSCRIPT GUIDELINES/COMMENTS:

The *International Journal of Government Auditing* is published quarterly (January, April, July, October) in Arabic, English, French, German, and Spanish editions on behalf of INTOSAI (International Organization of Supreme Audit Institutions). The *Journal*, which is the official organ of INTOSAI, is dedicated to the advancement of government auditing procedures and techniques. Opinions and beliefs expressed are those of editors or individual contributors and do not necessarily reflect the views or policies of the Organization.

Given the *Journal's* use as a teaching tool, articles most likely to be accepted are those which deal with pragmatic aspects of public sector auditing. These include case studies, ideas on new audit methodologies or details on audit training programs. Articles that deal primarily with theory would not be appropriate.

The *Journal* is distributed to the heads of all Supreme Audit Institutions throughout the world who participate in the work of INTOSAI. Others may obtain the journal on line at **www.intosaijournal.org**. Correspondence for all editions should be mailed to the *Journal's* administration office, GAO, 441 G Street, Room 7814, Washington D.C. 20548

Articles in the *Journal* are indexed in the Accountants' Index published by the American Institute of Certified Public Accountants and included in Management Contents. Selected articles are included in abstracts published by Anbar Management Services, Wembley, England, and University Microfilms International, Ann Arbor, Michigan, U.S.A.

International Journal of Management Theory & Practices

ADDRESS FOR SUBMISSION:

David C. Yen, Editor-in-Chief
International Journal of Management
   Theory & Practices
Miami University
Department of DSC/MIS
Oxford, OH 45056
USA
Phone: 513-529-4826
E-Mail: yendc@muohio.edu
Web: http://cmca.mis.ccu.edu.tw/acme/

CIRCULATION DATA:

Reader: Academics, Business Persons;
   Practitioners in Management
Frequency of Issue: Yearly
Sponsor/Publisher: Association of Chinese
   Management Educators (ACME)

PUBLICATION GUIDELINES:

Manuscript Length: 21-25
Copies Required: One
Computer Submission: Yes Email
Format: MS Word
Fees to Review: 0.00 US$

Manuscript Style:
   See Manuscript Guidelines

REVIEW INFORMATION:

Type of Review: Blind Review
No. of External Reviewers: 3
No. of In House Reviewers: 0
Acceptance Rate: 6-10%
Time to Review: 4 - 6 Months
Reviewers Comments: Yes
Invited Articles: 0-5%
Fees to Publish: 0.00 US$

MANUSCRIPT TOPICS:

Accounting Information Systems; Accounting Theory & Practice; Auditing; Behavioral Accounting; Cost Accounting; Econometrics; Economic Development; Economic History; Financial Services; Fiscal Policy; Government & Non Profit Accounting; Industrial Organization; Insurance; International Economics & Trade; International Finance; Macro Economics; Micro Economics; Monetary Policy; Portfolio & Security Analysis; Public Policy Economics; Real Estate; Regional Economics; Tax Accounting

MANUSCRIPT GUIDELINES/COMMENTS:

Call for Papers

The Editor-in-Chief invites prospective authors to submit original manuscripts for possible publication in this international journal.

Aims and Scope

International Journal of Management Theory and Practices is intended for senior managers in business and industry, managers and administrators in government and public service agencies, partners in professional organizations, teachers and trainers in management, public administration and related fields, information technology suppliers, service providers, information consultants, information scientists, systems analysts and researchers in business and information studies. It provides a focus and source of up to date information on the developing field of information management. Papers are welcomed in the areas of information systems, organizations, management, decision making, long-term planning, information overload, computer and telecommunication technologies, human communication and people in systems and organizations. The journal publishes original papers and review articles in the areas specified on the inside front cover, viewpoints, short reports, news from members/conferences, book reviews, conference reports, software reviews, publications received and a calendar of forthcoming events. *International Journal of Management Theory and Practices* is published annually and started with first publication in August 2000.

Refereed Procedure
Each submission will be reviewed by at least three selected reviewers. Track Editor will check the reviewers' comments and make a recommendation to Editor-in-Chief, who will then send the result to the senior author.

Copyright
Authors submitting articles for publication warrant that the work is not an infringement of any existing copyright and will indemnify the publisher against any breach of such warranty.

How to Submit
Original manuscripts that fit the aims and scope of *International Journal of Management Theory and Practices* should be submitted to the Editor-in-Chief.

International Journal of Management Theory and Practices is intended for senior managers in business and industry, managers and administrators in government and public service agencies, partners in professional organizations, teachers and trainers in management, public administration and related fields, information technology suppliers, service providers, information consultants, information scientists, systems analysts and researchers in business and information studies. It provides a focus and source of up to date information on the developing field of information management. Papers are welcomed in the areas of information systems, organizations, management, decision making, long term planning, information overload, computer and telecommunication technologies, human communication and people in systems and organizations.

Contributions
Those wishing to submit articles, viewpoints or reviews should send three copies to the Editor-in-Chief. Contributors should refer to the Notes for Authors on the inside back cover. The Editorial office encourages submissions to the journal on disk or sent via E-mail. Please contact the editorial offices for full guidelines.

General Information
International Journal of Management Theory and Practices is published semi-annually and will start with first publication August/September, 1999.

The journal publishes original papers and review articles in the areas specified on the inside front cover, viewpoints, short reports, news from members/conferences, book reviews, conference reports, software reviews, publications received and a calendar of forthcoming events.

Notes for Authors
It is a condition of publication that manuscripts submitted to this *Journal* have not been published and will not be simultaneously submitted or published elsewhere.

Original manuscripts that fit the aims and scope of *International Journal of Management Theory and Practices* should be submitted to the Editor-in-Chief using the above information.

Manuscripts should be submitted in triplicate (original and two copies). They should be typed, double-spaced, single-side, on International Standard Size A4 paper (or the nearest equivalent standard size in the USA) with a left-hand margin of 40 mm.

The title of the paper together with the name(s) and affiliation(s) of the author(s), and an abstract of 150-200 words should be given on a separate title page. The title should be repeated on page one of the manuscript. A brief biographical note covering the authors' interests, qualifications, and experience in the field of ACME should be given. Examples may be found in any issue of ACME.

All papers submitted will be refereed and must be written to a high standard of English. If referees require alternations to, or a revision of, an otherwise acceptable manuscript the author(s) will be responsible for retyping the paper. Papers should normally be 4-6,000 words long; longer ones will be considered by the editors but may be subject to editorial revision.

Table and illustrations should be given on separate sheets with their location noted in the next. Graphs and diagrams should be drawn in black ink in a form suitable for reproduction without retouching.

Footnotes should be kept to a minimum (where they cannot be avoided completely).

References in the text should be indicated by superior Arabic numerals, which run consecutively through the paper. The second or subsequent mention of the same author should be given the next consecutive number (and not the number given at the first mention).

References should be listed numerically at the end of the text and should on form to the following style:

Journal Articles (spell out journal titles completely and give the issue number when a volume is not continuously paged)
Ackoff, R.L. "Management Misinformation Systems," *Management Science* (USA), Vol. 14, No. 4, December 1961, pp. 147-156.

260

Books
Bonini, C.P. *Simulation of Information and Decision Systems in the Firm*, Prentice-Hall, Englewood Cliffs, NJ, USA, 1963, p. 137.

Book Chapters
R.H Chenhall, and Romano, C.A. "Formal Planning and Control Presence and Impact on the Growth of Small Manufacturing Firms," in *Job Generation by the Small Business Sector in Australia*, W. C. Dunlop and A.J. Williams (eds.), Institute of Industrial Economics, Newcastle, USA, 1989, pp. 71-89.

Papers From Conference Proceedings, etc.
Li, E.Y., Yen, D.C., and Chang, C.H. "A Profile of Marketing Information Systems in Small Million-Dollar U.S. Companies," *Proceedings of the First International Conference on POM/MIS*, Shatin, New Territories, Hong Kong, December 19-21, 1993, pp. 1-10.

Research Reports
PARKER, C.C., *Identification of patterns of information flow: user evaluation of the sources of supply*. School of Transportation (BLR&D Report No. 5288), University of Southampton, Southampton, 1997.

Page proofs will be supplied to the senior author of a paper but only errors in typesetting may be corrected at this stage. No changes in content will be permitted once the paper is set in type: consequently the author(s) should ensure that the paper is submitted in its final form.

The senior author will receive 10 complimentary offprints of the paper or copies of the Journal after publication and will be responsible for distributing an appropriate number to any fellow authors. Additional offprints/journals may be ordered. Inquires should be addressed directly to the Managing Editor, not the Editor-in-Chief. Managing Editor's information is listed as follows:

    Houn-Gee Chen, Chair and Professor
    Department of Information Management
    National Chung Cheng University, Chia-Yi, Taiwan ROC
    Phone: 05-2721500;   Fax: 05-2721501;   Email: **mishgc@ccunix.ccu.edu.tw**

Manuscripts will be accepted on the understanding that their content is original and that the manuscript has not been submitted for publication elsewhere. However, papers delivered at conferences and meetings may be acceptable if they are significantly extended or altered from their original presentation as a result of further work.

Text Preparation on Disk
Authors are encouraged to submit a computer disk (3.5" HD/DD disk) or e-mail copy containing the final version of the paper along with the final manuscript to the editorial office. Please observe the following criteria:
a.   Send hard copy in when the e-mail copy received cannot be opened by the Editorial office.
b.   When your paper has been refereed, revised if necessary and accepted, send a disk or e-mail copy containing the final version with the final hard copy.

c. The standard software used in the editorial office is Microsoft Word 6.0 or higher version.

d. The standard computer and OS used in the editorial office are IBM-compatible PC and Windows 95 or higher version.

e. Text, tables, and illustrations should be supplied as separate files. The standard software used in the editorial office is Microsoft Office—PowerPoint.

f. The file should follow the general instructions on style arrangement and, in particular, the reference style.

g. The file should use the wrap-around end-of-line feature (i.e. no returns at the end of each line). All textual elements should begin flush left, no paragraph indents. Place two returns after every element such as title, headings, paragraphs, figure and table callouts.

h. Keep a back-up disk for reference and safety.

International Journal of Strategic Cost Management

ADDRESS FOR SUBMISSION:

Il-Woon Kim, Managing Editor
International Journal of Strategic Cost
  Management
University of Akron
College of Business Administration
Building 262, Accountancy
259 South Broadway
Akron, OH 44325-4802
USA
Phone: 330-972-7461
E-Mail: ikim@uakron.edu
Web: www.wiley.com

PUBLICATION GUIDELINES:

Manuscript Length: 16-20
Copies Required: Three
Computer Submission: No
Format: N/A
Fees to Review: 0.00 US$

Manuscript Style:
  See Manuscript Guidelines

CIRCULATION DATA:

Reader: Business Persons
Frequency of Issue: Semiannually
Sponsor/Publisher: John Wiley & Sons, Inc.

REVIEW INFORMATION:

Type of Review: Blind Review
No. of External Reviewers: 2
No. of In House Reviewers: 1
Acceptance Rate: 21-30%
Time to Review: 2 - 3 Months
Reviewers Comments: Yes
Invited Articles: 0-5%
Fees to Publish: 0.00 US$

MANUSCRIPT TOPICS:
Cost Accounting

MANUSCRIPT GUIDELINES/COMMENTS:

Aims and Scope
The *International Journal of Strategic Cost Management* is directed to corporate financial executives with an interest in cost management, as well as consultants and academics. Areas that this *Journal* will focus on include: activity-based costing, activity-based management, performance measurement, benchmarking, best practices, target costing, continuous improvement, and total quality management.

Articles should address the readership and be informative, analytical, and practical. We seek material that will offer our readership new insights into and new approaches toward cost management issues. Manuscripts are considered for publication with the understanding that they represent original material, and are offered exclusively and without fee to the *International Journal of Strategic Cost Management*.

Articles must not have been published previously and may not be simultaneously submitted elsewhere.

Submission Instructions

A cover letter must accompany each submission indicating the name, address, telephone number, facsimile number, and e-mail address of the author to whom all correspondence is to be addressed. An affiliation must be supplied for each author. If the manuscript has been presented, published, or submitted for publication elsewhere, please inform the Editor.

Prospective authors should submit five copies of the complete manuscript, including tables and illustrations.

Format

Manuscripts should contain: title, names and complete affiliations of authors, including phone number, facsimile number, and e-mail address. Please provide an informative 100- to 200-word abstract at the beginning of your manuscript. The abstract should provide an overview of your paper and not a statement of conclusions only. If applicable, please provide keywords, contract grant sponsors, and contract grant number(s). Articles are normally about 15 published journal pages in length or shorter. Columns are generally no more than 10 journal pages in length.

Instructions for Typists

Manuscripts must be typed double-spaced on a single side only on standard 8 ½ x 11-inch (21.5 X 28-cm) white paper with one-inch margins. Material intended for footnotes should be inserted in the text as parenthetical material whenever possible.

All mathematical symbols, equations, formulas, Greek, or unusual symbols should be typed. If they must be handwritten, please write clearly and leave ample space above and below for printer's marks. When handwritten symbols are necessary, please provide a separate sheet listing and defining such symbols. This list will help to distinguish between characters that may otherwise be confused (e.g., b, B, β). If italic type is unavailable to the typist, underscore with a straight line anything to be printed in italic type. Note that the use of italics for emphasis should be used with extreme discretion.

References

Compile references on a separate sheet at the end of the main body of the text. References to published literature should be quoted in the text by giving author's name and year of publication, such as Smith (1995) or (Smith, 1995). The format for multiple references is either Smith (1997) and Jones and Black (1996), or (Smith, 1997; Jones and Black, 1996).

References should be listed alphabetically in the last section of the article titled "References." Journal references must be complete and include authors' initials, year of publication in parentheses, title of the paper, name of the journal, volume, and pages on which the article appears. Book references must include city of publication, publisher, and year of publication. Anthologies and collections must include names of editors and pages on which the reference appears. Books in a series must include series title and number/volume if applicable. Because of the many conference proceedings available, it is critical to give as much information as possible when citing references from proceedings. The complete title of the meeting, symposium, etc. (do not abbreviate titles), and the city and dates of the meeting must be included. If a proceeding has been published, provide the editors' names, publisher, city, year of publication, and pages on which the article appears. If a proceeding has not been published, indicate so. Examples follow:

Article in a Journal
Beatty, C.A., "Implementing Advanced Manufacturing Technology." *Business Quarterly* (Autumn 1990), 46-50.

Proceedings
Bessant, J. (1998). Organization Adaptation and Manufacturing Technology. Proc. *Final HASA Conf. CIM: Technologies, Organizations, and People in Transition* (Luxembourg, Austria), pp. 351-360.

Book
Usher, J.M., Roy, U., and Parsaei, H.R. *Integrated Product and Process Development: Methods, Tools, and Technologies.* (New York: John Wiley & Sons, 1998.)

Contributed Book
Kadirkamanathan, V, Niranjan, M., and Fallside, F. "Sequential Adaptation of Radial Basis Function Neural Networks and its Applications to Time-Series Prediction," in R. Lippman, J. Moody, and D. Touretzky, Eds., *Neural Information Processing*, Vol. 3, San Mateo, CA: Morgan Kaufman, 1991: 721-727.

Exhibits
Exhibits (such as tables and figures) should not be incorporated into the text, but grouped separately after the references. All exhibits should be numbered consecutively with Arabic numerals (1, 2, 3, etc.) and should include an explanatory heading. A list of exhibit captions on a separate sheet should be supplied.

Line Drawings. Figures should be professionally prepared and submitted in a form suitable for reproduction (camera-ready copy). Computer-generated graphs are acceptable only if they have been printed with a high-quality laser printer. Authors are cautioned to provide lettering of graphs and figure labels that are large clear, and "open" so that letters and numbers do not become illegible when reduced. Likewise, authors are cautioned that very thin lines and other fine details in figures may not successfully reproduce. Original figures should be drawn with these precautions in mind.

Halftones. High-quality photographs are necessary for clear halftone reproduction.

Electronic Submissions
In addition to providing hard copy, authors are requested to submit the final, accepted version of their manuscript on diskette to the Editor.

Text
Storage medium. 3 ½" high-density disk in IBM MS-DOS, Windows, or Macintosh format.

Software and format. Microsoft Word *6.0* is preferred, although manuscripts prepared using any other microcomputer word processor are acceptable. Sending a Rich Text Format (RTF) file will be very helpful also. Refrain from complex formatting; the Publisher will style your manuscript according to the *International Journal of Strategic Cost Management* design specifications. Do not use desktop publishing software such as Aldus Pagemaker or Quark XPress. If you prepared your manuscript using one of these programs, export the text to a word processing format. Make sure your word processing program's "fast save" feature is turned off.

File names. Submit the text and tables of each manuscript as a single file. Name each file with your last name (up to eight letters). Text files should be given the three-letter extension that identifies the file format. Macintosh users should maintain the MS-DOS "eight dot three" file-naming convention.

Labels. Label all diskettes with your name, the file name, and the word processing program and version used.

Paper copy. Accompany all electronic files with five identical printed paper copies.

Illustrations
Storage medium. Submit as separate files from text files, on separate diskettes or cartridges, 32" diskettes, Iomega Zip, and 5 ¼" 44- or 88-MB SyQuest cartridges can be submitted. At the author's request, cartridges and diskettes will be returned after publication.

Software and format. The preferred formats are TIFF or EPS with pict or tiff preview, although any format that is in general use that is not application-specific is acceptable.

Resolution. Journal-quality reproduction will require greyscale and color files at resolutions yielding approximately 300 ppi. Bitmapped line art should be submitted at resolutions yielding 600-1200 ppi. These resolutions refer to the output size of the file; if you anticipate that your images will be enlarged or reduced, resolutions should be adjusted accordingly.

File names. Illustration files should be given the 2- or 3-letter extension that identifies the file format used (i.e., TIFF, EPS, RGB, etc.).

Labels. Label all diskettes and cartridges with your name, the file names, formats, sizes, and compression schemes (if any) used. Hard copy output must accompany all files.

Authors of accepted papers will be asked to submit to the Editor three copies of their revised manuscripts, tables, original illustrations, floppy disk with an electronic copy of their material, copyright release form, and permissions. Additional information concerning this will be sent with acceptance letters.

Copyright Information
No article can be published unless accompanied by a signed publication agreement, which serves as a transfer of copyright from author to publisher. A publication agreement may be

obtained from the editor or the publisher. A copy of the publication agreement appears in most issues of the journal.

Only original papers will be accepted, and copyright in published papers will be vested in the publisher. It is the author's responsibility to obtain written permission to reproduce material that has appeared in another publication. A form for this purpose is sent with the manuscript acceptance letter.

International Tax and Public Finance

ADDRESS FOR SUBMISSION:

Michael Devereux & John D. Wils, Editors
International Tax and Public Finance
c/o Cheryl Knight
Kluwer Academic Publishers
101 Philip Drive
Norwell, MA 02061
USA
Phone: 781-871-6600
E-Mail: Cheryl.Knight@wkap.com
Web: www.wkap.nl

PUBLICATION GUIDELINES:

Manuscript Length: 26-30
Copies Required: Three
Computer Submission: Yes.
Format:
Fees to Review: 50.00 US$

Manuscript Style:
See Manuscript Guidelines

CIRCULATION DATA:

Reader: Academics
Frequency of Issue: Quarterly
Sponsor/Publisher: Springer

REVIEW INFORMATION:

Type of Review:
No. of External Reviewers: 2
No. of In House Reviewers: 0
Acceptance Rate: 21-30%
Time to Review: 4 - 6 Months
Reviewers Comments: Yes
Invited Articles: 21-30%
Fees to Publish: 0.00 US$

MANUSCRIPT TOPICS:

International Economics & Trade; Public Policy Economics; Tax Accounting

MANUSCRIPT GUIDELINES/COMMENTS:

Aims & Scope

Government finance is a vital aspect of public policy. With growing awareness of international and inter-regional dimensions, the analysis of public finance in open economies is fast becoming a leading area of economic research.

International Tax and Public Finance serves as an outlet for, and seeks to stimulate, first-rate research on both theoretical and empirical aspects of tax policy, broadly interpreted to include expenditure and financial policies. Special emphasis is on open economy issues: the coordination of policies across jurisdictions, for instance, or the effects of taxation on capital and trade flows. This international focus is not, however, an exclusive one: high quality work in any area of tax policy - single-country tax reform analysis, for instance - is also welcome.

A central feature of *International Tax and Public Finance* is the inclusion in each issue of a special section called the International Policy Watch, discussing a current policy issue, or reviewing some recent tax developments. Facilitating communication between academic work and tax practice in this way serves many purposes - researchers need to know priorities, for example, and policy-makers need to absorb the products of research.

International Tax and Public Finance is peer-reviewed. Reflecting the international focus, one editor is located in North America and the other in Europe. An active Editorial Board reinforces this diversity and, more important, plays a central role in establishing the journal as an essential resource for tax policy analysis.

Online Manuscript Submission

Kluwer Academic Publishers now offers authors, editors and reviewers of *International Tax and Public Finance* the use of our fully web-enabled online manuscript submission and review system. To keep the review time as short as possible, we request authors to submit manuscripts online to the journal's editorial office. Our online manuscript submission and review system offers authors the option to track the progress of the review process of manuscripts in real time. Manuscripts should be submitted to: **http://ITAX.edmgr.com**

The online manuscript submission and review system for *International Tax and Public Finance* offers easy and straightforward log-in and submission procedures. This system supports a wide range of submission file formats: for manuscripts - Word, WordPerfect, RTF, TXT, and LaTex; for figures - TIFF, GIF, JPEG, EPS, PPT, and Postscript. PDF is not an acceptable format.

Note. In case you encounter any difficulties while submitting your manuscript online, please get in touch with the responsible Editorial Assistant by clicking on "CONTACT US" from the tool bar.

Authors are requested to download the Consent to Publish and Transfer of Copyright form from the journal's website. Please send a completed and duly signed form either by mail or fax to the Editorial Office of *International Tax and Public Finance*. Authors should still follow the regular instructions for authors when preparing their manuscripts (see below).

The Editors
International Tax and Public Finance
c/o Cheryl Knight
Kluwer Academic Publishers
101 Philip Drive, Norwell, MA 02061, USA
Tel: (781)871-6600   Fax: (781)878-0449
E-mail: **Cheryl.Knight@wkap.com**

Submission Policy

Authors should be aware that there is a $50.00 submission fee. Along with your submission please include a check or payment by major credit card in the amount of US $50.00 made payable to the journal.

Submissions for the Policy Watch section should be indicated as such. Unless requested otherwise, the editors will consider all submissions for both the regular and Policy Watch sections.

Manuscript Preparation

Sections should appear in the following order: title page, abstract, text, notes, references, tables, figure legends, and figures. Comments or replies to previously published articles should also follow this format with the exception of abstracts, which are not required.

1. **Title Page.** The title page should include the article title, authors' names and permanent affiliations, and the name, current address, e-mail address and telephone number of the person to whom page proofs and reprints should be sent.

2. **Abstract.** The following page should include an abstract of not more than 100 words and a list of two to six keywords.

3. **Text.** The text of the article should begin on a new page. Section headings (including appendices) should be designated by Arabic numerals (1, 2, etc.), and subsection headings should be numbered 1.1, 1.2, etc. Figures, tables, and displayed equations should be numbered consecutively throughout the text (1, 2, etc.). Equation numbers should appear flush right in parentheses.

4. **Notes.** Acknowledgments and related information should appear in a note designated by an asterisk after the last author's name, and subsequent notes should be numbered consecutively and designated by superscripts (1, 2, etc.) in the text. All notes should be typed double-spaced beginning on a separate page following the text.

5. **References.** References in the text should follow the author-date format (e.g., Brown (1986), Jones (1978a, 1978b), Smith and Johnson (1983)). References should be typed double-spaced beginning on a separate page following the notes, according to the following samples (journal and book titles may be underlined rather than italicized). References with up to three authors should include the names of each author; references with four or more authors should cite the first author and add "et al." It is the responsibility of the authors to verify all references.

Sample References
- Becker, Gordon, Morris DeGroot, and Jacob Marschak. (1964). "Measuring Utility by a Single-Response Sequential Method." *Behavioral Science* 9, 226-232.
- Schoemaker, Paul. (1980). *Experiments in Decisions Under Risk: The Expected Utility Hypothesis.* Boston: Kluwer-Nijhoff Publishing.
- Smith, V. Kerry. (1986). "A Conceptual Overview of the Foundations of Benefit-Cost Analysis." In Judith Bentkover, Vincent Covello, and Jeryl Mumpower (eds.), *Benefits Assessment: The State of the Art.* Dordrecht: D. Reidel Publishing Co.

6. **Tables.** Tables should be titled and follow the references. Notes to tables should be designated by superscripted letters (a, b, etc.) within each table. Use descriptive labels rather than computer acronyms, and explain all abbreviations.

7. **Figures.** Lettering in figures should be large enough to be legible after half-size reduction. Figure legends should be typed double-spaced on a separate page following the tables.

270

Proofing

Please be sure to include your e-mail address on your paper. If your paper is accepted, we will be forwarding your page proofs via e-mail. Your cooperation is appreciated. The proofread copy should be received back by the Publisher within 72 hours.

Copyright

It is the policy of Kluwer Academic Publishers to own the copyright of all contributions it publishes. To comply with the U.S. Copyright Law, authors are required to sign a copyright transfer form before publication. This form returns to authors and their employers full rights to reuse their material for their own purposes. Authors must submit a signed copy of this form with their manuscript.

Offprints

Each group of authors will be entitled to 50 free offprints of their paper.

International Tax Journal

ADDRESS FOR SUBMISSION:

Walter F. O'Connor, Editor
International Tax Journal
Fordham University
Grad. School of Business Administration
113 West 60th Street
New York, NY 10023
USA
Phone: 212-636-6122
E-Mail: woconnor@fordham.edu
 woconnor@bschool.bnet.fordham.edu
Web:

PUBLICATION GUIDELINES:

Manuscript Length: 21-25
Copies Required: Three
Computer Submission: Yes
Format: WordPerfect 5.1 or ASCII
Fees to Review: 0.00 US$

Manuscript Style:
 See Manuscript Guidelines

CIRCULATION DATA:

Reader: Business Persons
Frequency of Issue: Quarterly
Sponsor/Publisher: Aspen Publishers

REVIEW INFORMATION:

Type of Review: Blind Review
No. of External Reviewers: 3
No. of In House Reviewers: 1
Acceptance Rate: 11-20%
Time to Review: 2 - 3 Months
Reviewers Comments: No
Invited Articles: 6-10%
Fees to Publish: 0.00 US$

MANUSCRIPT TOPICS:
International Economics & Trade; International Finance; Tax Accounting

MANUSCRIPT GUIDELINES/COMMENTS:

1. Articles should provide practical information and ideas about international tax practice. Articles should cover matters of importance to practitioners, and cover tax, legal, and business planning aspects affecting clients with international tax situations.

2. Be sure to include both your address and telephone number where you may be reached during business hours. While the utmost care will be given to all manuscripts, we cannot accept responsibility for unsolicited manuscripts. Article accepted for publication are subject to editorial revision. There is no payment for articles; authors will receive 10 copies (to be shared by multiple authors) of their published articles.

3. Type manuscript on one side of the paper only, on 8 ½" x 11" good-quality white bond. Please do not use "erasable" paper. Use one-inch margins and double spacing. Generally, article manuscript should be approximately 15 to 35 typed pages. On acceptance, submit a computer disk of the article in WordPerfect 5.1 or ASCII.

4. Within your article use headings and subheadings to break up and emphasize your points. Type headings and subheadings flush left.

5. Type footnotes separately, double spaced, at the end of the main manuscript. Footnote and reference citations should generally follow the *Harvard Blue Book.*

6. With your article, please include a brief biographical note.

7. Any artwork, e.g., flow charts, original drawings, or graphs, must be provided in camera-ready form. Typewritten or free-hand lettering is not acceptable; all lettering must be done professionally. Do not staple or paper clip illustrations and put all illustrations between sheets of cardboard before mailing, to prevent folds. Note: We will typeset tubular material, which you may provide in typewritten form as part of your manuscript.

8. Except in rare cases, *International Tax Journal* publishes articles only if they have not yet appeared or been accepted for publication elsewhere. If you are considering submission of previously published material, please correspond with the Editor first to determine if such submission is suitable. We will generally be pleased to consider articles for prior publication adapted from book-length works in progress but, again, request advance notice so that we may work out necessary copyright arrangements.

9. If you are reprinting any previously copyrighted material in your article, other than short quotations, you must submit with your manuscript letters of permission from the copyright holder and from the author (if he or she is not the copyright holder).

10. We will own and retain the copyright to all of the articles we publish, together with the right to reprint them in any republication of the *Journal* in any form or media. You may reprint your article for personal use, provided you do not do so for resale and provided the *Journal*, and Panel Publishers, a division of Aspen Publishers, Inc. as the *Journal's* publisher, are given appropriate credit if and when you reprint the article. We will be happy to provide you with appropriate credit-line language. (Should you wish to have your own article reprinted or reissued in a book or periodical to be sold or distributed by another publisher or organization, you must obtain prior written permission from us.)

Irish Accounting Review (The)

ADDRESS FOR SUBMISSION:

Hyndman, O hOgartaigh & Warnock, Eds.
Irish Accounting Review (The)
Phone:
E-Mail: n.hyndman@qub.ac.uk
ciaran.ohogartaigh@dcu.ie
keith.warnock@nuigalway.ie
Web: www.iafa.ie/irish_accounting_review/

CIRCULATION DATA:

Reader: Academics
Frequency of Issue: 2 Times/Year
Sponsor/Publisher: The Irish Accounting
and Finance Association / The Irish
Accountancy Educational Trust

PUBLICATION GUIDELINES:

Manuscript Length: 21-25
Copies Required: Three
Computer Submission: Yes Email
Format: MS Word or MS Word-compatible
Fees to Review: 0.00 US$

Manuscript Style:

REVIEW INFORMATION:

Type of Review: Blind Review
No. of External Reviewers: 2
No. of In House Reviewers: 1
Acceptance Rate:
Time to Review: 2 - 3 Months
Reviewers Comments: Yes
Invited Articles: 0-5%
Fees to Publish: 0.00 US$

MANUSCRIPT TOPICS:

Accounting Education; Accounting History; Accounting Information Systems; Accounting Theory & Practice; Auditing; Behavioral Accounting; Cost Accounting; Government & Non Profit Accounting; International Accounting; Managerial Accounting; Tax Accounting

MANUSCRIPT GUIDELINES/COMMENTS:

The Irish Accounting Review is published by the Irish Accounting and Finance Association as part of the process of fulfilling its objective to advance accounting and related disciplines in the education and research fields in the Republic of Ireland and Northern Ireland. The Review's policy is to publish suitable papers in any of the areas of accounting, finance and their related disciplines. Papers in all categories of scholarly activity will be considered, including (but not limited to) reports on empirical research, analytical papers, review articles, papers dealing with pedagogical issues, and critical essays.

All submissions that pass an initial editorial scrutiny will be subject to double-blind refereeing. Referees will be asked to assess papers on the basis of their relevance, originality, readability and quality (including, for empirical work, research design and execution). In determining relevance, the editors will be influenced by the Association's objectives; thus, papers reporting on empirical work will be viewed more favourably if they deal with data relevant to those working in Ireland. Similarly, papers that have previously formed the basis of a presentation at the Association's annual conference will be particularly welcomed. All submissions to *The Irish Accounting Review* should be made to either:

274

Noel Hyndman
School of Management & Economics
24 University Square
Queen's University of Belfast BT7 1NN

Keith Warnock
Department of Accountancy & Finance
National University of Ireland
Galway
Republic of Ireland

Notes for Contributors
1. Papers should be submitted electronically. Papers should not normally exceed 8,000 words.

2. There should be a separate file containing the title, author(s), affiliation(s) and one address to which correspondence regarding the paper (including proofs) should be sent. An abstract of not more than 100 words should be given at the beginning of the paper.

3. Citations in the text should be by author's name and year of publication, for example, Black (1972) or (Brown, 1972). In the case of citations of books or specific quotations, page numbers should be given, for example (White, 1992, pp. 10–11). Where more than one publication by the same author in a given year is cited, they should be distinguished by lower case letters after the year, for example (Green, 1987a, Green, 1987b). Where there are more than two authors, all names should be given in the first citation with 'et al.' used subsequently.

4. References should be listed alphabetically at the end of the manuscript in the following style:

DeAngelo, L.E. (1981). Auditor Size and Audit Quality, *Journal of Accounting and Economics*, Vol. 3, No. 3, pp. 183–199.
European Commission (1996). *Green Paper on the Role, the Position and the Liability of the Statutory Auditor within the European Union*, October, Brussels: European Commission.
Faulkner, R.R (1982). Improvising on a Triad, in *Varieties of Qualitative Research*, Vol. 5, Van Maanen, J., Dabbs, J.M. and Faulkner, R.R. (eds.), pp. 65–101, Beverly Hills, California: Sage Publications.
Fielding, N.G. and Fielding, J.L. (1986). *Linking Data: Qualitative Research Methods*, Beverly Hills, California: Sage Publications.

Only works referred to in the text should be listed, and a general bibliography should not be included.

5. Essential notes should be included as endnotes rather than footnotes.

6. In initial submissions, tables and diagrams may be either included at the appropriate point in the text or after the references with their positions indicated in the text. Do not submit any separate Excel documents. Any exceptional costs of artwork for diagrams will be charged to authors.

7. Mathematics should be used only if they contribute to clarity or economy of presentation. The conclusions of mathematical papers or elements of papers should be made intelligible to readers who are not mathematicians.

8. Papers should not be submitted while under consideration by any other journal.

9. Papers are accepted for publication on the understanding that they are subject to editorial revision and have not previously been published.

10. In the preparation of papers, authors must observe copyright rules and practices.

11. Authors should correct proofs quickly and should not make revisions on proofs.

12. Authors submitting a paper do so on the understanding that, if it is accepted for publication, copyright in the paper is assigned to the publisher. The Irish Accounting and Finance Association, as publisher, will not impose restrictions on the author(s) regarding the use of material from the paper in other published works.

Issues in Accounting Education

ADDRESS FOR SUBMISSION:

Sue Ravenscroft, Editor
Issues in Accounting Education
Iowa State University
College of Business
Department of Accounting
2330 Gerdin Building
Ames, IA 50011-135
USA
Phone: 515-294-3574
E-Mail: iae@iastate.edu
Web: www.bus.iastate.edu

PUBLICATION GUIDELINES:

Manuscript Length: 20
Copies Required: Five or Electronic
Computer Submission: Yes
Format: MS Word
Fees to Review: 75.00 US$
   100.00 US$ Non-members

Manuscript Style:
   See Manuscript Guidelines

CIRCULATION DATA:

Reader: Academics
Frequency of Issue: Quarterly
Sponsor/Publisher: American Accounting
   Association

REVIEW INFORMATION:

Type of Review: Blind Review
No. of External Reviewers: 2-3
No. of In House Reviewers: 1
Acceptance Rate: 15%
Time to Review: 2 - 3 Months
Reviewers Comments: Yes
Invited Articles: 0-5%
Fees to Publish: 0.00 US$

MANUSCRIPT TOPICS:

Accounting Education; Accounting Information Systems; Accounting Theory & Practice; Auditing; Capital Budgeting; Cost Accounting; Curriculum Issues; Government & Non Profit Accounting; Instructional Cases; Pedagogical Articles; Tax Accounting

MANUSCRIPT GUIDELINES/COMMENTS:

1. The purpose of *Issues in Accounting Education* is to provide useful information to accounting faculty to assist in the teaching of accounting courses and in the understanding of student and faculty performance and behavior. Papers that present research related to this purpose, that provide insights into the teaching function, or that describe methods or materials that can be used in the classroom will be considered for publication. Cases for classroom use are also welcomed. Authors should communicate in a direct and easily understood manner. Examples and illustrations are frequently helpful. Papers should contain descriptions of the methods used to support and validate the conclusions reached by the authors.

2. Electronic submission preferred. Please send two files – one for the manuscript and one for the cover page. Payment can be made directly to the American Accounting Association. If using hard copy, authors should submit five copies of their papers along with the submission

fee to the editor. Checks should be made payable to The American Accounting Association. A submission must provide a representation by the author that the paper is not currently under review by any other journal.

3. The editor will screen papers submitted to the journal. Those papers that are considered inappropriate or for which there appears to be a low probability of acceptance will be returned to the author promptly. The submission fee will not be returned.

4. Those papers that pass the initial screening will be sent to two to three reviewers for evaluation. A double blind review procedure is used. The reviewers are asked to provide a recommendation to accept or reject the paper, or to return it for revision. This review process takes approximately eight weeks. Approximately 15 percent of the papers submitted to the journal are eventually accepted for publication. Most of these papers are revised one or more times before acceptance. The lag between submission of a paper and publication generally is between eight and twelve months.

Authors are requested to use the following guidelines in preparing manuscripts for submission:
- An abstract of no more than 150 words should accompany the manuscript. The abstract should contain a concise statement of the purpose of the paper, the primary methods or approaches used, and the main results or conclusions.
- The paper should be double-spaced throughout, including abstract, notes, and references.
- Footnotes, references, tables, and figures should appear on separate pages.
- Tables and figures should be numbered serially using Arabic numerals. The table number (TABLE 1) and a title should appear at the top of the page in caps. The tables and figures should stand alone. Abbreviations should be avoided, and when used, should be explained in footnotes. Headings should be clear. Vertical lines normally should not be used. Horizontal lines should separate the title from the headings and the headings from the body. Figures should be prepared in a form suitable for printing.
- Headings and subheadings should be used throughout the paper. The title and major headings should be in caps, bold, and centered. Subheadings should be flush with the left margin, bold, and not in caps. Headings and subheadings should not be numbered.
- Notes should be used sparingly. References should be noted in the text using the date of publication in parentheses. For example: Wright (1986, 27). The reference list should use the following format:

Fleming, C.C., and B. von Halle. 1990. An overview of logical data modeling. *Data Resource Management* 1 (Winter): 5-15.

The title page should list the authors' names, titles, affiliations, telephone numbers, **email addresses** and any acknowledgements. The authors and their affiliations should not be identified anywhere else in the paper.

5. Permission is granted to reproduce any of the contents of *Issues* for use in courses of instruction, so long as the source and American Accounting Association copyright are indicated in any such reproductions.

6. Written application must be made to the Editor for permission to reproduce any of the contents of *Issues* for use in other than courses of instruction, e.g., books of readings. The applicant must notify the author(s) in writing of the intended use of each reproduction.

7. Except as otherwise noted, the copyright has been transferred to the American Accounting Association for articles appearing in this journal. For those articles for which the copyright has not been transferred, permission to reproduce must be obtained directly from the author.

Issues in Innovation

ADDRESS FOR SUBMISSION:

Martha L. Sale, Editor
Issues in Innovation
Sam Houston State University
Academic Accounting
POB 2056
Huntsville, TX 77341-2056
USA
Phone: 936-294-1254
E-Mail: msale@shsu.edu
Web: issuesininnovation.org

CIRCULATION DATA:

Reader: Academics
Frequency of Issue: 2 Times/Year
Sponsor/Publisher: Innovation Congress

PUBLICATION GUIDELINES:

Manuscript Length: 5-25
Copies Required: Electronic
Computer Submission: Yes Required
Format: MS Word
Fees to Review: 0.00 US$

Manuscript Style:
    American Psychological Association

REVIEW INFORMATION:

Type of Review: Blind Review
No. of External Reviewers: 2
No. of In House Reviewers: 1
Acceptance Rate: 21-30%
Time to Review: 1 - 2 Months
Reviewers Comments: Yes
Invited Articles: 0-5%
Fees to Publish: 0.00 US$

MANUSCRIPT TOPICS:

Accounting Information Systems; Cost Accounting; Industrial Organization; Operations Management

MANUSCRIPT GUIDELINES/COMMENTS:

All submissions should be electronic. *Issues in Innovation* encourage manuscripts dealing with any issue arising out of the rapidly changing business environment. Issues of interest include, but are not limited to emerging accounting practices relevant to e-Business, advanced manufacturing technologies, or changing paradigms.

Journal of 21st Century Accounting (The)

ADDRESS FOR SUBMISSION:

Walter B. Moore, Editor
Journal of 21st Century Accounting (The)
Nova Southeastern University
Huizenga Sch-Business & Entreprenership
Graduate Department of Accounting
3100 SW 9th Avenue
Fort Lauderdale, FL 33315
USA
Phone: 954-262-5101
E-Mail: walter@huizenga.nova.edu
Web: www.theaccountingjournal.org

PUBLICATION GUIDELINES:

Manuscript Length: 16-20
Copies Required: No Reply
Computer Submission: Yes
Format: MS Word
Fees to Review: 0.00 US$

Manuscript Style:
American Psychological Association

CIRCULATION DATA:

Reader: Academics, Business Persons,
    Students
Frequency of Issue: 2 Times/Year
Sponsor/Publisher: Nova Southeastern
    University

REVIEW INFORMATION:

Type of Review: Editorial Review
No. of External Reviewers: 1
No. of In House Reviewers: 1
Acceptance Rate: New J
Time to Review: 1 - 2 Months
Reviewers Comments: Yes
Invited Articles: New J
Fees to Publish: 0.00 US$

MANUSCRIPT TOPICS:

Accounting Education; Accounting Information Systems; Accounting Technology;
Accounting Theory & Practice; Auditing; Cost Accounting; Government & Non Profit
Accounting

MANUSCRIPT GUIDELINES/COMMENTS:

A journal published semi-annually by the graduate accounting department of the Huizenga
School of Business and Entrepreneurship of Nova Southeastern University.

The *Journal of 21st Century Accounting* is an exclusively online journal dedicated to providing
a forum for the accounting academic, practitioner and student. The purpose of the *Journal* is
to provide an outlet for topics interesting and useful to all segments of the accounting
community. One half of the *Journal* will be reserved for papers authored by students. Students
submitted manuscripts should be recommended by a faculty member. Co-authoring by faculty
and students is encouraged. Topics may include, but are not limited to the following:

- Financial
- Manager
- Auditing

- Governmental and nonprofit
- Ethics
- International
- Education
- Technology
- Public interest
- Information systems
- Professional practice issues

All manuscripts should follow APA guidelines. Papers will be reviewed and notification shall be made within approximately 30-45 days. Manuscripts should be submitted using Microsoft Word format and submitted as an attachment to an email cover letter. A short abstract and bibliography should accompany the submission. Fonts should be 12-pitch and double-spacing should be used.

Submissions and inquires should be directed to:
Editor Walter B. Moore
Editor, The Journal of 21st Century Accounting
Huizenga School of Business and Entrepreneurship
Nova Southeastern University
3100 SW 9th Avenue
Ft. Lauderdale, FL 33315
Phone: 1-800-672-7223, extension 5101
Email: **walter@huizenga.nova.edu** or **walter@nova.edu** (Computer submissions only.)

Journal of Academy of Business and Economics

ADDRESS FOR SUBMISSION:

Alan S. Khade & Cheick Wague, Editors
Journal of Academy of Business and
   Economics
International Academy of Business
   and Economics
983 Woodland Drive
Turlock, CA 95382-7281
USA
Phone: 209-667-3074
E-Mail: Review@iabe.org
Web: www.iabe.org

PUBLICATION GUIDELINES:

Manuscript Length: 10-20
Copies Required: Two
Computer Submission: Yes Disk, Email
Format: MS Word
Fees to Review: 0.00 US$

Manuscript Style:
   Chicago Manual of Style

CIRCULATION DATA:

Reader: Academics, Business Persons
Frequency of Issue: 2 Times/Year
Sponsor/Publisher: International Academy
   of Business and Economics (IABE) /
   South Stockholm University, Sweden

REVIEW INFORMATION:

Type of Review: Blind Review
No. of External Reviewers: 2
No. of In House Reviewers: 1
Acceptance Rate: 15-25%
Time to Review: 2 - 3 Months
Reviewers Comments: Yes
Invited Articles: 10%
Fees to Publish: 0.00 US$

MANUSCRIPT TOPICS:

Accounting Information Systems; Accounting Theory & Practice; Auditing; Cost Accounting; Forensic Accounting; Non-profit Organization; Tax Accounting

MANUSCRIPT GUIDELINES/COMMENTS:

Please follow the following Manuscript Guidelines for *Journal of Academy of Business and Economics (JABE)*.

The original, high-quality research papers and articles (not currently under review or published in other publications) on all topics related to business and economics will be considered for publication in *Journal of Academy of Business and Economics (JABE)*.

Papers are reviewed on a continual basis throughout the year. Early Submissions are welcome! Please email your manuscript to **Review@iabe.org**.

Copyright. Articles, papers, or cases submitted for publication should be original contributions and should not be under consideration for any other publication at the same time. Authors submitting articles/papers/cases for publication warrant that the work is not an infringement of any existing copyright, infringement of proprietary right, invasion of privacy, or libel and will indemnify, defend, and hold IABE/AIBE or sponsor(s) harmless from any damages, expenses, and costs against any breach of such warranty. For ease of dissemination and to ensure proper policing of use papers/articles/cases and contributions become the legal copyright of the IABE unless otherwise agreed in writing.

General Information. These are submission instructions for review purpose only. Once your submission is accepted you will receive submission guidelines with your paper acceptance letter. The author(s) will be emailed result of the review process in about 6-8 weeks from submission date. Papers are reviewed and accepted on a continual basis. Submit your papers early for full considerations!

Typing. Paper must be laser printed/printable on 8.5" x 11" white sheets in Arial 10-point font single-spaced lines justify style in MS Word. All four margins must be 1" each.

First Page. Paper title not exceeding two lines must be CAPITALIZED AND CENTERED IN BOLD LETTERS. Author name and university/organizational affiliation of each author must be printed on one line each. Do NOT include titles such as Dr., Professor, Ph.D., department address email address etc. Please print the word "ABSTRACT" in capitalized bold letters left justified and double-spaced from last author's name/affiliation. Abstract should be in italic. Please see the sample manuscript.

All other Headings. All other section headings starting with INTRODUCTION must be numbered in capitalized bold letters left justified and double-spaced from last line above them. See the subsection headings in the sample manuscript.

Tables Figures and Charts. All tables figures or charts must be inserted in the body of the manuscripts within the margins with headings/titles in centered CAPITALIZED BOLD letters.

References and Bibliography. All references listed in this section must be cited in the article and vice-versa. The reference citations in the text must be inserted in parentheses within sentences with author name followed by a comma and year of publication. Please follow the following formats:

Journal Articles
Khade Alan S. and Metlen Scott K. "An Application of Benchmarking in Dairy Industry" *International Journal of Benchmarking* Vol. III (4) 1996 17

Books
Harrison Norma and Samson D. Technology Management: Text and Cases McGraw-Hill Publishing New York 2002

Internet
Hesterbrink C. E-Business and ERP: Bringing two Paradigms together October 1999; PricewaterhouseCoopers *www.pwc.com*.

284

Author Profile(s). At the end of paper include author profile(s) not exceeding five lines each author including name highest degree/university/year current position/university and major achievements. For example:

Author Profile:
Dr. Tahi J. Gnepa earned his Ph.D. at the University of Wisconsin Madison in 1989. Currently he is a professor of international business at California State University Stanislaus and Managing Editor of Journal of International Business Strategy (JIBStrategy).

Manuscript. Absolutely no footnotes! Do not insert page numbers for the manuscript. Please do not forget to run spelling and grammar check for the completed paper. Save the manuscript on your diskette/CD or hard drive.

Electronic Submission. Send your submission as an MS Word file attachment to your Email to **Review@iabe.org**.

Journal of Accountancy

ADDRESS FOR SUBMISSION:

Sarah Cobb & Vince Nolan, Asst. Editors
Journal of Accountancy
American Institute of CPAs
Harborside Financial Center
201 Plaza Three
Jersey City, NJ 07311-3881
USA
Phone: 201-938-3290
E-Mail: scobb@aicpa.org
Web: www.aicpa.org

CIRCULATION DATA:

Reader: Business Persons, Accountants
(CPAs)
Frequency of Issue: Monthly
Sponsor/Publisher: American Institute of
CPAs

PUBLICATION GUIDELINES:

Manuscript Length: 8 Maximum
Copies Required: Five
Computer Submission: Yes Disks Only
Format: MS Word, WdPerfect, Most Others
Fees to Review: 0.00 US$

Manuscript Style:
Chicago Manual of Style

REVIEW INFORMATION:

Type of Review: Blind Review
No. of External Reviewers: 3+
No. of In House Reviewers: 1
Acceptance Rate: 11-20%
Time to Review: 2 - 3 Months
Reviewers Comments: Yes
Invited Articles: 50% +
Fees to Publish: 0.00 US$

MANUSCRIPT TOPICS:

Accounting Information Systems; Accounting Practice; Auditing; Cost Accounting; Econometrics; Ethics; Financial Reporting; Fiscal Policy; Fraud; Government & Non Profit Accounting; Industrial Organization; Insurance; International Economics & Trade; International Finance; Micro Economics; Personal Financial Planning; Portfolio & Security Analysis; Tax Accounting

MANUSCRIPT GUIDELINES/COMMENTS:

Author Guidelines
[A discussion of subject and content with a *JofA* editor is highly recommended]

The *Journal of Accountancy* is a monthly magazine for the accounting profession. It covers everything that accountants should know. The subjects include accounting, financial reporting, auditing, taxation, personal financial planning, technology, professional developments, ethics, liability issues, consulting, practice management, education and related business and international issues.

Because *JofA* readers have interests covering diverse subjects, articles should have broad appeal and focus on practical situations and applications. Those based on case studies—that is, real-life examples—or surveys should draw conclusions from the research, analyze the impact on the profession and offer insights or advice that will be useful to readers. Use many examples and case studies to illustrate points—readers want to read about other cpas' experiences. contact your editor to discuss case studies. Articles that present survey data without an accompanying analysis, are entirely theoretical or are derived wholly from secondary sources are rarely accepted.

It is recommended that prospective authors read several recent issues of the *Journal of Accountancy* and speak with one of its editors before writing an article.

Readers
Over 40% of *JofA* readers work in industry in positions from staff accountant to chief financial officer. Another 40% of readers are in public practice, in firms ranging in size from a sole practitioner to an international firm of several thousand; some 30,000 of our readers are sole practitioners and a great many others work in small or midsize firms. The remainder are government personnel, educators or students.

Most accounting issues affect CPAs in both industry and public practice. Therefore, articles should address the needs of both audiences when applicable. Authors should specify which segments of the readership their article addresses and their objectives in writing it. The more the editors know about the author's intent and targeted audience, the easier it is to judge an article's suitability. The larger the audience served, the more likely an article will be accepted.

Diversity
The CPA profession is increasingly young, female and nonwhite, and we want our magazine to reflect that diversity; make sure at least half of the sources you quote aren't white male partners at a Big Four firm. The more sources the merrier. Short, lively quotes are desirable. Please also provide contact information—mailing and e-mail address, and phone and fax number—for all persons profiled or quoted in your article.

Subject Matter
Articles in the *JofA* fall into several categories:

Practical. These discuss business problems and offer solutions—actual or hypothetical examples and case studies are required. See "CPAs as Audit Committee Members," Sept'03, page 32. "A Strategy for Finding the Right Accounting Software," Sept'03, page 39.

Corporate. These articles explore all aspects of management accounting—for staff accountants to CFOs. See "How to Profit by Safeguarding Privacy," May'03, page 47. "Regulation FD—Coping in the Trenches," Jun'03, page 53.

Technical. These articles usually cover new standards or best practices that affect all segments of the profession. They explain regulatory actions and their impact. See "Tax Relief—Chapter 2003," Oct'03, page 41.

Professional Issues. These articles address issues facing the profession. See "An Insider's View of the New, Computerized CPA Exam," Oct'03, page 11.

Future. These articles may be based on academic research or fast-moving trends that will have an immediate or very near future impact on the profession. Articles based on academic research must also focus on its practical applications. See "How Sarbanes-Oxley Will Change the Audit Process," Sept'03, page 49.

Length
Feature articles should be a maximum of 1,500 words (6–7 double-spaced, typed pages, sidebars not included in this word count). The *JofA* also accepts shorter, narrowly focused articles for its columns. There should be a maximum of 1,000 words. Such articles are particularly useful when based on the author's own experience.

Style
The first paragraph should say what the article is about and why the reader would be interested in it. Include essential background information on the topic here. Relate the rest of the article to subjects mentioned in the introductory paragraph. If you must include technical jargon or complicated terms in the text, follow them with brief explanations. Weave essential references into the narrative; do not use footnotes or endnotes.

Authors should supply numerical data or a fact to create at least one small graphic to illustrate an important element in the article or related to the background or history of the content. See "Niche Development Tips," Dec'03, page 45.

Manuscript Requirements
Double-spaced, one side only of white paper. Use black ink. Do not use any special formatting—such as boldface, underlining, subscripts, indents, italic, special margins. write special instructions for formatting in parenthesis.

The Editorial and Review Processes
Submit all manuscripts on an exclusive basis. If the *JofA* learns that a manuscript has been submitted to any other publication, it will not consider the article.

The *JofA* uses editorial advisers to assist in selecting material for publication. This group of advisers consists of about 60 professionals with broad experience, including those in public accounting firms of varying sizes, CPAs in commerce, industry, and education and those with particular expertise in various specialties.

Manuscripts undergo blind reviews. Authors receive acknowledgments before the manuscripts are forwarded to reviewers for evaluations and recommendations. Acceptance is based on practicality, readability, technical soundness, originality and interest to readers. The review process generally takes about eight weeks. All manuscripts receive a careful, judicious review, and the editors make every effort to assist the author in revising and editing a manuscript if, in the opinion of the reviewers, the subject is worth pursuing.

Once an article is accepted, an editor contacts the author to discuss any recommended changes. After revisions, the article is edited to conform to *JofA* style. The author receives a final manuscript for review and final approval. The author cannot rewrite at this time, but can make essential changes or corrections. Authors are given a tentative publication date. Regrettably, the *JofA* budget makes no provision for payment of honoraria for published articles. However, as a token of appreciation, authors of feature articles receive a specially bound copy of the magazine containing their article, as well as ten copies of the issue.

Submission Checklist
- Submit article on an exclusive basis
- Send 5 copies
- Place author's name on title page only
- Submit typewritten, double-spaced copy on plain paper with no logos or letterhead
- Send a disc along with the hardcopy
- Write on the disc label:
  1. Author's name
  2. Word processing program used
  3. Name of document
- Do not use special formatting in the text.
- Do not send electronic artwork unless it has already been discussed with a *JofA* editor.
- Include data for opening page graphic.
- Include examples and/or case study(s).

Editors
To discuss a manuscript or article idea with a *Journal* editor, contact:

Peter Fleming (201) 938-3286 **pfleming@aicpa.org**
[Senior Business and Industry Editor] Executive Compensation
and Employee Benefits/Financial Reporting/General Business/
Sarbanes-Oxley Compliance.

Michael Hayes (201) 938-3796 **mhayes@aicpa.org**
[Senior Business Development Editor] Assurance Services
(Practice Management)/Business Valuation/Career
Development/Consulting/Diversity/Legal Issues/Marketing/
Practice Management.

James Quaglietta (201) 938-3331 **jquaglietta@aicpa.org**
[Senior Tax Accounting Editor] Assurance Services (Technical)/
Education/Financial Reporting/Insurance/Investments/Not-for-
Profit/Personal Financial Planning/Quality Review/Retirement
Planning/Tax (includes Tax Briefs/Tax Cases/Tax News/Tax
Notes).

Robert Tie (201) 938-3412 **rtie@aicpa.org**
[Senior Editor] Accounting and Auditing/FDIC/Financial
Reporting/Government Accounting/Highlights/Inside AICPA/
International/Professional Issues/Technology/Venture Capital.

Stanley Zarowin **zarowin@mindspring.com**
[Technology Contributing Editor] E-Commerce/General Interest/
Golden Business Ideas/Technology/Technology Q&A.

Manuscripts or questions about editorial policy should be directed to:
Sarah Cobb/Sr. Asst. Editor
Journal of Accountancy
American Institute of CPAs
Harborside Financial Center
201 Plaza Three Jersey City, NJ 07311-3881
Phone: (201) 938-3290; Email: **scobb@aicpa.org**

or

Vince Nolan/Asst. Editor
Phone: (201) 938-3540; Email: **vnolan@aicpa.org**

Journal of Accounting & Organisational Change

ADDRESS FOR SUBMISSION:

Zahirul Hoque, Editor
Journal of Accounting & Organisational
  Change
Deakin University
School of Accounting, Economics & Fin.
Faculty of Business and Law
Waurn Ponds
Geelong, VIC 3217
Australia
Phone: 613-5227 2733
E-Mail: zahirul.hoque@deakin.edu.au
  hzahirul@yahoo.com.au
  shirin.hoque@deakin.edu.au
Web: www.deakin.edu.au

PUBLICATION GUIDELINES:

Manuscript Length: 26-30
Copies Required: Three
Computer Submission: Yes Email
Format: MS Word
Fees to Review: 0.00 US$

Manuscript Style:
  American Psychological Association,
  Chicago Manual of Style

CIRCULATION DATA:

Reader: Business Persons, Academics
Frequency of Issue: 3 Times/Year
Sponsor/Publisher: Emerald Group
  Publishing Limited

REVIEW INFORMATION:

Type of Review: Blind Review
No. of External Reviewers: 2
No. of In House Reviewers: 2
Acceptance Rate: 70%
Time to Review: 2 - 3 Months
Reviewers Comments: Yes
Invited Articles: 0-5%
Fees to Publish: 0.00 US$

MANUSCRIPT TOPICS:
Accounting Education; Accounting Information Systems; Behavioral Accounting; Cost Accounting; Economic Development; Government & Non Profit Accounting

MANUSCRIPT GUIDELINES/COMMENTS:

Aims, Scope and Editorial Policies
In today's business world, organisations experience dramatic change from time to time. The *Journal of Accounting & Organisational Change (JAOC)* represents a new emphasis on exploring how organisations change, and how the change process affects internal organisational processes. Organisational change often needs the adoption of innovative ideas and behaviour to achieve the desired change based on the strategic orientation of the organisation. The change process within the organisation frequently brings about changes in appropriate organisational structures and internal systems with different ramifications. New accounting and control systems can be essential to implement strategies in a change situation.

JAOC is a peer-reviewed, academic journal that publishes two volumes per year. It will publish high quality research on contemporary issues in organisational change and accounting. It provides a communication media between accountants and organisational experts, whether they work in industry, the public sector, in consulting, or in academic institutions. Contributions from HRM, organisational behaviour, industrial relations and organisational change and development researchers working in disciplines outside of accounting and finance are actively encouraged along with contributions from accounting and auditing academics.

Empirical and review papers are sought from a variety of theoretical and methodological perspectives. In addition to empirical and case study articles, *JAOC* also welcomes replication of previously published studies and review articles on advances in accounting and organisational change research. It welcomes manuscripts from any emerging and developed economies both in the public and private sectors. Emerging economies are defined broadly and may include those in transition to more market-based regimes.

The journal's aim is to be a primary source of literature on accounting, HRM, industrial relations, strategy and organisational change for both academics and their students. It will also be a valuable source for CEOs, CFOs and managers in both developed and developing countries.

Submission of Manuscripts
Manuscripts should be submitted via email to the Editor at **zahirul.hoque@deakin.edu.au** (Professor Zahirul Hoque). A cover page containing the name and affiliation of each author, complete addresses, phone and fax numbers, email addresses, any acknowledgements that the authors wish to make must accompany the manuscript. Files must be in Microsoft Word format. Principal authors are responsible for ensuring that co-authors agree to the inclusion of their names before submission of a manuscript to the journal.

Acceptance Criteria and Review Process
Manuscripts currently under consideration by another journal or other publisher should not be submitted. Subject matter must be of importance to the accounting and organisational change disciplines. Research questions must fall within the journal's scope. Presentation MUST conform to the journal's Manuscript Preparation and Style (see below).

All manuscripts submitted will normally only be considered for publication subject to a detailed blind review by at least two reviewers. In the interests of a fair review, authors should avoid the use of anything that would make their identity obvious. Using the reviewers' recommendations, the Editor will decide whether the particular manuscript should be accepted as is, revised, or rejected for publication.

Authors submitting a manuscript do so on the understanding that if it is accepted for publication, copyright in the article, including the right to reproduce the article in all forms and media, shall be assigned exclusively to the publisher. Revisions must be submitted within 12 months from request, otherwise they will be considered new submissions.

Manuscript Preparation and Style

English: Use Australian spelling rather than American spelling, and follow *The Macquarie Dictionary* recommendations generally. Words ending in –ise or –ize generally take –ise in Australian usage, e.g. realise, theorise, organise, etc. Use the original spelling in quoted material. Also note that the official spelling of an organisation's name should be retained, e.g. the World Health Organization.

Format. Authors MUST follow the following format when preparing their manuscripts for *JAOC*.

1. All manuscripts should be typed on one side of A4 (210mm x 297mm) and be double-spaced, except for indented quotations.

2. Margins should be at least 2.5cm (one inch) from top, bottom and sides to facilitate editing and duplication.

3. Manuscripts should be as concise as the subject and research method permit, generally not to exceed 8,000 words.

4. To assure anonymous review, authors should not identify themselves directly or indirectly in their papers. Single authors should not use the editorial 'we'.

5. A cover page should include the title of the paper, the author's name, title and affiliation, correspondence address, telephone number, fax number, email address, and any acknowledgements.

6. The first page of the paper should include the title of the paper, an **abstract** of 100-150 words, and three to six **keywords** which encapsulate the principal subjects covered by the paper.

7. All pages, including tables, figures, appendices and references should be serially numbered.

8. **Figures, charts** and **diagrams** should be kept to a minimum. They must be black and white with minimum shading and numbered consecutively using arabic numerals with a brief title and labelled axes. In the text, the position of the figure should be shown by typing on a separate line the words, "insert Figure 1 here".

9. **Tables** must be numbered consecutively with roman numerals and a brief title. In the text, the position of the table should be shown by typing on a separate line the words, "insert Table 1 here".

10. **Photos** and **illustrations** must be supplied as good quality black and white original half tones with captions. Their position should be shown in the text by typing on a separate line the words, "insert Plate 1 here".

11. For quotation within the text use only single quotation marks, and double marks for quotes within quotes.

12. Spell out numbers from one to ten, except when used in tables and lists, and when used with mathematical, statistical, scientific or technical units and quantities, such as distances, weights and measures. For example, *six days; 5 kilometres; 45 years.* All other numbers are expressed numerically.

13. Within text use the word percent; in tables, figures, and exhibits the symbol % is used.

14. Use a hyphen (-) to joint unit modifiers or to clarify usage. For example: a well-known author; re-form.

15. The following will be Roman in all cases: i.e., e.g., ibid., et al., op. cit.

16. Initials: T. M. Hopper (space between): Countries: U.S., U.K. (no space between).

17. Commas and periods are always placed inside the quotation marks. Colons and semicolons go outside the quotation marks. Questions marks and exclamation points go in or out, depending on whether they belong to the material inside the quote. If they belong to the quoted material, they go inside the quote marks and vice versa.

18. **Headings** must be short, clearly defined and numbered. Major headings should flush left, bold, and lower case. Second level headings should be flush left, italic, and lower case. Third level headings should be paragraph left, italic, and lower case. All headings must be numbered serially. For example:
A flush left, bold, and lower case, 1. First level heading
A left, italic, and lower case, 1.1. Second level heading
　　A paragraph left, italic, and lower case, 1.1.1. Third level heading

19. **Footnotes notes** should be used only if absolutely necessary and must be identified in the text by consecutive numbers, and placed at the bottom of the appropriate page of the article.

20. Manuscripts reporting on field surveys or experiments should include questionnaires, cases, interview schedule, or other instruments used in the study.

Citations. Citations are styled in the author–date (Harvard) system, as follows:
1. In the text, works are cited as follows: author's last name and date, with comma, for example, (Kaplan, 1984); with two authors (Kaplan and Norton, 1996); with more than two (Kaplan et al., 2001); with more than one source cited together (Kaplan, 1984; Kaplan and Norton, 1996); with two or more works by authors (Kaplan and Norton, 1992, 1996)

2. Use "p." or "pp." before page numbers: for example, (Kaplan and Norton, 1996, p. 25)

3. When the reference list contains more than one work of an author published in the same year, the suffix a, b, etc., follows the date in the text citation: for example, (Parker, 1999a, 1999b).

Reference list. At the end of the article a reference list in alphabetical order must be given, according to surname of the authors, followed by initials, as follows:

294

For books
Burrows, R. and Loader, B., 1994. *Towards a Post-Fordist Welfare State?* Routledge, London.

For edited books
Benyon, J. and Edwards, A., 1999. Community governance of crime control. In Stoker G. (Ed.), The *New Management of British Local Governance.* Macmillian Press, London.

For journal article
For one author: Parker, L.D., 2001. Back to the future: the broadening accounting trajectory. *The British Accounting Review*, 33(4), 421-454.

For two authors
Broadbent, J. and Guthrie, J., 1992. Changes in the public sector: a review of recent 'alternative' accounting research. *Accounting, Auditing and Accountability Journal*, 5(2), 3-31.

For more than two authors
Humphrey, C., Miller, P. and Scapens, R.W., 1993. Accountability and accountable management in the public sector. *Accounting, Auditing and Accountability Journal*, 6(3), 7-29.

For conference papers
Russell, P. and Sherer, M., 1991. Further discourse on the Thatcherism of the UK: illustrations of new accounting(s) and control(s) in the state sector. Proceedings of the Third Interdisciplinary Perspectives on Accounting Conference, University of Manchester.

Final Submission
Once accepted for publication, submit an electronic version of the final manuscript to the editor, either via email as an attached file (**zahirul.hoque@deakin.edu.au**) or on a 3.5" **disk** by ordinary mail in MS-WORD format labelled with: author name(s); title of article; journal title; file name. The authors must ensure that their article is complete, grammatically correct and without spelling or typographical errors.

Manuscripts not conforming to these guidelines will be returned to the author(s).

Journal of Accounting and Economics

ADDRESS FOR SUBMISSION:

Gail L. Pratt, Editorial Assistant
Journal of Accounting and Economics
University of Rochester
William E. Simon Graduate School
 of Business Administration
Rochester, NY 14627
USA
Phone: 585-275-4063
E-Mail: pratt@simon.rochester.edu
Web: www.elsevier.com

CIRCULATION DATA:

Reader: Academics
Frequency of Issue: Quarterly
Sponsor/Publisher: Elsevier Inc.

PUBLICATION GUIDELINES:

Manuscript Length: 20+
Copies Required: Electronic
Computer Submission: Yes Online
Format:
Fees to Review: 250.00 US$ Subscriber
 300.00 US$ Non-subscriber

Manuscript Style:
 See Manuscript Guidelines

REVIEW INFORMATION:

Type of Review: Blind Review
No. of External Reviewers: 1
No. of In House Reviewers: 0
Acceptance Rate: 11-20%
Time to Review: 1 - 2 Months
Reviewers Comments: Yes
Invited Articles: 0-5%
Fees to Publish: 0.00 US$

MANUSCRIPT TOPICS:
Accounting Information Systems; Accounting Theory & Practice; Auditing; Cost Accounting; Government & Non Profit Accounting; Tax Accounting

MANUSCRIPT GUIDELINES/COMMENTS:

Description
The *Journal of Accounting and Economics* encourages the application of economic theory to the explanation of accounting phenomena. The *Journal of Accounting and Economics* provides a forum for the publication of the highest quality manuscripts which employ economic analyses of accounting problems. Reading the *Journal of Accounting and Economics* provides the most accessible insight into the research that is influencing contemporary accounting scholars and students.

A wide range of methodologies are encouraged and covered:
* the determination of accounting standards;
* government regulation of corporate disclosure;
* the information content and role of accounting numbers in capital markets;
* the role of accounting in financial contracts and in monitoring agency relationships;
* the theory of the accounting firm;

- government regulation of the accounting profession;
- statistical sampling and the loss function in auditing;
- the role of accounting within the firm.

Guide for Authors

1. Papers must be in English.

2. Manuscripts are submitted electronically at: **www.ees.elsevier.com/jae/**

Submission fee is used to encourage quicker response from the referees who are paid a nominal fee if they return the manuscript within three weeks. The submission fee of US$ 250 must accompany all manuscripts submitted by authors who currently subscribe to the *Journal of Accounting and Economics* and US$ 300 for non-subscribers. The submission fee will be refunded for all accepted manuscripts (unless it was previously waived). There are no page charges. Cheques should be made payable to the *Journal of Accounting and Economics*.

Submission of a paper will be held to imply that it contains original unpublished work and is not being submitted for publication elsewhere. The Editor does not accept responsibility for damage or loss of papers submitted. Upon acceptance of an article, author(s) will be asked to transfer copyright of the article to the publisher. This transfer will ensure the widest possible dissemination of information.

3. Submission of accepted papers as electronic manuscripts, i.e., on disk with accompanying manuscript, is encouraged. Electronic manuscripts have the advantage that there is no need for rekeying of text, thereby avoiding the possibility of introducing errors and resulting in reliable and fast delivery of proofs. The preferred storage medium is a 5.25 or 3.5 inch disk in MS-DOS format, although other systems are welcome, e.g., Macintosh (in this case, save your file in the usual manner; do not use the option "save in MS-DOS format"). Do not submit your original paper as electronic manuscript but hold on to disk until asked for this by the Editor (in case your paper is accepted without revisions). Do submit the accepted version of your paper as electronic manuscript. Make absolutely sure that the file on the disk and the printout are identical. Please use a new and correctly formatted disk and label this with your name; also specify the software and hardware used as well as the title of the file to be processed. Do not convert the file to plain ASCII. Ensure that the letter 'I' and digit '1', and also the letter 'O' and digit '0' are used properly, and format your article (tabs, indents, etc.) consistently. Characters not available on your word processor (Greek letters mathematical symbols, etc.) should not be left open but indicated by a unique code (e.g. gralpha, alpha, etc., for the Greek letter α) Such codes should be used consistently throughout the entire text; a list of codes used should accompany the electronic manuscript. Do not allow your word processor to introduce word breaks and do not use a justified layout. Please adhere strictly to the general instructions below on style, arrangement and, in particular, the reference style of the journal.

4. Manuscripts should be double spaced, with wide margins, and printed on one side of the paper only. All pages should be numbered consequently. Titles and subtitles should be short. References, tables, and legends for the figures should be printed on separate pages.

5. The first page of the manuscript should contain the following information: (i) the title; (ii) the names. and institutional affiliations. of the authors; (iii) an abstract of not more than 100 words. A footnote on the same sheet should give the name, address, and telephone and fax numbers of the corresponding author [as well as an e-mail address].

6. The first page of the manuscript should also contain at least one classification code according to the Classification System for Journal Articles as used by the *Journal of Economic Literature*; in addition, up to five key words should be supplied.

7. Acknowledgements and information on grants received can be given in a first footnote, which should not be included in the consecutive numbering of footnotes.

8. Footnotes should be kept to a minimum and numbered consecutively throughout the text with superscript Arabic numerals.

9. Displayed formulae should be numbered consecutively throughout the manuscript as (1), (2), etc. against the right-hand margin of the page. In cases where the derivation of formulae has been abbreviated, it is of great help to the referees if the full derivation can be presented on a separate sheet (not to be published).

10. References to publications should be as follows: 'Smith (1992) reported that...' of 'This problem has been studied previously (e.g., Smith et al., 1969.)' The author should make sure that there is a strict one-to-one correspondence between the names and years in the text and those on the list. The list of references should appear at the end of the main text after any appendices, but before tables and legends for figures. It should be double spaced and listed in alphabetical order by author's name. References should appear as follows:

For monographs
Hawawini, G. and I. Swary, 1990, Mergers and acquisitions in the U.S. banking industry: Evidence from the capital markets (North-Holland, Amsterdam).

For contributions to collective works
Brunner, K. and A.H. Meltzer, 1990, Money supply, in: B.M. Friedman and F.H. Hahn, eds., Handbook of monetary economics, Vol. 1 (North-Holland, Amsterdam). 357-396.

For periodicals
Griffiths, W. and G. Judge, 1992, Testing and estimating location vectors when the error covariance matrix is unknown, Journal of Econometrics 54, 121-138.

Note that journal titles should not be abbreviated.

11. Illustrations will be reproduced photographically from originals supplied by the author; they will not be redrawn by the publisher. Please provide all illustrations in quadruplicate one high-contrast original and three photocopies. Care should be taken that lettering and symbols are of a comparable size. The illustrations should not be inserted in the text, and should be marked on the back with figure number, title of paper, and author's name. All graphs and diagrams should be referred to as figures, and should be numbered consecutively in the text in

Arabic numerals. Illustration for papers submitted as electronic manuscripts should be in traditional form.

12. Tables should be numbered consecutively in the text in Arabic numerals and printed on separate sheets.

Any manuscript which does not conform to the above instructions may be returned for the necessary revision before publication.

Page proofs will be sent to the corresponding author. Proofs should be corrected carefully; the responsibility for detecting errors lies with the author. Corrections should be restricted to instances in which the proof is at variance with the manuscript. No deviations from the version accepted by the Editors are permissible without the prior and explicit approval by the Editors; these alterations will be charged. Fifty reprints of each paper are supplied free of charge to the corresponding author; additional reprints are available at cost if they are ordered when the proof is returned.

Journal of Accounting and Finance Research

ADDRESS FOR SUBMISSION:

Roger Calcote, Editor
Journal of Accounting and Finance
   Research
American Academy of Accounting
   and Finance
220 Oliver Drive
Brookhaven, MS 39601
USA
Phone: 601-833-9741
E-Mail: calcote@cableone.net
Web: www.aaafonline.org

PUBLICATION GUIDELINES:

Manuscript Length: 21-25
Copies Required: Three
Computer Submission: Yes Disk Required
Format: MSWord, WordPerfect
Fees to Review: 100.00 US$ Per Author
   25.00 US$ Adt'l Per Co-Author

Manuscript Style:
   See Manuscript Guidelines

CIRCULATION DATA:

Reader: Academics
Frequency of Issue: Quarterly
Sponsor/Publisher: American Academy of
   Accounting and Finance

REVIEW INFORMATION:

Type of Review: Blind Review
No. of External Reviewers: 2
No. of In House Reviewers: 2
Acceptance Rate: 21-30%
Time to Review: 2 - 3 Months
Reviewers Comments: Yes
Invited Articles: 0-5%
Fees to Publish: 0.00 US$

MANUSCRIPT TOPICS:

Accounting Education; Accounting History; Accounting Information Systems; Accounting Theory & Practice; Auditing; Corporate Finance; Cost Accounting; Finance Education; Finance Research; Financial Institutions & Markets; Financial Services; Government & Non Profit Accounting; Insurance; International Economics & Trade; International Finance; Portfolio & Security Analysis; Real Estate; Tax Accounting

MANUSCRIPT GUIDELINES/COMMENTS:

Format Instructions

All instructions that follow are mandatory for the final copy of the paper you will submit by applicable deadline. These instructions are laid-out in the format you shall use. We are following the general style of *Accounting Horizons*. Please be advised that papers submitted not formatted as per these instructions will be returned.

Title

The title should be in Times New Roman point 16 font, bold, all capital letters, centered at the top of the first page, and beginning at the top margin (.75"). Titles of more than one line should be single spaced.

Authors
The author(s), name(s) and affiliation(s) should be centered and single spaced, beginning on the second line below the title. Do not use titles such as Dr. or Assistant Professor, etc. Do not include mailing addresses, telephone numbers, or e-mail addresses. Use Times New Roman point 14 font. The rest of the paper should be in Times New Roman point 12 font.

Mailing addresses and e-mail addresses for all authors and co-authors must be included on a separate page.

Headings
All headings should be in bold type. First-level headings should be centered and set in all caps. Second-level headings should be set flush left with initial caps. Do not use headings other than these two. Separate headings from preceding and succeeding text by one line space.

Abstract
Introduce the paper with an abstract of approximately 150-200 words. Begin the left column with the first-level heading, "**ABSTRACT**." Be sure the abstract is in columns and single spaced. Use Times New Roman point 12 font.

Body
The body of the paper should be single spaced and should follow the abstract. Use a first-level heading of some type after the abstract and before the first paragraph of the body of the paper to separate the two.

Figures and Tables
Figures and tables should be placed either "in-column" or at the top of the page as close as possible to where they are cited. First-level headings state the table or figure number and may be followed by second-level subheadings. Do not scale down the headings. A sample of a full page table and an "in-column" table are shown below.

Figures and tables must be inserted in the appropriate locations in the version of the paper submitted for publication. Do not leave figures and/or tables at the end of the paper.

Scalable fonts smaller may Times New Roman 12 may be used to fit a table "in-column" provided if, in the author's opinion, the data is still legible.

"In-Column" Table

TABLE 1		
May Include Multiple Columns		
Column	Column	Column
1	2	3

Table 2
Checklist for Papers

- Prepare using WordPerfect (any version) or Microsoft Word (any version).
- Submit disk copy 3.5" disk (final version only)
- Submit three (3) hard copies printed on 300 dot per inch (minimum) laser printer
- Use Times New Roman, point 12 (or the nearest thing to it available on your laser printer) for the body of the paper
- Title of paper: All caps, bold type, single-spaced, centered across both columns, Times New Roman, point 16 font
- Authors: include affiliations, no titles, bold type, single-spaced, centered across both columns, Times New Roman, point 14 font
- Headings: Only two allowed: 1st level- all caps, centered in column, bold type; 2nd level- initial caps, flush left, bold type, Times New Roman point 12 font
- Scale tables and figures to avoid use of paste, glue or tape
- Lay-out: Two columns, except for title, authors and figures and/or tables
- Margins: Top and bottom margins – 0.7500"
- Columns should be balanced newspaper with measurements set at 3.0" per column with .5" center space.
- Left and right margins – 1.00"
- Headers: Do not type in headers
- Page numbers: Do not type in: lightly pencil on back of pages
- Number of pages: Limited to 15
- Submit the final version of your paper by applicable deadline.

Calling References
Use *Accounting Review* style for calling references.

Footnotes
The use of footnotes is strongly discouraged.

Equations
All equations should be placed on a separate line and numbered consecutively, with the equation numbers placed within parentheses and aligned against the right margin.

$$R1 = f(X1) \tag{1}$$

References (Bibliography)
Since the bibliography should only include those references cited in the paper, it should be referred to as "**REFERENCES**", a first-level heading. References should be listed at the end of the paper and be in newspaper columns. Use a hanging indent of 0.3".

302

Appendices
An appendix should immediately follow the body of the paper, precede the references, and should be referred to as "**APPENDIX**", a first-level heading. If you have more than one appendix, number each consecutively with a second-level heading.

TYPING AND PRINTING INSTRUCTIONS
Word Processing Software and Type Size
Papers are to be prepared using WordPerfect (any version through 10) or Microsoft Word (any version). Submit the final version of your paper on a 3.5" disk or a compact disk. Also, submit three (3) laser printed hard-copies of the final version of the paper. The preferred type is Times New Roman point 16 font (title of paper), point 14 font (author) and point 12 font (body of paper). If not available on your laser printer, please use the type font that most closely matches Times New Roman.

Layout and Margins
Except for the title and author(s) information, papers are to be laid out using the Newspaper Columns feature. Set the column margins as follows:
Columns should be set at 3.0 each with .5" center.

All paragraphs should be indented 0.3". Set the top and bottom margins of the paper at 0.7500". Use "Full Justification" and do not use hyphenation. Do not skip a line between paragraphs.

Spacing
Single space the body of the paper. Double space before and after all headings. Double space after the last authors' name preceding the abstract heading.

Page Numbers
Do not type in (insert) page numbers. Keep pages in sequence and lightly pencil in the page number on the back of each page.

Headers
Do not include headers. Headers will be added after you submit your paper.

Note: All papers submitted using any format other than that described in these instructions will be returned.

Deadline for Submission of Papers
July 31, each year

Submissions Fees
$100 single author $25 each additional co-author

Submission fees must be included with original article submission.

Journal of Accounting and Public Policy

ADDRESS FOR SUBMISSION:

Lawrence A. Gordon, Editor-in-Chief
Journal of Accounting and Public Policy
Maryin P. Loeb, Editor
University of Maryland
Robert H. Smith School of Business
Acct. and Info. Assurance Department
College Park, MD 20742-1815
USA
Phone: 301-314-2255 or 301-405-2209
E-Mail: mloeb@rhsmith.umd.edu
lgordon@rhs.smith.umd.edu
Web: www.elsevier.com

PUBLICATION GUIDELINES:

Manuscript Length: Less than 40 Pages
Copies Required: Three
Computer Submission: Yes Email
Format:
Fees to Review: 0.00 US$

Manuscript Style:
    Chicago Manual of Style, & Journal
    Instructions

CIRCULATION DATA:

Reader: Academics, Business Persons
Frequency of Issue: Bi-Monthly
Sponsor/Publisher: Elsevier Inc.

REVIEW INFORMATION:

Type of Review: Blind Review
No. of External Reviewers: 2
No. of In House Reviewers: 1
Acceptance Rate: 11-20%
Time to Review: 2-4 Months
Reviewers Comments: Yes
Invited Articles: 0-5%
Fees to Publish: 0.00 US$

MANUSCRIPT TOPICS:

Accounting Information Systems; Accounting Theory & Practice; Auditing; Cost Accounting; Econometrics; Fiscal Policy; Information Security; Information Security Auditing; Micro Economics; Public Policy Economics

MANUSCRIPT GUIDELINES/COMMENTS:

Editor
    Martin P. Loeb
    Professor of Accounting and Information Assurance
    Deloitte & Touche Faculty Fellow
    The Robert H. Smith School of Business
    University of Maryland, College Park
    College Park, MD 20742-1815
    Phone: 301-405-2209, Fax: 301-405-0359, Email: **mloeb@rhsmith.umd.edu**

Description

The *Journal of Accounting and Public Policy* publishes research papers focusing on the intersection between accounting and public policy. Preference is given to papers illuminating through theoretical or empirical analysis, the effects of accounting on public policy and vice-versa. Subjects treated in this journal include the interface of accounting with economics, political science, sociology, or law. The *Journal* includes a section entitled Accounting Letters. This section publishes short research articles that should not exceed approximately 3,000 words. The objective of this section is to facilitate the rapid dissemination of important accounting research. Accordingly, articles submitted to this section will be reviewed within fours weeks of receipt, revisions will be limited to one, and publication will occur within four months of acceptance.

Guide for Authors

All manuscripts should be submitted to: Lawrence A. Gordon, and Martin P. Loeb, Robert H. Smith School of Business, University of Maryland, College Park, MD20742, USA. Manuscripts are submitted with the understanding that they are original, unpublished works, and are not being submitted elsewhere.

For additional information, see the *Journal of Accounting and Public Policy* web page within the Elsevier website: **http://www.Elsevier.com/inca/publications/store/5/0/5/7/2/1/index.htt**

Manuscript. Submit the original and three photocopies of the manuscript, typed double-spaced on 8½ x 11-inch bond paper. On the title page include names and addresses of authors, academic or professional affiliations, and the complete address of the author to whom proofs and reprint requests should be sent. Include an abstract of a maximum 200 words followed by a short list of key words. The text proper is to begin on the following page and ends with the acknowledgments, whenever appropriate. References, tables, figure captions, and footnotes to follow. Tables and figures are to be numbered, in order of appearance, with Arabic numerals, and each should have a brief, descriptive title. Footnotes to the text are numbered consecutively with superior Arabic numerals.

Typescripts should be carefully checked before submission to obviate alterations after acceptance.

Mathematical Notation. Use typewritten letters, numbers, and symbols whenever possible. Identify boldface, script letters, etc. at their first occurrence. Distinguish between number one and the letter "1" and between zero and the letter "O" whenever confusion might result.

References. Citation in text is by name(s) of author(s), followed by year of publication and page numbers in parentheses. For references authored by more than two contributors use first author's name and et al. For multiple citations in the same year use a, b, c after year of publication. The reference list should be typed alphabetically according to the following style:

Journal
Martens, S., Stevens, K., 1993. Positive accounting theory and the obligation for post-retirements benefits. Critical Perspectives on Accounting 4 (3), 275-295.

305

Daily
Lublin, J., Lopez, J., Jan. 15, 1993. Executive disclosures pay-off for advisers, The Wall Street Journal 221 (10), B1.

Book
Fleiss J., 1981. Statistical Methods For Rates and Proportions, 2nd edn. Wiley, New York.

Edited Book
Arens A., 1993. An academic's perspective of setting auditing standards. In: Mary Ball Washington Forum Series in Accounting Education, M. Usry (Ed.), University of West Florida, Pensacola, FL, pp. 36-47.

Institute Publication
Financial Accounting Standards Board (FASB), 1987. Recognition of depreciation by not-for-profit organizations. Statement of Financial Accounting Standards no. 93. Financial Accounting Standards Board, Stanford, CT.

Illustrations. Unmounted, glossy, black and white photographs or India ink drawings on white paper should accompany the original copy of the manuscript. Photocopies are acceptable for the other three copies of the manuscript. On the back of each figure write the number, first author's name, and indicate which the top. Captions appear on a separate page.

Proofs and Reprints. The corresponding author will receive proofs, which should be corrected and returned within ten days of receipt. The author is responsible for proofreading the manuscript; the publisher is not responsible for any error not marked by the author on proof. Corrections should be limited to printer's errors; no substantial changes are allowed at this stage. For each article 25 free offprints are supplied. Additional offprints may be ordered; the Publisher will send the order form to the corresponding author.

Copyright. Upon acceptance of an article by the journal, the author(s) will be asked to transfer copyright of the article to the publisher, Elsevier Science Inc. This transfer will ensure the widest possible dissemination of information under the U.S. Copyright law.

For publication data and offprints of your papers please contact Elsevier Science B.V., Author Support Department, P.O. Box 2759, 1000 CT Amsterdam, The Netherlands; fax no. +31 (20) 485.3752; email authorsupport@elsevier.ie. Information on the status of your paper may be found via the Internet at www.elsevier.com/oasis. You will find more information in the letter sent to you by the publisher upon arrival of your paper.

Author Enquiries. For enquiries relating to the submission of articles (including electronic submission where available) please visit the Author Gateway from Elsevier Science at http://authors.elsevier.com. The Author Gateway also provides the facility to track accepted articles and set up e-mail alerts to inform you of when an article's status has changed as well as detailed artwork guidelines, copyright information, frequently asked questions and more. Contact details for questions arising after acceptance of an article, especially those relating to proofs, are provided after registration of an article for publication.

Journal of Accounting Case Research

ADDRESS FOR SUBMISSION:

Eldon Gardner, Editor
Journal of Accounting Case Research
University of Lethbridge
Faculty of Management
4401 University Drive
Lethbridge, Alberta, T1K 3M4
Canada
Phone: 403-329-2726
E-Mail: gardner@uleth.ca
Web:

PUBLICATION GUIDELINES:

Manuscript Length: Any
Copies Required: Five
Computer Submission: No
Format: N/A
Fees to Review: 0.00 US$ Subscriber
    60.00 US$ Non-Subscriber

Manuscript Style:
    See Manuscript Guidelines

CIRCULATION DATA:

Reader: Academics
Frequency of Issue: 2 Times/Year
Sponsor/Publisher: University / Captus
    Press Inc.

REVIEW INFORMATION:

Type of Review: Blind Review
No. of External Reviewers: 2
No. of In House Reviewers: 0
Acceptance Rate: 21-30%
Time to Review: 2 - 4 Months
Reviewers Comments: Yes
Invited Articles: 0-5%
Fees to Publish: 0.00 US$ Subscriber
    60.00 US$ Non-Subscriber

MANUSCRIPT TOPICS:

Accounting Education; Accounting Information Systems; Accounting Theory & Practice; Auditing; Behavioral Accounting; Cost Accounting; Government & Non Profit Accounting; Tax Accounting

MANUSCRIPT GUIDELINES/COMMENTS:

Editorial Policy

The *Journal of Accounting Case Research* publishes cases on accounting and related topics, and educational manuscripts related to the use of case materials in accounting. Cases and Teaching Notes should be separated, and notes and references should appear at the end of the manuscript double-spaced manuscripts, on one side of the paper only, submitted with a diskette in WordPerfect or Microsoft Word containing all of the case material and teaching notes, are requested.

Cases submitted for review should have a separate title page with names and affiliations of all authors thereon. No names or references to the individuals involved in writing the case should be contained in the manuscript itself.

Cases should have a clear set of issues on which decisions are required, and they should be well written in the English or French language. Any exhibits, tables, graphs or charts should be prepared in camera-ready form on separate pages, preferably in Microsoft Word compatible form. A detailed teaching note is required, including some indication of courses in accounting for which the case is suitable; classroom format; other possible areas of use for the case; issues for discussion; directions for analysis, and any background material that would be relevant or appropriate for the case.

All cases submitted for review should be available for publication without restriction, unless a sponsoring agency (such as a research funding agency or post-secondary educational institution) also holds a copyright. Under such circumstances, the agency should be willing to allow publication in the *Journal of Accounting Case Research*, subject to minimal restrictions on use by subscribers.

A forwarding letter that contains either or both of the following, as applicable, should accompany cases submitted for review:

1. The source of the material and the authorization of the provider of the material for publication of the case in the *Journal of Accounting Case Research*.

2. A statement that any other material not provided by a specific source, as in (1), has been obtained from fictional or public domain sources, and that no copyrighted material has been used without permission.

It is the policy of the journal to have a minimum of two blind reviews, by qualified academic and/or professional reviewers, of all materials considered for publication. Reviewers are presented with guidelines, and their recommendations are given a careful and thorough consideration in publication decisions. The ultimate decision on publication, however, rests with the Editor and the Faculty of Management of the University of Lethbridge.

The Faculty of Management will hold the copyright on all published cases jointly with the author unless otherwise stated. Publication in other venues will be allowed by the journal if permission is requested in writing and a suitable royalty arrangement (if applicable) is made.

The following note is placed at the bottom of the first page of any case accepted for publication:

This case was prepared by John Doe of the University of Big City, Big City, State, and County as the basis for class discussion rather than to illustrate either effective or ineffective handling of a managerial situation. Distributed by the Faculty of Management, The University of Lethbridge, ©200x. All rights reserved to the author and to the Faculty of Management. Permission to use the case in classes of instruction, without restriction is provided to subscribers of the journal unless otherwise stated.

Submission of Cases

Five copies of cases and articles should be submitted (with teaching notes where applicable) to the Editor. Facsimile copies are not acceptable for publication, but authors may submit a copy in this manner for preliminary consideration by the editor.

Previously published material, or materials under review for publication elsewhere are not acceptable. Materials presented to workshops or in Proceedings are not construed to be previously published.

There is no submission fee for subscribers to *The Journal of Accounting Case Research*. Non-subscribers are required to pay the annual subscription fee, or demonstrate that it has been paid, prior to review of materials submitted.

For manuscript submissions and case copyright information, contact the Editor.

Journal of Accounting Education

ADDRESS FOR SUBMISSION:

James E. Rebele, Editor
Journal of Accounting Education
Robert Morris University
School of Business
6001 University Boulevard
Moon Township, PA 15108
USA
Phone: 412-269-4894
E-Mail: rebele@rmu.edu
Web: www.elsevier.com

PUBLICATION GUIDELINES:

Manuscript Length: None Required
Copies Required: Four
Computer Submission: No
Format: N/A
Fees to Review: 0.00 US$

Manuscript Style:
    See Manuscript Guidelines

CIRCULATION DATA:

Reader: Academics
Frequency of Issue: Quarterly
Sponsor/Publisher: Elsevier Inc.

REVIEW INFORMATION:

Type of Review: Blind Review
No. of External Reviewers: 3
No. of In House Reviewers: 0
Acceptance Rate: 11-20%
Time to Review: 2 - 3 Months
Reviewers Comments: Yes
Invited Articles: 0-5%
Fees to Publish: 0.00 US$

MANUSCRIPT TOPICS:
Accounting Education

MANUSCRIPT GUIDELINES/COMMENTS:

All submissions should be sent to the Editor at the above address.

1. The *Journal of Accounting Education* (*JAED*) is a refereed journal dedicated to promoting excellence in teaching and to stimulating research in accounting education. The *JAED* provides a forum for exchanging research results and instructional resources among accounting educators worldwide.

2. The *JAED* has three sections: a Main Section, a Teaching and Educational Notes Section, and a Case Section. Articles published in the Main Section are generally empirical and present in-depth analyses of the questions examined through the research. The Teaching and Educational Notes section includes instructional resources and ideas that would be interesting and useful to *JAED* readers. The Case Section includes classroom-tested cases that provide a valuable learning experience for students.

310

Manuscripts are sent to an associate editor who selects two individuals for a blind review. The reviewers use three criteria for evaluating papers: (1) readability, (2) relevance, and (3) reliability. The evaluation for readability is done to ensure that accounting educators can readily understand the paper. Poor readability can impede the ability of a reviewer to evaluate the contribution a paper makes to the literature, and may lead to rejection. All papers accepted for publication in the *JAED* must have a high level of readability. References should not impede the flow of the paper, and unnecessary or obscure jargon should not be used.

The second criterion is relevance. A paper is relevant if it has the potential to influence the process of educating accounting students. A paper that appeals to a broad spectrum of *JAED* readers or is unique or innovative has a better probability of influencing the process of educating accounting students, and is therefore more relevant than a paper without these features.

The third criterion is reliability. A paper is reliable if the conclusions of the paper can be reasonably inferred from the arguments or empirical results. Reliability is not hard to assess when a paper is statistical or involves empirical research. Authors can improve the probability that a manuscript will be accepted by including a section on the limitations of the research method. Reliability is harder to assess when a paper relies on verbal analysis. Reviewers have to depend on their own knowledge of the subject and the presentation in the paper to ensure that the arguments are relevant to the question addressed and that the paper is internally consistent.

The heart of a quality journal is the presentation of meaningful content in readable and usable form. The staff of the *JAED* is committed to ensuring that articles accepted for publication meet these high standards.

Manuscript Requirements. Authors should send four copies of their manuscript (and survey instrument, if applicable) for review. There is no review fee. All manuscripts should be typed double-spaced on 8 ½" x 11" bond paper.

A letter to the Editor must be enclosed requesting review and possible publication. The letter must also state that the manuscript has not been previously published and is not under review at another journal. The letter should include the corresponding author's address, telephone and FAX numbers, and e-mail address. This individual will receive all editorial correspondence. Upon acceptance for publication, the author(s) must complete a Transfer of Copyright Agreement form.

Title Page. The title page should list (1) the article title; (2) the authors' names and affiliations at the time the work was conducted; (3) corresponding author's address, telephone and FAX numbers; and e-mail address; (4) a concise running title; (5) an unnumbered footnote giving a complete mailing address for reprint requests; and (6) any acknowledgements.

Abstract. An abstract should be submitted that does not exceed 150 words in length. This should be typed on a separate page following the title page.

Style and References. Manuscripts should be carefully prepared using the *Publication Manual of the American Psychological Association*, for style. The reference section must be double-spaced and works cited in the paper must be included in the reference list.

Sample Journal Reference
Raymond, M.J. (1964). The treatment of addiction by aversion conditioning with
   apomorphine. *Behavior Research and Therapy*, 3, 287-290.

Sample Book Reference
Barlow, D.H., Hayes, S.C., & Nelson, R.O. (1984). *The scientist practitioner: Research
   and accountability in clinical and educational settings*. New York: Pergamon Press.

Tables and Figures. Do not send glossy prints, photographs or original artwork until acceptance. Copies of all tables and figures should be included with each copy of the manuscript. Upon acceptance of a manuscript for publication, original, camera-ready figures and any photographs must be submitted, un-mounted and on glossy paper. Photocopies, blue ink or pencil are not acceptable. Use black India ink, and type figure legends on a separate sheet. Write the article title and figure number lightly in pencil on the back of each.

Page Proofs and Offprints. Page proofs of the article will be sent to the corresponding author. These should be carefully proofread. Except for typographical errors, corrections should be minimal, and rewriting the text is not permitted. Corrected page proofs must be returned within 48 hours of receipt. Along with the page proofs, the corresponding author will receive a form for ordering offprints and full copies of the issue in which the article appears. Twenty-five (25) free offprints are provided; orders for additional reprints must be received before printing in order to qualify for lower publication rates. All coauthor reprint requirements should be included on the reprint order form.

Journal of Accounting Literature

ADDRESS FOR SUBMISSION:

Bipin Ajinkya & Stephen K. Asare, Co-Eds
Journal of Accounting Literature
University of Florida
Fisher School of Accounting
Graduate School of Business
PO Box 117166
Gainseville, FL 32611-7166
USA
Phone: 352-392-0229
E-Mail: kathy.murphy@cba.ufl.edu
Web: www.cba.ufl.edu

PUBLICATION GUIDELINES:

Manuscript Length: Any
Copies Required: One
Computer Submission: Yes Email
Format: See Guidelines
Fees to Review: 40.00 US$

Manuscript Style:
    See Manuscript Guidelines

CIRCULATION DATA:

Reader: Academics, Business Persons
Frequency of Issue: Yearly
Sponsor/Publisher: Fisher School of
    Accounting, University of Florida

REVIEW INFORMATION:

Type of Review: Editorial Review
No. of External Reviewers: 2
No. of In House Reviewers: No Reply
Acceptance Rate: 21-30%
Time to Review: 2 - 3 Months
Reviewers Comments: Yes
Invited Articles: No Reply
Fees to Publish: 0.00 US$

MANUSCRIPT TOPICS:

Accounting Information Systems; Accounting Research; Accounting Theory & Practice; Auditing; Cost Accounting; Government & Non Profit Accounting; International Accounting; Tax Accounting

MANUSCRIPT GUIDELINES/COMMENTS:

About the Journal

The *Journal of Accounting Literature* is published by the Fisher School of Accounting at the University of Florida. The objective of the *Journal* is to contribute to dissemination of knowledge through publication of (1) high quality state-of-the-art review articles, and (2) papers presented at University of Florida research conferences. Currently the *Journal* is published once a year.

Format

All manuscripts should be typed on one side of 8½" by 11" paper and be double-spaced throughout, including indented quotations, footnotes, bodynotes, and references. Margins should be appropriate to facilitate editing and duplication. In order to assure anonymous reviewing, authors should not identify themselves directly or indirectly in their papers.

A cover page should show the title of the paper, the author's name, title, and affiliation, and any acknowledgments. All pages, including tables, appendices, and references, should be spelled out, except where decimals are used. All others should be written numerically. Single authors should not use the editorial "we".

Tables and Figures
Each table and figure should appear on a separate page and bear an Arabic number and a title; each table and figure should be referenced in the text. The author should indicate on the manuscript where each table or figure should be inserted in the text.

Literature Citations
The name of the author and the year of publication of work cited should appear in square brackets in the body of the text: e.g., [Zeff, 1980]; [Gonedes and Dopuch, 1974]; [Burton, 1974, p. 64]; [Hakansson, 1977a]. If the name of the author is mentioned in the text, it need not be repeated in the citation; e.g., "Bedford [1981, p. 200] states that ..." All direct quotes must have a page citation.

If a reference has more than three authors, only the first name and et al. should appear in the citation. In the list of References, however, all of the names must be shown. As indicated in the Hakansson citation above, the suffix a, b ... should follow the year when the Reference list contains two or more publications by an author(s) in a single year.

Reference List
All references cited in the text, and *only* those cited in the text, should appear in the list of References. The references should be alphabetized by first author; articles with two or more authors are to be alphabetized by the second author. Multiple articles with the *same* author (or co-author) are then listed in chronological order.

Citations in the References list should conform to the following style:
- Date of publication follows author's name.
- Capitalize only the first letter of the main title and subtitle and any proper nouns in book or article titles.
- No quotation marks around article titles.
- Use periods after each main segment of entry.
- For further details and examples, see chapter 16 of *The Chicago Manual of Style* (13th ed.).

Footnotes
Textual footnotes should be used for digressions whose inclusion in the body of the manuscript might disrupt the continuity. Footnotes should be numbered consecutively throughout the manuscript with superscript Arabic numerals. Footnotes should follow the text of the manuscript.

Bodynotes
Bodynotes are to be used for presenting materials that are considered essential to the readers interested in technical details, e.g., equations, symbolic presentations of models, and statements of the underlying assumptions.

Bodynotes are to be double spaced and written in italics. They are to be presented within the text, but separated from other parts of the text by solid lines. The placement of bodynotes within the text should be consistent with two objectives: (1) they should be located where they will be most informative to interested readers, and (2) the logical flow of thought in the text must be possible both with and without reading the bodynotes.

Annotated Bibliography
In addition to the main synthesis article, the author should select a number of the most illustrative articles for annotating at the end of the survey. Each annotated article would include two main components: (1) identification: author, title, name of periodical of original source, date of original publication, and page numbers; (2) subject information: a brief statement of objective, method and results. Individual annotations should not exceed fifteen double-spaced lines.

Submission
Manuscripts should be e-mailed to **kathy.murphy@cba.ufl.edu** as a "WORD" attachment. A submission fee of $40.00 (U.S.), payable to the Journal of Accounting Literature, should be mailed to the Journal of Accounting Literature, Fisher School of Accounting, Graduate School of Business, University of Florida, P.O. Box 117166, Gainesville, FL 32611-7166.

Journal of Accounting Research

ADDRESS FOR SUBMISSION:

Managing Editor
Journal of Accounting Research
University of Chicago
Graduate School of Business
5807 S. Woodlawn Avenue
Chicago, IL 60637
USA
Phone: 773-834-4098
E-Mail: jar@ChicagoGSB.edu
Web: www.blackwellpublishing.com

PUBLICATION GUIDELINES:

Manuscript Length: Varies with Topic
Copies Required: One
Computer Submission: Yes Online
Format:
Fees to Review: 250.00 US$

Manuscript Style:
    Chicago Manual of Style

CIRCULATION DATA:

Reader: Academics
Frequency of Issue: 5 Times/Year
Sponsor/Publisher: Blackwell Publishing /
    Institute of Professional Accounting /
    Grad. Sch. of Bus., Unv of Chicago

REVIEW INFORMATION:

Type of Review: Editorial Review
No. of External Reviewers: Varies
No. of In House Reviewers: Varies
Acceptance Rate: 14%
Time to Review: No Reply
Reviewers Comments: Yes
Invited Articles: 0-5%
Fees to Publish: 0.00 US$

MANUSCRIPT TOPICS:
Accounting Theory & Practice; Auditing; Cost Accounting; Government & Non Profit Accounting; Monetary Policy; Tax Accounting

MANUSCRIPT GUIDELINES/COMMENTS:

Online Submission. http://services.bepress.com/jar/
Web Page. http://www.blackwellpublishing.com/journals/jar

1. The *JAR* accepts for review unpublished, original research in the fields of empirical, analytic and experimental accounting.

2. In a letter to the editors, the authors should clearly state the purpose of the paper and its expected contribution.

3. All material should be typed **double-spaced** including text, footnotes, references and appendices. Leave at least 1 ½ inch margins at top, bottom, and sides of each page. If you must submit a photocopy, please be sure all pages are clean and clear. Footnotes are to be typed **double-spaced** and placed together at the end of the manuscript. They should not appear at the bottom of pages within the text.

4. **References**. If references are given in the text or notes, the following form should be used: White [1970, p. 104] states, "...." or (see Green and Black [1975], White [1970; 1974]). Place dates of publication in square brackets, not in parentheses. References are to be typed **double-spaced** and placed at the end of the manuscript. Place references in alphabetical order and do not number them. Give place of publication as well as publisher and date of publication for books cited. Do not put the author's name in all capitals. Include in your references only those works that are cited in the text. And please double check that all references cited in the text appear in the References. (See a recent copy of the Journal for other questions of style in the references.)

5. **Mathematical Expressions**. Mathematical expressions should be indented or centered on the page. If they are numbered, the number should appear in parentheses at the right hand margin of the page.

The same format should be used consistently throughout the paper. Long equations may begin at the left margin and extend into the right margin. Vectors should be underlined to distinguish them from other expressions. Vectors will be set in boldface type. If an underbar is not a vector, please make a note on a separate sheet of paper for the copy editor.

6. **Enumerations**. Enumerations or lists should be displayed in paragraph form. Numbers and letters used to enumerate items should be set in parentheses. An example is given below:
Sample firms met the following criteria:
1. listed on the Compustat data base for the years 1970 to 1980,
2. market value of common equity greater than $200 million, and
3. earnings forecast data available in **value line**.

7. **Tables and figures**. Each table is to be typed on a separate sheet of paper. The information contained in the body of the table may be single spaced; textual material in the table (such as footnotes) should be double spaced. Tables are to be numbered with Arabic (not Roman) numerals. Example: TABLE 1, TABLE 2, etc. (note that TABLE is in capitals). The title of a table is to be typed in capitals and lowercase, not in all capitals. Example: Summary of Data from Period 1. Tables should avoid vertical rules and should have a double rule at the top and a single rule at the bottom, before the notes (if any).

8. The legends, labels and footnotes for all figures and tables should be sufficiently complete to make the table or figure self-contained. In other words, the reader should be able to understand the table or figure without reading the text. The following items should appear somewhere in the legend, column labels, row labels, axis labels, or footnotes:
1. Description of the content of the numbers or symbols in the body of the table or the content of the figure. This description should include the dimensions of all numbers, e.g., daily returns.
2. Sample description, including size, period and, if relevant, a subsample description.
3. Definition, in words, of the symbols, equations and terms used in the figure or table.

Journal of Accounting, Auditing & Finance

ADDRESS FOR SUBMISSION:

Bala K.A. Balachandran, Editor-in-Chief
Journal of Accounting, Auditing & Finance
New York University
Stern School of Business
40 West 4th Street, Suite 312
New York, NY 10012-1118
USA
Phone: 212-998-0029
E-Mail: kbalacha@stern.nyu.edu
Web: www.stern.nyu.edu

PUBLICATION GUIDELINES:

Manuscript Length: 20+
Copies Required: Electronic
Computer Submission: Yes Online
Format:
Fees to Review: 125.00 US$

Manuscript Style:
 See Manuscript Guidelines

CIRCULATION DATA:

Reader: Academics
Frequency of Issue: Quarterly
Sponsor/Publisher: Greenwood Publishing

REVIEW INFORMATION:

Type of Review: Blind Review
No. of External Reviewers: 1
No. of In House Reviewers: 1
Acceptance Rate: 10%
Time to Review: 2 - 3 Months
Reviewers Comments: Yes
Invited Articles: 0-5%
Fees to Publish: 0.00 US$

MANUSCRIPT TOPICS:

Accounting Information Systems; Accounting Theory & Practice; Auditing; Behavioral Accounting; Cost Accounting; Econometrics; Government & Non Profit Accounting

MANUSCRIPT GUIDELINES/COMMENTS:

1. Under new editorship, the *Journal of Accounting, Auditing, and Finance (JAAF)* has a new orientation. High quality, academic refereed articles will be accompanied by non-academic renderings of accepted manuscripts, and published simultaneously. These will be written in less technical language and directed to the practitioner.

2. The *Journal* will consider papers covering a broad spectrum of topics in finance. These may include, but are not necessarily restricted to, analytical or empirical contributions in areas such as theories of market equilibrium, concepts of "efficient markets", normative or descriptive theories of financial management, and investment decisions under uncertainty.

3. A serious attempt will be made to process manuscripts promptly. Upon acceptance of a paper, the author will be asked to provide a concise, non-academic version, describing the research problem, design, methodology, results and implications for practitioners. A professional editor will be available to assist the author in editing and styling the abbreviated

version. As a result, the work will be read by both academic peers and a wide audience of practitioners, the latter typically not having been exposed to research written in technical, academic language. Thus, the condensed version will provide the critical bridge between the academic and professional communities.

4. Three copies of each manuscript should be submitted to the editor.

5. Use only 8 ½" x 11" white bond paper. Do not use "erasable" paper. All manuscript copy, including text, footnotes, charts, quotations, etc., must be typed double-spaced, on one side of the paper only.

6. Sources of material should be numbered in brackets consecutively in the text throughout the article, starting with (1). These references are to be typed on a separate page entitled "References" at the end of the manuscript. Minor changes should be made between the lines of the typescript, not in the margins. That is, typographical errors and slight corrections of the text or footnotes may be written (please print) on the manuscript in pen. If corrections are lengthy or complex, retype the entire manuscript page.

7. Illustrations accompanying manuscripts should be numbered, provided with suitable legends (again, typed double-spaced on 8 ½" x 11" sheets), and market lightly in pencil on the back, with the name of the author and the title of the article. Illustrations such as original drawings or graphs are to be drawn in black India ink. Typewritten or freehand lettering is not acceptable. All lettering must be done professionally. Do not staple or paper clip illustrations. Put all illustrations between sheets of cardboard before mailing, to prevent folds. Tables and exhibits should be numbered consecutively. Center main headings within the article, type secondary headings flush with the left-hand margin.

8. A strong effort should be made to keep the punctuation simple. Most authors overuse parentheses, italics and quotation marks, which are simply edited out in the publication process.

9. If an article includes any previously copyrighted material (other than short quotation), the publisher must have letters of permission to reprint from the copyright holder and from the author if he or she is not the copyright holder. These letters must be submitted at the same time as the manuscript.

10. The *Journal* normally publishes articles only if they have not yet appeared or been accepted for publication elsewhere. There is generally no objection, however, to having articles that appear in the *Journal* reprinted in other publications at a later date, if appropriate permission is requested from the publisher at that time.

11. Authors of accepted papers will be furnished with copies of the issue in which their paper appears.

Journal of Accounting, Business and Management

ADDRESS FOR SUBMISSION:

Yousef Shahwan, Managing Editor
Journal of Accounting, Business and
   Management
Phone: 62 0341 491813
E-Mail: yousef40@hotmail.com
Web: www.stie-mce.ac.id

PUBLICATION GUIDELINES:

Manuscript Length: 26-30
Copies Required: Two
Computer Submission: Yes Disk, Email
Format: MS Word
Fees to Review: 0.00 US$

Manuscript Style:
   Chicago Manual of Style

CIRCULATION DATA:

Reader: Academics
Frequency of Issue: Yearly
Sponsor/Publisher: Malang School of
   Economics (MCE)

REVIEW INFORMATION:

Type of Review: Blind Review
No. of External Reviewers: 2
No. of In House Reviewers: 0
Acceptance Rate: 21-30%
Time to Review: 1 - 2 Months
Reviewers Comments: Yes
Invited Articles: 6-10%
Fees to Publish: 40.00 US$

MANUSCRIPT TOPICS:
Accounting Education; Accounting Information Systems; Accounting Theory & Practice; Auditing; Behavioral Accounting; Capital Market Based Accounting; Cost Accounting; Financial Reporting; Government & Non Profit Accounting; International Finance; Portfolio & Security Analysis; Tax Accounting

MANUSCRIPT GUIDELINES/COMMENTS:

Journal of Accounting, Business, and Management (*JABM*) is a journal that provides a scientific discourse about accounting, business, and management both practically and conceptually. The published articles in this journal cover various topics from the result of particular conceptual analysis, critical evaluation to empirical research. An aspect of social, organization, and philosophy as well as becoming one of the discourses of this publication.

This journal is published once a year: October. Publisher: BP STIE Malangkuçeçwara (MCE Publishing Board) - Jln. Terusan Candi Kalasan, Malang-Indonesia.

This journal accepts articles from the writers of MCE as well as other institutions through reviewing process organized by the board of editors under the following consideration: the originality, actualizing the cases, and contribution of articles for the advancement of science and empirical. In the editing process of the article, it might be possible to make a constructive study by the board of editors for its perfection.

This *Journal of Accounting, Business, and Management* of MCE has been accredited by Directorate of Higher Education No 134/DIKTI/Kep/2001

GUIDES TO WRITE ARTICLES
General Requirements
The article has to fulfill the following requirements:
1. The conceptual and research articles have not been published in another media;
2. Make it relevant to the fields of accounting, business and management;
3. Pay a publication cost of Rp. 250.000,- (no charge for the writers of MCE and board of editors' members).

Writing Technical Requirements
1. Articles must be written in English.
2. Writing systems for Conceptual Articles cover:
   - Abstract;
   - Introduction;
   - Content (which cover concepts or ideas of the writer);
   - Closure;
   - Conclusion; and
   - Bibliography
3. Writing systems for Research Articles cover:
   - Abstract;
   - Introduction;
   - Theoretical analysis;
   - Hypotheses (if any);
   - Research methods;
   - Data analysis;
   - Discussion and Conclusion;
   - Implication and Limitation;
   - Bibliography (Questionnaires and Attachment must be enclosed).
4. Articles must be typed by using MS-Word, font Times New Roman 11, spaces 1.5, number of pages 20-25 lembar, paper size: letter size. It should be submitted in the diskette 3.5" plus two print-out (hard copy);
5. Margin requirement: top=4 cm; bottom=4 cm; left=4 cm; right=4cm;
6. Topic of the article, the writer identity (without degree, but include the name of institution), abstract and keywords must be written in Indonesian Language or English;
7. The abstract should consist of 200-400 words in Indonesian Language or English;
8. Table and illustration are put into the content of article, followed by orderly numbers, title of table/illustration and quotation sources if necessary;
9. Statement of reference or quotation should be written in the page by mentioning the last name of the writer and the year between brackets. The page number could be put in if necessary;
10. Each article must cover bibliography (reference sources only).

Call for Papers

The *Journal of Accounting, Business, and Management* (*JABM*) welcomes articles in all areas of accounting and business related topics. Both theoretical and empirical manuscripts will be considered for publications. Article's formatting is not an important issue at the stage of submission. Once the article is accepted for publication, then the author is required to follow the prescribed format guidelines attached to the acceptance letter when appropriate. Each submission should have a cover page that includes the name, address, e-mail, telephone, and fax numbers of the author. In case of multiple authors, designate the corresponding author. Intended authors should submit their articles for possible publication via e-mail attachment directly to the Managing Editor at **yousef40@hotmail.com**.

The *Journal of Accounting, Business, and Management* is a double blind refereed academic journal. It was first published in 1998. It is published once a year that is in October of every year. The JABM is sponsored by Malangçeçwara College of Economics (MCE) in Indonesia with ISSN No. 0216-423X.

More information about *JABM* can be found by visiting the web site of the journal at:
www.stie-mce.ac.id.

Journal of Accounting, Ethics & Public Policy

ADDRESS FOR SUBMISSION:

Robert W. McGee, Editor
Journal of Accounting, Ethics & Public
    Policy
Dumont Inst. for Public Policy Research
Andreas School of Business
Barry University
Miami Shores, FL 33161-6695
USA
Phone: 305-899-3525
E-Mail: bob414@hotmail.com
Web:

PUBLICATION GUIDELINES:

Manuscript Length: 10-30+
Copies Required: Three
Computer Submission: Yes
Format: Law Review
Fees to Review: 0.00 US$

Manuscript Style:
    Uniform System of Citation (Harvard
    Blue Book), & Accounting Review
    Style

CIRCULATION DATA:

Reader: Academics
Frequency of Issue: Quarterly
Sponsor/Publisher: Dumont Institute for
    Public Policy Research

REVIEW INFORMATION:

Type of Review: Blind Review
No. of External Reviewers: 2
No. of In House Reviewers: 1
Acceptance Rate: 50%
Time to Review: 1 Month or Less
Reviewers Comments: Yes
Invited Articles: 11-20%
Fees to Publish: 0.00 US$

MANUSCRIPT TOPICS:
Accounting & Auditing in Developing Economies; Accounting Education; Accounting Ethics; Accounting Theory & Practice; Auditing; Behavioral Accounting; Cost Accounting; Economic Development; Fiscal Policy; Public Finance; Public Policy Economics; Tax Accounting

MANUSCRIPT GUIDELINES/COMMENTS:

Desired Length. The preferred length is 11-25 pages, double-spaced. However, we are more interested in quality than quantity, so a shorter or longer length will also be considered.

Blind Review. Yes, after the editor has determined that the paper is suitable for refereeing.

Selection Criteria. The paper must be well written and on a topic included under preferred subject matter.

Approximate Lead Time to Publication After Acceptance. An abstract will be posted on our website and perhaps other places within 30 days after final acceptance. The article will appear in paper form within 1-3 months thereafter.

Style Requirements. The cover page should include only the title of the paper and the names, addresses, institutional affiliations and telephone numbers of all authors. Acknowledgments, if any, should also be included here. The first page of the article should include the title and a 100 to 150 word abstract (indented). APA or *Accounting Review* style is acceptable. Alternatively, you may use law review style.

If you choose law review style, all references are to be by footnote. There is no reference section at the end of the article. The first time an article is cited, full particulars should be given. For example: Murray N. Sabrin, "Issues in Tax Reform," Northwestern Journal of Taxation, Vol. 14:2 (Fall, 1995), 422-437, at 425. Pages 422-437 represent the place where the article may be found. Page 425 refers to the page where the thought or quote may be found. Shorter citations may be given for subsequent references. For example, Sabrin at 436. Books should be cited as follows: Tibor R. Machan, Accounting Ethics (New York: Basic Books, 1996), 162. To cite items other than articles or books, use your best judgment.

Journal of American Academy of Business, Cambridge (The)

ADDRESS FOR SUBMISSION:

Senguder, Gordon & Scannell, Editors
Journal of American Academy of Business,
  Cambridge (The)
6051 N. Ocean Dr. #506
Hollywood, FL 33019
USA
Phone: 954-304-1655
E-Mail: drsenguder@aol.com
Web: www.jaabc.com

PUBLICATION GUIDELINES:

Manuscript Length: 16-20
Copies Required: Two
Computer Submission: Yes Disk, Email
Format: MS Word, English
Fees to Review: 0.00 US$

Manuscript Style:
  See Manuscript Guidelines

CIRCULATION DATA:

Reader: Academics, Professors,
  Researchers
Frequency of Issue: 2 Times/Year
Sponsor/Publisher: Senguder Press

REVIEW INFORMATION:

Type of Review: Blind Review
No. of External Reviewers: 2
No. of In House Reviewers: 2
Acceptance Rate: 36-38%
Time to Review: 1 - 2 Months
Reviewers Comments: Yes
Invited Articles: 31-40%
Fees to Publish: 495.00 US$

MANUSCRIPT TOPICS:
Auditing; Business Education; Business Information Systems; Economic Development;
International Economics & Trade; International Finance; Macro Economics

MANUSCRIPT GUIDELINES/COMMENTS:

How to submit a paper for the journal
Submissions may be made electronically via e-mail to **drsenguder@aol.com**. Electronic submissions are preferred. Submissions will be acknowledged within 48 hours. If submissions are mailed, please submit a paper or an abstract/proposal for a paper (follow the submission guidelines) to the attention of Dr. Turan Senguder and Dr. Jean Gordon, Co-Editors. The cover letter should include each author's name, institutional affiliation, complete mailing and e-mail addresses. Please also submit a résumé. See Web site for submission deadline.

General Information
The *Journal of American Academy of Business, Cambridge* (*JAABC*) invites you to participate in the journal. The *Journal of American Academy of Business, Cambridge* (*JAABC*) publishes articles of interest to members of the Business Community and will provide leadership in introducing new concepts to its readership. Because business is a diverse field, articles should address questions utilizing a variety of methods and theoretical perspectives.

The primary goal of the journal will be to provide opportunities for business related academicians and professionals from various business related fields in a global realm to publish their paper in one source. The *Journal of American Academy of Business, Cambridge* will bring together academicians and professionals from all areas related business fields and related fields to interact with members inside and outside their own particular disciplines. The journal will provide opportunities for publishing researcher's paper as well as providing opportunities to view other's work. Doctoral students are highly encouraged to submit papers to *JAABC* for competitive review. All submissions are subject to a two-person, blind-peer-review process.

The *JAABC* reserves the rights to amend, modify, add to, or delete its rules, policies, and procedures affecting its institutional relationship with authors (contributors) as deemed necessary by the administration. Any such amendment, modification, addition, or deletion shall not be considered a violation of the relationship between *JAABC* and authors (contributors). The submission gives *The Journal of American Academy of Business, Cambridge* exclusive rights to publish, copyright, and control reproduction of the manuscript. The final paper and registration fee must be submitted prior to submission deadline. When the paper is accepted, each author must pay the registration fee. There will be no refunds on cancellations received after the dead line

Submission Guidelines
Submissions may be made electronically via e-mail to **drsenguder@aol.com**. Electronic submissions are preferred. The manuscript should be in one file entirely in Microsoft Word. No other software may be used. The paper should be a maximum of eight pages including appendices, references, figures and tables. The paper must be singled-spaced, printed at 10-point with 1-inch margins in any Times font. Page numbers should begin with 1 and the paper should not exceed eight pages in length. In general, the paper must be the way you want it to look in the publication. Hence tables must be placed where you want them to appear. There will be a $55 charge for each published page exceeding the page limit. Papers are to be prepared in English and totally edited to avoid grammatical and typographical errors. Papers must be written in a clear, concise manner for ease of reading and interpretation.

Each submission should include the paper's title and the name, address and telephone number of the contact person for the paper.

Manuscript Format
Page number should begin with the number 1 and be centered at the bottom of the page in a Times font at 10-point. The manuscript must be single-spaced with 1-inch margins on all four sides and not exceed eight pages in length. The entire paper must be in any Times font at 10-point with the exception of the title, which must be at 16-point and bold. The paper should begin with title, author's information (10-point font and lower case), and the word "abstract" (10-point font, bold and capitalized), each of which must be centered. The balance of the paper should be fully justified.

As for line spacing, it should be title on the first line or lines and then author's information with one line per author and no blank lines between the title and author's information. The author's information line should contain first name, last name and institutional affiliation.

326

Leave two blank lines between author's information and the word abstract. Leave one blank line between the word abstract and the abstract itself. Leave two blank lines between the abstract and the body of the manuscript. There must be a blank line between paragraphs with the first line each paragraph indented. Please do not use columns. Please omit headers and footers. References need to be consistent and in a generally accepted format. Every sub-heading should be bold and capitalized. The manuscript should be in one file entirely in Microsoft Word. No other software may be used. View website for manuscript deadline.

Each submission should include the paper's title and the name, address and telephone number of the contact person for the paper. However, papers submitted earlier will be reviewed immediately and participants will be notified as soon as possible.

Journal of Applied Case Research

ADDRESS FOR SUBMISSION:

Alex Sharland, Editor
Journal of Applied Case Research
Barry University
Andreas School of Business
Andreas 207
11300 NE 2 Avenue
Miami Shores, FL 33161
USA
Phone: 305-899-3530
E-Mail: asharland@mail.barry.edu
Web: www.swcra.org/journal

PUBLICATION GUIDELINES:

Manuscript Length: 16-20
Copies Required: Four
Computer Submission: Yes Email
Format: MS Word prefered
Fees to Review: 65.00 US$

Manuscript Style:
American Psychological Association

CIRCULATION DATA:

Reader: Academics
Frequency of Issue: 1-2 Times/Year
Sponsor/Publisher: Southwest Case
Research Association (SWCRA)

REVIEW INFORMATION:

Type of Review: Blind Review
No. of External Reviewers: 2
No. of In House Reviewers: 1
Acceptance Rate: 21-30%
Time to Review: 2 - 3 Months
Reviewers Comments: Yes
Invited Articles: 0-5%
Fees to Publish: 0.00 US$

MANUSCRIPT TOPICS:
Accounting Education; Financial Services

MANUSCRIPT GUIDELINES/COMMENTS:

Style Requirements
Note to Authors. Please ensure that your revised case follows these guidelines. The case will not be published until it meets these criteria.

Font. Times New Roman (12 point)

Margins. 1.25 inch margins left and right. 1 inch margins top and bottom

Footnotes. Please do not footnote your references. Use citation style (Jennings 1997). For clarification points, either incorporate the information in the body of the text or refer to an Appendix.

Line Spacing. Single Spacing

Justification. Fully justified

Headings and Sub-Headings. Main headings should be centered, bold, and in CAPITALS. Subheadings should be left justified, bold and lower case.

Tables. Should be in Word (Tables) with Times New Roman Font

Appendices. Should be clearly labeled and clearly referenced in the body of the case

Graphs and Figures. Times New Roman font and graph details should be discernible in black and white print.

Teaching Notes. A full and complete set of teaching notes is required with your final manuscript. These notes will not be published but may be made available to those who purchase your case at a future date.

Journal of Business & Economic Studies

ADDRESS FOR SUBMISSION:

Luis E. Rivera-Solis, Editor
Journal of Business & Economic Studies
Dowling College
School of Business - Room 406
150 Idle Hour Boulevard
Oakdale, NY 11769
USA
Phone: 631-244-3214
E-Mail: riveral@dowling.edu
Web: www.dowling.edu

CIRCULATION DATA:

Reader: Academics
Frequency of Issue: 2 Times/Year
Sponsor/Publisher: Dowling College
   Northeast Buisiness and Economics
   Association

PUBLICATION GUIDELINES:

Manuscript Length: 21-25
Copies Required: Three
Computer Submission: Yes Strongly
   Recommend
Format: N/A
Fees to Review: 0.00 US$

Manuscript Style:
   American Psychological Association

REVIEW INFORMATION:

Type of Review: Blind Review
No. of External Reviewers: 2
No. of In House Reviewers: 1
Acceptance Rate: 11-20%
Time to Review: 4 - 6 Months
Reviewers Comments: Yes
Invited Articles: 0-5%
Fees to Publish: 0.00 US$

MANUSCRIPT TOPICS:
Accounting Theory & Practice; Auditing; Cost Accounting; Government & Non Profit
Accounting; Tax Accounting

MANUSCRIPT GUIDELINES/COMMENTS:

Submissions
Initial submissions must be made in triplicate with a cover letter stating that the manuscript is
not currently being considered at another publication. Send submission to:
   Editor-in-Chief, Luis Eduardo Rivera-Solis
   Journal of Business and Economic Studies
   Dowling College
   School of Business
   Idle Hour Boulevard
   Oakdale, NY 11769

All submissions are reviewed by at least two members of our peer-review board.

330

STYLE GUIDELINES
General Style Instructions
Margins
Top: 1.0
Bottom: 1.0
Left: 1.0
Right: 1.0
Gutter: 0
From Header: 0.5
From Footer: 0.5

Font
Times New Roman
Point Size: 12
Spacing: Double
Alignment Justification: Full

Formatting
Do not use the header/footer or the footnote/endnote features
Do not use any page or section breaks

Tabs
Default tabs set at 0.5

Tables and Figures. All tables and figures should appear at the end of the paper. Indicate in the paper, approximately, where the tables should go. Tables should be numbered in Arabic numbers, titled, and centered, e.g.,

TABLE 1. Percentage of Respondents

We strongly recommend using the Table feature of Word. However, if you prefer not to use the Table feature, the columns of the tables should be set using tab stops, NOT SPACES, to align.

Figures are numbered similarly to tables, e.g., FIGURE 1. The author will provide the figures on a disk in a Microsoft Word compatible program.

Equations. Default settings should be used. Set point size at 10 points; use Arabic numbers flush left in parenthesis.

Title, Sections, Subheads. Bold type the title and center it. Capitalize first letter of primary words only. On the next line down, (italicized) type the author's name(s) and affiliation. The abstract should follow. See below.

Exploring Options in Style
John A. Doe, Salem State College
Jane B. Smith, Fairfield University

Abstract
Sections of the paper, such as introduction, should be flush left with all capital letters, with one extra line between section head and text:

Introduction
Subheads should be in upper and lower case letters, flush left with one extra line above and no extra line of spacing below. For subheads below the first level subhead, indent one tab for the second subhead. Please restrict the subheads to no more than two. Please avoid using underlining and Roman numerals in the sections.

References. In-text references should include the author's last name and the year of publication in parentheses with no punctuation, e.g., (Underwood 1992).

The reference list should be in alphabetical order, and it should not be numbered. It should include the last name and first name of the author(s), the date of publication, the article title, the journal or book title, location, and the publisher, volume numbers and pages. See examples below:

Acs, Z. and D. Gerlowski. (1996). Managerial Economics and Organizations. Upper Saddle River, NJ: Prentice Hall.

Becker, G. (1965). A theory of the allocation of time. Economic Journal. 75: 493-517.

Miscellaneous
Please do not use the footnote/endnote feature. If notes are needed, use endnotes. Number the endnotes with superscript Arabic numbers in your text, and list them before the reference list.

Please avoid using the Bullet and Numbering feature in your text.

Please thoroughly review the manuscript for errors in spelling, grammar, and punctuation.

Accepted Papers. Style requirements for producing a finished submission include all of the above. An accepted paper must be Word compatible and submitted on a 3.5 floppy disk. Please submit a hard copy of your paper along with the disk. If there are changes or revisions on the latest paper that you submit, please mark it "revised" on the cover sheet. A brief autobiography will be requested upon acceptance.

JBES reserves the right to edit all accepted papers.

Journal of Business and Behavioral Sciences

ADDRESS FOR SUBMISSION:

Wali I. Mondal, Editor
Journal of Business and Behavioral
  Sciences
ASBBS
Box 502147
San Diego, CA 92150-2147
USA
Phone: 909-648-2120
E-Mail: mondal@asbbs.org
Web: www.asbbs.org

CIRCULATION DATA:

Reader: Academics
Frequency of Issue: 2 Times/Year
Sponsor/Publisher: American Society of
  Business and Behavioral Sciences

PUBLICATION GUIDELINES:

Manuscript Length: No Required Length
Copies Required: Four
Computer Submission: No
Format: N/A
Fees to Review: 20.00 US$

Manuscript Style:
  American Psychological Association

REVIEW INFORMATION:

Type of Review: Blind Review
No. of External Reviewers: 3
No. of In House Reviewers: 1
Acceptance Rate: 11-20%
Time to Review: Less than 6 Months
Reviewers Comments: Yes
Invited Articles: 0-5%
Fees to Publish: 200.00 US$ Minimum pg
  fee required

MANUSCRIPT TOPICS:

Accounting Education; Accounting Information Systems; Accounting Theory & Practice; Auditing; Behavioral Accounting; Cost Accounting; Econometrics; Economic Development; Economic History; Financial Services; Fiscal Policy; Government & Non Profit Accounting; Industrial Organization; Insurance; International Economics & Trade; International Finance; Macro Economics; Micro Economics; Monetary Policy; Portfolio & Security Analysis; Psychology; Public Policy Economics; Real Estate; Regional Economics; Tax Accounting

MANUSCRIPT GUIDELINES/COMMENTS:

Manuscripts in any area of Business and Behavioral Sciences will be considered for publication. Papers must be prepared in double space and must accompany an abstract not to exceed 250 words. Authors should follow the APA guidelines in preparing their manuscripts. Guidelines for final submission to the *Journal* will be sent only if a paper is accepted after review.

Journal of Business and Economic Perspectives

ADDRESS FOR SUBMISSION:

Bob Figgins, Editor
Journal of Business and Economic
   Perspectives
University of Tennesse at Martin
College of Business and Public Affairs
Martin, TN 38238
USA
Phone: 731-881-7226
E-Mail: bfiggins@utm.edu
  mprather@utm.edu
Web: http://www.utm.edu/departments/
  soba/

CIRCULATION DATA:

Reader: Academics
Frequency of Issue: 2 Times/Year
Sponsor/Publisher: University

PUBLICATION GUIDELINES:

Manuscript Length:
Copies Required: Four
Computer Submission: Yes
Format: MS Word
Fees to Review: 25.00 US$

Manuscript Style:
  Chicago Manual of Style

REVIEW INFORMATION:

Type of Review: Blind Review
No. of External Reviewers: 2
No. of In House Reviewers:
Acceptance Rate: 21-30%
Time to Review: 4 - 6 Months
Reviewers Comments: No
Invited Articles: 0-5%
Fees to Publish: 0.00 US$

MANUSCRIPT TOPICS:

Accounting Education; Accounting Information Systems; Accounting Theory & Practice; Auditing; Behavioral Accounting; Cost Accounting; Economic Development; Economic History; Financial Services; Fiscal Policy; Government & Non Profit Accounting; Industrial Organization; Insurance; International Economics & Trade; International Finance; Macro Economics; Micro Economics; Monetary Policy; Portfolio & Security Analysis; Public Policy Economics; Real Estate; Regional Economics; Tax Accounting

MANUSCRIPT GUIDELINES/COMMENTS:

Length of articles. Ordinarily, articles should not exceed **sixteen** double-spaced, typewritten pages, references and tables inclusive.

Mathematics. The use of mathematics and graphics should be kept at a minimum. Avoid technical jargon. Number equations. In identifying variables in formulas, capitalize only the initial letter of abbreviations - except where common usage indicates otherwise.

Submission of articles. Send four copies of all articles and $25.00 submission fee to:
Bob G. Figgins, Editor
Journal of Business and Economic Perspectives
College of Business & Public Affairs
The University of Tennessee at Martin
Martin, TN 38238
(731) 587-7226

We regret that we are unable to return or store manuscripts.

Review. Before publication, manuscripts are blind reviewed. On occasion, revisions may be suggested to the author to make the material of the greatest possible use to Journal readers. This process may take 3-4 months.

Typing. The manuscript should be double-spaced throughout. This applies to text, footnotes, references, and figure legends. Use standard 8 ½ X 11 white paper. Submit **four** copies and keep another for your own use. Type on one side only. Leave a 1 inch margin on all four sides of the text. Mathematical symbols must be clearly represented -- typed if at all possible. Make sure that final changes are made on all four copies.

Title page and summary. Use a cover page which shows the title of the paper, the name of the author(s) with their titles, institutional affiliations, and telephone numbers. Include on this page a summary of the article in 150 words or less. If appropriate, add as a footnote material about previous publications or other information which can be used to identify the author(s).

Corrections and insertions. Keep corrections in the manuscript to a minimum. Retype any page on which more than a few changes are necessary. Do not write in the margins. Type lengthy insertions on a separate page and mark the place in the text where the insertion is to appear. This page should also indicate that the insertion follows. (For example, number the insertion 12a. Page 12 should be marked "Followed by p.12a.")

Footnotes. Use footnotes sparingly. Number sequentially. Type footnotes double-spaced on a separate page at the end of the article. In general, avoid lengthy explanatory footnotes. This material can usually be incorporated in the text.

Section Headings. If sparingly used, section headings and subheadings enhance the readability of an article. Do not try to indicate typographical style, but show the relative weights by using all capital letters for the main headings (i.e., CONCLUSIONS) and initial capital letters (only) for words in the subheadings (i.e., Test Results).

Tables and charts. Avoid excessively long tables. Type tables and charts on pages separate from the text. Captions of all figures should be consistent. Capitalize the first letter in all words in main headings (i.e., Test Results). For captions of lesser importance in the column headings or subs, capitalize only the first letter of the initial word (i.e., Goodness of fit).

References. Type double-spaced with each item being flush left. For entries requiring more than one line, run-over lines should be indented. Authors in the references should be listed alphabetically: do not number the entries. Citations for books should contain author's last name, first name and middle initials followed by full title of the book, place of publication, publisher, and publication (copyright) date. The following example illustrates the desired form and punctuation.

Smith, Arthur G., Economics, New York: Godwin 1978.

Journal articles should include (in addition to author and title, as above) the name of the journal, date, volume, and page. For example:

Smith, Arthur G., "Teaching Economics," Journal of Economic Education, Spring 1976, 7, 4-12.

Vibhakar, Ashvin P., and Kennedy, Robert E., "Alternate Estimates of the Cost of Equity Capital: Electric Utilities Revisited," Journal of Business and Economic Perspectives, Fall 1982, 8, 1-22.

In referring to references in the text of the article, use the author's name, publication date, and page number (if needed). For example, "...as the data indicate (Smith, 1978, p. 456)" or, "...as Smith (1978) has stated..."

Journal of Business and Economics

ADDRESS FOR SUBMISSION:

Alan S. Khade, Managing Editor
Journal of Business and Economics
International Academy of Business
and Economics
983 Woodland Drive
Turlock, CA 95382-7281
USA
Phone: 209-667-3074
E-Mail: Review@iabe.org
Web: www.iabe.org

CIRCULATION DATA:

Reader: Academics, Business Persons
Frequency of Issue:
Sponsor/Publisher: International Academy
of Business and Economics (IABE)

PUBLICATION GUIDELINES:

Manuscript Length:
Copies Required: Two
Computer Submission: Yes Disk or Email
Format: MS Word
Fees to Review: 0.00 US$

Manuscript Style:
　　See Manuscript Guidelines

REVIEW INFORMATION:

Type of Review: Blind Review
No. of External Reviewers: 2
No. of In House Reviewers: 1
Acceptance Rate: 21-30%
Time to Review: 2 - 3 Months
Reviewers Comments: Yes
Invited Articles: 21-30%
Fees to Publish: 0.00 US$

MANUSCRIPT TOPICS:

Accounting Information Systems; Accounting Theory & Practice; Auditing; Cost Accounting; Econometrics; Economic Development; Financial Services; Fiscal Policy; Government & Non Profit Accounting; International Economics & Trade; International Finance; Macro Economics; Micro Economics; Monetary Policy; Portfolio & Security Analysis; Public Policy Economics; Real Estate; Regional Economics; Tax Accounting

MANUSCRIPT GUIDELINES/COMMENTS:

Please use following manuscript Guidelines for submission of your papers for the review. Papers are reviewed on a continual basis throughout the year. Early Submissions are welcome! Please email your manuscript to **Review@iabe.org**.

Copyright. Articles, papers, or cases submitted for publication should be original contributions and should not be under consideration for any other publication at the same time. Authors submitting articles/papers/cases for publication warrant that the work is not an infringement of any existing copyright, infringement of proprietary right, invasion of privacy, or libel and will indemnify, defend, and hold IABE or sponsor(s) harmless from any damages, expenses, and costs against any breach of such warranty. For ease of dissemination and to ensure proper policing of use papers/articles/cases and contributions become the legal copyright of the IABE unless otherwise agreed in writing.

General Information. These are submission instructions for review purpose only. Once your submission is accepted you will receive submission guidelines with your paper acceptance letter. The author(s) will be emailed result of the review process in about 6-8 weeks from submission date. Papers are reviewed and accepted on a continual basis. Submit your papers early for full considerations!

Typing. Paper must be laser printed/printable on 8.5" x 11" white sheets in Arial 10-point font single-spaced lines justify style in MS Word. All four margins must be 1" each.

First Page. Paper title not exceeding two lines must be CAPITALIZED AND CENTERED IN BOLD LETTERS. Author name and university/organizational affiliation of each author must be printed on one line each. Do NOT include titles such as Dr., Professor, Ph.D., department, address, email address etc. Please print the word "ABSTRACT" in capitalized bold letters left justified and double-spaced from last author's name/affiliation. Abstract should be in italic. Please see the sample manuscript.

All other Headings. All other section headings starting with INTRODUCTION must be numbered, in capitalized bold letters, left justified, and double-spaced from last line above them. See the subsection headings in the sample manuscript.

Tables Figures and Charts. All tables figures or charts must be inserted in the body of the manuscripts within the margins with headings/titles in centered CAPITALIZED BOLD letters.

References and Bibliography. All references listed in this section must be cited in the article and vice-versa. The reference citations in the text must be inserted in parentheses within sentences with author name followed by a comma and year of publication. Please follow the following formats:

Journal Articles
Khade Alan S. and Metlen Scott K. "An Application of Benchmarking in Dairy Industry" *International Journal of Benchmarking* Vol. III (4) 1996 17

Books
Harrison Norma and Samson D. Technology Management: Text and Cases McGraw-Hill Publishing New York 2002

Internet
Hesterbrink C. E-Business and ERP: Bringing two Paradigms together October 1999; PricewaterhouseCoopers *www.pwc.com*.

Author Profile(s). At the end of paper include author profile(s) not exceeding five lines each author including name highest degree/university/year current position/university and major achievements. For example:

Author Profile:
Dr. Tahi J. Gnepa earned his Ph.D. at the University of Wisconsin Madison in 1989. Currently he is a professor of international business at California State University Stanislaus and Managing Editor of Journal of International Business Strategy (JIBStrategy).

Manuscript. Absolutely no footnotes! Do not insert page numbers for the manuscript. Please do not forget to run spelling and grammar check for the completed paper. Save the manuscript on your diskette/CD or hard drive.

Electronic Submission. Send your submission as an MS Word file attachment to your Email to **Review@iabe.org**.

Other paper submissions may be sent by air mail to the following address: IABE, 983 Woodland Drive Turlock, CA 95382-7281, USA

Journal of Business Disciplines

ADDRESS FOR SUBMISSION:

A. Jay White, Chris E. Bjornson, Co-Eds.
Journal of Business Disciplines
Indiana University, Southeast
School of Business
Hillside Hall
4201 Grant Line Road
New Albany, IN 47150
USA
Phone: 812-941-2532
E-Mail: jwhite04@ius.edu
cbjornso@ius.edu
Web: www.abdwebsite.org/journal.htm

PUBLICATION GUIDELINES:

Manuscript Length: 1-20
Copies Required: Four
Computer Submission: No
Format: N/A
Fees to Review: 25.00 US$

Manuscript Style:
American Psychological Association

CIRCULATION DATA:

Reader: Academics
Frequency of Issue: 2 Times/Year
Sponsor/Publisher: Academy of Bus.
Disciplines, Indiana Univ. SE School of
Bus., Shippensburg Univ. School of Bus.

REVIEW INFORMATION:

Type of Review: Blind Review
No. of External Reviewers: 3
No. of In House Reviewers: 1
Acceptance Rate: 12-20%
Time to Review: 2 - 3 Months
Reviewers Comments: Yes
Invited Articles: 0-5%
Fees to Publish: 0.00 US$

MANUSCRIPT TOPICS:
Accounting Information Systems; Accounting Theory & Practice; Auditing; Cost Accounting; Tax Accounting

MANUSCRIPT GUIDELINES/COMMENTS:

Aim and Scope
The *Journal* is dedicated to publishing quality applied business articles designed to inform business practitioners and business academics. Articles should be of current importance and can be either empirical or theoretical in approach. General readability of the articles is of critical importance. (i.e. Manuscripts submitted should not be so technical or specialized that they are of interest only to specialists in that area. Manuscripts should be free of technical jargon or should define terms used. Also, manuscripts should not be focused on or overly dwell on an issue that is not of practical importance.) Possible application areas include:

Accounting	Finance	Applied Business Economics
Information Systems	Business History	International Business
Business Education	Management	E-Commerce
Marketing	Entrepreneurship	Small Business
Ethics		

Manuscripts will be subjected to external blind reviews.

Submit only original, unpublished manuscripts that are not under review elsewhere.

Manuscript Guidelines

Submit four copies of the manuscript on 8 ½ x 11 inch paper and a check for $25 payable to the *Journal of Business Disciplines*. If you are submitting an article, or if your article has been accepted for publication, please adhere to the following guidelines.

Guidelines Include

- Manuscripts are reviewed with the understanding that they have not been simultaneously submitted to any other journal, that they represent original work of the author(s), and that they have not been previously published.
- Manuscripts are evaluated anonymously. Names of authors should not appear on the article itself. Attach a separate cover page that includes the title, authors, and affiliation of each author to one (1) copy of the article. The title page should include the contact information for the corresponding author (for submission purposes only).
- Title page includes no personal titles for authors (for submission purposes only)
- Title should be limited to 8 words
- Body of the text starts on new page with title and no author identification (for accepted manuscripts, authors are listed below the title and the first footnote(s) should provide information about the author(s))
- Margins of 1 inch and full justification
- First level headings (title) centered, initial capitalization, bold 16 point font
- Second level headings (major captions, eg. Introduction . . .) centered, initial capitalization, bold 14 point font
- Third level headings, left justified, initial capitalization, bold 12 point font
- Fourth level headings, indented, initial capitalization, bold 10 point font
- The text should be in 10 point font
- Original submissions should be double spaced. (Single space text will be requested for accepted papers)
- Bullet points - consistency within each group of bullet points, no bold, italicize opening phrases of lengthy bullets
- Use footnotes
- Number tables sequentially, label and describe
- In-text references include (author, year, page) notation
- Reference section at the end of the text:
  - Reference only works cited in the text
  - Reference multiple works by the same author(s) using a, b, c

- Reference as follows: Author, Date, Title, Publisher (or if no identifiable authors) Title, Date, Publisher

Journal
Platt, ILD., Platt, M.B., 1991. A note on the use of industry-relative ratios in bankruptcy prediction. *Journal of Banking and Finance* 15 (6), 1183-1194.

Book
Wasserman, P.D., 1989. Neural Computing: Theory and Practice. Van Nostrand Reinhold, New York.

Institute Publication
US Congress, 1985. Public Law 99-198. 99 United States Statutes as Large 1325. US Government Printing Office, Washington, DC.

- Authors of accepted manuscripts may be asked to supply a camera-ready artwork for all charts and/or graphs. Camera-ready means a professional drawing on white paper or a clean, laser-printed copy of computer-generated charts/graphs.
- Authors of accepted works must supply an electronic copy of the paper in MS-Word format via e-mail.

Journal of Business Finance & Accounting

ADDRESS FOR SUBMISSION:

P. Pope, A. Stark & M. Walker, Editors
Journal of Business Finance & Accounting
ELECTRONIC SUBMISSION ONLY
Phone:
E-Mail:
Web: www.blackwellpublishing.com

PUBLICATION GUIDELINES:

Manuscript Length: 11-30
Copies Required: Electronic
Computer Submission: Yes Online
Format: MS Word or PDF
Fees to Review: 85.00 US$

Manuscript Style:
See Manuscript Guidelines

CIRCULATION DATA:

Reader: Academics
Frequency of Issue: 5 Times/Year
Sponsor/Publisher: Blackwell Publishing,
    Inc.

REVIEW INFORMATION:

Type of Review: Blind Review
No. of External Reviewers: 1
No. of In House Reviewers:
Acceptance Rate: 11-20%
Time to Review: 3-4 Months
Reviewers Comments: Yes
Invited Articles: 0
Fees to Publish: 0.00 US$

MANUSCRIPT TOPICS:
Accounting Theory & Practice; Econometrics; Portfolio & Security Analysis

MANUSCRIPT GUIDELINES/COMMENTS:

Topics Include. Accounting Choice; Accounting Theory; Asset Pricing; Capital Market Studies; Corporate Finance; Corporate Governance; Financial Disclosure; Financial Econometrics; Market Based Accounting Research; Risk Analysis; Valuation Theory and Practice.

Aims and Scope
The *Journal of Business Finance & Accounting* exists to publish high quality research papers in Finance and economic aspects of Accounting. The scope of the *Journal* is broad. It includes studies of the functioning of security and exchange markets through to the economics of internal organisation and management control. It also includes research papers relating to market microstructure, asset pricing, and corporate financial decision making. A distinctive feature of the *Journal* is that it recognises that adverse selection and moral hazard issues are pervasive in financial markets and business organisations, and that Accounting (both financial and managerial) plays a part in ameliorating the problems arising from such informational problems. Thus the editors see Accounting and Finance as being conceptually inter-linked. These linkages are especially apparent in the areas of corporate governance, financial

communication, financial performance measurement, and managerial reward and control structures.

The *Journal* welcomes both theoretical and empirical contributions, especially theoretical papers that yield novel testable implications, and empirical papers that are theoretically well motivated. The *Journal* is not a suitable outlet for highly abstract mathematical papers, or purely descriptive papers with limited theoretical motivation. The editors view Finance and Accounting as being closely related to Economics, and look for theoretical contributions and theoretical motivations that are based in economics. This includes mainstream neo-classical economics, as well as game theory and transaction costs economics. The *Journal* also welcomes papers in behavioural finance, which seek to advance our understanding of how the limits to human information processing ability influence financial decisions, and the framing and completeness of financial contracts.

The majority of papers in the *Journal* employ econometric or related empirical methods as a central feature of their research design. However, the editors welcome contributions that employ alternative empirical research methods, such as case studies. The *Journal* also publishes survey articles which present the current state of the art in Accounting and Finance. One issue each year is a special issue containing selected papers from the annual Capital Market Research conference.

Author Guidelines
All manuscripts should be submitted to **http://services.bepress.com/jbfa/**

Manuscripts are considered on the understanding that they are original, unpublished works not concurrently under consideration for publication elsewhere. The receipt of manuscripts will be acknowledged, but the editors and publishers can accept no responsibility for any loss or non-return of manuscripts. Suitable manuscripts will be given anonymous review, following which a copy of any review report will be supplied together with the editor's decision. As regards papers accepted for publication, the author(s) will be asked to transfer copyright to the publishers. Authors are requested to follow *JBFA's* manuscript and style requirements closely, to minimise later delay or redrafting. In particular, authors should draft their papers and footnotes etc. to avoid identifying themselves directly or indirectly, to help ensure a fair review.

Submission Fee. Each manuscript submitted for possible publication in *JBFA* (including rewritten and resubmitted manuscripts which had previously been rejected with advice that a rewritten paper could be reconsidered) must be accompanied by a submission fee. The fee is currently £36 for submission from UK addresses, and $75 USA (or the equivalent exchange value in other currencies) for submissions from all other addresses. However, please note that for designated authors who are paid-up personal subscribers to *JBFA* the submission fee is reduced to only one-half of the above rates. The rates of submission fees may alter with inflation: the latest rates are always printed on the inside front cover of the current issue of the journal. Submission fees should accompany the relevant manuscript, in the form of a cheque or draft made payable to the University of Manchester. If only the half-rate fee is sent, a cover note should give definite confirmation that the author is currently a paid-up subscriber.

344

Authors who wish to take out a subscription at the same time as submitting a manuscript must send a separate cheque for the subscription made payable to Blackwell Publishing Ltd.

Manuscript Requirements. Submit four photocopies of the manuscript (together with any submission fee) typed double-spaced (preferably on international-size A4 paper). On the title page include the names, titles and institutional affiliations of (all) the author(s) (if any), and also the complete address of the designated author to whom decisions, proofs and reprint requests should be sent. Also provide a running title of fewer than 50 characters and spaces, which will appear on alternate pages in the journal. If the paper is to include any acknowledgements these should be typed as a footnote on the title page. The second page should repeat the full title of the paper (but not the author(s) names) and contain the Abstract of the paper, not exceeding 100 words for full-length papers, or 60 words for shorter Notes, Comments, Replies or Rejoinders. The third page may repeat the full title of the paper (but not the author(s)' names) and here the text proper begins. The main text should be followed by any appendices, by any footnotes (which should be kept to the essential minimum identified in the text by superscript numerals and listed together at the end, not separately at the bottom of each page), and by the list of source references (see below). Tables and figures should be numbered in order of their appearance with Arabic numerals, and each should have a concise descriptive title (and source, where relevant).

References. Citation in the text is by name(s) of author(s), followed by year of publication (and page numbers where relevant) in parentheses. For references authored by more than two contributors use the first author's name and 'et al'. For multiple citations in the same year use a, b, c immediately following the year of publication. The source reference list should be typed in alphabetic order, and in accordance with the following examples of style: Amey, L. R. (1979), Budget Planning and Control Systems (Pitman, 1979) Budget Planning: a Dynamic Reformulation', Accounting and Business Research (Winter 1979), pp. 17-24. Lee, T. A. (1981), 'Cash Flow Accounting and Corporate Financial Reporting' in Essays in British Accounting Research, M. Bromwich and A. Hopwood, eds. (Pitman, 1981), pp. 63-78. Peasnell, K. V. , L. C. L. Skerratt and P. A. Taylor (1979), 'An Arbitrage Rationale for Tests of Mutual fund Performance', Journal of Business Finance & Accounting (Autumn 1979), pp. 373-400.

Mathematical and Statistical Material. Mathematical notation should be used only when its rigour and precision are essential to comprehension, and authors should explain in narrative format the principal operations performed. Preferably detailed mathematical proofs and statistical support should be relegated to appendices. Any equations used should be numbered sequentially in parentheses positioned flush with the right-hand margin. Whilst the journal does not wish to publish unnecessary mathematical or statistical detail, or specimen questionnaires, supplementary information of these kinds may be of assistance to the editors and reviewers in assessing papers, and authors are invited to submit such supporting evidence as separate documents clearly marked as being for information rather than publication.

Illustrations. All graphs, charts etc. submitted with papers must be referred to in the text, and be fully legible and clearly related to scales on the axes. If illustrations are numerous, a proportion may have to be deleted unless the author is able to supply artwork of camera-ready quality or to reimburse the journal for the cost of art-work.

Proofs, Offprints and Prices. The designated author will receive proofs, which should be corrected and returned within ten days of receipt. This author is responsible for proof-reading the manuscript: the editors/publishers are not responsible for any error not marked by the author on the proofs. Corrections to proofs are limited to rectifying errors: no substantial author's changes can be allowed at this stage unless agreement to pay full costs is communicated with the return of proofs. Similarly, offprints in excess of the twenty-five free copies automatically supplied to the designated author (for sharing among any co-authors) must be ordered at the time of return of proofs, in accord with the instructions and price list accompanying the proofs.

Comments and Replies. The journal welcomes non-trivial Comments on papers previously published in *JBFA*. To avoid publishing Comments based on misunderstandings, and to obtain Replies quickly so that they can be published simultaneously with the Comments, it is required that draft comments should be sent to the original authors for their reactions, prior to any formal submission to the editors for publication.

Journal of Business, Industry and Economics

ADDRESS FOR SUBMISSION:

Jim Couch, Editor
Journal of Business, Industry and
   Economics
University of North Alabama
Box 5141
Florence, AL 35632-5141
USA
Phone: 256-765-4412
E-Mail: jcouch@una.edu
Web:

CIRCULATION DATA:

Reader: Academics
Frequency of Issue: 2 Times/Year
Sponsor/Publisher: University of North
   Alabama

PUBLICATION GUIDELINES:

Manuscript Length: 6-10
Copies Required: Three
Computer Submission: Yes
Format: No Reply
Fees to Review: 100.00 US$

Manuscript Style:

REVIEW INFORMATION:

Type of Review: Blind Review
No. of External Reviewers: 2
No. of In House Reviewers: No Reply
Acceptance Rate: 20%
Time to Review: 2 - 3 Months
Reviewers Comments: Yes
Invited Articles: 0-5%
Fees to Publish: 0.00 US$

MANUSCRIPT TOPICS:

Accounting Information Systems; Accounting Theory & Practice; Auditing; Cost Accounting; Government & Non Profit Accounting; Tax Accounting

MANUSCRIPT GUIDELINES/COMMENTS:

For information regarding the manuscript guidelines, please contact the editor at the above address.

Journal of Corporate Accounting and Finance

ADDRESS FOR SUBMISSION:

Edward J. Stone, Editor
Journal of Corporate Accounting and
    Finance
John Wiley & Sons, Inc.
111 River Street
Hoboken, NJ 07030
USA
Phone: 201-748-6197
E-Mail: scho@wiley.com
Web: www.interscience.wiley.com/jpages

PUBLICATION GUIDELINES:

Manuscript Length:
Copies Required: Two
Computer Submission: Yes
Format:
Fees to Review: 0.00 US$

Manuscript Style:
    See Manuscript Guidelines

CIRCULATION DATA:

Reader: Business Persons
Frequency of Issue: Bi-Monthly
Sponsor/Publisher: John Wiley & Sons, Inc.

REVIEW INFORMATION:

Type of Review: Blind Review
No. of External Reviewers: 1
No. of In House Reviewers: 1
Acceptance Rate:
Time to Review: 1 Month or Less
Reviewers Comments: No
Invited Articles: 11-20%
Fees to Publish: 0.00 US$

MANUSCRIPT TOPICS:
Accounting Information Systems; Accounting Theory & Practice; Auditing; Cost Accounting

MANUSCRIPT GUIDELINES/COMMENTS:

Aims and Scope
The *Journal of Corporate Accounting and Finance* is directed to corporate accounting and financial executives and outside auditors and accountants working with corporations.

Articles should address this readership and be informative, analytical, and practical, but not highly technical. We seek material that will offer our readership new insights into, and new approaches to, corporate finance and accounting issues

Instructions to Authors
Manuscripts are considered for publication with the understanding that they represent original material, and are offered exclusively and without fee to the *Journal of Corporate Accounting and Finance.*

Articles must not have been published previously and may not simultaneously be submitted elsewhere.

An original and two copies of the manuscript must be submitted. Any accompanying artwork or exhibits must be submitted as black and white originals suitable for reproduction.

Articles should range from 3,700-7,500 words (15-30 pages), double-spaced on one side only of 8 ½" × 11" heavy-duty white bond paper.

Margins should be set to allow for 55 characters per line. A 1½" margin should be left at the top and bottom of each manuscript page.

Try to use as few footnotes as possible. If they are indispensable to the subject, they should appear double-spaced on a separate page at the end of the article. They should conform to the following style:

Journal article
Bento, R.F., White, L.F. (1998). Participants' values and incentive plans. Human Resource Management, 37(1), 47–60.

Book
Hopkins, B.R. (1998). The law of tax-exempt organizations (7th ed.) New York: John Wiley & Sons.

Send photocopies of the original source of lengthy quotations. This enables us to confirm the absolute accuracy of the quotation.

Please seek clarity, brevity, and pertinence. Titles of articles should be short and clear. All accepted manuscripts are subject to editing.

A brief—50 words or less—biographical sketch of the author should accompany the article. The sketch should name the author's position, company or other professional organization, and field of expertise.

A 100-to-125-word summary of the article should also be provided.

All unsolicited manuscripts must be accompanied by a self-addressed, stamped envelope. Otherwise, they cannot be returned to the author.

Address articles to: Edward J. Stone, Editor, The Journal of Corporate Accounting and Finance, c/o Sheck Cho, Managing Editor, John Wiley & Sons, Inc., 111 River Street, Hoboken, NJ 07030.

Disk Submission Instructions. Please return your final, revised manuscript on disk as well as hard copy. The hard copy must match the disk.

The *Journal* strongly encourages authors to deliver the final, revised version of their accepted manuscripts (text, tables, and, if possible, illustrations) on disk. Given the near-universal use of computer word-processing for manuscript preparation, we anticipate that providing a disk will be convenient for you, and it carries the added advantages of maintaining the integrity of your keystrokes and expediting typesetting. Please return the disk submission slip below with your manuscript and labeled disk(s).

Text

Storage medium. 3-1/2" high-density disk in IBM MS-DOS, Windows, or Macintosh format.

Software and format. Microsoft Word 6.0 is preferred, although manuscripts prepared with any other microcomputer word processor are acceptable. Refrain from complex formatting; the Publisher will style your manuscript according to the Journal design specifications. Do not use desktop publishing software such as Aldus PageMaker or Quark XPress. If you prepared your manuscript with one of these programs, export the text to a word processing format. Please make sure your word processing program's "fast save" feature is turned off. Please do not deliver files that contain hidden text: for example, do not use your word processor's automated features to create footnotes or reference lists.

File names. Submit the text and tables of each manuscript as a single file. Name each file with your last name (up to eight letters). Text files should be given the three-letter extension that identifies the file format. Macintosh users should maintain the MS-DOS "eight dot three" file-naming convention.

Labels. Label all disks with your name, the file name, and the word processing program and version used.

Illustrations

All print reproduction requires files for full color images to be in a CMYK color space. If possible, ICC or ColorSync profiles of your output device should accompany all digital image submissions.

Storage medium. Submit as separate files from text files, on separate disks or cartridges. If feasible, full color files should be submitted on separate disks from other image files. 3 ½" high-density disks, CD, and Iomega Zip disks can be submitted. At authors' request, cartridges and disks will be returned after publication.

Software and format. All illustration files should be in TIFF or EPS (with preview) formats. Do not submit native application formats.

Resolution. Journal quality reproduction will require greyscale and color files at resolutions yielding approximately 300 ppi. Bitmapped line art should be submitted at resolutions yielding 600-1200 ppi. These resolutions refer to the output size of the file; if you anticipate that your images will be enlarged or reduced, resolutions should be adjusted accordingly.

File names. Illustration files should be given the 2- or 3-letter extension that identifies the file format used (i.e., .tif, .eps).

Labels. Label all disks and cartridges with your name, the file names, formats, and compression schemes (if any) used. Hard copy output must accompany all files.

Journal of Cost Analysis & Management

ADDRESS FOR SUBMISSION:

David S. Christensen, Editor
Journal of Cost Analysis & Management
Southern Utah University
School of Business
351 W. Center Street
Cedar City, UT 84720
USA
Phone: 435-865-8058
E-Mail: christensend@suu.edu
Web: www.sceaonline.net

CIRCULATION DATA:

Reader: , Cost Analylists
Frequency of Issue: 2 Times/Year
Sponsor/Publisher: Society of Cost
   Estimating and Analysis

PUBLICATION GUIDELINES:

Manuscript Length: 16-20
Copies Required: Five
Computer Submission: Upon Acceptance
Format: N/A
Fees to Review: 0.00 US$

Manuscript Style:
   See Manuscript Guidelines

REVIEW INFORMATION:

Type of Review: Blind Review
No. of External Reviewers: 2
No. of In House Reviewers: 1
Acceptance Rate: 21-30%
Time to Review: 2 - 3 Months
Reviewers Comments: Yes
Invited Articles: 0-5%
Fees to Publish: 0.00 US$

MANUSCRIPT TOPICS:
Accounting Education; Accounting Information Systems; Accounting Theory & Practice; Auditing; Behavioral Accounting; Cost Accounting; Cost Analysis; Cost Estimate; Earned Value; Econometrics; Economic Development; Fiscal Policy; Government & Non Profit Accounting; Micro Economics; Production/Operations

MANUSCRIPT GUIDELINES/COMMENTS:

Statement of Editorial Policy
The *Journal of Cost Analysis & Management is* published by the Society of Cost Estimating and Analysis. It is a refereed journal dedicated to promoting excellence in cost estimating, cost analysis, and cost management. Its objective is to improve the theory and practice of cost estimating, analysis and management by promoting high quality applied and theoretical research. The *Journal* provides a forum for exchanging ideas, opinions, and research results among 'cost' educators and practitioners around the world.

The *Journal* seeks to publish research that is interesting, stimulating, and intellectually rigorous. Papers involving a variety of topics, settings and research methods are solicited. The methodology used in papers submitted for publication may be analytical or empirical. Manuscripts related to a broad range of cost topics for any sector of the economy –

manufacturing, service, retail, government, and not-for-profit – are desired. New theories, topical areas, and research methods are encouraged. Areas of interest include, but are not limited to, industrial engineering, economics, health care, operations/production management, construction management, business administration, and cost (managerial) accounting.

Manuscripts should be sent to either of the Editors who will initiate the review process. The review will use three criteria for evaluating papers: (1) readability; (2) relevance; and (3) reliability.

All papers accepted for publication in *JCA&M* must have a high level of readability. Poor readability can impede the ability of a reviewer to evaluate the contribution of a paper and may lead to rejection. It is necessary to ensure the paper can be readily understood by individuals involved in the area discussed in the paper. References should not impede the flow of the paper and unnecessary or obscure jargon should not be used. The details of the statistical methodology should be in an appendix rather than in the body of the paper if they are not central to the focus of the manuscript.

The second criterion is relevance. A paper is relevant if it has the potential to influence cost estimating, analysis, or management. A paper that appeals to a broad spectrum of readers or is unique or innovative has a better possibility of influencing costing practice and theory development and therefore, is more relevant than a paper without these features.

The third criterion is reliability. A paper is reliable if the conclusions of the paper can be reasonably inferred from the arguments. Reliability is not hard to assess when a paper is statistical or involves empirical research with which the reviewer is familiar. Authors can improve the probability of acceptance of a paper by including a section on the limitations of the research techniques.

When a paper relies on verbal analysis, reliability is harder to assess. Reviewers have to depend on their own knowledge of the subject to ensure the arguments are relevant to the question addressed and that the paper is internally consistent.

In summary, for a manuscript to be acceptable for publication, the research question should be of interest to the intended readership, the research should be well-designed and well-executed, and the material should be presented effectively and efficiently.

Submission Requirements
Authors should send five copies of their manuscript (and survey instrument, if applicable) for review. There is no review fee.

A letter to the Editor must be enclosed requesting review and possible publication.

The letter must also state that the manuscript has not been previously published and is not under review for another journal. The letter should include the corresponding author's address, telephone and FAX numbers, and E-mail address, if available (as well as any upcoming address change). This individual will receive all editorial correspondence.

352

Format
1. All manuscripts should be typed on one side of 8 ½ x 11 good quality paper and be double-spaced, except for indented quotations.

2. Manuscripts should be as concise as the subject and research methods permit.

3. Margins should be at least one inch from top, bottom and sides to facilitate editing and duplication.

4. To assure anonymous review, authors should not identify themselves directly or indirectly in their papers. Single authors should not use the editorial "we."

5, A cover page should include the title of the paper, the author's name, title and affiliation, email address, any acknowledgments, and a footnote indicating whether the author would be willing to share the data (see later paragraph in this statement).

6. All pages, including tables, appendices and references, should be serially numbered.

7. Headings should be arranged so that major headings are centered, bold and capitalize. Second level headings should be flush left, bold and both upper and lowercase. Third level headings should be flush left, bold, italic and both upper and lowercase. Fourth level headings should be paragraph indent, bold and lower case. Headings and subheadings should not be numbered. For example:

A CENTERED, BOLD, ALL CAPITALIZED, FIRST LEVEL HEADING
A Flush Left, Bold, Upper and Lower Case, Second Level Heading
A .Flush Left Bold, Italic, Upper and Lower Case, Third Level Heading
    A paragraph indent, bold, lower case, fourth level leading. Text starts....

Abstract
An abstract of 100 to 150 words should be presented on a separate page immediately preceding the text of the manuscript. The abstract page should contain the title of the manuscript but should not identify the author(s). Abstracts should contain a concise statement of the purpose of the manuscript, the primary method or approaches used, and the main results or conclusions.

Footnotes
Textual footnotes should be used only for extensions and useful excursions whose inclusion in the body of the manuscript might disrupt the continuity. Footnotes should be double-spaced, numbered consecutively throughout the manuscript with superscript Arabic numerals, and placed at the end of the text.

Tables and Figures
Authors should note the following general requirements:
1. Each table and figure (graphic) should appear on a separate page and should be placed at the end of the text. Each should bear an Arabic number and a complete title indicating the exact contents of the table or figure.

2. A reference to each table or figure should be made in the text.

3. The author should indicate by marginal notation where each table or figure should be inserted in the text, e.g., (Insert table X here).

4. Tables or figures should be reasonably interpreted without reference to the text.

5. Source lines and notes should be included as necessary.

6. When information is not available, use "NA" capitalized with no slash between.

7. Figures must be prepared in a form suitable for printing.

Mathematical Notation
Mathematical notation should be employed only where its rigor and precision are necessary, and in such circumstances authors should explain in the narrative format the principal operations performed. Notations should be avoided in footnotes. Unusual symbols, particularly if handwritten, should be identified in the margin when they first appear. Displayed material should clearly indicate the alignment, superscripts and subscripts. Equations should be numbered in parentheses flush with the right-hand margin.

Questionnaires and Experimental Instruments
Manuscripts reporting on field surveys or experiments should include questionnaires, cases, interview plans or other instruments used in the study.

Documentation
Citations. Work cited should use the: "author-date system" keyed to a list of *works in the* reference list (see below). Authors should make an effort to include the relevant page numbers in the cited works.

1. In the text, works are cited as follows: author's last name and date, without comma, in parentheses: for example, (Jones 1987); with two authors: (Jones and Freeman, 1973); with more than two: (Jones et al, 1985); with more than one source cited together (Jones 1987; Freeman 1986); with two or more works by one author: (Jones 1985 1987).

2. Unless confusion would result, do not use "p." or "pp." Before page numbers: for example, (Jones 1987,115).

3. When the reference list contains more than one work of an author published in the same year, the suffix a, b, etc., follows the date in the text citation: for example, (Jones 1987a) or (Jones 1987a; Freeman 1985b).

4. If an author's name is mentioned in the text, it need not be repeated in the citation; for example, "Jones (1987, 115) says..."

354

5. Citations to institutional works should use acronyms or short titles where practicable: for example, (GAO 1966); (AICPA Cohen Commission Report 1977). Where brief, the full title of an institutional work might be shown in a citation: for example, (ICAEW *The Corporate Report* 1975). 6. If the manuscript refers to statutes, legal treatises or court cases, citations acceptable in law reviews should be used.

Reference List. Every manuscript must include a list of references containing only those works cited. Each entry should contain all data necessary for unambiguous identification.

1. Arrange citations in alphabetical order according to surname of the first author or the name of the institution responsible for the citation.

2. Use authors' initials instead of proper names.

3. In listing more than one name in references (Rayburn, L., and B. Harrelson,...) there should always be a comma before "and."

4. Dates of publication should be placed immediately after authors' names.

5. Titles of journals should not be abbreviated.

6. Multiple works by the same author(s) should be listed in chronological order of publication. Two or more works by the same author(s) in the same year are distinguished by letters after the date.

Sample entries are as follows:

American Accounting Association, Committee on the Future, Content, and Scope of Accounting Education (The Bedford Committee). 1986. Future accounting education: Preparing for the expanding profession. *Issues in Accounting Education* (Spring): 168-195.

Ajzen, I:. 1987. Attitudes, traits, and actions: Dispositional prediction of behavior in personality and social psychology. In *Advances in Experimental Social* Psychology edited by L. Berkovitz, New York, NY: Academic Press.

Grizzle, J.E., C.F. Starmer, axed G:G. Koch, 1969. Analysis of categorical data by linear models. *Biometrics* 25: 489-504.

Notes. Notes are not to be used for documentation. As noted in a previous paragraph, textural notes should be used only for extensions and useful excursions of information that, if included in the body of the text, might disrupt its continuity.

Policy on Data Availability
Authors are encouraged to male their data available for use by others in extending or replicating results reported in their articles. Authors of articles which report data-dependent

results should footnote the status of data availability and, when pertinent, this should be accompanied by information on how the data nay be obtained.

Text Preparation on Disk
An electronic version on disk should be sent with the final accepted version of the paper to the Editor. The hard copy and electronic files must match exactly. All word processing packages are acceptable.

Page Proofs and Offprints
Page proofs of the article will be sent to the corresponding author. These should be carefully proofread. Except for typographical errors, corrections should be minimal, and rewriting of text is not permitted. Corrected page proofs must be returned with 48 hours of receipt.

Journal of Deferred Compensation: Nonqualified Plans and Executive Compensation

ADDRESS FOR SUBMISSION:

Bruce J. McNeil, Editor-In-Chief
Journal of Deferred Compensation:
   Nonqualified Plans and Executive
   Compensation
Leonard, Street and Deinard
150 South Fifth Street Suite 2300
Minneapolis, MN 55402
USA
Phone: 612-335-1783
E-Mail: bruce.mcneil@leonard.com
Web:

PUBLICATION GUIDELINES:

Manuscript Length: 21-25
Copies Required: Two
Computer Submission: Yes Disk, Email
Format: MS Word
Fees to Review: 0.00 US$

Manuscript Style:
   See Manuscript Guidelines

CIRCULATION DATA:

Reader: Business Persons, Academics
Frequency of Issue: Quarterly
Sponsor/Publisher: Aspen Publishers, Inc.

REVIEW INFORMATION:

Type of Review: Editorial Review
No. of External Reviewers: 1
No. of In House Reviewers: 1
Acceptance Rate: 11-20%
Time to Review: 1 Month or Less
Reviewers Comments: Yes
Invited Articles: 6-10%
Fees to Publish: 0.00 US$

MANUSCRIPT TOPICS:

Accounting Education; Accounting Theory & Practice; Employee Benefits; Executive Compensation; Government & Non Profit Accounting; Insurance; Options; Portfolio & Security Analysis; Stock Based Benefits; Tax Accounting

MANUSCRIPT GUIDELINES/COMMENTS:

Journal of Deferred Compensation (*JDC*) is devoted to providing practical information and ideas to professionals who deal with the tax, legal, and business planning aspects of nonqualified plans and executive compensation.

JDC emphasizes quality and clarity of exposition. Reviewers consider the following criteria in assessing submissions: value of the information to the *Journal's* audience, substantive contribution to the broadly defined field of nonqualified plans and executive compensation, and overall quality of manuscript. The decision to publish a given manuscript is made by the Editor-in-Chief, relying on the recommendations of the reviewers.

Submission of a manuscript clearly implies commitment to publish in the *Journal*. Papers previously published or under review by other journals are unacceptable. Articles adapted from book-length works-in-progress will be considered under acceptable copyright arrangements.

Manuscript Specifications. All textual material-including notes and references-must be double-spaced in a full-size nonproportional typeface (e.g., 12 pt. Courier), on one side only of 8½" x 11" good-quality paper, with 1½" margins all around. All pages must be numbered. References should be double-spaced and placed at the end of the text on a separate page headed "References." Notes must not be embedded in the text; they should be printed as double-spaced endnotes rather than footnotes. Improperly prepared manuscripts will be returned for repreparation.

Within the article, use short subheadings for organization and emphasis. Include a cover sheet with title, author's address and affiliations, mailing and e-mail addresses, and phone and fax numbers.

Artwork, including tables, charts, and graphs, must be of camera-ready quality. Each should be on a separate page placed at the end of the text, with proper placement indicated within text (e.g., "Insert Table 2 here").

Three high-quality copies of the manuscript should be submitted to the Editor-in-Chief. Include a biographical statement of 20 words or less.

Acceptance. Once an article has been formally accepted, the author must submit the article to the publisher in two formats: three high-quality manuscript copies and a Word 6.0 computer file on 3½" floppy diskette labeled with file type and name, soft ware version, article title, and author's name. No other software is acceptable.

Copyright is retained by the publisher, and articles are subject to editorial revision. There is no payment for articles; authors receive five copies of the issue in which the article is published. Manuscripts not accepted for publication are not returned. Authors should keep a copy of any submission for their files.

Manuscript submissions and inquiries should be directed to the Editor-in-Chief.

358

Journal of Derivatives Accounting

ADDRESS FOR SUBMISSION:

Mamouda Mbemap, Editor-in-Chief
Journal of Derivatives Accounting
Birkholweg 46
Frankfurt am Main
D-60433,
Germany
Phone: +49 179 534 5772
E-Mail: editor.jda@gmx.de
Web: www.worldscinet.com/jda/jda.shtml

CIRCULATION DATA:

Reader: Academics, Business Persons,
  Regulators and Standard Setters
Frequency of Issue: Quarterly
Sponsor/Publisher:

PUBLICATION GUIDELINES:

Manuscript Length: 16-25
Copies Required: Three
Computer Submission: Yes Disk, Email
Format: MS Word
Fees to Review: 0.00 US$

Manuscript Style:
  Uniform System of Citation (Harvard
  Blue Book), World Scientific Publishing

REVIEW INFORMATION:

Type of Review: Blind Review
No. of External Reviewers: 1-3
No. of In House Reviewers: 1-2
Acceptance Rate: 6-20%
Time to Review: 1 Month or Less
Reviewers Comments: Yes
Invited Articles: 6-20%
Fees to Publish: 0.00 US$

MANUSCRIPT TOPICS:
Accounting Standards; Accounting Theory & Practice; Asset and Fund Management; Assets and Liabilities; Audit and Assurance; Business Combination Agrements; Contingent Liabilities; Corporate Governance; Corporate Treasurey; Derivatives Documentation; Derivatives Instruments; Discolsure and Reporting; Financial Instruments; Foreign Exchange; Hedging and Trading Models; Models; Off-balance Sheet; Pricing; Risk Management; Securitization; Special Purpose Vehicle; Structured Products; Valuation and Pricing

MANUSCRIPT GUIDELINES/COMMENTS:

1. The initial manuscript should be sent to the Editor-in-Chief preferably via email (see: email address above or in the *Journal of Derivatives Accounting*).

2. Submission of a manuscript indicates a tacit understanding that the paper is not under consideration for publication with other journals.

3. Once the paper is accepted, authors are assumed to cede copyrights of the paper over to the *Journal of Derivatives Accounting*.

4. The authors should ensure that all materials in the paper are original and abide by all copyright rules. In order to facilitate the review process, authors should also ensure that

internet access and access through other outlets to submitted papers draft of papers and backup data cited in the papers is blocked or simply removed during the review.

5. All papers will be acknowledged and refereed. They will not be returned.

6. For reviewing purposes, the papers have to be prepared in the following manner:
- Apply double spacing and a 12-point font size for text.
- Supply diagrams at the back of the manuscript.
- Tables and figures should be numbered using Arabic numerals, with one table or figure to a page. All tables and figures should be self-contained.
- Headings and legends should be understandable without reference to the text.
- Refer to the *Webster's New Collegiate Dictionary* for spelling and *The Chicago Manual of Style* for punctuation and other points of style.
- Include the author's full titles, phone numbers, complete mailing and e-mail addresses.
- Provide a short concise executive summary of no more than 150 words, and between 5 and 10 keywords (eg, Workout, Turnaround, Distressed Debt etc...).
- Refer to the Harvard System [name (year)] for bibliographic reference. (Harvard System)
- Provide a text or prose description of all mathematical and statistical symbols. Preference should be given to text over Greek symbols.
- In order to facilitate editing and prompt publication, manuscripts accepted for publication will be prepared according to the Instructions for Typesetting Manuscripts of the publisher (on the web page of the *Journal*).

7. The first-named authors will be provided with 25 free reprints.

Journal of Digital Business

ADDRESS FOR SUBMISSION:

Rajendar K. Garg, Editor
Journal of Digital Business
  ELECTRONIC SUBMISSION ONLY
Phone: 724-357-4547
E-Mail: garg@iup.edu
Web:

CIRCULATION DATA:

Reader: Business Persons, Academics
Frequency of Issue: 2 Times/Year
Sponsor/Publisher:

PUBLICATION GUIDELINES:

Manuscript Length: 16-20
Copies Required: Three
Computer Submission: Yes Email Required
Format: MS Word, RTF format
Fees to Review: 0.00 US$

Manuscript Style:
  See Manuscript Guidelines

REVIEW INFORMATION:

Type of Review: Blind Review
No. of External Reviewers: 3
No. of In House Reviewers: 1
Acceptance Rate: New J
Time to Review: 2 - 3 Months
Reviewers Comments: Yes
Invited Articles: 0-5%
Fees to Publish: 50.00 US$ Plus pg fee
  beyond 8 pg limit

MANUSCRIPT TOPICS:
Accounting Information Systems; Auditing; Cost Accounting; Tax Accounting

MANUSCRIPT GUIDELINES/COMMENTS:

This "Manuscript Guidelines" are for papers that are accepted for publication in the *Journal of Digital Business*. All papers published in this journal are peer-reviewed, hence classifying these publications as "double blind peer-reviewed". Authors should follow the guidelines very closely in order to maintain the publication consistency in terms of style, appearance, and so forth. If authors fail to follow these guidelines, the Editor reserves the right to reject publication of those papers.

Please use the instruction sheet as an example or guide. Please note how the title and author information is displayed below:

ECONOMIC IMPACT OF DIGITAL BUSINESS IN CHINA
Steve Wolf, International University of Digital Business, USA, wolf@iudb.edu

(As shown above, for each author on one separate, single-spaced, centered line: First Name Last Name, Institution, Country, e-mail address. DO NOT INCLUDE TITLES, such as Dr., Professor, and Prof.)

Page Size. Preferably 8 ½" x 11" or nearest size (NO LEGAL SIZE or SMALLER THAN 8 ½ X 11)

Page Limit. All manuscripts are limited to eight (8) pages in the final printed format. (There will be a charge of $50 for each additional page which must be paid with your final camera ready submission. Your manuscript will not be published if you fail to pay for additional pages.)

Margins. 1" on all four sides (top, bottom, left and right).

Title. Preferably short manuscript title, centered, all capital letters, bold, 14 point Times New Roman

Author. Immediately following paper title, single-spaced, centered, bold, 10 point Times New Roman. On a separate line for each author: First Name, Last Name, Institution, Country e-mail address.

Headings. Preferably short. Left flushed, all capital letters, bold, 10 point Times New Roman.

Text/ Body. 10 point Times New Roman, left flushed, no indention. Paragraphs begin at left margin and right justified.

Do not number pages. Pages will be numbered consecutively at the time of publication by the Editor. However, use pencil lightly at bottom right corner to indicate page sequence/numbers that can be easily erased later on.

Spacing. All text SINGLE-SPACED, between paragraphs use Double Space.

Abstract. Begin your manuscript with an abstract of about 100 words, providing an overview of your research objectives, methodology, findings, etc. Include ABSTRACT as heading, left flushed and triple-spaced below the last author's name, affiliation, country, and e-mail.

Citations and References. The use of citations and references should be as limited as possible in order to save space. Only the most important sources should be cited and listed. Unlisted references should not be cited, and listed references must be cited in the body. Within your text, reference citations should consist of the author's last name and date of publication enclosed within parentheses. Example: (Agarwal, 2001). Do not use footnotes in your text.

All materials cited should be listed in an alphabetical order under the heading of REFERENCES starting at left margin. Do not number references. There should be double space between the REFERENCES heading and the first reference listing and between the two listings thereafter. However, each reference should be single-spaced.

Example of journal article
Garg, Rajendar K. (1996), "The Influence of positive and negative wording and issue involvement on responses to likert scales in Marketing Research", Journal of the Market Research Society, Vol. 38, No. 3, 235-246.

362

Example of a book
Turban, Efrain et al., (2004), Electronic Commerce, Prentice Hall, 2004

Tables and Figures. Tables and figures should be placed close to where they are cited, and they should be high quality and camera-ready They should be placed flush with the left-hand margin and have proper numbering, headings and other notations.

Journal of E-Business

ADDRESS FOR SUBMISSION:

Rajendar K. Garg, Editor
Journal of E-Business
Indiana University of Pennsylvania
Eberly College of Business
Department of Marketing
Indiana, PA 15705
USA
Phone: 724-357-4547
E-Mail: garg@iup.edu
Web: www.journalofe-business.org

CIRCULATION DATA:

Reader: Academics
Frequency of Issue: 2 Times/Year
Sponsor/Publisher: International Academy
of E-Business

PUBLICATION GUIDELINES:

Manuscript Length: 21-25
Copies Required: Three
Computer Submission: Yes Disk, Email
Format: MS Word
Fees to Review: 0.00 US$

Manuscript Style:
, Journal of Marketing

REVIEW INFORMATION:

Type of Review: Blind Review
No. of External Reviewers: 3
No. of In House Reviewers: 1
Acceptance Rate: 11-20%
Time to Review: 2 - 3 Months
Reviewers Comments: Yes
Invited Articles: 0-5%
Fees to Publish: 0.00 US$

MANUSCRIPT TOPICS:

Accounting Theory & Practice; E-Business; E-Management; E-Marketing; Industrial Organization; International Economics & Trade; International Finance; Tax Accounting

MANUSCRIPT GUIDELINES/COMMENTS:

Journal of E-Business invited manuscripts from authors relating to theory and practical aspects of electronic business. The *Journal of E-Business* will be published twice a year in June and December. The *Journal* will utilize a double blind review process.

Purposes/Objectives

- To enhance knowledge, understanding, training and scholarship in e-business/e-commerce that individuals must have to succeed in rapidly changing global, competitive environment
- To share and stimulate research in a variety of electronic commerce areas and topics
- To explore pedagogical/training approaches and issues
- To provide a dialogue between and among academicians, practitioners, and policy-makers
- To identify dynamic technological trends and their social, political and economic implications worldwide

- To create cross or interdisciplinary, integrated forums to benefit individuals in different business disciplines—marketing, finance, accounting, computer & information systems, production & operations management, purchasing & procurement, human resource management, R & D, etc.

Your paper may include topics listed below or any other relevant topic.
- E-Business Models/Theories/Conceptual Frameworks
- New & Old Economy—Similarities & Differences
- E-Commerce Strategies & Tactics
- E-Commerce Infrastructure & Technologies
- C2C (Consumer to Consumer)
- C2B (Consumer to Business)
- Nonprofit E-Commerce
- Intranet/Intra-Organizational E-Commerce
- Online Consumer & Business Behavior & Decision-Making
- Online Market Research/Data-Mining
- E-Communications and Advertising
- Relationship Marketing/One-2-One Marketing
- Web Design & Management
- Electronic Funds Transfer & Payment Systems
- E-Commerce Security
- Product/Service—Specific E-Business/Case Studies
- E-Commerce in Developed 16 Nations
- E-Commerce in Underdeveloped/Developing Nations
- Legal, Political, Ethical, Privacy Issues
- History of E-Commerce
- Future of E-Business—Trends, Forecasts, Prediction

Please submit three (3) copies of your manuscript on paper and an electronic version of the paper to the Editor. Please review the instructions to the authors prior to the submission of your paper.

Guidelines to Authors
The following instructions must be followed by authors for submitting their manuscripts to the *Journal of E-Business*.

Original Articles Only. Submission of a manuscript by authors to the *Journal of E-Business* represents a certification by them that the work contained in the manuscript is original, and that neither the manuscript nor any version of it has been previously published or under consideration by any other publication simultaneously.

Manuscript Length. Your manuscript may be no longer than 20-25 pages typed double-spaced. The limit of 25 pages includes figures, tables, references and abstract. More lengthy manuscripts may be considered, but only at the discretion of the Editor. The Editor will carefully assess the value and contribution of the article to the overall dissemination of knowledge in the field in making such a decision. Sometimes lengthier manuscripts may be considered if they can be divided into sections which may be submitted for publication under different titles in successive *Journal* issues.

Manuscript Style. References, citations, and general style of manuscripts submitted to the *Journal of E-Business* should follow the style used by American Marketing Association for its many journals such as, *Journal of Marketing*. References should be placed in alphabetical order at the end of the article.

Manuscript Preparation
- Margins. Leave at least a 1-inch margins on all four sides.
- Paper and/or Electronic Version. Authors are required to submit at least 3 copies of the manuscript on paper, and an electronic version via an email attachment using Microsoft Windows Word software (rtf format) and send it to **JEB@iup.edu**.
- Cover Page. Important Staple a cover page to the manuscript indicating only the article title (used for anonymous refereeing).
- Second "Title Page", which should not be stapled to the manuscript, should include full authorship information.
- ABSTRACT page should follow the second "Title Page" and should have 100-150 words abstract.
- The manuscript should be free of all spelling, grammar and punctuation errors.
- Inconsistencies: Please be sure that you are consistent in the use of abbreviations, terminology, and reference citations throughout your paper. When you use an abbreviation for the first time, please write it in full within brackets. For example, BEM (Big Emerging Markets).

Tables, Figures and Drawings. All tables, figures, illustrations, etc. should be embedded in the electronic version at the appropriate place within the text of the article. In the paper version, they should be appended to the article at the end.

Alterations. Often, a manuscript may be accepted by the Editor contingent upon satisfactory inclusion of changes mandated by anonymous referees and members of the Editorial Review Board. If the Editor returns your manuscript for such revisions, you are responsible for having the appropriate sections of the paper revised and altered.

Examples of References to Periods:
1. *Journal Article: One Author*
    Garg, Rajendar K. (1996), "The Influence of positive and negative wording and issue involvement on responses to liker scales in Marketing Research", *Journal of the Market Research Society*, Vol. 38, No. 3, 235-246.

2. *Journal Article: Multiple Authors*
    Kaynak, Erdner and Vinay Kothari (1984), "Export Behavior of small and medium sized manufacturers: Some policy guidelines for international marketers", *Management International Review*, Vol. 24, No. 2, 61-69.

Reprints. Upon publication, the senior author will receive one complimentary copy of the *Journal of E-Business* in the paper format. It would take approximately 10-12 weeks for the preparation of the reprints. For more copies, the authors would be able to download articles from the electronic version.

Copyright. If your manuscript is accepted for publication, copyright ownership must be officially transferred to the International Academy of E-Business. International Academy of E-Business retains all copyrights over all content published in the *Journal of E-Business*. The Editor's acceptance letter will include a form fully explaining this. This form must be signed by all authors and returned to the author at this time. Failure to return the copyright form in a timely fashion will result in delay of your manuscript in the *Journal*.

Journal of Educators Online

ADDRESS FOR SUBMISSION:

Matthew A. Elbeck, Editor
Journal of Educators Online
500 University Drive
Dothan, AL 36303
USA
Phone: 334-983-6556 ext. 356
E-Mail: melbeck@troy.edu
Web: www.thejeo.com

CIRCULATION DATA:

Reader: Academics
Frequency of Issue: 2 Times/Year
Sponsor/Publisher: Editorial Board

PUBLICATION GUIDELINES:

Manuscript Length: 16-25
Copies Required:
Computer Submission: Yes Disk, Email
Format: MS Word, Excel
Fees to Review: 0.00 US$

Manuscript Style:
    American Psychological Association

REVIEW INFORMATION:

Type of Review: Blind Review
No. of External Reviewers: 2
No. of In House Reviewers: 0
Acceptance Rate: 30%
Time to Review: 1 Month
Reviewers Comments: Yes
Invited Articles: 0-5%
Fees to Publish: 0.00 US$

MANUSCRIPT TOPICS:
Accounting Education; Accounting Information Systems; International Economics & Trade; International Finance

MANUSCRIPT GUIDELINES/COMMENTS:

Submit via e-mail attachment an MS Word copy of your manuscript to the editor Matthew Elbeck at **melbeck@troy.edu**. Maximum length of submission is twenty pages (A4 or Letter size with one inch margins), double spaced, including abstract, appendices, references, figures, and tables.

Include a cover letter with the paper's title and the name, address, telephone number, and e-mail address of the contact person; a brief bio (one paragraph) for each author; together with the statement "my/our paper entitled ------- has not been published and is not being considered for publication elsewhere."

Papers will be reviewed using a double-blind review process. Names of author(s) should appear only on the title page. Authors should not identify themselves or their institution elsewhere in the paper.

Submission indicates that the paper or a similar version of it has not been previously published, accepted for publication, and/or is not currently under consideration for publication elsewhere. Decisions by the editor are final.

All submitted papers will be reviewed and feedback sent to the author(s) within four weeks.

Journal of Emerging Technologies in Accounting

ADDRESS FOR SUBMISSION:

Miklos Vasarhelyi, Editor
Journal of Emerging Technologies in
  Accounting
Rutgers University
Rutgers School of Business
315 Ackerson Hall
180 University Ave.
Newark, NJ 07102
USA
Phone: 201-454-4377
E-Mail: miklosv@rutgers.edu
Web: aaahq.org

PUBLICATION GUIDELINES:

Manuscript Length:
Copies Required: Four
Computer Submission: Yes
Format:
Fees to Review: 25.00 US$

Manuscript Style:

CIRCULATION DATA:

Reader: Academics
Frequency of Issue: Yearly
Sponsor/Publisher: American Accounting
  Association - AIET

REVIEW INFORMATION:

Type of Review:
No. of External Reviewers: 3+
No. of In House Reviewers: 0
Acceptance Rate: 11-20%
Time to Review: 1 - 2 Months
Reviewers Comments:
Invited Articles: 0-5%
Fees to Publish: 0.00 US$

MANUSCRIPT TOPICS:
Accounting Information Systems; Auditing; Behavioral Accounting; Emergency Technology

MANUSCRIPT GUIDELINES/COMMENTS:

Note. *JETA* is published electronically and on paper. As soon as a paper is accepted it will be posted on the AAA website and when the issue is completed it is sent to the printer for the paper version.

Editorial Policy
The *Journal of Emerging Technologies in Accounting* is the academic journal of the Artificial Intelligence/Emerging Technologies Section of the American Accounting Association. The purpose of the this section is to improve and facilitate the research, education, and practice of advanced information systems, cutting-edge technologies, and artificial intelligence in the fields of accounting, information technology, and management advisory systems. The primary criterion for publication in *JETA* is the significance of contribution made to the literature.

JETA Mission
To encourage, support, and disseminate the production of a stream of high-quality research focused on emerging technologies and artificial intelligence applied or applicable to a wide set of accounting related problems.

Objectives
To provide an outlet for studies that are:
1. Forward-looking research regarding technologies and their impact on the accounting and business environments;
2. Discovery and exploratory research about technological environments, including artificial intelligence;
3. Conceptual research about the technological environment;
4. Field research of emerging and relatively new technologies;
5. Archival and retrospective studies of the life cycle of previously emerging technologies with a focus on a historical perspective of such technologies and the knowledge that can be gained in the current and future adoption and implementation of emerging technologies; and
6. Integrative plans for introducing, managing, and controlling emerging technologies in all areas of accounting (audit, financial, cost, tax, etc.), including both practice and curriculum issues.

To foster a community of ongoing scholarly discussions that emphasizes the concept that any singly published high quality research study will be but one extraction and culmination of knowledge in the overall research agenda of both the authors and researchers with similar interests. A refereed online discussion forum facilitates these ongoing scholarly discussions.

Review Process
The editorial review process is most efficient and effective when authors submit research papers that are polished and prepared for the review process. Such preparation should include subjecting the manuscript to critique by colleagues and others, for example, through participation in workshops and conferences. The paper should be revised to address comments raised by such colleagues and workshop and conference participants prior to submitting the manuscript to the journal. The *JETA* review process is not to be used as a means of obtaining feedback at early stages of developing the research. Reviewers and associate editors are responsible for providing critically constructive and prompt evaluations of submitted research papers based on the significance of their contribution and on the rigor of analysis and presentation. Associate editors also make editorial recommendations to the editor. The review is double blind. Authors should not intentionally and inadvertently identify themselves in the text of their manuscripts or in materials accompanying their manuscripts.

Manuscript Submission
Manuscripts currently under consideration by another journal should not be submitted. At the time of submission, the author must state that the work is not submitted or published in a journal elsewhere.

Electronic Submission

All manuscripts are to be submitted electronically to the journal editor. To preserve anonymity, two files should be submitted, one with the cover page, and one with the abstract, text of the paper, and tables, figures, and appendices. All documents should be submitted in Microsoft® Word format (.doc files). All tables, figures, and appendices must be placed in the same documents as the text of the paper. The two electronic files should be emailed to Miklos Vasarhelyi, Editor, at **miklosv@andromeda.rutgers.edu**. The submission fee is $25.00 in U.S. Funds. Payment may be made by credit card or check. For credit card payments, the electronic payment form is available on the AAA's web site. Checks should made payable to the American Accounting Association and mailed to Miklos Vasarhelyi, Editor, JETA, Rutgers School of Business, 315 Ackerson Hall, 180 University Avenue, Rutgers University, Newark, NJ 07102.

Manuscript Preparation

Manuscripts submitted to *JETA* should be prepared according the guidelines set forth in the B format of *The Chicago Manual Style* (14th edition, University of Chicago Press) with spelling in accordance with *Merriam-Webster's Collegiate Dictionary*.

Manuscript Format

All manuscripts should adhere to the following formats:
1. double-spaced, except for indented quotations
2. 12-point font
3. 8 ½ × 11" page set-up with margins of one inch from top, bottom, and sides to facilitate editing and comments
4. a cover page with the title of the paper, the author's name, title and affiliation, email address, any acknowledgments, and a footnote indicating whether the author would be willing to share the data. The cover page should be placed in a separate file from the abstract and manuscript.

Pagination

All pages, including tables, appendices, and references, should be serially numbered. Major sections should be numbered in Roman numerals. Subsections should not be numbered.

Numbers

Spell out numbers from one to ten, except when used in tables and lists, and when used with mathematical, statistical, scientific, or technical units and quantities, such as distances, weights, and measures. All other numbers are expressed numerically.

Abstract

An abstract of about 100 words should be presented on a separate page immediately preceding the text. The abstract should concisely inform the reader of the manuscript's topic, its methods, and its findings. The manuscript's title, but neither the author's name nor other identification designations, should appear on the abstract page.

372

Keywords
The abstract is to be followed by four keywords that will assist in indexing the paper. Text of Paper: The text of the paper should start with a section labeled "I. Introduction," which provides more details about the paper's purpose motivation, methodology, and findings.

Tables and Figures
The general requirements should be met:
1. All tables and figures must be placed in the same .doc file as the text of the manuscript in the proper order.
2. Each table and figure (graphic) should appear on a separate page and should be placed at the end of the text.
3. A reference to each graphic should be made in the text.
4. The author should indicate by marginal notation where each graphic should be inserted in the text. Equations: Equations should be numbered in parentheses, flush with the right-hand margin.

DOCUMENTATION
Citations
Work cited should use the author-date system keyed to a list of works in the reference list, for example, (Smith 1998), (Thompson and Gonzalez 1999), and (Wilson et al. 2000).

Reference List
Every manuscript must include a list of references containing only those works cited. Each entry should contain all data necessary for unambiguous identification. With the author-date system, use the following format recommended by *The Chicago Manual of Style*:
1. Arrange citations in alphabetical order according to surname of the first author or the name of the institution responsible for the citation.
2. Use author's initials instead of proper names.
3. Date of publication should be placed immediately after author's name.
4. Titles of journals should not be abbreviated.
5. Multiple works by the same author(s) in the same year are distinguished by letters after the date.
6. Inclusive page numbers appear as in the sample entries below, with a dash between to indicate their range.

Sample entries are as follows:

Greenstein, M., and H. Sami. 1994. The impact of the SEC's segment disclosure requirement on the bid-ask spread. *The Accounting Review* 69 (1): 179-199.

_____, and M. Vasarhelyi. 2002. Electronic Commerce: Security, Risk Management and Control. Second edition. Chicago, IL: McGraw-Hill.

Hunton, J. 2002. Blending information and communication technology with accounting research. *Accounting Horizons* 16 (1): 55-67.

O'Leary, D. 1999a. The impact of the euro on information systems. *Journal of Information Systems* 13 (2): 105-116.

_____. 1999b. REAL-D: A schema for data warehouses. *Journal of Information Systems* 13 (1): 49-62.

Policy on Reproduction

The mission of *JETA* is to encourage, support, and disseminate the production of a stream of high-quality research focused on emerging technologies and artificial intelligence. Thus, permission is hereby granted to reproduce any of the contents in *JETA* for use in courses of instruction as long as the source and American Accounting Association copyright are indicated in any such reproductions.

Written application must be made to the American Accounting Association for permission to reproduce any of the contents of *JETA* for use in other than courses of instruction, e.g., inclusion in books or readings or in any other publications intended for general distribution. In consideration for the grant of permission by *JETA* in such instances, the applicant must notify the author(s) in writing of the intended use to be made of each reproduction. Normally, *JETA* will not assess a charge for the waiver of copyright.

Except where otherwise noted in articles, the copyright has been transferred to the American Accounting Association. Where the author(s) has (have) not transferred the copyright to the Association, applicants must seek permission to reproduce (for all purposes) directly from the author(s).

Discussion Forum Editorial Policies

One of the objectives of the *Journal of Emerging Technologies in Accounting* is to foster a community of ongoing scholarly discussions that emphasizes the concept that any singly published high-quality research study will be but one extraction and culmination of knowledge in the overall research agenda of both the authors and researchers with similar interests.

The online forum of continuing discussion regarding accepted and digitally published *JETA* articles can be found on the AAA's web site: **aaa-edu.org**. This forum is facilitated, reviewed, and edited by the journal's Discussion Forum Editor. Postings are made monthly.

Examples of acceptable discussion comments include:

* specific critiques of experimental design, control groups, theoretical development (such critiques should be constructive and be followed with suggestions for improvement by future researchers);
* a list of additional, relevant published work and a discussion of why these works are relevant; and
* sharing of similar, relevant work-in-progress by other researchers.

374

Some examples appear below.

The Journal of Emerging Technologies in Accounting Web Site
Volume 1 Number 1

The Impact of Technology on Investors' Decisions
By John Doe and Jane Smith
Discussion Forum for This Article

Comment by Enrique Gonzalez - August 2002
This study would have been greatly enhanced by using a stronger control group. Such a group may be implemented by having a group of subjects that....

Comment by Mary Hill - December 2002
John Doe and I have expanded this study and we have included a control group as suggested by Gonzalez (2002). Also, we used larger experimental and control groups. We will be presenting this paper at the midyear XXX meeting. An abstract of the paper can be found at http://www.mysite.com.

Discussion Forum Submission Requirements
Discussion comments should be electronically submitted to the Andy Lymer, Discussion Forum Editor, **a.lymer@bham.ac.uk**. The submissions should include:

- submitter's name, affiliation, title, and email address
- title and issue number of the paper being critiqued
- discussion comments along with any diagrams and references all contained in a single word document.

Discussion Forum Editorial Policies
The Discussion Forum Editor has the sole discretion to review and accept or reject comments for posting to the discussion forum. The Discussion Forum Editor may suggest editorial changes before the posting of the comments. If the author of the comments does not wish to accept any or all of the proposed changes, then the Discussion Forum Editor has the right to reject the posting of the comments. Once comments have been accepted for posting to the discussion forum, the Discussion Forum Editor will send a copy of the comments to author of the original article that appeared in *JETA*.

Journal of Forensic Accounting

ADDRESS FOR SUBMISSION:

D. Larry Crumbley, Editor
Journal of Forensic Accounting
Louisiana State University
Department of Accounting
3106 A CEBA
Baton Rouge, LA 70803
USA
Phone: 225-578-6231
E-Mail: dcrumbl@lsu.edu
Web: www.bus.lsu.edu/accounting

CIRCULATION DATA:

Reader: Academics
Frequency of Issue: 2 Times/Year
Sponsor/Publisher: R.T. Edwards
(Philadelphia, PA)

PUBLICATION GUIDELINES:

Manuscript Length: 16-20
Copies Required: Three
Computer Submission: Yes Disk or Email
Format: IBM Compatible
Fees to Review: 35.00 US$

Manuscript Style:
, Academic

REVIEW INFORMATION:

Type of Review: Blind Review
No. of External Reviewers: 2
No. of In House Reviewers: 1
Acceptance Rate: 21-30%
Time to Review: 4 - 6 Months
Reviewers Comments: Yes
Invited Articles: 0-5%
Fees to Publish: 0.00 US$

MANUSCRIPT TOPICS:
Auditing; Fraud; Tax Accounting

MANUSCRIPT GUIDELINES/COMMENTS:

Aims & Scope
The *Journal of Forensic Accounting: Auditing, Fraud, and Taxation (JFA)* is dedicated to promoting excellence in forensic accounting. The journal is an independent international forum for the publication of significant research dealing with the models and methodologies of investigative and forensic accounting, seeking to establish a balance between theoretical and empirical studies, and striving to foster practitioner-academic dialogue and collaboration. Papers on fraud and forensic auditing; risk assessment; detection of financial statement fraud and tax evasion; bankruptcy and valuation studies; GAAP, GAAS and SEC violations; non-standard entries, structured transactions, earnings management, fair presentation and disclosure transparency; audit testing and evaluation; transaction reconstruction and accountability; litigation support and dispute avoidance; and the underground economy are solicited. In addition, papers on particular techniques and technologies, and preventative controls and improved standards are invited. Submitted research should be grounded in real-world business problems or litigation issues faced by practitioners and entity stakeholders. All papers are reviewed.

Intended Audience. Academic researchers and educators specializing in forensic accounting, as well as external and internal auditors, professional audit advisors, process security specialists, and legal, tax, and insurance personnel.

Information for Contributors
Submissions should follow the generally accepted conventions established in *Accounting Review*, with two important exceptions: 1) all entities must be identified with factitious names, and 2) an electronic version of the final article in PC-based Microsoft Word for Windows format is required. Style tips and conventions.

Please submit 3 copies of your manuscript, including photocopies of all artwork, along with a non-refundable processing fee of $35.00, to the Editor-in-Chief at the following address:

D. Larry Crumbley, Journal of Forensic Accounting
Dept. of Accounting, 3106A CEBA
Louisiana State University, Baton Rouge, LA 70803, USA
Phone: 225.388.6231, Fax: 225.388.6201, Email: **dcrumbl@ lsu.edu**

Please do not send your diskettes, permissions, transfer of copyright, or original artwork prior to notification of manuscript acceptance. Please include complete postal addresses, email addresses, phone and fax numbers for all authors of the article.

General Requirements
Journal of Forensic Accounting considers and accepts articles on the understanding that they are original works of the identified author(s), they have not been previously published or submitted elsewhere for publication; and that, if accepted, they will not be published elsewhere in any language without prior written consent of the publisher. It is a condition of acceptance that the publisher obtain exclusive copyright of the article in all languages and for all methods of delivery, throughout the world.

Style Tips and Conventions
- **Columnar data**. Align numerical columnar data on the decimal place, and ensure that all data items contain the same number of digits (e.g., zeros in the trailing places). Place footnotes or other callouts (e.g., asterisks) for columnar data elements in a separate column.
- **Use of italics**. Use of italics should be minimized. The house style of R.T. Edwards is to not italicize commonly used Latin phrases. These include, but are not limited to: e.g.; i.e.; per se; pro forma; de facto; etc.
- **Avoid "Double Headings."** Double headings (when a sub-level heading directly follows a superior level heading without any intervening text) should be avoided. At a minimum, the intervening text should explain how the idea(s) contained within the superior-level heading can be disassembled into the sub-headings.
- **Miscellaneous Conventions**. The stylistic conventions of R.T. Edwards, Inc. also include: 1) using the word "data" for both singular and plural instances (no "datum"); and, 2) treating the word "website" as a solid compound word, such as "farmhouse," "workplace," etc. (no "web site").

Journal of Government Financial Management (Government Accountants Journal)

ADDRESS FOR SUBMISSION:

Marie Force, Editor
Journal of Government Financial
   Management (Government Accountants
   Journal)
2208 Mount Vernon Avenue
Alexandria, VA 22301
USA
Phone: 800-242-7211
E-Mail: mforce@agacgfm.org
Web: www.agacgfm.org

PUBLICATION GUIDELINES:

Manuscript Length: 2,500 Words
Copies Required: Electronic·
Computer Submission: Yes
Format: MS Word
Fees to Review: 0.00 US$

Manuscript Style:

CIRCULATION DATA:

Reader: , Gov't Accountants, Auditors,
   Budget Analysts
Frequency of Issue: Quarterly
Sponsor/Publisher: Association of
   Government Accountants

REVIEW INFORMATION:

Type of Review: Blind Review
No. of External Reviewers: 2
No. of In House Reviewers: No Reply
Acceptance Rate: 40%
Time to Review: 1 - 2 Months
Reviewers Comments: Yes
Invited Articles: 0-5%
Fees to Publish: 0.00 US$

MANUSCRIPT TOPICS:
Accounting Information Systems; Accounting Theory & Practice; Auditing; Cost Accounting; Government & Non Profit Accounting; Tax Accounting

MANUSCRIPT GUIDELINES/COMMENTS:

About the Journal
Since 1950, the *Journal of Government Financial Management* has been providing valuable, in-depth information to decision-makers at all levels of government. A valuable research and information source, the *Journal* is published quarterly by the Association of Government Accountants (AGA). It is distributed to its membership of government financial managers as well as countless libraries across the nation and abroad.

Author Guidelines
The *Journal of Government Financial Management* is published quarterly by the Association of Government Accountants (AGA). Articles are submitted from all corners of the government financial management community. The purpose of the *Journal* is to contribute to the literature of the government financial management profession. The *Journal* staff appreciates the cooperation of the *Journal's* authors in following these guidelines.

Audience
The *Journal of Government Financial Management* is geared toward Association members who are involved at all levels of government financial management throughout the United States and its territories. The *Journal* can be found in more than 500 university libraries where it serves as a valuable research source for information about government financial management.

Content
The *Journal* will accept material that provides practical insights into any aspect of government financial management.

Article Submission Deadlines

Issue	Due Date
Summer (published June 1)	March 1
Fall (published September 1)	June 1
Winter (published December 1)	September 1
Spring (published March 1)	December 1

Process
Authors are encouraged to submit articles for review. The *Journal* Editorial Board is particularly interested in articles from practitioners. To be eligible for consideration, the author(s) must follow several guidelines. Submitted material must be:

- No more than 2,500 words;
- Original work that has not been previously published;
- Submitted via e-mail to the editor, Marie Force, MA, at **mforce@agacgfm.org**;
- Using end note rather than foot note format;
- Accompanied by a 50-word abstract and author biographies;
- Gender neutral;
- Accompanied (when applicable) by no more than four charts, graphs or boxes (provided in a separate file on the disk); and
- Accompanied (when applicable) by short, concise sidebars.

Articles that do not meet the above criteria will be returned.

Receipt of all manuscripts will be acknowledged. All submitted articles are initially reviewed by the *Journal* Editorial Board to determine whether the article is of interest to AGA members. Upon approval of the committee, articles are subjected to an anonymous review process involving members of the Association's esteemed peer review panel. The committee may also choose to reject the article and will provide an appropriate response to the author.

One possible outcome of the peer review process is a request for modifications. In this case, the author may or may not choose to make the suggested corrections or changes and return the manuscript for further consideration.

Another outcome of the peer review process is rejection of the article and again, the author will be provided with an appropriate response. Upon completion of the formal review process, all articles deemed acceptable are subjected to a final review from the chair of the *Journal* Editorial Board. The chair may choose to reject an article even after it has been revised. The decisions of the chair are final and are accompanied by an appropriate response to the author.

When an author is notified that his/her article will be published, the author will be asked to provide a professional photograph. Photographs must be in color. As a condition of publication, authors will be asked to sign a waiver affirming that the article has never before been published and confirming that the author understands that upon publication, the copyright will henceforth be held by the Association of Government Accountants and that all reprint requests must be made to the Association. Failure or refusal to sign this waiver will result in the cancellation of publication.

Articles scheduled for publication will be edited further by the *Journal's* editor and a copy editor for content, grammar and *Journal* style. These decisions are made by the editor and are usually final. However, authors of articles to be published will be offered the opportunity to comment on their edited articles as well as the final galley proof of the article. Authors are encouraged to carefully review their articles during this process. Upon publication, each author will receive five complimentary copies of the issue. Additional copies may be purchased for $24 each.

Journal of Information Systems

ADDRESS FOR SUBMISSION:

Brad Tuttle, Editor
Journal of Information Systems
University of South Carolina
Moore School of Business
Columbia, SC 29208
USA
Phone: 803-777-6639
E-Mail: jis@sc.edu
Web: http://accounting.utep.edu/jis/

PUBLICATION GUIDELINES:

Manuscript Length: 15-40
Copies Required: One
Computer Submission: Yes
Format: MS Word
Fees to Review: 25.00 US$

Manuscript Style:
    See Manuscript Guidelines

CIRCULATION DATA:

Reader: Academics
Frequency of Issue: 2 Times/Year
Sponsor/Publisher: American Accounting
    Association: Information Systems Section

REVIEW INFORMATION:

Type of Review: Blind Review
No. of External Reviewers: 3
No. of In House Reviewers: 0
Acceptance Rate: 11-20%
Time to Review: 2 - 3 Months
Reviewers Comments: Yes
Invited Articles: 0-5%
Fees to Publish: 0.00 US$

MANUSCRIPT TOPICS:
Accounting Information Systems; Business Information Systems; Electronic Commerce;
Technology/Innovation

MANUSCRIPT GUIDELINES/COMMENTS:

The content of the *Journal of Information Systems* (*JIS*) spans the organizational, behavioral,
economic, and technical aspects of information systems in organizations. *JIS* is a semi-annual
academic publication of the Information Systems Section of the American Accounting
Association, an organization whose members are interested in information systems education
and research.

JIS has three sections: an academic section for research findings with implications for
increasing knowledge about the development, use and effects of information systems; an
education section whose purpose is to enhance the teaching of information systems; and a
practice section for findings or analyses with implications for the effective practice of
information systems.

Topical areas are appropriate for *JIS* if they have the potential to influence subsequent thinking on information systems in research, education, or practice. Such areas include, for example:

1. Information systems modeling and related database management system issues, e.g., events-based, relational, or object-oriented approaches
2. Human-system interactions, including the effects of design choices
3. Internal control and auditing of information systems
4. Information use as a value-adding activity, and measuring the value added from information use
5. Implications of electronic commerce (EC) for business systems
6. Measurement, e.g., of quality, productivity, human performance, customer satisfaction, organizational learning, and innovation
7. Improving individual, group, and organizational responsiveness through information use
8. Socio-behavioral concomitants of information use, e.g., privacy, monitoring, and liability
9. Implications of enterprise resource planning (ERP) systems for business organizations
10. Effective use of data warehouses/datamarts in business systems
11. Knowledge management and expert systems

Journal of International Accounting Research

ADDRESS FOR SUBMISSION:

Lee H. Radebaugh, Editor
Journal of International Accounting
   Research
Brigham Young University
Research
516 TNRB
Provo, UT 84602-3068
USA
Phone: 801-422-4368
E-Mail: radebaugh@byu.edu
Web: http://aaahq.org/calls/JIAR_call.htm

PUBLICATION GUIDELINES:

Manuscript Length: 26-30
Copies Required: One
Computer Submission: Yes Email
Format: MS Word or PDF
Fees to Review: 50.00 US$ Non-Members
   25.00 US$ Members

Manuscript Style:
   Chicago Manual of Style

CIRCULATION DATA:

Reader: Academics
Frequency of Issue: 2 Times/Year
Sponsor/Publisher: International Section of
   the American Accounting Association

REVIEW INFORMATION:

Type of Review: Blind Review
No. of External Reviewers: 2
No. of In House Reviewers: 0
Acceptance Rate: 11-20%
Time to Review: 2 - 3 Months
Reviewers Comments: Yes
Invited Articles: 0-5%
Fees to Publish: 0.00 US$

MANUSCRIPT TOPICS:

Accounting Theory & Practice; Auditing; Behavioral Accounting; Cost Accounting; Econometrics; International Finance; Tax Accounting

MANUSCRIPT GUIDELINES/COMMENTS:

Topics Include. International Accounting, Cross-National Comparative Accounting, International Financial Statement Analysys, International Managerial Accounting, International Financial Reporting

The Journal of International Accounting Research publishes articles that increase our understanding of the development and use of international accounting and reporting practices or attempt to improve extant practices. International accounting is broadly interpreted to include the reporting of international economic transactions; the study of differences among practices across countries; the study of interesting institutional and cultural factors that shape practices in a single country but have international implications; and the effect of international accounting practices on users. The *Journal* has a diverse readership and is interested in articles in auditing, financial accounting, managerial accounting, systems, tax, and other specialties within the field of accounting. The *Journal* is open to research using a wide variety of research methods, including empirical-archival, experimental, field studies, and theoretical. The importance of the findings and the rigor of the analysis are the factors that determine acceptability. The *Journal* may include sections for Notes (shorter articles) and Commentaries.

Editorial Policy

All manuscripts are sent to two reviewers, although one or more additional reviewers may be consulted in some instances. Reviews will be double-blind (i.e., to both the author and reviewer). A strong effort will be made to complete the initial review within two to three months. The review process is intended to provide constructive comments that improve the quality of manuscripts by focusing on critical issues. The editorial team recognizes that the nuances of a paper are better left to the authors.

Submission of Manuscripts

1. Manuscripts currently under consideration by another journal or other publisher should not be submitted. At the time of submission, the author must state that the work is not submitted or published elsewhere.

2. To expedite the process, an electronic submission and review process can be employed. To preserve anonymity, place the cover page and the remainder of the document in separate Word or PDF files. In the case of manuscripts reporting on field surveys or experiments, the instrument (e.g., questionnaire, case, interview plan) should also be submitted in a separate file, with the identity of the author(s) deleted. E-mail the cover page, manuscript, and, if applicable, the instrument as attached files to Lee H. Radebaugh, Editor, at **Radebaugh@byu.edu**. The submission fee is $25.00 in U. S. funds for members of the AAA International Section, or $50.00 for others, made payable to the American Accounting Association. The submission fee is non-refundable. To charge the fee, the AAA website at:
   https://aaahq.org/AAAforms/journals/jiarsubmit.cfm

Alternatively, (although this is not encouraged) the submission fee also may be paid by check payable to the American Accounting Association, and mailed to Lee H. Radebaugh, Editor, 516 TNRB, Brigham Young University, Provo, UT 84602-3068

3. If electing to submit hard copy, one copy of manuscript should be mailed to Lee H. Radebaugh at the address above. In the case of manuscripts reporting on field surveys or experiments, one copy of the instrument (e.g., questionnaire, case, interview plan) should be submitted. Information that might identify the author(s) must be deleted from the instrument. The submission fee should be enclosed or charged at the AAA website (per above).

4. Revised manuscripts must be submitted within 12 months from request; otherwise they will be considered new submissions.

Manuscript Preparation Style

These practices are based on *The Accounting Review*. The primary difference is the acceptability of international standard size A4 paper and a 150 word abstract. For initial submission, any widely used style is acceptable.

The Journal of International Accounting Research manuscript preparation guidelines follow (with a slight modification) the B-format of *The Chicago Manual of Style* (14th ed; University of Chicago Press). Another helpful guide to usage and style is *The Elements of Style*, by William Strunk, Jr., and E.B. White (Macmillan). Spelling follows *Webster's International Dictionary*.

Format

1. All manuscripts should be typed in 12-point font on one side of 8 ½ x 11" or A4 good quality paper and be double-spaced, except for indented quotations.
2. Manuscripts should be as concise as the subject and research method permit, generally not to exceed 7,000 words.
3. Margins of at least one inch from top, bottom, and sides should facilitate editing and duplication.
4. To promote anonymous review, authors should not identify themselves directly or indirectly in their papers or in experimental test instruments included with the submission. Single authors should not use the editorial "we."
5. A cover page should show the title of the paper, the author's name, title and affiliation, email address, any acknowledgments, and a footnote indicating whether the author would be willing to share the data (see last paragraph in this statement).

Pagination. All pages, including tables, appendices and references, should be serially numbered. Major sections should be numbered in Roman numerals. Subsections should not be numbered.

Numbers. Spell out numbers from one to ten, except when used in tables and lists, and when used with mathematical, statistical, scientific, or technical units and quantities, such as distances, weights and measures. For example: *three days; 3 kilometers; 30 years.* All other numbers are expressed numerically.

Percentages and Decimal Fractions. In non-technical copy use the word percent in the text.

Hyphens. Use a hyphen to join unit modifiers or to clarify usage. For example: *a well-presented analysis, re-form.* See *Webster's* for correct usage.

Key Words. The abstract is to be followed by four key words that will assist in indexing the paper.

Abstract/Introduction

An Abstract of about 150 words should be presented on a separate page immediately preceding the text. The Abstract should concisely inform the reader of the manuscript's topic, its methods, and its findings. Key Words and the Data Availability statements should follow the Abstract. The text of the paper should start with a section labeled "I. Introduction," which provides more details about the paper's purpose, motivation, methodology, and findings. Both the Abstract and the Introduction should be relatively non-technical, yet clear enough for an informed reader to understand the manuscript's contribution. The manuscript's title, but neither the author's name nor other identification designations, should appear on the Abstract page.

Tables and Figures
The author should note the following general requirements:
1. Each table and figure (graphic) should appear on a separate page and should be placed at the end of the text. Each should bear an Arabic number and a complete title indicating the exact contents of the table or figure. Tables and figures should define each variable. The titles and definitions should be sufficiently detailed to enable the table or figure. Tables and figures should define each variable. The titles and definitions should be sufficiently detailed to enable the reader to interpret the tables and figures without reference to the text.
2. A reference to each graphic should be made in the text.
3. The author should indicate by marginal notation where each graphic should be inserted in the text.
4. Graphic should be reasonably interpreted without reference to the text.
5. Source lines and notes should be included as necessary.

Equations. Equations should be numbered in parentheses flush with the right-hand margin.

Documentation
Citations. Work cited should use the "author-date system" keyed to a list of works in the reference list (see below). Authors should make an effort to include the relevant page numbers in the cited works.
1. In the text, works are cited as follows: author's last name and date, without comma, in parentheses: for example, (Jones 1987); with two authors: (Jones and Freeman 1973); with more than two: (Jones et al. 1983); with more than one source cited together (Jones 1987; Freeman 1986); with more than one works by one author: (Jones 1985, 1987).
2. Unless confusion would result, do not use "p." or "pp." before page numbers: for example, (Jones 1987, 115).
3. When the reference list contains more than one work of an author published in the same year, the suffix a, b, etc. follows the date in the text citation: for example, (Jones 1987a) or (Jones 1987a; Freeman 1985b).
4. If an author's name is mentioned in the text, it need not be repeated in the citation; for example, "Jones (1987, 115) says..."
5. Citations to institutional works should use acronyms or short titles where practicable; for example, (AAA ASOBAT 1966); (AICPA Cohen Commission Report 1977). Where brief, the full title of an institutional work might be shown in a citation: for example, (ICAEW The Corporate Report 1975).
6. If the manuscript refers to statutes, legal treatises or court cases, citations acceptable in law reviews should be used.

Reference List. Every manuscript must include a list of references containing only those works cited. Each entry should contain all data necessary for unambiguous identification. With the author-date system, use the following format recommended by *The Chicago Manual*:
1. Arrange citations in alphabetical order according to surname of the first author or the name of the institution responsible for the citation.
2. Use author's initials instead of proper names.
3. Date of publication should be placed immediately after author's name.

386

4. Titles of journals should not be abbreviated.
5. Multiple works by the same author(s) in the same year are to be separated by letters after the date.
6. Inclusive page numbers are treated as recommended in Chicago Manual section 8.67.

Sample entries are as follows:

American Accounting Association, Committee on Concepts and Standards for External Financial Reports. 1977. Statement on Accounting Theory and Theory Acceptance. Sarasota, FL: AAA.

Demski, J. S., and D. E. M. Sappington. 1989. Hierarchical structure and responsibility accounting. Journal of Accounting Research 27 (Spring): 40-58.

Dye, R., B. Balachandran, and R. Magee. 1989. Contingent fees for audit firms. Working paper, Northwestern University, Evanston, IL.

Fabozzi, F., and I. Pollack, eds. 1987. *The Handbook of Fixed Income Securities*. 2nd edition. Homewood, IL: Down Jones-Irwin.

Kahneman, D., P. Slovic, and A. Tversky, eds. 1982. *Judgment Under Uncertainty: Heuristics and Biases*. Cambridge, U.K.: Cambridge University Press.

Porcano, T.M. 1984a. Distributive justice and tax policy. *The Accounting Review* 59 (October): 619-636.

----------. 1984b. The perceived effects of tax policy on corporate investment intentions. *The Journal of the American Taxation Association* 6 (Fall): 7-19.

Shaw, W. H. 1985. Empirical evidence on the market impact of the safe harbor leasing law. PhD. Dissertation, *The University of Texas at Austin*.

Sherman, T.M., ed. 1984. *Conceptual Framework for Financial Accounting*. Cambridge, MA: Harvard Business School.

Footnotes. Footnotes are not used for documentation. Textual footnotes should be used only for extensions and useful excursions of information that, if included in the body of the text, might disrupt its continuity. Footnotes should be consecutively numbered throughout the manuscript with superscript Arabic numerals. Footnote text should be double-spaced and placed at the end of the article.

Comments

Comments on articles previously published in *The Journal of International Accounting Research* will be sent to two reviewers at the same time. The first reviewer will be the author of the original article being subjected to critique. If substance permits, a suitably revised comment will be sent to a second reviewer to determine its publishability in *The Journal of International Accounting Research*. If a comment is accepted for publication, the original author will be invited to reply. All other editorial requirements, as enumerated above, also apply to proposed comments.

Policy on Reproduction

An objective of *The Journal of International Accounting Research* is to promote the wide dissemination of the results of systematic scholarly inquiries into the broad field of accounting.

Policy on Data Availability
An objective is to provide the widest possible dissemination of knowledge bases on systematic scholarly inquiries into accounting as a field of professional research, and educational activity. As part of this process, authors are encouraged to make their data available for use by others in extending or replicating results reported in their articles. Authors of articles, which report data dependent results, should footnote the status of data availability and, when pertinent, this should be accompanied by information on how the data may be obtained.

Journal of International Accounting, Auditing & Taxation

ADDRESS FOR SUBMISSION:

Kathleen E. Sinning, Editor
Journal of International Accounting,
  Auditing & Taxation
Western Michigan University
3182 Haworth College of Business
Kalamazoo, MI 49008-3899
USA
Phone: 269-387-5259
E-Mail: kathleen.sinning@wmich.edu
Web: www.elsevier.com

CIRCULATION DATA:

Reader: Business Persons, Academics
Frequency of Issue: 2 Times/Year
Sponsor/Publisher: Elsevier Inc.

PUBLICATION GUIDELINES:

Manuscript Length: 21-25
Copies Required: Three
Computer Submission: No
Format: N/A
Fees to Review: 25.00 US$

Manuscript Style:
  See Manuscript Guidelines

REVIEW INFORMATION:

Type of Review: Blind Review
No. of External Reviewers: 2
No. of In House Reviewers: 0
Acceptance Rate: 21-30%
Time to Review: 2 - 3 Months
Reviewers Comments: Yes
Invited Articles: 0-5%
Fees to Publish: 0.00 US$

MANUSCRIPT TOPICS:
Accounting Information Systems; Accounting Theory & Practice; Auditing; Behavioral Accounting; Cost Accounting; International Accounting; Tax Accounting

MANUSCRIPT GUIDELINES/COMMENTS:

Editorial Policy
The goal of the *Journal of International Accounting, Auditing, and Taxation* is to publish manuscripts that are relevant to the development of the field of international accounting. The journal publishes articles that deal with all areas of international accounting including auditing, taxation, information systems, management advisory services, and accounting education. Manuscripts appropriate for the journal include descriptions of research that applies rigorous methodologies and analytical techniques to accounting problems of interest to both academics and practitioners and critiques of current accounting practices and the measurement of their effects on business decisions.

All manuscripts received by *JIAAT* are sent to two reviewers for anonymous evaluation.

The journal is published semi-annually by Elsevier.

Manuscript Guidelines

1. Manuscripts currently under review by other publications or manuscripts that have been published should NOT be submitted. A statement indicating that the manuscript or an essentially similar manuscript is not submitted or published elsewhere MUST be included in the cover letter accompanying the submission.

2. Three copies of the manuscript must be submitted. In the case of manuscripts that report on field surveys or experiments, three copies of the research instrument (questionnaire, case, interview plan, etc.) should be included. Manuscripts should be copied single-sided on white paper.

3. Manuscripts should be double-spaced on 8 ½" by 11" paper. Indented quotations should be single-spaced. The margins should be one inch on the top, bottom, and sides. Do not indent paragraphs. Use double hard returns between paragraphs.

4. A separate title page must be included which indicates the author's name, address, affiliation, telephone number, fax number, and e-mail address. This information should not appear on any other page to assure anonymous review.

5. A separate abstract page should include the title of the manuscript, an abstract that does not exceed 200 words, and key words for referencing. The abstract should include a statement of the purpose of the manuscript, the methods used, the major results, and the conclusions. The abstract page should have the heading Abstract in boldface and flush with the left margin.

6. All pages, including tables, appendices, and references, should be numbered serially in the upper right hand corner.

7. In the body of the manuscript, major section headings should be in boldface, numbered with Arabic numerals, and flush with the left margin. The first letter of the first word in the heading should be capitalized.

Sub-section headings should be numbered with the section and subsection noted. The sub-section heading should be flush with the left margin, have only the first letter of the first word capitalized, and should not be in boldface.

Example:
5. Analysis and results

5.1. Results

8. Equations should be numbered in parentheses flush with the right-hand margin.

9. Explanatory notes should be used only for extensions of information that would disrupt the continuity of the paper if included in the body of the text. Notes should appear as footnotes at the bottom of the page on which they are noted.

10. Acknowledgements should not be included with a manuscript submitted for review. Acknowledgements in articles accepted for publication should be on a separate page that follows immediately after the conclusion of the article. The page should be headed with the word Acknowledgment in boldface and flush with the left margin.

11. Tables, figures, and exhibits must be prepared in a form suitable for printing. Each table, figure, and exhibit should be on a separate page and appear in the manuscript after the References page. Each table, figure, or exhibit should be numbered with Arabic numerals. The number should be flush with the left margin and should not be in boldface. The title of the table should appear on the line below the number. The title should be flush with the left margin and should not be in boldface. The first letter of the first word of the title should be capitalized. The table should be formatted from left to right.

    Example:
    Table 3
    Analysis of variance

The location of the tables in the text should be noted in the text by centering the following on a separate line:

[Table 1 About Here]

12. Three (3) copies of the manuscript and research instrument should be submitted to:
    Kathleen E. Sinning, Editor
    Journal of International Accounting, Auditing and Taxation
    3182 Schneider Hall
    Haworth College of Business
    Western Michigan University
    Kalamazoo, MI 49008-3899

Questions concerning manuscripts should be sent to **kathleen.sinning@wmich.edu**.

13. A revised manuscript must be submitted within 6 months of request or it will be considered a new submission.

14. To view an online sample copy of the journal and subscription information, see:
    www.elsevier.com/locate/intaat

Journal of International Business and Economics

ADDRESS FOR SUBMISSION:

Tahi J. Gnepa & Z. Radovilsky, Man. Eds.
Journal of International Business and
   Economics
Academy of International Business
   and Economics
PO Box 2536
Ceres, CA 95307
USA
Phone: 209-667-3074
E-Mail: akhade@aibe.org
   Review@aibe.org
Web: www.aibe.org

CIRCULATION DATA:

Reader: Academics, Business Persons
Frequency of Issue:
Sponsor/Publisher: Academy of
   International Business and Economics
   (AIBE)

PUBLICATION GUIDELINES:

Manuscript Length:
Copies Required: Two
Computer Submission: Yes Disk, Email
Format: MS Word
Fees to Review: 0.00 US$

Manuscript Style:
   Chicago Manual of Style

REVIEW INFORMATION:

Type of Review: Blind Review
No. of External Reviewers: 2
No. of In House Reviewers: 1
Acceptance Rate: 21-30%
Time to Review: 1 - 2 Months
Reviewers Comments: Yes
Invited Articles: 21-30%
Fees to Publish: 0.00 US$

MANUSCRIPT TOPICS:

Accounting Education; Accounting Information Systems; Accounting Theory & Practice; Auditing; Cost Accounting; Econometrics; Economic Development; Financial Services; Fiscal Policy; Government & Non Profit Accounting; Industrial Organization; Insurance; International Economics & Trade; International Finance; Macro Economics; Micro Economics; Monetary Policy; Portfolio & Security Analysis; Public Policy Economics; Real Estate; Tax Accounting

MANUSCRIPT GUIDELINES/COMMENTS:

Please use following manuscript Guidelines for submission of your papers for the review. Papers are reviewed on a continual basis throughout the year. Early Submissions are welcome! Please email your manuscript to Dr. Alan S. Khade at **Review@aibe.org**.

Copyright. Articles, papers, or cases submitted for publication should be original contributions and should not be under consideration for any other publication at the same time. Authors submitting articles/papers/cases for publication warrant that the work is not an infringement of any existing copyright, infringement of proprietary right, invasion of privacy,

392

or libel and will indemnify, defend, and hold AIBE or sponsor(s) harmless from any damages, expenses, and costs against any breach of such warranty. For ease of dissemination and to ensure proper policing of use papers/articles/cases and contributions become the legal copyright of the AIBE/IABE unless otherwise agreed in writing.

General Information. These are submission instructions for review purpose only. Once your submission is accepted you will receive submission guidelines with your paper acceptance letter. The author(s) will be emailed result of the review process in about 6-8 weeks from submission date. Papers are reviewed and accepted on a continual basis. Submit your papers early for full considerations!

Typing. Paper must be laser printed/printable on 8.5" x 11" white sheets in Arial 10-point font single-spaced lines justify style in MS Word. All four margins must be 1" each.

First Page. Paper title not exceeding two lines must be CAPITALIZED AND CENTERED IN BOLD LETTERS. Author name and university/organizational affiliation of each author must be printed on one line each. Do NOT include titles such as Dr., Professor, Ph.D., department address email address etc. Please print the word "ABSTRACT" in capitalized bold letters left justified and double-spaced from last author's name/affiliation. Abstract should be in italic. Please see the sample manuscript.

All other Headings. All other section headings starting with INTRODUCTION must be numbered in capitalized bold letters left justified and double-spaced from last line above them. See the subsection headings in the sample manuscript.

Tables Figures and Charts. All tables figures or charts must be inserted in the body of the manuscripts within the margins with headings/titles in centered CAPITALIZED BOLD letters.

References and Bibliography. All references listed in this section must be cited in the article and vice-versa. The reference citations in the text must be inserted in parentheses within sentences with author name followed by a comma and year of publication. Please follow the following formats:

Journal Articles
Khade Alan S. and Metlen Scott K. "An Application of Benchmarking in Dairy Industry" *International Journal of Benchmarking* Vol. III (4) 1996 17

Books
Harrison Norma and Samson D. Technology Management: Text and Cases McGraw-Hill Publishing New York 2002

Internet
Hesterbrink C. E-Business and ERP: Bringing two Paradigms together October 1999; PricewaterhouseCoopers *www.pwc.com*.

Author Profile(s). At the end of paper include author profile(s) not exceeding five lines each author including name highest degree/university/year current position/university and major achievements. For example:

Author Profile:
Dr. Tahi J. Gnepa earned his Ph.D. at the University of Wisconsin Madison in 1989. Currently he is a professor of international business at California State University Stanislaus and Managing Editor of Journal of International Business Strategy (JIBStrategy).

Manuscript. Absolutely no footnotes! Do not insert page numbers for the manuscript. Please do not forget to run spelling and grammar check for the completed paper. Save the manuscript on your diskette/CD or hard drive.

Electronic Submission. Send your submission as an MS Word file attachment to your Email to Dr. Alan S. Khade at **Review@aibe.org**.

Journal of International Business Research

ADDRESS FOR SUBMISSION:

Current Editor / Check Website
Journal of International Business Research
Digital Submission Through Website
Address other questions to:
 Jim or JoAnn Carland at # below
USA
Phone: 828-293-9151
E-Mail: info@alliedacademies.org
Web: www.alliedacademies.org

PUBLICATION GUIDELINES:

Manuscript Length: 16-20
Copies Required: Submit Through Web
Computer Submission: Yes
Format: MS Word, WordPerfect
Fees to Review: 0.00 US$

Manuscript Style:
 American Psychological Association

CIRCULATION DATA:

Reader: Academics
Frequency of Issue: Yearly
Sponsor/Publisher: Allied Academies, Inc.

REVIEW INFORMATION:

Type of Review: Blind Review
No. of External Reviewers: 3
No. of In House Reviewers: 2
Acceptance Rate: 21-30%
Time to Review: 3-4 Months
Reviewers Comments: Yes
Invited Articles: 0-5%
Fees to Publish: 75.00 US$ Membership

MANUSCRIPT TOPICS:
Global Business; International Business; International Economics & Trade; International Finance

MANUSCRIPT GUIDELINES/COMMENTS:

The journal publishes theoretical or empirical research concerning any of the Manuscript Topics.

Comments. All authors of published manuscripts must be members of the appropriate academy affiliate of Allied Academies. The current membership fee is $75.00 U.S.

Editorial Policy Guidelines
The primary criterion upon which manuscripts are judged is whether the research advances the disciplines. Key points include currency, interest and relevancy.

In order for a theoretical manuscript to advance the discipline, it must address the literature to support conclusions or models which extend knowledge and understanding. Consequently, referees pay particular attention to completeness of literature review and appropriateness of conclusions drawn from that review.

In order for an empirical manuscript to advance the discipline, it must employ appropriate and effective sampling and statistical analysis techniques, and must be grounded by a thorough literature review. Consequently, referees pay particular attention to the research methodology and to the conclusions drawn form statistical analyses and their consistency with the literature.

Journal of International Taxation

ADDRESS FOR SUBMISSION:

Robert Gallagher, Managing Editor
Journal of International Taxation
Warren, Gorham & Lamont/RIA Group
395 Hudson Street, 4th Floor
New York, NY 10014
USA
Phone: 212-807-2193
E-Mail: robert.gallagher@thomson.com
Web: http://ria.thomson.com/journals

PUBLICATION GUIDELINES:

Manuscript Length: 21-25
Copies Required: One
Computer Submission: Yes
Format: Word, WordPerfect
Fees to Review: 0.00 US$

Manuscript Style:
    See Manuscript Guidelines

CIRCULATION DATA:

Reader: , International
Frequency of Issue: Monthly
Sponsor/Publisher:

REVIEW INFORMATION:

Type of Review: Editorial Review
No. of External Reviewers: 0
No. of In House Reviewers: 1
Acceptance Rate: 50% +
Time to Review: 1 Month or Less
Reviewers Comments: No
Invited Articles: 50% +
Fees to Publish: 0.00 US$

MANUSCRIPT TOPICS:
Economic Development; Fiscal Policy; International Economics & Trade; International Finance; Tax Accounting; U.S./Foreign Tax Provisions

MANUSCRIPT GUIDELINES/COMMENTS:

1. We welcome the submission of articles offering practical information and ideas on tax planning for U.S. entities and individuals engaging in international transactions and foreign entities and individuals engaging in U.S. transactions. Articles should focus on matters of importance to practitioners and provide practical information on tax, legal, and business aspects affecting such taxpayers and transactions. Manuscripts for publication, and correspondence relating to them, should be sent to the Managing Editor.

2. All articles will be reviewed for acceptance by our Editor-in-Chief, or the *Journal's* Board of Advisors.

3. Articles should be submitted in one hardcopy version (typed, double-spaced, 8 ½" x 11") and one electronic version, either via e-mail or diskette, preferably WordPerfect. Length should be 15-35 double-spaced typed pages.

4. Within the article, please use some headings and subheadings to break up and emphasize your points. Type all headings flush with the left-hand margin, all capital letters for main headings but not secondary headings.

It is not necessary to use codes for different fonts, justification, line spacing, margin changes, tab settings, etc., as these will be deleted in the editorial process.

5. Footnotes and reference citations should generally follow the examples shown below.

1   Wyndelts and Fowler, "Avoiding Allocations to Goodwill Under the Asset-Acquisition Rules," 71 JTAX 392 (December 1989).

2   Bush Bros and Co., 87 TC 424 (1982), aff'd 670 F.2d 819 (CA-6, 1984), cert. den.

3   Morgenstern, 56 TC 44 (1971).

4   Rev. Rul. 75-223, 1975-1 CB 109; Rev. Rul. 89-121, 1999-47 IRB 25.

5   Hodel v. Va. Surface Mining and Reclamation Ass'n, 483 F. Supp. 425 (DC Ala., 1980).

6   H.R. 1313, 97th Cong., 1st Sess. § 11601 (1981).

7   H. Rep't No. 99-313, 99th Cong., 2d Sess. 719 (1987).

8   Temp. Reg. 1.132-5T(e).

9   GCM 38481, 3/5/81.

10 TD 8115, 12/16/86.

6. If you are reprinting in your article any previously copyrighted material other than short quotations, the publisher must have letters of permission to reprint from the copyright holder and from the author if he is not the copyright holder. These letters must be submitted at the same time as the manuscript.

7. Articles and columns published in *The Journal of International Taxation* will be copyrighted by the Publisher, which retains all reproduction, translation, and distribution rights in any media, including electronic reproduction, Except in rare instances, *The Journal of International Taxation* not yet appeared or been accepted for publication elsewhere. There is generally no objection to having articles that appear in *The Journal of International Taxation* reprinted in other publications at a later date if appropriate permission is requested from us at that time.

Journal of Libertarian Studies

ADDRESS FOR SUBMISSION:

Roderick T. Long, Editor
Journal of Libertarian Studies
Mises Institute
518 West Magnolia Avenue
Auburn, AL 36830
USA
Phone: 334-321-2102
E-Mail: jls@mises.org
Web: www.mises.org

CIRCULATION DATA:

Reader: Academics, Educated Laymen,
   Professionals
Frequency of Issue: Quarterly
Sponsor/Publisher: Ludwig von Mises
   Institute

PUBLICATION GUIDELINES:

Manuscript Length: 5-30
Copies Required: One
Computer Submission: Yes Preferred
Format: No Reply
Fees to Review: 0.00 US$

Manuscript Style:
   Chicago Manual of Style

REVIEW INFORMATION:

Type of Review: Blind Review
No. of External Reviewers: 1-2
No. of In House Reviewers: 1
Acceptance Rate: 40-50%
Time to Review: 1 - 2 Months
Reviewers Comments: Yes
Invited Articles: At times
Fees to Publish: 0.00 US$

MANUSCRIPT TOPICS:

Economic History; Fiscal Policy; Government & Non Profit Accounting; Industrial Organization; Insurance; International Economics & Trade; International Finance; Macro Economics; Micro Economics; Monetary Policy

MANUSCRIPT GUIDELINES/COMMENTS:

Topics Include. Philosophy, History of Thought, Political Science, Libertarianism, Austrian Economics, Education, Law, Anthropology, Public Policy, Classical Liberalism, Education, Sociology, History of Ideas

The mission of the *Journal of Libertarian Studies* is to advance the intellectual tradition of libertarianism, or the idea that individual liberty, with a strong presumption against state intervention in society, should be the first principle of political theory and practice. The journal explores libertarian themes not simply as a set of policy proposals, but as a wide-ranging interdisciplinary research program drawing upon each of the particular and seemingly isolated fields that study human action, including philosophy, political science, economics, history, law, sociology, geography, anthropology, education, and biology. To this end we solicit not only theoretical articles but, in addition, pieces that explore the history of ideas, or illustrate and apply the theory via analysis of history and current events. We also enthusiastically solicit contributions from across the ideological spectrum, both within and beyond the libertarian movement.

Submissions
The *Journal of Libertarian Studies* publishes both solicited and unsolicited manuscripts. Authors are encouraged to follow the *Chicago Manual of Style*. Manuscripts should: include an abstract of not more than 250 words; be double spaced; and be in MSWord, WordPerfect, or RTF format. Authors are expected to document sources and include a complete bibliography of only those sources used in the article. Author's name and email address must be included in a title page.

Manuscript submission implies that it is not under consideration with another journal and that it is an original work not previously published. It also implies that it will not be submitted for publication elsewhere unless rejected by the *JLS* editor or withdrawn by the author.

Submissions, correspondence, change-of-address, and permission requests should be sent to **jls@mises.org** or Judith F. Thommesen, Managing Editor, Journal of Libertarian Studies, 518 West Magnolia Avenue, Auburn, Alabama 36832-4528.

Journal of Management Accounting Research

ADDRESS FOR SUBMISSION:

Joan Luft, Editor
Journal of Management Accounting
  Research
Michigan State University
Eli Broad Graduate
  School of Management
East Lansing, MI 48824
USA
Phone: 517-432-2917
E-Mail: luftj@msu.edu
Web: http://aaahq.org/index.cfm

PUBLICATION GUIDELINES:

Manuscript Length: 16-20
Copies Required: Four
Computer Submission: Yes
Format:
Fees to Review: 50.00 US$

Manuscript Style:
  Chicago Manual of Style

CIRCULATION DATA:

Reader: Academics
Frequency of Issue: Yearly
Sponsor/Publisher: American Accounting
  Association / Management Accounting
  Section

REVIEW INFORMATION:

Type of Review: Blind Review
No. of External Reviewers: 2
No. of In House Reviewers: 0
Acceptance Rate: 15-20%
Time to Review: 2 - 3 Months
Reviewers Comments: Yes
Invited Articles: 0-5%
Fees to Publish: 0.00 US$

MANUSCRIPT TOPICS:
Cost Accounting; Management Accounting

MANUSCRIPT GUIDELINES/COMMENTS:

Objective. Improve theory and practice of management accounting "Management Accounting" is broadly defined:
- Variety of theoretical perspectives and research methods Innovations in management accounting practices
- Variety of topics, e.g.
  - internal reporting and decision making
  - incentives and performance evaluation
  - interface between internal and external reporting
- Variety of settings, e.g.
  - profit and not-for-profit
  - manufacturing and service organizations
  - domestic, foreign and multinational

Review process
- Editorial board includes diverse set of leading scholars
- Careful and constructive comments on papers
- Target turnaround time: two months
- Standard double-blind review by two reviewers

Editorial Policy
The Management Accounting Section of the American Accounting Association publishes the *Journal of Management Accounting Research* (*JMAR*). Its objective is to contribute to improving the theory and practice of management accounting by promoting high-quality applied and theoretical research. The primary audience for this publication is the membership of the Management Accounting Section of the American Accounting Association and other individuals interested in management accounting.

"Management Accounting" for purposes of this publication is to be broadly conceived. We will publish papers involving a variety of topics, settings, and research methods. The research methods used in papers submitted for publication may be analytical or empirical. We invite manuscripts related to internal reporting and decision making, the interface between internal and external reporting, profit and not-for-profit organizations, service and manufacturing organizations and domestic, foreign and multi-national organizations. New theories, topical areas, and research methods are encouraged.

As a publication of the American Accounting Association, the high standards applicable to the journals of the Association will be maintained. For a manuscript to be acceptable for publication, the research question should be of interest to the intended readership, the research should be well designed and well executed, and the material should be presented effectively and efficiently.

Review Process
Each paper submitted to *JMAR* is subject to the following review procedures:
1. The Editor will review the paper for general suitability for this publication.

2. For those papers that are judged suitable, a detailed blind review by two reviewers takes place.

3. Using the recommendations of the reviewers, the Editor will decide whether the particular paper should be accepted as is, revised, or rejected for publication.

The process described above is a general process. In any particular case, deviations may occur from the steps described.

Submission of Manuscripts
Authors should note the following guidelines for submitting manuscripts:
1. Manuscripts currently under consideration by another journal or other publisher should not be submitted. The author must state that the work is not submitted or published elsewhere.

2. Where firm- or organization-specific data released by a firm or organization are used in a manuscript, a signed release allowing identification of any person(s) or organization(s) in the manuscript must accompany the manuscript.

3. Manuscripts may be submitted electronically as e-mail attachments, or in hard copy. Four copies should be submitted if hard copy is sent. Submissions should be sent to Professor Joan Luft, Editor, Journal of Management Accounting Research, Broad School of Business, Michigan State University, East Lansing, MI 48824. (E-mail: **luftj@msu.edu**)

4. There is a non-refundable submission fee of $50, which may be paid by credit card through the AAA website (https://aaahq.org/AAAForms/journals/jmarsubmit.cfm) or by check. If payment is made by check, the check should be payable to the American Accounting Association and sent to the Editor along with the manuscript.

4. The author should retain a copy of the paper.

5. In the case of manuscripts reporting on field surveys or experiments, 4 copies of the instrument (questionnaire, case, interview plan, or the like), must be submitted.

6. Revisions must be submitted within 12 months from request, otherwise they will be considered new submissions.

Manuscripts not conforming to these guidelines will be returned to the author.

Comments
The journal does not have a regular section for Comments. Authors who wish to comment on articles previously published in *JMAR* should first communicate directly with the author(s) of the original article to eliminate any misunderstandings or misconceptions. If substantive issues still remain after the written exchange of views with the author(s), the Commentator may submit to *JMAR* the residue of the proposed Comment. Four copies of the correspondence between the Commentator and the author(s) of the original article should be submitted to the Editor together with four copies of the comment manuscript. All other editorial norms also apply to proposed Comments.

Manuscript Preparation and Style
The *Journal of Management Accounting Research's* manuscript preparation guidelines follow (with a slight modification) documentation 2 of the *Chicago Manual of Style* (14th ed.; University of Chicago Press). Another helpful guide to usage and style is *The Elements of Style*, by William Strunk, Jr., and E. B. White (Macmillan). Spelling follows *Webster's International Dictionary*.

Format
1. Manuscripts should be typed on one side of 8 ½ x 11" good quality paper and be double-spaced, except for indented quotations.

2. Manuscripts should be as concise as the subject and research method permit, generally not to exceed 7,000 words.

3. Margins should be at least one inch from top, bottom, and sides to facilitate editing and duplication.

4. To assure anonymous review, authors should not identify themselves directly or indirectly in their papers. Single authors should not use the editorial "we."

5. A cover page should include the title of the paper, the author's name, title and affiliation, any acknowledgments, and a footnote indicating whether the author would be willing to share the data (see last paragraph in this statement).

6. All pages, including tables, appendices and references, should be serially numbered.

7. Spell out numbers from one to ten, except when used in tables and lists, and when used with mathematical, statistical, scientific or technical units and quantities, such as distances, weights and measures. For example: *three days; 3 kilometers; 30 years.* All other numbers are expressed numerically.

8. In nontechnical text use the word *percent*; in technical text the symbol % is used. (See the *Chicago Manual* for discussion of the correct usage.)

9. Usage of hyphens and dashes
- Use a hyphen (-) to join unit modifiers or to clarify usage. For example: a well-presented analysis; re-form. See *Webster's* for correct usage.
- En dash (-) is used between words indicating a duration, such as hourly time or months or years. No space on either side.
- Em dash (—) is used to indicate an abrupt change in thought, or where a period is too strong and a comma is too weak. No space on either side.

10. The following will be Roman in all cases: i.e., e.g., ibid., et al., op. cit.

11. Initials: A. B. Smith (space between); States, etc.: U.S., U.K. (no space between).

12. When using "Big 6" or "Big 8," use Arabic figures (don't spell out).

3 Ellipsis should be used not periods, example ... not.

14. Use "SAS No. #" not "SAS #"

15. Use only one space after periods, colons, exclamation points, question marks, quotation marks - any punctuation that separates two sentences.

16. Usage of quotations and apostrophes
- Use real quotation marks—never inch marks: use " and ~' not " and."
- Use real apostrophes, not the foot marks: use not

17. Punctuation used with quote marks:
- Commas and periods are always placed inside the quotation marks.
- Colons and semicolons go outside the quotation marks.
- Question marks and exclamation points go in or out, depending on whether they belong to the material inside the quote. If they belong to the quoted material, they go inside the quote marks, and vice versa.

18. **Punctuation and parentheses**. Sentence punctuation goes after the closing parentheses if what is inside the parentheses is part of the sentence (as is this phrase). This also applies to commas, semicolons and colons. If what is inside the parentheses is an entire statement of its own, the ending punctuation should also be inside the parentheses.

19. Headings should be arranged so those major headings are centered, bold and capitalized. Second level headings should be flush left, bold and both upper and lowercase. Third level headings should be flush left, bold, italic and both upper and lower case. Fourth level headings should be paragraph indent, bold and lower case. Headings and subheadings should not be numbered. For example:

A CENTERED, BOLD, ALL CAPITALIZED, FIRST LEVEL HEADING

A Flush Left, Hold, Upper and Lower Case, Second Level Heading
A Flush Left, Bold, Italic, Upper and Lower Case, Third Level Heading
    A paragraph indent, bold, lower case, fourth level heading. Text starts....

Abstract
An abstract of no more than 150 words should be presented on a separate page immediately preceding the text. The abstract should be nonmathematical and include a readable summary of the research question, method and the significance of the findings and contribution. The title, but not the author's name or other identification designations, should appear on the abstract page.

Tables and Figures
The author should note the following general requirements:

1. Each table and figure (graphic) should appear on a separate page and should be placed at the end of the text. Each should bear an Arabic number and a complete title indicating the exact contents of the table or figure.

2. A reference to each table or figure should be made in the text.

3. The author should indicate by marginal notation where each table or figure should be inserted in the text, e.g., (Insert Table X here).

4. Tables or figures should be reasonably interpreted without reference to the text.

5. Source lines and notes should be included as necessary.

6. When information is not available, use "NA" capitalized with no slash between.

7. Figures must be prepared in a form suitable for printing.

Mathematical Notation
Mathematical notation should be employed only where its rigor and precision are necessary, and in such circumstances authors should explain in the narrative format the principal operations performed. Notation should be avoided in footnotes. Unusual symbols, particularly if hand-written, should be identified in the margin when they first appear. Displayed material should clearly indicate the alignment, superscripts and subscripts. Equations should be numbered in parentheses flush with the right-hand margin.

Documentation
Citations. Work cited should use the "author-date system" keyed to a list of works in the reference list (see below). Authors should make an effort to include the relevant page numbers in the cited works.

1. In the text, works are cited as follows: author's last name and date, without comma, In parentheses: for example, (Jones 1987); with two authors: (Jones and Freeman 1973); with more than two: (Jones et al. 1985); with more than one source cited together (Jones 1987; Freeman 1986); with two or more works by one author: (Jones 1985, 1987)

2. Unless confusion would result, do not use "p." or "pp." before page numbers: for example, (Jones 1987, 115).

3. When the reference list contains more than one work of an author published in the same year, the suffix a, b, etc. follows the date in the text citation: for example, (Jones 1987a) or (Jones 1987a; Freeman 1985b).

4. If an author's name Is mentioned in the text, It need not be repeated in the citation; for example, "Jones (1987, 115) says....

5. Citations to institutional works should use acronyms or short titles where practicable: for example, (AAA ASOBAT 1966); (*AICPA Cohen Commission Report* 1977). Where brief, the full title of an institutional work might be shown in a citation: for example, (*ICAEW The Corporate Report* 1975).

6. If the manuscript refers to statutes, legal treatises, or court cases, citations acceptable in law reviews should be used.

406

Reference List. Every manuscript must include a list of references containing only those works cited. Each entry should contain all data necessary for unambiguous identification. With the author-date system, use the following format recommended by the *Chicago Manual*:

1. Arrange citations in alphabetical order according to surname of the first author or the name of the institution responsible for the citation.

2. Use author's initials instead of proper names.

3. In listing more than one name in references (Rayburn, L., and B. Harrelson) there should always be a comma before "and."

4. Dates of publication should be placed immediately after authors' names. Titles of journals should not be abbreviated.

5. Multiple works by the same author(s) should be listed in chronological order of publication.

6. Two or more works by the same author(s) in the same year are distinguished by letters after the date.

Sample entries are as follows
American Accounting Association, Committee on Concepts and Standards for External Financial Reports. 1977. *Statement on Accounting Theory and Theory Acceptance*. Sarasota, FL: AAA.

Banker, R., G. Potter, and R. Schroeder. 1992. An empirical study of manufacturing overhead cost drivers. Working paper, University of Minnesota.

Berliner, C., and J. A. Brimson, eds. 1988. *Cost Management for Today's Advanced Manufacturing: The CAM-I Conceptual Design*. Boston, MA: Harvard Business School Press.

Cooper, R. 1 987a. The two-stage procedure in cost accounting: Part one. *Journal of Cost Management* (Summer): 43-51.

_____, 1987b. The two-stage procedure in cost accounting: Part two. *Journal of Cost Management* (Fall): 39-45

Einhorn, H. J., and R. Hogarth. 1981. Behavioral decision theory: Processes of judgment and choice. *Journal of Accounting Research* 19 (1): 1-31.

Horngren, C. T. 1962. Choosing accounting practices for reporting to management. *N.A.A. Bulletin* 19 (September): 3-15.

Kaplan, R. S. 1985. Accounting lag: The obsolescence of cost accounting systems. *In The Uneasy Alliance: Managing the Productivity-Technology Dilemma*, edited by K. Clark, R. Hayes, and C. Lorenz, 195—226. Boston, MA: Harvard Business School Press.

Takeuchi, H., and J. A. Queich. 1983. Quality is more than making a good product. *Harvard Business Review* 61: 139-145.

Footnotes. Footnotes are not used for documentation. Textual footnotes should be used only for extensions and useful excursions of information that if included in the body of the text might disrupt its continuity. Footnotes should be consecutively numbered throughout the manuscript with superscript Arabic numerals. Footnote text should be double-spaced and placed at the end of the article.

Policy on Reproductions
The objective of *JMAR* is to promote wide dissemination of the results of theoretical and applied research and other scholarly inquiries into the broad field of management accounting.

Permission is hereby granted to reproduce any of the contents of *JMAR* for use in courses of instruction, so long as the source and American Accounting Association copyright are indicated in any such reproductions.

Written application must be made to the Editor for permission to reproduce any of the contents of *JMAR* for use in other than courses of Instruction - e.g., inclusion in books of readings or in other publications Intended for general distribution. In consideration for the grant of permission by *JMAR* in such instances, the applicant must notify the author(s) in writing of the Intended use to be made of each reproduction. Normally, *JMAR* will not assess a charge for the waiver of copyright.

Except where otherwise noted in articles, the copyright interest has been transferred to the American Accounting Association. Where the author(s) has (have) not transferred the copyright to the Association, applicants must seek permission to reproduce (for all purposes) directly from the author(s).

Policy on Data Availability
The following policy, adopted by the Executive Committee of the AAA in April 1989, is applicable to all manuscripts submitted to *JMAR*:

> ...authors are encouraged to make their data available for use by others.... Authors of articles that report data dependent results should footnote the status of data availability and, when pertinent, this should be accompanied by information on how the data may be obtained.

Journal of Performance Management

ADDRESS FOR SUBMISSION:

Kevin Link, Editor
Journal of Performance Management
3895 Fairfax Court
Atlanta, GA 30339
USA
Phone: 770-444-3557
E-Mail: ami@amifs.org
Web: www.amifs.org

CIRCULATION DATA:

Reader: Business Persons
Frequency of Issue: 3 Times/Year
Sponsor/Publisher: National Association of
   Bank Cost and Management Accounting

PUBLICATION GUIDELINES:

Manuscript Length: 3,000-5,000 Words
Copies Required: Two
Computer Submission: Yes
Format: Any
Fees to Review: 0.00 US$

Manuscript Style:
   See Manuscript Guidelines

REVIEW INFORMATION:

Type of Review: Editorial Review
No. of External Reviewers: 4
No. of In House Reviewers: 1
Acceptance Rate: 90%
Time to Review: 3 - 4 Months
Reviewers Comments: No
Invited Articles: 50%
Fees to Publish: 0.00 US$

MANUSCRIPT TOPICS:
Accounting Information Systems; Accounting Theory & Practice; Auditing; Cost Accounting

MANUSCRIPT GUIDELINES/COMMENTS:

Call for Papers
The *Journal of Performance Management*, published by the Association for Management Information in Financial Services, seeks articles on issues relevant to management accounting in financial institutions. Articles should be on a subject of interest to practitioners in the field of bank cost and management accounting and should reflect the views of the author. Authors should not hesitate to submit articles that present a minority or unusual view as long as that view is effectively presented. A sample copy of the *Journal* will be provided to prospective authors upon request.

The *Journal* is published three times a year and distributed to 700 subscribers worldwide. The *Journal* generally publishes articles that have not appeared or been accepted for publication elsewhere. Exceptions to this policy may be approved if the author obtains a release from the copyright holder.

Authors of accepted papers will be furnished with twenty (20) copies of the issue in which their paper appears. Where multiple authors are involved, each author will be given four (4) copies. Complete address and telephone information for each author should be included with each article submitted.

Guidelines for Preparation of Manuscripts

Format. The entire manuscript, including text, footnotes, charts, and quotations, must be typed, double-spaced on plain 8 ½" x 11" paper, leaving one-inch margins on all sides. The title of the article and author's name and title should appear on page one of the manuscript. Headings should be used to give structure to the article and to order the text in a logical format. The premise of the article and the conclusion(s) should be clearly stated.

Length. Manuscripts may be of any length in the above format, generally over ten pages. The final determinant of an acceptable length is the subject matter of the article. The Editor reserves the right to edit manuscripts for length.

Style. Punctuation should be kept simple, adding to the readability of the article. Tables and exhibits should be numbered and printed on separate sheets of paper whenever possible; they should be clearly referenced in the body of the manuscript. Footnotes should include the author's name, title of reference, publisher, and date. Unless a direct quote is used, no page or volume numbers are required in the footnotes. References or bibliographies should be typed on a separate page, entitled "References", at the end of the manuscript.

Review and Editing

Submission. Authors are strongly encouraged to submit their manuscripts on computer disk in any major software program format; one clear paper copy of the manuscript must be included with each disk. (Call AMIFS with any questions about disk format.) Alternatively, two copies (one original, one photocopy) of each manuscript may be submitted to the Editor at the address shown above. If an article includes copyrighted material, (other than short quotations), submissions must be accompanied by a letter of permission to reprint from the copyright holder.

Review/Editing. Articles are screened by the Editor and may be sent out to reviewers for comment in certain cases. Manuscripts are evaluated based on coverage of the subject and whether it will be of interest to readers. Each manuscript is edited for grammar, punctuation, and structure, and may be returned to the author with suggestions for rewriting.

If a manuscript is accepted for publication, a release form will be sent to the author. The signed release form must be returned within 15 days. Published articles become the property of the AMIFS and may not be reprinted without the written permission of the publisher.

Journal of Public Budgeting, Accounting & Financial Management

ADDRESS FOR SUBMISSION:

Khi V. Thai, Editor
Journal of Public Budgeting, Accounting &
    Financial Management
Florida Atlantic University
111 E. Las Olas Blvd.
Fort Lauderdale, FL 33301
USA
Phone: 954-762-5635
E-Mail: thai@fau.edu
Web: www.pracademics.com

PUBLICATION GUIDELINES:

Manuscript Length: 20+
Copies Required: Three
Computer Submission: No
Format: N/A
Fees to Review: 0.00 US$

Manuscript Style:
    American Psychological Association,
    Modified

CIRCULATION DATA:

Reader: Academics, Practitioners
Frequency of Issue: Quarterly
Sponsor/Publisher: PrAcademics Press, Inc.

REVIEW INFORMATION:

Type of Review: Blind Review
No. of External Reviewers: 3
No. of In House Reviewers: 0
Acceptance Rate: 20-30%
Time to Review: 1-2 Months
Reviewers Comments: Yes
Invited Articles: 5-10%
Fees to Publish: 0.00 US$

MANUSCRIPT TOPICS:
Budget Deficits; Fiscal Policy; Government & Non Profit Accounting; Monetary Policy; Public Budgeting

MANUSCRIPT GUIDELINES/COMMENTS:

Editorial Policy
Published four times a year, *Journal of Public Budgeting, Accounting & Financial Management* is a refereed journal, which aims at advancement and dissemination of research in the field of public budgeting and financial management. The journal concentrates on the development of theories and concepts so that the field's boundaries can be established. The cognate areas constituting the focus of this publication are disciplines that concern how a budget is prepared, decided and implemented.

Practitioners and scholars are encouraged to submit manuscripts to the journal. Papers - whether empirical, field study, or conceptual - should help to serve the need for more active communication and greater exchange of thought, research and practical experiences among scholars and practitioners throughout the world. Appropriate topics for papers include various aspects of public budgeting and financial management such as (a) governmental accounting and financial reporting; (b) politics of budgeting, budgetary process and techniques; public financial management including cash management, risk management, debt management; (d) tax and expenditure policies, and (e) other issues related to governmental accounting, budgeting, financial management and fiscal policies.

Priority will be given to papers having carefully developed methods, insightful conceptual development, and practical and analytical solutions to government financial management problems. Interdisciplinary approaches are welcome.

Directions for Submission

1. Manuscripts can be submitted electronically to **thai@fau.edu** or in printed form (three copies) to the Editor.

2. A cover letter must accompany each submission indicating the name, e-mail address of the corresponding author.

3. Only original papers will be accepted, and copyright of published papers will be vested in the publisher. The general format of the manuscript should be as follows: title of article, names of author, abstract, and text discussion.

4. The abstract should not have more than 120 words. Whenever possible, the text discussion should be divided into such major sections as introduction, methods, results, discussion, acknowledgments, and references. Manuscripts should be submitted typed, double-spaced, on one side only. The entire typing area on the title page should be four and one-half inches wide by five and one-half inches long. The major headings should be separated from the text by two lines of space above and one line of space below. Each heading should be in capital letters, centered, and in bold. Secondary headings, if any, should be flushed with the left margin, in bold characters, and have the first letter of all main words capitalized. Leave two lines of space above and one line of space below secondary headings. All manuscripts should be left- and right-hand margin justified.

Acknowledgements of collaboration, sources of research funds, and address changes for an author should be listed on a separate section at the end of the paper after the section on References.

Explanatory footnotes should be kept to a minimum and be numbered consecutively throughout the text and aggregated in sequence under the heading notes, at the end of the text but before references.

References should be in the APA manuscript style of citation, and aggregated in the alphabetical order at the end of the manuscript under the heading, **References**.

5. For detailed guidelines, please visit **www.pracademics.com**.

Journal of State Taxation

ADDRESS FOR SUBMISSION:

James T. Collins, Editor-in-Chief
Journal of State Taxation
ELECTRONIC SUBMISSION ONLY
Phone: 843-525-6232
E-Mail: ebbtide2000@islc.net
Web:

PUBLICATION GUIDELINES:

Manuscript Length: 15-40
Copies Required: One
Computer Submission: Yes
Format: MS Word 6.0, WdPerfect, DOS
Fees to Review: 0.00 US$

Manuscript Style:
Chicago Manual of Style

CIRCULATION DATA:

Reader: Academics, Business Persons,
CPA, Attorney, Gov't
Frequency of Issue: Quarterly
Sponsor/Publisher: Commerce Clearing
House (CCH)

REVIEW INFORMATION:

Type of Review: Editorial Review
No. of External Reviewers: 1
No. of In House Reviewers: 1
Acceptance Rate: 50%
Time to Review: 1 - 2 Months
Reviewers Comments: No
Invited Articles: 6-10%
Fees to Publish: 0.00 US$

MANUSCRIPT TOPICS:
State & Local Taxation; Tax Accounting

MANUSCRIPT GUIDELINES/COMMENTS:

The *Journal of State Taxation* is devoted to articles that contribute to professional practice and provide timely analysis, creative strategies, and workable solutions to state tax problems. Articles should address tax strategies and tax legislation in a timely, up-to-date manner.

The *Journal* emphasizes quality and clarity of exposition. Reviewers will consider the following criteria in assessing potential contributions: the value of the information to the Journal's audience, the substantive contribution to the broadly defined field of state taxation, and the overall quality of the manuscript. The decision to publish a given manuscript is made by the Editor-in-Chief.

Submission of a manuscript implies a commitment to publish in the *Journal*. Previously published papers and papers under review by another journal are not acceptable. Articles for prior publication adapted from book-length works in progress will be considered, with attention given to the necessary copyright arrangements.

Manuscript Specifications. Manuscripts should not exceed the equivalent of 40 typewritten pages; the publisher also encourages the submission of shorter articles. All material should be double spaced, on one side only of 8 ½" x 11" with 1 ½" margins left, right, top, and bottom. References should be double spaced and placed at the end of the text, on a separate page headed "References." Notes may be left embedded in the text, but they should be printed as double-spaced endnotes rather than footnotes. Improperly prepared manuscript will be returned to the author for preparation.

Within the article, use headings and subheadings to break up text and emphasize points; type them flush left. Number all pages of text. Contributors should attach a cover sheet giving title, author affiliation, current mailing address, fax number, and phone number. To ensure anonymity in the review of manuscripts, the first page of the text should show only the title of the manuscript at the top of the page. Each table or figure should be positioned on a separate page at the end of the article; point of insertion should be indicated at the proper place in text (e.g., "Table 2 about here").

Tables should be in whatever program the article was written in, preferably Microsoft Word. Graphs or charts must be submitted as separate files in either Microsoft Word or Microsoft Excel and in black and white only. Embedded graphs or charts that have been prepared in another software program cause significant problems, as the editor and compositor cannot access them in order to key in editorial changes. Authors who cannot use Word or Excel should do one of the following: (a) supply a laser copy of black-and-white artwork (note, however, that color copies cannot be scanned, and that changes cannot be made on laser copies); (b) submit a copy of the graph as well as the data points that were used to create it (the compositor cannot recreate the graphs without these data); (c) submit as PowerPoint documents (these must be saved as .GIF files).

Routing and Handling Submissions. A disk should be submitted to the Editor-in-Chief and to the Legal Editor (at the email addresses indicated below). An abstract of 125 to 150 words and a biographical statement of no more than 50 words written in the third person, each one on a separate page, should accompany the manuscript.

Acceptance. Each disk must be labeled with software program and version, file name, author name, article title, and journal title.

The copyright will be retained by the publisher. Articles are subject to editorial revision. There is no payment for articles; authors receive two copies of the issue in which their article is published.

Manuscripts not accepted for publication will not be returned. Authors are advised to keep the original copies of their manuscripts for their files.

For business and production matters, contact the Managing Editor: Kurt Diefenbach, Managing Editor, Journals Department, Cch Tax and Accounting, 2700 Lake Cook Road, Riverwoods, IL 60015, 847-267-2415, **diefenbk@cch.com**

Article submissions and questions should be addressed to: James T. Collins, Editor-in-Chief, at **ebbtide2000@islc.net** and Sharon Brooks, Legal Editor, at **brookss@cch.com**

Journal of Taxation

ADDRESS FOR SUBMISSION:

Joseph I. Graf, Editor
Journal of Taxation
RIA Group
395 Hudson Street, 4th Floor
New York, NY 10014
USA
Phone: 212-807-2195
E-Mail: joseph.graf@thomson.com
Web: www.ria.thomson.com/riajournals

CIRCULATION DATA:

Reader: , Tax Accountants, Tax Attorneys
Frequency of Issue: Monthly
Sponsor/Publisher: RIA Group

PUBLICATION GUIDELINES:

Manuscript Length: 16-25
Copies Required: One
Computer Submission: Yes Required
Format: MS Word
Fees to Review: 0.00 US$

Manuscript Style:
See Manuscript Guidelines

REVIEW INFORMATION:

Type of Review: Editorial Review
No. of External Reviewers: 1 or 2
No. of In House Reviewers: 1
Acceptance Rate: 45%
Time to Review: 1 Month or Less
Reviewers Comments: No
Invited Articles: 60%+
Fees to Publish: 0.00 US$

MANUSCRIPT TOPICS:
Federal Income Taxation; Generation-Skipping Transfer Tax; Gift, Income, or Estate Taxation; Selected State & Local Tax Issues; Tax Accounting

MANUSCRIPT GUIDELINES/COMMENTS:

Articles intended for the *Journal of Taxation* should concentrate on practical information and tax-planning ideas. The target audience is the sophisticated tax professional. Articles should not be concerned with theoretical matters, or with policy discussions of how the law should be changed. (Constructive criticism of administrative or judicial interpretations of the law, however, is both acceptable and appropriate.) In general, the topic should be discussed with the editor beforehand to determine our interest.

To be considered for publication, an article must be sent to us on an exclusive basis. All manuscripts accepted for review are circulated to our editorial board for approval and comment. Once approved for publication in the print and electronic versions of the *Journal of Taxation*, every article is subject to editorial revision. Galley proofs will be sent to authors, and any corrections must be returned to us by the date indicated.

Manuscripts must be submitted in electronic form, preferably as an e-mail attachment. The file should be in MS Word.

Any questions should be addressed to the editor.

Journal of the American Taxation Association

ADDRESS FOR SUBMISSION:

Bryan Cloyd, Editor
Journal of the American Taxation
  Association
Virginia Tech
Pamplin College of Business
Dept of Accounting & Information Systems
3007 Pamplin Hall (0101)
Blacksburg, VA 24061
USA
Phone: 540-231-3181
E-Mail: bcloyd@vt.edu
Web: https://aaahq.org

PUBLICATION GUIDELINES:

Manuscript Length: Under 35
Copies Required: One
Computer Submission: Yes Required
Format: MS Word (.doc files)
Fees to Review: 75.00 US$

Manuscript Style:
  See Manuscript Guidelines

CIRCULATION DATA:

Reader: Academics
Frequency of Issue: 2 Times/Year
Sponsor/Publisher: American Taxation
  Association

REVIEW INFORMATION:

Type of Review: Blind Review
No. of External Reviewers: 2
No. of In House Reviewers: 0
Acceptance Rate: 11-20%
Time to Review: 2 - 3 Months
Reviewers Comments: Yes
Invited Articles: 0-5%
Fees to Publish: 0.00 US$

MANUSCRIPT TOPICS:
Fiscal Policy; Tax Accounting; Taxation

MANUSCRIPT GUIDELINES/COMMENTS:

Editorial Policies

JATA is a research publication of the American Taxation Association, an organization that promotes the study of, and the acquisition of knowledge about, taxation. The *Journal* is dedicated to disseminating a wide variety of tax knowledge and to fulfill this responsibility, the *Journal* considers research that employs quantitative, analytical, experimental, and descriptive methods to address tax topics of interest to its readership.

JATA solicits unpublished manuscripts not currently under consideration by another journal or publisher. Papers presented in connection with a formal program (regional or national) of the American Taxation Association, American Accounting Association, or similar organizations or societies may be submitted provided the manuscript does not appear in whole or in part (other than a brief abstract) in the proceedings of the event. Reference to its presentation should be made on the manuscript's title page at the time of submission. Each submission must be accompanied by a statement that the manuscript or a similar one has not been published and is not, nor will be, under consideration for publication elsewhere while being reviewed by *JATA*. Any violation of this exclusive submission and publication requirement is subject to one or more of the following sanctions: the manuscript will be rejected if not yet published; a subsequent issue of *JATA* will contain a disclaimer if the manuscript has been published; the editor of the other affected journal will be notified; and, for up to five years, the author and all co-authors of the manuscript will be barred from submitting and publishing any article or other materials in *JATA*, serving in any capacity with *JATA*, and serving as an officer or committee chairperson of the American Taxation Association. The sanctioned author(s) may appeal the editor's decision to the ATA Board of Trustees.

All manuscripts received by *JATA* are acknowledged and sent to two reviewers for evaluation. When the two reviewers are inconclusive about publication or rejection of a manuscript, one or more additional reviewers may be employed. The review process is designed to return all submissions within three months.

Submission of Manuscripts
Authors should note guidelines for submitting manuscripts:
1. Manuscripts currently under consideration by another journal or other publisher should not be submitted. All authors must state that the work is not submitted or published elsewhere.

2. In the case of manuscripts reporting on field surveys or experiments, three copies of the instrument (questionnaire, case, interview plan, or the like) should be submitted. If any of the dataset and/or results contained in the submitted research have been, or will be, reported in another publication, three copies of this other publication should also be submitted.

3. To expedite the review process, electronic submissions are required. To preserve anonymity, the cover page and the manuscript document should be submitted in separate Word files. In the case of research utilizing instruments (experimental material, questionnaires, cases, etc.) this material should also be submitted in a separate file. With the exception of the cover page, the identity of the author(s) should be deleted from the files. Files should be transmitted as email attachments to Professor Bryan Cloyd at: **JATA@vt.edu**. Contact Professor Cloyd if file compatibility or electronic submission presents a problem.

4. Beginning May 1, 2003 the submission fee is $75.00 in U.S. funds, which may be paid by credit card or check. To charge the fee, access the *JATA* site at the AAA web site: https://aaahq.org/AAAForms/journals/. Alternatively, the submission fee may be paid by check, made payable to the American Accounting Association and mailed to Professor Bryan Cloyd, Editor, Department of Accounting and Information Systems, 3007 Pamplin Hall (0101), Pamplin College of Business, Virginia Tech, Blacksburg, VA 24061.

5. Revisions must be submitted within 12 months from request, otherwise they will be considered new submissions.

Manuscript Preparation and Style
JATA manuscript preparation guidelines follow closely those used in *The Accounting Review*, another American Accounting Association publication. These guidelines follow (with a slight

modification) the Documentation 2 format of *The Chicago Manual of Style* (14th ed.; University of Chicago Press). Another helpful guide to usage and style is *The Elements of Style*, by William Strunk, Jr., and E. B. White (Macmillan). Spelling follows *Webster's International Dictionary.*

Format

1. All manuscripts should be typed on one side of 8½ x 11" good quality paper and be double spaced, except for indented quotations.

2. Manuscripts should be as concise as the subject and research method permit, generally not to exceed 7,000 words.

3. Margins of at least one inch on top, bottom, and sides to facilitate editing and duplication.

4. To assure anonymous review, authors should not identify themselves directly or indirectly in their papers. Single authors should not use the editorial "we."

5. A cover page should include the title of the paper, the author's name, title, affiliation, and any acknowledgements.

6. All pages, including tables, appendices, and references, should be serially numbered.

7. Spell out numbers one to ten, except when used in tables and lists, and when used with mathematical, statistical, scientific, or technical units and quantities, such as distances, weights, and measures. For example: *three days; 3 kilometers; 30 years.* All other numbers are expressed numerically. Generally when using approximate terms spell out the number, for example: *approximately thirty years.*

8. In nontechnical text use the word *percent*; in technical text the symbol % is used. (See the *Chicago Manual* for discussion of the correct usage.)

9. a. Use a hyphen (-) to join unit modifiers or to clarify usage. For example: *a well-presented analysis; re-form.* See *Webster's* for correct usage.
   b. En dash (–) is used between words indicating a duration, such as hourly time or months or years. No space on either side.
   c. Em dash (—) is used to indicate an abrupt change in thought, or where a period is too strong and a comma is too weak. No space on either side.

10. The following will be Roman in all cases: i.e., e.g., ibid, et al., op. cit.

11. Initials: A. B. Smith (space between); U.S., U.K. (no space between).

12. When using "Big 6" or "Big 8," use Arabic figures (don't spell out).

13. Ellipsis should be used, not periods: Example... not . . . .

14. Use "SAS No. #" not "SAS #."

15. Use only one space after periods, colons, exclamation points, question marks, quotation marks—any punctuation that separates two sentences.

16. a. Use real quotation marks—never inch marks: Use "and" not "and."
   b. Use real apostrophes, not the foot marks: Use ' and not '.

17. Punctuation used with quote marks:
a. Commas and periods are always placed inside the quotation marks.
b. Colons and semicolons go outside the quotation marks.
c. Question marks and exclamation points go in or out, depending on whether they belong to the material inside the quote or not. If they belong to the quoted material, they go inside the quote marks, and vice versa.

18. Punctuation and parentheses: sentence punctuation goes after the closing parentheses if what is inside the parentheses is part of the sentence (as this phrase is). This also applies to commas, semicolons, and colons. If what is inside the parentheses is an entire statement of its own, the ending punctuation should also be inside the parentheses.

19. Headings should be arranged so that major headings are centered, bold, and capitalized. Second level headings should be flush left, bold, and both upper and lower case. Third level headings should be flush left, bold, italic, and both upper and lower case. Fourth level headings should be paragraph indent, bold, and lower case. Headings and subheadings should not be numbered. For example:

A CENTERED, BOLD, ALL CAPITALIZED, FIRST LEVEL HEADING

A Flush Left, Bold, Upper and Lower Case, Second Level Heading
A Flush Left, Bold, Italic, Upper and Lower Case, Third Level Heading
A paragraph indent, bold, lower case, fourth level heading. Text starts....

Abstract
An abstract of not more than 150 words should be on a separate page immediately preceding the text. The abstract should be non-mathematical and include a readable summary of the research question, methodology, and principal findings and contributions. The style should be objective, without personal pronouns. The title, but not the author's name or other identification designations should appear on the abstract page and on the first page of the text.

Tables and Figures
The author should note the following general requirements:
1. Each table and figure (graphic) should appear on a separate page and should be placed at the end of the text. Each should bear an Arabic number and a complete title indicating the exact contents of the table or figure.
2. A reference to each table or graphic should be made in the text.
3. The author should indicate by marginal notation where each table or figure should be inserted in the text, e.g., (Insert Table X here).
4. Tables or figures should be reasonably interpreted without reference to the text.

420

5. Source lines and notes should be included as necessary.
6. When information is not available, use "NA" capitalized with no slash between.
7. Figures must be prepared in a form suitable for printing.

Mathematical Notation
Mathematical notation should be employed only where its rigor and precision are necessary, and in such circumstances authors should explain in the narrative format the principal operations performed. Notation should be avoided in footnotes. Unusual symbols, particularly if handwritten, should be identified in the margin when they appear. Displayed material should clearly indicate the alignment, superscripts, and subscripts. Equations should be numbered in parentheses flush with the right-hand margin.

Documentation
Citations. Work cited should use the "author-date system" keyed to a list of works in the reference list (as below). Authors should include the relevant page numbers in the cited works.

1. In the text, works are cited as follows: author's last name and date, without comma, in parentheses: for example, (Jones 1987); with two authors: (Jones and Freeman 1973); with more than two: (Jones et al. 1985); with more than one source cited together: (Jones 1987; Freeman 1986); with two or more works by one author: (Jones 1985, 1987).

2. Unless confusion would result, do not use "p." or "pp." before page numbers; for example: (Jones 1987, 115).

3. When the reference list contains more than one work of an author published in the same year, the suffix a, b, etc. follows the date in the text citation: for example, (Jones 1987a) or (Jones 1987a; Freeman 1985b).

4. If an author's name is mentioned in the text, it is not repeated in the citation; for example: "Jones (1987, 115) says ..."

5. Citations to institutional works should use acronyms or short titles where practicable; for example: (AAA ASOBAT 1966); (AICPA *Cohen Commission Report* 1977). Where brief, the full title of an institutional work might be shown in a citation; for example: (ICAEW *The Corporate Report* 1975).

6. Reference to a single regulation, government promulgation, or court case should be made in the form illustrated below. Generally, references to multiple works of the same type (e.g., two revenue rulings) or multiple works of different types (e.g., a revenue ruling and a court case) should be made through the use of a footnote unless they are of a brief nature which does not disrupt the flow of the text. The form for tax citations often encountered is presented below.

I.R.C. § 1248(a)   43 TC 1654 (1975)
Treas. Reg. § 1.1248-3(a)(4)   TC Memo 1943-496 (1943)
Rev. Rul. 82-1, 1982-1 CB 417   370 F. Supp. 69 (DC-Tx., 1974)
Rev. Proc. 82-1, 1982-1 CB 751   656 F. 2d 659 (CT. Cl., 1981)
LTR 8208047 (11/26/80)   411 F. 2d 1275 (CA-6, 1975)
                                    388 U.S. 1492 (1980)

Reference List. Every manuscript must include a list of references containing only those works cited. Each entry should contain all data necessary for unambiguous identification. With the author-date system, use the following format recommended by *The Chicago Manual*:

1. Arrange citations in alphabetical order according to surname of the first author or the name of the institution responsible for the citation.
2. Use author's initials instead of proper names.
3. In listing more than one name in references (Rayburn, L., and B. Harrelson) there should always be a comma before "and."
4. Dates of publication should be placed immediately after author's name(s).
5. Titles of journals should not be abbreviated.
6. Multiple works by the same author(s) should be listed in chronological order of publication. Two or more works by the same author(s) in the same year are distinguished by letters after the date.

Sample entries are as follows

American Accounting Association, Committee on Concepts and Standards for External Financial Reports. 1977. *Statement on Accounting Theory and Theory Acceptance.* Sarasota, FL: AAA.

Auerbach, A., and K. Hassett. 1990. Investment tax policy and the Tax Reform Act of 1986. In *Do Taxes Matter: The Impact of the Tax Reform Act of 1986*, edited by J. Slemrod. Cambridge, MA: MIT Press.

Bedard, J.C., and S. Biggs. 1990. Pattern Recognition, Hypothesis Generation, and Auditor Performance in Analytical Review. Working paper, University of Connecticut.

Boness, J., and G. Frankfurter. 1977. Evidence of non-homogeneity of capital costs within risk classes. *Journal of Finance* (June): 775-787.

Hendershott, P. H., and D. C. Long. 1984a. Trading and the tax shelter value of depreciable estate. *National Tax Journal* 37 (2): 213-224.

_____, and_____ 1984b. Prospective changes in the tax law and the value of depreciable real estate. *American Real Estate & Urban Economics Association Journal* 12 (Fall): 297-317.

Slemrod, J., ed. 1990. *Do Taxes Matter: The Impact of the Tax Reform Act of 1986.* Cambridge, MA: MIT Press

Taussig, M.K. 1967. Economic aspects of the personal income tax treatment of charitable contributions. *National Tax Journal* 20 (1): 1-19.

U.S. Congress, House. 1975. *Tax Equity Bill of 1975* [H.R. 1040]. 94th Cong., 1st Sess.

Witte, A.D., and D.F. Woodbury. 1985. The effect of tax laws and tax administration on tax compliance. *National Tax Journal* 38 (1): 1-14.

Footnotes. Footnotes are not to be used for documentation. Textual footnotes should be used only for extensions and useful excursions of information that if included in the body of the text might disrupt its continuity. Footnotes should be consecutively numbered throughout the manuscript with superscript Arabic numerals. Footnote text should be double-spaced and placed at the end of the article.

Policy on Reproduction

The object of *JATA* is to promote the wide dissemination of the results of research and other scholarly inquiries into the field of taxation. Permission is hereby granted to reproduce any of

Policy on Data Availability
An objective of *JATA* is to provide the widest possible dissemination of knowledge based on systematic scholarly inquiries into tax as a field of professional, research, and educational activity. As part of this process, authors are encouraged to make their data available for use by others in extending or replicating results reported in their articles. Authors of articles that report data-dependent results must provide the editor a statement indicating the status of data availability and, when pertinent, this should be accompanied by information on how the data may be obtained. The availability of data will not influence the decision to publish an article. The author's data availability statement will be included as a headnote to each article published in *JATA*. It remains the responsibility of the author and the person requesting the data to negotiate the terms of the release, use, publication, and protection of the author's data. A person using an author's data has a professional responsibility to comply strictly with the agreement negotiated with the author.

Journal of the International Academy for Case Studies

ADDRESS FOR SUBMISSION:

Current Editor / Check Website
Journal of the International Academy for
  Case Studies
Digital Submission Through Website
Address other questions to:
  Jim or JoAnn Carland at # below
USA
Phone: 828-293-9151
E-Mail: info@alliedacademies.org
Web: www.alliedacademies.org

CIRCULATION DATA:

Reader: Academics
Frequency of Issue: 6 Times/Year
Sponsor/Publisher: Allied Academies, Inc.

PUBLICATION GUIDELINES:

Manuscript Length: 16-20
Copies Required: Submit Through Web
Computer Submission: Yes
Format: MS Word, WordPerfect
Fees to Review: 0.00 US$

Manuscript Style:
  American Psychological Association

REVIEW INFORMATION:

Type of Review: Blind Review
No. of External Reviewers: 3
No. of In House Reviewers: 2
Acceptance Rate: 21-30%
Time to Review: 3-4 Months
Reviewers Comments: Yes
Invited Articles: 0-5%
Fees to Publish: 75.00 US$ Membership

MANUSCRIPT TOPICS:

Accounting Education; Accounting Information Systems; Accounting Theory & Practice;
Auditing; Behavioral Accounting; Cost Accounting

MANUSCRIPT GUIDELINES/COMMENTS:

Editorial Comment on Manuscript Topics

Our scope is broader than the topics listed above. The journal publishes Teaching cases in any
discipline or area. Cases must be accompanied by an Instructor's Note.

Comments. All authors of published manuscripts must be members of the appropriate
academy affiliate of Allied Academies. The current membership fee is $75.00 US.

Editorial Policy Guidelines

The primary criterion upon which cases are judged is whether the case, together with its
instructor's note, can be an effective teaching tool.

Cases need not conform to any guideline and may be in any discipline. Narrative cases are
acceptable as well as disguised field cases, library cases or illustrative cases. Each case must

be accompanied by an instructor's note and the note MUST conform to the editorial policy. This policy may be found on the website.

Referees require a decision point in a case and pay particular attention to readability and potential for student interest and involvement. Consequently, cases which DESCRIBE action are NOT generally acceptable. The important point is the use of a case in classroom teaching.

Journal of the International Society of Business Disciplines

ADDRESS FOR SUBMISSION:

Jason T. White, Editor
Journal of the International Society of
   Business Disciplines
24670 Interlude Road
Maryville, MO 64468
USA
Phone: 660-562-1764
E-Mail: jwhite@mail.nwmissouri.edu
  jwhite@isobd.org
  cacker@isobd.org
Web: www.isobd.org

PUBLICATION GUIDELINES:

Manuscript Length: 1-15
Copies Required: Three
Computer Submission: Yes Disk, Email
Format: MS Word
Fees to Review: 0.00 US$

Manuscript Style:

CIRCULATION DATA:

Reader: Academics
Frequency of Issue: Semi-Annual
Sponsor/Publisher: International Society of
   Business Disciplines

REVIEW INFORMATION:

Type of Review: Blind Review
No. of External Reviewers: 2
No. of In House Reviewers: 1
Acceptance Rate: 21-30%
Time to Review: 2 - 3 Months
Reviewers Comments: No
Invited Articles: 0-5%
Fees to Publish: 3.00 US$ per page to
   15, then $5 per page

MANUSCRIPT TOPICS:

Accounting Education; Accounting Information Systems; Accounting Theory & Practice; Auditing; Behavioral Accounting; Cost Accounting; Financial Services; Fiscal Policy; Government & Non Profit Accounting; Insurance; International Finance; Portfolio & Security Analysis; Tax Accounting

MANUSCRIPT GUIDELINES/COMMENTS:

The *Journal of the International Society of Business Disciplines* (*JISOBD*) seeks both theoretical and practitioner papers to be considered for publication. *JISOBD* is an international, refereed and double-blind reviewed scholarly journal. We seek articles promoting scholarship in applied, theoretical and practitioner research in all areas of business and economics. Case studies will also be considered for publication.

Articles presented at the semi-annual meeting of the International Society of Business Disciplines (ISOBD) received priority placement consideration in *JISOBD*, once accepted by the review team.

Submission Criteria

Articles should follow standard MLA citation guidelines. All articles must be double-spaced and not exceed 15 pages in length, including cover page and citations. If accepted, *JISOBD* charges $3.00 per page for compilation and distribution of the journal. An additional $5.00 per page surcharge will be assessed on those submissions in excess of 15.

The title page should include the article's title; author's names, affiliations and ranks; email address of primary contact person; and phone number for same.

All papers must be submitted in an electronic format that is readable by Microsoft Word. Tables, graphs and figures must be properly formatted within the Word submission, or they will not be accepted.

Only electronic submissions are accepted. For consideration, email your paper to:
   cacker@isobd.org

Editorial Review Process

To complete the double-blind review referee process takes approximately 8-12 weeks. Once that process is complete, the submitting author will receive an email indicating whether the article has been: 1) accepted for publication without change; 2) provisionally accepted for publication pending certain changes; 3) rejected for publication. We do require a signed binding copyright agreement from all authors, once the article has been accepted for publication in *JISOBD*. Electronic submission of these signatures is acceptable.

Journal of Theoretical Accounting Research (The)

ADDRESS FOR SUBMISSION:

Jeffry Haber, Editor
Journal of Theoretical Accounting Research
  (The)
Iona College
Hagan School of Business
715 North Avenue
New Rochelle, NY 10801
USA
Phone: 914-633-2244
E-Mail: jhaber@iona.edu
Web: jtar.org

PUBLICATION GUIDELINES:

Manuscript Length: 16-20
Copies Required: Three or 1 Electronic
Computer Submission: Yes·Email
Format: MS Word
Fees to Review: 100.00 US$

Manuscript Style:
  See Manuscript Guidelines

CIRCULATION DATA:

Reader: Academics
Frequency of Issue: 2 Times/Year
Sponsor/Publisher:

REVIEW INFORMATION:

Type of Review: Blind Review
No. of External Reviewers: 2
No. of In House Reviewers: 1
Acceptance Rate: New J
Time to Review: 1 Month or Less
Reviewers Comments: Yes
Invited Articles: 0-5%
Fees to Publish: 0.00 US$

MANUSCRIPT TOPICS:

Accounting Education; Accounting Information Systems; Accounting Theory & Practice; Auditing; Behavioral Accounting; Cost Accounting; Financial Services; Fiscal Policy; Government & Non Profit Accounting; Tax Accounting

MANUSCRIPT GUIDELINES/COMMENTS:

Mission

The goal of *The Journal of Theoretical Accounting Research* is to provide an academic outlet for research that does not include testing. Virtually all accounting journals expect quantitative analysis to be included. Researchers who prefer to remain in the theoretical realm have no publishing outlet for their work.

This journal will provide that outlet. There are many researchers who do like to do testing and apply quantitative methods. It is hoped that they will use this journal to get ideas for testable theories and apply their methods using the theories contained in the journal.

The journal is open source, so anyone can take the ideas and expand them to develop a testable model. It is also hoped that collaborations will be fostered between researchers who develop theory and those that will apply the testing.

Submissions

Submitting a manuscript for review is a simple process. Two Word files should be emailed the editor. The first file contains a single page, incorporating the title, author(s) and contact information. The second file contains the title and then the body of the paper, including abstract. The only reference to the authors should be in the first file.

There is no standard that has to be applied as far as margins, font, typeface, etc. The format and organization should reflect the subject matter, and the preferences of the author.

Payment may be made by mailing a check payable to Journal of Theoretical Research to the editor's address above or by logging onto Paypal and paying **editor@JTAR.org** the review fee (or an invoice may be generated if you prefer).

Review

All manuscripts will be submitted for double-blind review. The estimated turnaround time for a response is 45 days. The review fee is $100. If accepted for publication there is no page or publication fee.

All submissions will be reviewed for rigorous development for theory, implications for the profession, and timeliness of issue.

Editor

The editor is Jeffry R. Haber, Iona College. To contact the editor, email to **jhaber@iona.edu**. Submission fees are payable by check made out to the *Journal of Theoretical Accounting Research* or through Paypal.

Leaders' Edge (Michigan CPA)

ADDRESS FOR SUBMISSION:

Marla Janess, Editor
Leaders' Edge (Michigan CPA)
Michigan Association of CPAs
PO Box 5068
5840 Corporate Drive, Suite 200
Troy, MI 48007-5068
USA
Phone: 248-267-3700
E-Mail: macpa@michcpa.org
Web: www.michcpa.org

CIRCULATION DATA:

Reader: Business Persons, CPAs,
    Academics, Finance Professionals
Frequency of Issue: Bi-Monthly
Sponsor/Publisher: Michigan Association of
    Certified Public Accountants

PUBLICATION GUIDELINES:

Manuscript Length: 600-1,400 Words
Copies Required: One
Computer Submission: Yes
Format: Electronic
Fees to Review: 0.00 US$

Manuscript Style:
    American Psychological Association

REVIEW INFORMATION:

Type of Review: Editorial Review
No. of External Reviewers: 1
No. of In House Reviewers: 3
Acceptance Rate: 0-5%
Time to Review: 2 - 3 Months
Reviewers Comments: No
Invited Articles: 0-5% CPA Authored
Fees to Publish: 0.00 US$

MANUSCRIPT TOPICS:

Accounting Information Systems; Accounting Theory & Practice; Agribusiness; Auditing; Automobile Dealers & Suppliers; Construction Accounting & Taxation; Ethics; Financial Institutions; Financial Management; Financial Services; Government & Non Profit Accounting; Health Care Administration; Industrial Organization; International Economics & Trade; Tax Accounting

MANUSCRIPT GUIDELINES/COMMENTS:

Types of Manuscripts Sought

We publish original articles of interest to practitioners, those in business and in educational fields. Submitted articles should offer help in resolving questions that arise in practice, advice in implementing published standards and guidelines, insight to problems, with, preferably workable solutions, or report on the status of developing issues. Our articles should be of broad interest, although some could relate to specific industries or techniques. Articles should be of immediate interest and timely to the profession.

Manuscript Preparation

- Articles should be typed and double-spaced, ranging in length from one to two pages, and submitted electronically.

- Short biographies of each author should be submitted with the article. Authors should include their educational background, employment, professional associations and other relevant information.
- Authors should also submit a photo with their articles. Black-and-white photos are preferred, however color photos will be acceptable. Do not submit Polaroids. If you do not wish to have your photo in the newsletter, please make a note of that when sending in the article.
- Due to space constraints, it may not always be possible to run your article in the next issue. Please indicate if the content of your article may soon be outdated.
- Include both a headline and byline with your article.

Content
- Development of all articles should consider the questions who, what, when, where, why and how.
- Specific examples, case histories and quote should be an essential part of any article. Whenever possible, please illustrate your points with examples from your personal experience. Facts and figures are invaluable to the reader. Use them liberally.
- Write your article in the active voice using strong verbs. For example, "This situation demands your attention," rather than "Your attention is needed."
- Keep your copy relaxed; this isn't a scholarly magazine. Second person "you" in addressing members is acceptable. Avoid using the fist person "I."
- *Leader's Edge* does not use footnotes. Give attribution to your source within the copy of your article. For example, state, "According to a recent study by...," or "The Wall Street Journal reports..."
- Check your copy carefully before submitting. Have you duplicated any information? Are you repeating a word or phrase frequently throughout the article? Are your paragraphs or sentences too lengthy?

Review
- All articles are reviewed by the MACPA Editorial Board and, if appropriate, by the Column Editor in which the article would appear.

Graphics
- Charts and photographs can help emphasize and clarify points you believe should be made in the articles. Graphics should be done as neatly as possible with a description of what the graphic illustrates.
- The file size for graphics should be 20K or less and in .GIF file format (for faster download times). Other acceptable file formats include .JPEG or .BMP.

Editing
- The MACPA staff edits all manuscripts accepted for both content and style.
- Standards for style are set by the MACPA staff to follow professional publishing practices.

Management Accounting Quarterly

ADDRESS FOR SUBMISSION:

Kathy Williams, Editor
Management Accounting Quarterly
Institute of Management Accountants
10 Paragon Drive
Montvale, NJ 07645
USA
Phone: 201-474-1576
E-Mail: kwilliams@imanet.org
Web: www.strategicfinancemag.com

CIRCULATION DATA:

Reader: Business Persons
Frequency of Issue: Quarterly
Sponsor/Publisher: Institute of Management
   Accountants

PUBLICATION GUIDELINES:

Manuscript Length: 15-20
Copies Required: Four
Computer Submission: Yes
Format: MS Word
Fees to Review: 0.00 US$

Manuscript Style:
   Chicago Manual of Style

REVIEW INFORMATION:

Type of Review: Blind Review
No. of External Reviewers: 3
No. of In House Reviewers: 2
Acceptance Rate: 11-20%
Time to Review: 2-6 Months
Reviewers Comments: Yes
Invited Articles: 31-50%
Fees to Publish: 0.00 US$

MANUSCRIPT TOPICS:

Accounting Information Systems; Auditing; Corporate Finance; Cost Accounting; Fiscal Policy; Industrial Organization; Insurance; International Economics & Trade; International Finance; Monetary Policy; Portfolio & Security Analysis; Tax Accounting

MANUSCRIPT GUIDELINES/COMMENTS:

What should you write about?
Management Accounting Quarterly publishes only original material that contributes to the profession of management accounting and financial management.

We recommend that you study several issues of our magazine before you write and submit your manuscript. The best advice is to write only about the topics you know best and with which you've had experience.

Submitting Your Manuscript
We recommend submitting your manuscript via the online submission form. Files should be in Word or WordPerfect formats. We can also take .txt or .rtf files. Manuscripts must be accompanied by a submission form, so please don't e-mail files directly to us unless you have already submitted the form. Manuscripts will not be processed without a form.

If you need to submit your manuscript via hardcopy, it should be on plain white 8 ½" x 11" paper in a printed format. Leave sufficient margins on all sides (one inch is recommended). The text should be double-spaced. Include four copies of the manuscript along with a submission form. The form itself can still be submitted electronically, but include a copy with the manuscripts to ensure accurate processing. If your manuscript is accepted for publication, you will need to send us an electronic version via e-mail, 3.5" disk, or CD.

Write the title of your manuscript and the names of author(s) on a cover page. If there is more than one author, list the authors' names in the order you want them to appear in print. Number each page at the bottom. Do not put an author's name on anything but the cover page because all manuscripts are reviewed "blind." Using the author's name within the manuscript itself will cause delays in the manuscript processing and slow down the review process. If it must be used within the context of the article, black out the name. The editorial staff and reviewers will understand it is referring to the author. Names can also be used in citations and other references if there is no indication that the person listed is also the author.

The criteria for acceptable manuscripts are:
1. IMA is given exclusive publication rights.
2. Manuscripts must be accompanied by a Manuscript Submission form.
3. Manuscripts must not hale been previously published.
4. They must be submitted in English and in completed form for publication.
5. If authored by a nonmember, they must be accompanied by author's mailing address.
6. They must not be a poem outline, abstract, thesis, school term/research paper, unedited speech, or previously accepted manuscript.

The content of the manuscript must be timely.

Preparing Your Manuscript
Your manuscript must be accompanied by an official submission form. You can obtain the submission form from the website or through your chapter's manuscript director. Manuscripts without this form will be returned to the author.

Length of Manuscript. Most manuscripts we publish are approximately 15-20 typewritten double-spaced pages. Ideal length is about 3,000-4,000 words for *Management Accounting Quarterly*.

Abstract. Please provide an abstract or summary of your article on a separate sheet of paper. The editors use this abstract to summarize and introduce your article in the table of contents.

Tables and Figures. Your manuscript will be strengthened if you can illustrate your points. Graphic illustrations should be kept simple and in proportion to the manuscript's length. There should be a specific reference in the text to each table or figure in your manuscript, and put each table or figure on a separate sheet of paper.

Bio and Footnotes. Please include brief biographies of all authors with your manuscript, and make sure they contain a phone number and/or e-mail address for each author. Where necessary, footnotes should be on a separate page at the end of the manuscript. In references cited, please include author's full name, title of publication, name of publisher, date of publication, and page numbers where applicable.

The Review Process
All manuscripts submitted to *Management Accounting Quarterly* are reviewed in a two-stage process to determine if they are appropriate for publication. Each manuscript is assigned a control number when the Publications staff receives it. The author is notified of this control number via e-mail. When you want to know the status of your manuscript, please refer to this number when you contact the staff.

Technical Review. Each manuscript undergoes a blind review by three independent reviewers who have expertise in specific areas. All references to the author are deleted from the original and copies. Members of the manuscript appraisal committee base their evaluations on the following seven major criteria:

1. Is the topic of the manuscript relevant for our readers?
2. How well was the topic covered? Was it a thorough analysis and description of the topic? Were any assertions made that were not supported by the evidence and data supplied?
3. Is the manuscript original and not a rehash of what has been published previously?
4. Is it practical? Can our readers use the information to benefit their companies and careers?
5. Is it technically correct and, sound?
6. Is the topic timely? Does toe manuscript reflect the latest pronouncements and research? Does it represent, a new development or innovation of which our members should be aware?
7. Is the material presented clearly and concisely?

When these manuscript appraisal forms are returned to the editorial department after review, the three grades are then averaged to determine the overall grade assigned to the manuscript. Reviewers are asked to recommend that the manuscript be published, revised, or rejected and to provide reasons for their recommendations. We also ask them for suggestions on how the technical content of the manuscript can be improved. Based on the review committee's comments and further evaluation by the editorial staff of the magazine, manuscripts will either be considered for publication or rejected.

Publication
If your manuscript is selected for publication, you will be notified once the review process is complete and asked to submit an electronic version if you haven't already done so.

Once the editor has selected a publication date, a staff member will edit your manuscript and send you the edited version and a copyright permission form. Please review the editing, make any changes, sign the copyright form, and return all material within five days of receipt. During the editing process, an editor will contact you to discuss tables or figures to illustrate the article or any other matters pertaining to the content.

Return of Your Manuscript. If your manuscript is rejected, we'll let you know as soon as the decision is made. Remember to keep a copy of your article for your own records. The Publications Department can't be responsible for retaining rejected manuscripts.

Awards

The IMA member authors of the top manuscripts submitted, determined by the grade average, and published during the competition year are presented Certificates of Merit for their outstanding contributions to accounting and finance literature. IMA member authors of the top three manuscripts, as determined by an editorial advisory committee, will be presented Lybrand Gold, Silver, and Bronze Medals, respectively.

IMA Chapter Competition

As part of the yearly competition, chapters can earn credit in the Elective Activities category for submitting a manuscript to the magazines. An acceptable manuscript submitted on time is worth up to 300 points. There is also a bonus of 5% if one or more authors is an IMA member. There is a deduction of 10% for manuscripts submitted after the deadline. The deadline for full credit is November 20, of the competition year. No points will be awarded in the current competition year for manuscripts submitted after April 20.

To be eligible, manuscripts must meet the criteria listed above (see SUBMITTING YOUR MANUSCRIPT. A submission form, with chapter name and number in the proper fields, must accompany the manuscript. Failure to complete the form properly or follow any of the other submission criteria can result in a point deduction (if it needs to be resubmitted after the deadline) or the chapter may not get credit. The editorial decision to either accept or reject the manuscript far; publication does not affect the number bf points awarded to the chapter. As long as the manuscript meets the criteria and can be processed for review, the chapter will receive credit. See the Chapter Competition Guide for more information.

Tips for Effective Writing

Staff editors carefully edit every manuscript scheduled for publication. They follow a number of general principles in the editing process. Here are some suggestions for effective writing:

- Write punchy lead paragraphs that will "grab" readers and pull them into the article.
- Avoid long introductions. Get right to the point. Tell the reader exactly what you plan to do.
- Avoid jargon and acronyms. Readers don't like to go back and check their meaning.
- Don't pad your manuscript. It will be obvious to the editor and to the reader-if the editor lets the material stand.
- Avoid long, complex sentences. Break a complex thought into two or more sentences.
- Don't assume that the reader knows as much as you do. Carefully explain or define a term that isn't commonly used or was coined at your company.
- Use the active voice, not passive. Instead of writing "It was accomplished in 10 days," say "We finished the project in 10 days."
- Write a conclusion that sums up your major points and makes a statement on why the article is important to the reader.

Suggested Topics for Strategic Finance Authors
1. Treasury
2. Cash Management & Banking Relations
3. Corporate Development and Strategic Planning
4. Financing
5. Investor Relations
6. International Finance/IASC
7. Insurance (especially operational liability)
8. Financial Risk Analysis and Management (risks and opportunities)
9. Employee Benefits
10. Retirement Plans and Pension Administration
11. Leading
12. Investment Management and the Equity Market (IPO)
13. Management Information Systems
14. Other Technology Issues
15. Real Estate (such as valuation of private and public corporate enterprises)
16. SEC and FASB Regulatory Issues and other governmental regulations
17. Financial Reporting
18. Mergers & Acquisitions & Restructuring
19. Controllership
20. Budgeting & Planning
21. Capital Budgeting
22. Cost Accounting
23. AOM/Target Costing/Theory of Constraints
24. Corporate Taxes
25. Enterprise Resource Planning
26. Performance Measurement and Evaluation
27. Ethics
28. Intellectual Capital
29. R&D and New Product Development
30. Life-Cycle Product Analysis
31. Joint Ventures
32. Management of Human Resources/Employee Training and Education/Behavior
33. Communications and Presentation Skills
34. Internal Auditing
35. Awareness of External Auditing
36. Liquidation and Bankruptcy
37. Economical/Competitive Environment
38. Current Asset Utilization (AIR, Inventory Management)
39. Business Law
40. Bargaining Unit Negotiation
41. Outsourcing
42. Purchasing
43. Quantitative Analysis (statistics)
44. Industrial Engineering (factory floor optimization)

Management Accounting Research

ADDRESS FOR SUBMISSION:

Editorial Office
Management Accounting Research
Elsevier S&T Editorial Services Office
Stover Court
Bampfylde Street
Exeter, EX1 2AH
UK
Phone: 44 1392 285809
E-Mail: mar@elsevier.com
Web: www.elsevier.com

PUBLICATION GUIDELINES:

Manuscript Length: 26-30
Copies Required: Two
Computer Submission: Yes
Format:
Fees to Review: 0.00 US$

Manuscript Style:
See Manuscript Guidelines

CIRCULATION DATA:

Reader: Academics
Frequency of Issue: Quarterly
Sponsor/Publisher: Chartered Institute of
Management Accountants / Elsevier Inc.

REVIEW INFORMATION:

Type of Review: Blind Review
No. of External Reviewers: 2
No. of In House Reviewers: 1
Acceptance Rate: 21-30%
Time to Review: 3-4 Months
Reviewers Comments: Yes
Invited Articles: 0-5%
Fees to Publish: 0.00 US$

MANUSCRIPT TOPICS:
Accounting Information Systems; Cost Accounting; Management Accounting

MANUSCRIPT GUIDELINES/COMMENTS:

Submission of Manuscripts
Manuscripts for consideration should be submitted electronically to:
http://ees.elsevier.com/mar

If there are any problems with your internet connection or you experience problems with the upload, please e-mail your paper to: **mar@elsevier.com**

The corresponding author is responsible for ensuring that co-authors agree to the inclusion of their names before submission of a manuscript.

Acceptance Criteria
Submission of a paper to the Journal automatically implies that the manuscript is not concurrently under consideration for publication elsewhere. All papers submitted will normally only be published subject to double blind review. In the interests of a fair review, authors should try and avoid the use of anything which would make their identity obvious.

Referees are asked to comment upon the originality, authority, comprehensiveness, contribution, interest and usefulness of a submitted paper. All papers are also subjected to editorial review which, whilst covering style and quality of communication, may also cover academic and scholarly content. The editors make every effort to give a decision on manuscripts within 12 weeks of receipt.

Preparation of Manuscripts
Articles should be typed double-spaced throughout the text on A4 paper; with a margin of about 3 cm all round.

Table and Figure legends should be typed separately and placed at the end of the manuscript.

All pages should be numbered serially.

The title page should include the article title, authors' names and affiliations, the name and address of the person to whom proofs are to be sent, a running head of not more than 50 characters and any acknowledgements.

Articles should be arranged as follows:
(i) An abstract of about 150 words along with 3-6 key words
(ii) Main text in the sections, Introduction, Materials and Methods, Results, and Discussion (best presented as separate sections but may be combined).
(iii) References

Key words
Three to six key words or short phrases should be provided to assist indexers in cross-indexing the paper.

Illustrations
All illustrations must be cited in the text and in sequence. If line drawings are submitted they should be in black ink and drawn to approximately 1.5 to 2 times their required size for publication.

All authors wishing to use illustrations already published must first obtain the permission of author and publisher and/or copyright holders and give precise reference to the original work.

Tables
Tables should be numbered in series and must be cited in the text in sequence. Headings should be provided but otherwise the data should be self-explanatory.

References
In the text references should include the author's name, the year of publication, and the relevant page numbers if required; e.g. (Innes and Mitchell, 1990, p.6). For more than two authors, the reference should be abbreviated as follows: (Rickwood et al., 1990, p.37). Multiple references to works by the same author(s) in a single year should be distinguished in the text (and in the bibliography) by a, b, c, etc. following the year of publication.

438

The manuscript should include a bibliography containing only those references cited in the text and arranged in alphabetical order according to the surname of the first author. Full bibliographical details are required in the following style:

Examples
1. Bromwich, M., 1977. The use of present valuation models in published accounting reports, *The Accounting Review*, July, 587-596.
2. Broadbent, J., 1992. Change in organizations: a case study of the use of accounting information in the NHS, British Accounting Review, 24, 343-367.
3. Belkaoui, A., 1985. *Accounting Theory*, 2nd edition, San Diego, Harcourt Brace Jovanovich.

Footnotes
Footnotes should be numbered sequentially in the text and appear on a separate sheet at the end of the paper.

Proofs
Authors are expected to correct proofs quickly and not to make revisions on proofs; revisions made on proofs may be charged for. No payments are made to authors.

Copyright/Offprints
Authors submitting a manuscript do so on the understanding that if it is accepted for publication, copyright in the article in all forms and media, shall be assigned exclusively to the publisher. The Copyright Transfer Agreement, which may be copied from the pages following the Instructions to Authors or found on the journal home page [on website], should be signed by the appropriate person(s) and should accompany the original submission of a manuscript to this journal. The transfer of copyright does not take effect until the manuscript is accepted for publication. The written consent of the publisher must be obtained if any article is to be published elsewhere in the same form, in any language. It is the policy of the publisher that authors need not obtain permission in the following cases only: (1) to use their original figures or tables in their future work; (2) to make copies of their papers for use in their classroom teaching; and (3) to include their papers as part of their dissertation.

In consideration for the assignment of copyright, 25 offprints of each paper will be supplied. Further offprints may be ordered at extra cost; the offprint order form will be sent with the proofs.

Editor-in-Chief
R. W. Scapens, Accounting and Finance, Manchester Business School, Booth Street West, Manchester M15 6PB, UK. Tel. 44-161-2754020, Fax 44-161-2754023.
    Email: **robert.scapens@mbs.ac.uk**

Management Science

ADDRESS FOR SUBMISSION:

Wallace J. Hopp, Editor-in-Chief
Management Science
ELECTRONIC SUBMISSION ONLY
Northwestern University
Department of Industrial Engineering
and Management Science
Evanston, IL 60208
USA
Phone: 847-491-3669
E-Mail: hopp@northwestern.edu
Web: http://mc.manuscriptcentral.com/ms

PUBLICATION GUIDELINES:

Manuscript Length: 32 Pgs double-spaced
Copies Required: Submit Online
Computer Submission: Yes Required
Format: MS Word, PDF, TeX
Fees to Review: 0.00 US$

Manuscript Style:
    See Manuscript Guidelines

CIRCULATION DATA:

Reader: Academics
Frequency of Issue: Monthly
Sponsor/Publisher: INFORMS

REVIEW INFORMATION:

Type of Review: Editorial Review
No. of External Reviewers: 3
No. of In House Reviewers: 0
Acceptance Rate: 11-20%
Time to Review: 4 - 6 Months
Reviewers Comments: Yes
Invited Articles: 0-5%
Fees to Publish: 0.00 US$

MANUSCRIPT TOPICS:
Accounting Information Systems; Accounting Theory & Practice; Auditing; Cost Accounting; Government & Non Profit Accounting

MANUSCRIPT GUIDELINES/COMMENTS:

Editorial Statement
Management Science is a scholarly journal that publishes scientific research into the problems, interests and concerns of managers. Our scope includes articles that address management issues with tools from traditional fields such as operations research, mathematics, statistics, industrial engineering, psychology, sociology and political science, as well as cross-functional, multidisciplinary research that reflects the diversity of the management science professions. We also publish relevant articles and seek to stimulate research in emerging domains, such as those created by economic globalization, public policy shifts, technological improvements and trends in management practice.

Abridged Statement of Editorial Policies
Management Science seeks to publish articles that identify, extend, or unify scientific knowledge pertaining to management. Scientific paradigms can be drawn from a broad range

440

of disciplines, as reflected by the departmental structure of the journal. However, the unifying thread of all Management Science articles is a fundamental focus on improving our understanding of the practice of management. Within this scope, theoretical, empirical, prescriptive and descriptive contributions are welcome. In addition to managerial relevance, articles must meet high standards of originality and rigor. More detailed descriptions of editorial policies are given in the editorial statements of the individual departments. Authors seeking up-to-date information about specific department editorial objectives should send their requests to the appropriate department editor or to the editor-in-chief.

Clear exposition is an important criterion for publication in *Management Science*. Articles must be readable, well-organized, and exhibit good writing style. As much as possible, papers suitable for *Management Science* should be readable by those comfortable with undergraduate mathematics. We accept the use of graduate level mathematics only if it is essential for understanding. All articles and notes, if judged potentially suitable for Management Science, will be refereed by at least two competent readers.

The submission of a paper to *Management Science* for refereeing means that the author certifies the manuscript is not copyrighted; nor has it been accepted for publication (or published) by any refereed journal; nor is it being refereed elsewhere. If the paper (or any version of it) has appeared, or will appear in a non-refereed publication, the details of such publication must be made known to the editor at the time of submission, so that the suitability of the paper for *Management Science* can be assessed. *Management Science* requires that at least one of the authors of each accepted article sign a Copyright Transfer Agreement form. For further information write: Professor Wallace J. Hopp, Northwestern University, Department of Industrial Engineering and Management Science, Evanston, IL 60208-3119.

Management Science is dedicated to publishing papers that scientifically address the problems, interests and concerns of managers.

Manuscript Preparation
1. **Do innovative research** that generates insights of interest to a practicing manager. (The research itself need not be directly accessible to managers, but the motivation and results should be of interest to them.)

2. **Write a good paper** that:
- is consistent with *Management Science* length and style requirements.
- complies with ethical guidelines for academic publishing.
- has not been published elsewhere in violation with INFORMS copyright policy.
- includes full cover page with names of all authors and an abstract.

3. **Select a department** to review your manuscript. To do this, you should carefully examine the current Department Editorial Objectives. If you have any questions about fit, you may contact the appropriate Department Editor or the Editor-in-Chief. If you feel your paper falls between departments, you may note that on your submission. Departments Editors are being encouraged to handle interdisciplinary papers jointly.

Manuscript Submission

All submissions must be made electronically at **http://mc.manuscriptcentral.com/ms**. Details on how to do this are given in a PowerPoint tutorial. The basic steps are:

4. **Log in**. If you have not registered, you will be prompted to generate a new account that includes your personalized user ID. Please fill in the entire form; the email address is used for all correspondence related to your submission.

5. **Submit your paper on line**: Once logged in, the site walks you through ten steps for submitting a paper. The system accepts most word-processing formats, although MS Word or PDF are preferred. In addition to uploading your manuscript, you will be asked for an abstract, key words and a list of suggested referees who do not have any conflict of interest with you or your co-authors. All submissions to Management Science are expected to comply with INFORMS ethics and copyright guidelines.

6. **Get a manuscript tracking number** at the end of the submission. Please include this number in all subsequent correspondence regarding the paper.

Review Process

7. **Review for fit** is made by a Department Editor. Only if the paper is deemed consistent with journal and department objectives is it sent on for further review. This step should take less than two weeks.

8. **Review for significance** is made by an Associate Editor. If the paper is not judged to have the potential to make a significant contribution to the literature, it will be returned to the authors. This step should take less than two weeks.

9. **Detailed review** will be made by at least two qualified reviewers. Based on Referee and Associate Editor recommendations, the Department Editor will decide whether the paper should be accepted as is, revised or rejected.

10. **Timeline**. Our goal is to provide feedback to 75% of authors within 90 days and feedback to all authors within 180 days. If the paper goes beyond six months in the review process it is considered LATE. The on-line submission program is set up with automatic reminders to department Editors and Associate Editors to keep your manuscript moving through the system. But you are within your rights to inquire of the Department Editor concerning the status of a late paper.

Decision

11. **Email notification** will be sent to the corresponding author announcing that a decision has been made. You can access the decision and the supporting documents (e.g., referee reports) through your author center. The possible decisions are: Reject, Major Revision Required, Minor Revision Required, Accept.

12. **Revisions**, if suggested, will cause the manuscript to show up in the "Manuscripts to be Revised" area of your Author Center.

Post Acceptance

13. **Final submission.** If the paper is conditionally accepted for publication you will be requested to submit the final version of your manuscript in Word, Tex, Latex or WordPerfect format, along with a signed copyright form. Your paper will be transmitted directly to the Production editor at INFORMS. If any additional information is needed, you will be contacted.

As a condition of final acceptance of the paper for publication in *Management Science*, the author(s) must indicate if the paper is posted on a working paper website, other than their own. The author(s) are responsible for assuring that, if any part of the paper has been copyrighted for prepublication as a working paper, the copyright can and will be transferred to INFORMS when the paper has been accepted. This includes both print and electronic forms of the paper. On acceptance, the text, or any link to full text, must be removed from working paper websites, other the author(s)'s own website.

More Information. If you have any questions, are unable to access the ManuscriptCentral site, or are having trouble getting information on the status of your paper, please contact the Managing Editor.

Managerial Auditing Journal

ADDRESS FOR SUBMISSION:

Philomena Leung, Editor
Managerial Auditing Journal
Deaking University
School of Accounting, Economics
  and Finance
Burwood, Victoria,
Australia
Phone:
E-Mail: maj-admin@deakin.edu.au
Web: www.emeraldinsight.com

CIRCULATION DATA:

Reader: Business Persons, Academics
Frequency of Issue: 9 Times/Year
Sponsor/Publisher: Emerald Group
  Publishing Limited

PUBLICATION GUIDELINES:

Manuscript Length: 26-30
Copies Required: One
Computer Submission: Yes Email
Format: See Manuscript Guidelines
Fees to Review: 0.00 US$

Manuscript Style:
  See Manuscript Guidelines

REVIEW INFORMATION:

Type of Review: Blind Review
No. of External Reviewers:
No. of In House Reviewers:
Acceptance Rate: 47.1%
Time to Review: 1 - 2 Months
Reviewers Comments: Yes
Invited Articles: 6-10%
Fees to Publish: 0.00 US$

MANUSCRIPT TOPICS:
Accounting Information Systems; Accounting Theory & Practice; Auditing; Business Ethics; Computer Security; Cost Accounting; Government & Non Profit Accounting; Industrial Organization; Internal Auditing; Management

MANUSCRIPT GUIDELINES/COMMENTS:

About the Journal
The *Managerial Auditing Journal* uniquely addresses the changing function of the auditor, examining the managerial as well as the professional aspects of the role, and exploring the positive impact of auditing on company policy, corporate governance and organizational progress. Drawing together international, interdisciplinary contributions, this influential journal offers you a framework of explanation and guidance on the latest developments and research, and provides valuable insights into professional and career development.

JOURNAL OVERVIEW
Unique Attributes
The journal provides: a forum for those within a broad managerial as well as professional interest in audit to explore current practices, ideas and experience; a framework of explanation and guidance on developments and research; and perspectives on professional and career

development. Papers accepted for publication are double blind-refereed to ensure academic rigour and integrity.

Topicality

Auditors, once employed for the express purpose of checking the accounts for fraudulent practice, have now developed a more supportive role, guiding and maintaining continual improvement. This new approach is reflected in *MAJ*, which takes its readers beyond traditional conventions and looks at the ways in which contemporary auditors are improving both managerial and organizational performance.

Key Benefits

Managerial Auditing Journal presents a wide range of material with an emphasis on practical examples from expert practitioners, making it relevant to a broad readership. Its concentration on modern practice creates a useful forum for the development of new thinking and practice within the profession.

Key Journal Audiences

- Academics and researchers in the field
- Finance directors
- General managers
- Internal and external auditors
- Management consultants

Coverage

The journal's wide coverage includes:

- Career issues
- Communicating the results of audits
- Environmental auditing
- Ethical considerations
- Management theory and auditing practice
- People and assets auditing
- Social auditing processes

NOTES FOR CONTRIBUTORS
Copyright

Articles submitted to the journal should be original contributions and should not be under consideration for any other publication at the same time. Authors submitting articles for publication warrant that the work is not an infringement of any existing copyright and will indemnify the publisher against any breach of such warranty. For ease of dissemination and to ensure proper policing of use, papers and contributions become the legal copyright of the publisher unless otherwise agreed.

Editorial objectives

The journal will provide: a forum for those with a broad managerial as well as professional interest in audit to explore current practices, ideas and experience; a framework of explanation and guidance on developments and research; perspectives on professional and career development.

General principles

a. It is our intention to maintain a sound balance between theory and practice and to inform readers of current issues and new theoretical developments.
b. Contributors will be encouraged to concentrate on the practical implications of their work.
c. Articles based on experiences and evidence will receive particular encouragement.
d. A series of short articles on a linked theme appearing in successive issues would be particularly welcome.

The reviewing process

Each paper submitted is subject to the following review procedures:

1. It is reviewed by the editor for general suitability for this publication.
2. If it is judged suitable two reviewers are selected and a double blind review process takes place.
3. Based on the recommendations of the reviewers, the editor then decides whether the particular article should be accepted as it is, revised or rejected.

The process described above is a general one. The editor, however, may, in some circumstances, vary this process.

Emerald Literati Editing Service

The Literati Club can recommend the services of a number of freelance copy editors, all themselves experienced authors, to contributors who wish to improve the standard of English in their paper before submission. This is particularly useful for those whose first language is not English. **http://www.emeraldinsight.com/literaticlub/editingservice.htm**

Manuscript requirements

One copy of the manuscript should be submitted in Microsoft Word format by email only, with double line spacing with wide margins. All authors should be shown and author's details must be printed on a separate sheet and the author should not be identified anywhere else in the article.

Authors must supply a structured abstract set out under 4-6 sub-headings: Purpose; Methodology/Approach; Findings; Research limitations/implications (if applicable); Practical implications (if applicable); and, the Originality/value of paper. Maximum is 250 words in total. In addition provide up to six keywords which encapsulate the principal topics of the paper and categorise your paper under one of these classifications: Research paper, Viewpoint, Technical paper, Conceptual paper, Case study, Literature review or General review. For more information and guidance on structured abstracts visit:

http://www.emeraldinsight.com/literaticlub/editors/editorialadmin/abstracts.htm

Where there is a **methodology**, it should be clearly described under a separate heading. **Headings** must be short, clearly defined and not numbered. **Notes** or **Endnotes** should be used only if absolutely necessary and must be identified in the text by consecutive numbers, enclosed in square brackets and listed at the end of the article.

Figures, charts and **diagrams** should be kept to a minimum. They must be black and white with minimum shading and numbered consecutively using Arabic numerals with a brief title and labelled axes. In the text, the position of the figure should be shown by typing on a separate line the words "take in Figure 2". Good quality originals must be provided.

Tables should be kept to a minimum. They must be numbered consecutively with roman numerals and a brief title. In the text, the position of the table should be shown by typing on a separate line the words "take in Table IV"

Photos and **illustrations** must be supplied as good quality black and white original half tones with captions. Their position should be shown in the text by typing on a separate line the words "take in Plate 2".

References to other publications should be complete and in Harvard style. They should contain full bibliographical details and journal titles should not be abbreviated. For multiple citations in the same year use a, b, c immediately following the year of publication. References should be shown within the text by giving the author's last name followed by a comma and year of publication all in round brackets, e.g. (Fox, 1994). At the end of the article should be a reference list in alphabetical order as follows:

(a) *for books*
surname, initials and year of publication, title, publisher, place of publication, e.g. Casson, M. (1979), Alternatives to the Multinational Enterprise, Macmillan, London.

(b) *for chapter in edited book*
surname, initials and year, "title", editor's surname, initials, title, publisher, place, pages, e.g.Bessley, M. and Wilson, P. (1984), "Public policy and small firms in Britain", in Levicki, C. (Ed.), Small Business Theory and Policy, Croom Helm, London, pp.111-26. Please note that the chapter title must be underlined.

(c) *for articles*
surname, initials, year "title", journal, volume, number, pages, e.g.Fox, S. (1994) "Empowerment as a catalyst for change: an example from the food industry", Supply Chain Management, Vol 2 No 3, pp. 29-33

If there is more than one author list surnames followed by initials. All authors should be shown.

Electronic sources should include the URL of the electronic site at which they may be found, as follows:

Neuman, B.C.(1995), "Security, payment, and privacy for network commerce", IEEE Journal on Selected Areas in Communications, Vol. 13 No.8, October, pp.1523-31. Available (IEEE SEPTEMBER) http://www.research.att.com/jsac/

Notes/Endnotes should be used only if absolutely necessary. They should, however, always be used for citing Web sites. They should be identified in the text by consecutive numbers enclosed in square brackets and listed at the end of the article. Please then provide full Web site addresses in the end list.

Final submission of the article
Once accepted for publication, the final version of the manuscript must be provided by email with: author name(s); title of article; journal title; file name.

Each article must be accompanied by a completed and signed Journal Article Record Form available from the Editor or on http://www.emeraldinsight.com/literaticlub Authors should note that proofs are not supplied prior to publication.

The manuscript will be considered to be the definitive version of the article. The author must ensure that it is complete, grammatically correct and without spelling or typographical errors.

Technical assistance is available from Emerald's Literati Club on the website at http://www.emeraldinsight.com/literaticlub or by contacting Mike Massey at Emerald, e-mail mmassey@emeraldinsight.com.

A summary of submission requirements:
- Good quality hard copy manuscript
- A labelled disk
- A brief professional biography of each author
- An abstract and keywords
- Figures, photos and graphics electronically and as good quality originals
- Harvard style references where appropriate
- A completed Journal Article Record form

Massachusetts CPA Review Online

ADDRESS FOR SUBMISSION:

Kara Daszkiewicz, PR Coordinator
Massachusetts CPA Review Online
MA Soc. of Certified Public Accountants
105 Chauncy Street, 10th Floor
Boston, MA 02111
USA
Phone: 617-556-4000
E-Mail: kdaszkiewicz@mscpaonline.org
Web: www.mscpaonline.org

CIRCULATION DATA:

Reader: Business Persons
Frequency of Issue: Quarterly Electonic
Sponsor/Publisher: Massachusetts Society
of Certified Public Accountants

PUBLICATION GUIDELINES:

Manuscript Length: 1,500 Words
Copies Required: Electronic
Computer Submission: Yes
Format: MAC/PC, Text WP or ASCII
Fees to Review: 0.00 US$

Manuscript Style:
See Manuscript Guidelines

REVIEW INFORMATION:

Type of Review: Blind Review
No. of External Reviewers: 0
No. of In House Reviewers: 1-2
Acceptance Rate: No Reply
Time to Review: 2 - 3 Months
Reviewers Comments: No
Invited Articles: No Reply
Fees to Publish: 0.00 US$

MANUSCRIPT TOPICS:
Accounting Education; Accounting Information Systems; Accounting Theory & Practice; Auditing; Behavioral Accounting; Cost Accounting; Financial Services; Government & Non Profit Accounting; Industrial Organization; Insurance; Real Estate; Tax Accounting

MANUSCRIPT GUIDELINES/COMMENTS:

1. The editors often receive inquiries from CPAs and other who would like to write articles for the *CPA Review*, but aren't sure what we need or how to get started. Here are some hints and guidelines for authors on what the *CPA Review* editors are seeking.

2. Pertinent and interesting articles are the lifeblood of any magazine. Relevant articles are essential to the continuing quality of the *CPA Review*. We will always have a need for practical and suitable articles of interest to Massachusetts' professional accountants, financial executives, and educators.

3. The editors specifically consider the following questions in reviewing articles for publication in the *Review*:
- Is the topic suitable and of interest to our Massachusetts and New England readers?
- Does the article contribute new ideas or insights?
- Is the article concise and does the author cover the subject in sufficient depth?

4. The types of manuscripts that we are most likely to publish fall into three categories:
- articles that help solve practice problems or that advance "leading edge" management accounting techniques,
- penetrating analysis of important developments in taxation, education, computers, management advisory services, business, accounting and auditing, and
- insightful, pertinent opinion, interviews, letters, and short articles with a how-to-do-it or local Massachusetts slant. Highly theoretical papers are less desirable than practical, relevant articles primarily based on examples drawn from your experience.

5. The *Review* has had a generally favorable reaction to its series of interviews and roundtable discussions with prominent educators, business leaders, and political figures. We will continue to publish such articles from time to time.

6. A succinctly written article covering a suitable topic in depth will probably be published. The author's professional writing ability is a less important consideration.

7. Often, a brief and specific outline of a proposed manuscript can serve as a prompt means of obtaining a reaction to your ideas. Of course, the final acceptance of an article for publication can only be made after reading the completed manuscript.

8. There are, in short, numerous writing opportunities for prospective authors in the *CPA Review*. The editors are eager to assist anyone who would like to write for the magazine. We need you! The greater the number of quality manuscripts that we have to choose from the better we can achieve the primary goal of the *CPA Review*: to furnish useful, practical, and interesting information to our readers that will help them in their professional careers.

9. Clarity of thought and economy of words are two precious characteristics of well-written articles. Feature article treatment requires that the discussion of the topic be comprehensive. The *CPA Review* editors prefer articles of 1,500 words, or less.

Such brevity of expression might be difficult for some writers. The editors suggest that authors use the following style conventions and formats to help attain the appropriate level of topic coverage and article length:
- Write mostly in the active voice.
- Use relatively short sentences and paragraphs for most of the article. Keep it simple; make it forceful.
- Avoid the use of extensive checklists, footnotes, and tabulations.
- Review your manuscript for consistency of expression and format. (Eliminate any inconsistent or redundant material.)
- Don't overuse arcane jargon or technical lingo.

10. By adhering to the following minor "rules", you will make life less complicated for the CPA Review editors responsible for reviewing your manuscript:
- Include a cover page indicating the suggested article title, the author's name, address, and telephone number, and the date.

- Type your manuscript with double spacing and with generous margins. (Eight to ten typed pages, double spaced is about the maximum length for a feature article.)
- Submit manuscript electronically.
- Identify all borrowed or quoted material and identify sources in footnotes or references.
- Use brief titles and section subheadings.

11. Usually, two or three editors and staff members read each manuscript for editorial consideration and technical content. We attempt to complete the review process and notify authors regarding acceptance within 45 days.

12. There you have it - a few guidelines and suggestions for having your article published in the *CPA Review*. We wish you success. Our *CPA Review* readers and we look forward to reading your article.

Midwestern Business and Economic Review

ADDRESS FOR SUBMISSION:

James R. Owen, Editor
Midwestern Business and Economic
   Review
Midwestern State University
College of Business Administration
3410 Taft Blvd.
Wichita Falls, TX 76308
USA
Phone: 940-397-4661
E-Mail: james.owen@mwsu.edu
Web:

PUBLICATION GUIDELINES:

Manuscript Length: 16-25 Pages
Copies Required: Four
Computer Submission: Yes
Format: MS Word or RTF
Fees to Review: 0.00 US$

Manuscript Style:
   American Psychological Association

CIRCULATION DATA:

Reader: Academics, Business Persons
Frequency of Issue: 2 Times/Year
Sponsor/Publisher: Midwestern State
   University College of Business
   Administration

REVIEW INFORMATION:

Type of Review: Blind Review
No. of External Reviewers: 2
No. of In House Reviewers: 1
Acceptance Rate: 35-40%
Time to Review: 2 - 3 Months
Reviewers Comments: No
Invited Articles: 0-5%
Fees to Publish: 0.00 US$

MANUSCRIPT TOPICS:

Accounting Education; Accounting Information Systems; Accounting Theory & Practice; Auditing; Behavioral Accounting; Cost Accounting; Econometrics; Economic Development; Economic History; Financial Services; Fiscal Policy; Government & Non Profit Accounting; Industrial Organization; Insurance; International Economics & Trade; International Finance; Macro Economics; Micro Economics; Monetary Policy; Portfolio & Security Analysis; Public Policy Economics; Real Estate; Regional Economics; Tax Accounting

MANUSCRIPT GUIDELINES/COMMENTS:

The *Midwestern Business and Economic Review* invites submissions of original manuscripts and research by individuals in the public and private sector in the areas of economics and business administration Of particular interest are topics dealing with issues relevant to Texas and the Southwestern United States. Each manuscript submitted is anonymously reviewed by members of the Editorial Review Board and ad hoc reviews as needed. To meet the interest of a broad spectrum of the academic and business community, readability and expository clarity are considered essential in the review process.

All manuscripts submitted for review must meet the following guidelines:
- The manuscript should be double spaced, with 1" margins, and should not exceed twenty pages, including tables, figures, and references
- The first page should include the title of the article and an abstract not exceeding 100 words
- Endnotes are preferred over footnotes
- References should follow the American Psychological Association
- All tables and figures should be included on separate pages

A cover letter should be included with the submission containing the following:
- Title of manuscript
- Name, degree, rank, and affiliation of each author
- Contact information for each author (mailing address, telephone number, and email address)
- A brief biographical sketch of each author

It is preferred that each manuscript be accompanied by an electronic copy of the manuscript on a 3 ½" diskette, formatted in Microsoft Word or rich-text (RTF) formats. If an electronic copy is not submitted with the manuscript, one will be requested if the manuscript is selected for publication.

All manuscripts should be submitted to: Editor, Midwestern Business and Economic Review, Bureau of Business and Government Research, Midwestern State University, 3410 Taft Boulevard, Wichita Falls, Texas 76308-2099.

Multinational Business Review

ADDRESS FOR SUBMISSION:

Hongxi John Zhao, Editor
Multinational Business Review
Saint Louis University
Boeing Institute of International Bus.
John Cook School of Business
3674 Lindell Boulevard, Suite 332
St. Louis, MO 63108
USA
Phone: 314-977-3630
E-Mail: mbr@slu.edu
Web: mbr.slu.edu

PUBLICATION GUIDELINES:

Manuscript Length: 7,000 Words
Copies Required: Three
Computer Submission: Yes
Format: MS Word
Fees to Review: 50.00 US$
   30.00 US$ Journal Subscribers

Manuscript Style:
, Journal of International Business
Studies

CIRCULATION DATA:

Reader: Business Persons, Academics
Frequency of Issue: 3 Times/Year
Sponsor/Publisher: Boeing Institute of
   International Business / John Cook
   School of Business / St. Louis University

REVIEW INFORMATION:

Type of Review: Blind Review
No. of External Reviewers: 2
No. of In House Reviewers: 1
Acceptance Rate: 30%
Time to Review: 8 weeks
Reviewers Comments: Yes
Invited Articles: 0-5%
Fees to Publish: 0.00 US$

MANUSCRIPT TOPICS:
Accounting Information Systems; Auditing; International Accounting; Tax Accounting

MANUSCRIPT GUIDELINES/COMMENTS:

Multinational Business Review (*MBR*) solicits and welcomes articles of interest to academics as well as practitioners, with at least one "Practitioner Insights" article per issue. Collaborative papers between academicians and practitioners are encouraged, especially with corporate case studies with a global scope. All submissions should be original, not previously published, not accepted for publication, and not under consideration by another journal. The only exception is papers presented at a conference as a work-in-progress and subsequently published in conference proceedings. Specific formatting guidelines and submission instructions for email and mail are provided on the website. Should an article be accepted for publication, the author will receive special instructions for final submittal. *MBR* will have the copyright to all published articles – authors will be asked to sign a Copyright Release Form. Approval of a final proof will be required prior to publication.

National Accounting Journal (The)

ADDRESS FOR SUBMISSION:

W. Terry Dancer, Editor
National Accounting Journal (The)
8083 Highway 351
Jonesboro, AR 72401
USA
Phone: 870-935-1579
E-Mail: dancer@astate.edu
Web: Not yet available

CIRCULATION DATA:

Reader: Academics
Frequency of Issue: 2 Times/Year
Sponsor/Publisher: World Wide Publishing

PUBLICATION GUIDELINES:

Manuscript Length: 5-20
Copies Required: Three
Computer Submission: Yes
Format:
Fees to Review: 50.00 US$

Manuscript Style:
, Accounting Review Style

REVIEW INFORMATION:

Type of Review: Blind Review
No. of External Reviewers: 2
No. of In House Reviewers: 1
Acceptance Rate: 21-30%
Time to Review: 1 - 2 Months
Reviewers Comments: No
Invited Articles: 0-5%
Fees to Publish: 25.00 US$ Per Page

MANUSCRIPT TOPICS:
Accounting Education; Accounting Information Systems; Accounting Theory & Practice; Auditing; Behavioral Accounting; Cost Accounting; Government & Non Profit Accounting; Real Estate; Tax Accounting

MANUSCRIPT GUIDELINES/COMMENTS:

Statement of Policy
The *National Accounting Journal* (*NAJ*) is a refereed Accounting journal dedicated to the promotion of excellence in Accounting Education and the advancement of Accounting knowledge. The *Journal* provides a forum for the exchange of ideas, concepts, theories, and research results among college and university level educators. The journal will publish items ranging from brief educational notes to full length manuscripts. The intended readership of this journal is accounting academicians and accounting practitioners.

Manuscripts are subject to blind review. Reviewers will assess the professional quality with which the manuscript was prepared and evaluate the appropriateness for inclusion of the manuscript in the journal.

Manuscripts submitted to *IJBD* are expected to be free from grammatical and spelling errors. Authors are expected to have their manuscript examined by a grammarian before submitting a paper for review.

Manuscript Requirements
Three copies of each item submitted for review should be sent to: Dr. W. Terry Dancer, Editor, The National Accounting Journal, 8083 Highway 351, Jonesboro, AR., 72401. During the 2005-2006 year, the review fee for completed manuscripts will be $50.00, and the review fee for brief educational notes (three pages or less) will be $25.00. If a paper is accepted for publication, authors will be assessed a $25.00 per page publication fee.

The initial review process will require about six weeks. The focus on this initial review will be on the content of the item being reviewed. The format of your original submission is far less important than the content of the paper submitted. Authors of accepted papers will be given specific instructions for the appropriate format of the item to be published.

A letter of transmittal must accompany each paper submitted for review. The letter of transmittal should include the authors complete mailing address, affiliation, telephone number, fax number,, and E-mail address if available. Author names should be mentioned only on the title page.

Authors of accepted items will be required to submit a disk containing a file with the final version of the item keyboarded in Word perfect or Word and a hard copy of their final version. The Times New Roman 12pt font should be used exclusively, except where a special font is necessary. The table function should be used for all tables. Citations should be made in square brackets using the authors' last name, date, and where necessary, page number and a shortened form of the title. *The Accounting Review* should be referred to as an example of the correct style for citations.

By submitting a manuscript, the authors agree to transfer the right to the publisher to reproduce and distribute the item published. Authors may expect all items received by *NAJ* to be reviewed in a timely and efficient manner.

Subscription requests from libraries and individuals should be sent to the address noted above. The subscription rate for 2005-2006, is $100.00 per year.

National Tax Journal

ADDRESS FOR SUBMISSION:

Editor
National Tax Journal
Northwestern University
Kellogg School of Management
2001 Sheridan Road
Evanston, IL 60208
USA
Phone: 847-491-0257
E-Mail: NTJ@kellogg.northwestern.edu
Web: www.ntanet.org

PUBLICATION GUIDELINES:

Manuscript Length: 50 double-spaced Pgs
Copies Required: Four
Computer Submission: Yes
Format: MS Word, WordPerfect
Fees to Review: 0.00 US$

Manuscript Style:
    Chicago Manual of Style

CIRCULATION DATA:

Reader: Academics, Tax
    Practioners/Policymakers, Business
    Persons
Frequency of Issue: Quarterly
Sponsor/Publisher: National Tax
    Association

REVIEW INFORMATION:

Type of Review: Blind Review
No. of External Reviewers: 2
No. of In House Reviewers: 1
Acceptance Rate: 15%
Time to Review: 2-4 Months
Reviewers Comments: Yes
Invited Articles: 31-40 %
Fees to Publish: 0.00 US$

MANUSCRIPT TOPICS:
Fiscal Policy; Government Accounting; Public Economics; Public Policy Economics; Tax Accounting

MANUSCRIPT GUIDELINES/COMMENTS:

Submission Instructions
Hard copies of manuscripts should be submitted in quadruplicate and authors should retain their original copies. Alternatively, electronic submissions in MS Word or WordPerfect may be sent to **ntj@kellogg.northwestern.edu**. All submitted manuscripts should be accompanied by an abstract of 100 words or fewer and should not exceed 50 double-spaced pages (including tables, figures and appendices). The *NTJ* will consider only those manuscripts not currently under submission elsewhere.

Subscription
The annual subscription rate is US$90 (US$155 library) per year for domestic subscribers and US$100 (US$165 library) per year for foreign subscribers. Please order your subscription using the online form. Single back issues of the *Journal* are available for US$15, subject to availability.

The *National Tax Journal* (*NTJ*) is a refereed journal that is designed to be read by academics, tax administrators, businesspersons, lawyers, and accountants interested in government finance.

The *NTJ* is published quarterly by the National Tax Association as one method of fulfilling certain of the purposes of the organization, namely to encourage research in government finance by all interested persons and the dissemination of the resultant knowledge.

As a continuing editorial policy, the journal published contributions to knowledge in its area of concerns chosen by the editors from those submissions that have been positively evaluated by professional peers prior to publication, except when symposia proceedings are reported. Such contributions may be an addition to present knowledge whether institutional, empirical or analytical; a new methodology or administrative development; an evaluation of the pros and cons of a currently relevant policy problem; or a speculative and reflective treatment of an unsettled issue in government finance. All articles, whether administrative, economic, legal or policy in character, are refereed by practitioners or scholars in their particular fields prior to publication. As a matter of editorial policy, material previously published or scheduled for publication elsewhere will not be considered by the *NTJ*.

Within this policy framework, the journal seeks to present a broad spectrum of professional subject matter dealing with government finance and taxation to both members of the Association and others concerned with public sector finance and policy.

In preparing papers for the *Journal*, authors should bear in mind the diverse membership of the NTA—accountants, lawyers, business and government tax administrators and academicians—and write in a style that will communicate to them all. In particular, in every paper submitted to the *NTJ*, we require a self-contained summary and conclusions section fully accessible to the nonspecialist that, while brief, nevertheless is of sufficient size to communicate the substance and the significance of the paper to all readers. Technical and methodological discussions, kept to a minimum, should be placed in the appendix, whenever possible. Authors who wish to do so may note in their paper that additional data and/or explanation of methods and results are available on request.

New Accountant

ADDRESS FOR SUBMISSION:

Editor
New Accountant
3550 West Peterson
Chicago, Il 60659
USA
Phone: 773-866-9900
E-Mail: rencpublishing@earthlink.net
Web: newaccountantusa.com

CIRCULATION DATA:

Reader: Academics
Frequency of Issue: 6 Times/Year
Sponsor/Publisher: Profit Oriented Corp.

PUBLICATION GUIDELINES:

Manuscript Length: 6-10
Copies Required: One
Computer Submission: Yes
Format: Microsoft Word 6.0
Fees to Review: 0.00 US$

Manuscript Style:

REVIEW INFORMATION:

Type of Review: Blind Review
No. of External Reviewers: 5
No. of In House Reviewers: 2
Acceptance Rate: 21-30%
Time to Review: 3 Months or Less
Reviewers Comments: No
Invited Articles: 6-10%
Fees to Publish: 0.00 US$

MANUSCRIPT TOPICS:
Accounting Information Systems; Auditing; Capital Budgeting; Government & Non Profit Accounting; Insurance; International Finance

MANUSCRIPT GUIDELINES/COMMENTS:

Articles for *New Accountant* must appeal to students and the profession.

Oil, Gas & Energy Quarterly

ADDRESS FOR SUBMISSION:

Larry Crumbley, Editor
Oil, Gas & Energy Quarterly
Louisiana State University
Department of Accounting
3101 CEBA, #3106A
Baton Rouge, LA 70803
USA
Phone: 225-578-6231
E-Mail: dcrumbl@lsu.edu
Web: www.bus.lsu.edu/academics/accou
nting/faculty/lcrumbley/oilgas.html

PUBLICATION GUIDELINES:

Manuscript Length: 11 - 20
Copies Required: Two
Computer Submission: Yes
Format: Wordstar or WordPerfect
Fees to Review: 0.00 US$

Manuscript Style:
See Manuscript Guidelines

CIRCULATION DATA:

Reader: Business Persons
Frequency of Issue: Quarterly
Sponsor/Publisher: Profit Oriented Corp.

REVIEW INFORMATION:

Type of Review: Blind Review
No. of External Reviewers: 1
No. of In House Reviewers: 1
Acceptance Rate: 30-40%
Time to Review: 3 Months
Reviewers Comments: No
Invited Articles: 11-20%
Fees to Publish: 0.00 US$

MANUSCRIPT TOPICS:

Accounting Information Systems; Accounting Theory & Practice; Auditing; Cost Accounting; Fiscal Policy; International Finance; Natural Resources; Oil & Gas Accounting; Oil & Gas Taxation; Tax Accounting; Timber

MANUSCRIPT GUIDELINES/COMMENTS:

Articles by specialists and educators are needed on a quarterly basis. The manuscripts should explore the most significant current developments in oil and gas taxation, accounting, finance, and economics. Severance and excise tax issues and important state tax developments are appropriate topics. Other natural resources articles are also requested (e.g., coal, timber). Research studies derived from empirical and analytical methodologies are encouraged. Need 2 hard copies plus a computer disk.

Manuscripts should be sent to:
D. Larry Crumbley, Editor
Department of Accounting, Louisiana State University
3101 CEBA, #3106A, Baton Rouge, LA 70803
Phone: 225-578-6231; Fax: 225-578-6201; Email: **dcrumbl@lsu.edu**

Style Sheet
Authors. Please submit articles on both paper and word processing disks and indicate in a cover letter what software and version number were used to produce the disk. (e.g. WordPerfect 6.0, Microsoft Word 2.OA, etc.)

Heading Format
Article title should be centered and have initial caps. Below the article title, author's name should be centered and have initial caps. ("Initial caps" indicates that the first letter in each significant word is capped and the rest is in lower case.) Both article title and author's name should be boldfaced (precede with <BF> and follow with <RO>).
- **First level** - flush left, initial caps, precede heading with <BF> and follow with <RO>.
- **Second level** - beginning of paragraph, initial caps, precede heading with <BF> and end with a period and <RO>.
- **Third level** - beginning of paragraph, initial caps, precede heading with <IT> and end heading with a period and <RO>).
- **Fourth level** - indent one tab further than for normal paragraph, initial caps, underscore heading and end heading with a period.

Example of Heading Format:
<BF>Determining a Distributive Share of Property in Oil and Gas Finance<RO>
<BF>John J. Johnson<RO>
<BF>Property Values<RO>
<BF>Taxable Income from the Property.<RO> [Followed by text of paragraph.]
<IT>Gross Income<RO>. [Followed by text of paragraph.]

In General. [Followed by text of paragraph.]

Text
- Indent paragraphs five spaces.
- Use abbreviations sparingly.
- Acceptable illustrations: original artwork, glossy black-and-white photographs, ink drawings, printed forms and materials (Photocopies, unless very clear and legible, are usually not acceptable.)
- Reference first appearing in text should be written out, followed by a short form in parentheses. Later they should appear in the shortened form. For example:
  Internal Revenue Service (Service); subsequently: Service.
  Internal Revenue Code (Code) Section 331; subsequently: Code Section 331.
  Statement of Financial Accounting Standards (SFAS) No. 39; subsequently: SFAS No. 39.
- Quotations longer than 25 words should be block indented, but should still be surrounded by opening and closing quotation marks.

Footnotes
- Footnotes should be placed at the end of the article.
- Abbreviate wherever possible. Examples:
    I.R.C. §331
    Treas. Reg. §1.415-1(STRONG) (but: Temporary Treas. Reg.)
    Ltr. Rul.
- Abbreviate names of months and states.
- Case names are listed without underscores, unless they are incomplete or their citations do not immediately follow.
- Some common abbreviations in case citations:
    o   9th Cir., Fed. Reg., 2d Cir., 3d Cir.

Examples of references to periodical titles in footnotes:
Jones, "The Effect of the Tax Reform Act of 1978 on Limited Partnerships," **37 Harv. L. Rev.** 565, 570-573 (1980).

Blatz & Weirich, "Texas Oil and Gas Taxation," 31 **Oil & Gas Tax Q.** 249 (Sept. 1979).

Example of reference to books in footnotes:
Burke & Bowhay, **Income Taxation of Natural Resources** 1206 (1983).

Examples of footnotes in general:
1. Brown v. Green, 654 F. Supp. 309, 314-315(E.D. Cal., 1968), rev'd, 437 F.2d 594 (9th Cir. 1969).
2. ID. at 202.
3. 15 U.S.C. § 104(STRONG).
4. See note 1 supra.

Who Should Subscribe
- Accountants and attorneys in the energy industry.
- Financial and operating executives.
- Investment bankers, analysts, brokers, and traders.
- Bankers involved in energy financing.
- Major energy consumers and policy makers.
- Individuals with energy-related responsibilities (i.e., educators, legislators, reporters).

Operations Research

ADDRESS FOR SUBMISSION:

David Simchi-Levi, Editor
Operations Research
Massachusetts Institute of Technology
Department of Civil and Environmental
 Engineering
1-171
Cambridge, MA 02139
USA
Phone: 617-253-6160
E-Mail: dslevi@mit.edu
Web: http://or.pubs.informs.org;
  http://mc.manuscriptcentral.com/opre

PUBLICATION GUIDELINES:

Manuscript Length: Any
Copies Required: Four
Computer Submission: Yes Online
Format:
Fees to Review: 0.00 US$

Manuscript Style:
  Chicago Manual of Style

CIRCULATION DATA:

Reader: Academics
Frequency of Issue: Bi-Monthly
Sponsor/Publisher: Institute for Operations
 Research and Management Science
 (INFORMS)

REVIEW INFORMATION:

Type of Review: Editorial Review
No. of External Reviewers: 3
No. of In House Reviewers: 1
Acceptance Rate: 21-30%
Time to Review: 4 - 6 Months
Reviewers Comments: Yes
Invited Articles: 0-5%
Fees to Publish: 0.00 US$

MANUSCRIPT TOPICS:
Cost Accounting

MANUSCRIPT GUIDELINES/COMMENTS:

Topics Include. Computing and Decision Technology; Decision Analysis; Environment, Energy and Natural Resources; Financial Engineering; Manufacturing, Service and Supply Chain Operations; Marketing Science; Military OR; Optimization; OR Forum; OR Practice; Revenue Management; Simulation; Stochastic Models; Telecommunications and Networking; Transportation.

Subscription can be found at: **www.informs.org/Pubs/PubsIndividual.pdf**.

General Considerations
To submit a paper to *Operations Research*, the author should visit the online submission site at **http://mc.manuscriptcentral.com/opre**

Papers not in the fields covered by the Area Editors should besubmitted to the Editor.

Papers should **not** be sent to the Associate Editors.

Submission of a manuscript is a representation that the paper has neither been published nor submitted for publication elsewhere, and that, if the work is officially sponsored, it has been released for open publication.

Manuscripts will not be returned to an author unless specifically requested, or unless reviewers have provided annotations that will be of use to the author.

The text should be arranged as follows: title page, abstract, introduction, main sections, appendix, acknowledgment, and references. Appendices and an acknowledgment are optional. If a paper is accepted for publication, the Editor may request (or require) that supporting appendix material is placed online at the *Operations Research* web site. Authors should consider this either during the initial submission phase or during the final revisions of the paper and may wish to design their papers accordingly.

Personal Web Sites. Upon acceptance of a paper to *Operations Research,* the author must remove all copies of the paper from any web sites. The copyright belongs to INFORMS and placement of the paper on a web site is a violation of the copyright transfer agreement. Prior to publication in *Operations Research,* the authors must submit a signed copy of the Authors' Web Site Disclosure Form.

Observe the following points in preparing manuscripts. Papers not conforming closely to these instructions may be returned to their authors for appropriate revisions or may be delayed in the review process.

1. **Readability.** The abstract and the introduction of every paper must be free of unnecessary jargon and clearly readable by any INFORMS member. These sections should be written in an expository style that will be comprehensible to readers who are not technical experts in the subject matter.

2. **Title Page.** Each paper should have a title page that contains the author(s)' name(s) and address(es). The usual acknowledgments should be placed in a separate section at the back of the manuscript.

3. **Abstract.** Preface each article with a self-contained, one-paragraph abstract that summarizes the problem and the principal results and conclusions. It should not contain formulas, references or abbreviations, nor exceed 200 words.

4. **Introduction.** The introduction must clearly state the problem, the results to be found in the paper and their significance to the OR community. It should not contain equations or mathematical notation. Section numbering and headings begins here.

5. **Main Sections.** The main sections of the paper must be readable, the level of the mathematics and/or the terminology appropriate to the topic, and the material logically presented.

6. **Style**. The message of the paper will be enhanced if it is presented in active, forceful, and concise prose. Good writing is a craft at least as difficult as doing operations research. While the Editor and staff will correct minor lapses from good style in the manuscript, they cannot undertake wholesale revisions of poorly written papers. There is no set limit to the number of pages for a paper; however, conciseness and clarity of presentation are important publication criteria.

7. **Spacing and Format**. Double-space manuscripts throughout, including the abstract, subsidiary matter (list of captions, for example), and references. In general, keep figures and tables to a minimum. Each page of the manuscript should be numbered. Indent the first line of each paragraph.

8. **Footnotes**. *Operations Research* does not use footnotes; incorporate subsidiary material that would otherwise appear in footnotes in the main text, possibly in parentheses or brackets, or place it in a Notes section at the end of the text, before the Acknowledgment and References. Designate notes by using superscript numerals placed in serial order throughout the text.

9. **Acknowledgments**. Place acknowledgments of presentation, support, and assistance in a final section that precedes the References, not on the title page.

10. **References**. List only those references that are cited in the text. References in the text should be cited by the author's surname and the year of publication, for example, Flood (1962). If the reference has two or three authors, cite all of the authors' surnames and the year of publication—Flood, Smith and Jones (1982). If the reference has more than three authors, cite the first author's surname followed by et al. and the year of publication—Brown et al. (1985).

If there are more than one reference by the same author with the same year of publication, the first citation appearing in the text would read Flood (1962a), the second citation would read Flood (1962b), etc. Do not use parentheses or brackets for dates when the citation is already enclosed within parentheses.

At the end of the paper list references alphabetically by the last name of the first author. Do not number the reference list. Double-space this final section.

For journal references, give the author, year of publication, title, journal name, volume, and pages, for example:
FLOOD, M. M. 1962. New Operations Research Potentials. *Opns. Res.* 10,423-436.

For book references, give the author, year of publication, title, publisher, city, state, and pages, for example:
MORSE, P. M., AND G. E. KIMBALL. 1951. Methods of Operations Research. John Wiley, New York, 44-65.

For references to working papers or dissertations cite the author, title, type of document, department, university, and location, for example:

ROSENWEIN, M. 1986. Design and Application of Solution Methodologies to Optimize Problems in Transportation Logistics. Ph.D. Dissertation. Department of Decision Sciences, University of Pennsylvania, Philadelphia.

11. **Mathematical Expressions**. Within the text, use the solidus whenever possible in preference to built-up fractions: e.g., $a/(1-b)$ exponentials in the form $\exp(\ )$; avoid subscripts or superscripts on subscripts or superscripts; and, in general, minimize unusual typographical requirements. For displayed equations, use built-up fractions. Avoid lengthy equations that will take several lines to typeset (possibly by defining terms of the equations in separate displays).

Make subscripts and superscripts large and clear, and shown in a clearly inferior or superior position. The letter l and the numeral 1, and the letter O and the numeral 0, which are identical on most keyboards, should be identified. Symbols and Greek letters should be identified clearly. On their first occurrence, label unusual or ambiguous symbols by marginal notes. The difference between upper and lower case letters should be clear.

Display only those mathematical expressions that must be numbered for later reference or that need to be emphasized. Number displayed equations consecutively throughout the paper; do not number equations by section numbers. Appendix equations can be labeled A1, A2, etc. The numbers should be placed in parentheses to the right of the equation.

12. **Tables**. Tables should be numbered with Arabic numerals, have a title, and be referred to sequentially in the text. Column headings should be brief and not use abbreviations. Do not use vertical rules. The use of footnotes is encouraged; designate these by lower case letters. The submission of original tables suitable for reproduction is not necessary; all tables will be typeset for consistency. Each table should be on a separate sheet and not interleaved in the text.

13. **Figures**. Figures should be professionally drawn or laser-printed and suitable for photographic reproduction. All figures must be in black and white. Color figures will be printed in black and white and do not scan properly. The author is responsible for the quality of the final form of the figure(s). Figures are scanned and corrections on page proofs are costly. Do not clutter the figure with information that makes it difficult to read. To avoid an undesirable moiré effect when scanned, figures should be shaded with a coarse pattern rather than a fine screen. Line weights should be consistent and at least .25 points after reduction. Lettering in the body of the figure should be proportional to the graphic and be typed.

Most figures will be reduced to approximately 3¼" in width. For optimal quality, please submit final figures close to that size. All details on the figures should be checked carefully because correction on proofs necessitates reshooting.

Each figure must be cited and will be placed in the order mentioned in the text. Each figure must have a caption and a number (Arabic). Do not place the caption on the original of the figure. Place captions on a separate sheet. Do not differentiate between illustrations and figures.

14. **Subject Classification Scheme for the OR/MS Index.** Subject Classification Keywords Determine the appropriate subject classifications (up to 3) and accompanying descriptive phrases for all work submitted. Choose from one to three subject categories for each manuscript. For every category chosen, write a short phrase that puts the paper in context. (The phrase can be a concise rendering of the title, or it may specify some aspect of the paper that is import ant but not apparent in the title.) The length of each phrase, including spaces and punctuation, should not exceed 60 characters. This information will be printed on the title page of every article, technical note, and letter that is published.

Subject categories and phrases must appear on the title page of the manuscript.

15. **Reprints.** *Operations Research* does not have paper charges, nor does it supply free reprints. Authors of accepted articles may order reprints at reasonable rates at the time they submit their corrected galley proofs. Reprints of individual articles are not available from INFORMS.

Managing Editor. Janet Kerrigan, Department of Civil and Environmental Engineering, Massachusetts Institute of Technology 30 Wadsworth Street, 1-176 Cambridge, MA 02139, **kerrigan@MIT.EDU** Phone (617) 258-8409, Fax (617) 324-2546.

Pacific Accounting Review

ADDRESS FOR SUBMISSION:

van Zijl, Dunston, Lally & Brown, Co-Eds
Pacific Accounting Review
Victoria University of Wellington
School of Accounting & Commercial Law
The Business Manager
PO Box 600
Wellington,
New Zealand
Phone: 00 64 4 463 5078
E-Mail: See Guidelines
Web: www.par.ac.nz

CIRCULATION DATA:

Reader: Academics
Frequency of Issue: 2 Times/Year
Sponsor/Publisher: See Guidelines

PUBLICATION GUIDELINES:

Manuscript Length: 26-30
Copies Required: Four
Computer Submission: Yes Disk, Email
Format: MS Word (pdf)
Fees to Review: 18.75 US$
    30.00 NZ

Manuscript Style:
, A4 - double spaced

REVIEW INFORMATION:

Type of Review: Blind Review
No. of External Reviewers: 2
No. of In House Reviewers: 0
Acceptance Rate: 21-30%
Time to Review: 2 - 3 Months
Reviewers Comments: Yes
Invited Articles: 0-5%
Fees to Publish: 18.75 US$
    30.00 NZ

MANUSCRIPT TOPICS:

Accounting Education; Accounting Information Systems; Accounting Theory & Practice; Auditing; Behavioral Accounting; Cost Accounting; Government & Non Profit Accounting; International Finance; Portfolio & Security Analysis; Tax Accounting

MANUSCRIPT GUIDELINES/COMMENTS:

1. Manuscripts should be submitted to: **PacificAccountingReview@vuw.ac.nz**

Manuscripts are submitted with the understanding that they are original, unpublished works and are not being submitted for publication elsewhere. There is no submission fee for individual subscribers to the *Pacific Accounting Review*. A submission fee of $30.00, or the equivalent of a one-year subscription to the *Pacific Accounting Review*, will be charged to non-subscribers. For payment details, please refer to the *Pacific Accounting Review* website.

2. **Manuscripts** should be typewritten on one side of the paper only, double-spaced with wide margins. All pages should be numbered. References, tables, and figures should be typed on separate pages.

3. The **first page** of the manuscript should contain (i) the title, (ii) the name(s) and affiliation of the author(s), contact details including email address, and (iii) any acknowledgements.

4. Authors must supply an **abstract** not exceeding 150 words.

5. Major **headings** should be centralised, in bold capitals and given an Arabic numeral. Secondary headings should be centralised, in bold, lower case (except for the first letter) and numbered as shown. For example:

(1) MAJOR HEADINGS
1.1 Secondary Headings
Tertiary Heading

6. Important **formulae** should be numbered consecutively throughout the manuscript as (1), (2), etc on the right hand side of the page. Lengthy derivations should be included as an appendix.

7. **Tables, figures,** and **diagrams** must be titled and consecutively numbered in Arabic. The titles and legends on tables and figures must be sufficiently descriptive so that they are understandable with minimum reference to the text.

8. **References** should appear in the text as "Smith (1991) reports that" or "this has been examined elsewhere (Smith 1991, p. 32)". Footnotes should not be used for referencing. For references with three or more authors, cite the first author and et al. For multiple citations in the same year use "a,b,c," immediately following the year of publication. The full references should appear in alphabetical order, according to the last name of the first author, at the end of the manuscript. The following instructions apply:

Manuscript
Flint, D. (1988). *Philosophy and Principles of Auditing*, Macmillan Education Ltd, Hampshire, England.

Periodicals
Jensen, M.C. and W.H. Meckling (1976). Theory of the Firm: Managerial Behaviour, Agency Costs and Ownership Structure. *Journal of Financial Economics*, 3, 305-360.

Edited Books
Lichtenstein, S., B. Fischhoff and L.D. Philips (1982). Calibration of Probabilities: The State of the Art to 1980. In D. Kahneman, P. Slovic and A. Tversky (eds), *Judgement under Uncertainty: Heuristics and Biases*, Cambridge University Press, Cambridge.

9. **Endnotes** must be numbered consecutively in Arabic and appear as a separate page at the end of the manuscript.

10. If the paper is accepted for publication the authors are requested to email a single-spaced copy of the paper as well as provide a printed copy of the paper. The preferred word processing format is Microsoft Word. Proofs of the formatted article will be sent to the author(s).

This journal is sponsored by the following:
- Auckland University of Technology
- Lincoln University
- Massey University
- Manukau Institute of Technology
- UNITEC Institute of Technology
- University of Auckland
- University of Centerbury
- University of Otago
- University of Waikato
- Victoria University of Wellington

Pennsylvania Journal of Business and Economics

ADDRESS FOR SUBMISSION:

Leon Markowicz, Editor
Pennsylvania Journal of Business and
   Economics
Lebanon Valley College
Lynch 124A
Annville, PA 17003
USA
Phone: 717-867-6104
E-Mail: markowic@lvc.edu
Web:

CIRCULATION DATA:

Reader: Academics
Frequency of Issue: 2 Times/Year
Sponsor/Publisher: Association of
   Pennsylvania University Business and
   Economic Faculties (APUBEF)

PUBLICATION GUIDELINES:

Manuscript Length: 6-10
Copies Required: Three + Zip Disk
Computer Submission: Yes If Accepted
Format: MS Word
Fees to Review: 20.00 US$

Manuscript Style:
   American Psychological Association

REVIEW INFORMATION:

Type of Review: Blind Review
No. of External Reviewers: 2
No. of In House Reviewers: 1
Acceptance Rate: 35%
Time to Review: 2-4 Months
Reviewers Comments: Yes
Invited Articles: 0-5%
Fees to Publish: 0.00 US$

MANUSCRIPT TOPICS:

Accounting Education; Accounting Information Systems; Accounting Theory & Practice; Auditing; Behavioral Accounting; Cost Accounting; Econometrics; Economic Development; Economic History; Financial Services; Fiscal Policy; Government & Non Profit Accounting; Industrial Organization; Insurance; International Economics & Trade; International Finance; Macro Economics; Micro Economics; Monetary Policy; Portfolio & Security Analysis; Public Policy Economics; Real Estate; Regional Economics; Tax Accounting

MANUSCRIPT GUIDELINES/COMMENTS:

The *APUBEF Journal* is a refereed journal aimed at publishing the papers of faculty from the business and economics disciplines within the State System of Higher Education Universities in Pennsylvania, or from business and economics faculty at comparable institutions from within Pennsylvania and from surrounding states. While theoretical works are encouraged, most published papers are empirical or pedagogical in nature.

Send all paper submissions to Leon Markowicz, Pennsylvania Journal of Business and Economics, Lebanon Valley College, Lynch 124A, Annville, PA 17003, 717-867-6104, **markowic@lvc.edu**

Manuscript Style
1. Papers **must** be submitted on a zip disk using MS Word. Three high-quality, hard copies of the paper **must** accompany the disk: one with author information, two without. Printer setup should be HP LaserJet 4.

2. Use 10-point Times New Roman font for the body of the paper and all headings including the heading for **references**. Use 1" margins at top and bottom and 1.25 left and right.

3. Single-space the **text**. Double-space between paragraphs, and indent the first line five spaces using the tab key. Use full-justification.

4. Spell-check before sending the paper, and correct all grammatical errors. Also, edit the paper to address the comments and suggestions of the reviewers and editor.

Specific Requirements
1. Start the manuscript with the **full title**, centered in capitals, bold print. Following a space, each author and university should be identified, one author per line. No titles (Dr., Mr., Mrs., etc.) are to be used; nor should rank be indicated. Please, no fancy type styles other than ones specified. NO headers, footers or page numbers should be incorporated.

2. After the last author's name and affiliation, double-space, center, and type the heading **abstract**, bold and all caps. All papers **must** have an abstract of no more than 150 words, which provides a brief synopsis of the paper.

3. The next heading is **introduction**, bold and all caps. Double-space before and after. All major headings MUST follow this format. Secondary headings MUST be in bold print, left justified, first letter capitalized then lower case, with a space above and below each heading.

4. **Mathematical expressions and notations** should be used judiciously and all symbols should be identified.

5. **Tables** should be arranged sequentially in the order in which the tables are first mentioned in the text and placed at the end of the manuscript. Type the word Table and its Arabic numeral flush-left at the top of the table, double-space, then type the table title flush-left above the table. The explanatory notes to a table such as probability tables, explanations of acronyms, etc., should appear below the table. Use the same 10-point Times NewRoman font as used in the text and the tab function to construct the tables. If a "camera-ready" table is to be used, send the original and not a reduced copy for incorporation in the journal.

6. **Figures** (such as graphs, drawings, photographs, and charts) must be consecutively numbered in Arabic numerals, with their captions in the order they appear in the text. All illustrations must be camera-ready; photographs must be of professional quality, and drawings must be prepared in ink. Illustrations should be identified on the back in light pencil with the name of the author and the figure number.

7. Either **footnotes** or **endnotes** are permitted, but not encouraged. In most cases, the material they contain can be incorporated in the text. If footnotes are used, use the automatic footnote

472

function (Control F7), and specify a Times New Roman 10-point font for their text. Endnotes should be in the same 10-point Times New Roman font as the text and placed after the references.

References

1. When citing references in the text, please use parenthesis, author's name, comma and date of publication, i.e., (Wilson, 1996). For up to three authors, cite each and use the "&" for "and", i.e., (Dawes, Dowling & Peterson, 1992). For more than three authors, use the surname of the first author followed by "et al." comma and the year, i.e., (Cravens et al., 1988). Multiple reference citations in parentheses should be arranged alphabetically and a semi-colon used to separate them, i.e., (Cravens et al., 1988; Dawes, Dowling & Peterson, 1992; Wilson, 1996). Text citations must correspond accurately to the references in the reference list.

2. References should be listed alphabetically at the end of the manuscript. References with the same authors in the same order are arranged according to the year of publication, the earliest first.

3. An American Psychological Association format is used for the references.

For a Journal Article
Buzzell, R.D., Gale, B.T., & Sultan, R.G.M. (1975). Market share—a key to profitability. *Harvard Business Review, 75*(1), 97-106.

For a Book
Czepiel, J.A. (1992). *Competitive Marketing Strategy*. Englewood Cliffs, NJ: Prentice-Hall.

For more information and examples please refer to the *Publication Manual of the American Psychological Association*.

Petroleum Accounting and Financial Management Journal

ADDRESS FOR SUBMISSION:

Teddy L. Coe, Editor
Petroleum Accounting and Financial
   Management Journal
University of North Texas
Institute of Petroleum Accounting
PO Box 305460
Denton, TX 76203-5460
USA
Phone: 940-565-3170 / TDD 800-735-
   2989
E-Mail: coet@unt.edu
Web: www.unt.edu/ipa

PUBLICATION GUIDELINES:

Manuscript Length: 11-20
Copies Required: Three
Computer Submission: Yes
Format: IBM Compatible + Hard Copy
Fees to Review: 0.00 US$

Manuscript Style:
   Chicago Manual of Style

CIRCULATION DATA:

Reader: Academics, Industry Professionals
Frequency of Issue: 3 Times/Year
Sponsor/Publisher: University of North
   Texas

REVIEW INFORMATION:

Type of Review: Blind Review
No. of External Reviewers: 1
No. of In House Reviewers: 1
Acceptance Rate: 50%
Time to Review: 2 - 3 Months
Reviewers Comments: Yes
Invited Articles: 11-20%
Fees to Publish: 0.00 US$

MANUSCRIPT TOPICS:

Accounting Information Systems; Accounting Theory & Practice; Auditing; Corporate Finance; Cost Accounting; Econometrics; Economic Development; Industrial Organization; International Finance; Petroleum Accounting & Finance; Portfolio & Security Analysis; Public Policy Economics; Tax Accounting

MANUSCRIPT GUIDELINES/COMMENTS:

Managing Editor. Patti Balentine (same address as editor)

Editorial Policy Statement
The *Petroleum Accounting and Financial Management Journal* (formerly the *Journal of Extractive Industries Accounting* and then the *Journal of Petroleum Accounting*) is designed to communicate issues of interest to professionals, industry and academics involved with the oil and gas industry (especially as related to the extractive industries). With this broad spectrum of readership, several different classes of articles are suitable for publication in the journal. The primary criterion is that the article should contribute to knowledge about the industry. The different classes of acceptable articles are as follows:

Current Issues
Current issue papers cover discussion of accounting, tax, economic, or financial issues affecting the industry. These articles are frequently obtained by invitation. They should address an issue of interest, examine possible alternative solutions and support any suggestions with appropriate source materials, date, or other information.

Research Issues
Research papers that are of interest to the academic community as well as to industry and practice are also suitable for publication. These articles may be derived from empirical, analytical, behavioral, or other suitable methodologies. They may include replications of work done on broader data sets or they may be unique studies of interest to an understanding of the industry and the processes involved in it. Research papers may cover economic, public policy, and finance areas. They should be written in such a manner that those in practice can understand the contents. However, the use of high-level research methodology is encouraged. Papers in this category are reviewed by members of the editorial board before publication.

Other Papers
Other papers which present information of interest to the oil and gas industry are also considered for publication. These may include a variety of studies in such areas as public policy, taxation, statistical series or similar works. Case studies in the industry may also be included in this category.

Contact
For further information about publication or to inquire about submitting articles, contact Dr. Teddy L. Coe, Editor, or Ms. Patti Balentine, Managing Editor, Petroleum Accounting and Financial Management Journal, Institute of Petroleum Accounting, University of North Texas, P.O. Box 305460, Denton, TX 76203-5460, or call (940) 565-3164.

Style Sheet
1. **Manuscripts**. Contributors should submit two hard copies of the manuscript for review. The *Petroleum Accounting and Financial Management Journal* uses a blind review system; therefore, we prefer a separate title sheet showing authors and their affiliations so that we may remove the cover and all identifying marks before sending the article to the reviewer. In the case of multiple authors, please designate a contact person. All manuscripts should be on standard manuscript paper and may be either double- or single-spaced. Please number all pages.

2. **Diskettes**. If your article is accepted for publication, we will require a diskette copy for editing and formatting. The diskette should be in an IBM-compatible word processing program or in ASCII. Currently, all editing and formatting is done using WordPerfect 12. Please indicate either on the diskette label or in a covering letter what software program (including version, i.e., Microsoft Word 3.2) you have utilized in preparing your manuscript and include this information for any tables, spreadsheets, graphics, etc., for which you may have used a different program.

3. **Electronic Submissions**. You may send us your manuscript electronically if you would like. Send to **balentin@unt.edu**.

4. **Style**. The *Journal* adheres to the guidelines set out in *A Manual of Style*, University of Chicago Press, as regards questions of grammar, footnote and bibliographical styles, capitalization, emphasis, etc. As a general rule, we prefer that footnotes appear at the bottom of the page on which they occur. All formatting is done in house; therefore, no special treatment is required for headings, subheadings, page numbering, margins, etc., when preparing manuscripts for submission.

5. **Permissions and Authorizations**. Proper authorization for the use of any previously published material is the responsibility of the author. If you are using in your article any published chart, graph, figure, or other information, you should acknowledge the source and secure permission for re-use.

6. **Editorial Prerogative**. The editor reserves the right to correct grammatical mistakes, make recommendations, and adapt the format to *Journal* style. All authors receive an edited and formatted page proof showing exactly how their article will appear (including pagination, placement of tables, graphics, etc.) which they must approve before publication. If you have any further questions, please call the Institute of Petroleum Accounting, (940) 565-3164.

476

Practical Tax Strategies (Taxation for Accountants/Taxation for Lawyers)

ADDRESS FOR SUBMISSION:

Bob Scharin, Editor
Practical Tax Strategies (Taxation for
  Accountants/Taxation for Lawyers)
RIA
395 Hudson Street, 4th Floor
New York, NY 10014
USA
Phone: 212-807-2966
E-Mail: bob.scharin@thomson.com
Web: http://ria.thomson.com

CIRCULATION DATA:

Reader: Business Persons, Tax Accountants
  & Attorneys
Frequency of Issue: Monthly
Sponsor/Publisher: Warren Gorham &
  Lamont / RIA

PUBLICATION GUIDELINES:

Manuscript Length: 15-25
Copies Required: One
Computer Submission: Yes Email Preferred
Format: MS Word preferred/PC compatible
Fees to Review: 0.00 US$

Manuscript Style:
  See Manuscript Guidelines

REVIEW INFORMATION:

Type of Review: Editorial Review
No. of External Reviewers: 1
No. of In House Reviewers: 1
Acceptance Rate: 21-30%
Time to Review: 1 - 2 Months
Reviewers Comments: No
Invited Articles: 50% +
Fees to Publish: 0.00 US$

MANUSCRIPT TOPICS:
Federal Taxation; Tax Accounting

MANUSCRIPT GUIDELINES/COMMENTS:

Practical Tax Strategies welcomes articles offering practical information and planning strategies regarding federal income, estate, and gift taxes. Articles should focus on matters of importance to practitioners and provide guidance on structuring transactions to produce optimal tax consequences and satisfying compliance mandates with maximum efficiency. Articles should not discuss theoretical matters or how the law could or should be changed.

To be considered for publication, articles must be sent to us exclusively and are subject to review by our editorial board. If accepted for publication, the manuscript will be edited for stylistic conformity. Manuscripts should be double-spaced and submitted by e-mail, or as hard copy along with a computer disk. Typically, manuscripts run between 15 and 25 pages in length. Endnotes rather than footnotes should be used, and they should be restricted to citations (without textual explanations). When possible, illustrative examples and forms or lists should be included.

To submit articles, or for more information, please contact:
Practical Tax Strategies
Bob D. Scharin, Editor
RIA
395 Hudson Street, 4th Floor
New York, NY 10014
Phone: (212) 807-2966; Fax: (212) 337-4207
E-mail: **bob.scharin@thomson.com**

478

Public Fund Digest

ADDRESS FOR SUBMISSION:

Jesse Hughes, Editor
Public Fund Digest
1758 Carriage Drive
Hampton, VA 23664
US
Phone: 757-851-0525
E-Mail: jhughes@odu.edu
Web: www.icgfm.org

CIRCULATION DATA:

Reader: Business Persons, Government
    Financial Managers
Frequency of Issue: 2 Times/Year
Sponsor/Publisher: International
    Consortium of Government Financial
    Managers

PUBLICATION GUIDELINES:

Manuscript Length: 10-15
Copies Required: One
Computer Submission: Yes Disk, Email
Format: MS Word
Fees to Review: 0.00 US$

Manuscript Style:
    Chicago Manual of Style

REVIEW INFORMATION:

Type of Review: Editorial Review
No. of External Reviewers: 0
No. of In House Reviewers: 1
Acceptance Rate: 75%
Time to Review: 1 Month or Less
Reviewers Comments: Yes
Invited Articles: 11-20%
Fees to Publish: 0.00 US$

MANUSCRIPT TOPICS:
Accounting Education; Accounting Information Systems; Auditing; Economic Development; Financial Services; Fiscal Policy; Government & Non Profit Accounting; International Economics & Trade; International Finance; Public Policy Economics

MANUSCRIPT GUIDELINES/COMMENTS:

This is a practice oriented journal that solicits best practices in the areas of governmental financial management. The *Public Fund Digest* is issued at no charge to the members of ICGFM.

ICGFM Editorial Policy
To insure consistency in the handling of communications, the following editorial policies will apply to communications from the ICGFM:

Officers and Directors
All officers and directors will be responsible for identifying best practices and potential articles for publication in the ICGFM Newsletter, Digest, and web site. These will be referred to the Publication Editor for consideration in the next available publication. Preferably, Digest articles should be about ten single spaced pages in length.

Conference Coordinator(s)
The conference coordinator(s) will be responsible for providing a soft copy of the conference program, with name and email address of the presenters by subject title, to the Publication Editor within two weeks of the Conference. In addition, a soft copy of the presentations (in Word or PowerPoint format, to the maximum extent possible) will be provided to the Publication Editor for inclusion in the web site.

DC Forum Coordinator(s)
The DC Forum Coordinator(s) will be responsible for insuring that a summary of the presentations made at each DC Forum is provided to the Publication Editor for inclusion in the next Newsletter. The ICGFM member who invites the Forum speaker will be responsible for summarizing the presentation and submitting it to the Publications Editor within one week of the presentation.

Publication Editor
The Publication Editor will be responsible for encouraging all members to publish their best practices and leading edge issues in the ICGFM publications. All input provided will be reviewed by an officer or director to insure that it maintains the quality desired in the ICGFM publications. When the manuscript is accepted for publication, the Editor will be responsible for pulling the applicable publication together in a copy-ready format. This will be provided to the Layout Specialist who will be responsible for laying out the copy-ready material in final format and forwarding that material to the printer in the quantity specified.

Publication Schedule

	To Layout Specialist	Publication
Winter Newsletter	Nov. 1	Dec. 15
Spring Digest	Feb. 1	Mar. 15
Summer Newsletter	May 1	Jun. 15
Fall Digest	Aug. 1	Sep. 15

Funding and Distribution
The Public Fund Digest will be limited to approximately 100 pages and the Newsletter will be limited to no more than 12 pages. The printed copies will be sent to the following address:
    ICGFM, Suite 234
    444 North Capitol Street, NW
    Washington, DC 20001

The Secretariat will be responsible for distribution to the members based on the latest membership list. The bills associated with the publications will be send to the Editor for approval and then forwarded to the Treasurer for payment.

Public Money & Management

ADDRESS FOR SUBMISSION:

Michaela Lavender, Managing Editor
Public Money & Management
CIPFA
3 Robert Street
London, WC2N 6RL
UK
Phone: 001 561 218 8673
E-Mail: micky@mickylavender.com
Web: www.cipfa.org.uk/pt/pmm.cfm

CIRCULATION DATA:

Reader: Business Persons, Academics
Frequency of Issue: 5 Times/Year
Sponsor/Publisher: The Chartered Institute
of Public Finance and Accountancy
(CIPFA)

PUBLICATION GUIDELINES:

Manuscript Length: 26-30
Copies Required: Three
Computer Submission: Yes
Format: Any
Fees to Review: 0.00 US$

Manuscript Style:
, cod

REVIEW INFORMATION:

Type of Review: Blind Review
No. of External Reviewers: 2
No. of In House Reviewers: 2
Acceptance Rate: 11-20%
Time to Review: 2 Months or Less
Reviewers Comments: Yes
Invited Articles: 31-50%
Fees to Publish: 0.00 US$

MANUSCRIPT TOPICS:
Accounting Theory & Practice; Auditing; Cost Accounting; Government & Non Profit Accounting; Monetary Policy; Public Policy Economics

MANUSCRIPT GUIDELINES/COMMENTS:

Notes for Authors
Public Money & Management: Integrating Research with Policy and Practice particularly favours articles which contribute new knowledge as a basis for policy or management improvements, or which reflect on evidence from public service management and finance. The journal has a multidisciplinary readership, including officials in all types of public service organizations, academics, consultants and advisers working with the public services, politicians, journalists, and students on both academic and professional courses. Although this readership has been interested largely in British public management, there is an increasing interest in international developments. Accordingly, the editors welcome articles about developments outside the UK where they address generic issues or compare developments with British or other western experience.

The journal publishes core articles, new developments and contributions to debate. *Core articles* (about 5,000 words) are expected to meet high standards of intellectual argument, evidence and understanding of practice in public management. They are peer-refereed anonymously. New *Developments* (typically 2,500 words) focus on the evolution of contemporary public service policy, management or practice and convey the potential or actual impact of change in a detached, informed and authoritative way. These articles are not normally refereed, but are subject to editorial scrutiny. Contributions to the *Debate* section (typically fewer than 2,000 words) are personal statements about topical issues, expressing an argument, supported by examples or evidence. They, too, are subject to editorial scrutiny. Authors are advised to take into account the needs of the readership in drafting their articles and in particular to explain technical terms and avoid exclusive jargon.

Public Money & Management is published five times a year in January, April, June, August and October.

Submission
Manuscripts should be sent to the Managing Editor, Michaela Lavender: c/o Sandra Harper: Public Money & Management, CIPFA, 3 Robert Street, London WC2N 6RL. Five copies of each article should be submitted. Manuscripts can also be submitted by email, preferably in Microsoft Word, to Michaela Lavender: **micky@mickylavender.com**

Preparation
The following items should be included with manuscripts: title page, including full addresses of all authors; a two-line biography about each author; and a summary of around 50 words (core and new development articles). Spelling should follow the *Oxford English Dictionary*.

The journal uses the Harvard (name, date) system of referencing; references in the text should be given as (Brown, 1990), or Brown and Jones (1990), or Brown *et al.* (1992) if there are more than three authors. References should be given at the end of the article in a single alphabetical list:

To a journal: Stoker, G. (1996), The struggle to reform local government: 1970–95. *Public Money & Management*, 16, 1, pp. 17–22.

To a book: Margetts, H. (1996), Information technology in government. In Jackson, P. and Lavender, M. (Eds), *The Public Services Yearbook*, 1997/98 (Pitman Publishing, London).

Final Manuscripts and Proofing
After acceptance, authors are requested to submit their final manuscripts by email (preferably in Microsoft Word) to the Managing Editor, Michaela Lavender: **micky@mickylavender.com**.

Proofs for checking will be sent to authors by email and should be returned promptly by fax to Michaela Lavender on (001) 561 218 8673.

Copyright. Authors are requested, upon acceptance of their article, to transfer their copyright to CIPFA. This ensures that requests for permission to reproduce articles are handled systematically and in accordance with a general policy which is aware of the market and any relevant changes in international copyright legislation.

Real Estate Taxation

ADDRESS FOR SUBMISSION:

Robert J. Murdich, Editor
Real Estate Taxation
395 Hudson Street
New York, NY 10014
USA
Phone: 212-807-2894
E-Mail: robert.murdich@thomson.com
Web: http://ria.thomson.com/journals/
default.asp

PUBLICATION GUIDELINES:

Manuscript Length: 11-30
Copies Required:
Computer Submission: Yes Disk, Email
Format: MS Word or WordPerfect
Fees to Review: 0.00 US$

Manuscript Style:

CIRCULATION DATA:

Reader: , Accountants & Attorneys
Frequency of Issue: Quarterly
Sponsor/Publisher: RIA Group

REVIEW INFORMATION:

Type of Review: Editorial Review
No. of External Reviewers: 1
No. of In House Reviewers:
Acceptance Rate: Majority
Time to Review: 1 - 2 Months
Reviewers Comments: No
Invited Articles: 50% +
Fees to Publish: 0.00 US$

MANUSCRIPT TOPICS:
Real Estate; Tax Accounting

MANUSCRIPT GUIDELINES/COMMENTS:

Topics Include. Taxation of real estate, tax-free exchanges, partnerships, related areas

Real Estate Taxation welcomes articles offering practical information and tax planning ideas. Articles should focus on legal, tax, accounting, and finance issues of importance to real estate professionals and their advisors. When possible, illustrative examples and forms should be included. Articles should not discuss theoretical matters or how the law should or could be changed.

An article submitted for consideration must be sent to us exclusively to be reviewed by our editorial board. Once approved for publication in *Real Estate Taxation*, each article is subject to editorial revision. Authors receive galley proofs prior to publication and any corrections must be returned to us by the date indicated. There is generally no objection to having an article that appears in *Real Estate Taxation* reprinted in another publication at a later date, provided appropriate permission is requested from us and attribution given. Hard copy of the manuscript should be double-spaced, and typically will run between 15 and 25 pages; an electronic version is also required.

483

To submit articles, or for more information, please contact:
Real Estate Taxation
Robert Murdich, Managing Editor
RIA
395 Hudson Street
New York, NY 10014
Phone: (212) 807-2894 Fax: (212) 337-4207
E-mail: **robert.murdich@Thomson.com**

484

Regional Business Review

ADDRESS FOR SUBMISSION:

Janet Marta, Editor
Regional Business Review
Northwest Missouri State University
800 University Drive
Maryville, MO 64468-6001
USA
Phone: 660-562-1859
E-Mail: jmarta@mail.nwmissouri.edu
Web:

PUBLICATION GUIDELINES:

Manuscript Length: 16-20
Copies Required: Three
Computer Submission: Yes Disk, Email
Format: MS Word
Fees to Review: 0.00 US$

Manuscript Style:
    Chicago Manual of Style

CIRCULATION DATA:

Reader: Academics, Business Persons
Frequency of Issue: Yearly
Sponsor/Publisher: Melvin D. & Valorie G.
    Booth College of Business &
    Professional Studies

REVIEW INFORMATION:

Type of Review: Blind Review
No. of External Reviewers: 1
No. of In House Reviewers: 1
Acceptance Rate:
Time to Review: 1 - 2 Months
Reviewers Comments: Yes
Invited Articles: 0-5%
Fees to Publish: 0.00 US$

MANUSCRIPT TOPICS:
Accounting Theory & Practice; Behavioral Accounting; Economic Development; Economic History; Financial Services; Industrial Organization; International Economics & Trade; Macro Economics; Micro Economics; Regional Economics

MANUSCRIPT GUIDELINES/COMMENTS:

Authors should submit manuscripts electronically, as an attachment to an e-mail to the editor. Manuscripts must be double-spaced, with at least a one-inch margin on all sides; and about 15-25 pages in length. To assist in blind reviewing, the author's (authors') name(s) should appear on the title page only. In the case of multiple authors, please indicate in a cover letter the author with whom we should correspond.

Please avoid endnotes and footnotes and follow *Chicago* guidelines for references.

Research in Accounting Regulation

ADDRESS FOR SUBMISSION:

Gary John Previts, Editor
Research in Accounting Regulation
Case Western Reserve University
Weatherhead School of Management
461 Lewis Building
Cleveland, OH 44106-7235
USA
Phone: 216-368-2074
E-Mail: GJP@case.edu
Web: weatherhead.cwru.edu/rar

CIRCULATION DATA:

Reader: Business Persons, Academics,
  Professionals, Regulators
Frequency of Issue: Annual
Sponsor/Publisher: Elsevier Inc.

PUBLICATION GUIDELINES:

Manuscript Length: 10-20
Copies Required: Three
Computer Submission: Yes Preferred
Format: MS Word
Fees to Review: 0.00 US$

Manuscript Style:
  See Manuscript Guidelines

REVIEW INFORMATION:

Type of Review: Blind Review
No. of External Reviewers: 1+
No. of In House Reviewers: 1+
Acceptance Rate: 30%+
Time to Review: 8-12 Months
Reviewers Comments: Yes
Invited Articles: Infrequent
Fees to Publish: 0.00 US$

MANUSCRIPT TOPICS:
Accounting Theory & Practice; Auditing; Cost Accounting; Government & Non Profit Accounting; Public Policy Economics; Tax Accounting

MANUSCRIPT GUIDELINES/COMMENTS:

Research in Accounting Regulation's preferred method of submission is through electronic mail delivery. Submission of manuscripts through e-mail and other file transfer protocols speeds up delivery and reduces transaction costs for the authors and the editors. Compliance with these requests is greatly appreciated. Files may be delivered to Dr. Gary John Previts at **GJP@case.edu**. (NOTE: Please include a reference to *RAR* within the subject of the e-mail message.)

Because *Research in Accounting Regulation* uses extensive electronic publishing aides we ask our authors to make a few concessions to that process so that we can better meet our deadlines and get all our other work done as well!

Appearance
Your submitted paper must be completely re-formatted to conform with the publisher's technical and production requirements, thus, any formatting you have done will be lost. We

prefer you concentrate on the substance of the paper, not its appearance. With that in mind, we have developed the following guidelines to facilitate the process.

Typeface. Courier, 10-pitch, non-proportional.

Layout. Left and right one-inch margins.

Paragraphs. Block left. DO NOT INDENT the first line.

DO NOT JUSTIFY the body text.

Separate paragraphs with two carriage returns (hit the ENTER or RETURN key twice.)

Do not use "hanging indents."

Citation paragraphs are denoted with double quotes ("...paragraph")

Typing. Two (2) spaces after a period.

Indents, when necessary, with 4 or 5 spaces (not tabs). Please avoid, if possible. Do not use underlining to emphasize. Numbered items are typed with a period, then two spaces (NOT a tab).

Tables/Charts. Submit tables and charts on separate sheets (not included in the body text) in exactly the form you want them to appear. Create your tables and charts with other software applications such as Lotus or Harvard Graphics and submit the printouts directly from them. Try to avoid charts that necessitate a "landscape" (horizontal) format.

Bibliography/Endnotes. Bibliography and endnotes should adhere to *Accounting Review* style.

In general. If you use a clean, block left format with no centering, indenting, justification, or other appearance formatting you will find you can make a very presentable paper which is ready to go to the publisher.

Research in Governmental and Nonprofit Accounting

ADDRESS FOR SUBMISSION:

Paul Copley, Editor
Research in Governmental and Nonprofit
   Accounting
James Madison University
MSC 0203, 335 Showker Hall
Harrisonburg, VA 22807
USA
Phone: 540-568-3081
E-Mail: copleypa@jmu.edu
Web:

CIRCULATION DATA:

Reader: Academics
Frequency of Issue: Yearly
Sponsor/Publisher: Elsevier Inc.

PUBLICATION GUIDELINES:

Manuscript Length: 26-30
Copies Required: Three
Computer Submission: Yes Email
Format: MS Word
Fees to Review: 0.00 US$

Manuscript Style:
   , Accounting Review

REVIEW INFORMATION:

Type of Review: Blind Review
No. of External Reviewers: 1-2
No. of In House Reviewers: 0
Acceptance Rate: 21-30%
Time to Review: 1 - 2 Months
Reviewers Comments: Yes
Invited Articles: 0-5%
Fees to Publish: 0.00 US$

MANUSCRIPT TOPICS:
Government & Non Profit Accounting

MANUSCRIPT GUIDELINES/COMMENTS:

Purpose and Content
The basic purpose of *Research in Governmental and Nonprofit Accounting* is to stimulate and report high quality research on a wide range of governmental and nonprofit accounting issues.

The Editor strongly welcomes submission of original research papers which apply innovative theoretical analyses or empirical research designs and methods in a governmental or nonprofit accounting, auditing or reporting setting. Extensions of previous work with new samples, and improved empirical measures and analyses are also encouraged.

Additionally, *RIGNA* will continue to published high quality "state of the art" survey papers which synthesize existing research and provide directions for future research.

488

Submission Information

Submit three copies of the manuscript. The title page should include the names and addresses of the authors and clearly indicate who is to receive manuscript correspondence. The manuscript should include an abstract and complete list of references cited in the manuscript. Tables, illustrations or appendices should follow the references.

There is no submission fee. The submitting author should indicate that the submission is an original unpublished manuscript and is not under review at another journal. Before publication, the authors must transfer copyright to the publisher, JAI Press. A disk copy of the manuscript is required after the manuscript has been accepted for publication.

Manuscripts are submitted to blind review.

Correspondence

Paul Copley
James Madison University
MSC 0203 335 Showker Hall
Harrisonburg, VA 22807
Phone: 540-568-3081   Email: **copleypa@jmu.edu**

MANUSCRIPT GUIDELINES

General Instructions

Paper. Type or print the manuscript on one side of standard-size, or European equivalent paper. Do not use half sheets or strips of paper glued, taped, or stapled to the pages.

Type Element. The type must be dark, clear, and legible.

Double Spacing. Double space between all lines of the manuscript including headings, notes, references, quotations, and figure captions. Single-spacing is acceptable only on tables.

Permission To Reprint. If you are using material from a copyrighted work (e.g., tables, figures), you will need written permission from the copyright holder (in most cases the publisher) to use this material. It is the author's responsibility to obtain the reprint permission. A copy of the permission letter must accompany the manuscript.

Title Page. The title page includes 4 elements: (1) The title and subtitle, if any; (2) The author(s); (3) abbreviated title to be used as a running head consisting of a maximum of 70 characters, which includes all letters, punctuation, and spaces; (4) complete mailing address, email address, phone, and fax numbers of each author.

Text. Begin the text on a new page. The sections of the text follow each other without a break.

Appendices. Begin each Appendix on a separate page, with the word "Appendix" and identifying capital letters centered at the top of the page. If there is only one Appendix, it is not necessary to use an identifying letter.

Notes. Notes that are mentioned in text are numbered consecutively throughout the chapter. Begin notes on a separate page and double space them.

References. Reference style is the same as that appearing in *The Accounting Review*.

References cited in text must appear in the reference list; conversely, each entry in the reference list must be cited in text. It is the author's responsibility to be sure that the text citation and reference list are identical.

Important. Foreign language volumes, parts, numbers, editions, and so on must be translated into their English equivalents. Both the original language and the English translation will appear in the references. Authors must transliterate or romanize languages that do not use Latin characters (e.g., Greek, Russian, Chinese, Arabic, etc.), along with their English translation. A comprehensive resource for this is a publication issued by the Library of Congress, titled: ALA-LC Romanization Tables: Transliteration Schemes for Non-Roman Scripts.

Tables. Tables are numbered consecutively in the order in which they are first mentioned in text. Begin each table on separate page. Do not write "the table above/below" or "the table on p. 32" because the position and page number of a table cannot be determined until the page is typeset. In text, indicate the approximate placement of each table by a clear break in the text, inserting:

TABLE 1 ABOUT HERE

Set off by double-spacing above and below.

Editor: I prefer very detailed table headings. As an example, see Copley et al. (Accounting Review Jan. '94 pp. 249-250). I believe a reader should be able to look at a table heading and determine what information is being presented, about what type of entities, and from what time period. In addition, I prefer that the tables contain a definition of each variable. This holds for all the tables.

Figures. Figures are also numbered consecutively in the order in which they are first mentioned in text. Indicate the approximate placement of each figure by a clear break, inserting:

FIGURE 1 ABOUT HERE

Set off by double-spacing above and below. All figures must be submitted in a form suitable for reproduction by the printer without redrawing or retouching. Figures should be no larger than 4 x 6". If a figure exceeds this size, it should be large enough and sharp enough to be legible when reduced to fit the page.

Type all figure numbers and captions, double-spaced, on a separate page. When enclosing a figure in a box, please do not include the figure number and caption within the box, as these are set separately.

For identification by the production editor and the printer, please indicate your name and the figure number on the back of each figure. "Top" should be written on any figure that might accidentally be reproduced wrong side up. Staples nor paper clips should be used on any figure. Scotch tape should never be used to attach figure copy to another page as tape edges show up as black line in reproduction. Art will not be returned unless otherwise indicated.

Disk Preparation
(Required only after the manuscript has been accepted for publication)

1. Use a word processing program that is able to create an IBM compatible file.

2. Use 3 ½ inch, double (low) density or high density disks (preferably high density.
   NOTE: If you use double (low) density disks, be sure that the disk is formatted for double (low) density. If you use high density, be sure that the disk is formatted for high density. Unformatted or incorrectly formatted disks are unusable.

3. Structure the manuscript according to the Guidelines. Print one (1) copy for copy-editing/styling purposes. Be sure to DOUBLE-SPACE this copy. That includes the notes and references.

4. The entire chapter should be in one (1) file. Do not make separate files for text, notes, and references. If necessary, tables may go in a separate file.

5. All manuscripts must have numbered pages; all tables and figures must be placed at the end of the chapters; placement lines must be indicated for all tables and figures (e.g., PLACE FIGURE/TABLE X HERE).

6. Submit the word processing file with your printed copy. Please indicate on the disk which word processing program and version you have used (e.g.. MS Word, WordPerfect 5.1, 6.0, 7.0, etc. Word Star, WordPerfect for Windows, MS Word for Windows, etc.).

7. All text files must be spell checked and stripped of any and all graphics (graphs, equations, charts, line drawings, illustrations, or tables). Text files must be marked as to the placement of all graphics. Please send a separate graphics file as either tiff (tagged image file format) or eps (encapsulated postscript) and indicate which format has been used on the disk. We will require camera-ready copy, whether or not material is also supplied in a graphics file.

8. PLEASE be sure that the manuscript and disk submitted match. If the material on the disk has been updated, please print out a new copy of the manuscript to be sure you are submitting the correct version.

Research Journal of Business Disciplines

ADDRESS FOR SUBMISSION:

John Gill, Editor
Research Journal of Business Disciplines
PO Box 1399
Clinton, MS 39060-1399
USA
Phone: 601-877-6450
E-Mail: msabd@jam.rr.com
Web: www.msabd.org

CIRCULATION DATA:

Reader: Academics
Frequency of Issue: Yearly
Sponsor/Publisher: MidSouth Association
of Business Disciplines

PUBLICATION GUIDELINES:

Manuscript Length: Less than 26 Pgs.
Copies Required: Three
Computer Submission: Yes Email
Format: Adobe, MS Word, WordPerfect
Fees to Review: 90.00 US$

Manuscript Style:
, Accounting Horizons

REVIEW INFORMATION:

Type of Review: Blind Review
No. of External Reviewers: 2
No. of In House Reviewers: 2
Acceptance Rate: 41-50%
Time to Review: 1 - 2 Months
Reviewers Comments: Yes
Invited Articles: 0-5%
Fees to Publish: 25.00 US$ / Co-Author

MANUSCRIPT TOPICS:

Accounting Education; Accounting Information Systems; Accounting Theory & Practice; Auditing; Behavioral Accounting; Corporate Finance; Cost Accounting; Economic Development; Economic History; Finance Education; Financial Institutions & Markets; Financial Services; Fiscal Policy; Government & Non Profit Accounting; Industrial Organization; Insurance; International Economics & Trade; International Finance; Macro Economics; Managerial Accounting; Micro Economics; Monetary Policy; Portfolio & Security Analysis; Real Estate; Regional Economics; Tax Accounting

MANUSCRIPT GUIDELINES/COMMENTS:

The *Research Journal of Business Disciplines* is the official publication of the MidSouth Association of Business Disciplines.

To be eligible for submission to the *Journal*, manuscripts must have completed a documented process of public scrutiny by academic peers or practitioners. Papers presented at the Association's annual meeting meet this eligibility requirement. Under certain circumstances the Association may allow this requirement to be met by alternate methods. Such manuscripts must, in the editor's opinion, have receive sufficient, relevant feedback from academic peers and/or practitioners via some public forum to be eligible for submission to the *Journal*.

492

The Association's annual meeting is held at various locations in the southeastern or southwestern US during the first or second week of October. Information about the Association, the *Journal*, and the annual meeting can be obtained from our website www.msabd.org. Written requests for information on the Association, the *Journal*, and the annual meeting should be addressed to Vicky Gill, Executive Director, MSABD, P.O. Box 1399, Clinton, MS 39060-1399, USA. The email address is **msabd@jam.rr.com**.

Format Instructions
Papers submitted for initial review may be in practically any reasonable formatting schema. Accepted papers must be submitted in their final proof version to the *Research Journal of Business Disciplines* on 8.5 by 11.0 paper following the general style of *Issues in Accounting Education* and/or *Accounting Horizons*. MSABD will provide an MS Word template to format final submissions; contact the editor to obtain the template prior to making the final submission.

Submission Deadline
Papers presented at the annual meeting in October must be submitted to the *Journal* by January 15 of the year following presentation. Other submissions will be considered as they are received.

Research on Professional Responsibility and Ethics in Accounting

ADDRESS FOR SUBMISSION:

Cynthia Jeffrey, Managing Editor
Research on Professional Responsibility and
   Ethics in Accounting
Iowa State University
College of Business
3366 Gerdin Business Building
Ames, IA 50011-1350
USA
Phone: 515-294-9427
E-Mail: cjeffrey@iastate.edu
Web: ElsevierSocialSciences.com

CIRCULATION DATA:

Reader: Academics
Frequency of Issue: Yearly
Sponsor/Publisher: Elsevier Inc.

PUBLICATION GUIDELINES:

Manuscript Length: 16-25
Copies Required: Four
Computer Submission: Yes Email Preferred
Format: MS Word
Fees to Review: 40.00 US$
   Some May Be Waived

Manuscript Style:
   American Psychological Association

REVIEW INFORMATION:

Type of Review: Blind Review
No. of External Reviewers: 2
No. of In House Reviewers: 0
Acceptance Rate: 21-30%
Time to Review: 2 - 3 Months
Reviewers Comments: Yes
Invited Articles: 0-5%
Fees to Publish: 0.00 US$

MANUSCRIPT TOPICS:
Accounting Education; Accounting Ethics; Accounting Theory & Practice; Auditing; Behavioral Accounting

MANUSCRIPT GUIDELINES/COMMENTS:

Cynthia Jeffrey edits the re-titled *Research on Professional Responsibility and Ethics in Accounting*, beginning with volume 9. The broader scope encourages authors to submit papers on the topics of professional behaviour and professional responsibility in addition to the areas of moral development or sensitivity to ethical issues. See the aims and scope below.

Description
Research on Professional Responsibility and Ethics in Accounting (*RPREA*) seeks to publish high-quality research and cases that focus on the professional responsibilities of accountants and how they deal with the ethical issues they face. The professional responsibilities of accountants are broad-based; they must serve clients and user groups whose needs, incentives, and goals may be in conflict. Further, accountants must interpret and apply codes of conduct, accounting and auditing principles, and securities regulations. Compliance with these

494

professional guidelines is judgment-based, and characteristics of the individual, the culture, and situations affect how these guidelines are interpreted and applied, as well as when they might be violated. Interactions between accountants, regulators, standard setters, and industries also have ethical components. Research into the nature of these interactions, resulting dilemmas, and how and why accountants resolve them, is the focus of the annual volumes.

Theoretical papers, empirical studies, case studies, and teaching cases are particularly appropriate methodologies to address the focus of the annual volumes. They serve researchers, educators, policy makers, and practitioners by publishing research results and serving as a forum for the exchange of ideas.

Call for Papers
Research on Professional Responsibility and Ethics in Accounting seeks thoughtful and well-developed empirical or non-empirical manuscripts on a variety of current topics in accounting ethics, broadly defined. It examines all aspects of ethics and ethics-related issues in accounting including, for example, accountability, financial reporting, organizational control, gender issues, quality concerns, professionals codes, organization and culture, judgment and decision-making litigation, regulation, earnings management, professional responsibility, and social responsibility. Acceptable research methods for empirical work include action research, archival analysis, field based studies, financial statement analysis, laboratory experiments, mathematical modeling, psychometrics and surveys.

Non-empirical manuscripts should be academically rigorous. They can be theoretical syntheses, conceptual models, position papers, discussions of methodology, comprehensive literature reviews grounded in theory, or historical discussions with implications for current and future efforts. Reasonable assumptions and logical development are essential. Most manuscripts should discuss implications for research.

For empirical reports sound research design and execution are critical. Articles should have well articulated and strong theoretical foundations. In this regard, establishing a link to the non-accounting literature may be desirable. Replications and extensions of previously published works are encouraged. As a means for establishing an open dialogue, responses to, or comments on, articles published previously are welcomed.

Submission Information
Four copies are required. Submission Fee is US$40.00. Manuscripts should include a cover page which indicates the author's name and address and a separate lead page with an abstract not exceeding 250 words. The author's name and address should not appear on the abstract. In order to assure an anonymous review, authors should not identify themselves directly or indirectly. Submit manuscripts to the Editor. Electronic submissions are encouraged. Word documents should be sent as attachments in email to the Editor. Two attachments should be included in the submission. The first attachment should be a file with the title page and should include the author's name and address. The second file should include the abstract and the body of the paper.

Cases. Three copies of Cases and Proposed Teaching Notes should be sent directly to Steven Mintz, School of Business and Public Administration, California State University—San Bernardino, San Bernardino, CA 92407-2397.

Call for Reviewers
Individuals interested in being a members of the editorial review board should contact Professor Jeffrey by e-mail at **cjeffrey@iastate.edu**, and explain their interests.

Review of Accounting and Finance

ADDRESS FOR SUBMISSION:

Ahmed Riahi-Belkaoui, Editor
Review of Accounting and Finance
University of Illinois at Chicago
College of Business Administration
Department of Accounting (MC 006)
601 S. Morgan Street
Chicago, IL 60607-7123
USA
Phone: 312-996-4400
E-Mail: belkaoui@uic.edu
Web: www.uic.edu

PUBLICATION GUIDELINES:

Manuscript Length: 5,000 Words
  Maximum
Copies Required: Three
Computer Submission: Yes
Format:
Fees to Review: 0.00 US$

Manuscript Style:
  Chicago Manual of Style

CIRCULATION DATA:

Reader: Academics
Frequency of Issue: Quarterly
Sponsor/Publisher: Emerald Group
  Publishing Limited

REVIEW INFORMATION:

Type of Review: Blind Review
No. of External Reviewers: 2
No. of In House Reviewers: 1
Acceptance Rate: 11-20%
Time to Review: 2-4 Months
Reviewers Comments: Yes
Invited Articles: 10%
Fees to Publish: 0.00 US$

MANUSCRIPT TOPICS:
Behavioral & Finance; Behavioral Accounting; Innovative Empirical

MANUSCRIPT GUIDELINES/COMMENTS:

Topics Include. Including the Role of Accounting, Internal and External Communications on Market Valuation; Financial Statements Users' Behavior and public Policy; Special Interest in the examination of the International Ramification of Accounting and Finance Issues.

1. **Editorial Policy**
The *Review of Accounting and Finance* is a journal for publishing innovative articles reporting the results of accounting and finance research and explaining and illustrating related research methodology in less than 5000 words. The primary criteria for publication in the *Review of Accounting and Finance* are significance and innovativeness of the contribution an article makes to the literature.

2. **Manuscript Preparation and Style**
The *Review of Accounting and Finance's* manuscript preparation guidelines follow the B_ format of the *Chicago Manual of Style* (14th Ed: University of Chicago Press).

3. Format

1. All manuscripts should be typed on one side of 8 ½ x 11" good quality paper and be double-spaced, except for indented quotations.

2. Manuscripts should be as concise as the subject and research method permit, generally not to exceed 5,000 words.

3. Margins of at least one inch from top, bottom and sides should facilitate editing and duplication.

4. A cover page should show the title of the paper, the author's name, title, affiliation and any acknowledgments.

4. Pagination

All pages, including tables, appendices and references, should be serially numbered.

5. Abstract/Introduction

An Abstract of about 100 words should be presented on a separate page immediately preceding the text. The Abstract should concisely inform the reader of the manuscript's topic, its methods and its findings. Keyword and the Data Availability statements should follow the Abstract. The text of the paper should start with a section labeled "I. Introduction," which provides more details about the paper's purpose, motivation, methodology and findings. Both the abstract and the introduction should be relatively non-technical, yet clear enough for an informed reader to understand the manuscript's contribution.

6. Tables and Figures

The author should note the following general requirements:

- Each table and figure (graphic) should appear on a separate page and should be placed at the end of the text. Each should bear an Arabic number and a complete title indicating the exact contents of the table or figure.
- A reference to each graphic should be made in the text.
- The author should indicate by marginal notation where each graphic should be inserted in the text.
- Graphics should be reasonably interpreted without reference to the text.
- Source line and notes should be included as necessary.

Equations. Equations should be numbered in parentheses flush with the right-hand margin.

7. Documentation

Citations. Work cited should use the "author-date system" keyed to a list of works in the reference list (see below). Authors should make an effort to include the relevant page numbers in the cited works.

In the text, works are cited as follows: authors' last name and date, without comma, in parentheses: for example, (Riahi-Belkaoui 1987); with two authors: (Riahi-Belkaoui and Alvertos 1973); with more than two: (Riahi-Belkaoui et al. 1985); with more than one source cited together (Riahi-Belkaoui 1987; Alvertos 1986); with two or more works by one author: (Riahi-Belkaoui 1985, 1987).

Reference List. Every manuscript must include a list of references containing only those works cited. Each entry should contain all data necessary for unambiguous identification. With the author-date system, use the following format recommended by the *Chicago Manual*.

1. Arrange citations in alphabetical order according to surname of the first author or the name of the institution responsible for the citation.
2. Use author's initials instead of proper names.
3. Dates of publication should be placed immediately after author's name.
4. Titles of journals should not be abbreviated.
5. Multiple works by the same author(s) should be listed in chronological order of publication. Two or more works by the same author(s) in the same year are distinguished by letters after the date.

Inclusive page numbers are treated as recommended in *Chicago Manual* section 8.67.

Review of Accounting Studies

ADDRESS FOR SUBMISSION:

Review of Accounting Studies
ELECTRONIC SUBMISSION ONLY
Phone: 212-854-3832
E-Mail: rast@gsb.columbia.edu
Web: www.gsb.columbia.edu/rast

PUBLICATION GUIDELINES:

Manuscript Length: 26-50
Copies Required: Electronic
Computer Submission: Yes Online
Format:
Fees to Review: 175.00 US$

Manuscript Style:
  See Manuscript Guidelines

CIRCULATION DATA:

Reader: Academics
Frequency of Issue: Quarterly
Sponsor/Publisher: Springer

REVIEW INFORMATION:

Type of Review: Blind Review
No. of External Reviewers: 2
No. of In House Reviewers: 0
Acceptance Rate: 18-20%
Time to Review: 2 - 3 Months
Reviewers Comments: Yes
Invited Articles: No Reply
Fees to Publish: 0.00 US$

MANUSCRIPT TOPICS:
Accounting Theory & Practice

MANUSCRIPT GUIDELINES/COMMENTS:

Aims & Scope
Review of Accounting Studies Journal provides an outlet for significant academic research in accounting including theoretical, empirical and experimental work. The *Review of Accounting Studies* is committed to the principle that distinctive scholarship is rigorous. While the editors encourage all forms of research, it must contribute to the discipline of accounting. Theoretical models need not speak directly to current practice, but accounting information must surface in a major way. Similarly, empirical hypotheses or experimental predictions should relate principally to accounting issues.

Editorial Policy
The *Review of Accounting Studies* is committed to the principle of prompt turnaround on the manuscripts it receives. A new submission will generally not require more than three months with the journal. For the majority of manuscripts the journal will make an accept-reject decision on the first round. Authors will be provided the opportunity to revise accepted manuscripts in order to accommodate reviewer and editor comments; however, discretion over such manuscripts resides principally with the author(s). An editorial revise and resubmit

500

decision is reserved for new submissions which are not acceptable in their current version, but for which the editor sees a clear path of changes which would make the manuscript publishable.

A major advantage of our decentralized editorship is that expertise can be applied at the editor level across a broad array of research subjects. New submissions are assigned to an editor familiar with the research topic. This editor then selects reviewers for the manuscript and upon receiving the reviewer's comments, the editor communicates directly with the author(s).

Address for Contributors
New submissions must be submitted online at **www.gsb.columbia.edu/rast**. A $175 submission fee is payable online via credit card, money transfer or check made out to Columbia University. E-mail: **rast@gsb.columbia.edu**

Manuscript Preparation
Authors should follow the directions for online submission at:
  http://services.bepress.com/rast/

Final versions of accepted manuscripts (including notes, references, tables, and legends) should be typed double-spaced with 1" (2.5 cm) margins on all sides. Sections should appear in the following order: title page, abstract, text appendices, acknowledgements, notes, references, tables figure legends, and figures. Comments or replies to previously published articles should also follow this format with the exception of abstracts, which are not required.

Title Page. The title page should include the article title, authors' names and permanent affiliations, and the name, current address, telephone number, and e-mail address of the person to whom the page proofs and reprints should be sent.

Abstract. The following page should also include an abstract of not more than 100 words and double-spaced.

Text. The text of the article should begin on a new page. The introduction should have no heading or number. Subsequent headings (including appendices) should be designated by Arabic numerals (1, 2, etc.) and subsection headings should be numbered 1.1, 1.2, etc. Figures, tables, and displayed equations should be numbered consecutively throughout the text 1, 2, etc.). Equation numbers should appear flush right in parentheses.

Appendices. Appendices should appear as a separate section after the text.

Acknowledgements. Acknowledgements should appear as a separate section after the text or appendices and before any notes.

Notes. Notes should be numbered consecutively and designated by superscripts (^{1}, ^{2}, etc.) in the text. All notes should be typed double-spaced beginning on a separate page following the text or acknowledgements, and before the references.

References. References in the text should follow the author-date format (e.g., Brown (1986), Jones (1978a, 1978b), Smith and Johnson (1983)). References should be typed double-spaced beginning on a separate page following the notes, according to the following samples (journal and book titles may be underlined rather than italicized). References with up to three authors should include the names of each author, references with four or more authors should cite the first author and add "et al." It is the responsibility of the authors to verify all references.

Sample References
Becker, Gordon, Morris DeGroot, and Jacob Marschak. (1964). "Measuring Utility by a Single-Response Sequential Method." *Behavioral Science 9*, 226-232.

Schoemaker, Paul. (1980). Experiments of Decisions Under Risk: The Expected Utility Hypothesis. Boston: Kluwer-Hijhoff Publishing.

Smith, V. Kerry. (1986). "A Conceptual Overview of the Foundations of Benefit-Cost Analysis." In Judith Bentkover, Vincent Covello, and Jeryl Mumpower (eds.), Benefits Assessment: The State of the Art. Dordrech: D. Reidel Publishing Co.

Tables. Tables should be numbered and titled, and typed double-spaced, each on a separate page, following the references. Notes to tables should be designated by superscripted letters ([a], [b], etc.) within each table and typed double-spaced on the same page as the table. Use descriptive labels rather than computer acronyms, and explain all abbreviations.

Page Proofs and Reprints
Corrected page proofs must be returned within three days of receipt, and alterations other than corrections may be charged to the authors. Authors will receive 50 free reprints, and may order additional copies when returning the corrected proofs.

Review of Business Information Systems

ADDRESS FOR SUBMISSION:

Editor
Review of Business Information Systems
The Clute Institute For Academic
Research
PO Box 620760
Littleton, CO 80162
USA
Phone: 303-904-4750
E-Mail: staff@cluteinstitute.org
Web: www.CluteInstitute.org

PUBLICATION GUIDELINES:

Manuscript Length: 6-10
Copies Required: One
Computer Submission: Yes Email or Disk
Format: MS Word
Fees to Review: 0.00 US$

Manuscript Style:
    See Manuscript Guidelines

CIRCULATION DATA:

Reader: Academics, Consultants & CPAs
Frequency of Issue: Quarterly
Sponsor/Publisher: Clute Institute For
    Academic Research

REVIEW INFORMATION:

Type of Review: Blind Review
No. of External Reviewers: 2
No. of In House Reviewers: 1
Acceptance Rate: 11-20%
Time to Review: 2 - 3 Months
Reviewers Comments: Yes
Invited Articles: 0-5%
Fees to Publish: 30.00 US$

MANUSCRIPT TOPICS:
Accounting Information Systems

MANUSCRIPT GUIDELINES/COMMENTS:

The *Review of Business Information Systems* (*RBIS*) welcomes articles concerning any aspect of business information systems. Both theoretical and applied manuscripts will be considered for publication. Theoretical manuscripts must provide a clear link to important and interesting business information systems applications. The *RBIS* was recently ranked as the 6th most desirable publication outlet out of more than 50 information systems journals. This 2001 study, conducted by Lloyd D. Doney and Tim V. Eaton of Marquette University, was published in the Summer 2003 issue of *RBIS*. The *Review* is referenced in the *Author's Guide to Accounting and Financial Reporting*, the *Business & Economics Research Directory*, and all Periodical Directories. The overall acceptance rate for *RBIS* is 11% to 20%.

Review of Business Research

ADDRESS FOR SUBMISSION:

Bhavesh M. Patel & Eric Girard, Editors
Review of Business Research
PO Box 2536
Ceres, CA 95307
USA
Phone: 440-582-5978
E-Mail: Review@iabe.org
Web: www.iabe.org

CIRCULATION DATA:

Reader: Academics, Business Persons
Frequency of Issue: 2 Times/Year
Sponsor/Publisher: International Academy
of Business and Economics (IABE)

PUBLICATION GUIDELINES:

Manuscript Length: 11-15
Copies Required: One
Computer Submission: Yes Disk, Email
Format: MS Word
Fees to Review: 0.00 US$

Manuscript Style:
Chicago Manual of Style

REVIEW INFORMATION:

Type of Review: Blind Review
No. of External Reviewers: 2
No. of In House Reviewers: 1
Acceptance Rate:
Time to Review: 2 - 3 Months
Reviewers Comments: Yes
Invited Articles: 11-20%
Fees to Publish: 0.00 US$

MANUSCRIPT TOPICS:

Accounting Education; Accounting Information Systems; Accounting Theory & Practice; Auditing; Cost Accounting; Econometrics; Economic Development; Financial Services; Fiscal Policy; Government & Non Profit Accounting; Industrial Organization; International Economics & Trade; International Finance; Macro Economics; Micro Economics; Monetary Policy; Portfolio & Security Analysis; Public Policy Economics; Real Estate; Tax Accounting

MANUSCRIPT GUIDELINES/COMMENTS:

Please use following manuscript Guidelines for submission of your papers for the review. Papers are reviewed on a continual basis throughout the year. Early Submissions are welcome! Please email your manuscript to **Review@iabe.org**.

Copyright. Articles, papers, or cases submitted for publication should be original contributions and should not be under consideration for any other publication at the same time. Authors submitting articles/papers/cases for publication warrant that the work is not an infringement of any existing copyright, infringement of proprietary right, invasion of privacy, or libel and will indemnify, defend, and hold IABE or sponsor(s) harmless from any damages, expenses, and costs against any breach of such warranty. For ease of dissemination and to ensure proper policing of use papers/articles/cases and contributions become the legal copyright of the IABE unless otherwise agreed in writing.

504

General Information. These are submission instructions for review purpose only. Once your submission is accepted you will receive submission guidelines with your paper acceptance letter. The author(s) will be emailed result of the review process in about 6-8 weeks from submission date. Papers are reviewed and accepted on a continual basis. Submit your papers early for full considerations!

Typing. Paper must be laser printed/printable on 8.5" x 11" white sheets in Arial 10-point font single-spaced lines justify style in MS Word. All four margins must be 1" each.

First Page. Paper title not exceeding two lines must be CAPITALIZED AND CENTERED IN BOLD LETTERS. Author name and university/organizational affiliation of each author must be printed on one line each. Do NOT include titles such as Dr., Professor, Ph.D., department address email address etc. Please print the word "ABSTRACT" in capitalized bold letters left justified and double-spaced from last author's name/affiliation. Abstract should be in italic. Please see the sample manuscript.

All other Headings. All other section headings starting with INTRODUCTION must be numbered in capitalized bold letters left justified and double-spaced from last line above them. See the subsection headings in the sample manuscript.

Tables Figures and Charts. All tables figures or charts must be inserted in the body of the manuscripts within the margins with headings/titles in centered CAPITALIZED BOLD letters.

References and Bibliography. All references listed in this section must be cited in the article and vice-versa. The reference citations in the text must be inserted in parentheses within sentences with author name followed by a comma and year of publication. Please follow the following formats:

Journal Articles
Khade Alan S. and Metlen Scott K. "An Application of Benchmarking in Dairy Industry" *International Journal of Benchmarking* Vol. III (4) 1996 17

Books
Harrison Norma and Samson D. Technology Management: Text and Cases McGraw-Hill Publishing New York 2002

Internet
Hesterbrink C. E-Business and ERP: Bringing two Paradigms together October 1999; PricewaterhouseCoopers *www.pwc.com*.

Author Profile(s). At the end of paper include author profile(s) not exceeding five lines each author including name highest degree/university/year current position/university and major achievements. For example:

Author Profile:
Dr. Tahi J. Gnepa earned his Ph.D. at the University of Wisconsin Madison in 1989. Currently he is a professor of international business at California State University Stanislaus and Managing Editor of Journal of International Business Strategy (JIBStrategy).

Manuscript. Absolutely no footnotes! Do not insert page numbers for the manuscript. Please do not forget to run spelling and grammar check for the completed paper. Save the manuscript on your diskette/CD or hard drive.

Electronic Submission. Send your submission as an MS Word file attachment to your Email to **Review@iabe.org**.

Review of Derivatives Research

ADDRESS FOR SUBMISSION:

Jesikah Allison
Review of Derivatives Research
Journal Editorial Office
Kluwer Academic Publishers
101 Phillip Drive
Norwell, MA 02061
USA
Phone: 781-871-6300
E-Mail: Jesikah.Allison@wkap.com
Web: www.kluwer.com

PUBLICATION GUIDELINES:

Manuscript Length: No Reply
Copies Required: Four
Computer Submission: Yes All Stages
Format: MS Word, WordPerfect, ASCII
Fees to Review: 75.00 US$

Manuscript Style:
    See Manuscript Guidelines

CIRCULATION DATA:

Reader: Business Persons
Frequency of Issue: 3 Times/Year
Sponsor/Publisher: Springer

REVIEW INFORMATION:

Type of Review: Blind Review
No. of External Reviewers: No Reply
No. of In House Reviewers: No Reply
Acceptance Rate: 20-25%
Time to Review: 3-6 Months
Reviewers Comments: Yes
Invited Articles: 0-5%
Fees to Publish: 0.00 US$

MANUSCRIPT TOPICS:
International Finance; Portfolio & Security Analysis; Tax Accounting

MANUSCRIPT GUIDELINES/COMMENTS:

Topics Include. Derivative Markets; Theoretical, Empirical. Applications of Derivatives in all areas of Finance.

Editors
Menachem Brenner, Marti Subrahmanyam, Co-Editors
New York University, Management Education Center
44 West 4th Street, Suite 9-55, New York, NY 10012-1126
Phone: 212-998-0323, 212-998-0348   Fax: 212-995-4220
Email: **mbrenner@stern.nyu.edu   msubrahm@stern.nyu.edu**

Aims & Scope
The proliferation of derivative assets during the past three decades is unprecedented. With this growth in derivatives comes the need for financial institutions, institutional investors, and corporations to use sophisticated quantitative techniques to take full advantage of the spectrum of these new financial instruments. Academic research has significantly contributed

to our understanding of derivative assets and markets. The growth of derivative asset markets has been accompanied by a commensurate growth in the volume of scientific research.

The rapid growth of derivatives research combined with the current absence of a rigorous research journal catering to the area of derivatives, and the long lead-times in the existing academic journals, underlines the need for *Review of Derivatives Research*, which provides an international forum for researchers involved in the general areas of derivative assets. The *Review* publishes high quality articles dealing with the pricing and hedging of derivative assets on any underlying asset (commodity, interest rate, currency, equity, real estate, traded or non-traded, etc.). Specific topics include but are not limited to:

* econometric analyses of derivative markets (efficiency, anomalies, performance, etc.)
* analysis of swap markets
* market microstructure and volatility issues
* regulatory and taxation issues
* credit risk
* new areas of applications such as corporate finance (capital budgeting, debt innovations), international trade (tariffs and quotas), banking and insurance (embedded options, asset-liability management)
* risk-sharing issues and the design of optimal derivative securities
* risk management, management and control
* valuation and analysis of the options embedded in capital projects
* valuation and hedging of exotic options
* new areas for further development (i.e. natural resources, environmental economics).

Manuscript Submission
The *Review* has a double-blind refereeing process. In contrast to the delays in the decision making and publication processes of many current journals, the *Review* will provide authors with an initial decision within nine weeks of receipt of the manuscript and a goal of publication within six months after acceptance. Finally, a section of the journal is available for rapid publication on 'hot' issues in the market, small technical pieces, and timely essays related to pending legislation and policy.

Prospective authors are encouraged to submit manuscripts for consideration for publication in forthcoming issues of the *Review of Derivatives Research*. Four copies of the manuscript, together with a check or payment by major credit card for $75.00, should be sent to the following address:
Review of Derivatives Research/Journal Editorial Office
c/o Jesikah Allison, Kluwer Academic Publishers
101 Philip Drive, Norwell, MA 02061, USA
Phone: 781-681-0605; Fax: 781-878-0449
E-mail: **Jesikah.Allison@wkap.com**

Manuscript Preparation
Final versions of accepted manuscripts (including notes, references, tables, and legends) should be typed double-spaced on 8 ½" x 11" (22 x 29cm) white paper with 1" (2.5cm) margins on all sides. Sections should appear in the following order: title page, abstract, text,

notes, references, tables, figure legends, and figure. Comments or replies to previously published articles should also follow this format with the exception of abstracts, which are not required.

Title Page. The title page should include the title, authors' names and permanent affiliations, and the name, current address, e-mail address and telephone number of the person to whom page proofs and offprints should be sent.

Abstract. The following page should include an abstract of not more than 100 words and a list of two to six **keywords**. Also include **JEL** subject category number.

Text. The text of the article should begin on a new page. The introduction should have no heading or number. Subsequent headings (including appendices) should be designated by Arabic numerals (1,2, etc.), and subsection headings should be numbered 1.1, 1.2, etc. Figures, tables, and displayed equations should be numbered consecutively throughout the text (1, 2, etc.). Equation numbers should appear flush left in parentheses and running variables for equations (e.g.i =1,..., n) flush right in parentheses.

Notes. References in the text should follow the author-date format (e.g. Brown (1986), Jones (1978a, 1978b), Smith and Johnson (1983)). References should be typed double-spaced beginning on a separate page following the notes, according to the following samples (journal and book titles may be underlined rather than italicized). References with up to three authors should include the names of each author, references with four or more authors should cite the first author and add "et al." It is the responsibility of the authors to verify all references.

Sample References
Becker, Gordon, Morris DeGroot, and Jacob Marschak. (1964). "Measuring Utility by a Single-Response Sequential Method," Behavioral Science 9, 226--232.

Schoemaker, Paul. (1980.Experiments on Decisions Under Risk: The Expected Utility Hypothesis. Boston: Kluwer-Nijhoff Publishing.

Smith, V. Kerry. (1986). "A Conceptual Overview of the Foundations of Benefit-Cost Analysis." In Judith Bentkover, Vincent Covello, and Beryl Mumpower (eds.), Benefits Assessment: The State of the Art. Dordrecht: D. Reidel Publishing Co.

Tables. Tables should be titled and typed double-spaced, each on a separate sheet, following the references. Notes to tables should be designated by superscripted letters (a,b, etc.) within each table and typed double-spaced on the same page as the table. Use descriptive labels rather than computer acronyms, and explain all abbreviations.

Figures. Figures should be sharp, noise-free and of good contrast. We regret that we cannot provide drafting or art service. Each figure should be mentioned in the text and numbered consecutively using Arabic numerals. Specify the desired location of each figure in the text. Each figure must have a caption. Proper style for captions, e.g., "Figure 1. Model of entrepreneurial behavior in a network." All lettering should be large enough to permit legible reduction. Suggested figure formats: TIFF, GIF, EPS, PPT, and Postscript.

Electronic Delivery of Accepted Papers
IMPORTANT - Send hard copy (of ACCEPTED paper) via one of the methods listed above. Note, in the event of minor discrepancies between the electronic version and the hard copy, the electronic file will be used as the final version.

Kluwer accepts a wide range of file formats: for manuscripts - Word, WordPerfect, RTF, TXT, and LaTex; for figures - TIFF, GIF, JPEG, EPS, PPT, and Postscript. PDF is not an acceptable format.

Via electronic mail
1. Please e-mail electronic version to: **KAPfiles@wkap.com**
2. Recommended formats for sending files via e-mail:
   - Binary files - uuencode or binhex
   - Compressing files - compress, pkzip, or gzip
   - Collecting files - tar
3. The e-mail message should include the author's last name, the name of the journal to which the paper has been accepted, and the type of file. Our e-mail system can handle maximum file size of 20 MB. Please FTP large files.

Via anonymous FTP
ftp: ftp.wkap.com
cd: /incoming/production

Send e-mail to **KAPfiles@wkap.com** to inform Kluwer electronic version is at this FTP site.

Via disk
1. Label a disk with the operating system and word processing program along with the authors' names, manuscript title, and name of journal to which the paper has been accepted.

2. Mail disk to:
   Kluwer Academic Publisher
   Desktop Department
   101 Philip Drive
   Assinippi Park
   Norwell, MA 02061, USA

Any questions about the above procedures please send e-mail to: dthelp@wkap.com

Proofing
Please be sure to include your e-mail address on your paper. If your paper is accepted, we will be forwarding your page proofs via e-mail. Your cooperation is appreciated. The proofread copy should be received back by the Publisher within 72 hours.

510

Copyright
It is the policy of Kluwer Academic Publishers to own the copyright of all contributions it publishes. To comply with the U.S. Copyright Law, authors are required to sign a copyright transfer form before publication. This form returns to authors and their employers full rights to reuse their material for their own purposes. Authors must submit a signed copy of this form with their manuscript.

Offprints
Each group of authors will be entitled to 50 free offprints of their paper.

Schmalenbach Business Review

ADDRESS FOR SUBMISSION:

Wolfgang Ballwieser, Managing Editor
Schmalenbach Business Review
University of Munich
Munich School of Management
Ludwigstr. 28/RG
80539 Munich,
Germany
Phone: +49-89-2180-6309
E-Mail: sbr@bwl.uni-muenchen.de
Web: www.sbr-online.de

PUBLICATION GUIDELINES:

Manuscript Length: 26-30
Copies Required: Two
Computer Submission: No
Format:
Fees to Review: 0.00 US$

Manuscript Style:
    See Manuscript Guidelines

CIRCULATION DATA:

Reader: Academics, Business Managers
Frequency of Issue: Quarterly
Sponsor/Publisher:

REVIEW INFORMATION:

Type of Review: Blind Review
No. of External Reviewers: 1-2
No. of In House Reviewers: 1
Acceptance Rate: 37%
Time to Review: 2 - 3 Months
Reviewers Comments: Yes
Invited Articles: 0-5%
Fees to Publish: 0.00 US$

MANUSCRIPT TOPICS:
Accounting Theory & Practice; Auditing; Corporate Finance; Cost Accounting; Financial Institutions & Markets; Financial Services; Government & Non Profit Accounting; Insurance; International Finance; Portfolio & Security Analysis; Tax Accounting

MANUSCRIPT GUIDELINES/COMMENTS:

Call for Papers
The *Schmalenbach Business Review - SBR -* is the international edition of the oldest and most prestigious German journal of business, named "Schmalenbachs Zeitschrift für betriebswirtschaftliche Forschung" (zfbf). *SBR's* goal is to publish original and innovative research. The journal covers topics especially in accounting, finance, taxation, marketing and organisation, but is open for further subjects. Thus, *SBR* attempts to bring together the most important management areas. This approach of not specializing in one specific subject, such as accounting or finance, stands in the tradition of German business research journals.

Schmalenbach Business Review (SBR) publishes original research of general interest in business administration. Authors are invited to submit theoretical as well as empirical papers which are innovative.

SBR is soliciting contributions from all fields of business administration. Traditionally, most papers are in the field of:

* Accounting
* Finance
* Marketing
* Organization

but this list is by no means exhaustive.

Every submission is refereed by two referees, at least one review is double-blind. Every effort is made to ensure a quick turnaround time; usually the reviewing time does not exceed 90 days. The journal's internationally composed board of editors and ad hoc referees guarantee the high quality standard of the journal. The Editor conducts a desk rejection when he believes the probability of acceptance is insufficient to cause the authors to wait for the outcome of the full review. For example, the manuscript might be a poor fit with the journal or the manuscript might fail to provide new findings over the extant literature. A maximum of one referee report will be provided.

Manuscripts should be sent in duplicate, together with an data file without the author's name. The data file can be separately sent as an attachment of an e-mail. The address is:

Wolfgang Ballwieser; Managing editor of *SBR*
Munich School of Management; University of Munich
Ludwigstr. 28/RG; D-80539 Munich; Germany
Email: **sbr@bwl.uni-muenchen.de**

Information to Authors
Submission of a paper to *SBR* implies that the paper is unpublished original work by the author(s) and is not under consideration for publication elsewhere. Authors declare this explicitly.

PAPER GUIDELINES
General
Submissions should not exceed 25 pages/6000 words. Please print in Times New Roman, 12 point, 1.5 spaced, left and right margin 3 cm. Accentuation in the text and the footnotes should be made by italics. Do not use bold print.

Structure
1 ((bold))
1.1 (italics)
1.1.1 ((italics))
and so on

Do not use specific abbreviations in the main text. Exceptions can be made at usually abbreviated nouns such as USA, EU, p., km, or technical terms such as Ltd., API.

Add an abstract of approximately 10-15 lines to every paper, keywords and the *JEL*-Classification.

First Page
The names of the authors should be marked with an asterisk (*). In the footnote the profession and corresponding address should be given.

The first page should contain only the names and information about the authors, the title of the paper and the abstract. The second page should start with the title without reference to the authors and then commence with the text.

Tables and Illustrations
Tables and illustrations should be separated from the text as originals to allow a good quality of reproduction. Electronic submission is allowed.

Every table or illustration should have a heading, printed in italics. References in the text should be printed in italics and are not abbreviated [see table 3]

References
References in the body text should be reduced to a minimum.

Citations are made according to the author-year-principle directly in the body text. Footnotes should only contain additional sources and comments, should be numbered consecutively and placed at the bottom of the relevant page. They should be kept to a minimum (for example, no more than one per three or four pages) and should be concise (for example, no more than three lines long).

For citations, please cite only the last name [e.g. (Rappaport (1975, 179))]. If there is more than one author separate the names using a slash [e.g. Jensen and Meckling (1976, 156) say...or (Jensen and Meckling (1976))]. If there is more than one reference in a footnote, separate the references with a semicolon [e.g. (Mattessich (1995, 149); Watts/Zimmerman (1986, 139)]. As short form for several authors the abbreviation "et al." might be used. To ensure uniqueness of references in case of the same authors and publications in the same year, use letters to distinguish them (e.g., Bromwich (2004a, 2004b)).

List of References
Do not use abbreviations for journals.

The literature should be cited with last name, given name (not abbreviated), year of publication (in brackets), title, and source with place of publication according to the following examples:

Book
    title of the publication, place of publication: publishing company [e.g. Watts, Ross L. and Jerold L. Zimmerman (1986), *Positive Accounting Theory*, New Jersey et al.: Prentice-Hall.]

514

Journal article
    title of the article, name of journal volume, pages [e.g. Jensen, Michael C. and Wil-liam
H. Meckling (1976), Theory of the firm: Managerial behavior, agency costs and ownership
structure, *Journal of Financial Economics* 3, 305-60.]

Article in edited volume
    title of the article, in name(s) of the editor(s), title of the book, place of publication:
publishing company, pages [e.g. Grossman, Sanford J. and Oliver D. Hart (1982), Corporate
financial structure and managerial incentives, in John J. McCall (ed.), *The Economics of
Information and Uncertainty*, Chicago, Ill.: University of Chicago Press, 123-55.]

Unpublished work
    Theissen, Erik (2001), *Price Discovery in Floor and Screen Trading Systems*, Working
Paper, University of Bonn.

Southwest Business and Economics Journal

ADDRESS FOR SUBMISSION:

Syed M. Ahmed, Editor
Southwest Business and Economics Journal
Cameron University
School of Business
Business Research Center
2800 W. Gore Boulevard
Lawton, OK 73505
USA
Phone: 580-581-2430
E-Mail: syeda@cameron.edu
Web: http://www.Cameron.edu/academic/
business/brc/soce.html

PUBLICATION GUIDELINES:

Manuscript Length: 11-20
Copies Required: Three
Computer Submission: Yes
Format: MS Word
Fees to Review: 0.00 US$

Manuscript Style:
American Psychological Association

CIRCULATION DATA:

Reader: Academics, Business Persons
Frequency of Issue: Yearly
Sponsor/Publisher: Cameron University

REVIEW INFORMATION:

Type of Review: Blind Review
No. of External Reviewers: 1-2
No. of In House Reviewers: 0-1
Acceptance Rate: 30-35%
Time to Review: 2 - 3 Months
Reviewers Comments: Yes
Invited Articles: 0-5%
Fees to Publish: 60.00 US$

MANUSCRIPT TOPICS:

Accounting Education; Accounting Information Systems; Accounting Theory & Practice; Auditing; Behavioral & Finance; Behavioral Accounting; Corporate Finance; Cost Accounting; Econometrics; Economic Development; Economic History; Financial Institutions & Markets; Financial Services; Fiscal Policy; Government & Non Profit Accounting; Industrial Organization; Insurance; International Economics & Trade; Macro Economics; Micro Economics; Monetary Policy; Portfolio & Security Analysis; Public Policy Economics; Real Estate; Regional Economics; Tax Accounting

MANUSCRIPT GUIDELINES/COMMENTS:

Editorial Information
The *Southwest Business and Economics Journal* is published once a year by the Business Research Center, School of Business, Cameron University, Lawton. OK.

The *Southwest Business and Economics Journal* provides a bridge of communication between the business community and the academia. Articles related to all business areas and regional economic development are welcome. The journal publishes refereed articles from the academic community and an occasional invited article from business practitioners. The target audience includes both academics and the business and professional community. Priority will be given to subjects dealing with interpretations or new understandings, and solutions to problems faced by business and government leaders.

Author Guidelines

1. All submitted work must be original work that is not under submission to another journal or under consideration for publication in another form.

2. Authors must submit three double-spaced typewritten copies of their paper. Three copies of the paper should be submitted, in addition to the e-mail submission as an attached MS-WORD document.

3. The cover page shall contain the title of the paper, author's name, and affiliation. This page will be removed when the paper is sent to a referee. The first page of text should contain the title but not the name of the author.

4. A separate abstract of not more than 100 words should be included.

5. Each table and figure should be on a separate page at the end of the paper, with proper instructions about their placement in the paper.

6. Footnotes must be consecutively numbered and typed on a separate page and double-spaced.

7. Cite references in the text, placing the publication date in parentheses, e.g., "Banz (1981) was the first..." References should follow APA guidelines.

8. *Southwest Business and Economics Journal* will hold exclusive rights after acceptance.

9. Authors are advised to mention their office and residence telephone numbers and convenient times for contact.

10. The paper should be submitted to the Editor.

We accept computer submissions formatted in Word.

Spectrum

ADDRESS FOR SUBMISSION:

Darryl R. Matthews, Sr., Editor
Spectrum
7249 A Hanover Parkway
Greenbelt, MD 20770
USA
Phone: 301-474-6222
E-Mail: darrylmatthews@nabainc.org
Web: www.nabainc.org

PUBLICATION GUIDELINES:

Manuscript Length: 6-10
Copies Required: Four
Computer Submission: No
Format: N/A
Fees to Review: 0.00 US$

Manuscript Style:

CIRCULATION DATA:

Reader: Business Persons, Academic
Frequency of Issue: Yearly
Sponsor/Publisher: Professional Assn.

REVIEW INFORMATION:

Type of Review: Blind Review
No. of External Reviewers: 2
No. of In House Reviewers: 1
Acceptance Rate: 21-30%
Time to Review: 2 - 3 Months
Reviewers Comments: Yes
Invited Articles: 21-30%
Fees to Publish: 0.00 US$

MANUSCRIPT TOPICS:

Accounting Information Systems; Accounting Theory & Practice; Auditing; Cost Accounting; Econometrics; Fiscal Policy; Micro Economics

MANUSCRIPT GUIDELINES/COMMENTS:

This annual publication is the official journal of the National Association of Black Accountants, Inc. The journal is published with the intent of providing a communication mechanism whereby readers are kept abreast of key topics of interest within the accounting, finance, and business professions.

Technology updates, conferences and events, and updates relative to industry standards are among the items covered.

518

State Tax Notes Magazine

ADDRESS FOR SUBMISSION:

Carol Douglas, Editor
State Tax Notes Magazine
Tax Analysts
6830 N. Fairfax Drive
Arlington, VA 22213
USA
Phone: 703-533-4451
E-Mail: cdouglas@tax.org
Web: www.taxanalysts.com

CIRCULATION DATA:

Reader: Academics, Business Persons,
  Government
Frequency of Issue: Weekly
Sponsor/Publisher: Tax Analysts

PUBLICATION GUIDELINES:

Manuscript Length: Up to 30
Copies Required: One
Computer Submission: Yes
Format: MS Word
Fees to Review: 0.00 US$

Manuscript Style:

REVIEW INFORMATION:

Type of Review: Editorial Review
No. of External Reviewers: 0
No. of In House Reviewers: 1
Acceptance Rate: 50%
Time to Review: 1 Month or Less
Reviewers Comments: No
Invited Articles: 21-30%
Fees to Publish: 0.00 US$

MANUSCRIPT TOPICS:
Fiscal Policy; State & Local Taxation; Tax Accounting

MANUSCRIPT GUIDELINES/COMMENTS:

1. E-mail *Tax Notes* submissions to **taxnotes@tax.org** and *State Tax Notes* submissions to **cdouglas@tax.org**. Articles should be attached as Word files. Charts and tables should be attached as Excel files. Include the author's phone and fax numbers. Please do not send PDFs, even if the article has already been published in another journal or magazine. Our production process requires a Microsoft Word file.

2. Submissions for consideration as special reports should be no more than 100 double-spaced pages. Submissions for consideration as viewpoints, practice articles, or other commentary should be no more than 20 double-spaced pages.

3. Article titles and subheads should be as short as possible. If your article has more than one level of subheads, use the following system:
I. Level 1
A. Level 2
i. Level 3
a. Level 4

4. We use a modified *Blue Book* style of citations. Citations to articles that appear in *Tax Notes* and *State Tax Notes* should be as follows:

Jones, "Tax Reform Is Good," *Tax Notes*, Oct. 15, 2004, p. 253.

Doe, "Sales Tax Should Be Streamlined," *State Tax Notes*, Nov. 1, 2004, p. 123.

Citations to articles in newspapers and nonlegal journals (such as *The New York Times* or *Forbes*) should follow that style.

Citations to items in *Tax Notes Today* (*TNT*) and *State Tax Today* (*STT*) that do not appear in *Tax Notes* and *State Tax Notes* should always be cited as follows:

Letter to Treasury from John Q. Lawyer, *Doc 2004-12345, 2004* TNT 123-45 (Oct. 15, 2004).

For the Massachusetts Supreme Judicial Court's decision in *Sherwin-Williams*, see *Doc 2002-24629* or *2002 STT 213-20.*

If you are citing to something that appears in *Tax Notes*, use only the *Tax Notes* citation and not the doc number or *TNT* cite.

Citations to articles from law reviews and similar journals should be as follows: Smith, "Tax Reform Is Good," 56 *Tax Law Rev.* 345 (Jan. 2004).

Authors' names should be in roman, article titles should be in quotation marks, and book and journal titles should be in italics — all with initial caps only.

If you cite something more than once, use a shortened version in all footnotes after the first one. Example: Smith, *supra* note 1 at 352.

Do not use Roman numerals for footnote numbering.

Please try to keep footnotes to a reasonable minimum.

5. For all submissions, include a short (one or two sentences) bio of the author(s). For *Tax Notes* special reports only, include a one- or two-paragraph summary of the article.

6. If you have questions, please call:

Tax Notes Editor Bob Wells at 703.533.4684, Deputy Editor Jon Almeras at 703.531.4823, or Managing Editor John Bell at 703.533.4678.

State Tax Notes Editor Carol Douglas at 703.533.4451 or Managing Editor Dean Ahearn at 703.533.4464.

Strategic Finance Magazine

ADDRESS FOR SUBMISSION:

Kathy Willliams, Ediltor
Strategic Finance Magazine
Institute of Management Accountants
10 Paragon Drive
Montvale, NJ 07645
USA
Phone: 201-474-1576
E-Mail: kwilliams@imanet.org
Web: www.strategicfinancemag.com

CIRCULATION DATA:

Reader: Business Persons
Frequency of Issue: Monthly
Sponsor/Publisher: Institute of Management
   Accountants

PUBLICATION GUIDELINES:

Manuscript Length: 11-15
Copies Required: Four
Computer Submission: Yes
Format: MS Word
Fees to Review: 0.00 US$

Manuscript Style:
   Chicago Manual of Style

REVIEW INFORMATION:

Type of Review: Blind Review
No. of External Reviewers: 3
No. of In House Reviewers: 2
Acceptance Rate: 11-20%
Time to Review: 2-6 Months
Reviewers Comments: Yes
Invited Articles: 31-50%
Fees to Publish: 0.00 US$

MANUSCRIPT TOPICS:
Accounting Information Systems; Auditing; Corporate Finance; Cost Accounting; Fiscal Policy; Industrial Organization; Insurance; International Economics & Trade; International Finance; Monetary Policy; Portfolio & Security Analysis; Tax Accounting; Technology

MANUSCRIPT GUIDELINES/COMMENTS:

What should you write about?
Strategic Finance publishes only original material that contributes to the profession of management accounting and financial management.

We recommend that you study several issues of our magazine before you write and submit your manuscript. The best advice is to write only about the topics you know best and with which you've had experience.

Submitting Your Manuscript
We recommend submitting your manuscript via the online submission form. Files should be in Word or WordPerfect formats. We can also take .txt or .rtf files. Manuscripts must be accompanied by a submission form, so please don't e-mail files directly to us unless you have already submitted the form. Manuscripts will not be processed without a form.

If you need to submit your manuscript via hard copy, it should be on plain white 8 ½" x 11" paper in a printed format. Leave sufficient margins on all sides (one inch is recommended). The text should be double-spaced. Include four copies of the manuscript along with a submission form. The form itself can still be submitted electronically, but include a copy with the manuscripts to ensure accurate processing. If your manuscript is accepted for publication, you will need to send us an electronic version via e-mail, 3.5" disk, or CD.

Write the title of your manuscript and the names of author(s) on a cover page. If there is more than one author, list the authors' names in the order you want them to appear in print. Number each page at the bottom. Do not put an author's name on anything but the cover page because all manuscripts are reviewed "blind." Using the author's name within the manuscript itself will cause delays in the manuscript processing and slow down the review process. If it must be used within the context of the article, black out the name. The editorial staff and reviewers will understand it is referring to the author. Names can also be used in citations and other references if there is no indication that the person listed is also the author.

The criteria for acceptable manuscripts are:
1. IMA is given exclusive publication rights.
2. Manuscripts must be accompanied by a Manuscript Submission form.
3. Manuscripts must not hale been previously published.
4. They must be submitted in English and in completed form for publication.
5. If authored by a nonmember, they must be accompanied by author's mailing address.
6. They must not be a poem outline, abstract, thesis, school term/research paper, unedited speech, or previously accepted manuscript.

The content of the manuscript must be timely.

Preparing Your Manuscript
Your manuscript must be accompanied by an official submission form. You can obtain the submission form from the website or through your chapter's manuscript director. Manuscripts without this form will be returned to the author.

Length of Manuscript. Most manuscripts we publish are approximately 11-15 typewritten double-spaced pages. Ideal length is about 1,500-2,000 words for *Strategic Finance.*

Abstract. Please provide an abstract or summary of your article on a separate sheet of paper. The editors use this abstract to summarize and introduce your article in the table of contents.

Tables and Figures. Your manuscript will be strengthened if you can illustrate your points. Graphic illustrations should be kept simple and in proportion to the manuscript's length. There should be a specific reference in the text to each table or figure in your manuscript, and put each table or figure on a separate sheet of paper.

Bio and Footnotes. Please include brief biographies of all authors with your manuscript, and make sure they contain a phone number and/or e-mail address for each author. We do not use footnotes in *Strategic Finance* articles, so please include such material in the text of the article, and use it only when necessary. If you want to include a list of references, please put them on a separate page at the end of the manuscript. Please include author's full name, title of publication, name of publisher, date of publication, and page numbers where applicable.

The Review Process
All manuscripts submitted to *Strategic Finance* are reviewed in a two-stage process to determine if they are appropriate for publication. Each manuscript is assigned a control number when the Publications staff receives it. The author is notified of this control number via e-mail. When you want to know the status of your manuscript, please refer to this number when you contact the staff.

Technical Review. Each manuscript undergoes a blind review by three independent reviewers who have expertise in specific areas. All references to the author are deleted from the original and copies. Members of the manuscript appraisal committee base their evaluations on the following seven major criteria:

1. Is the topic of the manuscript relevant for our readers?
2. How well was the topic covered? Was it a thorough analysis and description of the topic? Were any assertions made that were not supported by the evidence and data supplied?
3. Is the manuscript original and not a rehash of what has been published previously?
4. Is it practical? Can our readers use the information to benefit their companies and careers?
5. Is it technically correct and, sound?
6. Is the topic timely? Does toe manuscript reflect the latest pronouncements and research? Does it represent, a new development or innovation of which our members should be aware?
7. Is the material presented clearly and concisely?

When these manuscript appraisal forms are returned to the editorial department after review, the three grades are then averaged to determine the overall grade assigned to the manuscript. Reviewers are asked to recommend that the manuscript be published, revised, or rejected and to provide reasons for their recommendations. We also ask them for suggestions on how the technical content of the manuscript can be improved. Based on the review committee's comments and further evaluation by the editorial staff of the magazine, manuscripts will either be considered for publication or rejected.

Publication
If your manuscript is selected for publication, you will be notified once the review process is complete and asked to submit an electronic version if you haven't already done so.

Once the editor has selected a publication date, a staff member will edit your manuscript and send you the edited version and a copyright permission form. Please review the editing, make any changes, sign the copyright form, and return all material within five days of receipt. During the editing process, an editor will contact you to discuss tables or figures to illustrate the article or any other matters pertaining to the content.

Return of Your Manuscript. If your manuscript is rejected, we'll let you know as soon as the decision is made. Remember to keep a copy of your article for your own records. The Publications Department can't be responsible for retaining rejected manuscripts.

Awards

The IMA member authors of the top manuscripts submitted, determined by the grade average, and published during the competition year are presented Certificates of Merit for their outstanding contributions to accounting and finance literature. IMA member authors of the top three manuscripts, as determined by an editorial advisory committee, will be presented Lybrand Gold, Silver, and Bronze Medals, respectively.

IMA Chapter Competition

As part of the yearly competition, chapters can earn credit in the Elective Activities category for submitting a manuscript to the magazines. An acceptable manuscript submitted on time is worth up to 300 points. There is also a bonus of 5% if one or more authors is an IMA member. There is a deduction of 10% for manuscripts submitted after the deadline. The deadline for full credit is November 20, of the competition year. No points will be awarded in the current competition year for manuscripts submitted after April 20.

To be eligible, manuscripts must meet the criteria listed above (see SUBMITTING YOUR MANUSCRIPT. A submission form, with chapter name and number in the proper fields, must accompany the manuscript. Failure to complete the form properly or follow any of the other submission criteria can result in a point deduction (if it needs to be resubmitted after the deadline) or the chapter may not get credit. The editorial decision to either accept or reject the manuscript far; publication does not affect the number bf points awarded to the chapter. As long as the manuscript meets the criteria and can be processed for review, the chapter will receive credit. See the Chapter Competition Guide for more information.

Tips For Effective Writing

Staff editors carefully edit every manuscript scheduled for publication. They follow a number of general principles in the editing process. Here are some suggestions for effective writing:

* Write punchy lead paragraphs that will "grab" readers and pull them into the article.
* Avoid long introductions. Get right to the point. Tell the reader exactly what you plan to do.
* Avoid jargon and acronyms. Readers don't like to go back and check their meaning.
* Don't pad your manuscript. It will be obvious to the editor and to the reader-if the editor lets the material stand.
* Avoid long, complex sentences. Break a complex thought into two or more sentences.
* Don't assume that the reader knows as much as you do. Carefully explain or define a term that isn't commonly used or was coined at your company.
* Use the active voice, not passive. Instead of writing "It was accomplished in 10 days," say "We finished the project in 10 days."
* Write a conclusion that sums up your major points and makes a statement on why the article is important to the reader.

Suggested Topics for Strategic Finance Authors
1. Treasury
2. Cash Management & Banking Relations
3. Corporate Development and Strategic Planning

4. Financing
5. Investor Relations
6. International Finance/IASC
7. Insurance (especially operational liability)
8. Financial Risk Analysis and Management (risks and opportunities)
9. Employee Benefits
10. Retirement Plans and Pension Administration
11. Leading
12. Investment Management and the Equity Market (IPO)
13. Management Information Systems
14. Other Technology Issues
15. Real Estate (such as valuation of private and public corporate enterprises)
16. SEC and FASB Regulatory Issues and other governmental regulations
17. Financial Reporting
18. Mergers & Acquisitions & Restructuring
19. Controllership
20. Budgeting & Planning
21. Capital Budgeting
22. Cost Accounting
23. AOM/Target Costing/Theory of Constraints
24. Corporate Taxes
25. Enterprise Resource Planning
26. Performance Measurement and Evaluation
27. Ethics
28. Intellectual Capital
29. R&D and New Product Development
30. Life-Cycle Product Analysis
31. Joint Ventures
32. Management of Human Resources/Employee Training and Education/Behavior
33. Communications and Presentation Skills
34. Internal Auditing
35. Awareness of External Auditing
36. Liquidation and Bankruptcy
37. Economical/Competitive Environment
38. Current Asset Utilization (AIR, Inventory Management)
39. Business Law
40. Bargaining Unit Negotiation
41. Outsourcing
42. Purchasing
43. Quantitative Analysis (statistics)
44. Industrial Engineering (factory floor optimization)

Tax Adviser (The)

ADDRESS FOR SUBMISSION:

Lesli S. Laffie, Editor
Tax Adviser (The)
American Institute of CPAs
Harborside Financial Center
201 Plaza Three
Jersey City, NJ 07311-3881
USA
Phone: 201-938-3445
E-Mail: llaffie@aicpa.org
Web: See Guidelines

PUBLICATION GUIDELINES:

Manuscript Length: 12-20
Copies Required: One
Computer Submission: Yes Email Preferred
Format: MS Word
Fees to Review: 0.00 US$

Manuscript Style:
　See Manuscript Guidelines

CIRCULATION DATA:

Reader: , CPAs, Tax Practitioners
Frequency of Issue: Monthly
Sponsor/Publisher: American Institute of
　CPAs

REVIEW INFORMATION:

Type of Review: Blind Review
No. of External Reviewers: 2
No. of In House Reviewers: 0
Acceptance Rate: 50%
Time to Review: 1 Month or Less
Reviewers Comments: Yes
Invited Articles: 50% +
Fees to Publish: 0.00 US$

MANUSCRIPT TOPICS:
Tax Accounting; Taxation

MANUSCRIPT GUIDELINES/COMMENTS:

The Tax Adviser covers a wide range of tax information. As an editorial objective, *The Tax Adviser* deals primarily with the technical aspects of Federal (and some state) taxation, providing practical, administrative and technical commentary through articles and regular departments. Thus, the material has a broad range of appeal, satisfying the needs of anyone who must keep informed on Federal tax matters. Qualified articles will be accepted from CPAs, lawyers, tax executives and professors.

We request that you submit your article exclusively to *The Tax Adviser*; articles are not considered on any other basis. Please note that our acceptance of a manuscript for Editorial Advisory Board review is not approval to publish the article. It is our practice to send the article to at least two of our Editorial Advisers for their opinion on publishing the article, technical advice and constructive comments. The reviewers are expected to submit their decision within about four weeks. Articles accepted for publication are subject to editorial revision. Regrettably, our budget does not provide for compensating authors of articles. However, as a token of our appreciation, an author will receive five copies of the issue containing his article. Also, 50 complimentary reprints of the article itself will be made available on request.

If you would like to have an article peer reviewed by an academic peer, please let us know.

General Suggestions. This section is devoted to providing guidelines for the selection of specific subjects for articles. By outlining several broad categories of articles, it may stimulate you or your colleagues to select a topic of interest. Certain articles are cited from *The Tax Adviser* to exemplify each approach.

1. Significant recent developments in a given area
This type of article separates fact from opinion. The ruling or court decision is discussed; the author's comments (e.g., analysis, tax planning hints) then follow.

See Whitlock, "Significant Recent Developments in Estate Planning" (September 2004).

2. In-depth treatment of a narrow point
No subject is too narrow to be a subject for a tax article—assuming that it requires (without padding) about 15 manuscript pages.

See Schell, "Proposed Regs. Shed Light on Income Forecast Method" (August 2004).

3. Estate planning articles
Because tax practitioners are, in general, not very sophisticated in estate planning, there is a greater latitude for selection of subjects in this area. The subject matter—but not the treatment—can be less sophisticated.

See Zupanc, Gaumnitz and Gaumnitz, "The Intricacies of Special-Use Valuation" (July 2004); Smith, "Navigating the Revised Gift Tax Return" (December 2003).

4. Analysis of current development(s)
This would include analysis and planning ideas under new legislation.

See Pannese and Iannone, "Post-JGTRRA Dividend Planning" (June 2004).

5. Community property articles
Despite the fact that affluent taxpayers are migrating to and from community property states in increasing numbers and the population of such states has been growing disproportionately, the national tax periodicals seem to provide insufficient coverage of community property issues. Therefore, this tax area should provide a fertile source of specific subjects for articles that will interest a number of common law (as well as community property) state practitioners.

See Rogers, Christensen and Cochran, "Overcoming the *Boggs* Dilemma in Community Property States," Part I (August 1999), Part II (September 1999).

6. Several articles covering one aspect of a broad area

This approach has been taken with respect to consolidated returns and ERISA, and could be applied to other areas, such as subpart F.

See Pannese and Iannone, "Post-JGTRRA Dividend Planning" (June 2004); Godfrey, "The Phaseout of the Federal State Death Tax Credit," Part I (February 2004), Part II (March 2004); Hegt, "JGTRRA Cuts Rates, Offers Some Deductions and Credits" (September 2003).

7. Trade or business profiles

Articles dealing with a particular type of business, such as a bank or insurance company, or a particular size of business.

See Altieri, "A Fringe Benefit Primer for the Closely Held C Corporation," Part I (October 2004), Part II (November 2004).

8. Tax policy

This type of article should deal with matters of policy on essentially a technical, rather than purely political, basis.

See Nellen, "The AICPA's 10 Guiding Principles" (February 2002).

9. Subjects requiring current coverage

Subjects that have been covered extensively in the not-too-recent past may still be worthy of coverage because of tax, accounting, economic or other reasons.

See Eyberg and Raasch, "FLP Planning after *Strangi, Kimbell* and *Thompson*" (December 2004); Wood and Daher, "Class Actions and the Attorneys' Fees Conundrum" (July 2004).

10. Proposed, temporary or final regulations

Articles on proposed, temporary or final regulations are always welcome, if the topic is of broad enough interest. Planning ideas under the rules should be included.

See Thompson, "Temp. Regs. Limit Duplicative Stock Losses" (January 2004); Schell, "Proposed Regulations Shed Light on Income Forecast Method" (August 2004).

11. Problems, pitfalls and planning opportunities

This type of article deals with the problems, etc., concerning a given tax subject, the general rules of which the reader is already familiar (or can become familiar) with. That is, technical explanations would be limited to that relevant to the problem, etc., at issue.

See Sunderman, "GRAT Planning with S Corp. Stock" (August 2004).

12. Checklists

See MacDonough, et al., "S Corporation Elections Guide" (September 2003).

528

13. New laws

Of course, new laws provide a fertile source of articles. *TTA's* experience with recent legislation shows that quality, rather than time, is of the essence to the publication of articles on new laws. Because the tax services can publish surveys of new laws more quickly, no real purpose is served by stressing time in publishing articles in *TTA*.

See Pannese and Iannone, "Post-JGTRRA Dividend Planning" (June 2004); Friske and Smith, "The Marriage Penalty after the JGTRRA" (May 2004); Godfrey, "The Phaseout of the Federal State Death Tax Credit," Part I (February 2004), Part II (March 2004).

Specific Topics. General subjects for articles suggested by *The Tax Adviser's* Editorial Advisers and staff.

Please note. At any given time, some topics are more "current" than others; *TTA* may have covered a topic recently or exhaustively; keep this in mind in selecting a subject to write about.

- AMT issues (individual or corporate)
- Accounting periods and methods
- Asset protection
- Bonds and exempt obligations
- Buy-sell agreements (from a CPA's perspective)
- Capital gains and losses
- Cash and currency reporting requirements
- Citizens living abroad
- Commuting expenses, deducting
- Compensation techniques planning
- Competent authority practice
- Compliance and penalties
- Confidentiality
- Consolidated return planning
- Corporate mergers & acquisitions
- Criminal tax penalties
- Current developments in depreciation
- Debt restructuring
- Deductions and credits
- Discharge of indebtedness income (Sec. 108(a)(1)(D))
- Earnings and profits problems
- Employee benefits
- Employee stock options
- Employee versus independent contractor issues
- Employing U.S. nationals abroad, compensation and tax issues
- Environmental cleanup costs
- Estate planning strategies (from a CPA's perspective)

- Ethics in tax practice
- Exempt organizations
- Family tax issues (divorce, community property, income-shifting, kiddie tax, etc.)
- Filing status
- Foreign corporations & nonresident aliens doing business in the U.S.
- Foreign income and taxpayers
- Fringe benefits and pass through entities
- Generation-skipping tax planning
- Hedging—rules and strategies
- Home office deductions
- Intangibles—depreciation, valuation
- IRS voluntary disclosure—does a policy exist?
- Imputed interest
- Inventory
- Life insurance in estate planning
- Life insurance issues
- LLCs and LLPs
- Lobbying expenses
- Offers in compromise
- OID issues
- PHC issues
- Partnership issues (including anti-abuse rule)
- Passive loss planning
- Payroll taxes: acquisitions & mergers
- Pensions
- Planning for Sec. 531 (AET)
- Post-mortem checklist
- Pre-publication costs (expenses accrued by authors, deductions)
- Real estate ownership
- Related-party transactions—accruals and sales
- S corporations
- SEPs
- Stock redemption agreements
- Tax aspects of bankruptcy
- Tax effect on the individual stockholder caught in a takeover, buyout, etc.
- Tax planning involving spreadsheet analysis
- Tax practice management
- Tax treaties—e.g., "permanent establishment" rules
- Taxation of financial institutions
- Taxation of life insurance companies
- Tax technology (software, hardware, the Internet, intranets)
- Trust use (from a CPA's perspective)
- Valuation of inventory
- Year-end tax planning

Preparing the Manuscript
It would greatly facilitate the processing of your article if you would observe the guidelines listed below for preparing your manuscript.

Title and Author. On a top sheet, give the title of the article, your name, professional affiliation, and contact information (phone/fax/e-mail).

Typing. All articles should be word-processed on one side of 8 ½" x 11" white paper, *double-spaced*, with a left hand margin of about two inches. Keep the formatting as simple as possible; do not use fancy typefaces or extra tabs.

Copies. Send two extra copies, if possible, for submission to the reviewing editorial advisers.

Footnotes. Keep footnotes to a minimum; cite Code sections and regulations in the text itself. Type all footnotes double-spaced and appropriately numbered at the *end* of the manuscript. Please do not embed the footnotes. See also *Citations*, below.

Length of Manuscript. Keep articles to a maximum of 12 pages (approximately four to five pages in the magazine).

Citations. Preferably, citations should be confined to footnotes. In any event, give only the "handle" (case name, etc.) in the text. (For example, if the *Schlude* decision is frequently referred to in the article, state: "In *Schlude*, the Supreme Court..."). In citations, exclude "Commissioner," "U.S." or the district director's name; they are unnecessary.

Tax Lawyer (The)

ADDRESS FOR SUBMISSION:

Jerald David August, Editor-in-Chief
Tax Lawyer (The)
American Bar Association
740 15th Street, N.W.
Washington, DC 20005
USA
Phone: 202-662-8681
E-Mail: dunna@staff.abanet.org
Web: www.abanet.org

CIRCULATION DATA:

Reader: Academics, Lawyers, Accountants,
Gov't Officials
Frequency of Issue: Quarterly
Sponsor/Publisher: American Bar
Association

PUBLICATION GUIDELINES:

Manuscript Length: 30+
Copies Required: Three
Computer Submission: Yes
Format: MS Word, ASCII
Fees to Review: 0.00 US$

Manuscript Style:
Uniform System of Citation (Harvard
Blue Book)

REVIEW INFORMATION:

Type of Review: Editorial Review
No. of External Reviewers: 3+
No. of In House Reviewers: 1
Acceptance Rate: 6-10%
Time to Review: 1 - 2 Months
Reviewers Comments: Yes
Invited Articles: 21-30%
Fees to Publish: 0.00 US$

MANUSCRIPT TOPICS:
Domestic Tax Issues; International Tax; Tax Accounting

MANUSCRIPT GUIDELINES/COMMENTS:

Statement of Editorial Policy
The Tax Lawyer endeavors to provide scholarly articles and student notes and comments on topics pertaining to taxation and other information that it believes to be of professional interest to members of the Section of Taxation of the American Bar Association and other readers.

The Tax Lawyer welcomes the submission of articles written by admitted members of the bar and by other professionals. Manuscripts by candidates for graduate degrees in law (e.g., LL.M. or M.L.T.) will be considered only if the author is admitted to the bar at the time of submission and will be considered student notes if the author is not admitted to the bar at the time of submission.

Although utmost care will be given to material submitted, *The Tax Lawyer* does not accept responsibility for unsolicited manuscripts. Authors are encouraged to submit articles electronically in the form of an e-mail attachment. Articles submitted as e-mail attachments must be formatted in MS Word. Please use standard formatting and fonts. E-mail submissions should be sent to: Assistant Staff Director, Publications, at **taxweb@staff.abanet.org**. Please refer to "The Tax Lawyer" in the subject line of the e-mail message. Authors who choose to send their manuscripts by regular mail should send three (3) copies, typewritten and double-spaced, to: Assistant Staff Director, Publications, ABA Section of Taxation, 740 15th Street, NW, Washington, DC 20005.

The Editorial Board of *The Tax Lawyer* reserves the right to accept or reject any article, note or comment and the right to condition acceptance upon revision of material to conform to its criteria. *The Tax Lawyer* does not publish material that has been previously published or is scheduled for publication elsewhere. Articles, notes and comments are accepted on the basis of merit, professional interest, appeal to the readership of *The Tax Lawyer*, timeliness of the topic, clarity of expression, and style. Notes and comments should consist of either analysis of recent developments in tax law or comments on important current tax cases.

Because issues of tax law and policy are frequently controversial, readers of *The Tax Lawyer* should understand that opinions expressed in its articles, notes and comments are solely those of the authors and may differ from those of the American Bar Association, the Section of Taxation, the Editorial Board of *The Tax Lawyer*, and the Student Editorial Board of *The Tax Lawyer*. An article contributed by a public official does not necessarily represent the views of that person's department or agency unless expressly stated in the particular instance. Nothing herein shall be construed as representing the opinions, views, or actions of the American Bar Association or of the Section of Taxation unless duly approved by the Association or the Section as the case may be.

Tax Management Real Estate Journal

ADDRESS FOR SUBMISSION:

Donald B. Reynolds, Jr., Editor
Tax Management Real Estate Journal
Buchanan Ingersoll PC Attorneys,
 Including the law firm of
 Silverstein and Mullens
1776 K Street, N.W., Suite 800
Washington, DC 20006
USA
Phone: 202-452-7958
E-Mail: reynoldsdb@bipc.com
Web: www.bnatax.com

PUBLICATION GUIDELINES:

Manuscript Length: 20+
Copies Required: One
Computer Submission: Yes
Format:
Fees to Review: 0.00 US$

Manuscript Style:
 See Manuscript Guidelines

CIRCULATION DATA:

Reader: Business Persons, Tax
 Professionals
Frequency of Issue: Monthly
Sponsor/Publisher: Tax Management, Inc.

REVIEW INFORMATION:

Type of Review: Editorial Review
No. of External Reviewers: 1
No. of In House Reviewers: 1
Acceptance Rate: 50%
Time to Review: 1 Month or Less
Reviewers Comments: Yes
Invited Articles: 50% +
Fees to Publish: 0.00 US$

MANUSCRIPT TOPICS:
Real Estate; Tax Accounting; Taxation

MANUSCRIPT GUIDELINES/COMMENTS:

1. Law journal quality original articles fully cited as to authorities used.

2. Short notes, reviews, letters welcomed.

3. Submission of MS with computer diskette or email attachment and hard copy appreciated.

4. *Uniform System of Citation* (17th Edition)

Information for Authors
The coverage and scope of the *Tax Management Real Estate Journal* is broad because of the numerous issues that arise in the taxation of real estate transactions. In addition to "typical" real estate subjects, it also includes such matters as partnerships and Subchapter S, tax shelters, low-income housing, tax-exempt bonds, real estate financing, installment sales, FIRPTA, tax-free exchanges of property, and transactional aspects of real estate. The *Journal*

534

strives to publish original articles of law journal quality, adequately researched and with the requisite citations of authorities, which will be of use to tax professionals involved in real estate transactions and sophisticated real estate investors.

Each monthly issue usually contains one or two principal articles of a length of from six to fifteen printed pages. Since one typeset page holds four to five double spaced manuscript pages, this means the typical article can vary from twenty-five to sixty typewritten pages. Longer articles are sometimes divided in two and printed in successive issues. The publisher's deadline is the last Wednesday of each month, so articles are needed as early in the month as possible in order that they may be fully reviewed and, if appropriate, discussed with the author by phone. Naturally, the sooner the manuscript is made available the better, since occasionally it is necessary to return one to the author for revision. The editor also welcomes shorter articles, commentaries and opinions, and reviews of books and real estate software.

Please include a two or three sentence **biography** that can be used as a non-numbered footnote on the first page and a one or two paragraph **abstract** that will precede the main body of the text. The abstract should state the subject and purpose of the article and major conclusions and recommendations.

Manuscripts should be typed double-spaced with a table of contents to assist in their review (and with footnotes at the end preferred). If possible, please include a 3 ½" diskette containing the article, marked to show the file name(s) and the name of the WP software. Alternatively, articles may be emailed to the editor at the above-mentioned address. No fee is paid for contributions submitted to the *Journal*, but incidental expenses, such as Federal Express, will be reimbursed on request. Ten extra copies of issues containing their published articles are routinely provided to authors with larger quantities being made available by advance arrangements.

Advisory board presentations. Twice a year (usually on the third Thursdays of December and June at 5:30 p.m. in the Waldorf Astoria Hotel) the Tax Management Real Estate Advisory Board meets in New York City for the presentation of three papers on real estate taxation. Papers presented at Advisory Board meetings are duplicated and mailed to board members about the first of the month during which the meeting is held. Authors are encouraged to make any revisions they wish subsequent to the board meeting and prior to publication. Such revised manuscripts are needed by the end of the month in which the meeting was held. The speakers are reimbursed for hotel, meal and travel expenses.

Sponsorship: Tax Management, Inc., The Bureau of National Affairs, Inc., Washington, DC

Tax Notes

ADDRESS FOR SUBMISSION:

Robert J. Wells, Editor
Tax Notes
6830 North Fairfax Drive
Arlington, VA 22213
USA
Phone: 703-533-4468
E-Mail: taxnotes@tax.org
Web: www.taxanalysts.com

CIRCULATION DATA:

Reader: Academics, Lawyers, Acountants,
   Policy Experts, Lawmakers
Frequency of Issue: Weekly
Sponsor/Publisher: Tax Analysts, Inc.

PUBLICATION GUIDELINES:

Manuscript Length: Any
Copies Required: One
Computer Submission: Yes Email Preferred
Format: Any
Fees to Review: 0.00 US$

Manuscript Style:
   See Manuscript Guidelines

REVIEW INFORMATION:

Type of Review: Editorial Review
No. of External Reviewers: 0
No. of In House Reviewers: 3
Acceptance Rate: 50 %
Time to Review: 1 Month or Less
Reviewers Comments: No
Invited Articles: 0-5%
Fees to Publish: 0.00 US$

MANUSCRIPT TOPICS:

Accounting Theory & Practice; Economic History; Tax Accounting; Tax History; Tax Policy; Tax Practice

MANUSCRIPT GUIDELINES/COMMENTS:

1. E-mail *Tax Notes* submissions to **taxnotes@tax.org** and *State Tax Notes* submissions to **cdouglas@tax.org**. Articles should be attached as Word files. Charts and tables should be attached as Excel files. Include the author's phone and fax numbers. Please do not send PDFs, even if the article has already been published in another journal or magazine. Our production process requires a Microsoft Word file.

2. Submissions for consideration as special reports should be no more than 100 double-spaced pages. Submissions for consideration as viewpoints, practice articles, or other commentary should be no more than 20 double-spaced pages.

3. Article titles and subheads should be as short as possible. If your article has more than one level of subheads, use the following system:
I. Level 1
A. Level 2
i. Level 3
a. Level 4

4. We use a modified *Blue Book* style of citations. Citations to articles that appear in *Tax Notes* and *State Tax Notes* should be as follows:

Jones, "Tax Reform Is Good," *Tax Notes*, Oct. 15, 2004, p. 253.

Doe, "Sales Tax Should Be Streamlined," *State Tax Notes*, Nov. 1, 2004, p. 123.

Citations to articles in newspapers and nonlegal journals (such as *The New York Times* or *Forbes*) should follow that style.

Citations to items in *Tax Notes Today* (*TNT*) and *State Tax Today* (*STT*) that do not appear in *Tax Notes* and *State Tax Notes* should always be cited as follows:

Letter to Treasury from John Q. Lawyer, *Doc 2004-12345, 2004* TNT 123-45 (Oct. 15, 2004).

For the Massachusetts Supreme Judicial Court's decision in *Sherwin-Williams*, see *Doc 2002-24629* or *2002 STT 213-20*.

If you are citing to something that appears in *Tax Notes*, use only the *Tax Notes* citation and not the doc number or *TNT* cite.

Citations to articles from law reviews and similar journals should be as follows: Smith, "Tax Reform Is Good," 56 *Tax Law Rev.* 345 (Jan. 2004).

Authors' names should be in roman, article titles should be in quotation marks, and book and journal titles should be in italics — all with initial caps only.

If you cite something more than once, use a shortened version in all footnotes after the first one. Example: Smith, *supra* note 1 at 352.

Do not use Roman numerals for footnote numbering.

Please try to keep footnotes to a reasonable minimum.

5. For all submissions, include a short (one or two sentences) bio of the author(s). For *Tax Notes* special reports only, include a one- or two-paragraph summary of the article.

6. If you have questions, please call:

Tax Notes Editor Bob Wells at 703.533.4684, Deputy Editor Jon Almeras at 703.531.4823, or Managing Editor John Bell at 703.533.4678.

State Tax Notes Editor Carol Douglas at 703.533.4451 or Managing Editor Dean Ahearn at 703.533.4464.

Tax Notes International

ADDRESS FOR SUBMISSION:

Cathy Phillips, Editor
Tax Notes International
Tax Analysts
6830 N. Fairfax Drive
Arlington, VA 22213
USA
Phone: 703-533-4492
E-Mail: cphillip@tax.org
Web: http://www.taxanalysts.com/

CIRCULATION DATA:

Reader: Business Persons, Academics, Tax
  Professionals
Frequency of Issue: 51 Times/Year
Sponsor/Publisher: Tax Analysts

PUBLICATION GUIDELINES:

Manuscript Length: 11-15
Copies Required: One
Computer Submission: Yes Email
Format: MS Word
Fees to Review: 0.00 US$

Manuscript Style:
  Chicago Manual of Style, Associated
  Press Stylebook

REVIEW INFORMATION:

Type of Review: Editorial Review
No. of External Reviewers: 0
No. of In House Reviewers: 2
Acceptance Rate: 80%
Time to Review: 1 Month or Less
Reviewers Comments: Yes
Invited Articles: 21-30%
Fees to Publish: 0.00 US$

MANUSCRIPT TOPICS:
Auditing; Financial Services; International Tax; Tax Accounting

MANUSCRIPT GUIDELINES/COMMENTS:

We publish articles of various lengths. In each magazine, we publish 1 to 3 long, analytical articles (special reports, viewpoints) and the rest are shorter news articles explaining the latest tax developments in a particular country. We are interested in receiving articles on new transfer pricing developments in most jurisdictions, as well as the following other subjects:

Tax-Related Articles in Local Newspapers. We would be interested in analysis of tax-related articles that are contained in local newspapers. Frequently, local newspapers report on tax developments in national level legislatures, court systems, or the executive branch of government. It also helps our subscribers if these developments are put into perspective by our contributors, the experts in their field in their country of expertise. We would appreciate it if you would provide analysis of such developments when you report on them.

Government-Issued Documents. National level courts, legislatures, and executive departments frequently issue tax-related documents. Legislatures usually have some annual tax-related bills, while courts routinely issue tax-related decisions and executive departments (finance and tax, generally) issue regulations, notices, circulars, press releases, etc. For these

538

documents, we would be interested in summaries that explain the contents of the documents and put those documents into perspective for our subscribers.

Documents Issued by Tax-Related Non-Government Organizations. Sometimes, nongovernment organizations issue tax-related documents. For example, local Chamber of Commerce Chapters frequently have tax committees that issue documents, such as recommendations on tax reform. We would be interested in summaries of these documents.

Tax Conferences and Meetings. We would be interested in news articles that review discussions at local tax conferences or general meetings that you have attended.

Other Country Developments With Affect on Your Country. As the world globalizes, developments in the tax system of one country has more of a readily apparent effects on the tax system of another country. For example, the OECD tax haven project has tax implications for every jurisdiction in the world with a tax system. We would be interested in news analysis stories on how specific changes in one jurisdiction may affect your jurisdiction.

Treaty Developments. We would be interested in news stories that report on tax treaty developments, including possible negotiations, renegotiations, amendments, etc.

General Subjects. We are frequently interested in articles that discuss various aspects of a country's tax system that we have not covered before. For example, we would be interested in articles that discuss the tax rules in effect in a country for e-commerce, tax havens, stock options, and other hot topics. Please propose topics to us to determine our level of interest in publishing.

Most articles range anywhere between 1 to 5 pages in length. The longer analytical articles we publish can be as long as 20 double-spaced, typed pages. Please e-mail us at **TNI-WTDContacts@Tax Analysts**

Taxation of Exempts

ADDRESS FOR SUBMISSION:

Robert J. Murdich, Managing Editor
Taxation of Exempts
295 Hudson St.
New York, NY 10014
USA
Phone: 212-807-2894
E-Mail: robert.murdich@thomson.com
Web: http://ria.thomson.com/journals/
default.asp

CIRCULATION DATA:

Reader: , Professionals, Accountants and
Attorneys
Frequency of Issue: 6 Times/Year
Sponsor/Publisher:

PUBLICATION GUIDELINES:

Manuscript Length: 11-30+
Copies Required:
Computer Submission: Yes Disk, Email
Format: MS Word or WordPerfect
Fees to Review: 0.00 US$

Manuscript Style:

REVIEW INFORMATION:

Type of Review: Editorial Review
No. of External Reviewers: 1
No. of In House Reviewers:
Acceptance Rate: Majority
Time to Review: 1 - 2 Months
Reviewers Comments: No
Invited Articles: 50% +
Fees to Publish: 0.00 US$

MANUSCRIPT TOPICS:

Government & Non Profit Accounting; Tax Accounting; Taxation of Tax-exempt
Organizations

MANUSCRIPT GUIDELINES/COMMENTS:

Taxation of Exempts provides tax analysis and guidance to members of the exempt
organization community. It is directed to the professional advisors of these organizations and
their contributors, as well as to members of the organizations' management. Provides the tax
information these organizations need to negotiate the rapid changes to new business and
regulatory environment.

Published bi-monthly, the Journal offers in-depth analyses and updates by leading
practitioners in an accessible and easy-to-read style. Articles cover such topics as:

- Intermediate sanctions
- Combinations and joint ventures
- Health care organizations
- Exemption and compliance
- Private foundations
- Political and lobbying activity

540

- The unrelated business income tax
- Charitable giving
- Compensation
- and much more

Taxation of Exempts goes behind the headlines to provide practical understanding and guidance on tax-related developments, such as knowing what to do in response and what is the best course of action.

Aspiring Authors

Taxation of Exempts welcomes articles offering practical information and ideas on legal, tax, accounting, and finance issues of importance to professionals in the field. Articles should provide guidance on structuring transactions and satisfying compliance requirements with maximum efficiency. Articles should not stress theoretical matters, or how the law could or should be changed, although analysis and critique of administrative or judicial decisions is acceptable and appropriate.

Articles submitted for consideration must be sent to us exclusively and are subject to review by our editorial board. If accepted for publication, the manuscript will be edited to conform with the journal's style, and authors will be asked to review galley proofs by a specified date. Manuscript typically runs 20 to 25 typed pages, double-spaced. Paper manuscript may be submitted for consideration, but an electronic copy is essential for publication.

To submit articles, or for more information, please contact:
Taxation of Exempts
Bob Murdich, Managing Editor
RIA
395 Hudson Street
New York, NY 10014
Phone: (212) 807-2894
Fax: (212) 337-4207
E-mail: **robert.murdich@Thomson.com**

Taxes - The Tax Magazine

ADDRESS FOR SUBMISSION:

Shannon Jett Fischer, Editor
Taxes - The Tax Magazine
CCH, Incorporated
2700 Lake Cook Road
Riverwoods, IL 60015
USA
Phone: 847-267-2243
E-Mail: taxes@cch.com
Web: http://tax.cchgroup.com

CIRCULATION DATA:

Reader: Business Persons
Frequency of Issue: Monthly
Sponsor/Publisher:

PUBLICATION GUIDELINES:

Manuscript Length: 6,500 Words
Copies Required: Two
Computer Submission: Yes
Format: 1 disk or E-Mail Attachment
Fees to Review: 0.00 US$

Manuscript Style:
    Uniform System of Citation (Harvard
    Blue Book), 17th Edition

REVIEW INFORMATION:

Type of Review: Editorial Review
No. of External Reviewers: 0
No. of In House Reviewers: 1
Acceptance Rate: 21-30%
Time to Review: 1 - 2 Months
Reviewers Comments: No Reply
Invited Articles: 11-20%
Fees to Publish: 0.00 US$

MANUSCRIPT TOPICS:
Federal Taxation; State & Local Taxation; Tax Accounting; Taxation

MANUSCRIPT GUIDELINES/COMMENTS:

Product Description
Taxes - The Tax Magazine has been a mainstay in professional journals since 1923. This monthly professional tax journal, written by top tax experts, provides thorough, accurate, and insightful analysis of current tax issues, trends, and legislative developments. It features succinct coverage of hot topics in legal, accounting, and economic aspects of federal and state tax—and alerts practitioners of planning opportunities and pitfalls, and rules being developed in Washington.

Each issue offers timely articles written by leading tax practitioners and educators. These articles provide in-depth coverage of important tax issues, along with tips on planning trends, opportunities, and pitfalls.

Taxes - The Tax Magazine publishes articles dealing with taxation issues that are timely and of national interest. In particular, we prefer analysis of new laws, cases, rulings, regulations, and areas of tax controversy in which the author presents his or her opinion concerning the validity, significance, and/or impact of the question in point, along with innovative tax planning ideas or strategies.

Submitted articles are viewed by the legal editor staff, according to topical expertise. The legal editing staff determines substantive value and general legal validity of submitted articles, and determines whether the article is in a form suitable for publication. Once accepted for publication, the articles are edited for content and style. Authors receive proofs for their comment prior to publication.

Articles should be approximately 6500 words in length. Authors should use endnotes and follow Blue Book (*Uniform Systems of Citation*, 17th Edition) style.

Submit one hard copy of the article along with an electronic version – either on diskette or via e-mail attachment to **fisChers@cch.com**. Hard copies and diskette may be mailed to the editor.

Consideration for publication may take approximately 4 – 6 weeks.

No commitment to publish an article is made until the final version has been reviewed. No compensation is provided for published articles. The magazine reserves the right to condition acceptance of an article upon revision of the article to conform to the magazine's guidelines.

Taxes - The Tax Magazine does not publish articles that have been previously published or are scheduled for publication elsewhere.

TAXPRO Quarterly Journal

ADDRESS FOR SUBMISSION:

Cindy Van Beckum, Production Editor
TAXPRO Quarterly Journal
NATP
720 Association Drive
PO Box 8002
Appleton, WI 54912-8002
USA
Phone: 800-558-3402 x1119
E-Mail: vcindyvb@natptax.com
Web: www.natptax.com

CIRCULATION DATA:

Reader: , Tax Professionals
Frequency of Issue: Quarterly
Sponsor/Publisher: National Association of
Tax Professionals (NATP)

PUBLICATION GUIDELINES:

Manuscript Length: 16-20
Copies Required: One
Computer Submission: Yes
Format: MS Word, RTF, TXT, among
others
Fees to Review: 0.00 US$

Manuscript Style:

REVIEW INFORMATION:

Type of Review: Editorial Review
No. of External Reviewers: 0
No. of In House Reviewers: 5
Acceptance Rate: 90%
Time to Review: 2 - 3 Months
Reviewers Comments: Yes
Invited Articles: 0-5%
Fees to Publish: 0.00 US$

MANUSCRIPT TOPICS:
Business Formation & Dissolution; Financial Services; Insurance; Portfolio & Security Analysis; Real Estate; Retirement Planning; Tax Accounting; Tax Law

MANUSCRIPT GUIDELINES/COMMENTS:

The NATP *TAXPRO Quarterly Journal* is written specifically for association members. Around 17,000 professionals currently belong to NATP. Members represent the tax profession in the following areas:

Individual— 41%	Accountants—18%	Enrolled Agents —25%
Attorneys—1%	CPAs—13%	Financial Planners—2%

Mission Statement. The *TAXPRO Quarterly Journal* provides a diverse group of tax professionals with the tools, information, and resources necessary to succeed in business while accurately and ethically applying the tax law to best serve their clients.

Editorial Concept
The intent of the publication is to inform members of current trends and developments within the tax preparation profession. Because their levels of expertise range from relatively

inexperienced to highly adept, our goal is to publish a wide variety of articles that focus on practical situations and applications, and yet maintain a broad level of appeal.

These professionals have no interest in academic studies, research reports, theoretical discussions or highly technical material. They do, however, appreciate articles that point out the opportunities and/or setbacks in the areas being discussed.

Such articles might include "how-to" approaches on practice management, increasing their bottom-line, applying government regulations, diversifying a tax practice, increasing tax knowledge, marketing a business, or negotiating with the IRS.

We encourage writers to submit material that focuses on approaches to the treatment of unusual tax problems, or service-oriented articles that offer hands-on advice to our readers. These are most useful when based on the author's own experience.

In addition to articles of this nature, the *Journal* will contain six or seven regular departments. These will feature short articles dealing with more topical issues such as general taxation, pending legislation, and changes being made within the IRS. The *Monthly* typically features only one practice management article per edition.

Choosing a Subject Matter

When choosing a subject, keep in mind that you should only write about the topics you know best. Members are interested in reading more on the following:

Roth IRAs	Tax Law Application	Insurance & Small Business
Liabilities	Bankruptcy & Insolvency	EA Status
Practice Management	Stress Management	Interim Reporting
Estate and Financial Planning	Consolidations, Mergers & Acquisitions	Meeting Needs for Future Generations
Auditing Issues	Offers in Compromise	Significant Others
Computers/Technology	Budgeting	Corporations
Accounting	Passive Activities	Collections
Pending Legislation	Client Representation	Partnerships
Professional Development	Amending Returns	Leases and Leasing
Small Business Practices	Extensions	Leadership
Pension Plans	Research Gathering	Volunteer Experiences
Government	Increasing Clientele	Office in Home
Marketing	Training Employees	Preparing for Tax Season
Consulting	Cafeteria Plans	Success Stories
Electronic Filing	Negotiating with the IRS	Case Studies
Processing Procedures	Social Security Benefits	Trade Tips
Professional Ethics	Commissioner's Advisory Group	Web Marketing

Writing Style

Proper organization is the most important key to writing a good article. By organizing your material and preparing an effective outline, you will eliminate some of the frustration usually involved in starting a new project. You will also be able to pinpoint the areas that may need researching to better support your ideas.

Once you have an outline on paper, you can begin your rough draft. It is not necessary to start with the introduction. Instead, begin with the easiest topic on your outline. Write down everything you know about the subject and then proceed to the next. Don't be too concerned about style, punctuation, and grammar for now. You can apply these later.

Once you have covered each topic on your outline, develop the first draft. Work on proper sentence structure, grammar, and style. Use the following three principles to help you in writing your first draft: 1) Use short words, sentences, and paragraphs. Avoid pretentious words, complicated terms, and technical jargon. 2) Write the way you talk, using the active voice. Instead of writing "the amendment was ratified by Congress," say, "Congress ratified the amendment." 3) Use strong nouns, verbs and phrases. For example, "Proposal bombs in Senate" sounds more exciting than "Proposal fails to win approval in Senate."

Next, go back and write the introduction. The opening paragraph should indicate exactly what the article is about and how an individual can benefit from reading it. Include any vital background information that pertains to your main theme. The final paragraph should mirror or summarize this, at the conclusion of the article.

Edit your manuscript a few days later. Define any weak areas and eliminate any irrelevant material. Cross out all the words that are not necessary. By doing so, you will make your article more concise and easier to read.

Here are some additional tips for more effective writing: 1) Avoid citations, footnotes, and quotations. 2) Avoid lengthy discussions about the topic's background. 3) Write "punchy" lead paragraphs that will grab the reader's attention. 4) Never assume the reader knows as much as you do. Explain complicated items in finer detail. 5) Write a conclusion that sums up your major points and explains why the article should be of interest to the reader.

Manuscript Requirements

Although there are no length requirements, most feature articles in the *Journal* run around 3,000 to 4,000 words. Departmental columns tend to be approximately 750 to 1,500 words. *TAXPRO Monthly* articles are about 1,000 words. Keep in mind that these are only guidelines. Write what you feel is necessary to efficiently cover the topic. When you have completed your manuscript, please e-mail it to the editor as a WordPerfect, Microsoft Word, Rich Text Format (RTF), or ASCII attachment. Include a brief biographical sketch (approximately 100 words). Contact us if there is a problem with this, as other formats are acceptable.

Editorial and Review Process

We assign deadlines to articles based on their anticipated date of publication. Normally, you will have six weeks to research your topic and write your manuscript. If you would like to

546

submit an article at any time for review or consideration, we encourage you to do so, and we will contact you if we decide to use your article for one of our publications or on the website. Shorter articles (900-1,500 words) should be sent to Char DeCoster at 800.558.3402 extension 1172, and longer articles (3,000-5,000 words) should be sent to Cindy Van Beckum. Some of the things we look for when considering an article for publication include: 1) Originality and timeliness of topic; 2) Technical soundness and readability; and 3) Practicality and applicability.

We will carefully review your manuscript to determine whether it contains all of these elements. If it does not, yet we feel your article would be a worthy contribution to our publication, we will make every effort to assist you in revising it.

After the editing and review process, we will e-mail or fax you a copy of your manuscript. Please review the revisions and notify us of any essential changes by the date specified.

Manuscripts are accepted on a gratis basis. In turn, being published will provide name recognition for you. Brief advertising for your business is allowed in the biography, as well. In appreciation, we will send you five complimentary copies of the issue in which your article appears.

If you have questions regarding your manuscript or our editorial policy, please contact the editor or Char DeCoster. Again, thank you for your interest in writing for NATP's professional tax publications. We hope this will be an enjoyable and rewarding experience for you.

Tennessee CPA Journal

ADDRESS FOR SUBMISSION:

Lori D. Druen, Editor
Tennessee CPA Journal
201 Powell Place
Brentwood, TN 37027
USA
Phone: 615-377-3825
E-Mail: ldruen@tscpa.com
Web: www.tscpa.com

CIRCULATION DATA:

Reader: Business Persons, Tennessee
 Certified Public Accountants
Frequency of Issue: 10 Times/Year
Sponsor/Publisher: Tennessee Society of
 CPAs

PUBLICATION GUIDELINES:

Manuscript Length: 6-10
Copies Required: Two
Computer Submission: Yes Disk, Email
Format: MS Word 97, 2000 or XP
Fees to Review: 0.00 US$

Manuscript Style:
 See Manuscript Guidelines

REVIEW INFORMATION:

Type of Review: Blind Review
No. of External Reviewers: 3
No. of In House Reviewers: 3-3+
Acceptance Rate: 21-30%
Time to Review: 2 - 3 Months
Reviewers Comments: Yes
Invited Articles: 21-30%
Fees to Publish: 0.00 US$

MANUSCRIPT TOPICS:

Accounting Education; Accounting Information Systems; Accounting Theory & Practice; Auditing; Cost Accounting; Economic Development; Financial Services; Government & Non Profit Accounting; International Economics & Trade; International Finance; Public Policy Economics; Real Estate; Regional Economics; Tax Accounting

MANUSCRIPT GUIDELINES/COMMENTS:

A publication of the Tennessee Society of Certified Public Accountants (TSCPA)

Content

Articles should be on issues relevant to CPAs practicing in Tennessee. Our audience is primarily accountants in public practice, although approximately 40 percent of our members also serve industry, government and education. Articles related to specific industries are acceptable.

Articles should be of a practical nature, offer guidance in complex situations, offer methods to improve practice, or help resolve questions arising in practice. We accept some articles which are based on questionnaires. References to specific statistical tests should be included in the footnotes. Our readers are primarily interested in the results of the questionnaire and conclusions which may properly be drawn from the results.

Factual accuracy is the responsibility of the author. Facts should be thoroughly checked before the manuscript is submitted.

Self-study questions
Authors should include two one-sentence True/False questions taken from the subject matter of each article submitted to the *Tennessee CPA Journal*. These questions will be used for possible inclusion in the CPE Self-Study Exam, which accompanies each issue of the *Tennessee CPA Journal*. (See form for submitting self-study CPE exam questions at http://www.tscpa.com/publicinfo/SelfStudy.pdf.)

Format
Manuscripts should be typed on 8 ½" x 11" paper, double spaced and use an 11pt. font size. Paragraphs should be indented three spaces. Quotations of more than three lines, footnotes, and references should be single-spaced and indented. Please allow one inch margins to facilitate editing.

The names(s) of the author(s) should not be on the manuscript itself. Numbers from one through nine should be spelled out, except where decimals are used or where the numbers are in tabular form. Numbers 10 and above should be written numerically. The manuscript should be written in third person and in non-sexist language.

We recommend *The Elements of Style* by William Strunk, Jr., and E. B. White (published in paperback by Macmillan Publishing Co., Inc.) as a guide to style and usage.

Biography of Author(s)
Names, title, education, employers and brief biographical information (e.g. professional memberships) should be on a separate cover page which includes the title of the manuscript. Also, please include a complete mailing address (no P.O. boxes please), business telephone number, and e-mail address.

Length
We accept manuscripts which will run from one to three pages of our publication (900 to 2,250 words).

Headings
Major headings should be centered. Subheadings should be flush left with the margin.

Tables and Figures
Each table or figure should be placed on a separate page and have a number and a title. Each table or figure must be referred to in the text. Indicate by a double row of dashes and an insert note where the table or figure should appear in the text:

= = = = = = = = = = = =
Insert Figure 1 here
= = = = = = = = = = = =

Footnotes
Textual footnotes should be used for definitions and explanations which might disrupt the reading continuity if placed in the body of the manuscript. Numerous footnotes and citations do not necessarily make for a better article and are not an indication of thorough research.

Reference List
When the manuscript cites other literature, a list of references must be included at the end of the text. References must be complete bibliography references, including page or paragraph numbers. Arrange entries alphabetically by surname of the first author. Works without authors should also be listed alphabetically. Multiple works by the same author(s) are listed in publication date order. Samples of entries are:

American Institute of Certified Public Accountants. Report of the Study on Establishment of Accounting Principles, *Establishing Accounting Principles* (1972).

Sprouse, R. T., "Accounting for What-You-May-Call-Its," *Journal of Accountancy* (August 1966), pp. 45-54.

Literature Citations
To cite sources of references, use square brackets in the body of the text to enclose the author's name and page number, if appropriate. If two references were published in one year, use a, b, c to indicate which work listed in the reference list is referred to, e.g. [Armstrong, 1977]; [Sprouse and Moonitz, 1962, p. 2]; [Hendriksen, 1973a]. Citations to professional publications should employ acronyms where practical, e.g., [APB Opinion No. 30]; (SFAS No 95]. If an author's name is mentioned in the text, it should not be repeated in the citation, e.g., "Armstrong [1977, p. 40] says . . ."

If a reference has three or more authors, list only the last name of the first author followed by "et al."

References to statutes, legal treatises or court cases should use citations acceptable in law reviews.

Submission of Manuscripts
Three copies of each manuscript should be submitted. TSCPA does not require copyright assignment or transfer from authors; however, TSCPA requests first publication rights. A Publication Release Form is required to be filled out by all authors upon submission. (http://www.tscpa.com/publicinfo/Publication_ReleaseForm.pdf)

Manuscripts should be sent to Tennessee Society of CPAs, Editor, 201 Powell Place, Brentwood, TN 37027. Each person submitting manuscripts will receive a letter of acknowledgement.

We also encourage the submission of manuscripts on disk or via e-mail using Microsoft Word versions 97, 2000 or XP. You may submit your manuscript as an attachment of an e-mail to **ldruen@tscpa.com**. Only one copy need be submitted with the disk or as an e-mail attachment.

550

Website Publication. All articles published in the *Tennessee CPA Journal* will be published on our Web site under the Members Only section. Each article will also be archived in our online Journal Archive, which is a searchable database for previously printed articles.

Review Process. Manuscripts are peer reviewed. This blind refereed process takes one to two months. Authors will be notified concerning acceptance, recommended revision or rejection of their manuscripts. Manuscripts will not be returned. TSCPA reserves the right to reject a manuscript at any time.

List of topic ideas we are looking for:
- Aging Issues
- Eldercare Legal Issues
- New IRS Audits
- Tax Fraud
- Business Fraud
- Insurance
- Taxpayer Advocacy Program
- Family Business Dynamics
- Contingency Planning/Risk Management
- Auditing Procedure Update
- Divorce: Transferring of Assets and Income
- Electronic Commerce: State Sales & Use Taxation
- Fixed Asset Management – Policies and Procedures
- Incentive Compensation Plans
- New Regulations
- Intellectual Capital (i.e. intangibles)
- Manufacturing Issues
- Marketing Your Firm's Services – Positioning Your Business for Growth and Prosperity
- New Governmental Issues
- Mergers and Acquisitions: Internal Auditor's Role
- Multiple State/Global Practice Issues
- Perception of CPAs in the Marketplace
- World Commerce – Financing, Letters of Credit
- Computer Software/Hardware Questions and Answers
- Ethics: Changes in Perceptions
- Streamlined Sales Tax in Tennessee
- Outsourcing
- Specialty Certifications
- Financial Reporting's Affect on the Market
- Compilation and Review Issues
- Mergers and Acquisitions of Accounting Firms
- Effects of New Overtime Laws
- Estate Planning
- Create your own topic

Today's CPA

ADDRESS FOR SUBMISSION:

DeLynn Deakins, Managing Editor
Today's CPA
14860 Montfort Drive, Suite 150
Dallas, TX 75254
USA
Phone: 972-687-8550
E-Mail: ddeakins@tscpa.net
Web: www.tscpa.org

CIRCULATION DATA:

Reader: Business Persons
Frequency of Issue: Bi-Monthly
Sponsor/Publisher: Texas Society of
 Certified Public Accountants

PUBLICATION GUIDELINES:

Manuscript Length: 2,100-3,000 Words
Copies Required: Electronic
Computer Submission: Yes Email Preferred
Format: Word or Text Document
Fees to Review: 0.00 US$

Manuscript Style:
 See Manuscript Guidelines

REVIEW INFORMATION:

Type of Review: Peer Review
No. of External Reviewers: 2
No. of In House Reviewers: 4
Acceptance Rate: 75%
Time to Review: 2 - 3 Months
Reviewers Comments: Yes
Invited Articles: 31-50%
Fees to Publish: 0.00 US$

MANUSCRIPT TOPICS:

Accounting Education; Accounting Information Systems; Accounting Theory & Practice; Auditing; Behavioral Accounting; Cost Accounting; Econometrics; Economic Development; Economic History; Financial Services; Fiscal Policy; Government & Non Profit Accounting; Industrial Organization; Insurance; International Economics & Trade; International Finance; Macro Economics; Micro Economics; Monetary Policy; Portfolio & Security Analysis; Public Policy Economics; Real Estate; Regional Economics; Tax Accounting

MANUSCRIPT GUIDELINES/COMMENTS:

Today's CPA is a peer-reviewed, bimonthly magazine of the Texas Society of Certified Public Accountants. It serves as the primary vehicle for conveying information to more than 27,000 CPAs statewide—one of the largest number of in-state CPAs participating in state accounting societies. This award-winning publication features articles and columns that focus on issues, trends, and developments affecting CPAs, their employers, clients, and employees. Always striving to keep CPAs abreast of the latest developments in all facets of business, *Today's CPA* endeavors to develop editorial content that challenges our readers while communicating items of importance.

Interested in writing for this or other magazines? We recommend e-mailing the managing editor and asking for both the guidelines for submissions and for the editorial calendar, which will tell prospective writers the topics the magazine or journal plans to address in the next few

Display Advertising
Requests for information about display advertising should be referred to DeLynn Deakins at 972-687-8550.

POLICIES
Advertising
All materials submitted as advertising are subject to acceptance for publication at the sole discretion of *Today's CPA*. Advertisers and advertising agencies assume liability for all content of advertisements printed and also assume liability for any claims arising there from. Requests for information about display advertising should be referred to DeLynn Deakins at 972-687-8550.

Letters to the Editor
Your comments on any article published in *Today's CPA* are welcome. Letters received will be published on a space-available basis. Address your letter to: Managing Editor, Today's CPA; Texas Society of CPAs; 14860 Montfort Drive, Suite 150; Dallas, TX; 75254-6705. You can also e-mail your letter to the editor to **ddeakins@tscpa.net**. Letters must be signed.

Manuscript Submission
Submit a synopsis work to the editor, or send your completed articles. Suggested article length is 2,100 to 3,000 words. It will be reviewed by the editor and technical editor. The magazine is peer-reviewed. Many articles are rejected. If your article is accepted, you may be asked to modify the copy, or to provide additional information, charts or graphic elements. We reserve the right to modify the story in any way necessary. *Today's CPA* retains the right of first publication. Do not submit your article or column to another publication until the review process is complete. Manuscripts or synopsis can be sent to: Editor, Today's CPA; Texas Society of CPAs; 14860 Montfort Drive, Suite 150; Dallas, TX; 75254-6705, or e-mailed to **ddeakins@tscpa.net**. Statements of opinions expressed are those of the authors and not necessarily those of the Texas Society of CPAs.

Troy University Business and Economic Review

ADDRESS FOR SUBMISSION:

Editor
Troy University Business and Economic
  Review
Troy University
102 Bibb Graves Hall
Troy, AL 36082
USA
Phone: 334-670-3524
E-Mail: glayton@troy.edu
Web: http://business.troy.edu/Publications/
  TSUBAER.aspx

PUBLICATION GUIDELINES:

Manuscript Length: 21-25
Copies Required: Three
Computer Submission: Yes
Format: MS Word
Fees to Review: 0.00 US$

Manuscript Style:
  American Psychological Association

CIRCULATION DATA:

Reader: Academics, Business Persons,
  Public Policy Influencers
Frequency of Issue: 2 Times/Year
Sponsor/Publisher: Troy University

REVIEW INFORMATION:

Type of Review: Blind Review
No. of External Reviewers: 2
No. of In House Reviewers: 1
Acceptance Rate: No Reply
Time to Review: 2-6 months
Reviewers Comments: Yes
Invited Articles: 6-10%
Fees to Publish: 0.00 US$

MANUSCRIPT TOPICS:
Accounting Education; Accounting Information Systems; Accounting Theory & Practice;
Auditing; Cost Accounting; Tax Accounting

MANUSCRIPT GUIDELINES/COMMENTS:

Publication Policy Statement
The mission of the *Troy University Business and Economic Review* is to publish research from
business scholars and practitioners that is meaningful to individuals with an interest in the
business community while, simultaneously, providing an outlet for Troy faculty research
activity and promoting the Troy University Sorrell College of Business.

All papers under consideration for publication will be subject to a "blind" review process;
papers will be reviewed by members of the editorial advisory board. Reviewers will be
selected to review individual articles based on their professional expertise. Individuals serving
on the review board will be approved by the Dean of the Sorrell College of Business. The
names of the reviewers associated with individual papers will remain confidential.

Criteria utilized in reviewing papers include the following:

- Quality of composition [writing style, grammar, and organization].
- Contribution of knowledge to the business community.
- Interest to Review readers.
- Timeliness of research and subject matter.
- Adequacy of literature review.
- Use of appropriate statistical techniques [if applicable].

Note. Review readership primarily is comprised of individuals in business, political, and professional positions within the State of Alabama and the Southeast U.S., Sorrell College of Business alumni, Business Advisory Council members, and business faculty at other universities throughout the U.S.

The review process will result in one of the following outcomes:

- Papers may be accepted as submitted [authors will be notified of a planned publication date].
- Papers may be accepted with revisions [as indicated by reviewers' comments to the author(s)].
- Papers may be rejected [comments also may be provided by reviewers to authors in this case].

Submission guidelines are as follows:

- Papers should cover a topic of general business or economic interest.
- The length should be no longer than 25 double-spaced, typed pages.
- Articles may be submitted by e-mail attachments in MS Word to **glayton@troy.edu**.
- Submissions should not endorse a particular product or service.
- References should be documented properly and listed using APA style titled "References."
- Paper titles should be in upper and lower case 14 point type and bold. Section headings should be centered, bold, all caps, and 12 point type. Subheadings should be left justified, bold, upper and lower case, and 12 point type.
- Notes should be included at the end of the paper (endnotes) titled "Notes."
- Paper should contain pictures and/or graphs when possible and suitable for black and white printing.
- Papers should **not** be submitted to [or published in] another publication while under consideration for publication in the *Review*.

Note. Articles also should be submitted with a picture of the author [black and white glossy or high quality electronic JPEG files] when possible. Pictures should be bust shots (head and shoulders) with males in coat and tie and females in business-appropriate attire. Backgrounds should be plain and in contrast to the individual featured.

Journal Name	Type Review	No. Ext. Rev.	Accept. Rate	Page
Accounting Education				
Abacus	Blind	2		1
Academy of Educational Leadership Journal	Blind	3	21-30%	6
Accounting and Business Research	Blind	2	11-20%	9
Accounting and Finance	Blind	2	21-30%	12
Accounting Education: An International Journal	Blind	3	21-30%	20
Accounting Educator's Journal	Blind	2	21-30%	24
Accounting Instructors' Report	Blind	1	21-30%	46
Accounting, Business and Financial History	Blind	2	40%	61
Advances in Accounting	Blind	2	11-20%	69
Advances in Accounting Education	Blind	2	21-30%	73
Advances in Public Interest Accounting	Blind	2	21-30%	86
Advances in Taxation	Blind	2	21-30%	89
American Journal of Business and Economics	Blind	2	21-30%	92
Australian Accounting Review	Blind	2	50%	99
Business Case Journal	Blind	3	11-20%	114
Business Education Forum	Editorial	1	6-10%	117
CAmagazine	Editorial	1	6-10%	130
Canadian Accounting Perspectives	Blind	2	11-20%	131
CASE Journal (The)	Blind	2	21-30%	135
Clarion Business and Economic Review	Blind	1	50%	144
CMA Management Magazine	Blind	1	21-30%	146
Contemporary Accounting Research	Blind	2	11-20%	157
Critical Perspectives on Accounting	Blind	3	6-10%	168
European Accounting Review	Blind	2	21-30%	183
Financial Accountability & Management	Blind	2	11-20%	189
Global Business and Economics Review	Blind	3+	0-5%	198
Global Perspectives on Accounting Education	Blind	2	11-20%	206
International Journal of Accounting, Auditing and Performance Evaluation		3	10-12%	240
International Journal of Business and Public Administration	Blind	2	10-20%	251
Irish Accounting Review (The)	Blind	2		273
Issues in Accounting Education	Blind	2-3	15%	276
Journal of 21st Century Accounting (The)	Editorial	1	New J	280
Journal of Accounting & Organisational Change	Blind	2	70%	290
Journal of Accounting and Finance Research	Blind	2	21-30%	299
Journal of Accounting Case Research	Blind	2	21-30%	306
Journal of Accounting Education	Blind	3	11-20%	309
Journal of Accounting, Business and Management	Blind	2	21-30%	319
Journal of Accounting, Ethics & Public Policy	Blind	2	50%	322
Journal of Applied Case Research	Blind	2	21-30%	327
Journal of Business and Behavioral Sciences	Blind	3	11-20%	332
Journal of Business and Economic Perspectives	Blind	2	21-30%	333
Journal of Cost Analysis & Management	Blind	2	21-30%	350

Accounting Information Systems

562   INDEX

Journal Name	Type Review	No. Ext. Rev.	Accept. Rate	Page
Journal of International Accounting Research	Blind	2	11-20%	382
Journal of International Accounting, Auditing & Taxation	Blind	2	21-30%	388
Journal of International Business and Economics	Blind	2	21-30%	391
Journal of Performance Management	Editorial	4	90%	408
Journal of the International Academy for Case Studies	Blind	3	21-30%	423
Journal of the International Society of Business Disciplines	Blind	2	21-30%	425
Journal of Theoretical Accounting Research (The)	Blind	2	New J	427
Leaders' Edge (Michigan CPA)	Editorial	1	0-5%	429
Management Science	Editorial	3	11-20%	439
Managerial Auditing Journal	Blind		47.1%	443
Massachusetts CPA Review Online	Blind	0		448
Midwestern Business and Economic Review	Blind	2	35-40%	451
National Accounting Journal (The)	Blind	2	21-30%	454
Oil, Gas & Energy Quarterly	Blind	1	30-40%	459
Pacific Accounting Review	Blind	2	21-30%	467
Pennsylvania Journal of Business and Economics	Blind	2	35%	470
Petroleum Accounting and Financial Management Journal	Blind	1	50%	473
Public Money & Management	Blind	2	11-20%	480
Regional Business Review	Blind	1		484
Research in Accounting Regulation	Blind	1+	30%+	485
Research Journal of Business Disciplines	Blind	2	41-50%	491
Research on Professional Responsibility and Ethics in Accounting	Blind	2	21-30%	493
Review of Accounting Studies	Blind	2	18-20%	499
Review of Business Research	Blind	2		503
Schmalenbach Business Review	Blind	1-2	37%	511
Southwest Business and Economics Journal	Blind	1-2	30-35%	515
Spectrum	Blind	2	21-30%	517
Tax Notes	Editorial	0	50 %	535
Tennessee CPA Journal	Blind	3	21-30%	547
Today's CPA	Peer	2	75%	551
Troy University Business and Economic Review	Blind	2		554

Auditing

Abacus	Blind	2		1
Academy of Accounting and Financial Studies Journal	Blind	3	21-30%	4
Accounting & Business	Blind		21-30%	8
Accounting and Business Research	Blind	2	11-20%	9
Accounting and Finance	Blind	2	21-30%	12
Accounting and the Public Interest	Blind	2	11-20%	15
Accounting Historians Journal	Blind	2	30%	33

Behavioral Accounting

Journal Name	Type Review	No. Ext. Rev.	Accept. Rate	Page
Critical Perspectives on Accounting	Blind	3	6-10%	168
Decision Sciences	Blind	3	11-20%	172
European Accounting Review	Blind	2	21-30%	183
Global Business and Economics Review	Blind	3+	0-5%	198
International Journal of Accounting	Blind	2	11-20%	234
International Journal of Accounting Information Systems	Blind	2	11-20%	236
International Journal of Accounting, Auditing and Performance Evaluation		3	10-12%	240
International Journal of Management Theory & Practices	Blind	3	6-10%	257
Irish Accounting Review (The)	Blind	2		273
Journal of Accounting & Organisational Change	Blind	2	70%	290
Journal of Accounting Case Research	Blind	2	21-30%	306
Journal of Accounting, Auditing & Finance	Blind	1	10%	317
Journal of Accounting, Business and Management	Blind	2	21-30%	319
Journal of Accounting, Ethics & Public Policy	Blind	2	50%	322
Journal of Business and Behavioral Sciences	Blind	3	11-20%	332
Journal of Business and Economic Perspectives	Blind	2	21-30%	333
Journal of Cost Analysis & Management	Blind	2	21-30%	350
Journal of Emerging Technologies in Accounting		3+	11-20%	369
Journal of International Accounting Research	Blind	2	11-20%	382
Journal of International Accounting, Auditing & Taxation	Blind	2	21-30%	388
Journal of the International Academy for Case Studies	Blind	3	21-30%	423
Journal of the International Society of Business Disciplines	Blind	2	21-30%	425
Journal of Theoretical Accounting Research (The)	Blind	2	New J	427
Massachusetts CPA Review Online	Blind	0		448
Midwestern Business and Economic Review	Blind	2	35-40%	451
National Accounting Journal (The)	Blind	2	21-30%	454
Pacific Accounting Review	Blind	2	21-30%	467
Pennsylvania Journal of Business and Economics	Blind	2	35%	470
Regional Business Review	Blind	1		484
Research Journal of Business Disciplines	Blind	2	41-50%	491
Research on Professional Responsibility and Ethics in Accounting	Blind	2	21-30%	493
Review of Accounting and Finance	Blind	2	11-20%	496
Southwest Business and Economics Journal	Blind	1-2	30-35%	515
Today's CPA	Peer	2	75%	551

Cost Accounting

Abacus	Blind	2		1
Academy of Accounting and Financial Studies Journal	Blind	3	21-30%	4

Journal Name	Type Review	No. Ext. Rev.	Accept. Rate	Page
Accounting & Business	Blind		21-30%	8
Accounting and Business Research	Blind	2	11-20%	9
Accounting and the Public Interest	Blind	2	11-20%	15
Accounting Historians Journal	Blind	2	30%	33
Accounting History	Blind	2	21-30%	36
Accounting Horizons	Blind	2	11-20%	39
Accounting Research Journal	Blind	2	21-30%	47
Accounting Review (The)	Blind	2	11-15%	50
Accounting, Business and Financial History	Blind	2	40%	61
Advances in Accounting	Blind	2	11-20%	69
Advances in Accounting Behavioral Research	Blind	2	11-20%	71
Advances in Environmental Accounting and Management	Blind	2	20-30%	77
Advances in International Accounting	Blind	2	50%	79
Advances in Management Accounting	Blind	2	21-30%	83
Advances in Public Interest Accounting	Blind	2	21-30%	86
American Journal of Business and Economics	Blind	2	21-30%	92
Australian Accounting Review	Blind	2	50%	99
Bank Accounting & Finance	Blind	2	50%	102
Behavioral Research in Accounting	Blind	2	15-20%	104
British Accounting Review (The)	Blind	2	10-15%	111
Business Case Journal	Blind	3	11-20%	114
California Business Review		2		121
California Journal of Business Research	Blind	2	25%	124
CAmagazine	Editorial	1	6-10%	130
Canadian Accounting Perspectives	Blind	2	11-20%	131
CASE Journal (The)	Blind	2	21-30%	135
Case Research Journal	Blind	3	11-20%	137
Catalyst: The Leading Edge of Ohio Business (Ohio CPA Journal)	Editorial	1	11-20%	139
Clarion Business and Economic Review	Blind	1	50%	144
CMA Management Magazine	Blind	1	21-30%	146
Coastal Business Journal	Blind	8	37.5%	149
Contemporary Accounting Research	Blind	2	11-20%	157
Corporate Taxation	Editorial	1	21-30%	161
CPA Journal	Blind	2	65%	163
Critical Perspectives on Accounting	Blind	3	6-10%	168
Decision Sciences	Blind	3	11-20%	172
European Accounting Review	Blind	2	21-30%	183
Global Business and Economics Review	Blind	3+	0-5%	198
Harvard Business Review	Editorial	0	0-5%	210
Intelligent Systems in Accounting, Finance and Management	Blind	2	11-20%	224
International Journal of Accounting	Blind	2	11-20%	234
International Journal of Accounting, Auditing and Performance Evaluation		3	10-12%	240

INDEX 581

Journal Name	Type Review	No. Ext. Rev.	Accept. Rate	Page
Strategic Finance Magazine	Blind	3	11-20%	520
Today's CPA	Peer	2	75%	551

Portfolio & Security Analysis

Academy of Accounting and Financial Studies Journal	Blind	3	21-30%	4
Accounting and Finance	Blind	2	21-30%	12
Accounting Research Journal	Blind	2	21-30%	47
American Journal of Business and Economics	Blind	2	21-30%	92
Bank Accounting & Finance	Blind	2	50%	102
British Accounting Review (The)	Blind	2	10-15%	111
Business Case Journal	Blind	3	11-20%	114
California Business Review		2		121
CAmagazine	Editorial	1	6-10%	130
CASE Journal (The)	Blind	2	21-30%	135
Catalyst: The Leading Edge of Ohio Business (Ohio CPA Journal)	Editorial	1	11-20%	139
CPA Journal	Blind	2	65%	163
Financial Counseling and Planning	Blind	3	25%	192
Global Business and Economics Review	Blind	3+	0-5%	198
International Journal of Management Theory & Practices	Blind	3	6-10%	257
Journal of Accountancy	Blind	3+	11-20%	285
Journal of Accounting and Finance Research	Blind	2	21-30%	299
Journal of Accounting, Business and Management	Blind	2	21-30%	319
Journal of Business and Behavioral Sciences	Blind	3	11-20%	332
Journal of Business and Economic Perspectives	Blind	2	21-30%	333
Journal of Business and Economics	Blind	2	21-30%	336
Journal of Business Finance & Accounting	Blind	1	11-20%	342
Journal of Deferred Compensation: Nonqualified Plans and Executive Compensation	Editorial	1	11-20%	356
Journal of International Business and Economics	Blind	2	21-30%	391
Journal of the International Society of Business Disciplines	Blind	2	21-30%	425
Management Accounting Quarterly	Blind	3	11-20%	431
Midwestern Business and Economic Review	Blind	2	35-40%	451
Pacific Accounting Review	Blind	2	21-30%	467
Pennsylvania Journal of Business and Economics	Blind	2	35%	470
Petroleum Accounting and Financial Management Journal	Blind	1	50%	473
Research Journal of Business Disciplines	Blind	2	41-50%	491
Review of Business Research	Blind	2		503
Review of Derivatives Research	Blind		20-25%	506
Schmalenbach Business Review	Blind	1-2	37%	511
Southwest Business and Economics Journal	Blind	1-2	30-35%	515
Strategic Finance Magazine	Blind	3	11-20%	520

Notes

Notes